The Modern Manager

The West Series in Management

Consulting Editors:
Don Hellriegel—*Texas A&M University*
    and
John W. Slocum, Jr.—*The Pennsylvania State University*

Burack	Personnel Management: Cases and Exercises
Burack and Smith	Personnel Management: A Human Resource Systems Approach
Costley & Todd	Human Relations in Organizations
Downey, Hellriegel & Slocum	Organizational Behavior: A Reader
Hellriegel & Slocum	Organizational Behavior, 2nd Edition
Hitt, Middlemist & Mathis	Effective Management
Hrebiniak	Complex Organizations
Huse	Organization Development and Change
Huse	The Modern Manager
Mathis & Jackson	Personnel: Contemporary Perspectives and Applications, 2nd Edition
Morris & Sashkin	Organization Behavior in Action: Skill Building Experiences
Newport	Supervisory Management: Tools & Techniques
Ritchie & Thompson	Organization and People: Readings, Cases, and Exercises in Organizational Behavior
Schuler & Huse	Case Problems in Management
Veiga & Yanouzas	The Dynamics of Organization Theory: Gaining a Macro Perspective
Whatley & Kelley	Personnel Management in Action: Skill Building Exercises

The Modern Manager

Edgar F. Huse
Boston College

WEST PUBLISHING COMPANY

St. Paul
New York
Los Angeles
San Francisco

A partially programmed study
guide with self-correcting
exercises has been developed to
assist you in mastering important
concepts that you will
encounter in this text. It is
available from your local
bookstore under the name,
Study Guide to accompany
Huse's *The Modern Manager*,
prepared by Pat Long and David
Gray.

COPYRIGHT © 1979
By WEST PUBLISHING CO.
50 West Kellogg Boulevard
P.O. Box 3526
St. Paul, Minnesota 55165

**Library of Congress Cataloging
in Publication Data**

Huse, Edgar F
The modern manager.
Bibliography: p.
Includes indexes.
1. Management. I. Title.

HD31.H825   658.4   78-24407
ISBN 0-8299-0197-3
1st Reprint—1979

To my family

Contents

Preface   xv

Part I   The Modern Manager

Chapter 1   The Importance of the Manager   2
Learning Objectives   4
Thought Starters   4
Jaws   4
Systems and the Manager   5
What Is a Manager?   7
Where Are Managers?   8
The Three Management Levels   9
Basic Characteristics of Managerial Work   12
The Personal Style of the Manager   16
Managing—A Rewarding Career   16
Implications for the Manager   18
Review   19
Frye Boots   19
Footnotes   20

Chapter 2   The Working Roles of the Manager   23
Learning Objectives   24
Thought Starters   24
A Day in the Life of Del Goetz   24
What Managers Do—Common Functions   25
The Working Roles of the Manager   26
The Interpersonal Roles of the Manager   28
The Informational Roles of the Manager   29
The Decisional Roles of the Manager   31
The Manager's Roles—A Contingency Approach   34
Implications for the Manager   36
Review   37
The Director of Social Work   37
Footnotes   39

Chapter 3   The Emergence of Management Thought   41
Learning Objectives   42
Thought Starters   42
The Great Pyramid of Cheops   42
Management and Management Techniques through the Ages   43
The Impact of the Industrial Revolution   45
The Rise of Scientific Management   46
The Rise of "Human Relations"   48
The Emergence of Structure—The "Classical" Approach   50
The Growing Importance of Technology and Environment   52
Current Integrative Trends   54
Implications for the Manager   56
Review   58
The Reorganization of the Roman Army   58
Footnotes   59

Part II   People at Work

Chapter 4   Individual Motivation and Performance   63
Learning Objectives   64
Thought Starters   64
The Young Foreman   64
The Content Models of Motivation   67
The Process Models of Motivation   71
Toward an Overall Model of Motivation   78
The Relationship between Job Satisfaction and Productivity   79
Implications for the Manager   79
Review   81
Making Hotplates   81
Footnotes   82

Chapter 5   Managing Effective Groups   87
Learning Objectives   88
Thought Starters   88
The Hovey and Beard Company   88
What Is a Group?   90
Activities, Interactions, and Sentiments   92
What Groups Offer Individuals   94
Characteristics of Effective Work Groups   95
Managing Effective Groups and Committees   99
Implications for the Manager   101
Review   103
Ajax Construction Company   103
Footnotes   104

Part III   Planning and Controlling

Chapter 6   Managerial Decision Making   109
Learning Objectives   110
Thought Starters   110
The Specialty Items   110
What Is a Decision?   112
Conditions under Which Decisions Are Made   114
Steps in the Rational Decision-Making Process   118
Some Psychological Factors in the Decision-Making Process   122
The Descriptive Approach to Decision Making   124
Effective Decision Making with Subordinates   125
Implications for the Manager   127
Review   129
The President's Decision   129
Footnotes   130

Chapter 7   Organizational Goals and Objectives   135
Learning Objectives   136
Thought Starters   136
General Hospital   136
The Importance of Goals and Objectives   137
Characteristics of Good Objectives   138
Organizations Have Multiple and Continuing Objectives   140
Hierarchy of Objectives   142

"Official" versus "Actual" Objectives   143
Objectives in a Changing World   145
Management by Objectives   146
Implications for the Manager   149
Review   151
The Marshall Company   151
Footnotes   152

Chapter 8   Strategic and Tactical Planning   **157**
Learning Objectives   158
Thought Starters   158
The Sears Story: The Best Laid Plans . . .   158
What Is Strategic Planning?   159
Who Does Planning?   162
The Importance of Planning   163
Types of Plans   166
Contingent Strategic Planning: Developing Scenarios   168
Steps in Long-Range Strategic Planning   169
Difficulties with Planning   173
Implications for the Manager   174
Review   176
Radio Shack International   176
Footnotes   177

Chapter 9   Controlling   **181**
Learning Objectives   182
Thought Starters   182
Lavelle's Private War   182
What Is "Controlling"?   183
The Basic Control Process   185
Steps in the Control Process   186
Ten Characteristics of Effective Controls   189
Extent and Pervasiveness of Controls   191
Indirect and Direct Control   193
Behavioral Aspects of Managerial Control Systems   194
Implications for the Manager   197
Review   198
Phantoms Fill Boy Scout Lists   198
Footnotes   199

Chapter 10   Analytical Aids to Decision Making,
**   Planning, and Controlling**   **203**
Learning Objectives   204
Thought Starters   204
National Airlines   204
Models   205
Operations Research (OR)   207
Tools and Techniques Used in Operations Research   209
Limitations of Operations Research   216
Implications for the Manager   217
Review   219
Decisions at B-Mart   219
Footnoes   220

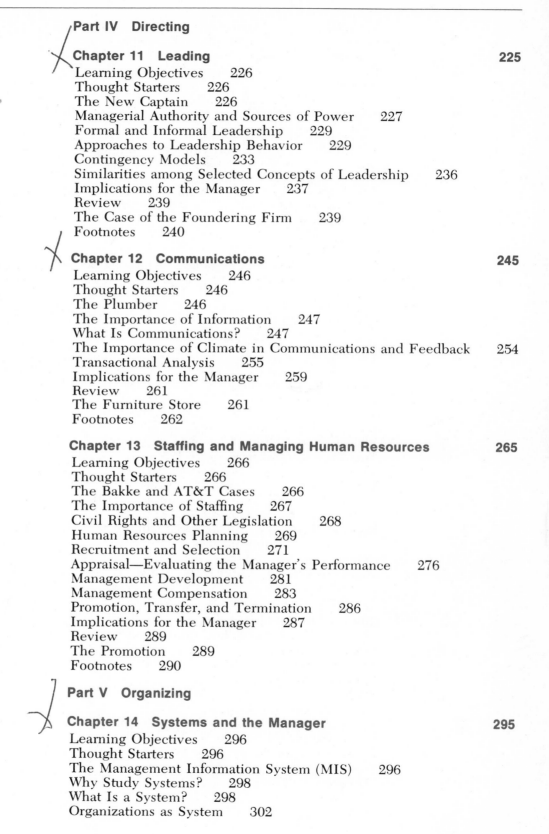

Part IV   Directing

Chapter 11   Leading   **225**
Learning Objectives   226
Thought Starters   226
The New Captain   226
Managerial Authority and Sources of Power   227
Formal and Informal Leadership   229
Approaches to Leadership Behavior   229
Contingency Models   233
Similarities among Selected Concepts of Leadership   236
Implications for the Manager   237
Review   239
The Case of the Foundering Firm   239
Footnotes   240

Chapter 12   Communications   **245**
Learning Objectives   246
Thought Starters   246
The Plumber   246
The Importance of Information   247
What Is Communications?   247
The Importance of Climate in Communications and Feedback   254
Transactional Analysis   255
Implications for the Manager   259
Review   261
The Furniture Store   261
Footnotes   262

Chapter 13   Staffing and Managing Human Resources   **265**
Learning Objectives   266
Thought Starters   266
The Bakke and AT&T Cases   266
The Importance of Staffing   267
Civil Rights and Other Legislation   268
Human Resources Planning   269
Recruitment and Selection   271
Appraisal—Evaluating the Manager's Performance   276
Management Development   281
Management Compensation   283
Promotion, Transfer, and Termination   286
Implications for the Manager   287
Review   289
The Promotion   289
Footnotes   290

Part V   Organizing

Chapter 14   Systems and the Manager   **295**
Learning Objectives   296
Thought Starters   296
The Management Information System (MIS)   296
Why Study Systems?   298
What Is a System?   298
Organizations as System   302

Organizational Subsystems   304
Implications for the Manager   309
Review   311
The Pajama Game   311
Footnotes   312

Chapter 15   Basic Propositions of Organizing   315
Learning Objectives   316
Thought Starters   316
The Osage Plant   316
Division of Labor   318
Horizontal Specialization (Departmentation)   319
Span of Control   322
Authority   324
The Dynamics of Specialization and Coordination—
   First-Level Supervisor   326
Classical Principles of Vertical Coordination   328
Organization Charts and Manuals   331
Implications for the Manager   333
Review   334
Benton's Department Store   334
Footnotes   335

Chapter 16   Designing the Organizational Structure   339
Learning Objectives   340
Thought Starters   340
The Electronics Products Division   340
Some Basic Factors in Organizational Design   342
A Contingency Model   346
A Contingency Approach to Organizational Design   349
Implications for the Manager   355
Review   357
Mangerial Choice   357
Footnotes   358

Part VI   Organizations and Change

Chapter 17   Managing Creativity   363
Learning Objectives   364
Thought Starters   364
Pet Rock   364
The Importance of Managing the Creative Process   365
Steps in the Creative Process   367
Managing Creativity   370
Techniques for Increasing Organizational Creativity   371
Creativity and Stability   373
The Process of Implementation   374
Implications for the Manager   375
Review   376
The Gunnery Problem   376
Footnotes   377

Chapter 18   Managing Conflict   381
Learning Objectives   382
Thought Starters   382

The President's Decision   382
Changing Philosophies about Conflict   383
Conflict, Competition, and Cooperation   385
Some Sources of Organizational Conflict   386
Managing to Reduce Conflict   388
Stimulating Constructive Conflict   391
Role, Role Conflict, and Role Ambiguity   394
Implications for the Manager   395
Review   397
The E. F. Howard Company   397
Footnotes   398

Chapter 19   Managing Change   **403**
Learning Objectives   404
Thought Starters   404
The Instrument Department   404
The Accelerating Pace of Change   405
Structural and Process Change   407
Change and Organization Development   410
Managing Change through Organization Development (OD)   412
Some Problems with Managing Change   418
Implications for the Manager   419
Review   420
A New Approach to Making Pet Food   420
Footnotes   421

Part VII   The Organization and the Environment

Chapter 20   Values, Power, and Ethics   **427**
Learning Objectives   428
Thought Starters   428
A Crisis of Conscience   428
The Importance of Values   429
The Importance of Power and Politics   432
The Importance of Ethics   435
Implications for the Manager   440
Review   441
To Tell or Not to Tell   441
Footnotes   442

Chapter 21   Managers and the Environment   **445**
Learning Objectives   446
Thought Starters   446
The Alaskan Pipeline   446
The Corporate Dilemma   447
Changing Concepts of the Economic System   449
The Interpenetrating Systems Model   451
Corporate Social Responsibility and the Social Audit   456
Implications for the Manager   459
Review   461
The Chevymobile   461
Footnotes   462

Chapter 22   The International Environment   **467**
Learning Objectives   468
Thought Starters   468

Coca-Cola   468
International and Multinational Firms   469
Comparative Management versus International Management   473
Environmental Constraints   475
Foreign Management Assignments   479
Implications for the Manager   479
Review   481
Laker Skytrain   481
Footnotes   482

Part VIII   A Conclusion and a Beginning

Chapter 23   Effective Managing—A Comparison and a Summary 487
Learning Objectives   488
Thought Starters   488
The Bureau of Vital Statistics   488
Managing Business Organizations (the Private Sector)   489
Managing in the Public Sector   493
Managing Third Sector Organizations   497
Managing—Some Common Functions   499
Effective Managing—A Review and a Summary   500
Implications for the Manager   503
Review   504
The College President   504
Footnotes   506

Chapter 24   Career Planning and Development   **509**
Learning Objectives   510
Thought Starters   510
The Interview   510
Career Consciousness   511
Career Stages   513
The First Job   517
Organizational Socialization   518
Equal Employment and Careers   519
The Dual-Career Family   520
Developing Initial Personal Career Plans   521
Implications for the Individual   523
Review   525
The Raymond Chemical Company   525
Footnotes   526
Careers: An Annotated Bibliography   529

Appendix: Operations Management   **531**
The Operations Functions   531
Organizational Processes   534
The Operations Function in Context   535
Planning and Operations Management   536
Operations Management in Relation to Other Functions   537
Designing Operating Systems   540
Planning and Control of Operations   543
An Operating System in Action—Book Publishing   547

Glossary   **553**

Name Index   **573**

Subject Index   **581**

Preface

The Purpose of the Book

This book is written with several purposes in mind: first, to acquaint students with basic concepts about organizations of all types, including private, governmental, and not-for-profit; second, to acquaint students with basic concepts and ideas about managers in organizations. The book begins at the supervisory level, where readers can more readily identify, and then moves up the ladder to the overall corporate point of view. The third primary purpose of this book is to teach students about the art and science of management. The book stresses the nature and function of management and management skills that are applicable in a wide variety of organizations and organizational levels.

Last, and perhaps significantly, the book is intended to be readable and enjoyable to the student. Management books tend to be of two kinds. One type gives the student only a superficial treatment of management. The book may be enjoyable but have little real content. Other books have a great deal of substantive content but quote so heavily from "esoteric" research that they are almost impossible to read or comprehend. This book is designed to strike a balance between the two. It draws heavily upon the research done in the field, but summarizes and synthesizes the material in a way that makes it easily understandable. Liberal use of cases and incidents helps the student to relate the concepts to personal experience.

The Teaching Approach of the Book

To be effective, a book must emphasize both the *content* of management (concepts, principles, tools) and the *process* of teaching management (learning objectives, cases, critical concepts). For this reason, each chapter begins with a case, frequently drawn from sources with which the student is already familiar. The case arouses interest, highlights the material contained in the chapter, and provides the student with a reference point based upon past experience and knowledge. Learning objectives at the beginning of the chapter establish the reason for reading besides just getting to the end. They highlight accomplishments expected from students. Presenting the critical concepts sets the stage for the presentation of the material on each topic. The student who can deal with the learning objectives and use the critical concepts has understood the basic content of the chapter. The thought starters are useful teaching tools as motivators and lively discussion points for student learners. Through the use of thought starters, the student is encouraged to use actual experience to help understand the textual material.

Within the chapter, examples from real life are liberally used to allow the student to relate the concepts to actual occurrences in the real world. Many of these are drawn from newspaper or popular journal articles and show the application of theory to a variety of different organizations. Again, the purpose is not only to highlight the material but to highlight it in a way that ties the ideas to the personal experience and knowledge of the student. Each chapter has a section called *Implications for the Manager*. More than a summary, this section contains recommendations for the modern manager to use the material in an effective manner. Review questions at the end of the chapter are designed to stimulate discussion or have the student engage in a project which will further increase knowledge of the textual material.

A case at the end of the chapter provides the opportunity for the student to again apply the knowledge learned from the text to specific situations. Many of the cases at the end of the chapters are taken from episodes published in newspapers or popular journals such as *Time* and *Business Week*.

The Plan of the Book

The book has eight parts, each with two to four chapters, as well as a major appendix on operations management. Part I describes the importance of the manager and examines managerial functions and tasks in a variety of organizations. This part also "debunks" some popular myths about managers and the evolution of management thought, including myths contained in Frederick Taylor's early book, *Scientific Management*. Part II describes people at work and provides the manager with tools to understand, predict, and manage the behavior of individuals and groups.

Part III describes the vitally important managerial functions of decision making, establishing organizational goals, planning, and controlling. The last chapter in Part III describes a number of analytical aids that can be used to improve the performance of these management functions.

Part IV describes how managers lead organizations, how they communicate, and how they staff organizations. This section provides guidelines for managers to become more effective in directing others.

In Part V, principles of organizing are examined. The organization can be analyzed from a systems point of view. Basic guidelines are given for organizing and improving organizational structure.

Organizations cannot remain static. As a result, Part VI describes how organizations and individuals can become more creative, how conflict can be productively handled, and how organizational change and development can be brought about.

Organizations do not exist in isolation. Rather, they affect, and are affected by, their environment. The first chapter in Part VII examines the crucial issues of ethics, power, and politics. The second chapter provides suggestions for the effective manager to understand and work with the environment outside the organization, and treats the growing importance of social responsibility. The final chapter in Part VII shows how the organization affects, and is affected by, the international environment.

Part VIII compares and contrasts management and managers in a wide variety of organizations and provides students with suggestions for personal career planning and development.

Many modern texts do not cover the subject of operations management in a complete fashion. This book covers operations management in a comprehensive appendix, tying the material back to the main body of the text.

Ancillary Materials

In addition to the book itself, there are a number of additional items available as aids to students and instructors.

1. *Study Guide.* This supplement, written by David Gray and Pat Long, outlines the key sections of *The Modern Manager*, provides students with self-testing questions for each chapter, and includes cases and experiential exercises.

2. *Casebook.* The book, *Case Problems in Management*, was prepared by Randall S. Schuler and Edgar F. Huse to accompany the text. It contains 39 cases, covering a variety of organizations and problems.

3. *Instructor's Manual.* A very complete, 220-page manual is available. It outlines the chapter, provides teaching suggestions, discusses the cases, and provides suggestions for end-of-chapter questions, as well as additional essay questions.

4. *Test Bank.* A comprehensive series of objective questions is available to users of the text. The questions have been class-tested, and include both multiple choice and discussion questions.

5. *Transparency Masters.* Transparency masters have been made of every figure and table in the text. Additional masters have also been included.

Acknowledgments   Writing, reviewing, editing, and producing a book is a complex process. Although only one name appears as author, many people made significant contributions to the publication of this book. A number of reviewers made valuable comments, recommendations, and suggestions about the content, structure, and style of the book. I would especially like to acknowledge the help of Don Hellriegel (Texas A&M University) and John Slocum (The Pennsylvania State University). Others who made significant comments include: Charles Beavin (Miami-Dade Community College); Nicholas J. Beltsos (Eastern Michigan University); Richard Chase (University of Arizona); Richard Cosier (Indiana University); Jeffrey D. Ford (Indiana University—Purdue University at Indianapolis); David Gray (The University of Texas at Arlington); David Gustafson (Boston University—Brussels); Douglas T. Hall (Northwestern University); Francine S. Hall; Ed Harrick (Southern Illinois University, Edwardsville); Jane Hass (University of Florida); Richard E. Kopelman (The Bernard M. Baruch College, CUNY); Alan H. Leader (Western Michigan University); Mary Lippitt (University of Minnesota); Kenneth M. Long (Bryant College); Pat Long (Tarrant County Junior College); Vincent Luchsinger (Texas Tech University); J. Stan Mendenhall (Oregon State University); Jack L. Mendleson (Arizona State University); Gail Miller (Otterbein College); James H. Morris (University of Alabama); Edward A. Nicholson (Wright State University); Joseph Nowlin (University of Wisconsin—Oshkosh); Chad Pierson (San Diego State University); James E. Post (Boston University); Karl G. Rahdert (Bowling Green State University); Robert Rosen (University of South Carolina); Vijay Sathe (Harvard University); Randall S. Schuler (Ohio State University); Leete Thompson (California State University, Sacramento); Paul Thompson (Brigham Young University); Warren A. Thrasher (University of Georgia); David D. VanFleet (Texas A&M University); and Daniel A. Wren (University of Oklahoma).

Colleagues at Boston College who gave generously of their time and ideas include: Jean Bartunek, James Bowditch, Thomas Dunn, Judith Gordon, Walter Klein, David Murphy, Charles Olivieri, Alan Thayer, and Arnold Weinstein; Pearl Alberts, reference librarian, who can find the most obscure references; Rand Macksamie and Bob Wehrmann, graduate students, for their assistance with the details of the book; Kim Bruyn, whose library research and other assistance was invaluable; Jean Kochis, for her editorial and many other skills; Geri Kenney, who gave secretarial support; and Betty Fast, who gave not only secretarial support but also held things together at crucial times. I would also like to thank John Neuhauser, Dean, for his support and comments; and the Reverends J. Donald Monan, S. J., and Charles Donovan, S. J., for their encouragement.

I would also like to express appreciation to the staff at West Publishing Co. for their help and encouragement in the undertaking. Last, but not least, I extend thanks and appreciation to my wife, Mary Huse, whose understanding, encouragement, and occasional harrassment made this book possible.

Conclusion

Management is, in a real sense, the cornerstone of effective organizations; good management is vitally important to the health of organizations, the nation, and the world. Because of its importance, management should be widely and thoroughly understood, but this is easier said than done. The field is highly complex, and is undergoing constant change through new knowledge and in response to economic conditions. I sincerely hope that *The Modern Manager* will contribute to a better understanding of organizations and the science and art of managing.

Edgar F. Huse
Chestnut Hill, Massachusetts
February, 1979

The Modern Manager

Part I

The Modern Manager

Chapter 1

The Importance of the Manager

Jaws

Systems and the Manager

What Is a Manager?

Where Are Managers?

The Three Management Levels
    The Operations Level
    The Managerial-Administrative Level
    The Strategic Level
    Distinguishing among the Levels

Basic Characteristics of Managerial Work
    A Variety of Activities
    Preference for Active and Nonroutine Tasks
    Preference for Oral Communications
    Involvement in a Series of Communications Networks and
        Contacts

The Personal Style of the Manager

Managing—A Rewarding Career
    Challenge and Meaningful Work
    Power
    Prestige and Self-esteem
    Opportunity for a Progressive Career
    Financial Reward

Implications for the Manager

Review

Frye Boots

Learning Objectives

When you have finished reading and studying this chapter, you should be able to:

1. Define the term *manager* and give examples of managers in several different types of organizations.
2. Identify the basic characteristics of an organization as a system.
3. Describe an organization in systems terms.
4. Give several examples of the importance of managers to organizations.
5. Identify major areas where managers work.
6. Describe the three management levels.
7. Describe the basic characteristics of managerial work.
8. Identify the rewarding aspects of a managerial career for yourself.
9. Define and be able to use the following concepts:

manager	technical level
system	managerial level
organization	strategic level

Thought Starters

1. How do you define the term *manager* now? What implications does the term have for you?
2. What do managers do that nonmanagers do not?
3. Where do managers generally work?
4. Is the conductor of an orchestra a manager? How about a movie director?

Jaws

Jaws, one of the most successful films ever produced, features a great white shark—one of nature's most efficient killing machines. *Jaws* is also an efficient entertainment machine and a great box office success. In the movie, a shark terrorizes the fictional town of Amity by attacking swimmers. Three men, including a police chief and a professional shark killer, attempt to kill the shark. The final battle is explosive.

Steven Spielberg was twenty-six when he was selected to direct the film. For four years, he had directed television productions, including episodes of *The Psychiatrist, Columbo,* and *Marcus Welby.* He progressed to directing (managing) movies, including a chiller called *The Sugarland Express*—the film that got him the job of directing *Jaws.* During the filming, he managed about 150 people, including the film crew, actors, technicians, scriptwriters, and the crews of ships and boats.

Although the movie was successful, its filming took twice as long as originally scheduled. The delay was due to a constant series of managerial problems that Spielberg had to solve.

One of the first problems was the location for shooting the movie. Martha's Vineyard, an island off the coast of Massachusetts, was picked because it closely resembled the fictional town of Amity. However, the choice was made in the winter. What Spielberg did not realize then was that in summer, when the filming was actually to take place, Martha's Vineyard is one of the most popular ports on the Atlantic coast. Literally hundreds of boats enter and leave the harbor each day.

During the filming, shots were frequently interrupted by curiosity seekers in small craft sailing too close to the cameras. How do you maintain suspense if a family of four is picnicking on a sailboat only fifty feet away from a "dramatic struggle"?

Another managerial challenge was Bruce, the mechanical shark. Actually, there were three sharks. Each weighed 1½ tons and cost about $150,000, and each was used for different movements (right-to-left, left-to-right) and different scenes. Thirteen technicians controlled the shark by means of a hundred-foot-long cable from a twelve-ton steel platform that had to be anchored to the ocean floor. The first time out, Bruce sank; the second time, the hydraulic system exploded. Only constant tinkering kept Bruce in action.

Planning and coordination were major managerial challenges. Each day, a flotilla set out to sea. One ship was for Bruce. Another was for the technicians handling the controls. Still others were for the camera crews and actors. There were even supply boats and an old ferry. The journey was made six days a week from May through October. Some days, the flotilla came back with no film at all. The failures were caused by Bruce, the weather, the small craft in the area, and a variety of other problems.

Organizing the script required constant work and tinkering. Versions were rewritten nightly before the next day's filming. Real sharks were hard to find; a dead one needed for the finale was finally flown up from Florida. It hung on the Edgartown dock for four days, creating a powerful stench. Local townsfolk retaliated by leaving dead fish on the doorsteps of the houses where the members of the cast were living.

Theft, curiosity seekers, weather, and a myriad of other problems aggravated the situation. Almost everything that could go wrong did. Spielberg had to reassure a despondent cast. Nevertheless, the daily trips continued until the last scenes were filmed in October.

Many members of the crew and cast took vacations off the island, but Spielberg never left. Although he put on a good front for the cast and crew, he was afraid that if he did leave, he would not come back. Finally, the job was done and he left the island, vowing firmly that he would never return. He has since directed *Close Encounters of the Third Kind*.[1]

Steven Spielberg illustrates the importance of the manager. Without his efforts, *Jaws* would never have been completed. Managers are important because they make certain that the activities of the organization are directed and coordinated, that the tasks are accomplished, and that the goals and objectives of the organization are reached.

In the rest of this chapter, we will examine the role of the manager in the organization, define what a manager is, and describe where managers work. We will then explore some basic characteristics of managerial work and look into the rewards of being a manager.

Systems and the Manager

Before discussing the manager as such, we should define *organization*, since managers do their work in organizations. What is an organization? It is easier to give examples than to define the term. General Motors is an organization. The local grocery store, bank, municipal water system, hospital, and TV station are organizations. The *TV Guide* is produced by an organization.

Organizations, which provide the goods and services we need, are all managed. Although they vary in nature and technology (for example, the technology of producing breakfast cereal is very different from that of directing a movie or creating electronic calculators), all organizations with which we come in contact have two things in common. They have managers to ensure that their objectives are reached, and they have a

Organization

common definition. For the purpose of this book, then, the formal **organization** is defined according to the classic questions of who, what, when, why, and how.

Who: Individuals and groups.
What: Human, financial, and other resources.
When: Over time.
Why: To achieve common goals and objectives by operating as a complex system.
How: By coordinating the operations and activities of a number of people.

One of the most important concepts in this definition is that of system. Stemming from general systems theory, an organization as a **system** can be defined as "a set of interdependent parts which together make up the whole because each contributes something and receives something from the whole, which in turn is interdependent with the larger environment. Survival of the system is taken to be the goal."[2]

The basic outline of a system is given in Figure 1.1. As this figure shows, organizations exist in the environment, are managed, and have inputs, operations, outputs, feedback, and boundaries. Although these are discussed in more detail in Chapter 14, they will be briefly described here to set the stage.

Inputs: Human or other resources coming into the system or subsystem, such as information, energy, and materials.

Operations: The process of transforming an input into a modified or different form. A manufacturing company, for example, has elaborate mechanisms for transforming incoming raw materials into finished goods.

Outputs: The results of what is transformed by the system. A bank may receive inputs (deposits), transform them (through record keeping), and export the output (money) to customers in the form of automobile and mortgage loans.

Feedback: Information regarding the actual performance or results of a system's activities. This information is used to control the future functioning of the system. Perhaps the most common example of feedback in operation is the house thermostat, which keeps the temperature of the house at a predetermined level.

Boundary: The borders or limits of the system. The boundary in Figure 1.1 is shown through dotted lines, since an organization is an *open system;* that is, it receives information, energy, material, and other resources from the external environment and exports finished goods, services, or ideas to it.

Subsystem: Part or unit of the system. For example, the registrar's office of a university can be considered a subsystem of the university. The university can in turn be considered a subsystem in interaction with other subsystems in the larger environment. Thus an organization can be considered a system in its own right, with a number of subsystems, or part of a larger system.

Synergism: The capability of the organization, as a system, to accomplish more than any of its subsystems. (The whole is more than the sum of its parts.) For example, supermarkets can provide shoppers with more ease and convenience than can individual specialty stores.

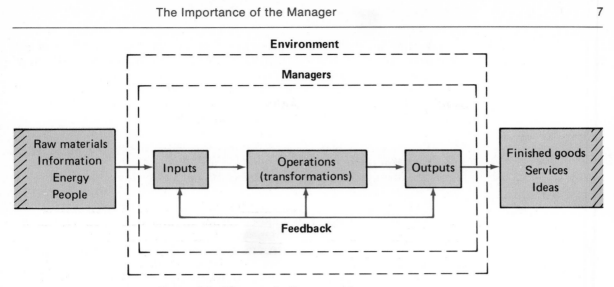

Figure 1.1 The organization as a system

Manager: The term itself is defined in the next section. But from a systems point of view, managers must coordinate the activities either of the larger system or of one or more subsystems within the organization. They serve as the important "linking pins" among the goods, services, and needs of society and among the financial, human, and other resources necessary to fulfill these needs. A capable manager is one who can provide effective coordination and guidance to meet the needs of both the organization and the society.

There is no doubt about the importance of managers to organizations. There is always a shortage of capable managers, whether the economy is up or down. All types of organizations, not only those in the profit-making sector, require managers. The constant and frustrating searches for welfare agency heads, school superintendents, college deans, city managers, and hospital administrators indicate that the nonprofit sector also realizes the importance of good managers.

For example, a newspaper report suggests that New York City is suffering from a loss of middle managers that is threatening the future delivery of services. Because of wage freezes, the uncertainty of continued employment, and other factors, many middle managers are quitting. The director of the city's Office of Budget and Management reports that the wrong people are leaving: those who are competent and capable. As a result, the effectiveness of the municipal government is being reduced. He explains: "The sense of continuity and institutional memory and context gets lost. You have to search all over for someone who remembers what was done and why."[3] As an illustration, the loss of good middle managers has forced the city's Health Department to substantially cut its services in a variety of areas.

What Is a Manager?

When asked the question "What is a manager?" many people reply, "A manager is a person who gets things done through other people." This response does not define the term *manager,* because it is too broad and vague. Salespeople, buyers, and others get things done through people but are not managers. Police directing traffic around the scene of an accident may be getting things done through people, but they are not managers.

A number of different terms are used synonymously for *manager*, including *director, administrator, supervisor*, and *president*. The term *manager* is used more frequently in profit-making organizations, while the terms *administrator* and *director* are used more widely in government and nonprofit organizations such as universities, hospitals, and social work agencies. (Some of the similarities and differences among managerial jobs in different organizations are described in Chapter 23.)

What, then, is a manager? When used collectively, the term *management* refers to those people who are responsible for making and implementing decisions within the system or subsystems (work units) in order to coordinate the activities of people in accomplishing the objectives of the organization. An individual manager is a person who works to accomplish the goals of the organization and who directly supervises one or more people in a formal organization. *Direct supervision* means that one or more people report to and work for the manager. One of the manager's basic functions is to establish and maintain the conditions under which the interdependent activities of individuals and groups can be coordinated to accomplish group and organizational goals.

A manager, then, can be a prime minister, an assembly line supervisor in a manufacturing company, the director of a symphony orchestra, a department head in a university, or a manager of a local service station. All supervise other people in a formal work unit (the entire organization—a system—or part of the organization—a subsystem). Salespersons, engineers, computer programmers, college instructors, and orchestra violinists make decisions and work toward accomplishing organizational goals. However, they are not managers, since they do not supervise others.

Where Are Managers?

Many people who think of managers in organizations picture the managers of large manufacturing corporations, such as General Motors, General Electric, and Westinghouse. When asked how many nonfarm U.S. businesses are in manufacturing, a number of people put the amount at greater than 50 percent; some suggest as high as 80 percent. Yet, reports put out by the U.S. government tell a different story, as the following figures indicate:

- In terms of nonfarm firms, about 5 percent are manufacturing; 16 percent are financial, real estate, and insurance; 29 percent are wholesaling and retailing; and a whopping 34 percent are service organizations.
- Of all U.S. businesses, about 86 percent had gross receipts of less than $100,000 per year, while only about 2 percent had gross receipts of more than $1 million.
- From 1970 to 1975 the number of laborers employed in manufacturing *decreased* by about 20 percent, the number of employees in service occupations increased by about 13 percent, and the number of professional and technical workers in health care increased by about 33 percent.
- Only about one-tenth of 1 percent of U.S. businesses employ 2,500 or more people.
- Approximately 90 percent of manufacturing firms employ 100 or fewer people.
- Approximately 98 percent of all U.S. firms employ fewer than 50 people.

The federal government is the single largest employer in the United States, with about 2,700,000 employees. State and local governments employ about 12,500,000 employees.[4]

Table 1.1 shows the number and percent of professional, technical, and managerial employees by organization category. Manufacturing employs about 19 million of the approximately 79 million professional and technical employees, for about 23 percent of the total. While 36 percent of all managers are employed in wholesale and retail organizations, only 14 percent are in manufacturing and 20 percent in public administration.

There are slightly more than 1 million businesses in the United States. Of these, about 980,000 are family owned or dominated, including some of the largest. For example, over 42 percent of the largest publicly-held corporations are controlled by either one person or a family, and another 17 percent are "possibly" under family control. In addition, there is another major category of large "privately"-owned companies: organizations with fewer than five hundred shareholders. These companies (which are not required to disclose financial figures) include Hallmark Cards, the Hearst Corporation, Cargill, and the Bechtel Corporation.[5] Some well-known family-managed firms include the H. J. Heinz Company, which has over $1 billion in sales; Triangle Publications, which owns the *Morning Telegraph*, *TV Guide*, and *Seventeen*; and Kaiser Industries.

A review of these figures indicates that statistically a college graduate is likely to work in a small firm rather than a big one; in a family-owned or controlled organization rather than a publicly-owned or controlled one; in government or wholesale or retail firms rather than in manufacturing.

The Three Management Levels

Every organization must function on at least three distinct but overlapping levels or subsystems, with each level having a somewhat different managerial focus and emphasis.[6] The three levels—operations, managerial, and strategic—are shown in Figure 1.2.

For example, a typical corporation will have a president and a group of vice-presidents or similar executives reporting to the president. The

Table 1.1 Location of professional, technical, and managerial employees by organization category

Organization category	Number of professional and technical employees (in thousands)	Percent of total	Number of managers and administrators (in thousands)	Percent of total
Manufacturing	18,956	23	1,270	14
Wholesale and retail	17,694	22	3,397	36
Public administration	14,948	19	1,854	20
Service	14,644	19	1,084	12
Transportation	4,509	6	419	4
Finance, real estate, and insurance	4,316	5	855	9
Construction	3,594	5	428	4
Mining	483	1	65	1

Source: Data compiled from U.S. Department of Labor, Bureau of Labor Statistics, *Handbook of Labor Statistics*, Bulletin 1966 (Washington, D.C.: Government Printing Office, 1977).

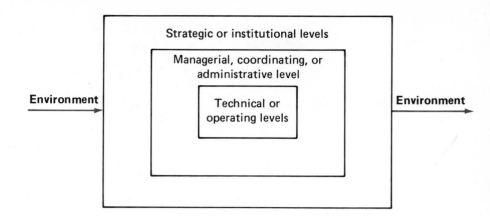

Figure 1.2 The three levels of management

vice-presidents may, in turn, supervise managers of departments or divisions. Lower down in the organization are managers who supervise specific functions or areas within departments. A typical school system will have a school committee, a superintendent of schools, and a staff of people who specialize in a single area, such as curriculum development. Below the superintendent are the principals of the various grade and high schools. The teachers in each school report to the principal and may or may not supervise teachers' aides and others.

In these two examples, the distinctions among levels can be seen in broad outline. The board of directors, the school committee, and probably the president and the superintendent are working at the strategic, or institutional, level. The managers of departments or divisions are working at the managerial, or coordinating, level. Managers of specialized functions or areas within a department are working at the technical, or operating, level, as are the various individual school principals. Those persons who work at relatively specific and routine tasks under the direction of a manager are usually called operative personnel and generally are not included as part of management. Although some vice-presidents of banks and insurance companies have no subordinates, they are still classified as part of management.

The technical, managerial, and strategic levels will be expanded upon and defined more clearly in the following sections.

The Operations Level

Every formal organization performs certain operations functions or operations in the actual production of goods and services. In an educational organization, the operations or technical function consists of the process of teaching. In a government bureau, it can consist of the administrative process that is directly related to the public. For example, the Social Security Administration produces and mails checks to social security recipients. The Internal Revenue Service collects taxes from individuals and organizations. A business organization physically produces goods or performs a service.

Therefore, in any organization there is a suborganization, the **technical level,** that concentrates on performing the operations function effectively. In the case of physical production, there is the processing of material and the supervision of those operations. The Social Security Administration must make certain that the checks are properly handled.

A state welfare department must try to make certain that only those who are qualified receive welfare checks.

Thus, the operations function is at the core of the organization, as Figure 1.2 suggests. It is concerned with the development, use, and interaction of resources (people, facilities, information, materials, money, and ideas) to provide the goods, services, or ideas for which the organization was established. The operations manager is involved in the managerial activities required to select, design, operate, control, and update the process. Thus, the operations manager is concerned with developing the best allocation and combination of resources in order to produce the desired product, service, or idea, in the proper amount, at the proper time, and at the desired level of quality. The topic of operations management is sufficiently important that it will be highlighted in the Appendix.

The Managerial-Administrative Level

As organizations get bigger and more complex, so also do their problems—especially those of coordinating the activities of people and determining which products will be made. In a school system, teachers must be selected and appointed to teach particular classes. Classrooms must be provided and courses scheduled for particular times. Maintenance and janitorial services must be scheduled so they do not interfere with teaching. The Social Security Administration does not mail out checks to just anyone; it mails them to specific categories of persons. The plant does not just produce a product; it produces a specific product for specific purposes. These and other problem areas are handled by the **managerial level** (sometimes called the **administrative level**), which performs two functions: administering and servicing the technical level and mediating between the technical level and those who use the "products,"—including customers, welfare recipients, and unhappy taxpayers. The parent who is dissatisfied with the teacher goes to the principal or the superintendent.

Decisions made at this level determine how the operations level operates. The payroll department of an organization does not determine how much salary a particular manager gets; it only makes out the checks.

This is, of course, a two-way process. For the operations level to do the work, the managerial-administrative level must satisfy "needs," such as the need for the right materials and the need of ensuring that the product is sold.

The Strategic Level

A formal organization must also operate in a wider social environment; thus it must be approved by society to achieve certain goals and objectives. As part of society, it is responsible to society. No organization is completely independent; all must be, in the large sense, guided and controlled by the structure and agencies of the community.

The **strategic level** controls the managerial level and mediates between the organization and the broader community served by the organization. Examples of the strategic level are the boards of trustees of nonprofit organizations, school boards that represent the community and guide the school superintendent, boards of directors of business corporations, and, in many cases, organization presidents or administrators.

The strategic level is concerned with making certain that the managerial level operates properly within the broader social systems—which, in the final analysis, are the source of legitimation and higher-level support that make it possible for the organization to attain its goals. The strategic level also determines the long-range direction of the organization and works to influence the larger environment. For example, an oil company may lobby to have laws changed in its favor, or a school board may impress on the public the need for a new school building.

Distinguishing among the Levels

Clearly, distinguishing among these three levels can help us understand the differing activities of the manager at different levels of the organization. Just as clearly, the division of an organization into only three levels is somewhat arbitrary, and many managers cannot be fitted neatly into only one level. For example, Stephen Spielberg was acting at the technical level when he helped to rewrite the script, at the coordinating or managerial level when he reassured and coordinated the work of the actors and technicians, and at the strategic level when he chose the location for the filming and dealt with the townspeople.

In larger organizations, there is a more clear-cut separation among the three levels. For example, as Figure 1.2 shows, the operations level is generally at the core of the organization. Its subsystems are relatively protected from the firm's external environment. The coordinating and strategic levels usually have more contact with and inputs from this environment. Indeed, the head of Coca-Cola spends about half his time visiting foreign countries to deal with other governments, understand local laws and customs, and expand the market for Coke, which sells 60 percent of its soft drinks overseas.[7]

Another set of terms used widely in business and other organizations includes *top management, middle management,* and *first-level management.* As Figure 1.3 shows, the term *top management* or *executive,* corresponds to the strategic, or third, level. The term *middle management* corresponds to the managerial and coordinating, or second, level. And the term *first-level management* corresponds to the operating or technical, or first, level. The line between each level is dotted to show that the distinction between each level is not always clear-cut, as we saw in the case of Stephen Spielberg.

Managers can also be described as functional or general. A *functional manager* has charge of a specialized area of operations, such as sales, production, purchasing, nursing, or university registration. A *general manager* has charge over more than one specialized area or function. For example, the assembly line supervisor or head nurse is usually a functional manager. The operating head of the Chevrolet Division of General Motors may have charge of a number of different units. Usually, but not always, technical or first-level managers tend to be functional managers; coordinating and strategic managers tend to be general managers.

Thus, the word *manager* is a broad one, covering all levels from the strategic to the operating—from the president or chairperson to the first-level supervisor, from top management to lower management. Since many first-level supervisors are promoted from the ranks, this book will concentrate more on the higher-level management jobs that ordinarily require a college degree.

Basic Characteristics of Managerial Work

In spite of the importance of the manager to the organization, relatively few studies have directly examined what managers really do. The total number of managers actually studied is still small, although the studies have included managing directors, top executives, middle- and lower-level managers and foremen.[8] Some basic characteristics seem to apply to managers in all types of organizations; they include hard work on a variety of activities, preference for active and nonroutine tasks,

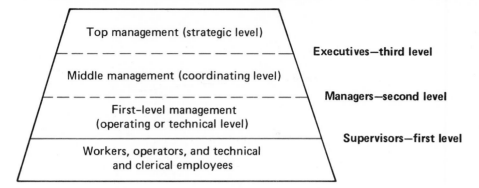

Figure 1.3   The different levels of management

direct personal relationships, and involvement in a series of communications networks.

A Variety of Activities

Many jobs require specialization. A machine operator may spend weeks making a single part; a computer programmer may spend months designing a single program. Most managers' activities are different, usually including more variety. For example, foremen may average almost six hundred different incidents each day (an average of one every forty-eight seconds)![9] As a result, they have to handle many pressing problems quickly. Often they have little time to plan, and sometimes their general lack of planning is the cause of the frenetic pace.

Managers' actions are also of short duration. For foremen the time span of activities may be on the order of seconds; for chief executives it may be somewhat longer. Half the activities are completed in fewer than nine minutes, and only a tenth take more than an hour. There is no question that managers work hard. A study of 160 managers found that they had little time to spend alone to think. On the average, during the four weeks of the study, the managers were alone only nine times for a half hour or more without interruptions. True breaks were seldom taken. Coffee was drunk during meetings, and lunchtime was almost always devoted to formal or informal meetings.[10]

Managing an organization or part of an organization is taxing. There is a lot to be done and relatively little time to do it. Faced with a variety of activities, the manager must be prepared to shift from one subject to another frequently and quickly.

One reason managers work hard is the challenge of the job, the responsibility for the success of the particular unit. There are few milestones along the way where the manager can say, "The job is done." The engineer can finish a particular design on a particular day, and the lawyer can win or lose a case at a specific time. But the manager's job is like "Old Man River"—it just keeps going. The manager can never be sure whether a little more effort might not contribute significantly to the success of the organization or its unit.

Preference for Active and Nonroutine Tasks

Managers seek out the more active, nonroutine elements of the job, particularly activities that are specific and current. They react to the "hot" information they receive informally and frequently from unscheduled meetings, the telephone, and similar sources. When such information comes in, it receives top priority. Managers will redesign their workdays or shift priorities immediately on the basis of this information. Because of their thirst for current information, mail and routine reports receive relatively little attention. Most reports deal mainly with the past, and the manager is more concerned with the here-and-now.

When a chief executive hears about a competitor's action, the response is immediate. When a factory supervisor hears of a possible parts shortage, the response is just as immediate. Because the manager wants "hot" information, there is a willingness to accept a high degree of uncertainty. Hearsay, gossip, and speculation are an important part of the manager's informational diet.

Managers react first to whatever is definite and concrete in their schedules. Thus it does little good to say to a busy manager, "I would like it next week," or "Let's get together to talk about the problem." Rather, specific times or deadlines should be established. For example, many executives carry appointment books with them. When they write down the appointment or meeting, they follow through on it. If they do not write it down, something else may take precedence.

Preference for Oral Communications

Managers strongly prefer oral communications. Almost all the research-based studies stress the high percentage of managerial time spent in such communications. Estimates are that about 60 to 80 percent of the manager's time is spent in conversation. Figure 1.4 indicates the amount of time and type of activities involving communications by top executives. The figure shows that scheduled meetings take up a high percentage of time. Such meetings can be held with individuals, small groups, or large groups, including people both within and outside the organization. Scheduled meetings tend to occur when a large amount of information needs to be transmitted, when the individuals are relatively unknown to the manager, or when scheduling a meeting is the only way to bring a number of people together.

Unscheduled meetings and telephone calls tend to be relatively short—the meetings usually lasting about twelve minutes and the phone calls about six. They are used to transmit information quickly, especially if the parties know each other relatively well. When problems suddenly arise, strategy is quickly developed or changed during a telephone call or unscheduled meeting. While these forms of communication take little time, they constitute about two-thirds of the manager's oral contacts.

Tours give the manager an opportunity to observe activity without prearrangement. However, while recognizing their importance and indicating that they want to increase the amount of time spent on tours, managers actually use them infrequently.

An important point is that, unlike other workers, the manager does not leave the meeting or the telephone to go back to work. These forms of communication are managerial work. The manager does not do research, assemble products, or develop computer programs. Rather, the manager's productive output is measured primarily in terms of using information to get the job done by other people.

One middle-level manager commented after a long and busy day, "What we have around here is wall-to-wall meetings." During that particular day, she had been able to spend about fifteen minutes at her desk. The rest of her time had been spent in meetings. On several occasions, she had been called out of meetings for telephone calls; and on the way to or from the meetings, she had spoken to perhaps a dozen other people. (The subject of communications is expanded on in Chapter 12.)

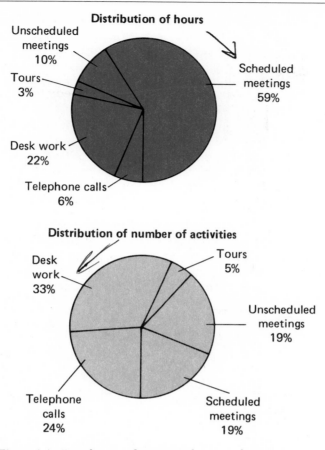

Figure 1.4 Distribution of managerial time and activities

Source: Fig. 4 (p. 39) from *The Nature of Managerial Work* by Henry
Mintzberg. Copyright © 1973 by Henry Mintzberg. Used by permission of
Harper & Row, Publishers, Inc.

**Involvement in a
Series of
Communications
Networks and
Contacts**

The manager is the center of a series of communications networks
involving superiors, subordinates, and people outside the work unit.
While the traditional literature concentrates on the relationship of managers to their own subordinates, actual research highlights the importance
of managers in dealing with horizontal work flow relationships. Managers do spend a considerable amount of time with their subordinates
(approximately one-third to one-half their time) but a surprisingly small
amount of time with their own supervisors. Studies of foremen indicate
that only about 10 percent of their time is spent with supervisors; this
appears to hold true for middle- and upper-level managers as well.

With whom, then, does the manager spend the workday? Much of it
is occupied with peers and others outside the actual work unit. The
average supervisor may be in contact with twenty-five to fifty different
individuals a day, including a wide variety of persons in the operating
and service departments.

The same phenomenon occurs in the middle and upper levels of
management, where there are constant and frequent contacts with
people both within and outside the organization. These people include
clients, business associates, suppliers, politicians, and consumers.

In dealing with the large variety and number of "outsiders," the manager acts as the hub of a series of communications networks. The conversations involve information giving and information receiving as well as a great deal of negotiating and bargaining with people over whom the manager has little or no direct authority. The amount and frequency of these lateral relationships have frequently been underestimated.

For example, most managerial job descriptions deal primarily with the manager's relationships with subordinates. Usually, at the end of the description, there is a sentence or so that ends, "and shall conduct such other relationships as are necessary to perform the job." Little attention is given in the average job description to the importance of these lateral interactions. (The subject of the manager in interaction with others is elaborated on in Chapter 2.)

The Personal Style of the Manager

In the immediately preceding sections, the manager was described as having a variety of functions, being involved in active and nonroutine tasks, relying heavily on oral communications, being part of extensive communications networks, working hard at a variety of different tasks.

Clearly, the style of one manager will vary from that of another. How a particular manager goes about doing the job depends in part on the job itself and in part on the nature and personality of the individual. Some managers tend to be calm and reflective; others tend to be impulsive and fast moving. While most managers prefer to be in direct oral contact with others, some prefer written communications. For example, Presidents Kennedy and Johnson appeared to enjoy meeting people face to face, while President Nixon appeared to prefer written memorandums that he could review in solitude. The manager's personality may thus have a strong influence on the way the job is done.

The type of job a manager has also influences behavior. A sales manager may take frequent trips throughout the region or the country, meeting customers, talking to salespeople, and the like. The manager of an accounting section may have far fewer contacts and take far fewer trips.

Sometimes, the manager's personality and the job do not mix. In one situation, a regional sales manager had been repeatedly passed over for promotion to marketing manager. In this particular organization, the marketing manager was expected to handle long-range planning and development of marketing strategy. The regional sales manager was highly impulsive and fast moving; in fact, someone had characterized him as an individual who was happiest when he had three phones on his desk, all ringing at the same time. When the marketing manager job was to be filled again, the company picked an individual who was good at long-range planning. But this time it promoted the regional sales manager to the position of assistant to the marketing manager. In this job, he had no direct supervisory responsibilities, but he handled all the emergency situations that would normally have required the marketing manager's attention. Finally, he was satisfied, as he constantly dashed off to cities such as Washington, Denver, and San Francisco, busily putting out fires. By essentially splitting the job into two parts, the company enabled the marketing manager to plan and gave the former sales manager the excitement and variety he craved.

Managing—A Rewarding Career

Certainly, managers work hard; yet managing is a rewarding career. The success of the organization is dependent on good management skills. This applies not only to those at the top of the organization but also to managers at all levels. Without good management, the organization will not survive. Indeed, many of the organizations that were giants fifty years ago are no longer in existence today or are much less successful. During the same time, other organizations have grown and prospered. Lockheed, Penn Central, Rolls-Royce, and W. T. Grant are examples of organizations that suffered because of poor management and the inability to change with the times. IBM, Polaroid, and Xerox are examples of organizations that have expanded far beyond anyone's expectations. (A less-than-astute manager once refused to rent an early Xerox machine, saying, "Nothing will ever replace carbon paper.")

Challenge and Meaningful Work

Many people have challenging jobs, but the job of the manager is especially challenging. Managers get a sense of accomplishment—a thrill—out of seeing their well-built product shipped, their school system producing well-educated children, or their electric utility functioning effectively and without breakdowns. Clearly, a sense of accomplishment is not limited to managers; probably everyone connected with, say, the moon landings or the Mars probes felt a sense of accomplishment. But the managers were essential in putting all the complex pieces together and for that reason could feel a special sense of accomplishment.

Typically, managers have a stronger need for challenge and accomplishment in meaningful work than many others do. This need can be satisfied through success in managing.

Power

Some people like to take orders; even the manager must take orders from higher-level supervisors. But managers enjoy seeing action being taken after they have made decisions. Their sense of power comes from their authority to use human, financial, and other resources. As one manager reported, "I really get a kick out of making things happen." Managers have the opportunity to make decisions and to influence people and events in accomplishing organizational goals. They have more opportunity and more leeway to effect objectives, policies, and practices than do nonmanagers. Capable managers are given more and more freedom and responsibility to exercise power and authority.

Prestige and Self-esteem

Self-confidence and the admiration of others are two other important motivating factors. The effective manager enjoys being well thought of by others, whether they are subordinates or supervisors, insiders or outsiders. A beginning manager in the lower levels does not have as much prestige as a company president but can still gain the admiration of others. In one situation, a young manager in a bank was asked by a vice-president to close out a bad debt from a company in bankruptcy. Rather than giving the folder to a clerk to follow the routine procedures for such cases, the manager riffled through the folder. She noticed that at the time of the loan application the company had listed a bank account in another state. She phoned the other bank, found that the account still existed, and was able to get the debt repaid. This independent action increased her own self-esteem and gained her the admiration of the higher-level bank managers.

Opportunity for a Progressive Career

Nobody can guarantee that a recent college graduate will become the president of an organization (unless the organization is family-owned). Only a few college graduates make it to the top, since there are many more graduates than there are chief executive officers or top administrators. Nevertheless, the effective manager can expect *opportunities* for a progressive career in management.

In one situation, a college graduate was placed in a training program that brought him into contact with capable, senior-level executives. The opportunity to observe and learn from these executives influenced the man greatly. He began to act and think like a top executive. When promotion did not come fast enough in the original company, he applied for, and got, the job of executive vice-president in a smaller company. When the president resigned to take over a larger company, the young man became president—seven years after his graduation from college.

Financial Reward

Money is both an essential ingredient of life and a measure of success. As a result, most managers expect their financial reward to increase as their level of achievement and responsibility increases. Sometimes, in two-career families, competition develops between spouses over the money each is bringing home. Also, women in management have traditionally been paid less than men. However, this inequity is being reduced, although not as quickly as might be hoped. Recent equal opportunity laws and regulations are more effectively reducing the pay gap between men and women managers.

In summary, most effective managers find that managing is a rewarding career. Not everyone wants to be a manager, and not every manager is motivated by the same needs. The tendency to equate movement into higher and higher ranks with success is sometimes a mistake. The regional sales manager described earlier in the chapter would have been unhappy if he had been promoted into the planning job. He was much happier—and more effective—as a high-level trouble shooter. (Ways of thinking about and planning for career development are described in more detail in Chapter 24.)

Implications for the Manager

Our society is composed of a variety of overlapping, interdependent organizations. We constantly come in contact with these organizations, directly or indirectly, from "simple" efforts such as getting a drink of water to complex actions such as surgery.

There are many different types of organizations, all of which need to be managed. The basic task of the manager is to establish and maintain the conditions under which individuals and groups can work together to accomplish organizational goals. Managerial talent is necessary not only for existing organizations but to help evolve new programs to solve social, environmental, and other problems.

Managers have a variety of titles. Among them are the simpler ones of supervisor, executive, administrator, director, and president and the more specialized ones of dean, department head, chief librarian, marketing manager, personnel director, credit manager, and head nurse.

To accomplish organizational goals, managers work hard at a variety of activities, prefer active and nonroutine tasks, direct personal relationships, and are involved in a series of communications networks. How the specific work is done depends, in part, on the personal style of the manager.

Managing can be a rewarding career because of the challenge of meaningful work, the prestige and self-esteem, the opportunity for progressing, the power, and the money it offers.

Review

1. What is a manager?
2. Explain the importance of the systems concept.
3. After reading the chapter, do you think the organizations to which you belong are managed effectively? Explain.
4. Explain why organizations are needed.
5. Give examples of the three management levels.
6. What are some basic characteristics of managerial work? Give some specific examples.
7. Do you think Stephen Spielberg is an effective manager? What information can you use to determine his effectiveness? What implications does this have for managers in other fields?
8. What would you find rewarding in being a manager? What aspects of being a manager might turn you off?
9. Observe an individual manager. How is the person's time spent? With whom? Does the manager keep busy? Are there ways in which the manager's workload can be reduced?
10. Read several issues of *Fortune* or *Business Week* and report back on what they indicate managers do.

Frye Boots

In 1969, few people except cowboys and members of motorcycle gangs wore boots. Then, it happened: Some California "hippies" came east to buy Frye boots for their leather shops in San Francisco, Sausalito, and Carmel. After these boots became popular in the counterculture, they were adopted by the establishment culture. They are now just the thing to wear with designer jeans or a Givenchy T-shirt. They have become de rigueur both here and abroad. Now, many manufacturers copy and/or compete with Frye.

Frye boots are made by the oldest continuously operated shoe manufacturer in the United States. The John A. Frye Shoe Company was founded in Marlborough, Massachusetts, in 1863, by John Frye, an English bootmaker. The firm is still located in part of the original factory, a five-story wooden building with a turret. During its more than one hundred-year lifespan, the company has manufactured footwear for early pioneers, Teddy Roosevelt's Rough Riders, thousands of actual cowboys, and servicemen during both world wars.

In 1949, the plant manager, Donald Ireland, bought the company from the Frye family. Since 1969, when the boom began, profits have soared. In 1969, the company had about 125 workers, many of whom were third and fourth generation bootmakers. Even though some 50 percent of the manufacturing is now automated, in 1977 the company employed more than 400 workers.

Frye boots are sold in about 4,000 retail stores, located in all fifty states of the United States and in fifteen other countries. About 1 million pairs of boots are sold each year. Proper styling is important at Frye, which has no permanent design staff. Frye boots are modified on the recommendations of retailers, who feed customer reactions back to the company. Sales are split about fifty-fifty between men and women, and most of the customers are about twenty-two to twenty-four years old. The company is now expanding into other products, such as women's bags, belts, and jeans.

Success has had its problems. For example, the company now has a number of competitors who imitate the design and styling of Frye boots. To counter this, Frye has used the advertising slogan, "When you ask for a Frye boot, be sure you get a Frye boot." Another problem is cost. The price of Frye boots keeps rising, and critics suggest that the company has increased prices more than the industry average. The company replies that prices are increased so it can continue to offer the same high-quality boot that it has been known for.

Customers' ages are also a problem. The age range is from about thirteen to the thirties, with the peak at about twenty-four. If people in their forties and older buy Frye boots, younger customers may be turned off. If demand picks up in the youngest age range, older customers may resent seeing "children" wearing "their" boots.

1. What makes Frye boots popular?
2. Do you think they will remain popular? (Styles can change rapidly, particularly in women's wear.)
3. In what ways are Frye boots and *Jaws* similar? How are they different?

Footnotes

1. "Summer of the Shark," *Time*, June 22, 1975, pp. 42–50; S. Spielberg, "Making It in Film," *Film Makers News Letter*, July 1975, p. 15; and C. Gottlieb, *The Jaws Log* (New York: Dell Publishing, 1975).
2. J. Thompson, *Organizations in Action* (New York: McGraw-Hill, 1967), p. 6.
3. L. Dembard, "Beame Is Losing Middle Managers," *New York Times*, September 12, 1976, p. E5.
4. U.S. Department of Commerce, Bureau of the Census, *Statistical Abstract of the United States*, 97th ed. (Washington, D.C.: Government Printing Office, 1976); U.S. Department of Labor, Bureau of Labor Statistics, *Handbook of Labor Statistics*, Bulletin 1905 (Washington, D.C.: Government Printing Office, 1976).
5. L. Barnes and S. Hershon, "Transferring Power in Nuclear Power Plants: The Family Business," *Harvard Business Review* 54 (July–August 1976): 105–114.
6. T. Parsons, *Structure and Process in Modern Societies* (Glencoe, Ill.: Free Press, 1960); E. Lawler, III, and J. Rhode, *Information and Control in Organizations* (Pacific Palisades, Calif.: Goodyear Publishing, 1976).
7. M. Jensen, "A Market Thirst Never Quenched," *New York Times*, April 9, 1978, Sec. 3.
8. J. Hemphill, *Dimensions of Executive Positions*, Research Monograph Number 98 (Columbus: Ohio State University, 1960); S. Carlson, *Executive Behavior* (Stockholm: Strongbergs, 1951); R. Stewart, *Managers and Their Jobs* (London: Macmillan, 1967); R. Guest, "Of Time and the Foreman," *Personnel* 32 (May 1956): 478–486; Q. Ponder, "The Effective Manufacturing Foreman," in E. Young, ed., *Industrial Relations Research Association Proceedings of the Tenth Annual Meeting*, Madison, Wis., December 1957, pp. 41–54; H. Mintzberg, *The Nature of Managerial Work* (New York: Harper & Row, 1973); H. Mintzberg, "The Manager's Job: Folklore and Fact," *Harvard Business Review* 53 (July–August 1975): 49–61; L. Sayles, *Managerial Behavior: Administration in Complex Organizations* (New York: McGraw-Hill,

1964); J. Horne and T. Lupton, "The Work Activities of 'Middle' Managers—An Exploratory Study," *Journal of Management Studies,* February 1965, pp. 14–33; S. Nealey and F. Fiedler, "Leadership Functions of Middle Managers," *Psychological Bulletin* 70 (November 1968): 313–329.

9. Stewart, *Managers and Their Jobs.*
10. Ibid.
11. M. Karagianis, "Frye Boots," *Boston Globe,* January 31, 1976, p. 17; and R. Weeks, sales manager, John A. Frye Shoe Company, personal communication.

Chapter 2

The Working Roles of the Manager

A Day in the Life of Del Goetz

What Managers Do—Common Functions

The Working Roles of the Manager

The Interpersonal Roles of the Manager
    The Manager as Figurehead
    The Manager as Leader
    The Manager as Liaison

The Informational Roles of the Manager
    The Manager as Monitor
    The Manager as Disseminator
    The Manager as Spokesperson

The Decisional Roles of the Manager
    The Manager as Entrepreneur
    The Manager as Disturbance Handler
    The Manager as Resource Allocator
    The Manager as Negotiator

The Manager's Roles—A Contingency Approach
    Levels in the Organization
    Types of Jobs
    Types of Organizations

Implications for the Manager

Review

The Director of Social Work

Learning Objectives

When you have finished reading and studying this chapter, you should be able to:

1. Identify the common functions of a manager.
2. Identify and give examples of how a manager serves as a nerve center for both the organizational unit and the environment.
3. Identify and give examples of the interpersonal roles of the manager.
4. Identify and give examples of the informational roles of the manager.
5. Identify and give examples of the decisional roles of the manager.
6. Specify how the managerial roles form an interrelated and interdependent system.
7. Specify how different types of managers emphasize different roles.
8. Define and be able to use the following concepts:

interpersonal roles   spokesperson
figurehead   decisional roles
leadership   entrepreneur
liaison   disturbance handler
informational roles   resource allocator
monitor   negotiator
disseminator

Thought Starters

1. In what ways do managers get work done?
2. How different are managers' jobs? How similar are they?
3. List what you think are the most important tasks of a managerial job.

A Day in the Life of Del Goetz

Located in Denver is a large warehouse cluttered with used tables, chairs, and couches. After filling a trash barrel, a woman in blue jeans dodges through the clutter to drag the barrel outside for later pickup. "Trash collection," she pants, "is one of the many 'joys' of owning a corporation."

As president of David's Moving & Storage, Del Goetz has many similar "joys." These include dealing with unhappy customers, unloading trucks, and even using a plunger on a stopped up toilet.

Goetz and her woman partner took over a failing moving and used furniture company in 1974. Within a year, sales were doubled and costs were cut considerably. During that first year, Goetz and her partner each put in approximately sixty hours per week, and the pace continues.

The business is now profitable. For it to reach that point, a number of changes were made. Goetz established good relationships with local real estate firms to get referrals. She contacted larger trucking firms in order to pick up their overflow business or business that did not interest them. She has become expert at negotiating prices for packing furniture prior to moving. She closely checks used furniture prices at other stores to make certain hers are competitive and has developed good sources for the furniture. She has centralized the used furniture business at the front of the warehouse, where there is a twelve-by-twelve foot door opening onto the sidewalk. This allows shoppers to come in and browse.

Goetz and her partner employ four men to move furniture and a woman to work part-time in the furniture store. In the peak season, the payroll may swell to thirteen movers—college students and others willing to work part-time.

During the day in question, Goetz arrived at the warehouse about 8 A.M. Technically, she is in charge of the moving operation, and her partner is in charge of the furniture store. But her partner frequently has to leave the warehouse and go to another building to inventory and price furniture. As a result, Goetz often takes over both jobs and answers the telephone. She also spends a lot of time with actual or potential customers, since they are the lifeblood of the business.

In the course of an hour, Goetz gave specific instructions to a moving crew about a special customer and informed them of the moving schedules for the next two days. She also called a florist to order flowers for the birthday of a local real estate agent, supervised the loading of two used chairs for delivery to a customer, helped one of the men move a dresser to make room for a couch, and answered questions from two customers.

Later in the afternoon, she began making out the payroll. This work was interrupted by customers and phone calls. Goetz is pleased with the volume of the moving business and the profitability of furniture sales. Still, she knows that the hectic pace is not likely to let up. She left the warehouse about 6:30 P.M.

Besides her business, Goetz is active in a number of different organizations, including an association that helps women get jobs and loans for starting businesses.[1]

This case shows the varied activities of a manager of a small business. Using it as a base, the chapter will examine some of the common functions performed by managers as they accomplish the goals and objectives of the organization. For example, managers must plan how the objectives will be accomplished or changed if necessary and must coordinate the different parts of the work to make it flow smoothly. The chapter will also examine managers' actual behavior in performing these functions.

What Managers Do—Common Functions

The manager's basic purpose is to supervise individuals or groups in order to accomplish the goals of the organization. In 1916, Henri Fayol, a French businessman, suggested that the manager's job had five basic functions: planning, organizing, coordinating, commanding, and controlling.[2] Later, management author Luther Gulick expanded these major functions to seven, as described below.[3]

Planning: Developing in broad outline the things that need to be done and ways of doing them that will accomplish the objectives of the organization.

Organizing: The activities necessary to develop the formal structure of authority through which work is subdivided, defined, and coordinated to accomplish the organization's objectives.

Staffing: The personnel function of employing and training people and maintaining favorable work conditions.

Directing: The continuous process of making decisions and conveying them to subordinates in general and/or specific instructions and orders so they will know what to do.

Coordinating: The functional activity of interrelating the various parts of the work to be done so it will flow smoothly.

Reporting: Keeping supervisors, managers, and subordinates informed as to what is going on within the manager's area of responsibility through records, research, inspection, or other methods.

Budgeting: Handling budgets, fiscal planning, accounting, and control.

Although POSDCORB—the acronym created from the names of these functions—was originally used to describe the work of a chief executive, most writers use it to describe the job of manager at all levels. Almost all modern texts on management also include additional functions, such as communicating and motivating, but these are generally fitted into the basic framework described above.

POSDCORB, then, is widely accepted as describing the basic framework of the manager's job. Nevertheless, managerial activities cannot always be neatly fitted into these overall basic dimensions. For example, consider a manager who attends the funeral of a subordinate's mother; or an executive who must visit a customer because, as executive, he has more status than the salesman (who may actually know more about the product and the customer); or a manager who gives a subordinate some useful information gathered while attending a dinner sponsored by the local chamber of commerce.

Clearly, these activities cannot be neatly classified as planning, organizing, directing, coordinating, and so on. They all go on continuously and are highly interrelated in the whole job. However, the general concepts can still be used to describe the overall objectives of managerial work: "They are just ways of indicating what we need to explain."[4]

In other words, concepts such as planning and organizing are helpful in providing broad classification of managerial work. They are less helpful in describing what managers actually do on a day-to-day basis to get the job done.

The systems approach is helpful in understanding the interdependence of and interrelationships among these essential functions. For example, coordination is dependent on proper organizing. Organizing is dependent on planning, which determines the broad direction of the organization. Planning in turn is dependent on some prior organizing, although the way the organizing function is carried on is affected by the need for coordination.

Thus the managerial subsystem is concerned with controlling, coordinating, and directing the other subsystems of the organization. In the next section, we will examine the roles that help managers successfully accomplish the basic functions of their job.

The Working Roles of the Manager

A number of studies have examined what managers actually do and how they spend their time. Many of the studies, briefly referred to in the previous chapter, were concerned with positions such as foreman, hospital administrator, company president, supervisor, and field sales manager.[5] The studies included managers in the United States, Canada, Great Britain, and Sweden. In some instances, questionnaires were used to ask managers what they do. More productive information has been obtained by actually observing managers at work.

Henry Mintzberg has not only studied a variety of managerial jobs but has also comprehensively synthesized the empirical studies of managerial roles. He suggests that ten clusters, or roles, can be used to describe the basic ways managers go about accomplishing the job.[6]

Much of the following discussion of managerial roles is based on his synthesis of the literature.

A *role* is a set of systematically interrelated and observable behaviors that belong to an identifiable job or position. Each role, then, is a subsystem. The level of the job affects the emphasis placed on different roles; and the manager's style affects how a role is performed (but not whether it needs to be performed).

From a systems point of view, there are ten different but highly interrelated roles. They can be separated into three different groupings: (1) those primarily concerned with interpersonal relationships (the **interpersonal roles**), (2) those primarily concerned with the transfer of information (the **informational roles**), and (3) those essentially involving decision making (the **decisional roles**). Figure 2.1 shows all ten roles.

Before the ten roles are discussed in more detail, several points should be understood. First, every manager's job consists of some combination of roles. Second, each role can be observed; a person can actually watch the manager perform it. Third, the roles account for the variety of activities engaged in by different managers. Fourth, the roles can be described individually but cannot be isolated; they form an integrated system. Finally, the stress and emphasis vary with the job and the managerial level—technical, administrative, or strategic.

Authority and status allow the manager to act in the interpersonal roles of figurehead, leader, and liaison. By assuming these roles, the manager is able to move into the informational roles. These in turn lead directly to the decisional roles. The results of decisions provide feedback to the manager about adjusting activities to changing conditions or to the results of the decision-making activities.

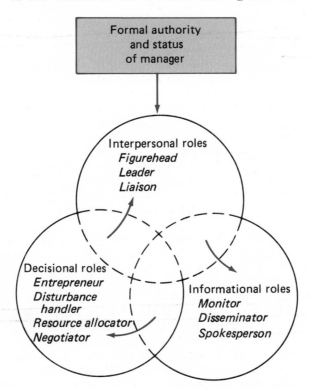

Figure 2.1 The interlocking and interrelated roles of the manager

The Interpersonal Roles of the Manager

As already mentioned, the three interpersonal roles of figurehead, leader, and liaison develop from the manager's formal authority and status.

The Manager as Figurehead

As head of the organization or one of its units, the manager represents it in formal matters, including ceremonial and symbolic activities; this is the figurehead role.

All managerial jobs require some duties that are symbolic in nature—involving interpersonal activity but not significant information processing or decision making. The president of a university gives out the diplomas at commencement. The factory supervisor attends the wedding of one of the workers. The mayor of the town gives the keys of the city to a returning hero.

At first glance, these duties do not appear to be central to the job of manager. Yet, they are expected, and effective managers are involved in them. (In some cases the task is made necessary by internal or external rules, as when the university president or chairperson of the board signs the diplomas.) While little attention has been paid to the figurehead role, it is an important one.

In January 1977 the federal government approved financing for the "Westway," a new road intended to replace New York City's collapsing West Side Highway. The project was expected to cost at least $1.6 billion. Because of the importance of the decision, the federal Secretary of Transportation, William T. Coleman, delivered the message personally. Present at the press conference were, among others, Governor Hugh Carey and Mayor Abraham Beame. Coleman, Beame, and Carey were all there in the figurehead role.

The Manager as Leader

The **leadership role** involves responsibility for directing and coordinating the activities of subordinates to accomplish organizational goals. A highly important role, it is dealt with in depth in Chapter 11.

Some aspects of the leadership role have to do with staffing—making certain that hiring, training, promotion, dismissal, and related activities are performed properly. Other aspects have to do with motivating subordinates—especially trying to ensure that the needs of the organization and the needs of subordinates are integrated. For example, the manager may give special praise to a subordinate for a task done well, may reassure other subordinates who are unsure of their work, or may fight subordinates' battles with higher-ups. Sometimes, the leadership role may be unpleasant, involving firing or other disciplinary actions.

Still other aspects of the leadership role have to do with controlling—inquiring into the activities of subordinates to make certain things are going well, probing for problems that need attention. Is the part being made properly? Is the unit performing within the budget? Is the social worker helping the clients? Is the new college instructor getting the material across to students?

The Manager as Liaison

The **liaison role** involves the manager in contacts outside the vertical chain of command in an effort to bring information into the unit and gain favors from others. It includes interacting in a network of contacts with peers and others in order to get that information. An effective manager spends an appropriate amount of time in this role.

The liaison role deals with the tremendous number of relationships the manager must maintain with individuals and groups outside the organization or unit (subsystem). It often consumes about half the manager's time. For example, the assembly line supervisor may have contact with twenty-five or more individuals from outside the unit during the work day. The same has been found true for middle- and upper-level managers.

The further up in the organization the manager is, the more likely it is that the liaison contacts are outside the organization itself. At the strategic level, for example, a member of the board of directors, the president, or the top administrator is much more likely to be a member of trade associations, the chamber of commerce, and other such groups than is the supervisor of the keypunch operation or the assembly line. At the lower, technical levels of the organization, the liaison tends to be outside the specific unit but inside the organization. The emphasis tends to be focused more directly on maintaining the work flow.

The purpose of the liaison role is to establish better contacts with those who send work into the subsystem and with those to whom the subsystem sends its goods and services. The role may involve selling, purchasing, innovation, lobbying, and advisory activities. Getting to know the proper person to contact is an essential part of the manager's job.

The interpersonal roles of figurehead, leader, and liaison are frequently combined in actual life. For example, a manager may attend a ceremonial dinner in the figurehead role but may meet someone who is important as a future contact. Del Goetz, for example, belonged to a number of outside organizations. She also sent flowers for the birthday of a local real estate agent and established good relationships with real estate and trucking firms.

The Informational Roles of the Manager

In the interpersonal roles, the competent manager builds a network of interpersonal contacts. By the nature of these contacts, the manager becomes the nerve center of the unit—the central focus for the receiving and sending of nonroutine information. Three roles characterize the manager as a nerve center: monitor, disseminator, and spokesperson. In this set of roles, information is received, transmitted, or recombined.

President Franklin D. Roosevelt was good at gathering information. The essence of his technique was competition. One of his aides reported:

> He would call you in and ask you to get the story on some complicated business. After a couple of days of hard labor, you would come back and present the juicy morsel you'd uncovered under a stone somewhere, and then you'd find out he knew all about it, together with something else you didn't know. Where he got his information from he wouldn't usually mention, but after he had done this to you once or twice you got damn careful about your information.[7]

The Manager as Monitor

In much the same way as a radar set, the manager in the **monitor role** continually scans the environment to receive and collect information. The manager must not only check continually to see that the unit is operating properly but must also check continually inside and outside the unit to ensure that possible changes are identified and problems and opportunities detected and to determine when information has to be given to others and decisions made.

In the monitor role, the manager makes use of the formal and informal contacts developed in the liaison role and of the reports generated by the organization, such as current sales and expense figures. At the strategic level, much of the monitoring is external to the organization itself. The successful president of a company must know as much as possible about what competitors are doing; he or she cannot wait to take action until after a competitor has introduced a new product. The manager also must know what effect pending or upcoming legislation or new regulations may have on the organization and what effect the rise or fall of the dollar will have on it. As already mentioned, the head of Coca-Cola spends about half his time in countries outside the United States determining what is happening in places like Moscow and Cairo.

At the administrative level the manager uses operating reports to determine how the organization is functioning, constantly reviews how well specialized functions are operating in conjunction with each other, and obtains outside information from those who use the "products." For example, the dean of a school of management may spend considerable time meeting with other deans and with outside business people. At the operating level, the assembly line supervisor may use production schedules and similar internally generated information along with informal communications to make certain that parts are available before the assembly is to start. The department head in a university may check with the bookstore to make certain the textbooks are available before classes start.

In the *Jaws* case described in Chapter 1, Steven Spielberg had to continually monitor what was going on. How was the script coming along? Was there trouble with the townspeople? Was Bruce working properly? Were the weather conditions right for filming? Only on the basis of up-to-date information obtained from a variety of sources could he film the picture.

The effective manager designs a personal information system, largely informal rather than formal, largely oral rather than written. The manager then pieces together all the incoming information into a mental image or "model" of the unit and its interaction with the external environment or other units.

A manager in one organization made a special effort to cultivate and make friends with the maintenance supervisor. The close interpersonal contact helped ensure that the equipment in the unit was maintained properly. Furthermore, the manager was among the first to know that the maintenance supervisor was resigning to join another company. Long before the official announcement of the resignation, the manager began cultivating the supervisor's replacement, who did not even know yet that his boss was leaving.

The Manager as Disseminator

The **disseminator role** involves passing along special or privileged information that subordinates will not otherwise be able to obtain. When subordinates do not have quick and easy contact with each other, the manager also passes information among them.

A change in the manufacturing schedule must be quickly transmitted to the appropriate supervisor, who will in turn pass the information on to subordinates. The president informs a vice-president that he has just heard that Company X, a supplier, is going bankrupt. The vice-president immediately tells the purchasing agent, since the situation may affect orders that have been placed with Company X.

A significant problem of the disseminator role is delegation. As the nerve center for the unit, the manager has a good deal of information "stored in memory" (to use a computer term). There is little problem in delegating tasks that are specialized or that involve only one function. A different situation occurs when tasks cut across specialties or involve the manager's special information. As the nerve center, the manager has most of the relevant information and is thus best suited to handle these tasks. But no individual person can do everything, so some tasks must be delegated. The problem is that the manager cannot easily pass all relevant information on to subordinates. Much of it was received orally, and passing it along is difficult and time-consuming.

The Manager as Spokesperson

In the **spokesperson role**, the manager speaks for the unit and represents it to others. The nature of the role is highly varied. At the strategic level, the president of an organization or a member of its board of directors may, for example, be asked to appear before a congressional committee conducting a hearing. During the oil crisis in 1973 and 1974, presidents of several major oil companies were asked to explain their organizations' position and the steps they were taking to help the situation.

At the technical level, the first-line supervisor in a manufacturing organization may be told by a subordinate that there is a parts shortage. The immediate response is to contact someone in purchasing to see if parts can be expedited. The person in the purchasing department may in turn contact a supplier.

As can be seen from these illustrations, the spokesperson role requires that the manager keep a number of groups informed. The first of these groups is the unit's key influencers. For the company president, this may mean the board of directors; for the city's mayor, it may mean the city council.

A second series of groups is the organization's "public." For the chief executive the public may include government agencies, customers, suppliers, and the press. For example, a chief executive may "lobby" for the organization, give a speech to a trade association outlining the firm's plans, and oversee the preparation of the annual report to stockholders. The first-level supervisor in a manufacturing unit may interact with engineers, inspectors, purchasing people, and a variety of others primarily within the organization. The head nurse, on the other hand, may have extensive contact with visitors and others outside the formal unit.

A key concept of the spokesperson role is that of representation. The manager must act as an advocate for subordinates. A sales manager may respond to complaints from salespersons about slow delivery time by asking the manufacturing supervisor for faster delivery. Managers must recommend pay increases for their subordinates. A department head may convince a dean and an academic vice-president that more faculty members are needed to handle an influx of new students.

In summary, the informational role involves the manager in gathering and receiving information in the monitor role and transmitting that information in the disseminator and spokesperson roles. Further, the manager uses this information in the decision-making roles—the subject of the next section.

The Decisional Roles of the Manager

Developing interpersonal relationships and gathering information are not ends in themselves. They are the basic inputs to decision making. The third and perhaps most important of the manager's roles are the decisional roles—entrepreneur, disturbance handler, resource allocator, and negotiator. (Chapter 6 deals more specifically with the decision-making process itself.)

The Manager as Entrepreneur

In the **entrepreneur role**, the manager works to improve the unit, to bring about planned, voluntary, controlled change for the better. The effective manager is constantly looking for new ideas to help in doing a better job. After a new idea is identified, the manager considers whether it will be helpful to the unit. If it is both helpful and simple, it may be put into action immediately. For example, Del Goetz centralized the used furniture business at the front of the warehouse and opened a twelve-by-twelve foot door facing the sidewalk to make it easier for shoppers to come in and browse.

If the new idea is complex or difficult to implement, a development project may be started. Many of these projects are supervised directly by the manager, while others are delegated until their completion, at which point the manager approves or modifies them. (Chapters 17 and 19 explore these concepts more extensively.)

A few years ago, Eastern Airlines instituted a new service between Boston, New York, and Washington. The "shuttle service" was very different from previous scheduled flights. Planes left every hour. No reservation was required. Passengers could board the plane directly and purchase tickets in flight. Every passenger was guaranteed a seat. If the airplane was filled, another was brought out, even for a single passenger (which actually happened). This project took a number of years to implement, since the necessary capital had to be raised, the operating procedures had to be established, and the approval of a number of regulatory agencies had to be gained. Once implemented, however, the project was an instant success. (Indeed, the shuttle service is still a success.)

The Manager as Disturbance Handler

In the **disturbance handler role** the manager takes corrective action to respond to pressure and change that are beyond personal control. At the strategy level, the disturbance may be new legislation. At the administrative level, it may be a wildcat strike or a supplier's failure to fulfill a contract. At the technical level, it may be a machine breakdown or the illness of key employees.

There are many other types of disturbances. A subordinate may quit. An airplane crash may create an emergency for both the airport and the local hospitals. A protracted storm may delay delivery of vital parts. A competitor may unexpectedly come out with a new, innovative product.

By their very nature, disturbances must be handled quickly; the manager's disturbance handling role must take priority over other roles. When a disturbance occurs, the manager must shift activities and work to find at least a short-term solution. For example, if a wildcat strike occurs, the first priority is to get people back to work. Solving the longer-term problem is put off to "buy time." After the strike is over, there will be time to explore the deeper reasons and take long-term corrective action.

As sociologist Leonard Sayles phrases it:

> The achievement of . . . stability, which is the manager's objective, is a never-to-be attained ideal. He is like a symphony orchestra conductor, endeavoring to maintain a melodious performance in which the contributions of the various instruments are coordinated and sequenced, patterned and paced, while the orchestra members are having various personal difficulties, stage hands are moving music stands, alternating excessive heat and cold are creating audience and

instrument problems, and the sponsor of the concert is insisting on irrational changes in the program.[8]

In summary, the disturbance handler role is a highly significant one. Not only does the manager have to cope rapidly with unforeseen problems, but also decisions made under pressure can affect longer-term strategy because of the precedents they set.

The Manager as Resource Allocator

In the **resource allocator role**, the manager decides who will get what resources in the unit. The resources can include time, money, material, equipment, people, and the unit's reputation. Almost all organizations have limited resources; few can accomplish everything they hope for. Choices must be made continually as to how the resources will be allocated.

Resource allocation is one of the most vital of the manager's decisional roles. The decision to allocate resources to one area automatically means that they cannot be allocated to another. (Many chapters of this book are directly or indirectly related to resource allocation. Establishing organizational goals, planning, controlling, and staffing, for example, all involve resource allocation.)

At the strategy level, resource allocation determines the organization's long-range direction. Should greater national priority be placed on cancer research, aid to emerging nations, or a landing on Mars? Should time and effort be spent on buying or merging with other organizations? How much effort should be expended on influencing the larger environment? Should the university build a new library or a theatre arts center? In the local municipality, should street improvement or a new sewage disposal plant receive the greater priority?

At the managerial or administrative level, should the dean push for more faculty members or more books in the library? Should money be spent for renovating the old plant or building a new one? What should be the design of the next year's automobile? What proportion of money should be put into advertising and what proportion into improving an existing product? Should police and fire department personnel get bigger raises than other municipal employees? What procedures should be established to service the products manufactured and sold by the organization?

Questions of resource allocation at the operating level are also vitally important. With a tight manufacturing schedule, which products should have priority? Should the machine be stopped for maintenance, or should it continue running in order to get the product out? Should a second shift be put on, or should time and a half be paid for overtime? Given limited faculty, which courses should be offered next semester? Given a limited budget, should the welfare department concentrate more on counseling welfare clients or on catching chiselers?

Decisions on resource allocation are not made completely on the basis of objective facts. To illustrate: After doing a thorough cost and feasibility analysis, a large multinational company approved the installation of a computer in Europe. The computer was to be placed at the company's office in Switzerland, since this was a central (and effective) location. The installation was to involve additional staff to program and operate the computer. The London manager strongly objected to the choice of Switzerland, feeling that this was a reflection on his own status and prestige. Because he made such a fuss, the organization eventually installed two computers, one in Switzerland, as originally intended, and one in London , to satisfy the well-respected and capable London manager.

The Manager as Negotiator

The fourth and final decision-making role is that of **negotiator**. In this role the manager discusses and bargains with other units to obtain advantages for his or her own unit. The owner of a football team may negotiate with a superstar who is holding out for more money. The first-line supervisor may negotiate with the maintenance department to get machines repaired faster. The purchasing agent may negotiate with vendors for lower cost or faster delivery. The sales manager may negotiate price with a large customer.

Sayles suggests that negotiation is at the core of the manager's relationships with others:

> *Sophisticated managers place great stress on negotiations as a way of life. They negotiate with groups who are setting standards for their work, who are performing support activity for them, and to whom they wish to "sell" their services. . . . It is also worth noting that the realistic manager recognizes that the terms of any agreement are not fixed but always are subject to reopening.*[9]

Thus, as with the other roles, the manager as negotiator is frequently dealing with uncertainty and change. Negotiations are duties that cannot be shirked, since only the manager has the nerve center information that many negotiations require and the formal authority to commit the organization to action.

The Manager's Roles—A Contingency Approach

Although described separately, the manager's ten roles form an integrated whole. No specific one can be taken from the others if the managerial job is to remain intact. For example, the manager who has no liaison contacts does not develop sufficient external information to pass on important information to others. The manager who does not monitor the internal and external environment cannot do an adequate job of planning. The purchasing manager who remains blissfully unaware that a major supplier is involved in a long and bitter strike is headed for trouble. The company president who does not plan to meet or stay ahead of competition may not have the job for long. (The organization that makes last year's calculators at last year's prices may soon be out of business.)

Managers do not give equal attention to each of the roles. Each manager is an individual with a personal style. In addition, the roles emphasized depend on managers' organizational levels, the type of organization in which they work, and the types of jobs they hold. Thus, much of the role variation depends not only upon the individual managers but also on the varying situations in which they are placed.[10]

Levels in the Organization

As already pointed out, much of the differing emphasis on managerial roles stems from the manager's level in the organization. In fact, the organizational level appears to be more important than the type of organization.[11] For example, the president of the United States, the president of a company, the head of a school committee, and others at the strategy level may spend proportionately more time in the figurehead role than does a supervisor at the technical level.

Chief executives gather information to be used in broad strategy making. Administrative-level managers gather information that helps implement the broad strategy. Technical-level managers gather information to keep the work process going.

Chief executives may negotiate acquisitions or mergers. Managers at the coordinating level may negotiate delivery dates on orders or sales. Assembly line supervisors may negotiate with production engineers about redesigning a part to make the assembly process easier. The supervisor of a keypunch unit may negotiate with upper-level managers about the priority of materials to be prepared for the computer.

Types of Jobs

In general, managerial jobs at the strategy level tend to be broader and to have greater scope than jobs at the coordinating or technical levels. The lower the level, the more likely the manager's job is to be specialized and narrow in scope.

In addition, managers at the same level tend to concentrate their time on different sets of roles as a function of the job itself. For example, manufacturing managers appear to spend the majority of their time in the negotiator and disturbance handler roles. They also spend more time with subordinates and work more at troubleshooting than do other types of managers.[12]

Sales managers too are concerned with people, although they tend more toward the interpersonal roles in dealing with external contacts (the liaison and figurehead roles) and in developing and training the sales force (the leadership role). Once a salesperson's training has been completed, however, the sales manager of a national or international firm may see the person only infrequently, perhaps at an annual sales meeting. Because of the nature of the job, sales managers spend much more time than other managers outside the organization. It is not unusual for some sales managers to spend more time with customers than with people inside the company.

Managers of specialists—such as accountants, personnel specialists, and industrial engineers—form another distinct group. On the whole, these managers often tend to work alone and to be heavily involved with paperwork, although they also advise others in peer and lateral relationships. These managers spend a great deal of time within the specialty function of their units. As a result, the monitor and spokesperson roles appear to be the most important to them.

Types of Organizations

The size of the organization appears to affect what managers do.[13] The larger the firm, the more the separation into strategic, coordinating, and technical levels. In smaller organizations, this separation is not as clear and distinct (as the Del Goetz case shows).

The chief executives of large firms spend a good deal of time in the figurehead and liaison roles. In smaller organizations, there is more informality and a greater concern for internal operating issues. Managers of smaller firms may deal directly with suppliers, associates, and clients. As a result, the heads of smaller organizations may spend more time in the leader, information processing, and negotiator roles than do executives of larger organizations.

The managers of public organizations, such as school systems and state and federal agencies, deal more directly with the general public than do managers of privately owned organizations. Since there are political issues, problems, and choices in the public organization, the liaison, spokesperson, and negotiator roles are generally important for managers in public life. Whether or not the stereotype is true, managers in profit-making organizations are seen as relatively more involved in the entrepreneur role.

In summary, there is evidence that each managerial job contains interpersonal, informational, and decisional roles. The emphasis on each role differs by managerial level, type of job, and type of organization.[14] The difference is one of emphasis and scope. The chief executive is concerned about and responsible for the effectiveness of the entire organization and obtains a great deal of information from an environment external to the organization. The supervisor at the technical level gathers and disseminates information of a more specific, concrete type, usually primarily from within the organization itself.

Implications for the Manager

This chapter describes the basic activities a manager engages in to accomplish the common managerial functions of POSDCORB— primarily planning, organizing, and directing. It also identifies ten managerial roles that vary by the level of the organization, the type of job, and so on.

The manager's ten working roles can be observed. (For example, we can see the president of an organization acting as a figurehead in giving a gold watch to a retiring employee.) They can also be grouped into three basic categories: interpersonal relationships, information processing, and making significant decisions. The three categories can be further divided into the ten observable roles. The interpersonal roles are those of figurehead, liaison, and leader. The informational roles are those of monitor, disseminator, and spokesperson. The decisional roles are those of entrepreneur, disturbance handler, resource allocator, and negotiator.

These roles form an interrelated, interdependent whole. Although they can be described individually, they cannot exist in isolation. Each is dependent on the others.

The manager is in a unique position to act as a "nerve center" for information of the organization. Contacts with subordinates and with those outside the unit help the individual develop a powerful data base of internal and external information. As a result, the manager is the organization's generalist, with the best store of nonroutine information.

Much of the manager's information is tangible, current, and oral. It is used to detect changes, to inform outsiders and subordinates, to identify both problems and opportunities, and to build a base for decision making.

The manager makes or approves the significant decisions for the unit. Some of the decisions bring about change and improvement; others handle unexpected problems that come up. The manager also oversees the allocation of the unit's resources, including both money and personnel. Finally, the manager negotiates with other organizations or units.

In summary, the manager is the nerve center of the organization or organizational unit—a key link between the unit and the environment and between subordinates and others within the unit. Even though the work of the unit is usually specialized, the manager must not only know all about it but also be able to perform the ten observable roles. Managers in different jobs may emphasize different roles but must perform all of them well.

Review

1. How did the material covered in this chapter correspond to your own knowledge of managers?
2. Select a variety of managers to observe, such as the manager of a service station, the manager of a clothing store, a head nurse, and a manufacturing supervisor. What roles do they appear to emphasize?
3. Identify and discuss as many different roles as you can from the case "A Day in the Life of Del Goetz."
4. Explain how the ten roles of the manager form an interrelated and interdependent whole.
5. Explain what is meant by the statement "The basic managerial roles are observable."
6. Discuss the concept of *nerve center.* In what way is the idea important?
7. Can one be an effective manager without getting oral information? Discuss.
8. From your own experience, give examples of the different roles of the manager. Does the emphasis seem to vary with the organization? Explain.
9. Interview other students for their ideas of what a manager does. Do you agree with their explanations? Discuss.
10. What roles does a department head emphasize? A college dean? An editor of a school newspaper? A football coach? Which roles does each seem to spend the most time on?

The Director of Social Work

Mercy Hospital is a 225-bed general hospital. Helen Strauss, director of social work for the hospital, has a master's degree in social work and is a certified member of the National Association of Social Workers. Her primary training is in psychotherapy, and she has held several previous supervisory jobs.

The department of social work has about twenty professional and paraprofessional workers. Its primary task is to help patients and their relatives in a number of ways. The help ranges from psychotherapy, to counseling patients on how to pay their bills, to working on teams with physicians and nurses to provide complete health care, to arranging for placement in nursing homes.

On a particular day, Strauss left home about 7:45 A.M. On her way to the hospital, she dropped off a revised transfer agreement at a nursing home. While there, she chatted briefly with the director about the agreement and paid a quick visit to a patient recently transferred from the hospital.

Arriving at her office about 9:30, she found six phone messages on her desk. While taking off her coat, she talked to one of the social workers, who reported that the relatives of a patient admitted the day before had been located. The phone rang. The director of fiscal affairs asked Strauss to attend a meeting about collections from patients not covered by insurance. The meeting was set for 1:00 P.M. After finishing that phone call, Strauss called back several of the people who had left messages. One call was to a person in the Veterans Administration and dealt with a recent change in medical benefits to veterans. Another was to an irate wife concerned about her husband; this matter was referred to one of the social workers. While talking on the telephone, Strauss opened some of her mail, much of which she threw into the wastebasket after a quick look at it. Between phone calls, her secretary and several other workers dropped in with questions or to give or get information.

At 10:30, she left her office to attend a regularly scheduled mental health workers meeting of the medical, surgical, and pediatric wards, bringing her proposed revision of a medical record form (one of the items to be discussed at the meeting). On her way back from the meeting, she dropped into the office of the personnel director to discuss potential secretarial candidates, since her secretary was leaving.

So the day went. Lunch was with the chief of the psychiatric unit and several other administrators. One of the agenda items was new admissions to the in-patient psychiatric unit.

At 1:00, Strauss attended the meeting on patients not covered by insurance. She reported on the results of her phone call to the individual from the Veterans Administration and found out that several patients had been admitted that morning who would require social service help.

As she returned to her office, she received a call from a nursing home indicating that it now had a bed for a patient. She relayed the information to the appropriate social worker. From 2:00 to 2:10, she talked by phone to the director of volunteers, negotiating taxi fares for the volunteer worker in social service who could not walk to the hospital on snowy days.

For a few minutes, she worked on the fiscal budget for her department. The meeting was a week away, but she had been working on the budget, off and on, for a month. The budget request would recommend some needed improvements in the department. Again, the phone rang. It was a graduate student from a local university conducting a survey. The call was cut short by another one, this time from the manager of the city infirmary. Following that, a new worker came in for advice about a dying patient and how best to work with the patient and relatives.

Leaving the office, Strauss attended the social service rounds on the surgical floor. (Although there was a social worker assigned to surgery, she attended to keep herself informed.) Before returning to her office, she stopped briefly at a good-bye party for the head nurse in pediatrics. She waited until the gift (to which she had contributed) was presented and then left. While at the party, she talked to a number of other hospital workers and mentioned to a social worker some results of the 1:00 P.M. meeting.

After she returned to her office, several people dropped in. One was a mental health worker who was applying to graduate schools of social work and wanted her to write letters of recommendation. Meanwhile, her desk was again covered with messages about incoming calls. She began returning the calls but stopped at 5:30 since her car pool was waiting.

Twenty minutes after she returned home, she received a call from the head nurse in the emergency room. The police had brought in an incoherent eighty-six-year-old man. After several calls to nursing homes and other potential sources of information, she joined in the decision to admit the individual and attempt to do a thorough psychiatric workup the next day.

1. What concepts of the manager's job described in Chapters 1 and 2 can you identify in the job of director of social work?

2. How many of the managerial roles can you identify? Are the roles always clear-cut? Specify how the roles you identified are interdependent with each other.
3. Specify how the roles you identified are observable from Helen Strauss's actual behavior.

Footnotes

1. J. Libman, "Going It Alone, Female Entrepreneurs Like Del Goetz Make 'Man's Work' Pay Off," *Wall Street Journal,* August 22, 1975, p. 1. Reprinted with permission of The Wall Street Journal, © Dow Jones & Company, Inc. 1975. All rights reserved.
2. H. Fayol, *General and Industrial Management,* trans. C. Storrs (London: Sir Isaac Pitman and Sons, 1949). Originally published in French in 1916.
3. L. Gulick, "Notes on the Theory of Organization," in L. Gulick and L. Urwick, eds., *Papers on the Science of Administration* (New York: Columbia University Press, 1937).
4. D. Braybrooke, "The Mystery of Executive Success Re-examined," *Administrative Science Quarterly* 8 (1964): 537.
5. R. Stewart, *Managers and Their Jobs* (London: Macmillan, 1967); R. Stewart, "The Jobs of the Manager," *Management Today,* July 1976, pp. 64–67; R. Stewart, "To Understand the Manager's Job: Consider Demands Constraints, Choices," *Organizational Dynamics* 4 (Spring 1976): 22–32; W. Tornow and P. Pinto, "The Development of a Managerial Job Taxonomy: A System for Describing, Classifying and Evaluating Executive Positions," *Journal of Applied Psychology* (in press).
6. H. Mintzberg, *The Nature of Managerial Work* (New York: Harper & Row, 1973); H. Mintzberg, "The Manager's Job, Folklore and Fact," *Harvard Business Review* 53 (July–August 1975): 49–61; H. Mintzberg, "Managerial Work: Analysis from Observation," *Management Science* 18 (October 1971): B-97 to B-109.
7. R. Neustadt, *Presidential Power: The Politics of Leadership* (New York: Wiley, 1960), p. 157.
8. L. Sayles, *Managerial Behavior: Administration in Complex Organizations* (New York: McGraw-Hill, 1964), p. 162.
9. Ibid., p. 131.
10. F. Aguilar, *Scanning the Business Environment* (New York: Macmillan, 1967); R. Davis, *Performance and Development of Field Sales Managers* (Boston: Division of Research, Harvard Business School, 1957); S. Nealey and F. Fiedler, "Leadership Functions of Middle Managers," *Psychological Bulletin* 70 (April 1968): 313–329.
11. C. Shartle, *Executive Performance and Leadership* (Englewood Cliffs, N.J.: Prentice-Hall, 1956).
12. Mintzberg, *Nature of Managerial Work*; Stewart, *Managers and Their Jobs*; and Stewart, "To Understand the Manager's Job."
13. I. Choran, "The Manager of a Small Company" (MBA thesis, McGill University, 1969); H. Stieglitz, "The Chief Executive's Job—and the Size of the Company," *Conference Board Record* 7 (September 1970): 38–40.
14. Mintzberg, *Nature of Managerial Work.*

Chapter 3   The Emergence of Management Thought

The Great Pyramid of Cheops

Management and Management Techniques through the Ages
    Accounting and Records
    Laws, Rules, and Regulations
    Civil Service

The Impact of the Industrial Revolution

The Rise of Scientific Management
    The Development of Scientific Management
    Taylor's Report on Bethlehem Steel (a Myth)
    The Gilbreths

The Rise of "Human Relations"
    The Background of the Hawthorne Studies
    The Hawthorne Studies Themselves
    The Results of the Hawthorne Studies (a Myth)

The Emergence of Structure—The "Classical" Approach

The Growing Importance of Technology and Environment

Current Integrative Trends
    The Growing Importance of the Systems Concept
    The Contingency Approach

Implications for the Manager

Review

The Reorganization of the Roman Army

Learning Objectives

When you have finished reading and studying this chapter, you should be able to:

1. Demonstrate the historical relationships among management, culture, and managerial practices.
2. Discuss the contribution of scientific management to management thought.
3. Discuss the contribution of human relations to management thought.
4. Identify two major myths that have affected today's management thought.
5. Describe how some management practices grew out of the prevailing culture.
6. Identify and describe the potential impact of technology and environment on organizations.
7. Compare and contrast the effect of stable and turbulent environments.
8. Discuss current integrative trends in management thought.
9. Define and be able to use the following concepts:

society   types of technology
culture   stable environment
Industrial Revolution   turbulent environment
scientific management   system
Hawthorne effect   contingency approach

Thought Starters

1. How far back does the history of management go?
2. Has there always been a need for managers? Explain.
3. Can a knowledge of history help in understanding today's world?

The Great Pyramid of Cheops

The Great Pyramid was built as a tomb for Cheops, a Pharaoh of Egypt, about 2000–3000 B.C.[1] It has been studied perhaps more intensively than any other building in history. Extensive management skill was required to plan, schedule, and coordinate its building. For example, the rock base is less than half an inch from being perfectly level. Exactly how the construction was managed is still uncertain and subject to a great deal of debate.

When originally built, the pyramid measured 755 feet on each side at the base and was 482 feet high. It covers thirteen acres and contains about 2.5 million stone blocks, each weighing from about 2.5 to 15 tons. The blocks were cut to size from quarries along the Nile River and moved by barge or raft to the construction site. The specifications were such that each block could be fitted into place with only slight adjustments. The blocks were fitted together so well that a knife cannot be inserted in the joints.

Cheops commissioned the project. The architect, probably after a number of conferences with Cheops, selected the specific site and drew up the plans. Many problems had to be overcome. For example, a number of changes were made in the design during the course of construction. A well coordinated schedule had to be developed to ensure that each individual stone arrived at the construction site at the proper time. Too many blocks would be in the way; too few would slow construction.

The planning and coordination involved many different activities. These included quarrying the stone, moving the stone to the Nile, loading and unloading barges or rafts, transporting the stone to the construction site, building ramps, building the pyramid itself, building and decorating the inside galleries and funeral chamber, making and maintaining timber tracks and rollers, making clay bricks, making baskets for the transport of the fill to the ramps, baking, cooking, and supplying sanitary services.

Scholars disagree as to where the stone was quarried, how it was moved, how it was put into place, how long the project lasted, and how many workers were involved. Some scholars have suggested that a ramp was built to the top of the pyramid. Engineers argue that a ramp could be built only about halfway up. How could blocks weighing up to 15 tons be lifted hundreds of feet into the air? Block and tackle, cranes and similar lifting devices had not yet been invented.

This case shows an early problem in management. Were the Great Pyramid to be built today, the approach would undoubtedly be different, but many of the problems of planning, coordination, and decision making would still be present. In this chapter, we will examine some of the ways in which management thought has evolved over the centuries. As with other types of knowledge, there has been an explosion of ideas and thoughts about management in recent years. Nevertheless, the same basic management problem exists today as in Cheops's time: What is the best way to go about attaining the goals of the enterprise? History can be helpful in understanding and working toward the solution of this problem. By looking to where we have come from, we can better see where we should be going.

First, we will look at some examples of management thought developed thousands of years ago. Then, we will review the impact of the Industrial Revolution on modern society and modern organizations. Finally, we will take a look at several of the ideas that have been developed since the turn of this century. In the process, we will debunk some outstanding myths.

The main thrust of the chapter will be to demonstrate the historical interaction (and interdependence) of society and culture with organizations, management, and managerial techniques and practices. <u>Society is the totality of social relationships among human beings. Culture is the totality of socially transmitted ideas, beliefs, and values within a society.</u> For example, in early Egyptian society, a prevailing cultural belief was that the Pharaoh was a deity. In some cultures it is believed that women should not uncover their faces in public. In the United States, an important cultural belief is that the best form of government is a democracy.

Management and Management Techniques through the Ages

Chapter 2 showed that formal organizations consist of three levels: the strategic or institutional level, the managerial or coordinating level, and the technical or operating level. Figure 3.1 shows the influence of culture and society on these three levels, thereby adding a fourth level.

In the case of the Great Pyramid, the Egyptians firmly believed in a life after death. The culture also encouraged the belief that the Pharaoh was a deity and needed a suitable home after death. The society thus demanded the building of a suitable tomb. The size of the tomb certainly affected the strategic level of organization. The best estimates are that

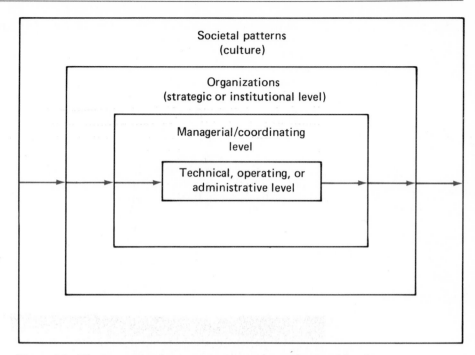

Figure 3.1   The interaction between society and organizational levels

the adult male population of Egypt at the time was no more than about half a million. Therefore, the pyramid required a great deal of resource commitment and an organization for the actual construction. It also required a great deal of coordination, as well as a variety of administrative and operating techniques. Clearly, much of the actual management was at the technical level—supervision of the many different crews at work on different tasks. In addition to the operating techniques used in building the tomb, the Egyptian managers kept meticulous documents. They knew exactly how much was received, from whom, when it arrived, and how it was used.

Accounting and Records

Written accounting systems date back many years. For example, the temple records of the Sumerian civilization date back to about 3000 B.C.[2] Separation of church and state was not as important as it is now. The priests of the Sumerian temple collected and controlled a large variety of worldly goods. The religious tax gave them ownership of vast revenues, estates, flocks, and herds. Some people felt that individual priests might be lining their own pockets. As a result, an elaborate accounting system was developed. The chief priest got a regular accounting from the lesser priests of their income and expenses. This is one of the early instances of managerial control through organizational accounting.

Thus one of the earliest sets of written documents in the world are the five-thousand-year-old accounts of the Sumerian priests. The documents were not used for religious purposes (as we consider them) but stemmed from managerial needs.

Laws, Rules, and Regulations

About 2000 B.C., King Hammurabi united the cities along the Euphrates and Tigris rivers into one powerful nation, Babylon.[3] He then developed the Code of Hammurabi, a set of laws covering trade, business, real estate, personal property, labor, and the family. Most of the laws were of a business nature, dealing with partnerships, sales, loans, contracts, promissory notes, and other agreements. The code described in specific detail the legal procedures to be followed in such business transactions as minimum wages, control, and responsibility.

About fifteen hundred years later, another strong manager came to the helm of Babylon. Nebuchadnezzar not only reunited the Babylonians but also led them to new heights, both militarily and domestically. For example, it was during his rule that color-coding methods of production control were used in the textile mills. The different types of yarn entering the mills were identified by colored tags. Incentive wage payments were introduced; the wages paid to the women who were spinning and weaving were determined by their amount of production.

The color-coding system was also used in the granaries. Harvested grain was stored in large pottery jars. When the jars were sealed, a colored reed was placed in the seal, indicating the age of the grain.

Thus laws, regulations, production scheduling, and color coding were all established before the rise of capitalism as we know it.

Civil Service

China

The first known job descriptions for Chinese civil servants were written about 1100 B.C.[4] These descriptions existed for all civil servants, from the prime minister down to the most humble household servant. The duties, responsibilities, and limitations of each job were spelled out in clear language.

About 120 B.C., the Chinese developed the first civil service examination system.[5] Many clerks and administrators were unable to read and thus were unable to fully understand government laws and regulations. Somewhat irked by this, Prime Minister Kin-Sun Hung established a system of examinations whereby those who scored highest were given government jobs. About three hundred years later, the system was expanded. Civil servants were classified into nine different grades, depending on such factors as knowledge, experience, ability, and character. The grading was done by an impartial judge. Over time, the judging became less impartial and more political. In 606 A.D., the system was again replaced by government examinations (after the "impartial judge" approach had been tried for four hundred years).

In each of these cases, managerial practices grew out of the culture in which they were needed. It was not until the Industrial Revolution that the modern organization as we know it began to emerge.[6]

The Impact of the Industrial Revolution

England

The development of the steam engine made possible the modern organization as we know it. The steam engine brought power for factories, ships, and trains. The economy began to shift its emphasis from land and labor to power and industrialization. The interactions among culture, organization, coordination, and administration were particularly clear.

The cultural climate in England favored the growth of commerce and industry. The English government was more open and sensitive to the development of commerce than were the governments of many other countries, especially France. The social values favored achievement and profit making. In addition, England had ample supplies of coal and iron, essential ingredients for an industrialized society. Before the development of the steam engine, England had had a number of small but thriving industries in such areas as textiles and iron products.

The introduction of the steam engine made possible the vast expansion of these industries by lowering production costs, which in turn increased markets. As the markets expanded, the need grew for more production, more machines, more workers, and more capital to finance the expansion. Division of labor became more common. These shifts in administrative practices required new and different management practices and new types of organizations. Thus the **Industrial Revolution** involved economic and social changes brought about when the mechanization of production resulted in a major shift from home manufacturing to large-scale factory production.

For example, the Industrial Revolution destroyed *cottage industry*, work done in the home by a domestic artisan who generally owned all the tools of the trade. The new machines were much too expensive to be owned by individuals, so it became necessary to bring machines and workers together in large factories where the building, the machinery, and the materials were owned by a few people. In addition, as the work was simplified and the use of machinery grew, women and children began to be employed on a large scale. Thus the building of large factories, the use of expensive equipment, and the employment of large numbers of relatively unskilled people forced changes in the way work was done.

Discipline became necessary for those unused to factory work. Planning and coordination became more necessary. Different methods of training and of wage payment were required. There was a sharper distinction between the "capitalist" and the "worker."

According to management historian Daniel Wren, "The Church could organize and manage its properties because of dogma and the devotion of the faithful; the military could control large numbers of men through a rigid hierarchy of discipline and authority; and governmental bureaucracies could operate without having to meet competition or show a profit."[7] The managers in the new and expanding commercial organizations and factories could not use these approaches. As the culture fostered the growth of industry and trade, the need for better organizations and improved administrative techniques also increased. As England shifted from an agricultural economy to an industrial one, there was a shortage of both skilled managers and skilled workers. Farm workers or those used to small cottage industries did not want to work in the factories; those who did want to work there were unskilled.

The Industrial Revolution emerged from a society and culture that encouraged business and commerce. In turn, the society and culture were changed by the new organizations and administrative practices. With increasing industrialization came the need for a higher and more capable level of managers. As manufacturing techniques changed, the need for a trained, motivated work force increased. Operating techniques changed. England shifted from an agricultural economy to an industrial one. The age of management had emerged.

Moving away from the Industrial Revolution, the rest of the chapter will focus more on a few events shaping managerial thought since 1900.

The Rise of Scientific Management

Some people passively accept the world around them. Others have a striving sense of urgency; they constantly question the existing state of affairs and try to bring about change. They are the "movers and shakers." Such a person was Frederick Taylor, who is known as the founder of "scientific management."[8] Taylor felt that a scientific approach (experimentation and observation) was essential to management.

The Development of Scientific Management

A person who constantly looked for a better way, Taylor is reported to have revolutionized baseball by developing the overhand pitch.[9] An avid baseball player, he believed that the underhand pitch was slow and inefficient and began to throw overhand instead. Other players protested, but there were no rules against such a delivery. Soon, all pitchers were throwing overhand.

Taylor devoted much of his life to promoting the principles of **scientific management**. His basic approach was to observe the separate elements or motions of each task a worker performed. After carefully analyzing the job, he would redesign it to develop the "one best way" for all workers. His approach included developing standard methods, times, and equipment; rest periods; and even time for unavoidable delays. The worker would then be selected and trained. Both the company and the worker would benefit—the organization through greater productivity and the worker through higher pay.

Perhaps you have observed that shovels come in different shapes and sizes. Taylor is reported to have discovered that the optimum size shovel enabled the user to lift twenty-one pounds—hence, one size shovel for coal, another for sand, and a third for grain.

Taylor's Report on Bethlehem Steel (a Myth)

Perhaps the best-known of Taylor's work was his report on Bethlehem Steel at around the turn of the century. Taylor reported that the company had about seventy-five men employed to load pig iron into freight cars. Each "pig" weighed about ninety-two pounds. Taylor found a Pennsylvania Dutchman named Schmidt and offered to increase his pay from $1.15 per day to $1.85 per day if he would follow orders with "no back talk." Schmidt agreed. Taylor claimed that he then trained other workers until the entire crew had raised their productivity.

Unfortunately, later research into Bethlehem Steel's actual records, Taylor's published and unpublished revisions of his own work, and other sources indicate that this report is more fiction than fact—almost completely a lie. A recent study suggests also that writers on management thought have, since 1911, uncritically accepted Taylor's account as true and thereby continued the myth about his work.[10] However, in his writings and speeches, Taylor did impress on management the need to study operating practices to increase worker efficiency.

The Gilbreths

use of motion pictures to analyse motions of workers

Many others followed Taylor's example in increasing efficiency. Two of the most famous, Frank and Lillian Gilbreth, refined and advanced the scientific approaches made popular by Taylor. For instance, Frank Gilbreth identified seventeen basic motions or thought processes by which a job could be analyzed (such as search, find, grasp, transport, and position). These basic units of behavior were called "therbligs," a slightly altered, backward spelling of the Gilbreth name. Their identification allowed jobs to be analyzed in finer detail.

Whereas Taylor had studied relatively gross bodily motions, Gilbreth developed the use of motion pictures in studying work; each picture of an action included a large-faced clock with the hands moving through fractional parts of a minute. Gilbreth also developed the cyclograph, which used small electric bulbs fastened to the fingers of the operator and flashing at regular intervals. When pictures were taken with a stereoscopic camera, the work was recorded in three dimensions. This approach made it possible to determine more precisely the time and motion involved in the work itself, thus increasing the accuracy of the analysis.

In opposition to Taylor, who contended that a worker should follow orders "with no back talk," the Gilbreths involved the workers and used their comments in studies. Thus they actually inaugurated both the scientific method of analyzing work and fatigue and the study of worker psychology and participation. (Although the Gilbreths began their work independently of Taylor, the three later joined forces and helped found the American Society of Mechanical Engineers.)

Made popular by Taylor and systematized by the Gilbreths, time and motion studies are still used as a way of determining what the times and costs of making a product should be. Further, the interest in worker psychology and participation is growing at an accelerating pace, as will be seen in later chapters. For example, a recent newspaper headline reads, "GM [General Motors] Finds Advantages in Giving Workers Decision-Making Role."[11]

The story is told that the Gilbreths applied scientific management not only to industry but also to their household and their twelve children. Taking a bath was seen as both a necessity and an "unavoidable delay." As a result, a Victrola (a hand cranked record player) was installed in the bathroom so the family could listen to German and French language instruction while bathing. In the bathroom, the boys were shown the most efficient way of bathing before the record was completed. The girls were given "dry run" demonstrations by Frank Gilbreth while he sat in the middle of the living room with his clothes on.[12]

The Rise of "Human Relations"

In the early 1920s, a textile plant near Philadelphia was having serious problems. In one area of the factory the turnover rate was 250 percent a year. Scientific management had been tried but with little success. In desperation, the plant management called in Elton Mayo from the University of Pennsylvania.

When he came into the plant, Mayo and others interviewed the workers, who complained about fatigue and about feeling solitary and depressed. Mayo's recommendations for improvement included establishing rest periods. This and other physical improvements reduced turnover and increased productivity. As the interviews continued, Mayo concluded that something even more significant was happening. Because of the interviews, the discussions about rest periods, and the general management interest, the workers no longer felt solitary. They formed social groups; and the more they felt part of a group, the fewer their complaints and the lower their turnover rate—which dropped to 5 percent a year.[13]

Shortly thereafter, Mayo went to the Harvard School of Business Administration. There he worked with Fritz Roethlisberger and others in what became the most famous series of research studies in the human relations movement—the Hawthorne studies, done at the Hawthorne plant of the Western Electric Company near Chicago.

The Background of the Hawthorne Studies

Before describing the work itself, some additional historical background is needed. Around the turn of the century, manufacturers of gas and electrical fixtures struggled for control of industrial and residential lighting. Industry tended to use gas because it was cheaper. But then came the development of the more modern tungsten filament lamps, which were more efficient (and thus cheaper) than the older style lamps.

Since the new lamps were more efficient, the electric companies were concerned about less electrical current being used. Advertising started to stress that better illumination increased productivity. From

1918 to 1923, a number of "studies" were conducted showing that better lighting resulted in higher productivity. Because the tests were financed by the electrical industry, management remained skeptical.

To overcome the skepticism, several large electric companies decided to finance a series of additional studies that would not appear to be connected in any way to their companies. The Committee on Industrial Lighting was established, with Thomas Edison as its honorary chairman. The CIL was officially sponsored by the National Research Council of the National Academy of Sciences. Its working chairman and headquarters were situated at the Massachusetts Institute of Technology. The chairman, an MIT professor, recommended that studies be conducted at the Hawthorne plant of Western Electric—hence the name Hawthorne studies.[14]

The Hawthorne Studies Themselves

In all, seven studies took place at the Hawthorne plant between 1924 and 1932. One of the best-known of the early studies involved a highly repetitive task—assembling telephone relays—done by six women. Accurate records were kept of such factors as light intensity, room temperature, humidity, and production. Production was measured by a continuously running output recorder, and information about the rate of production was available to the individual workers. As the research continued, the results became more and more puzzling; production rates kept rising no matter what was done. The researchers decided that illumination was not an important variable and began examining other factors—among them weather conditions, wage payments, rest periods, and the workers' physical and emotional condition. It became clear that no single factor—least of all the level of lighting—could account for productivity levels.

Another widely reported study was done in the bank wiring observation room, where no changes were made in physical working conditions, methods of payment, or anything else. The workers were simply observed. There were only fourteen men in this department, and they were divided into three semiautonomous but interdependent work groups. The men did piecework, and their output was easily measured. The study indicated that the group had a clear-cut standard for production levels—a standard established by the group itself, not by management. Men who exceeded the norm were called "slaves," "rate busters," or "speed kings"; men who did not come up to it were called "chiselers." Workers were hit on their biceps (a practice called "binging") as a means of enforcing the standards. One of the findings for this small group was that its production standard was more important than wage incentives in affecting output. Another finding, given little or no emphasis at the time, was that the workers did *not* increase productivity because of the observer's "interest."[15]

The Results of the Hawthorne Studies (a Myth)

For years, several important findings of the Hawthorne studies were reported in the literature as fact. Some of the major findings were that workers' individual characteristics and the social characteristics of both the work and its environment are highly important. "Solitary" people do not behave the same as people who belong to a group. The group itself is important; a group's production is better predicted by the standards or norms of the group than by incentive pay. Those who violate the group standards of productivity are likely to be punished in some way.

One of the most widely-known "facts" about the studies is the "Hawthorne effect." A research or work situation is said to involve the **Hawthorne effect** when workers' behavior changes and productivity increases because the workers are aware that persons important in their lives are taking an interest in them.

There have been a number of criticisms of the Hawthorne studies, including charges of scientific illiteracy, clinical bias, promanagement bias, and drawing unwarranted conclusions from groups as small as two to six workers. One specific example of an unwarranted conclusion is that output did not increase under all conditions; rates of output dropped when piecework was eliminated, when the workday was lengthened, and when rest periods were eliminated. Furthermore, the researchers gave little attention to the importance of piecework rates, although in one of the studies an increase in piecework payment alone increased productivity by 12 percent in a few months. And the conclusion that interest in the worker increases productivity clearly did not apply to the bank wiring observation room.[16]

Probably the major contribution of the Hawthorne studies (however poorly designed) was that they generated a great deal of interest in individual and group behavior. The studies were a counterbalance to the ideas being fostered by proponents of scientific management, particularly in the 1930s and later. The notion of people as strictly economic beings began to be questioned, and assumptions about human nature began to be changed. The pendulum began to swing away from the view of workers as stupid and phlegmatic toward a more personalized view of them.

The Hawthorne studies stemmed from the prevailing culture, which focused on such impersonal aspects of work as illumination. In turn, the studies affected the culture, as evidenced by the growing emphasis today on motivation, group dynamics, and quality of working life. They also profoundly affected administrative practices, thereby demonstrating the interrelationships among the four levels shown in Figure 3.1. (Further attention is given to individual motivation and group dynamics in Chapters 4 and 5.)

The Emergence of Structure—The "Classical" Approach

Organizations have always been structured, as the Babylonian and Egyptian examples show. The major impact on the modern organization came from the Roman military model and from the design and structure of the Catholic Church. Modern writing about organizational design and structure started shortly after the beginning of the Industrial Revolution, and it continues to this day. *Organizational structure* refers to how the organization is designed and how the parts are interrelated.

One of the chief concerns of organizational structure, division of labor, was described by Adam Smith in 1776, in his *The Wealth of Nations*. Smith noted that a single worker could make about 20 pins a day. When the task was subdivided into a number of operations, he reported, ten workers could produce 48,000 pins a day—240 times what a single worker could produce alone.

Some of the more influential works on organizational design came shortly after the turn of this century. One of the important factors in the development of structural thought was its international flavor. Similar ideas were propounded almost simultaneously (and independently) in France, Germany, Great Britain, and the United States.

Imagine being in France about 1915, visiting a large coal mine. You might have had the opportunity to meet Henri Fayol, the president and one of the more modern writers on industry. Fayol's first book, published originally in a French journal in 1916 as *Administration industrielle et*

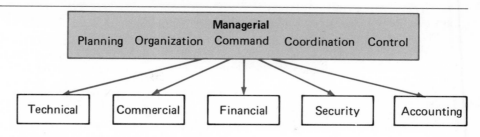

Figure 3.2   The activities of a business

générale received considerably more attention when its title was translated as *General and Industrial Management.*[17]

Fayol distinguished among six different activities of a business, as shown in Figure 3.2. These included technical activities, which involve areas such as manufacture and production; commercial activities, which include buying, selling, and exchange; financial activities, which include the search for and best use of capital; security activities, which include the protection of persons and property; accounting activities, which include costs, balance sheets, and statistics; and managerial activities, which include planning, organization, command, coordination, and control. Fayol put primary emphasis on managerial functions, since he felt that managerial skills had been the most neglected of the business operations.

To emphasize the managerial function, Fayol developed fourteen principles of management, shown in Table 3.1. Fayol was careful to use the term *principles* rather than *rules* or *laws*, since he believed that organizations need to adapt to changing situations and that principles must therefore be flexible. By drawing up these principles, Fayol paved the way for others to follow, to change, and to modify as they learned more about management.[18]

Subsequently, an American author, Luther Gulick, expanded on Fayol's managerial functions and developed POSDCORB (which was described in Chapter 2). For Gulick the basic managerial functions are planning, organizing, staffing, directing, coordinating, reporting, and budgeting.[19]

Max Weber, a German sociologist, argued that bureaucracy represented the ideal to which the design of organizations should proceed. He believed that rules and regulations are necessary not only to make the organization function but also to protect its members from favoritism. According to Weber, the bureaucratic organization should have certain basic characteristics: (1) a division or specialization of labor, (2) a well-developed hierarchy, (3) a system of procedures that defines and protects the rights and duties of employees; (4) interpersonal relationships based on position rather than personality, and (5) promotion and selection based on technical competence rather than on "knowing someone." Weber clearly stated that bureaucracy, with its well-defined rules and expertise, was an effective way of getting rid of organizational favoritism, arbitrary authority, payoffs, kickbacks, and incompetence. He also stated that the resultant job security would promote innovation.[20]

(Incidentally, one of the "causes" of the growth of unions and union insistence on the need for seniority was the need to protect workers from arbitrary decisions by relatively untrained low-level managers. It is

Table 3.1 Fayol's fourteen principles of management

1. Division of work: The specialization of workers, including management, to improve efficiency and increase output.
2. Authority and responsibility: The right to give orders and the power to exact obedience (p. 12). Authority leads to responsibility.
3. Discipline: Obedience, application, energy, and behavior (p. 22) given to the organization, depending on the leaders.
4. Unity of command: No person should have more than one boss.
5. Unity of direction: There should be only one plan for accomplishing goals (an extension of the unity of command principle).
6. Subordination of individual to general interest: The concerns of the organization placed ahead of individual concerns.
7. Pay: Arrangements for pay that are fair and satisfactory to all and competence rewarded but not overrewarded.
8. Centralization: The consolidation of the management function according to the circumstances surrounding the organization.
9. Hierarchy: The lines of authority should run clearly from the top of the organization to the lowest level.
10. Order: People and materials should be in the right place at the right time and people should be in the jobs most suited to them.
11. Equity: Loyalty should be encouraged by justice, kindliness, and fairness.
12. Stability: High employee turnover both causes and is the result of inefficiency and good organizations have stable managements.
13. Initiative: The necessity of "thinking out a plan and ensuring its success (p. 39)" and of giving subordinates the opportunity to perform.
14. Esprit de corps: Oral communications should be used to keep teams together.

Source: Henri Fayol, *General and Industrial Management*, trans. C. Storrs (London: Sir Isaac Pitman and Sons, 1949). Note that individual page numbers are given with the items in the table. *Administration industrielle et générale* first appeared in French in 1916 in the third issue for that year of the *Bulletin de la Société de l'Industrie Minerale*. It was published in book form in 1925 by Dunod Frères of Paris.

unfortunate that today the term *bureaucracy* has become associated with red tape, inefficiency, slowness, and waste.)

Fayol's, Gulick's, and Weber's approaches were quite similar. All three suggested that there was an ideal way to design an organization, and all three emphasized a single chain of command and clear lines of communication. Indeed, all three had experience only with organizations that produced a single, relatively simple product. For this reason, at least, the three may not have been completely correct in their approach. Nevertheless, many of their ideas have clear applications to modern business. For example, they pointed out the importance of the managerial job, and they got people thinking systematically about organizational structure.

The Growing Importance of Technology and Environment

Early in the century, Taylor made a distinction between the organization that produces large quantities of the same product and the organization that produces special products to customer order. He suggested that management needed to be different in the two cases, but his suggestion was largely ignored by both the classical writers on structure (such as Fayol and Weber) and the human relations writers.

Eventually, however, Taylor's distinction was found to be valid. Joan Woodward studied a hundred firms in England to find out whether the "classical" structural principles of organization held true in all cases. In analyzing her data she found that the principles suggested by people like Fayol and Weber did not always hold up. She discovered unexplained organizational differences among successful firms. Puzzled, she reexamined her data and began to identify the importance of a new concept—*technology*. The differences among firms made sense when the organizations were classified by the technology used in their production processes.

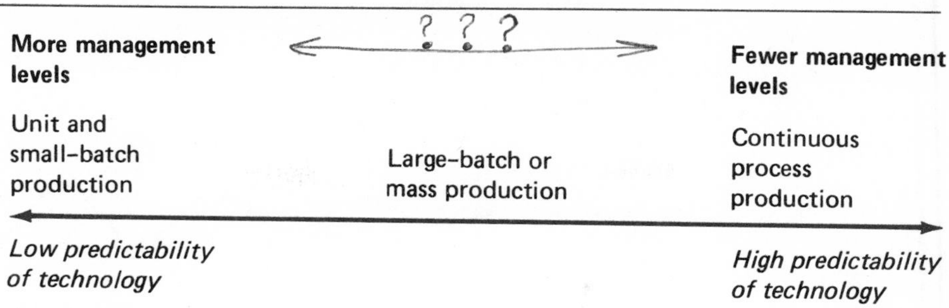

More management levels ← ? ? ? → Fewer management levels

Unit and small–batch production	Large–batch or mass production	Continuous process production

Low predictability of technology   High predictability of technology

Figure 3.3 The continuum of predictability of technology

Woodward distinguished three broad groupings—three **types of technology**—according to production techniques and the complexity of production: (1) unit and small-batch production, such as custom-tailored clothing, or products manufactured in small quantities, such as machine parts; (2) mass or large-batch production, such as automobiles on an assembly line or large quantities of standard electronic components; and (3) continuous or process production, such as that done in chemical and oil-refining plants.

As Figure 3.3 shows, unit and small-batch production is the least sophisticated technologically; large-batch or mass production is intermediate; and continuous process production is the most sophisticated.

In general, the firms could be placed on a scale according to the predictability of results and the degree of control over the production process. Unit production had the lowest predictability, and continuous process production had the highest predictability. The more successful firms had a type of management that varied along the scale of predictability. For example, the more complex the technology, the greater the number of managers and management levels; and the greater the technological complexity—from unit to continuous process—the greater the number of clerical and managerial people involved. Firms that did not follow these and other "principles" were less successful. In other words, Woodward found that each of the three different technologies had specific types of organizational structures that were associated with success.[21]

Shortly after Woodward's studies, two other researchers came up with similar results. They found that successful firms had two basic types of organizational structures, depending on the nature of the environment. Different organizations, or subunits of organizations, can be placed at different points on a continuum, as shown in Figure 3.4.

A **stable environment** shows little or no unexpected or sudden change; that is, the few product changes that do occur generally can be predicted well in advance. (Organizations making cotton string, burlap, and manhole covers, for example, exist in a relatively stable environment.) Successful organizations existing in a stable environment, called "mechanistic" organizations, have well-defined procedures, rules, and functional roles. They follow a bureaucratic model of organization characterized by a high degree of reliance on task specialization, clear rules, precise job descriptions, and an understanding of rights and responsibilities.

A **turbulent environment** has many sudden, rapid, and frequently unpredictable product changes. (Organizations in the computer and medical instrument fields, for example, exist in this kind of environ-

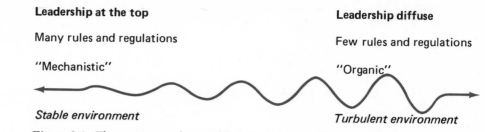

Figure 3.4 The continuum from stable to turbulent environment

ment.) Successful organizations in a turbulent environment are designed differently from those in a stable environment; for these organizations an "organic" structure seems more effective. This structure emphasizes taking and giving orders and places great value on the use of special knowledge from lower levels of the organization. In mechanistic organizations, leadership is centered at the top; in organic organizations, leadership and decision making are diffuse and the emphasis is on consultation and decision making by consensus.[22]

The classical management thoughts about organizational structure emerged from a society and culture in which there was relatively little change. (When Ford brought out the first mass-produced car, it was said, "You can have any color, so long as it is black.") Now the culture is more attuned to rapid change, and organizations and administrative techniques also change. As a computing device, the abacus has been used in Asia for hundreds of years, unchanged. But in our culture, last year's pocket electronic calculator is obsolete this year. (Further attention is paid to evolving organizational structure in Chapters 15 and 16.)

Current Integrative Trends

In the past thirty years a tremendous body of knowledge about management and organizations has been built up. Research in the field is still expanding, as is shown by the large number of books, journals, and journal articles dealing with management. Interest in this area is growing partly as a result of our shift from a relatively unchanging society to one that is undergoing constant change and becoming more interdependent. Two particular integrative trends are important to our society—the systems concept and the contingency approach.

The Growing Importance of the Systems Concept

The idea of relationships and interdependence has always been implicit in management thought. In recent years, however, the idea has become more central, has received greater emphasis, and has moved toward the concept of a system. As derived from general systems theory, a system can be defined as a series of interrelated and interdependent parts such that the interaction or interplay of any of the parts affects the whole. As used in this book, the word *system* applies to the entire organization, and the word *subsystem* applies to the integrated groups or units of the organization. Thus the organization as a system is composed of a number of interrelated and interdependent components, each of which affects the other; and the organization can in turn be considered a subsystem of the larger culture.

To illustrate: American Airlines recently reached an out-of-court settlement with some of its stewardesses, agreeing to pay them a total of more than $2.7 million. Between 1964, when the Civil Rights Act was passed, and 1970, the airline had dismissed approximately three

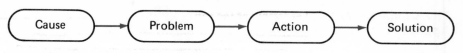

Figure 3.5   Single-cause linear thinking

hundred stewardesses because they had become pregnant. In 1977, the airline agreed that these dismissals were wrong and further agreed to rehire the women, pay them for the time they had lost from work, and make Social Security payments for them for the time the case was in the courts. The airline apparently had considered the stewardesses only subsystems within the company. But the airline itself is a subsystem within the larger society, which, at the stewardesses' request, decided not to treat the dismissal as strictly an internal matter.

Managers have always been aware of the interdependence of the organization's subsystems as well as of the interdependence of the entire organization and its environment. But they have often lacked full appreciation of the concept of system. Thus they have tended to use the "single cause habit of thinking."[23] Those involved with the dismissal of the stewardesses, for example, were thinking primarily of the pregnancies and not of the larger culture.

The way out of the dilemma of single-cause thinking is to assume that events occur as a result of many forces acting in a complex relationships to each other. In fact, the word *system* itself contains the ideas of multiple causes and complex interrelationships of a large number of forces. If managers assume that actions have both intended and unintended consequences, they are shifting from single-cause or linear thinking to systems thinking.

Under single-cause or linear thinking, a problem has a single cause requiring a single solution that can be evaluated solely in terms of its impact on the problem. Once found, the solution stays put, as shown in Figure 3.5.

Under systems thinking, a problem is embedded in a situation. The problem still requires a solution, but the solution may have multiple components and may itself be a system. Any solution will have both intended and unintended effects, and these effects should be identified, if possible. Once implemented, the solution does not stay put, since the situation itself may change, as shown in Figure 3.6.

When a manager takes action, the action affects more than the problem to be solved. The decision infiltrates the system and has both intended and unintended consequences—some of which are more significant than what was intended (as was the case with the airline).

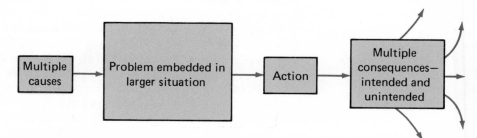

Figure 3.6   Multiple-cause systems thinking

The Contingency Approach

The second integrative trend, the **contingency approach**, is the idea that the best way to lead, plan, organize, and conduct managerial activities is not fixed but depends on the situation.[4] As we have seen in this chapter, approaches or techniques that are highly effective in one situation may be less effective in other situations or cultures. The construction of the pyramids would be managed differently today. Management processes appropriate during the Industrial Revolution would not be appropriate today. The way to organize a firm engaged in small-batch production is not the way to organize a firm engaged in continuous process production.

Therefore, the major task of managers is to determine which decision, or approach, under which circumstances will best help reach the goals of the organization. In his book, Taylor reported his statement to a worker that "a high-priced man takes orders with no back-talk." Such an approach to leadership would not be appropriate with today's work force.

Research indicates that the contingency approach needs to prevail in almost every managerial action. The effective manager must continually ask, "Which method will work best here?" Managing unskilled workers is very different from managing highly-trained professionals. In addition, managers trained in systems and contingency thinking take the entire organization into consideration in making decisions. A decision that may be helpful for one subunit of the organization may not be helpful in reaching the goals and objectives of the entire organization. Properly used, systems thinking and contingency thinking should help achieve the overall goals of any organization within the larger environment and culture.

Implications for the Manager

Knowledge is steadily accumulating in both the "hard sciences" and management. We know more about organizations, management, and managers than we did even a few years ago. Building the pyramid was a complex task but not nearly so complex as designing and managing many modern organizations. Building a supersonic jet or sending a probe to Mars requires more planning and coordination and closer tolerances than moving a stone block down the Nile.

Managing is receiving more systematic attention now than ever before. Yet, the fundamental need of management and managers—the need to plan, direct, and organize work activities to accomplish the goals of the organization—remains essentially unchanged.

This chapter has attempted to select a few samples of management thought through the ages and to show how this thought has affected and been affected by the larger society and culture. Without the cultural beliefs and approval of society, the Great Pyramid could never have been built. Later, the stress on the effect of lighting on individual productivity led to larger issues bearing on motivation, group dynamics, and the quality of working life.

The major movements of scientific management and human relations have had great influence on current management thought. Both Taylor's early work and the conclusions of the Hawthorne studies turn out, after careful examination, to be based primarily on myth. Yet, both "studies" had, and still have, a profound impact on today's thinking.

For example, Taylor was responding to a need to prevent waste by making work more systematic. His widely acclaimed work led to intensive study of prevailing work patterns. As the focus on the job increased, there was a corresponding decrease of interest in the worker. Then came the Hawthorne studies, which counteracted the overly enthusiastic claims of some proponents of scientific management by placing greater attention on workers, both individually and in groups.

As organizations became more complex, there was a greater need to look at them as a whole. Fayol, Weber, and others responded to the need to systematize organizations and to provide a way of guiding organizational structure. Although these people were influenced by their knowledge of organizations that had a relatively simple technology and stable environment, the principles they laid down permeate much of management thought and practice today. Of course, some of their work is now inappropriate, but Fayol himself warned that he was propounding "principles," not "laws."

Finally, managers must understand that there is no set of clear, unified principles that can be applied unthinkingly to all management problems; there are instead only guidelines that must be applied selectively to any particular situation. The effective manager needs to use both systems and contingency thinking to select the proper approach for any situation.

Review

1. Assume that you are in charge of building the Great Pyramid of Cheops. Knowing what you know today, how would you go about designing the organization structure; recruiting, training, and paying employees; and handling other details?
2. Explain how the myth of Taylor's work at Bethlehem Steel and the conclusions of the Hawthorne studies came to be so widely believed.
3. Why is it important for you to learn about and understand the development of different management theories?
4. What was Mayo's principal contribution to management knowledge?
5. Which of Fayol's principles and functions of management do you believe still apply today?
6. How much do you think writers such as Fayol and Weber were influenced by the culture in which they lived?
7. Do you think Fayol would describe organizations now as he did when his book was first published (in 1916)?
8. Does the systems approach seem more appropriate for our time and culture than for Fayol's? Explain.
9. According to the contingency approach, what is the major task of the manager?
10. Read about and report on the life and work of one of the following: Chester Barnard, Ralph C. Davis, Harrington Emerson, Mary Parker Follett, Luther Gulick, Hugo Munsterberg, Robert Owen, Fritz Roethlisberger, Herbert Simon, or Max Weber.
11. If you were able to have a conversation with any person from the past, whom would you pick? What would you choose as the subject of conversation?

The Reorganization of the Roman Army

As a popular and successful general, Caius Marius had been elected Consul of the Roman republic five times. In 102 B.C., at the height of his popularity, he reorganized the Roman army—a reform that had been needed for about fifty years. The structural reorganization was relatively simple. The Roman legion consisted of about six thousand men. Marius divided them into sixty centuries (one hundred men), each under a centurian. He grouped each century into ten cohorts, and he had the heads of the cohorts report directly to the general of the legion. This division made the army more efficient, but the real reorganization was based on changes in society.

Before the reorganization, the army was based on the draft; and under the Roman constitution, the draft applied only to citizens who owned a certain amount of property. But over time, the rich landowners, merchants, and others who were eligible no longer had either the aptitude or the taste for military service. The draft was kept, but Marius allowed the poor and unemployed to volunteer. Soon the reluctant farmers and merchants disappeared from the army. The volunteers were those who saw service under a successful general as a prospect for adventure or escape from poverty.

Then, the army began to supply equipment to the soldiers, instead of having each individual furnish his own. This meant fewer distinctions based on wealth and ensured that both equipment and training were more standardized.

The bulk of the volunteers were farm laborers or small farmers so heavily in debt that they were in danger of losing their farms. In addition to the prospect of prizes from a successful campaign, a general in search of recruits could promise that, if the army were disbanded, the soldiers would be given an allotment of land. Thus the new Roman army gave more prominence to generals with established reputations whose names would bring in recruits.

The common soldier began to shift allegiance from the republic or the senate to the general. The senate might back down or delay on promises, but the soldiers could count on their generals to fight political battles for them. This made it almost impossible for one general to take an army from another or to remove another general from command.

Thus the army fell more and more under the control of the generals. In turn, the generals became servants of their own armies. They could not retire from public life if their own army were disbanded, since they had to fulfill the promises by which they had obtained volunteers.

Although the Roman soldier respected the constitution, the armies would not hesitate to support their generals against the government if the generals had good reason for attacking it. In 51 B.C., approximately fifty years later, Julius Caesar and Pompeius Magnus (Pompey) began a political struggle. In 50 B.C. Pompey violated the constitution, and Caesar's soldiers enthusiastically followed him. Caesar crossed the Rubicon and invaded Italy, and the civil war began. It ended in 44 B.C. with Caesar being voted a perpetual dictatorship. This was the beginning of the downfall of the Roman republic.[25]

1. How do societal patterns, organizations, managing, and the operating levels interact in this case? In the short run? In the long run?
2. Given hindsight, could the army have been reorganized differently?
3. What implications might this historical information have for the world we live in today?
4. What similarities and dissimilarities do you see in this case to such areas as scientific management, the emergence of human relations, and organizational structure?
5. What effect might systems thinking have had?

Footnotes

1. A. Erman, *Life In Ancient Egypt,* trans. H. Tirard (London: Macmillan & Co., 1894); F. Bratton, *A History of Egyptian Archaeology* (New York: Crowell, 1968).
2. M. Childe, *Man Makes Himself* (New York: New American Library, 1951).
3. G. Contenau, *Everyday Life in Babylon.* (London: Edward Arnold Publishers, 1954).
4. U. Kuo-Cheng, *Ancient Chinese Political Theories* (Shanghai: Commercial Press, 1928).
5. A. Lepawsky, *Administration* (New York: Knopf, 1949).
6. G. Filipetti, *Industrial Management in Transition* (Chicago: Richard D. Irwin, 1949); C. George, Jr., *History of Management Thought,* rev. ed. (Englewood Cliffs, N.J.: Prentice-Hall, 1972); D. Wren, *The Evolution of Management Thought* (New York: Ronald Press, 1972).

7.   Ibid., p. 43.

8.   F. Taylor, *The Principles of Scientific Management* (New York: Harper & Bros., 1944).

9.   W. J. Duncan, *Essentials of Management* (Hinsdale, Ill.: Dryden Press, 1975), p. 37.

10. C. Wrege and A. Perroni, "Taylor's Pig-Tale: A Historical Analysis of Frederick W. Taylor's Pig-Iron Experiments," *American Management Journal* 17 (March 1974): 6–27; C. Wrege, personal communication; J. Gillespie and H. Wolle, "Report on the Establishment of Piecework in Connection with the Loading of Pig-Iron at the Works of the Bethlehem Iron Co., South Bethlehem, Pennsylvania," in Wrege and Perroni, "Taylor's Pig-Tale," p. 17.

11. "GM [General Motors] Finds Advantages in Giving Workers Decision-Making Role," *Hartford Courant*, November 24, 1977, p. 1.

12. F. Gilbreth, Jr., and E. Carey, *Cheaper by the Dozen* (New York: Crowell, 1948).

13. E. Mayo, *The Political Problems of an Industrial Society* (Cambridge, Mass.: Division of Research, Graduate School of Business Administration, Harvard University, 1947).

14. C. Wrege, "Solving Mayo's Mystery: The First Complete Account of the Origin of the Hawthorne Studies—The Forgotten Contributions of C. E. Snow and H. Hilbarger," *Academy of Management Proceedings*, Kansas City, Missouri, August 11–14 1976; C. Wrege, personal communication.

15. F. Roethlisberger and W. Dickson, *Management and the Worker–An Account of a Research Program Conducted by the Western Electric Company, Hawthorne Works, Chicago* (Cambridge, Mass.: Harvard University Press, 1939); Wrege, "Solving Mayo's Mystery"; H. Parsons, "What Happened at Hawthorne?" *Science* 183 (March 1974): 922–932; E. Mayo, *The Human Problems of An Industrial Civilization* (New York: Viking Press, 1960).

16. Parsons, "What Happened at Hawthorne?"; A. Carey, "The Hawthorne Studies: A Radical Criticism," *American Sociological Review* 32 (June 1967): 403–416; D. Miller and W. Form, *Industrial Sociology* (New York: Harper & Bros., 1951); Wrege, "Solving Mayo's Mystery."

17. H. Fayol, *General and Industrial Management*, trans. C. Storrs (London: Sir Isaac Pitman and Sons, 1949).

18. Fayol, *General and Industrial Management*.

19. L. Gulick, "Notes on the Theory of Organization," in L. Gulick and L. Urwick, eds., *Papers on the Science of Administration* (New York: Columbia University Press, 1937).

20. M. Weber, *The Theory of Social and Economic Organization* (New York: Oxford University Press, 1947).

21. J. Woodward, *Management and Technology* (London: Her Majesty's Printing Office, 1958).

22. T. Burns and G. Stalker, *The Management of Innovation* (New York: Barnes & Noble, Social Science Paperbacks, 1961).

23. J. Seiler, *Systems Analysis in Organizational Behavior* (Homewood, Ill.: Dorsey Press, 1967), p. 11.

24. F. Luthans, "The Contingency Theory of Management: A Path out of the Jungle," *Business Horizons* 15 (June 1973): 447–465; F. Kast and J. Rosenzweig, eds., *Contingency View of Organization and Management* (Chicago: Science Research Associates, 1973).

25. G. Ferrero, *The Greatness and Decline of Rome* (London: William Heinemann, 1909); F. Marsh, *A History of the Roman World* (New York: Barnes & Noble, 1963).

Part II

People at Work

Chapter 4

Individual Motivation and Performance

The Young Foreman

The Content Models of Motivation
    The Need Hierarchy Model
    The Motivation-Hygiene Model
    The Relationships among the Content Models

The Process Models of Motivation
    The Positive Reinforcement Model
    The Expectancy Model

Toward an Overall Model of Motivation

The Relationship between Job Satisfaction and Productivity

Implications for the Manager

Review

Making Hotplates

Learning Objectives

When you have finished reading and studying this chapter, you should be able to:

1. Describe what is meant by a "model" of motivation.
2. Identify the steps in the need hierarchy.
3. Compare and contrast the need hierarchy with the two-factor approach to motivation.
4. Compare and contrast the positive reinforcement and expectancy approaches to motivation.
5. List the five basic rules for using positive reinforcement.
6. Compare and contrast the content and process models of motivation.
7. Identify and utilize techniques for increasing motivation.
8. Discuss the relationship between job satisfaction and productivity.
9. Redesign a situation to allow for increased need satisfaction.
10. Define and be able to use the following concepts:

motivation	ERG
performance	positive reinforcement
intrinsic rewards	model
extrinsic rewards	continuous reinforcement
content models	partial reinforcement
process models	expectancy model
need hierarchy model	choice
motivation-hygiene	expectancy
model	preference
self-actualization	situation

Thought Starters

1. What motivates you in a work situation? What motivates other people?
2. Explain this statement: "People work only for money."
3. What made you decide to read this question?

The Young Foreman

Tom, a recent college graduate, was made foreman of an assembly line that put together automatic transmissions for an automobile company. The assembly line was located in a relatively isolated part of a large factory. Twenty men stood at predetermined work stations; their jobs had been carefully designed by industrial engineers so that fifty automatic transmissions could be produced each hour. This number was the "standard" for men working at a normal pace, and it included a ten-minute rest break in the morning and another one in the afternoon. According to factory rules, the assembly line could be shut down only during those breaks and the lunch hour.

Tom soon realized that the standard was not being met. Rather than fifty units per hour, only thirty-seven were being produced. New to the job, he was concerned that he would be criticized for failing to meet the standard. He checked the production records and found that the standard had never been met; in fact, the average of thirty-seven transmissions per hour had been maintained since the last design change of the transmission (more than a year ago), when the standard of fifty had been established.

While in college, Tom had studied the effects of participation and feedback on employee motivation. So he decided to call a meeting and ask for suggestions from the workers. The first meeting was not very productive, but Tom did get a few suggestions. One was that the men wanted stools, so they sometimes could sit down. Tom got the stools and allowed each worker to stand or sit as he desired.

The second meeting was much more productive. Tom brought up the difference between the thirty-seven units being assembled and the standard of fifty and asked for suggestions. The men said that the job was boring and that an occasional break beyond the scheduled ones would be helpful. Forgetting the factory rule that the assembly line could be shut down only during prescribed times, Tom made a deal with the workers. When they completed fifty units in a given hour, they would get the rest of that hour off for a cigarette or coffee break. Within two weeks the men were taking only thirty-five minutes to produce the standard; the other twenty-five minutes were spent on breaks.

Tom and the workers realized that this situation could not continue. Although the assembly line was relatively isolated, Tom was getting complaints from other foremen that his men were sitting around too much. They renegotiated their deal. This time productivity went to sixty-five units per hour with a ten-minute break every hour. Things went well until the plant superintendent, who had heard of the increased production, decided to pay an unannounced visit. Unfortunately, he came just when the line was being shut down (at an unauthorized time, according to factory rules). After watching the men on their break for about ten minutes, he became angry and shouted that assembly lines should not stop and that the men were being paid to *work* eight hours a day.

As a result, the men went back to "working" their eight hours, and production went back to thirty-five units per hour. Tom was eventually able to convince the superintendent that if the men produced fifty units an hour, they could take some time off; but the superintendent insisted that they at least had to give the appearance of being busy. Production again rose to fifty units, and Tom and his workers developed ways of "looking busy" during their breaks.

This case illustrates several points that will be covered in more detail in the chapter. First, managers are responsible for getting things done through people (motivating them). They must provide the right conditions for people to work together, and they must coordinate the workers' efforts. Second, different people have different ideas about motivation. Third, as the situation changes, people's behavior also changes. Finally, people are always motivated; they behave in ways that are intended to satisfy needs and to reduce the tension of these needs, as Figure 4.1 shows.

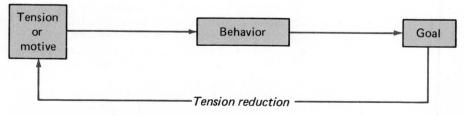

Figure 4.1   Motivation to achieve a goal

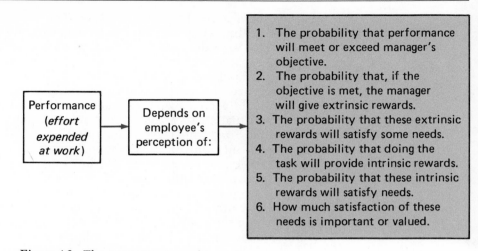

Figure 4.2   The motivation to work

Motivation can be defined as "conditions responsible for variation in the intensity, quality, and direction of ongoing behavior."[1] Performance is the behavior that a person selects on the job to meet or achieve personal goals. Motives, which are internal, can be distinguished from external conditions and forces that determine how a person acts in a given situation. In the case of the new foreman, the motivation shifted as the external conditions changed, and the behavior changed as the motivation changed. Individuals perform in ways that help satisfy needs, and they avoid activities that do not satisfy needs or that result in punishment. The individual's performance as based on perception of the situation can be seen in Figure 4.2.

Work performance is a function of the individual's perception of the probability of attaining the objectives set by the manager and of receiving both extrinsic and intrinsic rewards. Extrinsic rewards are rewards given by the organization, such as pay, promotion, praise, tenure, and status symbols. Intrinsic rewards cannot be given by the organization; they must originate and be felt within the person.[2] Intrinsic rewards—which include feelings of accomplishment, achievement, and self-esteem—are controlled and given by the individuals themselves.

Extrinsic and intrinsic rewards motivate performance only if they appear to depend on the performance. Organizations can *directly control* extrinsic rewards such as pay; they can only *influence* when and how individuals experience intrinsic rewards by the way they structure the work environment.

Managers cannot change people; they can only change behavior. To do this they usually must change the *work situation*—the place and/or circumstances of work—so it will provide the opportunity for people to satisfy work-related needs through performance. The balance of the chapter will look at some of the needs people have and will examine how work situations can be changed to satisfy these needs. In order to do this, several different "models" of motivation will be described. As used in this chapter, a *model* is a mental representation or idea of why people behave as they do. (Clearly, Tom and the plant superintendent were using different models.) The chapter will differentiate between "content" and "process" models, although the basic difference is only their relative focus; that is, there is considerable overlap between the two

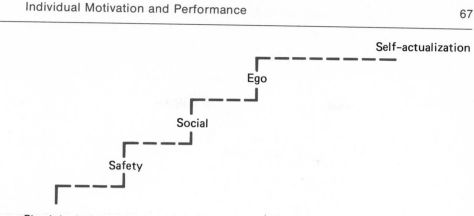

Figure 4.3 The need hierarchy

models. The **content models** tend to focus more on the wants and needs that individuals are trying to satisfy (achieve) within the situation. The **process models** tend to focus more on how managers can change the situation to better tie need satisfaction to performance. Clearly, the manager must focus on both the individual and the situation if performance is to be improved.

The Content Models of Motivation

Two content models of motivation are discussed in this section. The first, the **need hierarchy model**, describes a hierarchy of needs existing within people. The second, the **motivation-hygiene model**, describes factors in the workplace that dissatisfy people and factors that motivate them.

The Need Hierarchy Model

The need hierarchy model, developed by psychologist Abraham Maslow and adapted for use in management by psychologist Douglas McGregor, suggests that:

1. Adult motives are highly complex. No single motive affects behavior; rather, a number of motives operate at the same time.
2. Needs form a hierarchy. In general, lower-level needs must be at least partially satisfied before higher-level needs emerge.
3. A satisfied need is not a motivator. If a lower-level need is satisfied, a higher-level need emerges. In a sense, humans are always "wanting."
4. There are many more ways to satisfy the higher-level needs than the lower-level needs.

The five need levels are physiological, safety, social, ego, and self-actualization (or developmental).[3] Their sequence and relative importance are shown in Figure 4.3.

The *physiological* level includes the universal needs for food, clothing, and shelter. These needs usually must be met before people become concerned with higher-level needs. When an individual has at least partially satisfied the physiological needs, other needs emerge.

The *safety* level originally involved freedom from physical harm, but recent writers have included freedom from job layoffs and loss of income. In most Western countries, the first two levels of needs are satisfied for most people. The importance of these needs can be seen in the widespread emphasis on job tenure, savings accounts, and various types of insurance.

The *social* level includes the need to belong—to be accepted by others and to give and receive friendship and love. In the case at the beginning of the chapter, Tom may have been tapping into social needs in his discussions with the workers on how fast they should work and how they could "appear busy."

The *ego* level involves the need to have a firm, stable, and usually high evaluation of oneself. This level has both internal and external aspects. The internal aspects include personal feelings of self-worth, such as self-confidence, achievement, knowledge, and competence. The external need for a good reputation involves status, appreciation, recognition, and respect. At the social level the person wants only to be accepted as an individual; at the ego level the person wants to be seen as competent and capable. Tom probably increased the ego satisfaction of the assembly line workers, while the plant superintendent probably threatened it.

At the fifth and highest level, **self-actualization**, individuals are concerned with developing their full potential through self-development, creativity, and psychological health; their need for self-actualization cannot be completely satisfied by any job. Most people never achieve this level of need satisfaction; instead they remain preoccupied with satisfying the lower-level needs. Maslow estimated some years ago that in the United States 85 percent of physiological needs, 70 percent of safety needs, 50 percent of social needs, 40 percent of ego and esteem needs, and only 10 percent of self-actualization needs were being satisfied.[4] Although the percentages may have changed, they probably are very similar.

The need hierarchy has been modified by later research indicating that the five levels can be reduced to three levels of core needs: existence, relatedness, and growth (**ERG**).[5] The first level—*existence*—includes the physiological (survival) and safety categories, among them fringe benefits, pay, and working conditions. The second level—*relatedness*—includes the social and esteem levels. The basic ingredient of this need is mutuality, or sharing, with such significant persons as family members, co-workers, subordinates, supervisors, and friends. The third level—*growth*—involves the individual's desire to be self-confident, productive, and creative. It includes the desire to engage in tasks that require full utilization of abilities and that develop additional capabilities or skills. As Table 4.1 shows, there is an overlap between the growth need and Maslow's ego and self-actualizing needs.

The need hierarchy is a general proposition supported by only a few studies; indeed, some studies do not support the proposition.[6] Managers using the theory should try to determine the motivational state of their employees before attempting to develop better performance. For example, are the basic needs being satisfied? Do the employees seek or want opportunities to take on greater responsibilities, thereby increasing growth or self-esteem?

Care should be taken not to overgeneralize from the model. A number of different needs may be in operation at any one time, and not all of them can be satisfied simultaneously. Some aspects of the job may

Table 4.1 A comparison of the need hierarchy and the existence, relatedness, and growth models

Maslow/McGregor	ERG
Self-actualization Self-esteem	Growth
Social esteem Social affiliation Interpersonal safety	Relatedness
Material safety Physiological needs	Existence

be more satisfying than others; and although some motives are involved only with job behavior or performance, others may be reserved for behavior off the job. For example, as mentioned earlier, it is impossible to completely satisfy the self-actualization or growth needs in the job situation.

A few years ago, people were enjoying themselves at a popular Boston nightclub called the *Coconut Grove*. We can assume that they were satisfying social, status, and esteem needs. Suddenly a fire broke out, threatening their physiological and safety needs. People rushed to the exits in a panic, only to find that the doors opened inward rather than outward. Their rush was so great and their panic so strong that the people could not move back to allow the doors to be opened. They literally clawed, fought with, and trampled each other in their panic. Relatedness gave way to the struggle for existence, and the result was that hundreds of people died. This incident is an example of what can happen when one set of needs is suddenly threatened. (By the way, the *Coconut Grove* disaster is the primary reason that doors on most modern buildings now open outwards.)

The Motivation-Hygiene Model

Herzberg

About twenty years ago, Frederick Herzberg and his associates asked engineers and accountants what they liked and disliked about their work. After analyzing the data, Herzberg suggested that there were two vital kinds of factors in any job: hygiene and motivation. The motivation-hygiene model is based on the idea that one set of job characteristics leads to worker dissatisfaction (hygiene) and another set leads to satisfaction at work (motivation). The *hygiene factors* involve the context in which the work is performed; they include company policy and administration; job security; interpersonal relations with supervisors, peers, and subordinates; salary; and working conditions. Herzberg's findings suggested that if these conditions were poor, they could lead to physical or psychological withdrawal from the job. The improvement of conditions is a little like vaccination; it can keep someone from getting sick, but it doesn't make the sick person well—hence the term *hygiene*. The hygiene factors suggest that conditions surrounding the job must be adequate before a person is motivated to work.

According to Herzberg, the *motivation factors* include achievement, recognition, advancement, the work itself, the possibility of growth, and responsibility. These factors tend to increase productivity by increasing job satisfaction (and motivation) and improving mental health.

To briefly summarize Herzberg's findings: What motivates employees toward effective work is a job that is challenging and that allows feelings of achievement, growth, responsibility, advancement, earned recognition, and enjoyment of the work itself. What turns them off are primarily factors that are not directly part of the job itself, such as poor working conditions, bad lighting, insufficient coffee breaks, lack of opportunity to socialize, unpleasant work rules, unneeded titles, a rigid seniority system, low wages, and a lack of fringe benefits.[7]

A 1971 *Atlantic Monthly* quotes a supervisor who is describing assembly line workers, "You don't think. . . . You're just an automated puppet." A worker adds, "That's all I'm working for—my paycheck and retirement." The article goes on to describe an employee who began shooting "at everybody in white shirts" with an M-1 carbine. In a few minutes, three men were dead. At his trial, the worker was found innocent because of temporary insanity. After viewing the factory where the man worked, one juror was heard to remark, "Working there would drive anyone crazy." The worker was reinstated (although not in the same job)![8]

The motivation-hygiene model has been extensively criticized.[9] One of the most serious criticisms is that the way in which the information was gathered (interviews) may have affected the findings. Since people usually attribute good results to their own efforts and blame others for bad results, it is possible that this human tendency predetermined the findings. The more the research approach varies from Herzberg's, the more likely it is that the conclusions will also vary.

Nevertheless, the model shows that not all factors in the workplace have the same potential for motivating behavior. It also presents a useful generalization. From the viewpoint of the employee, any job has both satisfying and dissatisfying features. Furthermore, it suggests that increasing pay or improving working conditions will not automatically increase motivation; they may decrease dissatisfaction but may not affect work performance at all. The model has many weaknesses, but it has been used successfully as a practical guide for redesigning some jobs.[10] (The subject of job design is discussed in greater detail in Chapter 19.)

The Relationships Among the Content Models

Although the models discussed so far have different sources, they show marked similarities, as Table 4.2 indicates. The left-hand column is the need hierarchy, with the higher-order needs (starting with self-actualization) at the top and the lower-order needs at the bottom; the middle column is the ERG model; and the right-hand column is the motivation-hygiene model.

As can be seen, there are some obvious likenesses. The hygiene factors are roughly equivalent to the lower-level hierarchy needs, and the motivational factors are roughly equivalent to the upper-level hierarchy needs. All the models are slanted toward humanistic concerns; that is, they assume that most people want more self-esteem, which is achieved through greater opportunity for achievement, advancement, and responsibility. This assumption is clearly not true for all people. For example, some children who have been severely abused or who come from deprived homes may have learned to avoid advancement and responsibility.

The manager using the content approaches should carefully analyze the working conditions and other circumstances surrounding the job to determine if they are satisfactory. If they are, the manager should try to provide opportunities for interesting work, earned recognition, and additional responsibility for those willing to accept it. In the case at the beginning of the chapter, Tom could not change the design of the

Table 4.2 A comparison of the Maslow/McGregor, ERG, and Herzberg models

Maslow/McGregor need hierarchy model	ERG model	Herzberg motivation-hygiene model
Self-actualization		Motivation factors
		Growth potential
	Growth	Work itself
Self-esteem		Achievement
		Advancement
Social esteem		Responsibility
		Recognition
	Relatedness	
		Hygiene factors
Social affiliation		Relationships with supervisor, peers, and subordinates
Interpersonal safety		Company policy and administration
Material safety		Pay
		Job security
		Working conditions
	Existence	
Physiological needs		

assembly line, but he was able to improve some of the working conditions (rest breaks) and provide additional responsibility and recognition. For example, he gave the men a say in how many units they would produce, and he recognized and rewarded them when they achieved the production goal.

The Process Models of Motivation

The content models of motivation provide some idea of the needs people are trying to satisfy. However, they are not very explicit in showing how people attempt to satisfy needs at work or how managers can change the work situation to enable employees to satisfy needs through improved job performance.

The process models are more explicit in these areas. This section examines two of the process models of motivation: the positive reinforcement model and the expectancy model.

The Positive Reinforcement Model

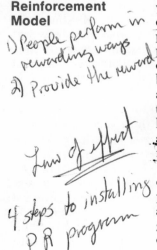

The **positive reinforcement model** involves the use of positive rewards to increase the frequency or probability of occurrence of the desired performance. It is based on two fundamental principles: (1) people perform in ways that they find most rewarding to them; and (2) by providing the proper rewards, it is possible to improve performance. The emphasis in a positive reinforcement (PR) program is on the desired job behavior that leads to job outcomes or results rather than the results alone, on the use of positive reinforcement rather than punishment or the threat of punishment, and on providing direct links between job behavior and rewards. According to the *law of effect*, behavior that leads to a positive result tends to be repeated, while behavior that leads to a neutral or negative result tends not to be repeated.

Therefore, the base of the positive reinforcement approach is the direct linking of behavior and its consequences. The installation of a PR program requires four basic steps, as shown in Figure 4.4: (1) conducting a performance audit, (2) establishing performance standards or goals, (3) giving feedback to employees about actual performance, and (4) offering employees praise or other rewards tied directly to performance.[11]

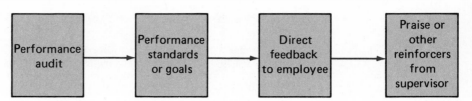

Figure 4.4   Steps in a positive reinforcement program

Conducting a Performance Audit

Performance audits examine how well jobs are currently being performed. Without them, many managers believe that their operations are going better than they actually are; thus the results of such audits are usually surprising. To illustrate: Emery Air Freight Corporation conducted a performance audit on the way it was shipping packages. The cost of freight is considerably reduced if all the small packages going to a particular city are put in large containers. The managers involved in this part of the operation predicted that large containers were used in shipping about 90 percent of the time. The audit showed, however, that the actual figure was only 45 percent.[12] If possible, workers should be involved in establishing performance audits, since they know more about the job than anyone else.

Establishing Performance Standards or Goals

Standards are accepted minimum levels of performance. It is important that they follow directly from the performance audit and that they be tied directly to the job. The goals should be measurable and attainable, and the standards should be challenging but not impossible to reach; perfection is never possible. Standards generally should be set on the basis of observation and common sense, and they should be as precise as possible. "Better identification with the organization" and "increased job satisfaction" are too general to be standards.

Where possible, the workers should be involved in establishing their standards. In the case at the beginning of the chapter, the standard of fifty automatic transmissions per hour was not accepted by the workers until they participated in the decision to take a break after making that number of units. Production eventually climbed to sixty-five units. It would have been impossible for Tom to set a higher standard, such as eighty units. Indeed, when the plant manager simply enforced the rules, productivity dropped. At Emery Air Freight, the employees in the Chicago customer service department set and reached a standard higher than the one management would have set for giving customer answers within a specified time period.[13] However, giving employees all the information they need to establish a reasonable standard—a time-consuming process—is not always possible.

Giving Feedback to Employees about Actual Performance

The third step in a positive reinforcement program is to give workers the basic data they need in order to keep track of their own work. The standards of performance for many jobs are not clearly stated; and even when clearly stated, they are seldom available to the worker. A woman in an insurance company described her routine as follows: "I glance through the form to see if it is completely filled out. Then I separate the blue copies from the yellow copies and put them in different piles." When asked the purpose of the form, how it was used, and where the different colored copies went, she reported that she didn't know. She had no idea if the information on the form was accurate, and she did not know the consequences if the form was incompletely or incorrectly filled out. All she knew was that each line of the form had to have something on it or be returned to another department.

Performance standards are ineffective without constant measurement and feedback. The feedback should be neutral rather than evaluative or judgmental and, if at all possible, should come directly to the worker rather than to the supervisor. Prompt, direct feedback refers, of course, to knowledge of results, one of the most important learning principles. Feedback allows the worker to know whether performance is improving, remaining the same, or getting worse.

To illustrate: In the relay assembly test room described in connection with the Hawthorne studies in Chapter 3, operators assembled small relays for telephone equipment. Continuously operated recorders counted each relay assembled by each worker. Readings were taken every half hour , and "at the end of each day, a report specified the total number of relays each worker had completed, type of relay, total time for sets of 50, and time breaks."[14] The workers freely discussed their performance. For example, on April 19, 1929, at about 4:30 P.M., Operator 3 said, "I'm about 15 relays behind yesterday." Operator 5 reported, "I made 421 yesterday and I'm going to make better today."[15] It has since been suggested that this prompt feedback was one of the reasons for the increased productivity revealed in the Hawthorne studies.

Offering Employees Praise or Other Rewards Tied Directly to Performance

As defined earlier, positive reinforcement involves the use of positive rewards to increase the frequency or probability of occurrence of the desired performance. The fourth step in a positive reinforcement program—offering employees praise or other rewards tied to performance—is the most important one. The behavior should be rewarded and the praise expressed in specific quantitative terms. "Keep up the good work, Chris" is too general. A better form of praise is: "Mickey, I liked the imagination you used in getting the product packed. You are running fairly consistently at 97 percent of standard. After watching you, I can understand why."

One of the most common rewards is money. Although money has a great deal of impact, many organizations are not sufficiently flexible to use it as a motivator. However, other rewards can be just as effective. These rewards include specific praise and recognition tied to the specific job behavior, the opportunity to choose activities, the opportunity to personally measure work improvement, and the opportunity to influence both coworkers and management.

Rewards for specific performance should be given as soon as possible after the behavior has taken place. Reinforcement should be more frequent at the beginning but can become less frequent and more unpredictable after the desired performance level is reached.

There are several different types of reward schedules, among them continuous reinforcement and partial reinforcement. Under **continuous reinforcement** the employee is reinforced every time the correct performance occurs. When this schedule is used, performance improves rapidly but can regress just as rapidly when the reinforcement is removed. In addition, managers find it difficult or impossible to continuously reward performance. Therefore, managers should use **partial reinforcement**, rewarding correct behavior only part of the time. There are a number of partial reinforcement schedules, perhaps the most effective being the variable ratio schedule. Under this schedule, reinforcement is given after an average number of desired responses, but the actual reinforcement varies around the average rather than being given at the exact point.[16] In practice, pay usually occurs on a fixed interval schedule, such as once a week or once a month; pay increases and promotions occur on a variable interval schedule; and praise, recognition, and similar rewards occur on a partial reinforcement schedule.

There are six basic rules for using reinforcement:

Rules for using reinforcement

1. *Do not reward everyone the same way*. Using a defined objective or standard, give more rewards to the better performers.
2. *Recognize that failure to respond also has reinforcing consequences*. Managers influence subordinates by what they don't do as well as by what they do; lack of reward thus can also influence behavior. Managers frequently find the job of differentiating among workers unpleasant but necessary.
3. *Make certain to tell people what they must do to be rewarded*. If employees have standards against which to measure the job, they can use their own built-in feedback system to let them make self-judgments about the work. They can then adjust their work patterns accordingly.
4. *Make certain to tell people what they are doing wrong*. Few people like to fail; most want to get positive rewards. A manager who withholds rewards from subordinates should give them a clear idea of why the rewards are not forthcoming. The employees can then adjust their behavior accordingly rather than try to search out what behavior will be rewarded.
5. *Do not punish anyone in front of others*. Constructive criticism is useful in eliminating undesired behavior; so also is punishment, when necessary. However, criticizing or punishing anyone in front of others lowers the individual's self-respect and self-esteem. Furthermore, other members of the work group may sympathize with the punished employee.
6. *Be fair*. Make the consequences equal to the behavior. Do not cheat an employee out of just rewards; if someone is a good worker, say so. Some managers find it difficult to praise; others find it difficult to counsel or tell an employee about what is being done wrong. A person who is overrewarded may feel guilty, and one who is underrewarded may become angry.[17]

In the case at the beginning of the chapter, the reward for specific performance was closely related to the performance itself. As soon as the agreed-upon units were assembled, the men took their break. When the managers and employees at Emery Air Freight understood that only 45 percent of the packages were being shipped in containers, and feedback and positive reinforcement were given, the workers soon hit the standard of 95 percent. The change resulted in savings of about $65,000 per year.[18]

The manager using the positive reinforcement model should first carefully examine the job (audit the performance) to determine standards, preferably with the assistance of the employees. Then, the manager should establish methods of getting direct feedback to employees about individual or group performance (as in the case at the beginning of the chapter). Finally, the manager should provide positive reinforcement as employees come closer to the standard, shifting perhaps from a continuous to a partial reinforcement schedule as they get very close to the standard. (At the beginning, the manager might have

Manager
① examine job
② direct feedback
③ PR as s

to look carefully for even small changes in behavior in order to give positive reinforcement; otherwise behavior might not improve.)

The Expectancy Model

V. Vroom

The expectancy model of motivation, designed by Victor Vroom, has been the subject of a great deal of research and attention since its original development. The **expectancy model** suggests that people are motivated at work to choose among different behaviors or intensities of effort if they believe their efforts will be rewarded and if the rewards they expect to get are important to them. The three primary factors in this model are choice, expectancy, and preference.[19] **Choice** involves the freedom to select from among different possibilities or alternatives. People can usually choose among a wide range of behaviors. They, for example, choose to come to work or to call in sick and to work hard on the job or to take it easy. The men in the case at the beginning of the chapter initially "chose" to hold productivity down to thirty-seven automatic transmission assemblies per hour and later "chose" to increase productivity to sixty-five units per hour. Working harder led to rest breaks (positive outcomes) but may also have led to more fatigue while working (negative outcome). A student may decide to study hard to get a good grade in a particular course (positive outcome) but may have to pass up going to a party (negative outcome). Sometimes the choice is relatively simple, as in these examples. At other times it is more difficult, as in choosing a career or shifting from one organization to another.

Expectancy is the belief, expressed as a subjective estimate or odds, that a particular act will or will not be successful. Individuals who want to attain a particular goal must usually expend some effort to do it. However, people have certain expectations or beliefs about whether their behavior will be successful. If they see the odds as zero, they will not even try.

To illustrate: The expectancy model was being explained to a group of managers meeting in a conference room with a twenty-foot ceiling. A thousand dollars was offered to anyone who could, without special help, kick the ceiling with either foot. Nobody even tried. The individuals wanted the thousand dollars, but they subjectively estimated that their odds of kicking the ceiling were zero and they made their choice on the basis of this expectancy.

As with positive reinforcement, the standards should be seen as realistic, challenging, and attainable. For example, to obtain a feeling of achievement, the probability of accomplishing the task must be relatively low but not impossible.

Preferences involve valuing some rewards more highly than others and avoiding punishment. In the case at the beginning of the chapter, the opportunity to take a break was a valued reward for which the men were willing to work harder. In another situation, a work group became so involved in meeting production schedules that they found themselves discussing a problem in the plant cafeteria after work hours. As one women said: "Isn't this silly? I really should be home making dinner." From her behavior, however, it was clear that her preference was to stay and discuss the problem.

The expectancy model of behavior suggests that people have needs and will work (behave) in a way that accomplishes goals that satisfy those needs. The goals may be either ends in themselves or means to further ends. For example, an engineer became so involved in solving a technical problem that he worked even on Saturdays and Sundays until the problem was solved. Coming to work on the weekend was his choice, based on the expectation that he would solve the problem. He preferred working to watching television.

The process of choice, expectancy, and preference can be expressed in five propositions:

1. Behavior is directed toward satisfying needs by achieving goals or other outcomes. The outcomes may be valued for themselves or because they lead to still other outcomes, such as passing a course to get a diploma to get a better job.

2. The behavior must be seen as making it possible to achieve a particular outcome. Working harder resulted in a rest break for the factory workers in the earlier case. Working on weekends helped the engineer solve a difficult problem more quickly. Studying harder usually results in higher grades.

3. In most circumstances, individuals can choose among a range of different behaviors to reach certain outcomes. For example, assume that a student wants high grades. One way to achieve the grades is to study hard; another way is to take easy courses; a third way is to cheat; and a fourth way is to join a study group. There are, of course, a number of different mixtures of alternatives; the student can, for example, take easy courses, study hard, and cheat.

4. The more the individual perceives that the desired goals or outcomes are a direct result of personal behavior, the greater the motivation. For example, if everybody has job security for minimum effort, there is little motivation to work hard for that outcome. But hard work may lead to other important outcomes, such as a pay increase, promotion, or increased recognition and praise from the boss.

5. Most behaviors have both positive and negative outcomes. Working harder, as in the case of the engineer working on weekends, may lead to solving the problem quicker (positive outcome) but may also lead to fatigue (negative outcome) or loss of social life (negative outcome). However, the engineer clearly felt that there was a greater positive outcome than negative outcome in working hard to solve the problem. There was little payoff for the men assembling the automatic transmissions to work harder until they got rest breaks as the positive outcome of their hard work.

The model can be summarized by stating that performance at work and the outcomes that people work for are both a function of the expectancy that the outcome will be achieved and the preference for the particular outcome. People are constantly making choices based on the subjective probability that what they do will have a payoff, as can be seen in Figure 4.5, where the individual has an unsatisfied need for status (that is, he would like to be held in higher esteem by others). He has a number of choices. Clearly, one choice is to work harder. This may get him increased income, which will allow him to buy a bigger house or to gain status in other ways. Hard work may also get him promoted. However, working hard also has some negative outcomes, one of which is fatigue.

Another way the individual can gain status is by his leisure time practicing to become a better golfer. If he does get better at this activity, he will gain more status and recognition from his friends; but he may have to forego increased income at work. What will he do?

Individual motivation   **Behavior**   **Outcome**

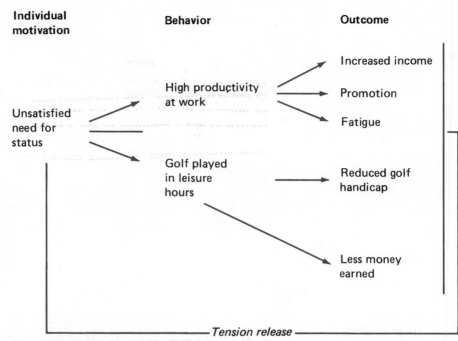

Figure 4.5 An expectancy model of motivation

Probably he will work out the subjective answers to a series of questions before making a choice: What is the probability or expectancy that harder work will really lead to increased income? What is his preference for increased income versus improvement in his golf game? What is the probability (expectancy) of his actually improving his golf game? Although the individual may not be consciously aware that he is mentally calculating the value of these different choices, the calculations are indeed going on.

In other words, the question he is constantly asking is, "What is the payoff for me?" The diagram in Figure 4.5 is, of course, oversimplified. People are very complex, and a number of their needs are usually in operation at the same time. Nevertheless, the model suggests that needs are considered along with the best subjective probabilities and that particular behaviors will bring about outcomes that satisfy the needs. From the behavior choices available, the individual will choose the one that has the greatest perceived reward.

Thus the expectancy model forces the manager to focus on a fundamental managerial problem. If workers are to be motivated to perform satisfactorily on the job, they must see a clear-cut payoff. The manager's responsibility is to either change the situation or help the workers more clearly see the path to the goal. (Some specific suggestions for solving this problem are made at the end of the chapter; other suggestions—referred to as the "path-goal" approach—are described in Chapter 11.)

Neither the positive reinforcement nor the expectancy theory models have been subjected to a great deal of rigorous research in business and similar organizations. However, both show promise, and both are currently being examined by researchers.

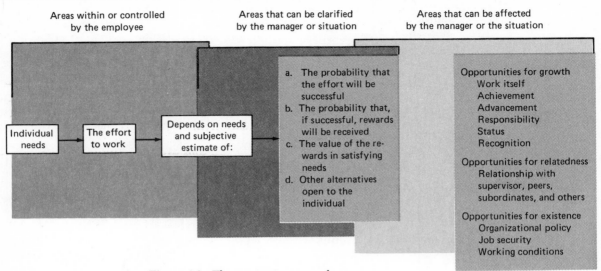

Figure 4.6 The motivation to work

Toward an Overall Model of Motivation

There are some similarities and some differences among the four basic models of motivation we have discussed.[20] Figure 4.6 shows the basic similarities, and this section will stress these similarities, which are of more value to the reader than are the differences.

Some areas of motivation are controlled by individuals, each of whom comes into any situation with different needs and abilities. Individuals decide whether to put forth the effort to work, basing their decision not only on their needs and abilities but also on their subjective estimates. They decide what rewards they value and then whether the effort is worth the reward. These are subjective perceptions.

Managers, on the other hand, have greater control of the situation. When the managers at Emery Air Freight learned that the percentage of packages shipped in larger containers was only 45 instead of the 90 they had predicted, they were able to take precise corrective action and bring the percentage up to their standard.

Managers often are inaccurate in their estimate of the relative importance to employees of various rewards and working conditions. Frequently, they spend large sums of money to "motivate" employees without really knowing how the employees see the world. The Christmas turkey given to everyone has little effect on performance throughout the year; the gift simply is not tied to any kind of performance.

A classic example of misjudgment occurred in the dietary department of a hospital. The majority of the department's employees were women, and most of the women were about fifty years old. Each Christmas the head dietician of the hospital gave out mesh Christmas stockings filled with such goodies as hard candies, chocolates, and oranges. The employees solemnly lined up, received their Christmas stockings, and said "thank you and a Merry Christmas" to the dietician. What she never knew was that this gift actually embarrassed the employees; they felt they were being treated like children, but they were too polite to say so.

The employees' estimates of effort, reward, and the value of reward are subjective. Nevertheless, the manager can be influential in helping to clarify the relationship between effort and reward. The manager can, for example, establish situations where the goals are clearer and the feedback on performance is faster and more direct. Thus, the right-hand column of Figure 4.6 is more directly affected by the manager or the organization than by the employee. The manager can (1) provide opportunities for making certain that the standards are clear and that the employee receives feedback regarding performance, (2) create opportunities for the work itself to be more intrinsically interesting, (3) design jobs so that they contain more opportunities for responsibility or achievement, and (4) provide recognition or establish the opportunity for the employee to obtain gratification from the work itself or from the reward system.

A sales manager can make certain that the sales quotas are clear and attainable (perhaps by setting the quotas in conjunction with the salespeople). When a quota is reached, the manager can give praise and recognition to the salesperson that goes beyond the gratification the individual may receive from reaching or exceeding the quota.

A survey of a manufacturing situation showed that skilled machinists were not receiving recognition for good work. Their supervisor commented, "Why should I praise them? They are getting paid for it." Unbelievable but true.

Individuals have available a wide range of behaviors that they do not use because they are not rewarded in the environment. Therefore, the importance of the interaction between the individual and organizational conditions cannot be overstressed. For example, the opportunity for meaningful relationships with others may be important to some people. The manager can certainly foster or bring about greater opportunity for the satisfaction of social needs on the job, particularly when satisfaction of such needs is tied directly to job performance. One of the reasons for increased productivity in the case at the beginning of the chapter may have been the increased opportunity of the workers to satisfy social needs after reaching the agreed-upon standard. Finally, the manager (and the organization) affect job security and working conditions through organizational policy and its administration.

The Relationship between Job Satisfaction and Productivity

The relationship between job satisfaction and productivity is not completely clear. For a long time, people felt that high levels of satisfaction "caused" high productivity. Then, studies began to suggest that there was no consistent relationship between job satisfaction and productivity. Still later work suggests that while performance is related to intrinsic satisfaction, extrinsic rewards such as pay, praise, and recognition lead to higher performance levels.[21] In other words, paying someone well or giving praise and recognition tends to increase the performance level. The increase in performance in turn increases the intrinsic satisfaction.

Thus the manager should be less concerned about having "happy" workers and more concerned about creating conditions that enhance productivity. Out of increased productivity will usually come increased job satisfaction.

Implications for the Manager

Motivation has been defined as the conditions responsible for the intensity, quality, and direction of ongoing behavior. These conditions are both intrinsic and extrinsic to the individual. Performance at work is a result of the individual's needs, beliefs, and attitudes and of the situation in which the person works. Since most people who work are mature adults, there is relatively little managers can do to change the people themselves. However, managers do influence the conditions under which the people work, and changing the work situation frequently has a powerful effect on people's performance.

The different models of motivation overlap considerably. The content models tend to focus directly on people's needs, while the process models tend to focus more on behavior and the work situation. Clearly, attention must be paid both to the person and the situation. There is no single, comprehensive, well-supported model to which all subscribe; yet, there is enough agreement among the different approaches to give the effective manager some overall guidelines.

Adults are complex and have many needs. No single motive affects behavior; rather, a number of motives may be operating at the same time. Satisfied needs are not motivators, but when lower-level needs are satisfied, higher-level needs emerge. In this sense, people are always "wanting" beings, each with a unique set of needs that are satisfied or unsatisfied at any particular time. Therefore, managers should work hard at understanding their own motives. The better they understand themselves, the better they can understand others.

The individual has a wide choice of behaviors in most work situations; among them are the choices of whether to come to work or not and whether to work hard or take it easy. The decision to engage in one behavior results from a conscious or unconscious choice among different probabilities that needs will be satisfied. These choices are affected by many factors, including the work situation, other people, and the individual's own past experiences. Some behaviors are motivated by avoidance of loss; for example, the individual may come to work to avoid being fired. Other behaviors, especially those involving better-than-average performance, result from attempts to satisfy such complex needs as relatedness, status, and growth.

The manager should examine carefully the range of choices within the work situation. What alternatives do people have? Which alternatives may lead to increased performance?

Behavior changes as the situation changes. Although there are always technological and other constraints, the manager does have some control over work situations. Within limits of the company, the manager should carefully examine what can be done in any job situation to allow for more direct need gratification that will lead to better performance. The manager can help motivate employees by clarifying their subjective perceptions that specific behaviors will lead to specific rewards. To whatever extent possible, the manager should ensure that reward systems are closely tied to performance.

In summary, for performance to improve and effort to increase, the manager must strive to define superior performance by rewarding superior performers more than others. The link between superior performance and reward must be as clear and well understood as possible. High performance also requires that employees know what is expected of them and that rewards be those that satisfy needs.

Review

1. What is a "model" of motivation?
2. List and give examples of the levels in the need hierarchy.
3. What are some difficulties in applying the need hierarchy model?
4. What are the basic differences between the hygiene and motivational factors?
5. Describe the basic relationships among the content models of motivation.
6. What are the basic differences between the content and process models of motivation?
7. Describe and give examples of the basic characteristics of the positive reinforcement model of motivation.
8. What are the basic steps in the positive reinforcement model?
9. Describe and give examples of the basic features of the expectancy model of motivation.
10. What can the manager do to motivate people?
11. Interview a number of managers (such as managers of pharmacies, grocery stores, service stations, fast food restaurants, and the like). Ask them what motivates their subordinates.
12. Ask the same managers to describe a time when they felt especially good about their jobs and a time when they felt especially bad about their jobs. How do their answers relate to what you have learned in this chapter?
13. Ask the same managers to describe their own motivation. Is there a difference between what they answer about their subordinates' motivation and what they answer about their own motivation? If there is a difference, how would you explain it?
14. Take a work situation with which you are familiar, and assume you are the manager. How would you change the situation to provide more opportunity for need gratification on the job?

Making Hotplates[22]

This is a two-part case. You should not read the second part until your instructor tells you to.

Part I

A group of ten workers were responsible for assembling hotplates (instruments for heating solutions to a given temperature) for hospital and medical laboratory use. A number of different models of hotplates were being manufactured. Some had a vibrating device so that the solution could be mixed while being heated. Others heated only test tubes. Still others could heat solutions in a variety of different containers.

With the appropriate small tools, each worker assembled part of a hotplate. The partially completed hotplate was placed on a moving belt to be carried from one assembly stage to the next. When the hotplate was completed, an inspector would check it over to ensure that it was working properly. Then, the last worker would place it in a specially prepared cardboard box for shipping.

The assembly line had been carefully "balanced" by industrial engineers, who had used a time and motion study to break the job down into subassembly tasks, each requiring about three minutes to accomplish. The amount of time calculated for each subassembly had also been "balanced" so that the task performed by each worker was supposed to take almost exactly the same amount of time. The workers were paid a straight hourly rate.

However, there were some problems. Morale seemed to be low, and the inspector was finding a relatively high percentage of badly-assembled hotplates. Controllable rejects—those "caused" by the operator rather than by faulty materials—were running about 23 percent.

After discussing the situation, management decided to try something new. The workers were called together and asked if they would like to build the hotplates individually. The workers decided they would like to try this approach, provided they could go back to the old program if the new one did not work well. After several days of training, each worker began to assemble the entire hotplate.

1.   What do you think will happen in Part II of this case?
2.   How has the situation been changed? What "motivators" were in effect before? What "motivators" are in effect now?

Part II

The change was made at about the middle of the year. Productivity climbed quickly. By the end of the year, it had leveled off at about 84 percent higher than during the first half of the year, although no other changes had been made in the department or its personnel. Controllable rejects had dropped from 23 percent to 1 percent during the same period. Absenteeism had dropped from 8 percent to less than 1 percent. The workers had responded positively to the change, and their morale was higher. As one person put it, "Now, it is *my* hotplate." Eventually, the reject rate dropped so low that all routine final inspection was done by the assembly workers themselves. The full-time inspector was transferred to another job in the organization.

1.   What changes in the work situation might account for the increase in productivity and the decrease in controllable rejects?
2.   What might account for the drop in absenteeism and the increase in morale?
3.   What were the major changes in the situation? Which changes were under the control of the manager? Which were controlled by the workers?
4.   What might happen if the workers were to go back to the old assembly line method?
5.   Can you think of other situations where an approach like this might be useful?

Footnotes

1.   W. Vinake, "Motivation as a Complex Problem," in M. Jones, ed., *Nebraska Symposium on Motivation* (Lincoln: University of Nebraska Press, 1962), p. 3.
2.   E. Lawler, III, and J. Rhode, *Information and Control in Organizations* (Pacific Palisades, Calif.: Goodyear Publishing, 1976).
3.   A. Maslow, *Motivation and Personality* (New York: Harper & Bros., 1954); and D. McGregor, *The Human Side of Enterprise* (New York: McGraw-Hill, 1960).
4.   Maslow, *Motivation and Personality.*

5. C. Alderfer, *Existence, Relatedness and Growth: Human Needs in Organizational Settings* (New York: Free Press, 1972); L. Waters and D. Roach, "A Factor Analysis of Need Fulfillment Items Designed to Measure Maslow Need Categories," *Personnel Psychology* 26 (Summer 1973): 185–190; D. Hall and K. Nougaim, "An Examination of Maslow's Need Hierarchy in an Organizational Setting," *Organizational Behavior and Human Performance* 4 (February 1968): 12–35.

6. Ibid.

7. F. Herzberg, B. Mausner, and B. Snyderman, *The Motivation to Work* (New York: Wiley, 1959); F. Herzberg, "One More Time: How Do You Motivate Employees," *Harvard Business Reivew*, 46 (January–February 1968): 53–62.

8. W. Serrin, "The Assembly Line," *Atlantic Monthly*, October 1971, pp. 62–68.

9. B. Hinton, "An Empirical Investigation of the Herzberg Methodology and Two-Factor Theory," *Organizational Behavior and Human Performance* 3 (August 1968): 286–309; E. Locke, "Satisfiers and Dissatisfiers among White-Collar and Blue-Collar Employees," *Journal of Applied Psychology* 58 (February 1973): 67–76; and D. Ondrak, "Defense Mechanisms and the Herzberg Theory: An Alternate Test," *Academy of Management Journal* 17 (March 1974): 121–147.

10. R. Ford, *Motivation through the Work Itself* (New York: American Management Association, 1969); M. Myers, *Every Employee a Manager* (New York: McGraw-Hill, 1970); and W. Paul, K. Robertson, and F. Herzberg, "Job Enrichment Pays Off," *Harvard Business Review* 41 (March–April 1969): 61–78.

11. A. Bandura, *Principles of Behavior Modification* (New York: Holt, Rinehart and Winston, 1969); W. Nord, "Beyond the Teaching Machine: The Neglected Area of Operant Conditioning in the Theory and Practice of Management," *Organizational Behavior and Human Performance* 4 (November 1969): 375–401; W. Hamner, "Worker Motivation Programs: Importance of Climate, Structure and Performance Consequences," in W. Hamner and F. Schmidt, eds., *Contemporary Problems in Personnel: Readings for the Seventies* (Chicago: St. Clair Press, 1974), pp. 280–401; R. Beatty and C. Schneier, "A Case for Positive Reinforcement," *Business Horizons* 2 (April 1975): 57–66; and H. Wiard, "Why Manage Behavior? A Case for Positive Reinforcement," *Human Resources Management*, Summer 1972, p. 18.

12. E. Feeney, "At Emery Air Freight: Positive Reinforcement Boosts Performance," *Organizational Dynamics* 1 (Winter 1973): 41–50.

13. Ibid., pp. 47–48.

14. H. Parsons, "What Happened at Hawthorne?" *Science* 183 (March 1974): 924.

15. F. Roethlisberg and W. Dickson, *Management and the Worker* (Cambridge, Mass.: Harvard University Press, 1961), p. 74.

16. W. C. Hamner, "Reinforcement Theory and Contingency Management in Organizational Settings," in H. Tosi and W. C. Hamner, eds., *Organizational Behavior and Management: A Contingency Approach* (Chicago: St. Clair Press, 1974), pp. 86–111.

17. Ibid.

18. Feeney, "At Emery Air Freight," p. 42.

19. V. Vroom, *Work and Motivation* (New York: John Wiley, 1964); and L. Porter and E. Lawler, III, *Managerial Attitudes and Performance.*, Homewood, Ill.: Dorsey Press, 1968).

20. Nord, "Beyond the Teaching Machine."

21. A. Brayfield and W. Crockett, "Employee Attitudes and Employee Performance," *Psychological Bulletin* 52 (November 1955): 396–424; J. Wanous, "A Causal-Correlational Analysis of the Job Satisfaction and Performance Relationship," *Journal of Applied Psychology* 59 (April 1974): 139–144; and J. Dermer, "The Interrelationship of Intrinsic and Extrinsic Motivation," *Academy of Management Journal* 18 (March 1975): 125–129.

22. E. Huse and M. Beer, "An Eclectic Approach to Organizational Development," *Harvard Business Review* 49 (September–October 1971): 103–112; M. Beer and E. Huse, "A Systems Approach to Organization Development," *Journal of Applied Behavioral Science* 8 (January–February 1972): 79–101; and "The Drive to Make Dull Jobs Interesting," *U.S. News & World Report*, July 17, 1972, p. 50.

Chapter 5　Managing Effective Groups

The Hovey and Beard Company

What is a Group?

Activities, Interactions, and Sentiments

What Groups Offer Individuals
    Safety and Security
    Relatedness
    Higher-Level Needs
    Accomplishing Organizational Objectives

Characteristics of Effective Work Groups
    Group Norms
    Group Cohesiveness
    Group Leadership

Managing Effective Groups and Committees
    Content
    Process

Implications for the Manager

Review

Ajax Construction Company

Learning Objectives

When you have finished reading and studying this chapter, you should be able to:

1. Define and illustrate the concept of *group*.
2. Explain why people join groups.
3. Identify characteristics of effective work groups.
4. Compare and contrast group content and process.
5. Identify and give examples of ways of increasing group or committee effectiveness.
6. Learn how groups can help or hinder the manager in achieving organizational goals.
7. Understand the processes of effectively managing a group or committee.
8. Increase self-awareness of how to be an effective group member.
9. Define and be able to use the following concepts:

emergent activities	group
pivotal group norms	formal group
relevant group norms	command group
group cohesiveness	committee
leadership	task force
content	informal group
process	required activities
group task activities	required interactions
group building activities	sentiments
self-serving activities	emergent interactions

Thought Starters

1. How old were you when you first joined a group?
2. How many different groups do you belong to?
3. How would you identify a group leader?
4. Does your behavior change when you are with different groups?
5. Have you ever "led" a group? In what sense were you the leader? What were the results?

The Hovey and Beard Company

The Hovey and Beard Company manufactured a variety of wooden toys, including animals and pull toys.[1] After the toys were cut, sanded, and partially assembled in one area, they were sent to the paint room; here, they were individually dipped in shellac and painted by eight workers. The toys were usually two-colored; but since only one color could be applied at a time, the process had to be repeated for each additional color. Most toys therefore had to go through the paint room at least twice.

For many years, the toys were made almost entirely by hand. However, sales increased; and to meet the demand, the painting operation was changed. The eight painters were now lined up alongside an endless chain of continuously moving hooks that carried the toys into a long oven. Each worker sat at an individual painting booth, which was designed to be a backstop for excess paint and to carry away fumes. The worker would take a toy from a tray, place it in a jig (a holding device) inside the paint booth, spray on the proper color, and then hang the toy on the hook passing by. The engineers had carefully calculated the rate at which the hooks moved so that when each person was fully trained, the chain going into the oven would have a toy on each hook.

The paint room workers were on a group bonus plan; they received additional pay when the standard, or quota, was exceeded. However, the engineers calculated that the workers would not reach full productivity for about six months. As a result, the workers were given a learning bonus that was scheduled to be reduced regularly until it stopped completely at the end of the six months. In this way the workers would not initially lose any income; but as their productivity went up, they also would not need the supplement.

At the end of the second month, trouble was obvious. Production was low, and there were bitter complaints that the speed of the line was too fast. The workers were angry at both the engineers and the supervisor, and several of them quit. One worker, Helen, appeared to be the leader in complaining to the supervisor. (Management saw Helen as a "ringleader" who was holding back the group's productivity.)

The supervisor asked the personnel department for advice, and they suggested a general meeting with the painters. After several such meetings, Helen made the point clear. The painters felt they could keep up the pace some of the time but not all day long. Eventually, the workers were given the authority to regulate the speed of the line, and a control was installed in Helen's booth. The workers also had a number of meetings of their own to discuss how the speed of the line should be varied during the day.

Productivity soared. Two months before the scheduled ending of the learning bonus, the group was painting toys at a level about 40 percent above what had been expected under the original arrangement. Bob, one of the painters, remarked, "I always knew we were the best group in the plant!"

Now, the painters were earning more than many skilled workers in the rest of the plant. Management was besieged by complaints that something be done. Finally, the plant superintendent, without consulting anyone, revoked the learning bonus and removed the control from Helen's booth. The hooks moved again at the constant speed. Helen and Bob objected, but the decision stuck. Within a month, six of the eight painters left, including Helen and Bob; the supervisor quit in about two months. Production dropped well below the previous levels, and some members of the group were no longer speaking to each other.

What happened in the Hovey and Beard case? Why did the eight painters first complain, then increase productivity, and finally reduce productivity? Understanding group behavior and the properties of groups is essential to being both a good manager and an effective member of groups, and this chapter will explain both. However, before we examine some of the concepts of groups, we will see how earlier chapters can be applied to the situations dealt with here.

Chapter 1 showed that about half a manager's time is spent in either scheduled or unscheduled meetings. Almost all these meetings are group meetings—a group of people getting together to solve problems or make plans. Thus the manager is frequently a member of a group with other managers or peers. The eight painters in the Hovey and Beard case also attended meetings—some of them formal, such as those with the supervisor, and some of them informal, such as those where they decided how fast the hooks should move—and also were members of a group.

Chapter 3 examined early studies of the Hawthorne plant of Western Electric; these studies demonstrated that groups have a powerful effect on human behavior. Chapter 4 suggested that people are motivated to act a certain way within a given situation. For their behavior to change, the situation must be changed. However, any change has both intended and unintended consequences. For example, in the Hovey and Beard case, the supervisor focused primarily on the painters' complaints. The actions he took increased their productivity, but they also resulted in the unintended consequence of higher than normal pay for the workers.

The superintendent unilaterally changed the situation again for a number of reasons: (1) the wage structure of the plant was upset, (2) the prestige of the engineers had suffered, and (3) some of management's prerogatives were apparently being taken over by employees. His decision essentially ignored the group and focused on the larger organization; and while it "solved" some of the organizational problems, it had unintended consequences for the group of painters (the supervisor and most of the painters quit, and productivity dropped) and ultimately for the organization.

Small groups are very important in affecting behavior. A 1972 bibliography listed more than five thousand articles and books on the subject, and more work has been done since.[2] It is clear that knowledge about group dynamics and behavior is tremendously important to the effective manager, who must know when to make unilateral decisions and when to rely on groups (including meetings and committees). The effective manager is also an effective group member. Approximately half a manager's time is spent interacting with others—including peers, other managers, specialists, and others in the work flow process—at a lateral level.

In one organization, sales districts were divided into fourths in terms of total sales. The least effective sales teams (the bottom fourth) cost the organization about $1 million in profits each year when compared to the highest-performing teams. The two big differences between the highest- and lowest-performing sales teams were "team cohesion" and "leadership."[3]

In the rest of this chapter, we will examine some principles of group dynamics in order to develop two main objectives: (1) to better understand how to manage a group, and (2) to learn how to become a more effective group member. In accomplishing these objectives, we will need to keep in mind that a group is a part of the larger organization with which it interacts.

What Is a Group?   A group is "any number of people who: (1) have a common purpose or objective, (2) interact with each other to accomplish their objective, (3) are aware of one another, and (4) perceive themselves to be a part of the group."[4] Throughout our lives we belong to many different groups. Families are groups; so are scouts and similar organizations. Friendship clubs, chess clubs, and drama and music organizations are all groups.

This text concentrates primarily on groups at work. In most organizations, getting the work done requires group efforts. Managing an individual requires an understanding of individual dynamics, and managing a group requires understanding of group dynamics.

In the definition of a group, "any number of people" cannot be taken too literally, since, at some point, the number of people may become too large to fit the rest of the definition. (Clearly, all the people in the United States cannot interact with each other.) Each group has a common objective, but the individuals belonging to it may have other personal objectives. (An insurance salesperson may join the high school PTA to help promote the school's welfare. But belonging to the PTA may also provide contacts for insurance sales.)

Perhaps it is the awareness of each other that most clearly differentiates between a group and an aggregation of people. Unless people are aware of each other and of the fact that they are a group, they remain a collection rather than a group. They must see themselves as a group in order to interact to accomplish the common objective.

The interaction can be over a long or a short period of time. To illustrate: A line of people were waiting to purchase tickets for a rock concert. Although the people had a common purpose, buying tickets, they were not a group. Suddenly, two people tried to crash the line. About eight of the people in line immediately banded together to stop the gate crashers. At that moment, a group was formed. After the group succeeded in repelling the invaders, they continued talking to each other; but the common purpose, keeping out the gate crashers, was gone, and the group reverted to an aggregation. In this example, the "aggregate" of people had suddenly perceived themselves as being part of a group.

There are many different kinds of groups and many different ways of classifying them. For the purpose of this text, we will concentrate on both formal and informal groups existing in organizations. **Formal groups** are established by the organization to accomplish specific tasks. These groups include **command groups** which consist of managers and their direct subordinates; and **committees** and **task forces**, which are created to carry out specific organizational assignments or activities. Command groups and committees usually continue in existence, while task forces usually are established to solve a particular problem and then are disbanded.[5] Committees and task forces frequently cut across organizational lines, as Figure 5.1 shows.

For example, the boards of directors of large organizations usually have committees to review worker compensation and public policy issues. Audit committees to review financial considerations are now almost universal; in fact, organizations whose shares are sold on the New York Stock Exchange are required to have them. Approximately 80 percent of top management people are members of one or more committees, as are some 75 percent of middle-level managers and 50 percent of lower-level managers; over 30 percent of nonmanagement personnel belong to committees.[6]

As already mentioned, task forces (or project teams) are usually formed to work on a particular problem or activity and are then disbanded. The problem is usually one that cuts across a number of organizational subunits. In one organization, for example, task forces composed of managers and technical experts from the research, development, marketing, production, and purchasing departments are formed to make certain that each new product is moved smoothly from the idea stage through the production stages and into the marketplace.

Informal groups are those formed within the organizational structure but by the individuals themselves rather than by management. Indeed, they may or may not be approved by management. Many informal groups are formed to satisfy social needs on the job. Sometimes, they are formed to hold production at a certain level; at other times, they attempt to accomplish a certain task better. In one rigid bureaucratic organization, for example, a group of middle- and lower-level managers meet approx-

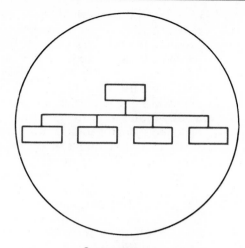

Command group

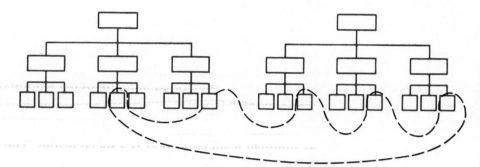

Task force or committee

Figure 5.1 A command group and a task force or committee

The individuals within the dotted lines belong to both a command group
and a task force.

imately once a week to cut through the company's red tape and coordinate their efforts more effectively.

**Activities,
Interactions, and
Sentiments**

The eight painters in the Hovey and Beard case constituted a formal
task group established by management. The three terms defined here—
activities, interactions, and sentiments—will help in understanding the
behavior of the group. **Required activities** are the assigned tasks at which
people work. **Required interaction** takes place when a person's activity
follows or is influenced by the activity of another; the interaction can be
either verbal or nonverbal. **Sentiment** is the feelings or attitudes a person
has about others, such as like or dislike and approval or disapproval.
Activities and interactions can be seen, while sentiments must be inferred from behavior.[7] At the beginning of the Hovey and Beard case, the
activity is clear—hand painting of toys—but little is known about interactions or sentiments. After the activity changed (to spray painting for an
automated operation), the interactions changed. **Emergent interactions**
are informal interactions beyond those required; they result from

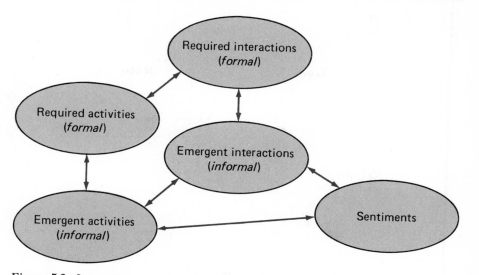

Figure 5.2 Interactions among required and emergent activities, required and emergent interactions, and sentiments.

changed activities and sentiments. For example, when the painters began to talk to each other about working conditions, their interactions were emergent because they were beyond the activities and interactions required by the organization. These interactions led to changed feelings or sentiments about each other and the organization. Helen emerged as the informal leader and Bob as a social leader. The group began to have more positive feelings about themselves and more negative ones about their supervisor. **Emergent activities**—informal actions, beyond those required, that result from changed sentiments—began to be seen. Deliberately or not, the painters' productivity did not at first reach the level desired by management.

Figure 5.2 shows the interactions among required and emergent activities, required and emergent interactions, and sentiments. In the painters' situations, when the change in required activities allowed the group to control the speed of the line, their activities, interactions, and sentiments changed again. Their discussions focused less on complaints and more on how to increase productivity; their interactions—both required and emergent—focused on what the speed of the line should be. Their sentiments also changed; the painters felt better about themselves and about their supervisor. When the superintendent stepped in to make a unilateral change in their required activities, the painters' interactions and sentiments changed again.

To summarize Figure 5.2, required activities lead to required interactions, which in turn lead to sentiments. Sentiments then affect emergent (informal) activities and emergent (informal) interactions, which in turn lead to changed sentiments. For example, after the last change, the supervisor and six painters quit (changed activities and sentiments); and some members of the group were no longer speaking to each other (changed sentiments). As the figure indicates, it is difficult to determine cause and effect. Rather, from a systems point of view, the activities, interactions, and sentiments are both causes and effects of each other.

What Groups Offer Individuals

As Chapter 4 suggested, we have a number of needs, only a few of which can be satisfied in isolation in our complex modern society. In theory, if we are hungry, we can satisfy our need for food by eating. However, this need is usually involved with others. We need money to buy food; but in order to have money, we must work for it or have someone give it to us. Very few people can live in isolation. (*Robinson Crusoe* is an excellent illustration of the unusual struggle of a person completely alone.) Most needs can be satisfied only with or by other people. What are some of the needs that groups help individuals to satisfy?

Safety and Security

Belonging to a group is important for safety and security. Clearly, the newborn infant must be protected from a hostile world. But children soon learn to protect each other. A grade school teacher who asks a class, "Who did that?" will probably receive no answer. Even young groups protect their members, and to be a tattletale is a serious social mistake. Teenagers struggling for individual independence use the group as a source of social support to protect them from an uncertain world.

Group support is just as necessary to the individual in an organization. Both formal and informal groups serve to protect individual workers and to help them deal with the formal organization or the environment. Union membership, seniority, and other such measures help satisfy safety and security needs. The need for physiological and psychological support from groups can be seen most clearly by individuals in dangerous jobs such as coal mining or fire fighting. Coal miners depend heavily on each other for support and protection. Shortly after World War II, there was an attempt in England to combine small work teams into larger crews with more technical equipment. The result was a reduced output of coal until the small group concept was reintroduced in a modified form. Fire fighters depend on each other for protection; an individual who cannot be relied on to work with his "buddies" is ostracized.

One of the chief causes of casualties among untrained troops in battle is "bunching up." People who are in danger need to be physically close to one another, even if they know that this increases their collective danger. Studies of soldiers in World War II showed that men who belonged to cohesive groups were more confident of being able to perform well in battle, less fearful, more responsible for carrying out their duties, and less likely to surrender under stress than were men who did not belong to such groups. The studies also showed that, as a determinant of behavior, the group was more important than loyalty to country or orders received from military supervisors.[8] In recognition of this fact, the U.S. Army instituted the "buddy system," whereby at least two people work together.

Relatedness

People are social beings. Belonging to groups satisfies a number of social needs. Many studies have shown that high turnover, absenteeism, and alienation are closely related to the inability to belong to groups. Emotional support from a group is especially helpful when people are under stress. The importance of relatedness needs was highlighted in both the Korean and Vietnam conflicts. U.S. prisoners of war who were in solitary confinement tended to talk to their captors much more than the official policy (soldiers were to give only name, rank, and serial number) specified.[9] Many prisoners seemed to have an overwhelming compulsion to talk when taken to an interrogator, even knowing that the questioner was the enemy. A person isolated from human communication and companionship simply loses touch with reality.

Higher-Level Needs   Groups can also satisfy higher-level needs such as status, esteem, and growth. For example, recognition can be given only by others. In the case of the eight painters, a great deal of pride in accomplishment was generated when the workers were allowed to determine their own pace. Productivity soared, only to drop dramatically when the superintendent took that responsibility away from them.

Accomplishing Organizational Objectives   Most organizational tasks require the coordinated effort of a number of people to maintain productivity and reach organizational goals. The formal or informal group can be extremely helpful in solving specific work problems or in keeping the individual from making mistakes on the job.

     Groups perform a number of functions in accomplishing organizational objectives. One major function is training new members in how to get the job done. In theory, the organization is responsible for training employees to do new tasks or jobs. But company training is usually not sufficient. The effective work group helps the employee learn how to interact with the rest of the organization and how to get the job done. Sociologist William F. Whyte describes work groups in the restaurant industry:

> *In restaurants we studied, management trained the waitresses to work together and help each other. They were taught to consider two, three, or more stations as a unit and to divide the work among themselves in the most efficient manner. . . . The waitresses help only those girls who will return the favor. . . . The girl who helps nobody can get nobody to help her, and she drops behind and has trouble with her service. The girl who gives help gets help in return.*[10]

     The group, together with the manager, can also help clarify the job to be done. *Goal clarity* exists when the task of the group is clearly identified, and *goal-path clarity* exists when the manner of completing the task is clearly defined. The individual's motivation to work is situation dependent and affected by both informal and formal groups. The individual subjectively estimates whether an effort will be successful and bring forth rewards. The manager must clarify the goal and the manner of attaining it, but the groups to which the individual belongs also serve as a powerful force on the subjective estimates and on the clarity of the work goal. Studies have shown that groups with clearly specified goals are more highly motivated and work more effectively than groups where the goal is not clear.[11] Groups operate to both reach goals and to establish or clarify them.

Characteristics of Effective Work Groups   An effective work group clearly develops goals, maintains adequate resources to accomplish them, and functions as a team whose members can participate fully in group discussions. Some of the factors that influence group effectiveness are norms, cohesion, and leadership.

Group Norms   Over time, groups tend to develop norms, or standards of behavior. A *norm* is a rule that tells the individual how to behave in a particular group. To understand the idea of norms, one need only watch an individual who belongs to a number of different groups. The person should behave somewhat differently in each of the following groups: a church group, a family group, a bowling group, and a task group.

Some rules are formal, dictated by the organization; they become norms only when accepted by the group. In one organization, for example, there was a formal rule that workers had to wear safety glasses at all times. The rule was constantly violated until the manager held a group meeting. The group decided that safety glasses should be worn in particular areas and when working on particular machines. The rule then became an accepted norm and was followed by all the workers. Other rules are informal, emerging from the interactions and sentiments of the group members. For example, in the Hovey and Beard case, the group of painters developed a rule (norm) of high productivity when they were allowed to regulate the speed of the line of hooks.

Norms have certain characteristics. First, norms are developed for behavior that is significant for the group. Although interactions and activities are prescribed by the organization, the emergent activities, interactions, and sentiments combine to influence the development of norms. For example, one group may have a norm of high productivity, while another has a norm of low productivity.

Second, norms can apply to all members of a group or to certain members only. A norm that states how one person will interact with others is called a role; to phrase it another way, a role is the behavior expected of an individual in a given position by the other members of the person's group. For example, the manager is expected to behave differently than the other members of a work group. A new member of a work group may be expected to follow the norms more closely than a more senior and liked member.

Third, some norms are of central importance—accepted by almost everyone in the group—while other norms are of less importance.[12] A pivotal group norm is a norm to which every member of the group must conform. For example, a manager or worker who does not show up for work or does not do anything while on the job will not last long in the organization. A relevant group norm is not as central as a pivotal norm; following it is seen as not absolutely essential but as worthwhile and desirable. Since norms vary from group to group, a norm that is pivotal to one group or organization may be only relevant to another.

Each group member (whether new or old) has several choices about behavior. One choice is complete conformity, where the individual accepts all the norms of the group. Another is creative individualism, where the individual accepts only pivotal norms and accepts or rejects specific relevant norms. The third choice is rebellion, where all the group's values and norms are rejected. Creative individualism appears to be the best choice for both the individual and the group. Rebellion causes the individual to leave or to be expelled from the group, and complete conformity reduces the individual's ability to influence the group.

A norm among most blue-collar workers is that they wear work shirts rather than white shirts to work. The story is told of one worker who began wearing a white shirt and a tie to work (a norm of most management people). Puzzled and uncertain how to treat this "deviant" behavior (creative individualism), management eventually promoted the individual to assistant foreman (thereby legitimating the white shirt and tie).

Conformity to norms is not usually blind, slavish, and unthinking; nor is it only a function of the norm's centrality. Conformity also depends on the group itself, the individual and situational factors. For example, intelligent persons are less likely to conform to norms than those who are less intelligent. Conformity can also be affected by the size of the group. For example, larger groups (more than four or five people) tend to have less uniform conformity than smaller groups. The larger the group, the more likely that subgroups or cliques will form.

Fourth, norms allow a range of possible deviations from the base. But when an individual deviates too far from a norm, there is usually some form of punishment for the behavior. The range of deviation and the punishment vary with the situation and the individual. In an organization that had periodic union strikes, one member of a work group would cross the picket line and go to work. When they had resumed work, the other members punished the deviant by never speaking to him and by causing occasional "accidents" in his vicinity. Sometimes a piece of heavy metal would be dropped close enough to the deviant worker that he only narrowly escaped injury. Periodically, the organization would have to buy him a new toolbox because the old one would be "accidentally" crushed by a heavy object dropped by someone who had tripped in just the right place.

A manager coming into an organization is a formal leader of one group and a member of many groups. Among the manager's most important tasks are learning the norms of the different groups, finding out which are central and which are not, and determining the degree of conformity required and the degree of nonconformity allowed. Detecting norms can be done through observation. Do people at a meeting wait for the boss to speak first? Are they on an first-name basis? Do they arrive on time for meetings? Is disagreement or controversy encouraged, or are people overly courteous? What style of clothing is preferred? The manager can also ask discreet questions, such as, "How do we usually handle this?"

The effective manager works to change norms that hinder the accomplishment of organizational goals. For example, if a work group has a norm of low productivity, the manager will explore the reasons for this norm and will look for ways of changing the situation in order to change the norm. Most importantly, the new manager attempts to develop trust among subordinates. A high level of trust increases the manager's influence and ability to change or modify norms.

Group Cohesiveness

Group cohesiveness is the degree to which group members are motivated to remain within the group and, in consequence, to behave in similar ways (as shown in Figure 5.3). A cohesive group is able to act as one body to attain its goals. In addition, the more cohesive the group, the more likely it is to satisfy the individual needs of its members. Group cohesiveness develops out of the activities, interactions, and sentiments shown in Figure 5.2. A number of factors affect the degree to which a group is cohesive.

size

The *size* of a group affects its cohesion. If the group consists of only two or three people, it may not have enough available skill to accomplish a complex task; consequently, the group may "break down" in failure. On the other hand, if the group becomes too large, communications within it may become less effective, and individual members may not have enough opportunity to satisfy their own needs. The larger the group, the greater the tendency to form subgroups, thereby lowering the cohesiveness of the larger group.

proximity

The *proximity* and *geography* of a group also influences cohesiveness. Groups that work closely together in the same geographical location tend to be more cohesive and effective than groups that are geo-

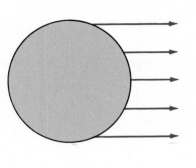

Behavior of cohesive group　　　　　　　**Behavior of group with
low cohesiveness**

Figure 5.3　Norms and cohesiveness affect behavior

graphically separated. The opportunity for face-to-face contact is highly important. The more a group is isolated from other groups, the more likely that the group will be cohesive and will work toward its common goals. This is particularly true when it is easy for group members to communicate with each other. Under these conditions, a small, isolated work group can become highly cohesive and demand a great deal of conformity from its members.

Outside pressure is another important aspect of group cohesiveness. Banding together against a common enemy is one of the best ways known to make a group forget its common differences and become cohesive. In many work groups, outside pressure can come from union-management conflict, competition with other groups, reaction against a supervisor, or mistrust between two groups. In the Hovey and Beard case, group cohesiveness first began to build as the painters banded together against the supervisor and the engineers who redesigned the job.

It was earlier said that the more cohesive the group, the more its members are motivated to accomplish the group's goals and to behave in similar ways. *Accomplishing group goals* increases group cohesion; failure to accomplish them reduces group cohesion. In the Hovey and Beard case, high productivity helped increase cohesion. When the situation was changed and the group could no longer control the speed of the moving hooks, it lost its cohesiveness, and many of the workers quit.

From the manager's point of view, group cohesiveness can sometimes be helpful and sometimes harmful. A cohesive group is necessary to accomplish organizational goals; however, it may decide to work *against* management (by establishing group norms of low productivity, for example).

When a group is too cohesive, or "clubby," new ideas may be rejected too quickly. As group members become excessively close, they may generate a feeling of "we know best." In this stage, called "groupthink," there may be a tremendous desire for unanimity. The feelings of solidarity and loyalty to the group may override the motivation to evaluate different courses of action logically and realistically. The principles of groupthink have been used to explain a number of unfortunate and highly significant decisions made by top-level government administrators.

Outside Pressure

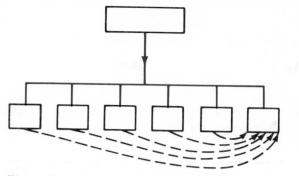

Formal leader

(official instruction, help, guidance, and supervision)

Informal leader

(informal, unofficial help, guidance, and support)

Figure 5.4   The formal and informal leader

The effective manager works at building a cohesive group whose energies are directed toward accomplishing organizational goals. Passing along information, getting the resources for the group to accomplish the task, and holding frequent open meetings are some of the ways the manager can build cohesiveness. Groupthink can be avoided by encouraging open discussion and conflicting points of view.[13]

Group Leadership

ability to influence others

An effective work group wants to accomplish a task, gain some sort of social satisfaction, and have a sense of contribution and growth. In other words, the group needs to attain both unit or organizational goals and individual or personal goals. To reach these objectives requires **leadership**—the ability to influence the behavior of others. (Leadership is so important that Chapter 11 is devoted entirely to it.) The task of the leader is to help the group reach both organizational and personal goals.

Since this perfect match of leaders and goals seldom occurs, informal leaders often emerge from the activities, interactions, and sentiments of the ongoing group. These informal leaders may focus on helping the group accomplish its work tasks or its more social goals. Formal instructions come from the supervisor, and informal help comes from the informal leader, as Figure 5.4 shows. The informal leader may be lower in "official" status than the formal leader. For example, during World War II a lieutenant commander in the U.S. Navy was put in charge of a major repair installation. He tried to run the installation, but he had had relatively little experience in this area. He found that his chief petty officer knew all the details of the work to be done, and soon he had delegated most of the actual supervision to the enlisted man.

Informal leadership emerges to bring about balance in the group and to help the group satisfy both organizational and personal goals. If the formal leader can accomplish both goals, an informal leader may not emerge. If an informal leader emerges to help accomplish *organizational* goals, then both the formal and informal leaders are task oriented, and the chances are good that a *social* leader will emerge to maintain a balance between organizational and personal needs. The effective manager recognizes the existence of informal leaders and works with them to help the group develop norms of high productivity, to build more cohesion, and to enable the group to satisfy social and other needs.

Managing Effective Groups and Committees

The purpose of a work group is to perform a task—to accomplish a specific objective. The task can be a temporary one performed by a task force established to solve the particular problem. It can also be ongoing, performed by a manager and subordinates who have regular staff meetings or a standing committee. The individuals in the group have unique personal needs and varying commitments to the task. Therefore, the group has a multiplicity of objectives, some organizational and some personal. Not all groups are productive; frequently, managers come away from committee meetings believing that they have been a waste of time. There is a way of diagnosing some of the factors that make groups effective. However, before explaining these factors, we will discuss two concepts necessary for understanding them—content and process.

Content

Content involves the subject of the meeting or of the task being performed. The effective chairperson of a problem-solving committee, for example, has a number of tasks to perform if the committee is to work effectively.

[margin note: goals & authority of comm. should be defined]

1. The goals and authority of the committee should be clearly defined and specified. What should the activities be? Can the committee make decisions, or can it only advise and recommend?

[margin note: size & content of comm. should be defined]

2. The size of the committee should be determined, based in part on its authority and responsibility. If the task is difficult or complex, the committee should have enough "experts" to be able to approach the problems from several angles. Generally, fewer than five members reduce the committee's effectiveness, while more than fifteen tend to break down into subgroups. The committee probably should have from five to ten members.

[margin note: agenda must be distributed before meeting]

3. The chairperson should make certain that the agenda for the meeting, together with any supporting information, is distributed before the meeting. This gives committee members an opportunity to study and think about the material before the meeting and reduces "off the cuff" comments.

[margin note: specific time]

4. Specific times should be announced for starting and stopping the meeting, and these times should be kept if at all possible.

[margin note: encourage participation]

5. During the meeting, the chairperson should encourage members to present their ideas. In addition, the chairperson should avoid dominating the meeting and should encourage relatively quiet persons to participate by asking them for their ideas or comments. The chairperson should be alert for the tendency to pick the first feasible solution presented and should encourage the generation of as many feasible alternatives as possible, thereby avoiding premature majority votes or other approaches that reduce constructive conflict.

[margin note: summarize & restate]

6. The chairperson should periodically summarize the discussion and restate what appears to be the current position of the committee so as to make certain that the task remains clear and the discussion does not wander. [14]

Process

Process involves how the content is handled or discussed by the group. A number of different approaches have been developed to describe group process. One of the more effective is an approach that distinguishes among group task activities, group building activities, and self-serving activities [15]

Group task activities are activities directed at helping the group accomplish its goals. They include initiating, orienting the group to its goals, coordinating, and giving and seeking information. In the Hovey and Beard case, Helen was the most involved with group task activities.

[left margin, vertical: Know content vs. Process]

Initially, she complained about the working conditions, and later she controlled the speed of the line from her booth.

Group building activities are any activities that allow the group to maintain itself by helping to satisfy members' needs and by fostering cooperation among members. A group can become more effective by using humor to reduce tensions, by harmonizing ("I don't think you two are really as far apart as you think"); and by encouraging people to participate. All these activities are attempts to build better group relationships so the group can maintain itself. In the Hovey and Beard case, Bob was the social or group building leader.

Sometimes, group members satisfy their needs through **self-serving activities**, activities that satisfy individual needs at the expense of the group. Among these activities are dominating, attention-getting, aggression, and withdrawal. They can all be very disruptive and reduce the ability of the group to attain its formal or primary objectives. The person who engages in these types of activities may be more involved in serving personal interests than in helping the group accomplish its objective.

Managers need to understand the difference between content and process in order to help the group become more effective. If a group is engaged in too much task activity and not enough group building activity, its effectiveness can be reduced. Conversely, too much maintenance activity can detract from the task. Self-serving activities are usually symptoms of nonconstructive satisfaction of valid personal needs, and the manager should try to understand and deal with them.

The difference between content and process is also important because people are emotional as well as rational and cannot completely separate the two. A sure sign that a group is in trouble is when someone suggests, "Let's leave emotions out of this and stick with the facts." Emotions *are* facts. The neglect of group building activities is probably one of the most important factors in reducing the effectiveness of many group and committee meetings. The effective manager is one who can pay attention to both content and process.

Implications for the Manager

A manager is, by definition, a formal leader of a work group as well as a subordinate reporting to an upper-level manager (and thus a member of another formal work group). In addition, a manager is a member of many different formal or informal groups at the lateral or peer level. Indeed, managers may be involved with as many as forty or fifty different groups, both inside and outside the organization. As a leader of one group and a member of others, an effective manager needs to have a clear understanding of group dynamics and the characteristics of effective and ineffective groups.

The effective manager is aware that prescribed activities and interactions lead to emergent activities, emergent interactions, and sentiments. As a result, the manager must try to set up situations in such a way that the prescribed activities and interactions promote a cohesive group. This requires establishing goals for the group or using the group to help establish goals, depending on the situation.

Group norms have a powerful effect on behavior. The effective manager observes and watches for group norms and builds trust in order to be able to influence them. Cohesive groups can do a better job than uncohesive groups of attaining organizational goals. Thus the manager should work at establishing conditions that promote group cohesiveness while avoiding groupthink. The manager may also be able to change the geography of the group if that is needed. Lacking the ability to do this, the effective manager may have frequent meetings and promote open discussion and honest differences of opinion.

The effective manager (1) understands clearly the difference between content and process and uses the knowledge to diagnose why a group is not performing as effectively as it could; (2) works hard at understanding the norms of different groups in order to behave more effectively within them; (3) helps new members understand the norms and standards so they can be effectively integrated into the group; and (4) is aware of the interface between groups. (The supervisor in the Hovey and Beard case worked only with one particular group and lost sight of the consequences of that group's behavior on the other groups in the organization.)

All organizations have informal groups. The effective manager recognizes this and works with such groups and with their informal leaders. The manager cannot personally satisfy the needs of all members. (Indeed, the norms of many groups require that the manager maintain a certain psychological distance from members.) Thus the manager should help the informal leaders satisfy the needs of individuals in the group. Furthermore, the manager should try to keep formal activities from unnecessarily disrupting the informal organization and should draw on the influence of the informal group by integrating its objectives with those of the formal group.

Review

1. What are the key elements in the definition of a *group*?
2. What is the basic difference between command groups and committees?
3. How does a formal group differ from an informal one?
4. Explain the interdependence of activities, interactions, and sentiments.
5. Explain the importance of understanding the idea of group norms and cohesiveness.
6. Distinguish between formal and informal leadership. Are both necessary? Explain.
7. In what ways does group process affect the tasks of the group?
8. List some group building activities.
9. List some self-serving activities.
10. Under what circumstances might a work group have low productivity as its norm? Under what circumstances might it have high productivity?
11. What are the major characteristics of effective groups? Think of the effective and ineffective groups you have known about. Can you identify some reasons for their effectiveness or ineffectiveness?
12. Think of a group with which you have been familiar over a period of time. Explain the relationships among its activities, interactions, and sentiments.
13. When you were in high school, did your parents affect your behavior more or less than your peer group did? Explain.
14. Observe a work group of some kind. Can you identify specific group task, group building, and self-serving activities?

Ajax Construction Company

Since Ajax's construction work usually increased during the summer, the company normally employed extra help for that time. This year, one of the extra workers was Bill Marston, an architectural design student who was interested in gaining practical construction experience. Ajax needed some college graduates on its permanent staff and planned to consider him for employment after he graduated college if he worked out well that summer. Marston had an athletic scholarship at his university and was in good enough physical condition to do the heavy construction work demanded of summer employees.

After he was hired, Marston was interviewed by Scott Drake, one of the construction foreman. Drake was impressed by Marston and agreed to assign him to one of his own crews. After several days of orientation, all new employees were assigned to work teams, each of which had an experienced group leader. The foreman usually saw little of the new employees after that, since he gave assignments to the group leaders.

In about three weeks, Marston approached Drake. He was upset and told Drake that he would either have to quit or else take a chance of being fired or hurt. He explained that the harder he worked on the job, the less popular he was with the others in the work crew. No one would eat lunch with him or talk to him. He had gone to the group leader to ask if his work was unsatisfactory or if there was some other problem. The group leader explained that his work was satisfactory but that the pace he was setting was too high and was going to put someone else out of a job. He then advised Marston to either slow down to the rate of the others or take the chance of an "accident" happening to him.

1. How does a group exert pressure on a newcomer to conform to group norms?
2. Should Marston take the group leader's advice seriously?
3. How does an organization get into a situation where employees dictate productivity rates?
4. What should you do if you were Scott Drake and had a number of different work teams under your management?

Footnotes

1. Adaptation from pp. 90–96 in *Money and Motivation: An Analysis of Incentives in Industry* by William Foote Whyte. Copyright 1955 by Harper & Row, Publishers, Inc. Reprinted by permission of the publisher.
2. M. Knowles and H. Knowles, *Introduction to Group Dynamics*, rev. ed. (New York: Association Press, 1972).
3. J. Zenger and D. Miller, "Building Effective Teams," *Personnel* 52 (March–April 1974): 20–29.
4. E. Huse and J. Bowditch, *Behavior in Organizations: A Systems Approach to Managing*, rev. ed. (Reading, Mass.: Addison-Wesley, 1977), p. 160.
5. D. Cartwright and D. Lippitt, "Group Dynamics and the Individual," in *Organizational Psychology: A Book of Readings*, rev. ed., ed. D. Kolb, I. Rubin, and J. McIntyre (Englewood Cliffs, N.J.: Prentice-Hall, 1974). R. Napier and M. Gershenfeld, *Groups: Theory and Experience* (Boston: Houghton Mifflin, 1974); R. Likert, *New Patterns of Management* (New York: McGraw-Hill, 1961); R. Likert, *The Human Organization: Its Management and Value* (New York: McGraw-Hill, 1967); and G. Farris, "Organizing Your Informal Organization," *Innovation* 25 (October 1971): 2–11.
6. R. Tillman, "Committees on Trial," *Harvard Business Review* 40 (May–June 1960): 8.
7. J. Seiler, *Systems Analysis in Organizational Behavior* (Homewood, Ill.: Dorsey Press 1967); G. Homans, *The Human Group* (New York: Harcourt, Brace and Co., 1950); and M. Shaw, *Group Dynamics: The Psychology of Small Group Behavior* (New York: McGraw-Hill, 1976).
8. S. Stouffer et al., *The American Soldier: Combat and Its Aftermath* (Princeton, N.J.: Princeton University Press, 1949); and E. Shils, "Primary Groups in the American Army," in *Continuties in Social Research: Studies in the Scope and Method of the American Soldier*, ed. R. Menton and P. Lazarsfeld (New York: Free Press, 1954), pp. 16–39.
9. W. Dean, *General Dean's Story* (New York: Viking Press, 1954); E. Schein, "The Chinese Indoctrination Program for Prisoners of War," *Psychiatry* 19 (May 1956): 149–172; and E. Kinkead, *In Every War but One* (New York: Norton, 1959).
10. W. Whyte, *Human Relations in the Restaurant Industry* (New York: McGraw-Hill, 1948), p. 124.
11. A. Cohen, "Situational Structure, Self-esteem and Threat-Oriented Reactions to Power," in *Studies in Social Power*, ed. D. Cartwright (Ann Arbor, Mich.: Institute for Social Research, 1959); and B. Raven and J. Rietsema, "The Effects of Varied Clarity of Group Goal and Group Path upon the Individual and His Relation to the Group," *Human Relations* 10 (February, 1957): 29–44.
12. E. Schein, "Organizational Socialization and the Profession of Management," in *Organizational Psychology: A Book of Readings*, rev.

ed., ed. D. Kolb, I. Rubin, and J. McIntyre (Englewood Cliffs, N.J.: Prentice-Hall, 1974), pp. 1–15.

13. C. O. O'Donnell, "Ground Rules for Using Committees," *Management Review* 50 (October 1961): 63–67; and A. Filley, "Committee Management: Guidelines from Social Science Research," *California Management Review* 13 (Fall 1970): 13–21.

14. Zenger and Miller, "Building Effective Teams"; O'Donnell, "Ground Rules for Using Committees."

15. K. Benne and P. Sheats, "Functional Roles of Group Members, *Journal of Social Issues* 4 (Spring 1948): 41–49.

Part III

Planning and Controlling

Chapter 6

Managerial Decision Making

The Specialty Items

What Is a Decision?

Conditions under Which Decisions Are Made
 The Importance of the Decision
 Programmed versus Unprogrammed Decisions
 Decisions under Certainty, Risk, and Uncertainty
 Limits to Rational Decision Making
 The "Politics" of the Situation

Steps in the Rational Decision-Making Process
 Recognizing That a Problem Exists
 Identifying and Defining the Problem
 Developing Alternative Solutions
 Evaluating the Relative Worth of the Alternatives
 Selecting the Best Solution
 Implementing the Solution
 Evaluating the Results

Some Psychological Factors in the Decision-Making Process
 The Person versus the Situation
 "Facts" versus Emotions

The Descriptive Approach to Decision Making

Effective Decision Making with Subordinates

Implications for the Manager

Review

The President's Decision

Learning Objectives

When you have finished reading and studying this chapter, you should be able to:

1. Define a decision and show the importance of decision making in accomplishing organizational goals and objectives.
2. Describe the different conditions under which managers make decisions.
3. Compare and contrast decisions made under certainty, risk, and uncertainty.
4. Explain why managers frequently look for a satisfactory decision rather than the ideal one.
5. Explain why personal values and politics affect decisions.
6. List and give examples of the seven basic steps in the rational decision-making process.
7. Compare and contrast the rational and the descriptive approach to decision making. Explain why the rational approach is preferable.
8. Describe the conditions under which managers should involve subordinates and others in the decision-making process.
9. Explain how decisions can range from emotionally based to logically based.
10. Define and be able to use the following concepts:

decision	conditions of risk
choice	conditions of uncertainty
alternatives	satisfice
organizational goals	bounded rationality
programmed decisions	decision-making steps
unprogrammed decisions	rational
conditions of certainty	emotional

Thought Starters

1. How do you define the term *decision*?
2. How many decisions do you make in the course of a day?
3. Was reading this question a decision?
4. What are some factors that would cause you to read this chapter?
5. What is a "good" decision?

The Specialty Items

Oil companies produce a large number of different products, including the familiar ones of gasoline, jet fuel, heating oil, and lubricants. In addition, each company makes a variety of specialty items, generally designed for industrial uses; some of these goods are made for only one industrial customer.

The finance manager of a relatively small company operating only in a few states found that the organization consistently lost money on many specialty items, the number of which had been increasing over the years. After a detailed study, the manager identified a number of items that were expensive for the organization to produce and that were sold at a large loss. For example, the organization manufactured one barrel of special lubricating oil per year for a single company. The finance manager recommended to the president that three hundred of the most expensively produced specialty items be dropped. The study had shown that raising the price to cover costs on these items would be more upsetting to customers than dropping the items altogether.

The sales manager and the salespeople insisted that they had to have all the specialty items in order to keep customers buying the larger items. The sales manager pointed out that the organization purchasing the single barrel of special lubricating oil also purchased large quantities of fuel oil, gasoline, and other standard products. Refusal to make the lubricating oil might therefore result in the loss of a major account (and the salespeople worked for both salary and commission).

In these discussions, a number of alternatives were explored, among them: (1) to discontinue selling the large-loss products (the basic recommendation of the finance manager); and (2) to continue selling the products, since there seemed to be no way to tell if dropping them would substantially reduce sales on other products (the basic recommendation of the sales manager).

The problem was explained to the salespeople at the annual sales meeting. After considerable discussion, they still felt that all but a few of the specialty items should continue to be sold; thus management decided to drop only about fifty of the specialty items. Since the sales force strongly felt that a greater drop could result in considerable loss of goodwill and of other sales, management did not want to impose that decision. It concluded also that the drop could result in a great deal of hostility and resentment among the salespeople, and it wished to avoid that problem.

After still further discussion, another alternative was brought up and agreed upon: No commission would be paid on the remaining heavy-loss specialty items. The salespeople agreed that it was not fair for the organization to take a substantial loss and to pay sales commissions for those items at the same time.

Over a period of two years, the "demand" for specialty items dropped by almost 85 percent; more than half the remaining items were no longer sold at all, and the number was being reduced each year. With awareness of the problem and with no commission, the salespeople were no longer "pushing" the products; and frequently they suggested alternate standard products to their customers. Although the company was relatively small as oil companies go, the reduction in the sale of specialty items saved it more than a million dollars per year.

This case illustrates some important aspects of decision making. The separate decisions to make specific specialty items originally appeared satisfactory, but in the aggregate they proved extremely costly. The finance manager showed that the best alternative to the problem was to drop three hundred items. But although his decision was based on a detailed study, it did not take into account the strong resistance of the sales manager and salespeople. Therefore, the politics of the situation required developing new alternatives that could be accepted by other powerful people in the organization. In this sense, the original decision was a poor one, although it did highlight the problem.

This chapter examines the decision-making process and suggests how to make better decisions. Good decisions, which are forward looking to achieve organizational goals, involve problem identification, choice, and alternatives; and they have both intended and unintended consequences. They can be relatively certain or can involve a great deal of risk and uncertainty. (Some of the more qualitative aids to decision making, planning, and controlling are discussed in detail in Chapter 10.) Poor decisions are frequently the result of (1) not thinking carefully enough about whether the decision actually furthers the organization's objectives, (2) the tendency to ignore problems in the hope they may go away, (3) insufficient examination of alternatives, and (4) the avoidance of risk.

What Is a Decision?

A **decision** is a choice made from among alternative courses of action that are available. The purpose of making a decision is to establish and achieve organizational goals and objectives. The reason for making a decision is that a problem exists; goals or objectives are wrong, or something is standing in the way of accomplishing them.

Thus the decision-making process is fundamental to management. Almost everything a manager does involves decisions; indeed, some suggest that the management process is decision making.[1] Although managers cannot predict the future, many of their decisions require that they consider possible future events. Often managers must make a best guess at what the future will be and try to leave as little as possible to chance; but since uncertainty is always there, risk accompanies decisions. Sometimes the consequences of a poor decision are inconsequential; at other times they are substantial.

The process of decision making has been studied for many years. The more we understand the mental processes of human beings, the more we understand decision making. Four basic elements within the decision-making process can be identified: choice, alternatives, goals, and consequences.

Choice is the opportunity to select among alternatives; If there is no choice, there is no decision to be made. Decision making is the process of choosing, and many decisions have a broad range of choice. For example, a student may be able to choose among a number of different courses in order to implement the decision to obtain a college degree. For managers, every decision has constraints based on policies, procedures, laws, precedents, and the like. These constraints exist at all levels of the organization.

Alternatives are the possible courses of action from which choices can be made. If there are no alternatives, there is no choice and, therefore, no decision. If no alternatives are seen, often it means that a thorough job of examining the problem has not been done. For example, managers sometimes treat problems in an either/or fashion; this is their way of simplifying complex problems. But the tendency to simplify blinds them to other alternatives, which never get known or formulated.

At the managerial level, decision making includes limiting alternatives as well as identifying them, and the range is from highly limited to practically unlimited. In the case at the beginning of the chapter, before the meeting with the salespeople, the alternative of not paying commissions on the heavy-loss items had not been considered.

Decision makers must have some way of determining which of several alternatives is best—that is, which contributes the most to the achievement of organizational goals. An **organizational goal** is an end or a state of affairs the organization seeks to reach. Because individuals (and organizations) frequently have different ideas about how to attain the goals, the best choice may depend on who makes the decision. Frequently, departments or units within an organization make decisions that are good for them individually but that are less than optimal for the

very profound

larger organization. Called *suboptimization,* this is a tradeoff that increases the advantages to one unit or function but decreases the advantages to another unit or function. For example, the marketing manager may argue effectively for an increased advertising budget. In the larger scheme of things, however, increased funding for research to improve the product might be more beneficial to the organization.

These tradeoffs occur because there are many objectives that organizations wish to attain simultaneously. Some of these objectives are more important than others, but the order and degree of importance often vary from person to person and from department to department. Different managers define the same problem in different terms. When presented with a common case, sales managers tended to see sales problems, production managers saw production problems, and so on.[2]

The ordering and importance of multiple objectives is also based, in part, on the values of the decision maker.[3] Such values are personal; they are hard to understand, even by the individual, because they are so dynamic and complex. Certainly, many value judgments were made in the Watergate cover-up leading to President Nixon's resignation. In many business situations different people's values about acceptable degrees of risk and profitability cause disagreement about the correctness of decisions.

People often assume that a decision is an isolated phenomenon. But from a systems viewpoint, problems have multiple causes, and decisions have intended and unintended consequences, as Figure 6.1 shows. An organization is an ongoing entity, and a decision made today may have ramifications far into the future. Thus the skillful manager looks toward the future consequences of current decisions. In the specialty items case, to unilaterally reduce the manufacture and sale of all the heavy-loss specialty items could have alienated the sales force and reduced sales of other items. After three years, the positive consequences of the group decision were still apparent; besides the achieved savings, the number of specialty items sold was still being gradually reduced.

Decisions made by a subunit of an organization frequently can have unforeseen effects on other parts of the organization. As a result, there are constant renegotiations and new decisions. For example, the number of specialty items manufactured by the company described earlier had slowly increased over the years as the sales force had responded to customer needs for special products. In the same way, the number of specialty items was reduced after the sales meeting.

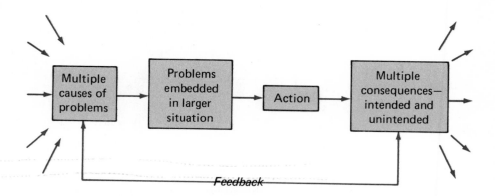

Figure 6.1   Multiple causes and consequences

Conditions under Which Decisions Are Made

Managers make many different kinds of decisions under different circumstances.[4] Decisions of such magnitude as building a new plant may require the approval of the board of directors as well as outside financing. Bringing out a new product may involve a great deal of uncertainty. In an organization with a union, the decision of what to pay a new employee may be highly certain, programmed in advance. In this section, we will describe some of the conditions under which managers make decisions.

The Importance of the Decision

Decisions for the organization range from relatively unimportant to crucial. A decision to buy a different brand of ink for the mimeograph machine may be relatively unimportant. But the decision by the R. J. Reynolds Tobacco Company to spend $40 million dollars in six months to introduce a new cigarette was a major one. REAL cigarettes were introduced in June 1977. For almost four years, fewer than fifty people at Reynolds had been involved in the secret project to gather an additional 1 to 2 percent of the highly profitable $15 billion cigarette market in 1977 and 1978 [5]

A manager can determine whether a decision is important by asking a series of questions:

1. What effect will the decision have on the goals and objectives of the organization?
2. How many people will be affected? A decision affecting ten people in a small organization will have a relatively greater effect than one involving the same number of people in a large organization.
3. How much money is involved? Again, the answer to this question is relative to the size of the organization. A $100,000 expenditure for a local grocery store might be crucially important, while the same amount of money for a supermarket chain might be unimportant.
4. What is the relative frequency of this type of decision? Decisions that are made frequently tend to be routine. For example, the decision to buy paper clips is made often—and routinely—in many organizations; but the decision to build a new plant is made infrequently and is very important.
5. What is the time pressure? Decisions made under conditions of urgency may be important, but the time allotted to them may be minimal. Frequently, deadlines are set by circumstance or by people other than the manager. A sudden breakdown of the assembly line may force quick decisions and action; later, there may be time to study the situation in more detail and determine ways to reduce such breakdowns.[6]

Programmed versus Unprogrammed Decisions

A major aspect of decision making is consideration of whether the decision can be programmed or whether it is unique and unprogrammable.[7] (The terms are borrowed from computer language, where a program is a series of steps for the automatic solution of a problem, such as a statistical analysis.)

Programmed decisions are repetitive and routine because definite systematic procedures have been established for making the choice. A high percentage of the decisions made in any organization are programmed in that they are covered by policies, procedures, and rules. There are standard methods for computing payrolls, for making out sales orders, for admitting patients to hospitals, for assembling instruments, and for registering students. The manager's chief concern in the decision-making process is to determine when decisions are routine enough to be programmed and then to ensure that the "programs" are running properly. (Aids to programmed decision making are discussed in Chapter 11.)

Unprogrammed decisions are more unique and unstructured than programmed decisions. (Indeed, a completely unprogrammed decision is unique, with no rules or guidelines.) Buying a car, purchasing stocks or bonds or a house, arranging a merger, developing a new product—all are examples of unprogrammed decisions. Such decisions have fewer rules, procedures, and guidelines; and they require more judgment on the part of the manager. Often the objectives or goals are not clear.

Both programmed and unprogrammed decisions can be minor or major in terms of their consequences. For example, while decisions involving inventory purchases are usually programmed, they often involve substantial sums of money. Yet, a minor decision such as choosing the design of the company stationery is usually unprogrammed. The more important the decision and the more unprogrammed it is, the more the manager may want to follow the steps in the rational decision-making process (described later in this chapter).

Programs are constantly being developed for previously unprogrammed decisions. For example, investment decisions made by bank officers are generally considered to be a mixture of experience, knowledge, personal contacts, and intuition; over time, investment officers develop rule of thumb guidelines for making investments. But in one study, a computer program was constructed to duplicate a bank officer's investment decisions. An investigator observed the decisions the officer made, interviewed him, and then developed a computer program to imitate the decisions as closely as possible. The model was tested by comparing the computer selection with decisions made by the officer on four different investment accounts. Although not identical, the two sets of decisions were very similar.[8]

Thus one factor in the decision-making process involves the manager seeking out ways to turn unprogrammed decisions into programmed ones. Programmed decisions require relatively little managerial time, which can then be spent on major, unprogrammed decisions.

Decisions under Certainty, Risk, and Uncertainty

Managers make decisions to establish and accomplish desired future objectives. The objective may be immediate, such as asking someone to work overtime to complete a particular assembly. It may also be long term, such as the decision of Freddy Laker to start his Skytrain service between the U.S. and England, which took a number of years and numerous court battles. Unfortunately, the future is not always safe and predictable. Still, managers who make decisions on the basis of available information frequently find the information sufficient for a confident prediction of the future. In general, managers make decisions regarding the future under three possible conditions: certainty, risk, and uncertainty.[9] Figure 6.2 shows the continuum from certainty to uncertainty.

Conditions of Certainty

Under conditions of **certainty**, the manager has enough information to be able to closely predict the outcome of decisions. The alternatives are known, and the decision can maximize the outcome desired by the manager. Some decisions under certainty are very simple. If the manager decides to have a meeting with a subordinate in the afternoon, the

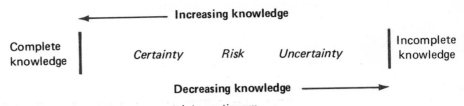

Figure 6.2 The certainty-uncertainty continuum

chances are good that the subordinate will attend the meeting. If a foreman decides that certain parts should be assembled, the foreman can be reasonably certain that power failure will not interrupt the assembly operation. Of course, the future is never completely certain; the subordinate may become ill, or a power failure may stop the assembly operation. However, under conditions of certainty, we behave as though such problems will not occur. Other decisions made under certainty may be highly complex, such as the scheduling of a number of different machines and products to be manufactured and assembled. In such situations, complex mathematical models, such as linear programming, may be used (see Chapter 10).

Conditions of Risk

Under **conditions of risk**, the manager can develop alternatives and estimate the probability of their leading to the desired outcomes. (*Probability* is defined as the percentage of times a specific outcome would occur if an action were taken a large number of times.) Insurance companies, for example, charge different premiums for people of different ages. Frequently automobile insurance for men under twenty-five costs more than for men over twenty-five, since the probability of younger drivers having accidents is greater than that of older drivers, all other things being equal.

In some cases, the probability is not known but can be estimated on the basis of past experience. In risk situations, mathematical tools such as decision trees (graphic representations of decision-making models) can help reduce the risk.

Conditions of Uncertainty

We can never be completely sure of predictions of the future; but under **conditions of uncertainty, the probabilities attached to the available alternatives are even less well known than those for risk.** If there are a large number of factors to consider and if the factors are not similar to each other and are in a constant state of change, the manager must use judgment, experience, and intuition to assign approximate probabilities to the different alternatives.

For example, it may be very difficult to establish a selling price for a product that has never been marketed before. In the same way, it may be impossible to predict just how valuable a new piece of equipment may be when actually installed. For example, one organization that purchased a number of computerized machines found that the productivity level was only about 25 percent of what the original estimates had been.

Under conditions of uncertainty, the manager can use several group techniques to develop alternatives and to establish approximate probabilities. With the *Delphi method*—one technique for forecasting developments (especially technological ones)—the members of the group do not meet face to face. With the *nominal group* method—another such technique—members of the group are physically together but do not directly interact. (Both techniques are discussed in more detail in Chapter 17.)

Limits to Rational Decision Making

In uncertain conditions, the manager may finish working on a problem as soon as a "satisfactory" solution is found. Of course, since not all the alternatives may have been either identified or analyzed, the solution may not be the best. This approach to decision making, called **satisficing,** is the practice of striving for a "satisfactory" rather than an "optimum" decision. Since not all alternatives are considered in the most rational manner, it has also been called the science of "muddling through."[10]

With complex problems, however, managers cannot possibly evaluate all the alternative solutions available to them, even using the most sophisticated computers. As a result, they reduce the complexity of a problem to the level at which they can handle the possible alternatives; this technique is known as **bounded rationality.**

It is important to distinguish between satisficing and bounded rationality. Bounded rationality is a natural limit on the human ability to handle complex situations, but satisficing is a deliberate choice to limit the alternatives considered to reach a satisfactory solution. The first is naturally imposed; the second is purposefully selected.

If we were to look for the "optimum" decision in all situations, we probably would not make very many decisions because each one would take so much time. Instead, we usually decide things quickly and then move on to the next problem. Value judgments also play a part in our decisions; often we "don't like" some alternatives and, therefore, don't consider them thoroughly.

The "Politics" of the Situation

Decisions are not always made on the "facts" of the case, as a casual reading of any newspaper will show. Many decisions in the Arab-Israeli or the Southern Ireland–Northern Ireland conflicts are made on a political basis. Government officials frequently make decisions that are influenced by how the voters feel or by pressures from other sources. Generally, the more important the decision, the more politics are involved. Business organizations are also influenced by politics.[11] For example, Kermit Vandivier, a newspaper reporter, describes a major problem with politics at the B. F. Goodrich Company. In 1967, the company had received a contract to build brakes for a new Air Force plane, the first contract from the Air Force in ten years. The original brake design was bad; but through a series of intricate "politics," the design was never changed. Instead, the Air Force was given glowing reports of the success of the brake. More and more people became involved in the situation, and eventually the final qualifying reports contained inaccurate and misleading data. Kermit Vandivier was involved in writing the final report. When the brakes failed in the actual test flight, Vandivier went to his lawyer, who suggested that Vandivier was part of a conspiracy to defraud and strongly recommended that he report the details to the Federal Bureau of Investigation. Vandivier resigned his position and ten months later, in 1969, was the chief witness before a Senate subcommittee looking into the brake situation. Goodrich eventually redesigned the brake properly. But Vandivier concludes his report by indicating that several of those involved in the situation have since been promoted.[12]

Granted, this illustration is an extreme case. Yet, it does point out that managerial decisions are affected by the politics of the situation. That politics are involved does not mean that managerial decisions are dishonest; it simply means that others' wishes must be taken into consideration in decision making.

Steps in the Rational Decision-Making Process

Particularly for important, unprogrammed decisions involving risk, the decision-making process can be complex. Managers have limited time and knowledge, and frequently there is pressure to make decisions quickly. There are some clear, rational steps to decision making that can both improve the process and help the manager avoid some pitfalls. The manager might not want to follow these steps under all circumstances, but they are a guide for action in important decisions. The rational decision-making process can be divided into the following prescribed steps: (1) recognizing that a problem exists, (2) identifying and defining the problem, (3) developing alternative solutions, (4) evaluating the relative worth of the alternatives, (5) selecting the best solution, (6) implementing the solution, and (7) evaluating the results.

Throughout these steps, the manager needs to constantly collect and analyze information. Does a problem really exist? Is the problem really a symptom of another problem? Are all the alternatives really developed? Which alternative appears to best contribute to the goals and objectives of the organization? Do the results contribute to the organization? Are there unintended as well as intended consequences? Figure 6.3 shows this process in diagrammatic form.

These steps seem simple and obvious, but when managers are rushed for time, they frequently skip through the process or overlook one of the steps. This is why some offices hang on the wall a placard that reads, "Why is there never time to do it right the first time and always time to do it over?"

Recognizing That a Problem Exists

Something goes wrong. A critical part does not arrive. Profits are down. A new law is passed. Some problems arise quickly and some grow over time. To make good decisions the manager needs to recognize that something should be done differently or that something is being done differently that should not be. Thus a good decision maker is aware of the problem situation and of the factors leading up to the need for a decision.

The situation is not always clear-cut, however; the "problem," for example, may be only a hunch that something is not quite right. Further, most managers have more problems than they can handle at any one time. Good managers learn to pick out the key situations on which to focus attention and determine the amount of time, effort, and expense that can be devoted to them.

Identifying and Defining the Problem

What usually leads the manager to recognize that a problem exists? Frequently, it is a symptom of the actual problem. For example, a manager may notice that many employees are quitting. Although this can be called a "turnover problem," the turnover is probably a symptom of a more fundamental problem. Thus the problem to be solved is the one that is causing people to quit. Proper identification of the problem is critical.

Problem identification is a matter of locating deviations from objectives and then looking for the reasons behind them.[14] Information can come from a number of different sources; among them are *historical data*, which may show that the performance of the unit or organization is declining relative to past performance; *planning data,* which suggest that results are not meeting planned objectives; and *criticism* from outsiders, which may show poor organizational performance. Still another

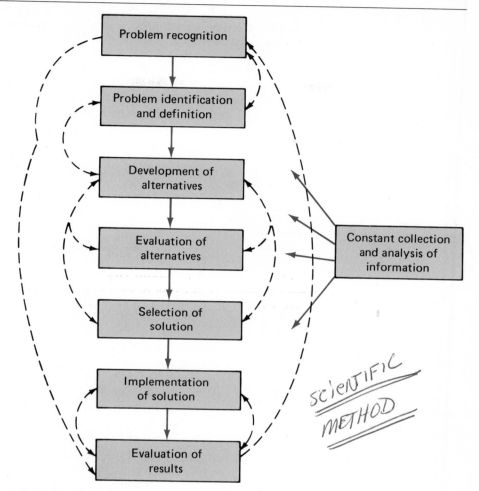

Figure 6.3   Steps in the decision-making process—the rational approach

source of information is newspapers, which describe what the U.S. Congress is doing, what executive moves are being announced, and what competitors are doing.

Problem identification is hindered by people's reluctance to recognize that a problem exists, by their feeling that the cure may be worse than the disease, by their tendency to rationalize and to postpone decisions, and by their reluctance to make "unpopular" decisions. In Vandivier's organization, many executives simply did not want to admit that the original aircraft brake was poorly designed and would never work. Managers also tend to stick to the "tried and true" rather than collecting and analyzing information to really identify a problem. The following example illustrates the importance of proper problem identification and of thorough data collection.

An organization was making an electrode used in medical instruments. Suddenly, a leak was discovered in a piece of platinum tubing used to hold a fluid within the electrode. The tubing was crimp welded (that is, the end of the tubing was crushed together to seal it). For weeks, attempts were made to improve the crimp welder, which had been identified as the problem. There was some improvement, but leakage continued. Finally, someone began asking questions that led to their diagnosis. A metallurgist who was finally consulted explained that a crimp weld could work only if the platinum was "pure." Since the welding was done after the fluid was inserted, it would never work properly. A new method was found for welding the platinum tubing shut by heating it until it melted. Thus the real "problem" was not the crimp welder on which so much time had been spent.

Diagnosis requires a clear definition of the problem. This means avoiding traditional responses, sifting out all the relevant information, and distinguishing clearly between problems and symptoms. It also means identifying the reasons for the need for a decision and the possible obstacles in the path of achieving the goal.

Developing Alternative Solutions

Once we know what the problem is, we can look for solutions. The range of alternatives depends on a variety of related issues, among them: How important is the problem, and how expensive is it? The more important the problem, the more time the manager will spend developing alternatives.

Identifying alternatives can be sabotaged by managers who stick to the tried and true and never look for newer, more creative ways of doing things. It is particularly important that decision makers attempt to develop alternatives. Often groups are particularly helpful at this stage, since they offer a diversity of viewpoints and ideas. In a creative atmosphere they can develop novel ways of handling problems. (This is discussed further in Chapter 4 and at the end of this chapter.)

Evaluating the Relative Worth of the Alternatives

Evaluating the relative worth of alternatives is closely related to developing alternative solutions. For example, there is usually a tentative evaluation of alternatives as they are being developed. (However, a premature evaluation may reduce the number of alternatives generated.)

Evaluation of the effectiveness of each alternative can be done by asking two basic questions: How realistic is each alternative in terms of the goals, objectives, and resources of the organization? How well will the alternative help solve the identified problem? An alternative may seem logical; but if it does not appear feasible, it is not a useful alternative. For example, a problem may be identified as a failure to meet profit objectives. Several solutions immediately come to mind. One is to cut costs. But if costs have already been cut or if further cutting may reduce the quality of the product or service, then this alternative is not very useful. Also, alternatives that are too costly or that strain other resources of the organization are not desirable. For the problem at hand a useful alternative may be to redesign the product to make it more attractive to the purchaser, thereby allowing the price to be raised.

Another pitfall is to use the wrong criteria or standards. Often decisions are based on an alternative's contribution to overall profit. But if return on investment is the ultimate goal of the organization, looking only at the profit contribution may lead to the selection of the wrong alternative. It is critical that the criteria used for evaluating be consistent with the objectives or goals the decision maker wishes to attain.

When the alternatives have been evaluated, they should be ranked in terms of realism and of how well they will solve the identified problem.

Selecting the Best Solution

It is often assumed that if a good job has been done in identifying and evaluating alternatives, then selection of the best one should be fairly easy. However, managers know that they cannot always get all the facts. Thus, under circumstances of uncertainty and risk, the decision maker may not really know, for example, how large a market will develop for a new product or if the competition will be heavy or light. To further compound the problem, it is often not known what impact a particular alternative will have.

As a result, the "best" alternative is based on the amount and degree of information available at the time the decision must be made. Frequently, it is the result of a compromise among a number of different factors, each with its own tradeoffs. Furthermore, since managers have a tendency to make use of bounded rationality and to satisfice (as discussed earlier in the chapter), it is often impossible for them to reach the "optimum" solution.

Finally, managers may wish to try out the solution to determine how it works. For example, many organizations test market new products in specific geographical areas before going ahead with national or international distribution. This tentative approach allows managers to anticipate problems that may occur when the decision is finally implemented.

Implementing the Decision

On the one hand, implementing a decision is the easiest part, since the manager need only trigger the mechanism to get things going. On the other hand, the manager must be concerned with the effects of the decision—and these are not always predictable.

One troublesome aspect of decision making is the way others view the decision. What a manager thinks and believes and what subordinates or peers think and believe can be very different. Therefore, another decision to be made is the acceptance or rejection of change resulting from a decision. The effective implementation of a decision depends on whether it is accepted by the people involved. This acceptance in turn depends on agreement about problem identification and diagnosis, alternative solutions, and selection of the best alternative. When any of these steps are seen differently, some people may disagree with the decision; thus some managers keep the appropriate people informed of the reasons for a decision, since this usually will help them accept it. Since decision making is a combination of both information and value judgments, people can disagree with either or both.

The "best" decision can sometimes be the wrong decision. Often people choose an alternative that cannot be implemented or that causes newer problems. And, of course, since human nature is complex, there is seldom consensus among leaders and followers except for the simplest of decisions. Still, the job of the manager is to make decisions, however unpleasant the task can sometimes be.

Evaluating the Results

Evaluating results is difficult because managerial decisions are seldom completely right or wrong. In picking among alternatives, who knows whether another alternative might not have been better? However, there are methods of evaluating the quality of decisions, especially of those that are clearly "wrong." A classic wrong decision was the introduction of the Edsel automobile by the Ford Motor Company in the late 1950s. The car did not sell, and the fiasco cost the company a small fortune. On the other hand, the first Mustang was a great success. Would another type of car have sold even better? The answer to this question will never be known, since alternatives were never tried.

Most managers agree that the best time to evaluate a decision is at the time the decision is made.[15] Situations change so rapidly that an excellent decision at one time might later turn out poorly because of unknown and unforeseeable events. (Of course, a poor decision might turn out well under other conditions.)

There are two basic criteria by which the potential effectiveness of a decision can be evaluated: (1) the objective quality of the decision, and (2) the acceptance of the decision by those whom it involves or who have to implement it.[16]

The objective quality of the decision can be determined by asking the question: How well did the manager carry out the formal decision-making steps? If the problem was fully diagnosed, if available information was gathered and evaluated, and if alternatives were developed and evaluated, the resulting decision should have a high objective quality. If the problem is a technical one, then looking only at the objective quality of the decision may be sufficient.

If, on the other hand, people are involved in the decision, the second question needs to be asked: How well was the decision accepted by those involved? Sometimes a decision can have high "objective" quality but not be accepted. In the case at the beginning of the chapter, the quality of the finance manager's original decision was reduced because of resistance by the sales force; and the sales force resisted at least partly because there were alternatives that had not been thoroughly considered in the original analysis. Although the final responsibility for a decision rests with the manager, acceptance by others is clearly better than their passive or overt resistance.

The "rational" decision-making steps explained here frequently are not followed in actual practice. To find out why, we will first look at several psychological factors and then examine a more descriptive approach.

Some Psychological Factors in the Decision-Making Process

Earlier in the chapter, we mentioned that decisions have value judgments attached to them. There are also several other psychological factors to consider. Two such factors are the distinction between the decision and the person and the distinction between facts and emotions.[17]

The Person versus the Decision

Since decisions involve both facts and judgments, they tend to be personal in nature, even when they are made by a committee. Yet, a distinction can be made between the decision and the decision maker. The decision is "external" to the individual; that is, people should be able to accept the individual while disagreeing with or rejecting the individual's decision. Many people, however, are unable to make this distinction. As a result, they often reject the decision maker. It is therefore important that people try to understand why decision makers arrive at their decisions; this can be done through exploring their values, assumptions, and objectives.

"Facts" versus Emotions

One reason we do not always make the "best" decision is that value judgments and emotions enter into the decision-making process. Since we cannot eliminate them, we need to be aware of them—especially if they seem to be in opposition to the data. This is necessary because we need to be clear about our assumptions. The following example illustrates how emotional factors and values can enter into decision making. A large company maintained a fleet of company cars for its employees. Whenever possible, people driving somewhere on company business were required to drive one of these cars rather than their personal car in order to reduce insurance risks. The fleet manager wanted to trade in the cars every two years. To make such a policy change he was required to use the company index, a mathematical formula for computing return on investment (ROI). Using the complete records that were kept on each automobile, the manager found that no matter how he looked at it, the index showed it was cheaper to maintain the same cars for several years rather than to trade them in every two years. One day, someone suggested that he had "forgotten" two essential variables—company image and employee morale. Driving a new car, the person said, would be better for both image and morale than driving a car six or seven years old. Several weeks later, the manager triumphantly reported, "The index shows that I should trade cars every two years." He had been able to insert new "numbers" to get the results he wanted.

A modern-day tragedy is that we often make a stereotyped value judgment about managers, seeing them as emotionless machines. Indeed, many managers have been told not to exhibit or to consider feelings, that all their decisions should be rational, impersonal, and controlled. This is nonsense. Humans are not computers; their feelings and emotions are important. Thus an important part of the decision-making process is recognition of the part that feelings and emotions play in decision making.

Figure 6.4 shows the continuum between "emotional" and "rational" decisions. A completely rational decision is based solely on objective facts, while a completely emotional decision is based solely on subjective feelings. At the far left are decisions made from an "emotional" state, such as fear, anger, or joy. Next on the continuum are decisions based primarily on intuition. Although not emotional, these decisions have little data to back them up. Such decisions are frequently made under conditions of uncertainty when the probabilities attached to the available alternatives are relatively unknown and the manager needs to rely on intuition and judgment. At the far right of the continuum are purely rational decisions based completely on fact. For example, a customer may enter a store and purchase a number of items. The sales clerk adds up the prices and announces, "That will be $25.42." This is a decision, but it is so closely bound by rules and regulations that the conclusion is inevitable. However, if the customer is a friend, the clerk may decide to give the person a "discount," which involves much more judgment and emotionality.

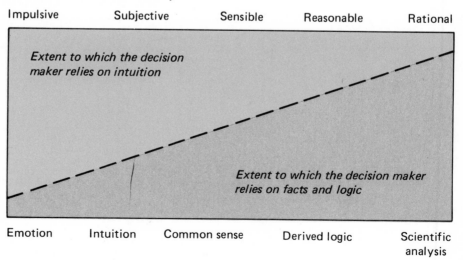

Figure 6.4 Approaches to decision making

The Descriptive Approach to Decision Making

Figure 6.3 showed seven steps in the decision-making process—seven rational steps for coming up with an optimal solution. But people do not always decide by the rules. In fact, often they do not even act when they see a problem. Instead they procrastinate (which is also a decision).

Even when people do attempt problem solving, they tend to take shortcuts. First, they think they see a problem. As soon as they tentatively identify it, they come up with a possible solution. If the solution does not work, or if somebody objects to it, they begin to redefine the problem, usually coming up with another possible solution. If that works, they stop. If it does not, they further redefine the problem, coming up almost immediately with another solution (as shown by Figure 6.5).

This figure illustrates several important points. First, it shows a process by which people "finish" working on a problem as soon as a "satisfactory" solution is found. Rather than seeking the optimal solution, the busy manager frequently wants one that is only "good enough." (This is called "satisficing," and it was described earlier in the chapter.) Second, because not all the alternatives can be identified, particularly under conditions of uncertainty, the manager often reduces the complexity of the problem through bounded rationality (also described earlier in the chapter). Finally, managers are sometimes more concerned about avoiding risks or losses than about making gains, more concerned about the personal consequences of the decision than about the organization's goals. As a result, decisions tend to be more conservative than they should be, as the following example shows.

A company president learned about a small company available for purchase that had a good chance to make a large profit. After considering the matter, he decided not to bring the decision up to the board of directors, who would have to approve the purchase. His reasoning was that if his company bought the small company and the decision turned out well, he would be seen only as doing a good job as president. Although the odds were small, if the purchase did not turn out well, he might be seen as having made a highly visible mistake. Thus he himself had nothing to gain by recommending the purchase; and even though it probably would have helped the company, he chose not to take the risk. The board of directors never knew.

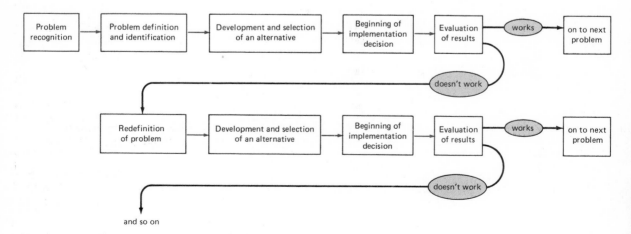

Figure 6.5 Steps in the decision-making process—the descriptive approach

Comparing the descriptive model of decision making (Figure 6.5) with the rational model (Figure 6.3) the differences become apparent. The objective of the descriptive model is to explain how individuals and organizations tend to make decisions. The objective of the rational model is to prescribe techniques for accomplishing a specific end and to explain how managers should behave to maximize goal accomplishment.

Both approaches are important. The rational model gives managers guidelines for efficient action. However, it makes some unrealistic assumptions about the world. The descriptive model shows that the real world is far more complex than theory would suggest, and it helps managers learn to appreciate the usefulness of judgment. Thus both approaches help managers deal with the realities of organizational life.

The effective manager generally will use the rational approach in areas that are relatively programmed and simple and the descriptive approach in complex, unprogrammed situations. Of course, the manager should also understand that the decision-making process ideally will approach the rational model whenever possible and should be aware of any deviations from that model.

Effective Decision Making with Subordinates

As Chapter 1 showed, much of a manager's time is spent working with other people, and much of what the manager does is therefore influenced by others. Decision making usually is not a solitary process. Most decisions involve others, and many are arrived at through some sort of group process.[18] The groups generally are called committees, conferences, task forces, and staff meetings—although some have no name at all.

At times, it is appropriate for a manager to handle the entire decision-making process alone. Usually, however, even where an individual manager has the responsibility for solving a specific problem, getting the decision put into effect requires the involvement and participation—and therefore the commitment—of others. For example, in the case at the beginning of the chapter, any attempt by the finance manager to unilaterally reduce a large number of specialty items would have been strongly resisted by the sales manager and the sales force.

Some suggested guidelines for involving individual subordinates or groups in the decision-making process are based on three assumptions: (1) that the decision-making style should vary with the situation, (2) that the amount of participation by subordinates should vary with the situation, and (3) that no single decision-making style is appropriate to all situations.[19] Therefore, the manager should pick the decision-making style that is most appropriate and effective in the situation. Table 6.1 lists five styles for decision-making under different conditions.

Table 6.1 Decision-making styles

1. The manager makes the decision, using the information available at the time.
2. The manager gets necessary information from subordinates and then makes the decision. Subordinates may or may not be told about the problem or the decision.
3. The manager shares the problem with subordinates on an individual basis, requesting their suggestions and ideas without bringing them together as a group. The manager then makes the decision, which may or may not be influenced by the subordinates.
4. The manager discusses the problem with a group of relevant subordinates, requesting their collective ideas and suggestions. The manager then makes the decision, which may or may not be influenced by the group of subordinates.
5. The manager shares the problem with subordinates as a group. The group generates and evaluates alternatives and attempts to reach agreement on the proper solution by consensus. The manager accepts the decision that has the support of the entire group.

The manager should then ask a number of questions to determine which decision-making style is most appropriate to the situation. The questions are listed below and are illustrated by a **decision tree** (a graphic representation of the decision-making process) in Figure 6.6. The questions, which can be answered on a yes-no basis, are arranged across the top of the figure. To use the model for any situation, one starts at the left side and works toward the right, asking the question immediately above any box in the figure. The basic questions are:

1. Is there a quality requirement such that one solution is likely to be more rational than another? If the answer is no, the manager can use decision style 1 from location A.
2. Is there sufficient information to make a good decision? If the answer is no, then decision style 1 will probably not be appropriate.
3. Is the problem structured? Is it clear what information is needed and where it can be obtained? If the answer is no, then styles 2, 4, or 5 may be appropriate, depending on the need for acceptance by subordinates.
4. Is acceptance of the decision by subordinates critical to its implementation? If the answer is yes, then styles 1 and 2 will not be appropriate, and style 5 may be the most appropriate.
5. If the manager makes the decision, is it reasonably certain to be accepted by subordinates? If the answer is yes, then style 1 or 2 may be appropriate, depending on the information available to the manager. If the answer is no, then styles 4 or 5 may be more appropriate, depending on the situation.
6. Can subordinates be trusted to base their solutions on the achievement of organizational goals? If yes, decision style 5 may be most appropriate.
7. Is conflict among subordinates likely to occur if the preferred solution is chosen? If the answer is yes and if a good decision needs to be reached, style 5 will probably not be appropriate, and styles 3 or 4 should probably be used.

This approach to decision making provides simple guidelines for when to involve subordinates. For example, if the problem is known and structured, if the manager has the necessary information, and if there is little or no problem with subordinate acceptance, decision style 1 is probably most appropriate. On the other hand, if there are a variety of potentially good solutions, if subordinates can be trusted, and if the problem is complex (with no single person having all the information), decision style 5 may be most appropriate. When different styles seem equally appropriate, the manager should select the one that is least costly in terms of time and resources.

Group decision making may be highly important when more than one organizational unit is involved. In such a case, a "decision" made by one unit is frequently resisted by another unit affected by the decision. Therefore, if a decision affects more than one organizational unit—particularly if the units are organized under different managers—representatives of all the units should help in the decision making. Failure to involve all units will almost automatically mean opposition.[20]

To avoid unnecessary complexity, the decision tree used in Figure 6.6 was limited to subordinates. But decision making can also be improved by the involvement of peers. There are also several other ap-

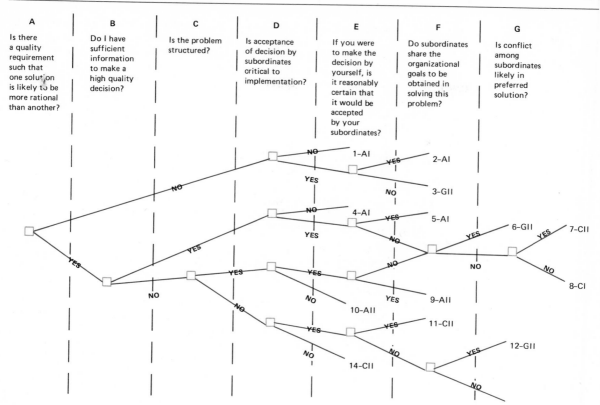

Figure 6.6 Effective decision making with subordinates

proaches to using groups in decision making, two important ones being nominal and delphi groups. A *nominal group* is physically together, but the members do not directly interact. A *Delphi group* is composed of a panel of people who are not physically together but who interact through the use of questionnaires. Both groups are described in detail in Chapter 17, and mathematical and quantitative aids to decision making are described in Chapter 10.

Implications for the Manager

This chapter has examined the importance of the decision-making process in accomplishing the goals and objectives of the organization. The manager may make hundreds of decisions a week. Some relatively certain and unimportant ones require only a few seconds to make. Major ones, however, may require a great deal of time. Some decisions are highly programmed and require little thought. Others, especially those which are important and made under conditions of uncertainty, may require innovative approaches. The decision to purchase mimeograph ink is very different from the decision to spend $40 million to promote a new cigarette.

To help managers improve the decision-making process, a number of rational steps were outlined. Unfortunately, many people do not follow these steps very well. One of the reasons for this is that they are in a hurry to move on to other things; another is that they make value judgments that are not based on fact. Because people are in a hurry and because they have a lot to do, they seldom try for the "best" solution; rather they satisfice—that is, they develop a solution that is only satisfactory. There are also some psychological reasons for satisficing. One is the tendency to make decisions that minimize personal risk. Another is the tendency to procrastinate in the hope that the problem will go away.

Emotions have a great influence on decisions, although many people believe in the myth that managers are like computers, making decisions on facts only. All people are affected by their own and others' emotions. Thus they need to become more aware of their own and others' values and emotions rather than trying to ignore them.

A decision is good if it contains a quality solution and if it is accepted by those whom it affects. Thus it is important for managers to involve subordinates in the decision-making process at appropriate times and places.

Review

1. Why is it suggested that decision making is the most important managerial function?
2. What are the different conditions under which managers make decisions?
3. Should a manager make a decision differently under conditions of certainty, risk, and uncertainty? Explain.
4. In what ways do values and politics affect decisions?
5. What are some of the reasons that managers look for satisfactory decisions rather than ideal ones?
6. Explain the basic difference between *satisficing* and *bounded rationality*.
7. What are the steps in the rational decision-making process?
8. What are some of the reasons why these steps are not always followed?
9. What are the basic differences between the rational and the descriptive approaches to decision making?
10. What are the conditions under which managers should involve subordinates and others in the decision-making process?
11. Observe the manager of a local business or organization. What kinds of decisions are made? How are they made? What suggestions can you offer to improve the decision-making process?
12. Do you follow the steps given in the chapter for making rational decisions, or do you tend to jump from problem identification to tentative solutions and then back again?
13. Try following the steps for better decision making on an important problem. Do you think you will get a better solution? Explain.

The President's Decision

A small firm had about twelve secretaries reporting to managers. Working hours were 9 A.M. to 5 P.M. One morning, the president of the company was looking out his office window, which was directly above the entrance to the building. He noticed that his own secretary was about ten minutes late to work and that the others were coming in as much as ten to fifteen minutes late. Angrily, he called in his secretary and dictated a memorandum to all the secretaries.

The memo stated essentially that working hours were from 9 to 5 and that each secretary was expected to arrive promptly on time or to be docked pay for the lost time. The memo was hand delivered to each secretary.

The next morning all the secretaries arrived exactly at 9 A.M. The president was pleased. His decision had been effective.

That afternoon, he called in his secretary about 4:30 P.M., as was his usual custom, to begin dictating letters to be typed the next day. (Frequently, the dictation would take about an hour.) The secretary arrived with her steno pad, and the president began dictating. Normally, he would continue dictating until all the letters were finished. This particular day, however, his secretary stood up at 4:45 and closed her notebook even though a considerable amount of dictation remained.

She gently reminded the president that working hours were from 9 to 5 and that she would need the remaining time to clear up some unfinished business. Throughout the organization, all the other secretaries were doing much the same thing. Promptly at 5, every secretary left the building.

Within a few weeks, everything was back to normal. The secretaries were again coming in a few minutes late, and the work was getting done.

1. How effective was the president's decision?
2. What inferences had he made?
3. Had he considered all the alternatives? the consequences?
4. What would you have done in his place?
5. What was the problem the president was trying to solve?
6. Did he properly evaluate the alternative he chose?

Footnotes

1. P. Drucker, *The Practice of Management* (New York: Harper & Bros., 1954); J. Forrester, "Managerial Decision Making," in *Management and the Computer of the Future* ed. M. Greenberger (New York: Wiley, 1962); H. Simon, *The Shape of Automation for Men and Management* (New York: Harper Torchbooks, 1965); H. Simon, *Administrative Behavior*, 3rd ed. (New York: Free Press, 1976).
2. D. Dearborn and H. Simon, "Selective Perception: A Note on the Departmental Identification of Executives," *Sociometry* 21 (January 1958): 140–144.
3. G. England, "Personal Value Systems of American Managers," *Journal of the Academy of Management* 10 (March 1967): 53–68; W. Guth and R. Tagiuri, "Personal Values and Corporate Strategy," *Harvard Business Review* 43 (September–October 1965): 123–132.
4. R. Morrell, *Managerial Decision-Making: A Logical Approach* (Milwaukee: Bruce Publishing, 1960); C. Kepner and B. Trego, *The Rational Manager* (New York: McGraw-Hill, 1965); C. Gremion, "Toward a New Theory of Decision Making," *International Studies of Management and Organization* 2 (Summer 1972): 125–141.
5. A. Crittenden, "$40 Million for a Real Smoke," *New York Times*, May 15, 1977, Sec. 3.
6. See F. Shull, A. Delbeque, and L. Cummings, *Organizational Decision Making* (New York: McGraw-Hill, 1970); D. Miller and M. Starr, *Executive Decision and Operations Research* (Englewood Cliffs, N.J.:Prentice-Hall, 1960); S. Beer, *Brain of the Firm* (London: Penguin Books, 1973).
7. H. Mintzberg, D. Raisinghani, and A. Theoret, "The Structure of Unstructured Decision Processes," *Administrative Science Quarterly* 21 (June 1976): 246–265; T. Burns and G. Stalker, *The Management of Innovation* (London: Tavistock Publications, 1961); D. Heenan and R. Addleman, "Quantitative Techniques for Today's Decision-Makers," *Harvard Business Review* 54 (May–June 1976): 32–62; D. Rados, "Selection and Evaluation of Alternatives in Repetitive Decision Making," *Administrative Science Quarterly* 17 (June 1972): 196–206; P. Soelberg, "Unprogrammed Decision-Making," *Proceedings of the 26th Annual Meeting of the Academy of Management,* December 27–29 1966, 3–16.
8. G. Clarkson, "A Model of Trust Investment Behavior" in *A Behavioral Theory of the Firm,* ed. R. Cyert and J. March (Englewood Cliffs, N.J.: Prentice-Hall, 1963), pp. 265–266.

9. S. Archer, "The Structure of Management Decision Theory," *Academy of Management Journal* 7 (December 1964): 269–287; K. MacCrimmon, "Managerial Decision-Making," in *Contemporary Management: Issues and Viewpoints* ed. J. McGuire (Englewood Cliffs, N.J.: Prentice-Hall, 1974), pp. 445–495.

10. H. Simon, *Administrative Behavior* (New York: Macmillan, 1957); C. Lindblom, "The Science of 'Muddling Through,'" *Public Administration Review* 19 (Spring 1959): 79–88; J. Thompson and A. Truden, "Strategies Structures and Processes of Organizational Decision," in *Readings in Managerial Psychology*, ed. H. Leavitt and R. Pondy, (Chicago: University of Chicago Press, 1964).

11. R. Hall and J. Clark, "Problems in the Study of Interorganizational Relationships," *Organization and Administrative Sciences* 5 (January 1974): 45–65; S. P. Sethi, *Up Against the Corporate Wall* (Englewood Cliffs, N.J.: Prentice-Hall, 1974); S. Midlin and H. Aldrich, "Interorganizational Dependence," *Administrative Science Quarterly* 20 (September 1975): 382–392.

12. K. Vandivier, "The Aircraft Brake Scandal," *Harper's Magazine,* April 1972, pp. 45–52; K. Vandivier "Why Should My Conscience Bother Me?" in *In the Name of Profit*, ed. R. L. Heilbroner (New York: Doubleday, 1972), pp. 3–31.

13. C. Watson, "The Problems of Problem-Solving," *Business Horizons* 19 (August 1976): 88–94; C. Kepner and B. Tregoe, *The Rational Manager: A Systematic Approach to Problem Solving and Decision Making* (New York: McGraw-Hill, 1965).

14. W. Pounds, "The Process of Problem Finding." *Industrial Management Review,* Fall 1969, pp. 1–19.

15. A. Elbing, *Behavioral Decisions in Organizations* (Glenview, Ill.: Scott, Foresman, 1970); N. Maier, *Problem-Solving Discussions and Conferences: Leadership Methods and Skills* (New York: McGraw-Hill, 1963).

16. Ibid.

17. D. Emery and F. Tuggle, "On the Evaluation of Decisions," *SMU Business Topics* 24 (Spring 1976): 42–48; N. Hill, "Self-Esteem: The Key to Effective Leadership," *Administrative Management* 37 (August 1976): 24–36; J. Pfeffer, G. Salancik, and H. Leblebuci, "The Effect of Uncertainty on the Use of Social Influence in Organizational Decision-Making," *Administrative Science Quarterly* 21 (June 1976): 227–246; R. Lauer and R. Thomas, "A Comparative Analysis of the Psychological Consequences of Change," *Human Relations* 29 (March 1976): 239–248; J. Dickson, "The Adoption of Innovative Proposals as Risky Choice: A Model and Some Results," *Academy of Management Journal* 19 (June 1976): 291–303.

18. N. Maier, *Problem-Solving and Creativity in Individuals and Groups* (Belmont, Calif.: Brooks-Cole Publishing, 1970); C. Argyris, "Interpersonal Barriers to Decision-Making," *Harvard Business Review* 44 (March–April 1966): 84–97; J. Gibb, G. Platts, and L. Miller, *Dynamics of Participative Groups* (St. Louis, Mo.: Swift, 1959); M. Shaw, *Group Dynamics* (New York: McGraw-Hill, 1976); B. Baker, D. Fisher, and D. Murphy, "Project Organization: Factors Affecting the Decision Environment," Paper Presented to the Midwest Conference, American Institute for Decision Sciences, Minneapolis, Minnesota, May 1974.

19. V. Vroom and P. Yetton, *Leadership and Decision Making* (Pittsburgh: University of Pittsburgh Press, 1973); V. Vroom, "A New Look at

Managerial Decision-Making," *Organizational Dynamics* 1 (Spring 1973): 66–80; V. Vroom and P. Yetton, "A Normative Model of Leadership Style," *Readings in Managerial Psychology,* 2d ed, ed. H. Leavitt and L. Pondy (Chicago: University of Chicago Press, 1973).

20. E. Huse, "The Behavioral Scientist in the Shop," *Personnel* 42 (May–June 1965): 50–57.

Chapter 7   Organizational Goals and Objectives

General Hospital

The Importance of Goals and Objectives

Characteristics of Good Objectives
    Specific and Well Understood
    Balanced
    Expected Results Identified
    Internal and External Constraints Considered
    Measurable and Quantitative in Nature
    Within the Power of the Individual Manager or Work Unit
    Acceptable to People in the Organization

Organizations Have Multiple and Continuing Objectives

Hierarchy of Objectives

"Official" versus "Actual" Objectives

Objectives in a Changing World

Management by Objectives

Implications for the Manager

Review

The Marshall Company

Learning Objectives

When you have finished reading and studying this chapter, you should be able to:

1. Define and specify what an organizational objective is.
2. Illustrate the importance of objectives to organizations.
3. Describe and give illustrations of the characteristics of good objectives.
4. List and give illustrations of the continuing objectives of organizations.
5. Define and give examples of the levels in the hierarchy of objectives.
6. Explain the difference between "official" and "actual" objectives, and describe their importance.
7. From your personal experience, give five examples of different interests affecting organizational objectives, and describe these interests.
8. Compare and contrast the reasons for a successful and unsuccessful management by objectives (MBO) program.
9. Define and be able to use the following concepts:

goals   "operating" goals
objectives   "actual" objectives
continuing objectives   influence group
hierarchy of objectives   management by objectives (MBO)
"official" objectives

Thought Starters

1. What objectives do you have in reading this book?
2. Do the learning objectives at the beginning of the chapter coincide with your own personal objectives?
3. How do the objectives of the instructor seem to fit with your own personal objectives and the objectives of the text?
4. What personal objectives do you have in reading this chapter?

General Hospital

A general hospital with about four hundred beds had four areas of general performance, which were broken down into twelve specific objectives for the hospital. The performance areas and objectives are shown in Table 7.1.

Nurses, senior physicians, and junior physicians were asked to rank the first eleven of the twelve objectives in terms of importance. (The twelfth objective was not used in the rankings.) Each of the three groups agreed among themselves as to the importance of different objectives but disagreed with the other two groups. For instance, nurses ranked "comfort level" and "considering both psychosocial and medical condition of the patient" as the most important and "keeping high bed occupancy" the least important. These rankings suggest that the nurses are primarily concerned with creating an environment in which specialized health care can be carried out.

The senior physicians were also oriented toward the patient but in a very different way. Senior staff gave greatest weight to such objectives as "providing full information to patient," "using hospital resources efficiently," and "not keeping patients waiting for admission."

The junior physicians took a position between the positions of the nurses and senior staff. However, they also gave much more importance to "good training and teaching" than did the other two groups. The three groups agreed in placing least importance on "bed occupancy" and

Table 7.1   Performance areas and specific objectives for a general hospital

General Performance Areas	Specific Objectives
Resource utilization (efficiency)	
	1. Keeping stay of patient as short as possible.
	2. Using time of senior medical staff efficiently.
	3. Using all resources efficiently.
	4. Keeping high bed occupancy.
Innovation and adaptiveness to environment	
	5. Making certain patients have minimum wait before admission.
	6. Keeping a good community reputation.
	7. Providing a high comfort level for patients.
	8. Maintaining high morale for staff.
	9. Considering both psychosocial and medical condition of patient.
	10. Providing full information to patient about illness and treatment.
Goal achievement (effectiveness)	
	11. Providing good training and teaching.
	12. Providing high-quality nursing and medical care.

"length of hospital stay." However, these two items were considered the most important by an outside agency that rated the effectiveness of the hospital.[1]

Although they were not included in the survey, we can guess that the people in the hospital's business office might stress "keeping high bed occupancy" and "hospital stay" more important than "providing good teaching and training." One of the reasons the business office might stress "hospital stay" is that many insurance plans, including Medicare, will not pay for a patient who does not medically need to remain in the hospital. At the same time, the hospital staff may be searching frantically for an available bed in a nursing home for a patient who needs this type of care rather than hospitalization. In one situation, a patient remained in a hospital for almost forty days because a nursing home bed was not available. The hospital had to absorb the cost.[1]

This case illustrates the importance of organizational goals and objectives as a guide to managerial action. Without clear, strategic goals, an organization cannot have clear objectives; and if the objectives are not clear, they may never be reached. Because of the complexity of many modern organizations, a hierarchy of objectives exists. Broad strategic objectives are found at the top management level, frequently in the form of continuing objectives. Objectives become narrower at each lower management level. Also since organizations are composed of people with differing values, expectations, and beliefs, there is a difference between "official" and "actual" objectives. Because organizations exist in a changing world, the effective manager needs to continually reassess objectives to ensure that they achieve organizational goals and at the same time satisfy individual needs.

The Importance Of Objectives

All organizations (and individuals) need a sense of direction. Can you imagine someone arriving at the ticket counter of an airline and asking, "Will you sell me a ticket?" The first question the bewildered ticket clerk will ask is, "To where?" The clerk will be even more bewildered if the individual responds, "I don't know. Where do you go?" The usual approach is to decide on the destination and then plan how to get there.

Organizational goals are "desired states of affairs which the organization attempts to realize." [2] They are levels of aspiration that are relatively timeless. For example, in the case at the beginning of the chapter, "providing high-quality nursing and medical care" can be considered a goal that will probably not change in the foreseeable future and that most, if not all, the employees will agree with. Organizational goals can include such areas as survival, efficiency in the use of resources, employee satisfaction, and the production of goods and services desired by consumers.

Organizational **objectives** are ideas or statements that help steer the activities of the organization toward the attainment of goals. They are levels of aspiration that are more time-bound than goals. For example, commercial organization may have as one of its goals "a fair return to stockholders." During a period of prosperity, a fair return may be a 6 percent dividend on the shares. During a period of recession, a fair return may be the attempt not to cut the dividend rate below 3 percent because of decreased profits.

Thus goals and objectives are closely related through the key concepts of "a desired state" that the "organization attempts to realize." The organization may or may not reach the desired state, but the chances of doing so are greater if the objectives are clearly spelled out. One of the most common causes of organizational failure is the lack of a carefully considered and clear-cut statement of objectives to attain goals. Without such objectives, planning cannot take place. Of course, both goals and objectives vary with the nature and type of the organization. A profit-making organization may well have a different set of goals and objectives than a municipality or a university.

Figure 7.1 shows the relationships among goals, objectives, planning, control, decision making, and the environment. Organizational goals affect and are affected by the environment. Laws, rules, regulations, and the shifting, changing values of society affect the "desired state of affairs." Objectives stem from the overall organizational goals; these in turn affect the planning and control processes, which exist to ensure that the organization accomplishes its objectives. Decision making is involved in establishing goals, determining objectives, planning to accomplish the objectives, and controlling to ensure that the activities of the organization are directed toward overall goals.[3]

Characteristics of Good Objectives

Objectives for the entire organization are necessarily broader than objectives for a department or work group. Nevertheless, good objectives have certain common characteristics. [4] They should be specific, well understood, and balanced and should identify expected results, be measurable, take into consideration internal and external constraints, be within the power of the individual manager or work unit, and be acceptable to people in the organization. (See Table 7.2.)

Specific and Well Understood

The organization must be clear about its identity; only in this way can objectives be understood by those who are part of it. As we will see later, organizations have a hierarchy of goals. The goals at the top of large organizations are broader and more strategic than goals lower in the

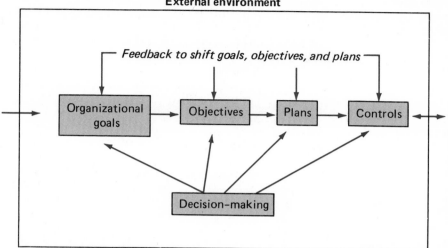

External environment

Feedback to shift goals, objectives, and plans

Organizational goals → Objectives → Plans → Controls

Decision-making

Figure 7.1 The relationships among goals, objectives, plans, controls, decision making, and environment

organization, which tend to be more specific, tangible, and technical in nature. Nevertheless, the objectives of the individual unit need to be well understood and tied in to the objectives of the larger organization.

Balanced

Clarity and understanding are not enough; objectives must also be balanced. Since objectives are used as guides to action, they need to help integrate the activities of the different units, functions, and departments toward common goals. Many organizations run into trouble because their customer service objectives are not properly related to their profit objectives. In other organizations, too many college graduates are recruited by the personnel department to be consistent with objectives of the organization. Since there is no real opportunity to use all of these high-potential individuals, the result is high turnover after a few years. As one noted writer put it, "Every organization and every part of every organization must be an expression of the purpose of the undertaking concerned or it is meaningless and therefore redundant." [5]

Expected Results Identified

In the case at the beginning of the chapter, "high quality medical care" can be considered a broad organizational goal; and as such it is difficult to measure. Objectives must clearly identify the results expected if they are to commit individuals to action. Goals such as "high quality medical care" or "to make profits" do not represent meaningful guides to action, whereas "keeping the bed occupancy rate at or above 85 percent" or "making a 10 percent profit after taxes" do.

Table 7.2   Characteristics of Good Objectives

1. Specific and well understood
2. Balanced
3. Expected results identified
4. Internal and external constraints considered
5. Measurable and quantitative in nature
6. Within the power of the individual manager or work unit
7. Acceptable to people in the organization

Internal and External Constraints Considered

Most organizations operate within a framework of external constraints, including legal, environmental, and competitive restrictions. They also have internal constraints, such as limitations of financial and other resources. As the environment changes, the objectives and expected results of organizations need to change as well. The overall goals of General Motors may not have changed over the years, but more stringent laws regarding automobile exhaust systems have caused many specific objectives within the organization to change.

Measurable and Quantitative in Nature

At all levels in the organization, objectives should be measurable in order to identify expected results and determine whether they have been obtained. Many objectives can be stated in terms of quantity, quality, cost, and time. However, there is also the danger of overmeasurement. When managers are faced with two objectives, one easily measurable and the other not, they tend to focus more sharply on the measurable one and neglect the other.

Within the Power of the Individual Manager or Work Unit

Objectives should be attainable. For an organization to grow and prosper, objectives should contain a certain amount of "reach" or "stretch." If they are too low, there is little challenge. If they are too high, people may not even attempt to achieve them—or they may become frustrated if they try but fail to achieve them.[6]

Acceptable to People in the Organization

An objective that is not accepted by people in the organization does not result in changed behavior or action toward attaining it. For objectives to be accepted, the needs of the individual should be integrated with those of the organization. Furthermore, the organization should have ways to use and control conflict productively. One way of gaining employee acceptance is for the manager to involve employees in deciding how to achieve objectives.

In an actual situation, a manufacturing plant received orders from corporate headquarters to reduce the work force by 20 percent because of a drop in sales during a recent recession. The plant manager felt that the reduction would be temporary, but he could not be sure. He and his immediate subordinates discussed a number of different approaches to the problem. Finally, he decided to present it to the workers themselves, giving them the facts and some alternative approaches. After considerable discussion, the 20 percent reduction was achieved. Some workers went on a four-day work week, while others continued on five. Some workers took unpaid vacations. Others asked for an official layoff notice so they could collect unemployment. There was never any question about achieving the objective of a 20 percent reduction, since this was decided by corporate management. In implementing management's decision, however, the workers themselves decided how the objective was to be achieved. Both managers and workers felt positive about the way it was finally implemented.

Organizations Have Multiple and Continuing Objectives

A **continuing objective** is one that is relatively unchangeable over time. The case at the beginning of the chapter described twelve major and continuing objectives, among them "making certain patients have minimum wait before admission." Clearly, this objective is a desired one, but its specific implementation can change in differing situations. For example, in a time of disaster, such as a plane crash, the minimum wait for patients in the emergency room will be longer than at less rushed times.

Some continuing objectives that apply to all organizations are:

1. *Identification.* The organization should be clear about its identity and have a commitment to organizational objectives.
2. *Integration.* The needs of the individual and the organization should be integrated.
3. *Collaboration.* The organization should have mechanisms for the productive use and control of conflict.
4. *Adaptation.* The organization should be able to respond quickly and appropriately to changes in the environment.
5. *Revitalization.* The organization should be able to continually renew itself so as to be able to deal with problems of both growth and decay.[7]

These five primary objectives help steer the activities of any organization toward the attainment of its goals. Of course, objectives that are specifically for business organizations tend to be more result oriented. For example, most people who think about business organizations suggest that profit is a primary business objective. As management consultant Peter Drucker points out, this is an oversimplification. Drucker suggests than an organization needs to have result oriented objectives in at least eight key areas.[8] Although the eight key performance areas were originally identified for use in profit-making organizations, many of them also apply to public sector and service organizations.[9] The eight areas are described below.

1. *Market standing*—the share of the market the organization has when compared with competitors. For example, one organization may have an objective of increasing its share of the market by 5 percent each year. Another organization, one with a large market share, may decide that to increase its market share might bring about an antitrust action. In the public sector, the client is frequently "built in." There is relatively little competition for Medicare, the local post office, or the local police and fire departments. In such circumstances, the concern for "market standing" may be directed at examining carefully how well the client is being served. AT&T, for instance, has elaborate indexes to determine how well the public is being served.
2. *Productivity*—the amount of input (such as labor, materials, and funds) to output necessary to produce a given amount of goods or services. Organizations of all types need to be continually concerned about productivity. Two of the continuing objectives of the hospital discussed at the beginning of the chapter were "using time of senior medical staff efficiently" and "using all resources efficiently."
3. *Profitability*—the ratio of outputs to inputs. While organizations in the private sector are concerned about profits as an objective, nonprofit organizations or organizations in the public sector are concerned about keeping costs down and balancing funds for the greater public good. For example, the Secretary of Health, Education and Welfare (HEW) is responsible for keeping a proper balance among such different programs as delivering hot meals to the elderly, determining eligibility for Medicaid benefits, funding cancer research, and supporting elementary school curriculum development.

4. *Physical and financial resources.* Organizations need adequate financial reserves. They also need to protect and maintain equipment, buildings, and inventory. A hospital must maintain enough cash on hand to pay its bills and to meet the payroll. After an automobile is built and sold, the manufacturer must maintain an inventory of parts so that the car can be maintained and repaired.

5. *Innovation.* For an organization to stay in operation, it must bring out new products and services or improve existing ones. The organization manufacturing electronic pocket calculators cannot just rest on its laurels. If it does, a competitor will very likely bring out a new calculator that will make the current one obsolete. Serious questions are always arising in this area. In cancer research, for example, should the innovation be aimed at funding for research into the causes of the disease or at treatment of those who already have the disease?[10] Given limited resources, should a hospital try for improved teaching or the purchase of specialized new equipment? What is the proper balance between differing but important objectives?

6. *Manager performance and development.* The organization, public or private, that does not develop its most critical resource—management—will not long continue to exist. To develop this resource the organization must provide the tools and the opportunities that allow its managers to do a good job.

7. *Worker performance and attitudes.* The organization must be continually concerned about worker performance and attitudes, since it is through people that the work gets done.

8. *Public and social responsibility.* More and more organizations in the private sector must be concerned with social and public responsibility, with the improvement or deterioration of the environment and of the quality of life.[11] One of the primary purposes of organizations in the public sector is the fulfillment of public and social responsibility goals. Thus public health may be a goal rather than an objective.

Drucker developed the eight key performance areas as a result of his consulting work with General Electric. At the time, GE was measuring managerial success primarily on the basis of a single objective— the rate of return on investment. A clever manager could make high profits by neglecting long-term considerations, such as innovation, equipment maintenance, and employee attitude. Because of the apparent "success" the manager might be quickly promoted, but the next manager would be faced with major problems. To avoid this, Drucker recommended that the single objective of return of profit be expanded to the eight key areas listed above. As he reported, "Objectives are needed in every area where performance and results directly and vitally affect the survival and prosperity of the business."[12]

Hierarchy of Objectives

To make certain that objectives are accomplished it is important to distinguish among the levels of management. The three overall levels (strategic, managerial, and operating) were described in detail in Chapter 2, and will be briefly repeated here. The strategic level of management mediates between the organization and the wider social environment, determining the strategy and overall direction of the organization. The managerial or administrative level coordinates activities within the organization. The operating level is concerned with the actual production of goods and services.

Thus there is a hierarchy of objectives that corresponds to the three broad managerial levels, as demonstrated in Figure 7.2. The **hierarchy of objectives** is a graded series in which the organization's objectives are supported by each succeeding managerial level down to the level of the individual. The example used in the figure is that of market standing. The strategic marketing decision is to increase the market share of widgets by 10 percent during the year. In turn, the managerial objective is to produce and sell 2,775,610 of all types of widgets. In order for this number of widgets to be manufactured and sold, the purchasing department must develop a comprehensive parts list—which must include the time of ordering and the time needed for the order to be processed and shipped, manufacturing will have certain essential items earlier than other less essential ones. Finally, the buyer who specializes in purchasing electronic parts must make certain that the specific parts are within the factory ten working days before needed. (Previous study has shown that inventory costs are greatly increased if the material arrives more than ten days in advance).

"Official" Versus "Actual" Objectives

Almost all organizations have "official" objectives.[13] Such official objectives can be defined as the "general purpose" of the organization. They are used in annual reports and other authoritative pronouncements. Actually, although they are called objectives, they are frequently

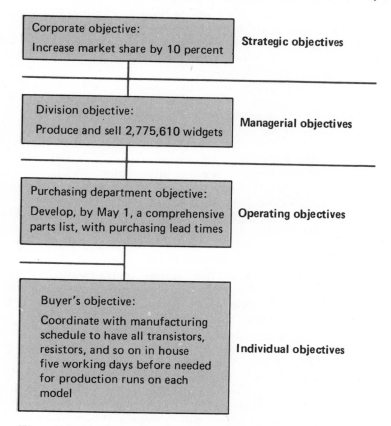

Figure 7.2 The hierarchy of objectives

philosophical statements. Examples are "to provide high quality medical care to the patient," "to promote employee welfare and morale," and "to fulfill the organization's social responsibility to the community." These official objectives are often drawn up for public consumption by a special blue-ribbon committee; they are then signed by the president or the chairperson of the board of directors, framed, and hung on the walls of executive offices and in the lobby of the main office. They are seldom reexamined or changed. Unfortunately, they are often so general as to be of little practical use. Furthermore, they are like "home, motherhood, and the flag" in the sense that nobody can really be against them. "Operating" goals, on the other hand, guide the activities of the organization, "regardless of what the official goals say are the aims." [14] To illustrate: Several years ago, a manufacturing plant with an "official" goal of social responsibility to the community received complaints about polluting a small river. A waste by-product of the firm turned the water a reddish color. To actually remove the reddish discharge would be expensive, so the company's plant manager "solved" the problem by putting in a storage tank and dumping the waste only at night, when the color could not be seen. Such cases are probably rare, but this one is a specific example of the difference between actual and official objectives. The plant manager was proud of his "solution" to the problem; top management was unaware of the solution.

While there is little conflict with regard to official objectives, there can be a great deal of it with operating objectives. For example, a university school of management may have an overall goal to which all the faculty subscribe: "to provide quality education to the student." The conflict may come about in terms of the required courses a student may have to take. Competition may occur among departments wanting to maintain their own power bases and to attract the better students to major in their areas.

Although little actual research has been done on the effect of objective incompatibilities among individuals or units of the organization, it is clear that conflict can come about from different interpretations of the objectives and from the desire to gain resources or to preserve power and freedom of action for organizational units. Conflict over interpretation of objectives may increase the quality of decisions, while conflict over resources may decrease the quality. [15]

It is important to note that organizations themselves do not actually have objectives. Instead, *people* have objectives stemming from their own views and motivations. Thus "organizational objectives" are really shifting and uneasy compromises among the individuals within the organization and the changing demands made by the outside environment. As social psychologist Robert Katz says: "Every strategic action must strike a balance between so many conflicting values, objectives and criteria that it will always be suboptimal from any single viewpoint. Every decision or choice affecting the whole enterprise has negative consequences for some of the parts."[16]

It is commonly assumed that objectives are developed at the top and then passed down and accepted by each of the lower levels. However, there are forceful arguments against this assumption. For example, some individuals within the organization may be totally unconcerned about profits. The research and development department may focus on elegant and excellent designs. Marketing may want a large variety of different products to attract the customer. Manufacturing may want fewer and simpler high-volume products to reduce costs. The president may want to minimize risks, and the director of research may want to make a name for himself by developing an esoteric new product or writing articles. Certainly, none of these conflicting desires shows any development from the top down of organizational objectives.

Nonindustrial organizations have the same types of conflicts. University administrators may seek to reduce costs by having each faculty member carry a full teaching load. Individual faculty members may prefer to spend more time on their own consulting, research, or writing. Thus the "actual" objectives of the organization are a result of a continuing series of compromises and negotiations among "constituencies." In the hospital case at the beginning of this chapter, some objectives of importance to the hospital administrators and insurance agencies were given little weight by nurses, senior physicians, and junior staff, each of whom stressed different objectives.

These multiple and conflicting objectives emerge from continuous bargaining among the organization's personnel, and the bargaining occurs because people are not satisfied. (A satisfied need is not a motivator.) Each person has a list of needs or demands that may pop up at different times. Thus many organizations have goals that are highly contradictory but that are not so recognized because they are held by different members or groups and are rarely considered simultaneously.

As Chapter 2 described, many managers do not have the time to fully inform their subordinates. In addition, as situations change, managers keep general objectives in mind but constantly shift priorities.

Objectives In A Changing World

More and more, the manager must maintain a delicate balance in trying to develop continuing objectives that satisfy a number of different "influence" groups. An **influence group** is any person or persons who exert pressure on an organization. [17]

As Figure 7.3 shows, before taking action, managers must deal with a multitude of different influence groups. These include employees, creditors, customers, suppliers, the public at large, special interest groups, and stockholders—all of whom may have valid claims (although the claims are often conflicting). For example, managers who are concerned with the organization's future may feel they must satisfy the desires of public interest groups concerned about pollution. Shareholders, on the other hand, may worry more about the impact of pollution control on

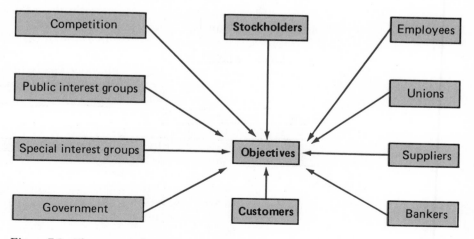

Figure 7.3 The many influences on the organization

current dividends and the price of their stock. Furthermore, if a supplier raises prices sharply, managers may choose to absorb some of the direct costs rather than raise prices, since price increases may send customers to competing products. Since this action reduces earnings, the managers may then have to defend the action to bankers when it is time to negotiate a new loan.

Government and government regulations are having a profound impact on organizations. In 1977, the concept of equal employment opportunity was broadened when the Department of Health, Education and Welfare (HEW) announced new regulations forbidding employment discrimination against 3.5 million handicapped people. The change in mandatory retirement from sixty-five to seventy has tremendous consequences for individuals as well as organizations.

These are only a few examples of how different influence groups affect organizations of all kinds. Managers must be alert to the "politics" of such situations. General objectives may not change, but the emphasis and priority given to different objectives may change quickly and unexpectedly. The modern manager needs to actively "sense" changes in both the internal and external environment and to make appropriate adjustments in objectives.

A recent study shows that managers feel strongly that objectives need to be balanced among the interests of groups such as consumers, stockholders, and labor. According to this study, most modern managers desire to earn only a "reasonable" or "fair" profit for stockholders and are highly conscious of the social responsibilities of business.[18]

Some organizations seem better able to adapt and shift objectives and priorities than others. For example, du Pont makes fluorocarbons, which include Freons, the principal gases used as aerosol propellants. There is some evidence that Freons affect the ozone layer that shields the earth from dangerously excessive ultraviolet radiation. When the federal government recommended a gradual phaseout of aerosol sprays propelled by fluorocarbons, du Pont agreed to cooperate.

Management By Objectives (MBO)

As Chapters 4 and 5 have pointed out, managers' needs must be satisfied in order for them to achieve high performance in meeting the organization's goals and objectives. This section is intended to pull together a number of issues already covered in the chapter. It will indicate how organizational objectives can best be achieved through the use of a hierarchy of objectives, ranging from the strategic down to the administrative and technical levels.

Many large organizations are using an approach known as management by objectives (MBO) as a way of implementing top management or company objectives. The approach enables lower levels of management to understand, accept, and work toward the attainment of these objectives. An effective MBO program consists of periodic manager-subordinate meetings designed to accomplish organizational goals by mutual planning of the work, periodic review of accomplishments, and mutual solving of problems that arise in the course of getting the job done.[19] There are three basic steps in this process:

1. The manager and the subordinate jointly determine the subordinate's specific areas of responsibility. An essential part of this process is mutual agreement about the tasks to be accomplished.
2. The manager and the subordinate agree on the priorities, standards of performance, and the like for each area of responsibility.

3. The manager and the subordinate agree on a general work plan for achieving the desired results in each broad area of responsibility—the results tying in with the overall objectives of the organization or unit.

Failure to go through the steps carefully can cause problems. In one instance, the president and vice-president of a company had agreed on a major task for the vice-president—to find a company that their firm could either purchase or merge with. The vice-president worked on the problem for about six months, with little success. Although he located several companies, he and the president didn't seem to be agreeing on the choices; and they were not clear about why they disagreed.

At this point, the company was considering installation of an MBO program. In the process, the two men were asked independently to write down the vice-president's major activities. They disagreed on some major issues (Step 1); but after discussing them, they reached agreement. The two were then asked, again independently, to write down the standards of performance of a particular task—the purchase or merger (Step 2). They did so and again found areas of disagreement. The president, for example, expected the vice-president to locate an organization relatively close to any major airport. The vice-president, on the other hand, was examining only organizations within a two-hour driving radius of his own company. This major area of disagreement did not emerge until the two actually began going through the steps outlined above, even though they had been "discussing" the project for six months.

The MBO process is a cyclical one of work planning, review, and new planning. It is based on three psychological principles, shown in Figure 7.4. These principles indicate that subordinates can best improve their performance on the job when they:

1. *Know what is expected of them.* The planning process gives subordinates better information about priorities, expected results, the methods by which results will be measured, and resources available to do the job.
2. *Receive feedback about how they are doing.* Knowledge of results is the most basic of the three principles. Appropriate and timely feedback is essential for improving job performance.
3. *Can obtain coaching and assistance as needed.* The process must be changed from management by crisis to planning ahead, so the manager can act as a helper rather than a judge.

When properly installed, MBO can have positive effects on goal achievement as well as on subordinate development. One research project compared managerial groups using MBO with groups not using it (control groups). Subordinates of the managers using MBO reported greater goal involvement, achievement, and accomplishment, together with greater agreement with the supervisor about the job to be done and ways of improving job performance.[20] A number of studies in a variety of organizations report similar findings.[21]

Not all MBO programs are successful in their implementation and application. One of the problems is that MBO has two historically and philosophically different forms. One form is based almost completely on the organization, stressing the need for highly quantitative measurement to reach organizational objectives.[22] Little attention is paid to the individual or to individual differences, and a great amount of attention is

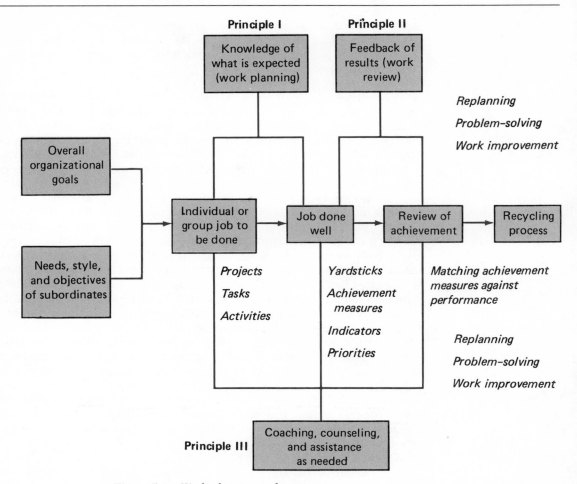

Figure 7.4 Work planning and review

Adapted with permission from E. Huse and E. Kay, "Improving Employee
Productivity through Work Planning," in *The Personnel Job in a Changing
World,* ed. J. Blood (New York: American Management Association, 1964),
p. 305.

directed toward specific techniques (such as the use of the proper forms,
specific times for discussions to take place, and the following of certain
prescribed approaches). This form usually has a great deal of top management support, but little opportunity exists for lower-level subordinates to modify or have any effect on the process.

The second form is concerned about organizational goals but emphasizes the growth and development of subordinates. [23] It ties organizational goals to individual goals, strengths, and potential for growth.
Supervisors and subordinates work together in a freer and more open
fashion, discussing and ultimately agreeing on broad job responsibilities. Subordinates are free to develop short-term performance goals,
specific action plans, and criteria for self-appraisal, all subject to the
overall approval of the immediate supervisor. They discuss their self-
appraisals with the supervisor, and both then develop a mutually agreed
upon set of new performance goals and plans. The second form of MBO

appears to be the more successful of the two in terms of both individual and company goals.

A properly installed MBO program motivates subordinates for three main reasons:

1. It allows satisfaction of the need for achievement and accomplishment—a need that appears to be greater for lower-level than for higher-level managers.
2. It allows managers to clarify the path to personal rewards on the part of subordinates.
3. It allows managers increased opportunities to provide subordinates with a better "fix" on the job and on the relationship of performance to goal attainment.[24]

An incorrectly applied MBO program can have unintended and highly negative results.[25] If it is based on a power-backed, reward-punishment psychology, the result can be damage to employee self-esteem. If the establishment of subordinates' goals is intended to make the manager or unit look good rather than to contribute to the overall objectives of the organization, the effectiveness of the program can be reduced. As one foreman said: "Just tell me what you want my boss to look good on, and I'll make it happen, even if I have to cheat on something else." If tangible measurements are overemphasized, they can have serious negative consequences for long-term goals and for employee competence. For example, managers who emphasize profits to the detriment of, say, management development and worker attitudes may fail to develop the potential of their subordinates (an important objective for most organizations). If quantity is overemphasized, quality of work may be reduced.

The successful MBO program should meet four criteria:

1. It should be individually designed to fit the needs of each organization.
2. It should give equal attention to training processes and training content.
3. It should avoid destructive competitiveness.
4. It should be implemented slowly and should involve all departments.[26]

Implications For The Manager

Objectives are necessary for any organization. They determine the direction in which the organization will go, and they point to a desired state of affairs that the organization is attempting to realize. As a result, they form the basis for planning, organizing, and controlling the nature and future of the organization.

Frequently, those who are not familiar with organizations assume that objectives are set at the top, are relatively fixed and unchangeable, and are agreed on by all members of the organization. As we saw in the hospital case at the beginning of the chapter, these assumptions are misleading. Effective managers know that objectives are shifting and even slippery concepts. In our fast-moving society, the manager must be able to keep the overall goals in mind even as the relative importance of specific objectives changes.

Managers must also be politicians. Operating or actual objectives come about from a constant series of negotiations among both internal and external groups. Effective managers are therefore adept at partially satisfing each of the groups. (None of the "influence groups" is ever fully satisfied; thus managers can only strike a balance among their conflicting demands.)

Effective managers are also aware that people—not organizations—have objectives. As a result, such managers do not expect the different individuals or groups within the organization to subscribe fully to all the organization's objectives. For example, the manager of the hospital in the case at the beginning of the chapter should be aware of the differing perceptions of the nurses, the senior physicians, and the junior physicians.

Management by objectives is one important way of bringing together organizational, individual, and group objectives. When properly used, MBO provides a method for transmitting objectives throughout the hierarchy while allowing for individual differences. Some individuals follow orders almost blindly; others need a fair amount of latitude in carrying out their job. MBO makes certain that managers and their subordinates agree in advance on what is expected and what criteria they will use to determine how well a job has been done. Later chapters will describe other approaches to ensuring the accomplishment of objectives; but MBO, when appropriately used, can be a most effective tool.

Review

1. What is an organizational goal? How is it different from an organizational objective?
2. Describe the importance of objectives.
3. What are the characteristics of good objectives?
4. In what way are organizational goals, objectives, plans, and decision making interrelated?
5. What is meant by *hierarchy of objectives*?
6. What are the differences between "official" and "actual" objectives? Explain.
7. Why is it sometimes necessary to change objectives?
8. What is meant by the term *management by objectives*?
9. What are some reasons for the success or failure of MBO programs?
10. Do the learning objectives at the beginning of this chapter agree with your personal objectives? How might they be changed if you were to discuss them with your instructor? with the author?
11. Are there any similarities between the learning objectives and an MBO program?
12. Select organizations of different sizes and interview several members of these organizations. What is their perception of the organizational objectives? How much agreement is there? Does the size of the organization affect people's responses?
13. In the case at the beginning of the chapter, different groups placed different importance on specific objectives. Is it a good idea to try to get everyone to place equal importance on each objective? Explain.

The Marshall Company

The Marshall Company manufactured automobile shock absorbers (among other items). These were sold as replacement parts by dealers, service stations, auto repair shops, and other retailers. Competition was growing intense, and the Marshall Company was losing some of its share of the market. After extensive discussion and analysis, the president and the board of directors decided that the price of the shock absorbers needed to be reduced by 5 percent to keep up with competition. Since the profit margin was small, a corresponding increase in productivity would be necessary. The manufacturing manager agreed that the productivity increase was necessary, and he explained the situation to his subordinates.

After about two weeks, productivity had gone down by 7 percent rather than up by 5 percent. The manufacturing manager called a meeting with the unit manager of fabrication, the unit manager of assembly, and the unit manager of quality control. (Quality control ensured that parts passed inspection before being assembled and that the assembled shock absorbers met established standards before being shipped.)

Manufacturing Manager: "I've called you together because we have a serious problem. As you know, two weeks ago we agreed to raise productivity by 5 percent because of increased competition and the need to lower prices. Since then, productivity has *decreased* by 7 percent, rather than being increased."

Unit Manager of Fabrication: "I can tell you what the problem is, and it's a simple one. Pat [the unit manager of assembly] is sending back more parts than ever before to be reworked. We are making the parts to the same tolerance as we always have; yet about two out of five parts are coming back."

Unit Manager of Assembly: "Unless we get better quality parts, we can't maintain our present production level, much less increase by 5 percent. We don't mind taking time to try to get the parts to fit together when we are not under pressure to get production out. If we are going to increase productivity, we have to have parts that fit like they are supposed to. That's why we are sending them back."

Unit Manager of Quality Control: "I can tell you one thing. My inspection foreman and inspectors are under more pressure from Chris' [unit manager of fabrication] and Pat's people than ever before. They are trying to get substandard parts and shocks approved. If we are going to continue to put out a quality product, we have to hold to the standards. My people are not going to give in under pressure. We have to maintain high quality standards."

Just then, the telephone intercommunication system buzzed. The manufacturing manager picked up the telephone and asked the secretary: "Yes, what is it?" The secretary answered: "The union business agent is on the telephone. He wants to see you right away. Something about a union problem with a speedup."

1. What is happening in this case? Why has people's behavior changed?
2. Is the objective clear and measurable? Has everyone agreed to it?
3. What should the manufacturing manager do? What should he tell the other managers? The union agent?
4. Could the situation have been avoided?

Footnotes

1. Adapted, by permission of the publisher, from "The Many Dimensions of Performance Measurement" by C. Davies and A. Francis, *Organizational Dynamics*, Winter 1975, © 1975 by AMACOM, a division of American Management Associations. All rights reserved.
2. A. Etzioni, *Modern Organizations* (Englewood Cliffs, N.J.: Prentice-Hall, 1954), p. 6.
3. J. Carrington and L. Aurelio, "Survival Tactics for Small Business," *Business Horizons* 19 (February 1976): 13–24; T. Leavitt, *The Third Sector* (New York: Amacon, 1973); and A. Frank, "Goal Ambiguity and Conflicting Standards: An Approach to the Study of Organization," *Human Organization* 17 (Winter 1958–1959):8–13.
4. C. Granger, "The Hierarchy of Objectives," *Harvard Business Review*, 42 (May–June 1964): 63-74; S. Elion, "Goals and Constraints, "*Journal of Management Studies* 8 (October 1971): 292–303; G. Latham and G. Yukl, "A Review of Research on the Application of Goal Setting in Organizations," *Academy of Management Review* 18 (April 1975): 824–845; and G. England, "Organizational Goals and Expected Behavior of American Managers," *Academy of Management Journal* 11 (June 1967): 107–111.
5. L. Urwick, *Notes on the Theory of Organization* (New York: American Management Association, 1952), p. 19.
6. V. Vroom, *Work and Motivation* (New York: Wiley, 1964).

7. W. Bennis, *Organizational Development* (Reading, Mass. Addison-Wesley, 1969).

8. P. Drucker, *The Practice of Management* (New York: Harper & Bros., 1954), p. 62.

9. M. Murray, "Comparing Public and Private Management: An Exploratory Essay," *Public Administration Review* 35 (July–August 1975): 371–374; N. Long, "Public Policy and Administration: The Goals of Rationality and Responsibility," *Public Administration Review* 14 (Winter 1954): 18–34; and L. Lynn, Jr., and J. Siedl, " 'Bottom-line' Management for Public Agencies," *Harvard Business Review* 55 (January–February 1955): 145–153

10. F. Greve, "The Big Cancer Oversell," *Boston Globe*, April 25, 1978.

11. Drucker, *The Practice of Management*, p. 62.

12. Ibid., p. 63.

13. L. Barnes and S. Hershon, "Transferring Power in the Family Business," *Harvard Business Review* 54 (July– August 1976): 105–114; W. Turcotte, "Control Systems, Performance and Satisfaction in Two State Agencies," *Administrative Science Quarterly* 19 (March 1974): 60–73; B. Buchanan II, "Government Managers, Business Executives and Organizational Commitment," *Public Administration Review* 34 (July– August 1974): 339–347; and Frank, "Goal Ambiguity and Conflicting Standards."

14. C. Perrow, "The Analysis of Goals in Complex Organizations," *American Sociological Review* 26 (December 1961): 854–866.

15. T. Kochan, L. Cummings, and G. Huber, "Operationalizing the Concepts of Goals and Goal Incompatabilities in Organizational Behavior Research," *Human Relations* 29 (June 1976): 527–544; and R. Cosier and G. Rose, "Cognitive Conflict and Goal Conflict Effects on Task Performance," *Organizational Behavior and Human Performance* 19 (August 1977): 378–391.

16. Robert L. Katz, *Management of the Total Enterprise* (Englewood Cliffs, N.J.: Prentice-Hall, © 1970), p. 13.

17. S. Hunt, "Conducting a Social Inventory," *Management Accounting* 55 (October 1974): 15–22; M. Anshen, ed., *Managing the Socially Responsible Corporation* (New York: Macmillan, 1974); J. Paluszek, *Business and Society: 1976–2000* (New York: American Management Association, 1976); and D. Aaker and G. Day, "Corporate Responses to Consumerism Pressures," *Harvard Business Review* 50 (November–December 1972): 114–124.

18. C. Edmonds III and J. Hand, "What are the Real Long-run Objectives of Business?" *Business Horizons* 19 (December 1967): 75–81.

19. E. Huse, *Organization Development and Change* (St. Paul: West Publishing, 1975); E. Huse and E. Kay, "Improving Employee Productivity through Work Planning," in *The Personnel Job in the Changing World*, ed. J. Blood (New York: American Management Association, 1964), pp. 300–330; D. DeFee, "Management by Objectives: When and How Does It Work?" *Personnel Journal* 56 (January 1977): 32–38; and H. Weihrich, "Management by Objectives: Does It Really Work?" *University of Michigan Business Review* 28 (July 1976): 27–35.

20. Huse and Kay, "Improving Employee Productivity."

21. A. Raia, "Goal Setting and Self-Control," *Journal of Management Studies* 2 (February 1965): 34–58; H. Tosi and S. Carroll, "Management Reaction to Management by Objectives," *Academy of Management Journal* 11 (December 1968): 415–426; and J. Ivancevich, "Changes in

Performance in a Management by Objectives Program," *Administrative Science Quarterly* 19 (December 1974): 574–593.

22. Huse, *Organization Development and Change.*
23. H. Levinson, "Management by Whose Objectives?" *Harvard Business Review* 48 (July–August 1970): 125–134; V. Ridgway, "Dysfunctional Consequences of Performance Measurements," *Administrative Science Quarterly* 1 (June 1956): 240–247; G. Morrisey, "Without Control, MBO Is a Waste of Time," *Management Review* 64 (February 1975): 11–17; J. Bucalo, "Personnel Directors. . . . What You Should Know before Recommending MBO," *Personnel Journal* 56 (April 1977): 176–178; H. Weihrich, "An Uneasy Look at the MBO Jungle: Toward a Contingency Approach to MBO," *Management International Review* 16 (September 1976): 103–109.
24. D. McClelland, *The Achieving Society* (Princeton, N.J.: Van Nostrand, 1961), 36–62; E. Huse, "Putting in a Management Development Program That Works," *California Business Review* 8 (Winter 1966): 73–80; R. House, "A Path Goal Theory of Leader Effectiveness," *Administrative Science Quarterly* 16 (September 1971): 321–338.
25. W. Mahler, "A Systems Approach to Managing by Objectives," *Systems and Procedures Journal* 17 (October 1966): 1; S. Kerr, "Some Modifications in MBO as an OD Strategy," *Academy of Management Proceedings,* August 13–16, 1972, p. 40
26. R. Byrd and J. Cowan, "MBO: A Behavioral Science Approach," *Personnel* 51 (March–April 1974): 42–50.

Chapter 8

Strategic and Tactical Planning

The Sears Story: The Best Laid Plans . . .

What Is Strategic Planning?

Who Does Planning?

The Importance of Planning
    Coping with Change
    Reaching or Changing Organizational Objectives
    Helping Organizations Succeed
    Helping Day-to-day Decision Making
    Maintaining an Effective Control Process

Types of Plans
    Breadth
    Use
    Time

Contingent Strategic Planning: Developing Scenarios

Steps in Long-Range Strategic Planning

Difficulties with Planning

Implications for the Manager

Review

Radio Shack International

Learning Objectives

1. Define the terms *strategic planning,* and describe its importance.
2. Compare and contrast planning activities at different levels of management.
3. Explain the difference between strategic planning and tactical planning.
4. Explain why planning is important.
5. Describe three different classifications of plans.
6. List the steps in strategic planning.
7. Identify difficulties with planning.
8. Show why managers should plan even though they may not like to.
9. Describe the relationships among decision making, goals, objectives, planning, and control.
10. Define and be able to use the following concepts:

plan	rules
strategic planning	standing plan
organizational strategy	single-use plan
organizational policy	program
control	budget
tactical planning	project
procedures	scenario

Thought Starters

1. What does the term *plan* mean to you?
2. Do all organizations plan? Do you plan?
3. Is organizational planning different from personal planning?
4. How is planning related to decision making? To organizational goals and objectives?

The Sears Story: The Best Laid Plans . . .

Sears, Roebuck is a giant among retailers. Its 1977 sales were over $17 billion, an increase of 16 percent over the previous year. The $2.3 billion increase is greater than the total sales of many large retail firms, such as the R. H. Macy Co.

However, although Sears itself was profitable, the profit from retailing dropped off substantially as compared to profits from such organizations as Allstate, Sears's property and casualty insurance subsidiary. In fact, Sears did not make a penny on the the extra $2.3 billion in retail sales. Instead, its overall profit from retailing dropped by about 13 percent. This drop can be compared to J. C. Penney's increase of about 28 percent and Montgomery Ward's increase of 17 percent in the same year. Needless to say, the stockholders were not happy.

Sears has consistently been one of the most successful retailing organizations in the world. The company pioneered the first honest mail-order catalogue. In the 1920s, Sears recognized the growing importance of the automobile and changed its long-range plans. The company began building shopping centers and became a leader in retail chains. Sears's success was originally based on its image as a low-cost merchandiser.

In 1967, however, Sears changed its strategic plans and began to sell higher-priced merchandise, attracting more affluent shoppers. More of its profits came from the higher-priced items. The strategy worked, but over time its image as a merchandiser of low-priced goods was gradually eroded; and competitors (such as K mart and Penney) began taking over the image, especially during the inflationary period of the early 1970s.

Recognizing the trend, Sears reorganized in 1975, centralizing more decisions at corporate headquarters in Chicago. In 1976, it developed a strategic plan for increasing sales the following year. The plan contained several different approaches: (1) many more "promotional" sales than usual, (2) price slashes on many items, (3) longer sales (which were to last as long as three to four weeks as opposed to the normal three to nine days), (4) more money spent on advertising (approximately $1 million more than the previous year), (5) more advertising in the national magazines (which have a more lasting effect than newspaper advertising), and (6) increased compensation bonuses for store managers (an increase in the amount of the bonus based primarily on volume of sales).

One of the purposes of the strategic plan was to get customers into the store. It was assumed that once in the store, they would buy other items as well as the "promotional" ones. For the first nine months, the strategy seemed to work. About a quarter of new business came from the marked-down merchandise. In fact, in November and December 1977 and January 1978 more than 40 percent of the new business came from markdowns. But during those three months Sears's profits declined by 30 percent.

As a result, Sears is reorganizing once again. The company now has a vice-president of logistics (to keep inventory levels down) and a new vice-president of planning. It has changed the bonus for executives so there is less weight on volume. Sears is also opening more stores and is considering broadening its base by purchasing other companies.[1]

Sears has generally been successful over the years. First, it was a giant mail-order house. Then it shifted to retail stores and shopping centers. Later it modified its strategic planning again, putting in higher-priced merchandise. As Penney and K mart began taking away economy shoppers, however, Sears once more changed strategy. And when the new emphasis on high-volume sales cut into profits, it reevaluated strategy yet another time.

With this case as a base, we will now examine the importance of strategic planning. Planning in organizations is an essential activity. Only after direction has been established can managers decide "what is to be done, when it is to be done, how it is to be done, and who is to do it."[2]

All managers plan. At the top level, they determine overall strategic goals and continuing objectives. At the lower levels, their plans are more detailed and tactical, directed toward accomplishing the goals set at the top.

What Is Strategic Planning?   In the simplest sense, a **plan** is anything that involves selecting a course of action for the future. A football team plans for the season by observing how the opposing teams play and then mapping out strategies and specific plays. During the game itself, the quarterback plans the next play, which depends on what has happened during the game itself, the team's position on the field, the score, and a multitude of other variables.

Planning looks to the future to determine the direction in which an organization or its subunits should be going. It helps bridge the gap from

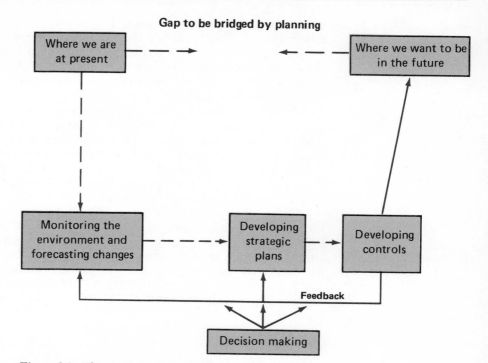

Figure 8.1 The strategic planning process

"where we are" to "where we want to be," as Figure 8.1 shows. Decision making occurs at each of three levels on the way from the present to the future: monitoring and forecasting, developing plans, and developing controls. In the case of Sears, monitoring of the environment showed that Sears's image as a low-cost merchandiser was being eroded. Plans were developed to increase the volume of sales, but the controls showed that the volume increase was also causing reduced profits. As a result, new plans had to be made. Each step, of course, involved decision making.

Top-level **strategic planning** is a process that begins with goals and objectives and that creates strategies, policies, and detailed plans and controls to achieve them.[3] Each of these terms can be examined in detail. (In Chapter 7, organizational goals were described as desired states of affairs that the organization attempts to realize, and organizational objectives were described as ideas or statements that help steer the activities of the organization toward the attainment of those goals.)

An **organizational strategy** is a broad course of action selected from among alternatives as the best way to obtain major objectives, with due regard for relative capabilities, major functions, policies, and resources. The purpose of the strategy is to maintain a position of advantage, particularly in relation to competitors, by capitalizing on strengths and minimizing weaknesses. For example, in 1945, when J. Peter Grace took over the W. R. Grace Company from his father, his review of the environment in which the company existed indicated that the organization was involved in too many risky ventures, particularly in South America. By 1950 he had developed a broad long-term strategy to move the company toward greater corporate security and to make it into one that would prosper no matter what the circumstances. His examination of the environment suggested that chemicals would be less risky than sugar

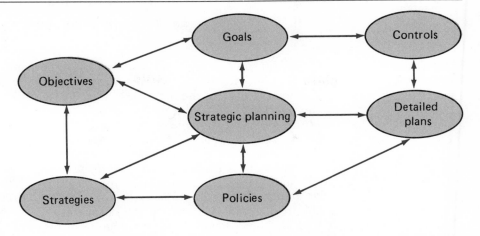

Figure 8.2 The interrelationship of the strategic planning process to other processes

plantations (which might be nationalized). He saw that the widespread use of airplanes for overseas travel made the passenger service of the company's steamships less attractive. As a result, he got the company out of South America and out of the passenger steamship business and diversified into such areas as chemicals, restaurants, and sporting goods stores. By 1977, not a single piece of the old W. R. Grace Company was left. Sales have risen from $200 million in 1950 to about $4 billion in 1977.[4] Apparently, Peter Grace's long-term strategic planning has been successful.

An **organizational policy** is a "standing decision" made in advance, and covering a set of prescribed circumstances—the limitations and/or guidelines for action. **Control** is the process that allows managers to determine whether activities conform to the plan and the objectives and to make adjustments when necessary. In the case of Sears, the policy was to increase promotional sales and bonus pay for managers. The control process showed, however, that although this policy increased sales, it did so at the expense of profits. This knowledge allowed top management to make adjustments, such as tightening up on inventory levels and modifying bonuses dependent on sales volume.

From a systems point of view, decision making, goals, objectives, strategic plans, strategies, and policies are highly interrelated, as Figure 8.2 shows. For example, Peter Grace's decision to diversify the company for greater security (a goal) led to strategic plans to move out of risky businesses into safer ones. This in turn led to a change in overall strategy that affected specific policies and plans.

Goals are the end points of planning; their establishment provides the basic direction for more specific planning (such as strategies, policies, detailed plans, and controls). Strategic planning assists in bridging the gap between the present and the future. Specific plans help identify and activate the organizational behavior needed for attainment of the ends. Leadership, communications, and control assure that the planned behavior becomes reality.

To illustrate, the goal of an electronics firm can be to grow and achieve leadership in its field. An accompanying objective can be to achieve a 15 percent compound rate of growth in sales over the next ten years to place its performance in the top 4 percent of the industry. To accomplish this, strategic plans are necessary to bridge the planning gap.

Without such plans, neither the goal nor the objective are likely to be reached.

Who Does Planning?

Planning is done at all levels of the organization, as shown in Table 8.1.[5] At the top level the planning is strategic, directed toward the general position of the organization in the environment. What should be the overall goals of the organization? What is its basic mission or purpose? What is the overall strategy? What should be the continuing objectives? A greater degree of uncertainty exists at this level than at lower levels, since the probable outcomes are less known. The relevant environment is primarily external to the organization—including political, social, legal, and financial issues. As a result, the criteria for making decisions are mainly subjective. Top management must rely more heavily on qualitative standards for determining the effectiveness of plans than do those lower in the management hierarchy.[6]

At the middle or coordinating level of management, planning is directed toward implementing the strategic plans by coordinating the work of different organizational units. Planning at this level, sometimes called **tactical planning**, "involves deciding specifically how the resources of the organization will be used to help the organization achieve its strategic goals."[7] Managers develop alternatives and estimate the probability of their leading to desired outcomes. Both certainty and uncertainty are involved in their decisions; although they can rely heavily on the past performance of the organization, some decisions will cover entirely new ground. The environment at the middle level is more internal than that at the top, and the manager is constrained by top-level decisions about continuing objectives and the implementation of strategy and policy. The degree of risk can be reduced at this level by the introduction of quantifiable techniques, such as market research and forecasting.

At the lowest or operating level of management, the managers must follow the tactical plans established by the middle level of management to achieve the strategic plans formulated at the top. Operational plans are generally specific and tangible. They involve risk, but usually enough information is at hand for the manager to closely predict the outcome of decisions. Environmental constraints are primarily internal, consisting of objectives, policies, budgets, procedures, and rules. Thus plans at this level can be more automatic, and decisions can be quantitative (such as creating production schedules and adhering to costs and budgets).

In reality, the differences among the three managerial levels is not clear-cut. Information is continually flowing both up and down. (Strategic planning is also called top-down planning because it provides the middle and lower levels with information they need to use in de-

Table 8.1 Planning at different levels of the organization

Levels of management	Types of plans	Degrees of certainty
Top or strategic management	Strategic planning	Primarily uncertainty, with some degree of risk
Middle or coordinative management	Coordinative planning (tactical plans)	Primarily risk, but both certainty and uncertainty involved
First level or operating management	Operational planning	Some risk, but moderate degree of certainty

veloping operational, or bottom-up, plans.) It is through the interchanging, reviewing, and recycling of top-down and bottom-up plans that the planning activity in general is coordinated and the plans themselves sorted into long-range and short-range categories. In the Sears case, information from the lower level indicated that the strategic plan to increase volume of sales also needed to take into account the amount of profit that would be generated.

The Importance of Planning

Planning is important for at least five reasons:

— 1. It enables the organization to cope with change.[8]
— 2. It helps ensure that organizational objectives are reached or changed when necessary.
— 3. It helps the organization succeed.
— 4. It helps in day-to-day decision making.
— 5. It enables the organization to maintain an effective control process.

Coping with Change

A phenomenon of our time is the increased emphasis placed on planning by all sorts of organizations—business, education, government, and others. The primary reasons for this phenomenon are that the world is more turbulent than it used to be, change is more rapid than ever before, and problems are more complex. Organizations know that without good plans, they will be caught by surprise (as many were during the oil embargo of 1973).

Organizations today are involved with innumerable problems, including inflation, recession, resource shortages, government regulations, and greater worldwide interdependence. Individuals, institutions, and nations are interrelated by so many threads of communication, ideas, economics, and cultures that it is sometimes difficult for them to understand how a tug on one thread affects others in the fabric. If the Organization of Petroleum Exporting Countries (OPEC) raises prices of crude oil, the impact is felt immediately throughout the world. Established in 1960 by representatives from Iraq, Iran, Kuwait, Saudi Arabia, and Venezuela, OPEC supplies 80 percent of the oil entering world trade. In 1973, it adopted the strategy of regulating production by way of an oil embargo. The embargo led to long lines at service stations, debates in Congress over energy policy, balance of payments problems for the United States and many underdeveloped nations, and increased investments in the United States by OPEC nations.

Planning used to involve primarily economic and technological factors; now it must give weight to social and political factors as well. A change in government structure in Japan, India, or Israel would affect stock market prices in the United States almost immediately. Business executives, university presidents, and school superintendents are becoming concerned about the growing number of federal rules and regulations. E. I. du Pont, which has annual sales of more than $8 billion, reports "spending $5 million and 180 man-years of work annually to file 15,000 reports to the Federal Government."[9] Clearly, managerial planning must be directed to the impact of social and political forces as well as economic and technological forces. (See Chapter 21.)

Organizations that consider social, political, economic, and technological trends in their planning can face the future with some confidence. They stand less chance than others of being surprised by legislative or administrative actions of government, by shifting public moods, or by the changing aspirations of customers or employees. A good illustration of the failure to develop "anticipatory management" involves the recent discrimination lawsuits against AT&T. Fines and compensatory damages resulting from AT&T's discrimination against women have run into millions of dollars. If management had properly perceived the growing influence of the women's movement, the organization could have changed its practices with respect to the promotion and compensation of women and avoided the lawsuits and fines.

Reaching or Changing Organizational Objectives

Planning helps managers and employees see where they are and points the way for them to achieve organization and unit objectives. Without planning, activities become ends in themselves rather than means to ends.

Planning, especially strategic planning, also affects objectives and goals. Effective planning often discloses information about the future environment that indicates which objectives may need to be changed. The profit objective was not reached by companies who developed plans for making horseshoes or buggy whips when the long-range predictions showed that the automobile was taking over the roads.

Helping Organizations Succeed

A number of studies have examined the results of planning, either directly or indirectly. In most of them, organizations with formal planning programs were compared with similar organizations that did not have these programs. The planners outperformed the nonplanners in such areas as sales, growth rates, stock prices, and earnings per share. This was particularly true for organizations in rapidly changing environments, such as drugs and plastics.[10] Planning is not a guarantee of success, but it certainly helps. In the Sears case, planning—and the follow-up on planning—showed what changes were needed over the years to keep the firm profitable.

A recent study compared the growth of General Electric and Westinghouse. It pointed out that "since the mid-1960's, the two companies have been heading in distinctly different directions, impelled by divergent management and operating philosophies."[11] The study attributes much of GE's rapid growth to meticulous planning and a strategy of risk containment and Westinghouse's lag to two basic failures—"an *absence of strategic planning* and a depth of financial controls."[12]

GE has been a pioneer in the development of strategic planning and environmental forecasting. Since 1970, the starting point for any planning cycle at GE has been a long-term environmental forecast that attempts to predict the entire economic-technological-social-political environment for a time period of ten years. The social-political portion of the forecast attempts to identify the key issues arising from changing societal expectations and to analyze their relevance and importance to the organization. The findings are integrated with those of the more traditional economic and technological forecasts to form the overall environmental forecast. Hence, at GE there is talk of a "four-sided framework" for planning (which is shown in Figure 8.3).

The environmental forecast provides premises for top-down corporate-level strategic planning at GE and for operational, or bottoms-up, planning that goes on in some forty strategic business units (SBUs) there. The planning system was designed to ensure the logical progression from long-range environmental forecast, to corporate objectives and strategies, to specific forecasts, strategies, and policies for each SBU. Hence, it is not surprising that GE, a pioneer in environmental

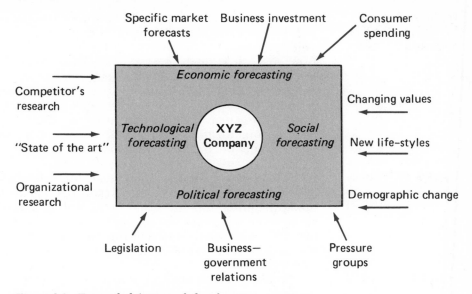

Specific market forecasts   Business investment   Consumer spending

Competitor's research

"State of the art"

Organizational research

Economic forecasting

Technological forecasting   **XYZ Company**   Social forecasting

Political forecasting

Changing values

New life-styles

Demographic change

Legislation   Business— government relations   Pressure groups

Figure 8.3   Four-sided framework for planning

Adapted from Ian H. Wilson, "Socio-Political Forecasting: A New Dimension to Strategic Planning," *Michigan Business Review*, July, 1974, pp. 19–20. Reprinted by permission from the July, 1974, issue of the *University of Michigan Business Review*, published by the Graduate School of Business Administration, The University of Michigan.

forecasting and strategic planning, is already marketing a complete line of compact electric ovens that use considerably less energy than do full-size ovens. It is also interesting to note that since at least 1956, one of GE's objectives has been "to lead in research in all fields of science and in all areas of work relating to the business, *including managing as a distinct and a professional kind of work*."[13]

Helping Day-to-Day Decision Making

Managers are busy people. They are constantly interacting with others in the roles of entrepreneur, disturbance handler, resource allocator, and negotiator (see Chapter 2). Because they are busy, they must frequently make quick decisions on the basis of relatively little information. For that reason they need guides on how to make good decisions. Otherwise, their decisions may not help the organization or unit move in the planned direction.

To illustrate: A manager was working to develop a cohesive work group as part of an organizational plan. When the manager found he needed more storage space for the group, he called on an engineer to design the storage unit. Unaware of the manager's plans for developing a cohesive work group, the engineer decided to place the storage unit in the "logical" place—right in the middle of the work group. Placing the unit in that particular spot would have severely reduced group interaction and probably would have resulted in the creation of two subgroups. When the manager saw the proposed location, he immediately asked that the unit be moved to an area that would not reduce the group's cohesiveness. Without the original plan, the manager would not have been aware of the effect of putting the storage unit in the midst of the work group.

Maintaining an Effective Control Process

The final reason for good planning is that planning and control are highly interrelated.[14] After objectives and plans to meet them are developed, controls are necessary to ensure that resources are properly used and individuals perform so as to achieve the objectives of the organization. Many texts indicate that the purpose of planning is to control the behavior of subordinates. This is an oversimplification. The purpose of control is to enable management to achieve plans; thus control is a means, not an end in itself. Control systems are created to help an organization achieve its plans and accomplish its objectives. (The subject of control is discussed more fully in Chapter 9.)

Types of Plans

There are a number of ways of describing plans.[15] This is already obvious, since passing references have been made to strategic and operational planning, top-down and bottom-up planning, and long-range and short-range planning. In this section, three other ways of classifying plans are discussed: (1) according to scope or breadth, (2) according to use or function, and (3) according to time or duration.

Breadth

Strategic plans are the broadest in scope. Successively narrower plans are strategies, policies, procedures, and rules (as shown in Figure 8.4). Strategic plans are integrated, comprehensive, and unified; they are designed to make certain that the organization's basic goals are achieved and to change the goals when necessary.

Strategies, which have less scope, are directed toward attaining major objectives. Sears, for example, changed strategies to gain a greater share of the market, and Peter Grace changed strategies to make his company more secure. According to a noted professor, "Strategies do not attempt to outline exactly how the enterprise is used to accomplish its major objectives; this is the task of a multitude of major and minor supporting programs."[16]

Policies, which are even narrower in scope than strategies, are standing decisions intended to serve as overall guidelines to thinking and decision making. They can be specified in writing or developed out of common practice. For example, an organization may have either a written or unwritten policy of "hiring from within." Policies are usually developed by executive committee or by the organization's board of directors. Normally they do not change very rapidly. For example, when trucks began to be used for handling freight, railroad policy was to fight their use. Railroads saw themselves as being in the railroad business, not in the transportation business. In the same way, the motion picture companies opposed the coming of television. Only after television had become popular did these companies discover that it was a good market for their films.

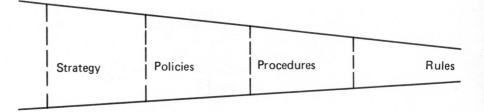

Figure 8.4   The narrowing scope of strategy policies, procedures, and rules

Procedures are plans that establish a customary method of handling future activities. They are narrower than policies because they are guides to action rather than to thinking. Unlike policies, which usually involve the entire organization, procedures tend to be intradepartmental or interdepartmental in scope. Even when they cut across departmental lines, they stress departmental functions. For example, a manufacturing company may have procedures for handling orders (sales department), procedures for manufacturing (production department), procedures for receiving payment (finance department), and procedures for shipping goods (shipping department). Each major department can change its procedures to some degree without necessarily affecting the other departments, but a change in policy affects all departments. The amount of vacation time an employee gets may be organizational policy. How vacations are scheduled in a particular department is probably regulated by procedures.

Rules are the simplest type of plan and the narrowest in scope; they describe or require that definite, specific actions be taken (or not taken) in a given situation. Sometimes they are related to procedures. For example, a rule requiring the wearing of safety glasses in a certain area of a plant may have a related procedure that outlines how employees or visitors to the area can obtain and return the glasses. Procedures may incorporate rules, but rules do not incorporate procedures or policies. They serve as guides to behavior, and there is generally no discretion in their use.

Use

The two major use plans are standing plans and single-use plans. A **standing plan** is a plan established to guide organizational actions that are repeated frequently. For example, organizations pay employees; banks make repeated automobile loans; hospitals routinely admit patients; retail stores routinely accept returned merchandise. For each of these activities a standing plan can be developed that establishes guides to action and ensures that the action is taken in a consistent manner. Policies, procedures, and rules are successively narrower and more detailed standing plans.

Single-use plans are plans specifically developed to carry out courses of action that are relatively unique and unlikely to be repeated. A new plant is needed; a space vehicle is sent to Mars; a customer orders a one-of-a-kind piece of equipment. In each of these circumstances, existing plans are insufficient for the job to be done, because the job requires a specific plan tailored to the circumstances. An organization may have built plants in the past; but zoning laws, construction costs, specific terrain and location problems, and union restrictions may require a unique plan to be developed for a particular plant. There are three basic types of single-use plans: programs, projects, and budgets.

A **program** is a single-use plan that involves a large number of interrelated and interdependent activities. An example of a program is the installation of management by objectives in a large organization. As a plan, the program must specify (1) the major steps required to complete the overall task, (2) the order and timing in which the steps will be accomplished, and (3) the unit or individual responsible for each step. For example, in building a new plant, architectural plans must be drawn that are specific to that building, and the work of such varied groups as steelworkers, plumbers, painters, and carpenters must be coordinated.

A **project** is a single-use plan that is either a subset of a program or less complex than a program. For example, one project might be to improve the effectiveness or durability of a particular product, such as revising a textbook to bring it up to date. Another project might be a task force established to develop and follow through on plans to install a new machine in a manufacturing plant.

Budgets are plans for a given future period that are stated in numerical (usually financial) terms. To some degree, budgets are a control device, since they govern a variety of different activities. For example, expense budgets control expenses; and capital expenditure budgets control what will be spent for new plants, machinery, and equipment.

Budgets are important aspects of both programs and projects. However, they can also be considered single-use plans, since budget making is clearly a form of planning. The preparation of a budget is a means of deciding in advance how resources will be allocated among different activities. As a single-use plan, the budget must take strategic objectives into account. If it does not, the overall strategy will have only a limited effect on actual activities. For many organizations, the budget is the planning mechanism around which other activities are planned. Many organizations wind up in financial trouble because they do not develop well-planned and executed budgets.

Time

A third way of classifying plans is by **duration**. Some plans have a very short-range effect and others have a long-range effect. For example, when faced with a parts shortage, a first-level supervisor may suddenly shift plans and begin assembling some other item. In this case, the planning may involve only a few minutes or a day or two. However, short-range planning need not involve only problems. A certain hospital employs a financial manager who works full-time planning how to temporarily invest surplus funds before they need to be used. The investments seldom last longer than ninety days.

All organizations do short-range planning. However (as Chapters 1 and 2 showed), there is a tendency for managers to concentrate on immediate and specific problems and fail to consider the need for long-range plans. As one prominent consultant put it, "In the large majority of companies, corporate (long-range) planning tends to be an academic, ill-defined activity with little or no impact."[17] This failure is particularly true with regard to long-range plans (five to twenty years or more) that establish the strategy of the organization.

One study suggests that top management should spend about 10 percent of their time thinking about the next five to ten years and about 50 percent of their time thinking about the next two to five years. Middle management should spend about 50 percent of their time thinking about the next six months to a year, while first-level management should devote little time to the future—concentrating on a span of a week or less.[18]

Clearly, this "ideal" state varies with the type of organization. For a utility company, five to ten years might be a relatively short time span. On the other hand, in the quickly changing garment industry, three months may be a relatively long time span.

Contingent Strategic Planning: Developing Scenarios

In the past, planning usually involved choosing one "most probable" future or environment as a basis for developing a strategy. Now there is growing awareness that organizational planning must be prepared to deal with uncertainty—with events that cannot be predicted in advance. This means that organizations must develop contingency plans for a number of different environments or "alternative futures." These alternative futures are called "**scenarios**."[19] Each plan is based on a different scenario—that is, a different set of assumptions about the future. Thus the organization may decide:

1. If the actual future environment is like Scenario A, follow Plan 1.
2. If the actual future environment is like Scenario B, follow Plan 2.
3. If the actual future environment is like Scenario C, follow Plan 3.

Building a scenario includes: (1) identifying key variables affecting an organization, (2) developing different sets of assumptions, (3) estimating the interactions between the key variables and the assumptions, and (4) developing a written description of the future under different sets of predicted environments. Although a large number of potential scenarios can be identified, probably no more than three or four should be fully developed; more than four may not be markedly different in their characteristics. But if only one or two are developed, probably not enough attention is being paid to the different future possibilities.

Each scenario should be plausible. One way of doing this is to include realistic variables; another way is to look at the "mix" of variables. For example, high rates of inflation, considerable economic growth, high rates of unemployment, and low gasoline prices might each be possible. It is highly unlikely, however, that all four would occur simultaneously.

Each scenario should be kept neutral in tone. It should be written from the viewpoint of someone living in the future and describing what it is like and how it developed. A scenario for an independent oil company might describe better fuel consumption, slower growth in market demand, and a need for fewer outlets providing lower prices through the use of self-service pumps. Another might consider the impact of electrically-powered automobiles. Yet another might consider the elimination of private automobiles because of an energy shortage.

In one situation, sixty MBA students were asked to develop a scenario that would consider the impact of social responsibility for organizations in the future. In Round 1, each student suggested an estimate (probability) of certain actions occurring in the future. These results were then combined and returned to the students, together with selected pro and con arguments. In Round 2, each student reestimated the probabilities and presented further arguments. After four rounds, some tentative conclusions were as follows (combined probabilities are given in parentheses):

> *It is likely (.60) that corporations will become more socially responsible, but it is doubtful (.47) that the public will think any more of them for it. . . . Public ferment will be evidenced probably (.63) in increased activist group pressure to curb corporate powers. . . . Perhaps one effect that the concern for social responsibility will have is an increased ability (.55) of the public to judge accurately the degree of social responsiveness by a corporation.[20]*

Steps in Long-Range Strategic Planning

Quickly changing, uncertain environments are forcing organizations to prepare better for the future. The primary reason is that in a fast-moving, increasingly complex environment, decisions based entirely on present-oriented considerations are obsolete almost as soon as they are made. A future-oriented organization needs to take responsibility for adapting to change when necessary and, more importantly, to shape the future when possible.

More and more emphasis is being placed on long-range planning.[21] This emphasis is usually provided by the organization designing its own formal planning system. It was stated earlier that establishing objectives could come first in planning. Yet, a long-range environmental forecast was the first element in the planning cycle at General Electric. Is this contradictory? Not really. GE has formalized, institutionalized, and integrated environmental forecasting into its planning process. This guarantees that the organization will pay sufficient attention to external pressures when establishing objectives.

As Figure 8.5 shows, there are eight long-range planning steps for a relatively small organization: (1) identifying organizational objectives, (2) determining the time span of plans, (3) identifying organizational strengths and weaknesses, (4) identifying key elements, (5) developing scenarios, (6) selecting the best strategy, (7) developing specific policies, plans, and programs, and (8) measuring and controlling progress. Larger organizations can and do use the same approach, but they also have more resources, such as a planning and forecasting staff and highly sophisticated, computerized mathematical techniques (some of which are described in Chapter 10).

Step 1: *Examining and determining explicit organizational objectives, policies, and basic mission.* What is the organization's basic mission? Who are its clients and its competition? These and other questions should be answered in writing. Unless the organization is clear about what it is and where it is, planning is of little use.

Step 2: *Determining the time span of plans.* The time span of planning depends somewhat on the organization and the product's life span. For example, utility companies planning the construction of power generators need to have longer time spans than do manufacturers of women's clothing.

Step 3: *Identifying organizational strengths and weaknesses.* When Ford Motor Company took over Philco a few years ago, it made a fundamental error. Ford purchased Philco in order to diversify, expecting to rehabilitate the ailing company through an infusion of managerial talent and capital. Within a short time, all but three of the top twenty-five managers had left Philco. Ford brought in eighteen managers in the first six months, but these people knew the automobile rather than the appliance business. Within four years, there were about fifty Ford executives in the Philco business, and they all had the same fundamental weakness. Eventually Ford had to get managers who knew the appliance business.[23]

Step 4: *Identifying the key elements of consequence to the organization.* What has been important to the organization, and what will be important in the future? Almost all organizations use indicators such as employment rate, inflation rate, and the Gross National Product (GNP) in their planning. (The GNP is the nation's output of goods and services—expressed in terms of dollars—during a period of one year.) Universities can plot the potential pool of college undergraduates to predict enrollments. The GNP, inflation rates, and employment rates can be used to predict the number of new car sales. While many of these elements cannot be predicted exactly, it is possible to find a reasonable range for key variables that includes both a middle ground and the extremes. For

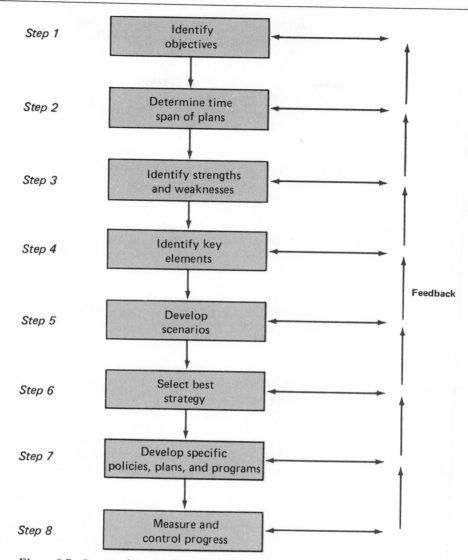

Figure 8.5 Steps in long-range planning for a small organization

example, the inflation rate might be predicted to vary from 5 percent to 20 percent.

Step 5: *Developing scenarios in which the organization may operate.* As described earlier, scenarios show alternative futures in which an organization may operate.

Step 6: *Selecting or modifying the "best" strategy.* For each scenario, the strategy that has the most likely opportunity for achieving organizational objectives should be developed. Examination of the scenarios and their underlying assumptions and strategies frequently leads to a "compromise" strategy. The strategy finally adopted should be adaptable to changing situations or different environments. It should be flexible and more attractive in the near future than the long range, since the near future is more accurately predicted.

Step 7: *Developing medium- and short-range policies, plans, and programs.* Long-range strategy is implemented by developing specific medium- or short-range plans, policies, and programs—usually at the middle management level or below—to ensure that the overall strategy is attained.

Step 8: *Measuring and controlling the progress of the plan.* The process of controlling is critical to any plan. Managers need to continually check the progress of plans so they can either take remedial action if necessary or change the original plan if it is unrealistic. The primary advantage of contingency planning is that managers need not start from scratch each time. Controls can take many forms. One of the most used is the budget; another is the profit and loss statement. (The subject of controlling is sufficiently important to be discussed in more detail in Chapter 9.)

Although a number of straightforward steps have been listed for the planning process, such a neat and orderly approach is rare in actuality. Since the outside world changes constantly, planning is a continuous process, and most managers can be engaged in several of the planning steps at the same time. Rather than updating a five-year plan on an annual basis, plans are often updated quarterly, monthly, or even weekly. Arizona Public Service Company has a "dynamic" approach that looks ahead two years but is reexamined every month. At Ralston Purina Co., a 1 percent change in the price of an important commodity triggers a change in the organization's cost models. After reexamination, the whole corporate plan may change accordingly.[24]

Continuous feedback from the environment and from within the organization is necessary both for control and for evaluation. Are the plans on target? Do short-range plans need to be revised because of environmental changes? Are the control procedures operating properly? Relatively little is known about the evaluation of planning. Is a 5 percent underestimate of sales or of hospital bed occupancy a major or minor error? Should an underestimate be treated in the same way as an overestimate? For example, many managers underestimate what they can actually do so they can look good by doing more than expected. Is this good or bad? Should the numbers be held to rigidly, as in the following example?

Richard Beeson, president of Canada Dry, is describing what he heard from David Mahoney, who was chief executive at Norton Simon, Inc. (which controls Canada Dry):

> "I had been on the job only a couple of weeks," Beeson says, "when we had a Canada Dry board meeting." I said to Mahoney, "Dave, we're a little bit below budget now, and I think we can hold that for the rest of the year."
>
> Dave looked at me, smiled, and said, "Be on budget by the six-month mark; be on by the year."
>
> "But Dave," I said, "there isn't enough time to get on by the half. I inherited this situation, after all."
>
> Still smiling, Dave looked at me and said, "Do I pay you a lot of money? Do I argue with you over what you want to spend? Do I bother you? Then don't tell me what the goals should be. Be on by the half; be on by the end of the year."
>
> "What if can't, Dave?", I asked.
>
> "Then clean out your desk and go home."
>
> Beeson . . . says he began running through the reasons why he

could not meet the goals, but Mahoney said, "Not interested. My board and my stockholders want me to make my numbers. The way I make my numbers is for you guys to make your numbers. Make your numbers!"[25]

Clearly, Mahoney is overstating the case. Clearly, it is also important to him to make certain that the overall plan is adhered to. More would have to be known about his managerial style to determine whether he was being too inflexible. However, the existence of a clear set of plans enabled Beeson and Mahoney to identify each other's positions.

Thus the eight basic steps can provide an organization with a series of flexible long-range plans that allow it to shift strategies and tactics as circumstances change. Furthermore, these steps can be modified so that lower-level managers can use them to do unit planning within the organization. In this case the time span will be shorter and the scenarios will be laid primarily within the organization.

Difficulties with Planning

There are many problems of long-range planning.[26] Some of them will be briefly described below.

Concentration on the Present

One problem is the short time frame under which many managers operate. As Mahoney told Beeson, "Be on budget by the six-month mark; be on by the year." This attitude creates a strong tendency to concentrate on today's problems and crises. Stockholders and upper-level managers are often very interested in short-run performance. Many management information systems and financial analyses are focused primarily on the present rather than the future. Most control measures are based on the present rather than the long-term future (as the conversation between Beeson and Mahoney shows). Under these conditions, managers may feel that there is no time for long-range planning and no immediate reward for it—that their most important objective is to meet the budget for short-range performance. For this reason, it is imperative that long-range planning be tied directly to immediate performance.

Confusing Planning Studies with Plans

Many larger organizations have planning departments; frequently, however, these departments work in isolation, apart from the line managers who are responsible for both day-to-day and long-range operation of the organization. Lacking participation in the planning process, line managers are not committed to the plans that are formulated. Even worse, the plans themselves are frequently unrelated to the line manager's major problems. As a result, many organizations have stacks of planning studies and no real plans implemented. For a study to become a plan, a decision must be made to commit the organization to the use of certain resources or to a particular direction.

Lack of Clear, Attainable, and Specific Objectives

Unless the objectives of the organization are clear, effective planning cannot take place; the organization has to decide where it wants to go before making plans to get there. And unless the objectives are verifiable, it will be impossible to tell whether they have been achieved. Many objectives can be quantified (for example, dollars of sales and profits), but many cannot. When objectives cannot be quantified, they can be described in qualitative terms.

**Too Heavy
Concentration on
Economic and
Technological
Factors**

Most planning takes into consideration primarily economic factors (such as inflation and employment rates) and technological factors (such as new products or equipment). Few plans really examine in detail the organization's internal and external political and social factors. For example, the oil embargo of 1973, which was primarily a political factor, came as a complete surprise to many organizations. As another illustration, most plans assume that everyone in the organization subscribes equally to organizational objectives, which is not usually the case.

**Planning Perceived
as Being Concerned
Only with the Future**

"Long range planning is not planning for future decisions, but planning the future impact of present decisions."[27] Many managers do not recognize the truth of this statement. As a result, they do not think about the future consequences of present decisions. Managers must try to forecast as much as possible the impact of today's decisions on the future. And, since most of us tend to base our decisions on our past experience, plans should take into account the past as well as the future.

**Implications for
the Manager**

This chapter has developed the basic concepts of planning. At Sears, for example, the overall strategic planning of the company has caused it to change directions through the years. In general, Sears has become a giant in its field through good strategic planning. Yet, even in large, well-run organizations, errors can be made; and at Sears the error was an overemphasis on volume that reduced retailing profits.

As discussed in Chapters 1 and 2, managers are busy people who tend to deal with the here and now. They are more excited about immediate problems than about future ones. Yet, in their various roles, they must monitor the external and internal environment, disseminate information to subordinates and others, and act as entrepreneurs and resource allocators. These roles require planning of a high order. Planning is also necessary for the organization to adapt to future changes, accomplish its objectives, and control the utilization of resources.

Planning involves developing a course of action for the future. At the higher levels of the organization it tends to be broader in scope and less detailed than at the lower levels, but managers at all levels must plan. Effective planning reduces the extent of "management by crisis," and effective organizations encourage their managers to plan.

Managers should involve others in the planning process. Although the managers are ultimately responsible for the success or failure of the units, divisions, or organizations, they must have the support and assistance of subordinates. Involving subordinates in planning is a way for managers to get better results. Subordinates can be of considerable help in developing better plans. For one thing, several people can come up with more ideas than one person can. For another, research indicates that employees will try harder to accomplish plans that they have helped establish. The effective manager should get suggestions and recommendations from key subordinates before implementing important plans.

There is increasing emphasis on developing contingency plans or scenarios for future environments. Although larger organizations usually have formal planning departments that use sophisticated techniques, many smaller organizations do not. Thus this chapter has described a number of steps in the long-range planning process for use in organizations that do not have such techniques. The eight steps described here can be easily modified, however, to apply to a small unit of a large organization. Finally, lower-level managers can build scenarios based on unit goals and objectives.

Perhaps the most important advice that can be given to managers is that they should constantly be asking the question "What if . . . ?" when making decisions. As indicated earlier in the chapter, long-range planning is really assessing the future impact of present decisions.

Review

1. How many ways can the idea of planning be used?
2. At what levels of the organization should planning take place?
3. Are plans that are best for one unit or department always best for the entire organization? Explain.
4. Do you think the planning done by Sears, Roebuck was realistic? Would you have done anything differently?
5. How are the concepts of decision making, planning, objectives, and control interrelated?
6. Should all plans cover the same length of time? Discuss.
7. Interview members of different organizations, including both large and small ones. Do the people you have talked to know the objectives for their organizations? How much planning is done in each organization? Are the people you talked to involved in the planning process? Describe their involvement.
8. Assume you are to develop long-range plans for a local service station, pharmacy, jewelry store, barbershop, or similar organization. What information will you need to know? Will it be different for each organization? How will you go about building scenarios for the future?
9. Can a lower-level manager develop long-range plans? Discuss.
10. What effect does participation have on planning? Discuss.

Radio Shack International

In 1973, Radio Shack opened its first European store in Belgium. In 1977, the organization had 459 overseas outlets but had not added a new store in eighteen months. In addition, it had lost $21 million from its European operations in the previous three years.

Charles D. Tandy had spent thirteen years building Radio Shack into the leading merchandiser of amateur electronic gear in the United States. He bought Radio Shack Corporation in 1963 when it was in trouble. In the first nine months of fiscal 1977, the six thousand store chain had earnings of $56.2 million on revenues of $732.6 million—respective increases of 14 percent and 32 percent. Retail stores accounted for 95 percent of the company's earnings and revenues.

Radio Shack's success in the United States appears to be a combination of well-located stores, discount prices, a wide product mix, and heavy advertising. Charles Tandy believes that this approach will work in Europe and that the four years of heavy losses are only temporary. Basically, he says, "I see nothing different about the people in Europe from the people in the U.S." As a result, he plans to continue with the same strategies.

Others suggest that the problem is more fundamental—that discounting methods that work in the United States will not attract Europeans, who are highly brand and quality conscious. In a blitz operation, the European market was blanketed with hundreds of stores, many in poor locations.

In many cases, local laws and customs were overlooked or disregarded. When the first store was opened in Belgium, for example, Tandy overlooked a law that requires a government tax stamp on window signs. In Holland, the first Christmas promotion was geared to December 25. The company was not aware that the Dutch exchange holiday gifts on St. Nicholas Day, usually celebrated on December 6. In Germany, one of the biggest losses occurred when Radio Shack gave away flashlights to promote its stores—and was served with an injunction for violating German sales laws.

In the United States, citizens band radios are Radio Shack's best-selling item, accounting for 22 percent of sales. Belgium, Britain, and Holland bar citizens band radios; and various laws have curbed the sale of other items as well.

European competitors suggest that Europeans are willing to pay premium prices for top quality items and that Radio Shack's image as a discount house keeps customers away. The quality image is especially strong in France, where Radio Shack has only eight stores (none of which is in Paris).

Despite the losses, sales are slowly increasing; and Tandy is optimistic that his basic strategy will work. In fact, he predicts that the foreign operation will be profitable in two years.[28]

1. How might planning be different in Europe than in the United States?
2. What recommendations would you have for Tandy after reading this chapter? Is he being optimistic or realistic in his planning?
3. What steps would you take to increase sales and profitability? What would you want to know about the different European countries?
4. What implications does this case have for other international operations?

Footnotes

1. W. Robertson, "How Sears' Retailing Strategy Backfired," *Fortune*, May 8, 1978, pp. 103–104; "Sears Net Fell 19% in Quarter Ended January 31," *Wall Street Journal*, March 22, 1978, p. 2; and "Sears Starts Program to Improve Gross Profit Margins," *Household Furniture Daily*, February 27, 1978, p. 1.
2. G. Steiner, *Top Management Planning* (New York: Macmillan, 1969), p. 7.
3. Ibid., p. 20.
4. P. Bernstein, "Peter Grace's Long Search for Security," *Fortune*, May 8, 1978, pp. 117–133.
5. R. Anthony, *Planning and Control Systems: A Framework for Analysis* (Cambridge, Mass.: Harvard University Press, 1966); Steiner, *Top Management Planning;* and P. Lorange and R. Vancil, *Strategic Planning Systems* (Englewood Cliffs, N. J.: Prentice–Hall, 1977).
6. Anthony, *Planning and Control Systems,* p. 19.
7. J. Stoner, *Management* (Englewood Cliffs, N. J.: Prentice–Hall, 1978), p. 97.
8. Lorange and Vancil, *Strategic Planning Systems,* p. 5.
9. "Rage over Rising Regulation," *Time*, January 2, 1978, p. 48.
10. J. Eastlack and P. McDonald, "CEO's Role in Corporate Growth," *Harvard Business Review* 48 (May–June 1970): 150–163; D. Herold, "Long Range Planning and Organizational Performance: A Cross-Validation Study," *Journal of the Academy of Management* 15 (March 1972): 91–102; S. Schoeffler, "Impact of Strategic Planning on Profit Performance," *Harvard Business Review* 52 (March–April 1974): 137–145; R. Stagner, "Corporate Decision Making," *Journal of Applied Psychology* 53 (February 1969): 81–87; and S. Thune and R. House,

"Where Long Range Planning Pays Off," *Business Horizons* 13 (August 1970): 80–87.

11. "The Opposites: G. E. Grows while Westinghouse Shrinks," *Business Week*, January 31, 1977, p. 60.

12. Ibid., p. 60.

13. Ibid., p. 61.

14. W. Newman, *Constructive Control: Design and Use of Control Systems* (Englewood Cliffs, N. J.: Prentice–Hall, 1975); and E. Lawler III and J. Rhode, *Information and Control in Organizations* (Pacific Palisades, Calif.: Goodyear Publishing, 1976).

15. W. Newman, *Administrative Action: The Techniques of Organization and Management*, 3rd ed. (Englewood Cliffs, N.J.: Prentice–Hall, 1964); H. Koontz and C. O'Donnell, *Principles of Management* (New York: McGraw–Hill, 1976); and Stoner, *Management.*

16. H. Koontz, "Making Strategic Planning Work," *Business Horizons* 19 (April 1976): 38.

17. L. Gerstner, "Can Strategic Planning Pay Off?" *Business Horizons* (December 1972): 5.

18. Steiner, *Top Management Planning*, p. 26.

19. B. Nanus, "The Future-Oriented Corporation," *Business Horizons* 18 (February 1975): 5–12; F. Foreland, "Dialectic Methods of Forecasting," *The Futurist* 5 (August 1971): 169–170; and B. Cazes, "The Future of Work: An Outline of a Method for Scenario Construction," *Futures* 8 (October 1976): 405–410.

20. J. Diffenbach, personal communication.

21. W. King and D. Cleland, "Information for More Effective Strategic Planning," *Long Range Planning* 10 (February 1977): 59–64; R. Linneman and J. Kennell, "Shirt Sleeve Approach to Long-Range Plans," *Harvard Business Review* 55 (March–April 1977): 141–151; and H. Mintzberg, "Planning on the Left Side and Managing on the Right," *Harvard Business Review* 54 (July–August 1976): 49–58.

22. D. Schoen, "Responsibilities of Corporate Planning—A Checklist," *Management Review* 66 (March 1977): 26–27; E. Wrapp, "Good Managers Don't Make Policy Decisions," *Harvard Business Review* 39 (September–October 1967): 91–99; and F. Gilmore, "Formulating Strategy in Smaller Companies," *Harvard Business Review* 49 (May–June 1971): 168–178.

23. P. Siekman, "Henry Ford and His Electronic Can of Worms," *Fortune,* February 1966, p. 116.

24. "Corporate Planning: Piercing Future Fog," *Business Week*, April 28, 1975, pp. 46–54.

25. "The Way I Make My Numbers Is for You Guys to Make Your Numbers," reprinted by permission of *Forbes* Magazine from the February 15, 1972 issue, p. 26.

26. E. Warren, *Long-Range Planning: The Executive Viewpoint* (Englewood Cliffs, N. J.: Prentice–Hall, 1966); Steiner, *Top Management Planning;* P. Stonich, "Formal Planning Pitfalls and How to Avoid Them–Part I," *Management Review* 64 (June 1975): 5–6; and "Part 2" *Management Review* 64 (July 1975): 29–35.

27. Koontz, "Making Strategic Planning Work," p. 39.

28. "Radio Shack's Rough Trip," *Business Week,* May 30, 1977, p. 55.

Chapter 9   Controlling

Lavelle's Private War

What Is "Controlling"?

The Basic Control Process

Steps in the Control Process
    Step 1: Establishing Standards
    Step 2: Measuring the Results of Activities against Standards
    Step 3: Correction of Deviations

Control as a Feedback Process

Ten Characteristics of Effective Controls

Extent and Pervasiveness of Controls
    Organizational Structure and Design
    Production Control
    Inventory Control
    Quality Control
    Budget Control

Indirect and Direct Control
    Indirect Control
    Direct Control

Behavioral Aspects of Managerial Control Systems
    Relating Controls to Accepted and Meaningful Goals
    Determining Who Gets Control Information and How It Is Used
    Ensuring That One Set of Measurements Is Not Overly Stressed
    Recognizing That Conflict over Goals, Plans, and Controls Will
        Always Exist

Implications for the Manager

Review

Phantoms Fill Boy Scout Lists

Learning Objectives

When you have finished reading and studying this chapter, you should be able to:

1. Demonstrate the relationships among decision making, establishing objectives, planning, and controlling.
2. Compare and contrast directing and controlling.
3. Recognize the importance of forward-looking controls.
4. Define and give examples of the basic types of controls.
5. List and give examples of the characteristics of effective control systems.
6. Give examples of the pervasiveness of control systems.
7. Compare and contrast direct and indirect control.
8. Identify (by giving examples) some of the intended and unintended consequences of control systems.
9. Demonstrate why objectives, plans, and controls are not accepted by everyone in the organization.
10. Define and be able to use the following concepts:

control   inventory control
directing   quality control
pre-controls   budget control
steering control   indirect control
yes-no control   direct control
post-action control   positive response
standard   passive response
deviation   negative response
production control

Thought Starters

1. What does the term *control* mean to you? Does it have a positive or negative tone to you?
2. How many "controls" are you already familiar with? What are some of them?
3. Have you ever ignored or objected to a control? If so, what are some of your reasons for doing so?

Lavelle's Private War

In August 1971, General John Lavelle took command of all the U.S. Air Force units in the Vietnam conflict. At the time, bombing raids in North Vietnam could be conducted only with White House approval or as "protective reaction strikes." Such strikes could take place only if a target, usually a missile battery, had fired or was preparing to fire on a U.S. plane.

General Lavelle watched the North Vietnamese building up their forces along the border. Opposed to the build-up and unable to get approval to bomb selected targets, Lavelle decided to take matters into his own hands. From November 1971 to March 1972 (when he was recalled), he secretly sent his planes north to bomb selected but unauthorized targets. The official report of each unauthorized mission was falsified, and the strike was referred to as a protective reaction strike.

The White House and the Pentagon might never have heard of Lavelle's private war except for the fact that an Air Force sergeant in Vietnam heard his immediate commander say that even the president did not know what was going on. The sergeant wrote Iowa Senator Harold Hughes to find out "if this falsification of classified documents is legal and proper." Within hours, the Air Force inspector general was on a plane to Saigon.

The inspector general pinpointed 147 unauthorized raids in which Lavelle had chosen his own targets, and there may well have been many more. During the four months in question, Lavelle's planes reported 1,300 "protective reaction strikes." How had General Lavelle managed to conduct at least 147 that were in violation of White House rules before he was caught? The general and his subordinates had developed a double accounting system. The Air Force required reports on all missions, which were checked to make certain that the rules had not been violated. However, Lavelle and his subordinates completed two sets of reports for each strike—one true and the other false. The true reports detailed damage done to North Vietnamese airfields, supply dumps, and the like. The false reports detailed "protective reaction strikes" and were forwarded to the Pentagon. Both sets were kept in South Vietnam—some in Lavelle's office.

In November 1971, Henry Kissinger began secret peace talks in Paris. In that same month the general began his extracurricular activities with strikes at three North Vietnamese airfields. Thus the White House and Pentagon lost control of air activities at the same time that negotiations began. Indeed, there was the haunting possibility that Lavelle's raids might have contributed to the mysterious breakdown of the secret peace negotiations. When delicate coordination was most needed between the civilian and military areas of government, it was not effective because a vital series of controls was not functioning effectively.

Lavelle, by the way, was removed from command and given the choice of retiring from the Air Force or taking a lesser position at the pay and rank of a major general (two stars). He chose to retire. The Department of Defense kept silent of the real reason for this retirement, making the announcement on April 7, 1972, that the general was "retiring for personal and health reasons."[1]

This case shows both the need for information and control systems and the difficulty of coordinating and controlling the different activities within an organization. The overall policy was clear: There must be civilian control over the military. The established procedure was clear: All but protective reaction strikes had to be approved in advance by Washington. The rule was specific: Detailed reports were to be sent to Washington for review. But, as the case indicates, the elaborate control system was ineffective for four months. In fact, if an individual sergeant had not blown the whistle, the deception might never have been discovered. The important issues to be covered in this chapter are the need for information and control systems in organizations, the purposes they serve, the design of effective controls, the types of controls, and some of the reasons for the ineffectiveness of controls.

What Is "Controlling"?

Establishment of organizational objectives and plans is of little value if the plans are not adequately carried out to achieve objectives.[2] Any plan is only as effective as management's ability to carry it out; planning itself is not an end. To be effective, management must be able to measure performance, determine if and where deviations from the plan are occurring, and take corrective action when necessary. Knowing how effectively the planned activities are being carried out is essential to

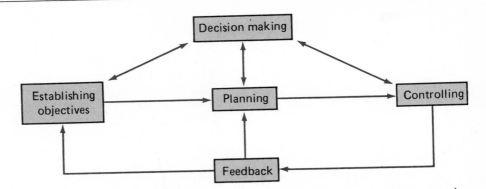

Figure 9.1 The relationships among decision making, establishing objectives, planning, and controlling

achieving the plan's objectives. Therefore, decision making, establishing objectives, planning, and controlling are highly interrelated activities—as Figure 9.1 shows.

The development of computers has made possible faster and more effective control processes. For example, one objective of airlines is to fill all seats for every flight but not to "overbook." Hotels and motels want to fill all their rooms but not have more guests than available rooms. The computerized reservation systems of airlines and major hotel and motel chains allow ticket clerks, reservation clerks, and managers to determine immediately whether a seat or room is available and to confirm a reservation in seconds. This ability is taken for granted today, but a few years ago such an approach to control was not possible.

The examples given here help show the difference between managerial controlling and controlling done by nonmanagers. According to two management researchers, "In the literature relating to organizational behavior, there is ambiguity in the use of the word control. The confusion arises largely because to control can also mean to direct. Precisely defined, **control** refers solely to the task of ensuring that activities are producing the desired results."[3] (Boldface added.) Although managers set objectives, many other people control activities or processes. For example, the airline reservation clerk who tells a potential passenger that all the seats are booked is controlling behavior. The technician who sits at the console of an automated refinery is controlling process.

In contrast, the manager performs two different, but closely related, tasks in controlling. One is **directing,** which includes leading, developing, training, and motivating subordinates. The other is controlling itself, which means ensuring that activities are producing the desired results. Figure 9.2 shows the difference between the two concepts.

As the figure shows, one common use of *control* refers to directing, which can be performed only by managers. The second use of *control* refers to the evaluation of the desired outcome of an activity and to making necessary corrections. Clearly, there is an overlap, since establishment of any monitoring approach usually means directing the activities of another person. There is also a difference, since one tends to stress impersonal approaches, such as "controlling" the output of a refinery, while the other places greater emphasis on personal factors, such as supervisor-subordinate responsibility, discretion, and autonomy.

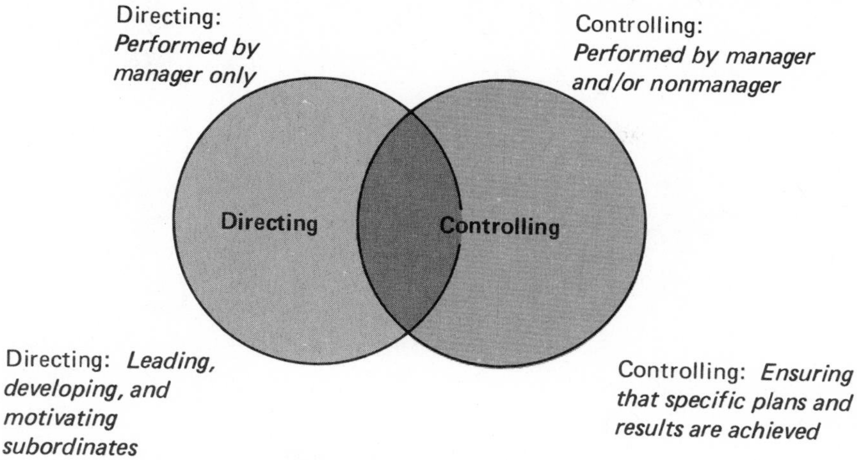

Directing:
*Performed by
manager only*

Controlling:
*Performed by manager
and/or nonmanager*

Directing   **Controlling**

Directing: *Leading,
developing, and
motivating
subordinates*

Controlling: *Ensuring
that specific plans and
results are achieved*

Figure 9.2 The relationship between directing and controlling

The Basic Control Process

The basic purpose of control is positive in that it focuses on achieving organizational goals and objectives.[4] The best control process is forward looking; it prevents deviations from plans or objectives by anticipating their potential occurrence. The next best process detects variations as they occur. The poorest process points up problems after they have developed. The latter process is one of the reasons why control is sometimes seen as a "negative" function. Controls that catch deviations only after they have occurred can lead to casting blame.

To illustrate: Most organizations have as one of their objectives the safety of employees. In one firm, a tank had to be cleaned periodically. Even when empty, the tank contained potentially dangerous fumes. Specific rules covered the actual cleaning. The employee cleaning the tank had to wear a gas mask. He also had to wear a rope around his body under his arms. Another employee, at the top of the tank, held the rope; thus, if the worker cleaning the tank were overcome by fumes, he could be quickly pulled out. One day, the foreman noticed that someone was cleaning the tank. The person was wearing the rope, but there was nobody standing at the top of the tank to pull it up in an emergency. The foreman immediately rushed off to find the "culprit." What he did not realize was that his action in leaving was a clear violation of the rule that someone had to be in attendance at the tank at all times while it was being cleaned. The foreman had lost sight of the positive side of controlling—in this case the goal of safety.

There are at least four basic types of controls: pre-controls, steering controls, yes-no controls and post-action controls.[5] Although the four are related, they will be described separately.

Pre-controls are forward looking controls established before an activity takes place. For example, an organization may wish to bring out a new product. Market research indicates that, to be competitive, the product must not cost more than a certain amount. Standard cost control information can be used to determine how much labor and other costs will be involved. If the predicted cost is too high, steps can be taken to reduce the cost before the product goes into production.

Steering controls are controls in which results are predicted and corrective action is taken while the operation or task is being performed.

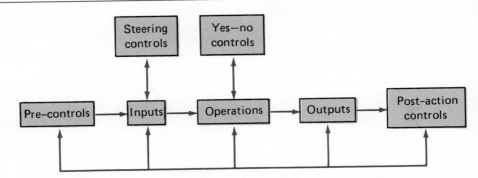

Figure 9.3   The interrelationships among the different types of controls

In the Mars landings and Venus probes, in-flight corrections were made while the spacecrafts were in progress to their destinations. Steering controls offer perhaps the greatest opportunity for bringing actual results close to desired results, because they provide a way to take corrective action while the activity is still going on.

Yes-no controls indicate that the work is either acceptable or unacceptable. Quality inspection and legal approval of contracts are examples of such controls, which are essentially safety devices. A parachute is either properly packed or not. Yes-no controls would be unnecessary if steering controls were always effective. But steering controls may be too expensive or not fully reliable, so yes-no controls are frequently needed.

Post-action controls compare results to a standard when the action or task is completed. School report cards, budgetary controls, and final inspections are examples of these controls. While post-action controls come "after the fact," they can be an effective way to reward individuals for good performance and to provide planning data for pre-controls and steering controls.

All four types of controls are necessary for an effective control system; each has purpose and reason. (Figure 9.3 shows the interrelationships among the four types of controls.) Because steering controls appear to be the most forward looking and effective, more emphasis will be placed on them than on the other three in the rest of this chapter.

Controlling is a universal management function.[6] Therefore, its basic process is similar no matter what is being controlled. The basic control process involves three steps: (1) establishing standards, (2) measuring the results of activities against these standards, and (3) taking necessary corrective actions when deviations from standards occur. Figure 9.4 shows these basic steps.

Step 1: Establishing Standards

Standards are the units of measurement that serve as reference points against which actual results can be compared. The planning process establishes the general objectives for the organization or unit, and each objective needs one or more standards. The basic purpose of control is to make certain that plans and goals are achieved. Unless there are standards against which the results can be compared, control is impossible. Thus the development of standards is a vital first step in controlling.

The standards can be physical—representing, for example, quantities of products, units of output or service, number of clients seen, time, turnover, absenteeism, or hours of work. They can also be expressed in

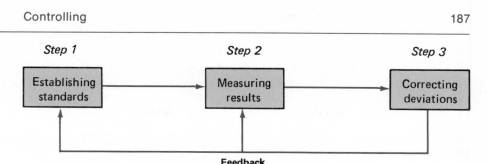

Step 1   *Step 2*   *Step 3*

Establishing
standards   Measuring
results   Correcting
deviations

Feedback

Figure 9.4   The basic steps in the controlling process

monetary terms, such as costs, investments, or revenues. If possible, standards should point to key result areas. For example, the J. C. Penney department stores measure productivity in two key areas—sales per square foot and sales per labor hour. Using computerized cash registers, Penney's can provide managers with almost instant information on total sales and type of sales. These data can then be directly related to square footage and hours of labor. Managers can use the information to decide if slow-selling goods should be replaced with faster-moving items or to pinpoint areas of high and low productivity.[7]

Step 2: Measuring the Results of Activities against Standards

Ideally, the measurement of results against standards should involve pre-controls or steering controls. This would allow **deviations**—variations from a plan—to be detected in time to make corrections. Frequently, alert managers can predict possible deviations from information gained through their information-gathering role. News that a competitor is bringing out a new product or that a vendor's employees are planning to strike is a warning signal that plans may have to be changed.

Measurement of actual results is made easier if a scale of performance has been developed. Indeed, this step in controlling often requires two different phases—collecting the data and then comparing them with the control standards. When the planning function has been performed well and objectives are tangible, developing such a scale is generally easy. When the data collection has been done well, comparison of actual results to standards can be done by simply looking at the two sets of data.

But clear measurements are not always possible. For example, the goals of an organization can include increasing management development. Although the number of people attending management development courses can be counted, the count may not indicate how well the managers have been trained. Sometimes, clear measurements are too costly. For example, a large department store chain developed an elaborate procedure for controlling returned merchandise, but examination showed that the cost of maintaining the system was far greater than the cost of simply taking back any returned merchandise.

Measurement of results for tangible activities, such as the rate or quality of production of a mass-produced item, may require relatively little effort. For other activities, particularly interpersonal ones, measurement is much more difficult. What standard can a manager use to determine the overall competence of the social work director of a hospital? How does the social work director measure the results of a psychiatric social worker who is working with the family of a mental patient? Managers can take several approaches in such situations. They can, for example, discuss the standards with their subordinates in an effort to develop better (even though still relatively intangible) standards. They can also use management by objectives to develop mutual agreement about the job and about how well it is being done. Of course, in many instances, "managerial controls over interpersonal relationships must continue to be based upon intangible standards, considered judgment . . . and even, on occasion, sheer hunch."[8]

Step 3: Correction of Deviations

The final step in the control process is correcting significant deviations of actual results from planned results. This step actually includes both a decision-making and an action-taking phase. If there are deviations, there must first be an analysis and a decision about what is wrong and what corrective action should be taken. Care must also be taken at this stage to separate symptoms from causes.

The second phase of correcting for deviations is initiating the corrective action, which may involve redrawing plans, modifying the goal or objective, or changing the general situation. In the case of General Lavelle, the corrective action, which came months after the deviation began, consisted of recalling the general.

Control as a Feedback Process

Thus far, for the purpose of clarity, we have described the three steps in sequence, as though they were independent of each other. In reality, however, the steps are highly interrelated through the principle of feedback, as shown in Figure 9.5.[9] In a furnace system, the principle of feedback is used to "inform" the thermostat when the furnace should be turned on or off. In many respects, managerial control follows the same process—a process that is found in physical, biological, social, and other systems.

Control processes need not be highly complex. Indeed, effective controls can be very simple and still include the basic steps of establishing standards, measuring results, and taking corrective action. To illustrate: A restaurant owner suspected that the night watchman was both stealing liquor and drinking it on the job. Neither activity was allowed. Controlling the drinking was probably not possible, but reducing the theft (establishing standards) certainly was. The restaurant manager decided to introduce a control process. Every night, just before leaving the restaurant, he would turn every two whiskey bottles behind the bar at a 45 degree angle to each other. The next morning, he could look at the collection of bottles and immediately tell which had been moved (comparing results against standards). For several days, the manager remarked to the night watchman: "Hobby, how was the Four Roses last night?" or "I see you had Canadian Club this time." (Corrective action.) The control process stopped Hobby from stealing whiskey, but it did not stop him from continuing to drink. Eventually, he was fired for drinking on the job (whiskey that he had bought elsewhere). Thus the final corrective action was discharge.[10]

There are no catalogs of controls to be followed, because organizations, departments, and units are different; they all have a variety of products and services to be measured and innumerable policies, procedures, and rules. For example, revenue can be measured by such different standards as profits as a percentage of sales, return on investment (ROI), or profits before and after taxes. Financial soundness can be measured by standards for working capital, cash availability, inventory levels, reserves for depreciation, and many different ratios available for analyzing balance sheets (including the ratio of current assets to current liabilities, net worth to debt, and net quick assets to short-term liabilities). Costs can be measured in terms of individual activities, units,

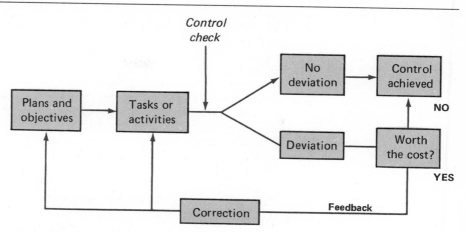

Figure 9.5 Control as a cybernetic process

or varying lots. Production can be measured in rates for such varying periods of time as minutes, hours, shifts, days, months, or years. Different measurements of performance exist for personnel selection and training, supervision, public relations, advertising, purchasing, and all the other activities of any organization.

Ten Characteristics of Effective Controls

Managers want to have effective and adequate control systems to help them make certain that results conform to plans. Much of the time and effort spent on accounting, statistics, and other planning approaches in an organization is devoted to furnishing them such information. Each organization is different, and each has unique and special control designs. In designing control systems, managers should keep in mind the ten basic characteristics of effective controls, which follow.[11]

1. *Controls must be tied to the needs and nature of the activity.* The control system must be based on the area in which results are expected and the job they are expected to perform. A marketing department, for example, may use pre-controls for product introduction and yes-no controls for specific advertisements. A vice-president in charge of manufacturing may generally use more sophisticated and broad-ranging controls than a shop floor supervisor. Large businesses need different control systems than small ones. The closer controls are designed to reflect the specific nature of plans and expected results, the more effective they are.
2. *Controls must indicate deviations promptly.* The ideal control system detects potential deviations before they become actual ones. Although it is important to know when things are going wrong, it is even more important to know beforehand that they are likely to go wrong.
3. *Controls must be forward looking.* Closely related to the last characteristic is the concept of using forecasting as a method of control. Uusally there is a time lag between a deviation and a corrective action. For example, although accounting reports are usually accurate, they occur after the fact. The manager may, however, want to forecast the future (with all its potential for error) rather than wait for an accurate report about which little can be done.

4. *Controls must point out critical exceptions at important points.* The manager cannot watch everything. The "exception principle" must therefore be applied to factors that are critical in comparing results against predicted plans. The more the manager concentrates on *important* exceptions, the more effective are the control results. A manager may not worry if the cost of postage stamps is over budget by 20 percent but may be very concerned if the cost of office labor is 10 percent higher than expected.

5. *Controls must be reliable.* Accuracy in reporting results is essential. As computers are used more widely in organizations, information transferral becomes less of a problem and good data more of one. One way of insuring the reliability of data is to make certain that those reporting it do not perceive the ultimate use as being punitive to them. We all hate to testify against ourselves.

6. *Controls must be valid.* The validity of a measurement refers to the degree to which it actually measures what it is supposed to measure. Counting the number of different clubs used by a golfer gives no idea of the person's score. One of the best examples of deliberate mismeasurement occurred a few years ago. Two cars were entered in an international road trial. One was from Russia, and the other was from the United States. The U.S. car won, but the Russian press reported that "while the Russian car had finished second, the American car came in next to last."[12] Although the figures were accurate and the reporting reliable, the conclusion was not valid.

7. *Controls must be flexible.* As Chapter 8 has shown, we live in an uncertain world. Because of this, it is dangerous to make controls too objective and inflexible; there are always going to be changed plans and unforeseen circumstances to alter any situation. One way of maintaining flexibility is to have alternative plans (and controls) for various possible situations. A sure sign of an organization that has inflexible controls is the failure to remove obsolete ones. For example, a large insurance company handles pension plans for a number of organizations. On one such plan is the notation, "Before taking any action on this plan, see John Doe." At one time, there had been a problem with the pension program, and the control of seeing John Doe was instituted. John Doe eventually left the company, but five years later, the "control" was still officially in force (though obviously ignored).

8. *Controls must be economical.* Controls are a means to an end, not an end in themselves. A control process that costs more than the results it controls is not worth having. The effective manager carefully reviews control systems to ensure that they are cost effective, and one way of doing this is to control only critical and important areas. In one company, an executive vice-president spent many hours a week reviewing expense accounts of salesmen and other employees. In two years, he changed not a single expense account, but he continued the reviews anyway. From the viewpoint of the total organization, his time could have been more profitably spent in other activities.

9. *Controls must be understandable.* In the age of complex mathematical formulas, charts, and computer printouts, a tendency has arisen to develop "controls" that are not understandable by those who use them or those who are "controlled" by them. In one organization, although foremen indicated that they

understood the budget and cost systems, it was clear from questions they asked at a meeting "that the foremen who had indicated to us that they understood the system did not understand it at all. Furthermore, since the answers that they received to their questions were invariably phrased in technical engineering and accounting terms, it is doubtful that their comprehension had increased very much by the end of the meeting."[13] If the control system cannot be understood and easily used by those involved, it is a liability rather than an asset.

10. *Controls must indicate corrective action.* An adequate control must indicate not only that deviations are occurring but also what corrective action should be taken. A control is of value only if it allows decisions to be made before a crisis develops. This means that the control system must show where failures are occurring, who is responsible for them, and what should be done about them.

Extent and Pervasiveness of Controls

We are all aware to some degree of the extent and pervasiveness of control systems. Every time we stop for a traffic light, we are affected by a process for controlling traffic. The checkout counter at the local supermarket is a control process for ensuring that the company is paid for the goods it provides. Registration for courses at a university is a control process to ensure that accurate records are kept of students' classes to guarantee that the students' degrees and transcripts will be valid (and that tuition will be paid).

Some control systems are simple, and some are complex. All are established to eliminate surprises and to accomplish certain objectives. They take a number of forms, including: (1) organizational structure and design, which determines reporting relationships and job design; (2) production control, which is concerned with the timing and routing of any product—from peanut butter to movies; (3) inventory control, which is concerned with the number of things produced; (4) quality control, which ranges from services to goods; and (5) budgetary control, which involves income, expenses, and similar matters.[14] Each of these areas will be described briefly.

Organizational Structure and Design

Organizational structure involves the overall design of the organization, including reporting relationships and job design. It influences the work flow, the information flow, and the behavior of people on the job. In the past, there was little solid research to indicate the best way of designing organizations or subunits, including individual jobs. However, there is a growing body of knowledge indicating that not only is organizational design a powerful control mechanism but also that organizations (or their subunits) can often be better designed.[15] When this happens, the organization becomes more effective, individuals become more highly motivated, and tension and frustration are lessened. (This topic is covered in more detail in Chapter 16.)

Production Control

Production control, an essential part of any organization, is concerned with the functions necessary to produce goods or services. Classes are scheduled to ensure that students and faculty come together at the right time and place. For manufacturers, production control is a complex process involving many aspects of the work flow, including the sequence in which operations are to be performed and making certain that the right parts are ready at the right time and that machines are properly loaded.

Inventory Control

Inventory control, which is used by all organizations, is concerned with making certain that the right amount of raw materials, work in progress, and finished goods are available. A supermarket manager who orders too little milk runs the risk of losing sales; one who orders too much milk runs the risk of spoilage and waste. Universities know that not all the students they admit will actually enroll. As a result, the admissions office admits more than the university can actually handle, using pre-controls based on past experience to try to get the right number actually admitted. Airlines, hotels, and motels have a complex inventory control process to ensure maximum use of facilities.

In large, complex organizations, inventory control is clearly more difficult than it is in small ones. However, sophisticated methods have been developed for determining the proper level of inventory for literally hundreds of thousands of different parts.

Quality Control

Quality control is concerned with the quality of goods and services provided. It ranges from the relatively simple to the highly complex. A relatively simple quality control model is a student's grade point average. A university sets a minimum standard and reviews the student's average to ensure that he or she is performing in an academically satisfactory manner. A slightly more complex example of quality control is the McDonald's hamburger. McDonald's uses a computer to maintain tight quality control of the size and content of their hamburgers, each of which must be 1.6 ounces in weight, .221 inches thick, and 3.875 inches wide when raw.

Budget Control

Every organization has financial controls. Perhaps the best-known of these controls is the budget—a statement of the future revenues and expenses of the organization. Budgets represent perhaps the clearest quantification of the organization's plans. These single-use plans are also used to control financial and other resources.

The budget for most organizations is usually a composite of five subsidiary budgets: a revenue budget, an operations budget, a financial budget, a capital expenditures budget, and an expense budget.

The *revenue budget* is a forecast of expected receipts. In business, it is based on sales forecasts. In universities, it is often based on the total amount of money coming in from tuition, room and board, state and federal assistance, the campus bookstore, laboratory fees, and so on. The *operations budget* covers expenses such as labor, materials, heat, and light. The *financial budget* covers both cash receipts and payments of all kinds. The *capital expenditures budget* covers new buildings, additions to old buildings, other construction, and new equipment. The paving of a parking lot is included in a capital expenditures budget, while the painting of an office is included in an operations budget. The *expense budget* covers expenses not included in other budgets, such as advertising and other market costs.

Budgets are one of the most widely used control mechanisms. Because they require putting plans down on paper in dollar amounts, they force decisions to be made and priorities to be established. No organization has unlimited resources; if the forecast is that X dollars will be received in receipts, then it is difficult to project spending more money than X dollars. For profit-making organizations, some amount lower than X dollars must be spent if they are to show a profit.

Budgets are often resisted. Some managers feel a need to spend more money than is available to them. As a result, there is always negotiation over this scarce resource. In addition, budgetary planning is difficult because of the changes always occurring in our society. However, although budgets have their faults, most modern, complex organizations would be unable to operate without them.

Indirect and Direct Control

There are two basic ways of making certain that future action is corrected or improved—indirect and direct control.[16] **Indirect control** traces the cause of an unsatisfactory result to the responsible person so that activities or practices can be corrected. **Direct control** is the practice of developing better managers to more skillfully use concepts, principles, and techniques to reduce the amount and degree of undesirable results. So far, this chapter has discussed indirect controls.

Indirect Control

Most organizations have thousands of different standards for comparing output with plans; these standards include time, cost, quality, and quantity. Deviations from them may require indirect control, as defined above. However, there are at least two causes of deviations: uncertainty and lack of experience, knowledge, or judgment.

Uncertainty

As described in Chapter 6, the elements of a plan can include certainty, risk, and uncertainty. Under conditions of certainty, the facts are known; under conditions of risk, probabilities must be used. Many decisions are made under conditions of uncertainty through the use of hunch, intuition, and judgment. In these situations, indirect control is ineffective, since errors caused by unknown and unforeseeable events cannot be corrected. Thus, tracing the cause to the responsible person is of little real help.

Lack of Experience, Knowledge, or Judgment

Human errors do occur. Lack of experience in a particular job may cause deviations from plans, especially under conditions of uncertainty. Furthermore, years of experience in a specialized job may be insufficient to qualify an individual as a general manager. Good judgment requires maturity and the application of both education and experience to managerial problems. When a manager lacks experience or knowledge, steps can be taken to make up for the lack. The person can be transferred into a position that will provide the necessary experience or can receive further training. Continuing errors of judgment, particularly at the lower levels, may require transfer, demotion, or separation.

Part of the problem with indirect controls is that they are based in part on some questionable assumptions. One such assumption is that performance can always be measured. But under some conditions, particularly those of uncertainty, measurement may be difficult. Another questionable assumption is that personal responsibility can always be pinpointed. Government action, sudden moves by competitors, or unforeseeable disasters (such as the burning of a plant) can disrupt the best plans and controls. Still other invalid assumptions are that the time and expense of controls are always warranted and that mistakes can always be discovered in time. Thus, besides indirect controls, which are always necessary, emphasis should also be placed on direct controls.

Direct Control

Direct control is based on the principle that there is no substitute for the correct application and use of fundamental management principles at all managerial levels: "The higher the quality of managers and their subordinates, the less will be the need for indirect controls."[17] Improving direct control means improving the quality of managers and their subordinates. This approach is forward looking in that it stresses reducing the amount and degree of undesirable results.

There are a number of ways of improving the quality of performance, including planned manager development programs, multidisciplinary trouble-shooting task forces, special project assignments, cross-functional task force study teams, ongoing appraisal, management by objectives, and planned job rotation.

For example, one company determined that a salesman had the potential to become a general manager. To give him the broad experience needed for this job, the company planned a series of job rotations to various functional areas. First, he was made accountant for a small plant. Although he had had no actual accounting experience, he was trained for two weeks by the current plant accountant (who was in turn being rotated to a different job).

After working as plant accountant for about a year and a half, the young man was moved to the position of first-level manufacturing supervisor in a larger plant. The intent of these carefully planned transfers was to give him broad experience and background before his salary grew too large for these positions.

Combining direct control with indirect control also has a number of advantages. Improved managerial and subordinate effectiveness creates a more competent work force in which fewer errors or deviations will occur. The control process itself is more internalized, encouraging self-control. Through ongoing appraisal and management by objectives, subordinate managers have more knowledge of what is expected of them, gain a better understanding of objectives, and see the close relationship of measurement to performance.

Behavioral Aspects of Managerial Control Systems

Control has so far been viewed as making sure that the results achieved are in line with those planned. The emphasis has thus been on the impersonal aspects of control systems. However, the separation of impersonal control and personal direction is to some extent artificial, since the two often overlap (as Figure 10.2 shows). Control, for example, has behavioral consequences—both intended and unintended—and many controls deal with people rather than inanimate objects.

Organizations spend a great deal of time and effort designing control systems to ensure that the results attained by the organization conform with its plans. Frequently, however, the control process is ineffective. Sometimes the process is designed without regard to behavioral consequences, and sometimes managers misuse the controls.[18]

From a behavioral point of view, a number of reasons exist for control processes being effective or ineffective (or between the two). Among them are:

1. People are motivated to satisfy needs. Sometimes, these needs are satisfied in ways that are of benefit to the organization. But at other times, they are satisfied in ways that are harmful to the organization (although satisfying to the individual).

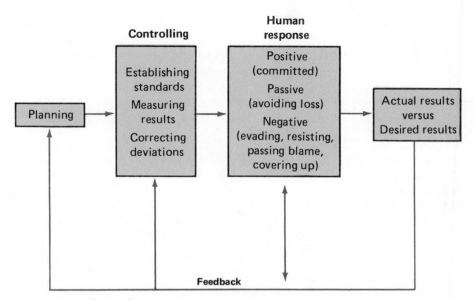

Figure 9.6   Behavioral responses to control processes

2. Group or peer pressure can have a powerful effect on behavior. The social or work norms of a group are tremendously important in shaping what individuals do at work.
3. Organizational objectives are frequently a matter of uneasy compromise between conflicting individual and group interests. That is, organizations do not have objectives; people do. And given that there is often disagreement about objectives, it is easy to see why control processes are not always fully accepted by the individuals and groups within an organization.

As Figure 9.6 shows, there are three basic ways in which individuals or groups can respond to a particular set of controls. The first is a **positive response**; the control process is accepted because the individual feels that the goals and plans are worthy, relevant, and appropriate, or that they may bring rewards or punishments.

The second response is a **passive** one; the individual recognizes the objective of the control as being part of the job responsibility but is personally indifferent about the actual or desired results. A cab driver, for example, takes passengers to their destinations but is unconcerned with why the trips are being made.

The third response is a **negative** one; the individual or group actively resists the control process. The resistance need not be overt or blatant. In the case of General Lavelle, his resistance to the control process was sufficiently strong that he directly, but secretly, disobeyed the rules.

The negative responses to control systems can be reduced in several ways. Following are some of the more important ones.

Relating Controls to Accepted and Meaningful Goals

Controls are better accepted when they are seen as reflecting a valuable part of a job. This means that the goals being aided by the control process must be meaningful and must be developed in terms that are understandable and valuable to the individual workers. When an individual gains personal satisfaction from attaining a result that is also desired by the organization, that person's feeling about control is positive.

Frequently, worker participation is used to obtain prior understanding and acceptance of goals, plans, and controls. However, standards are sometimes set with little or no knowledge about or participation of those whose behavior is being controlled. This top-down approach can lead to unreasonable, unreliable, and invalid standards because it ignores information that employees have about the job and about what is to be accomplished.

Determining Who Gets Control Information and How It Is Used

Control information can be given to any of the following: (1) staff units, (2) high-level line managers, (3) the manager of the organizational unit being measured, and (4) the individuals in the groups being measured. Control processes must be tailored to specific organizations, so there is no single description or prescription of who should get specific data. In general terms, the individual or group who can make the most meaningful use of the data should receive the information directly.[19] The principle of immediate feedback is one of the most important learning principles. In many organizations, however, those directly involved are the last to know when a job has been done well or poorly.

The motivational theory on self-control suggests that commitment will be higher and corrective action better when the individual or group obtains the data first. Immediate feedback of results directly to the affected individuals, departments, or groups may eliminate the resentment that often is felt when data are first made available at higher levels.

How the information is used is of vital importance. When data are going to be used to help solve problems, there is generally a higher degree of commitment to make sure the data are valid. But when data are used to control or to punish people, there is a strong tendency for the workers to play the "numbers game." Although controls are not usually established to catch people, this approach sometimes can slip in. An inspector was once asked whether his job was to pass good parts or to screen out bad parts. He responded, "To pass good parts." When asked, "What would happen if a week or two went by and you found no bad parts?" he answered "Oh, I couldn't do that! My boss would think that I wasn't doing my job."

This tendency toward self-protection is increased when controls and measurements are developed by specialists or staff groups who then obtain the data before management or employees. In such cases the information is often used to make the individual staff unit look good at the expense of the manager or organizational unit. Data developed and used in this way are frequently distorted. Managers and employees all know how to play the game, which drastically reduces the usefulness of the control process.

Ensuring That One Set of Measurements Is Not Overly Stressed

Control systems have a direct effect on how much energy workers put into their tasks. When one area of measurement is stressed above the others, there is a tendency for workers to expend more time and effort in that area than in others. For example, a bank teller may have available a number of control measures, including accuracy of the cash count and attitude toward customers. If the accuracy of the cash count is stressed and no mention is made of politeness to the customer, the teller will tend to ignore customer relations.

Sometimes, of course, control measures can be used to guide behavior in the desired direction. The oil company discussed in Chapter 6 was losing money on its "specialty" products. When the salespeople fought against dropping the products, the company (with input from the sales group) instead dropped the sales commission on these products. Over a period of time, sales of the specialty products were reduced to the point where the organization was able to eliminate many of them from the line of goods sold.

Recognizing That Conflict over Goals, Plans, and Controls Will Always Exist

There will never be unanimity on objectives, plans, and controls; some conflict will always exist in organizations. The effective manager knows this and is prepared to handle the conflicts in productive ways. (See Chapter 19 for a more detailed discussion of the subject.)

Implications for the Manager

The effective manager knows that establishing objectives, planning to meet those objectives, and controlling to ensure that the results of plans are on target are the essential functions of the job. Objectives, plans, and controls are linked together by a number of complex and interrelated decisions made on the basis of an uncertain and turbulent environment. The manager must be able to adjust to any contingency and be ready to change plans, objectives, and controls.

The manager must also be aware that controls pervade the entire organization in many different forms (from how people are paid to how the organization is designed) and that almost any organizational change will affect them. Thus managers must know the characteristics of good control systems and must constantly review controls to ensure that they are well designed.

The astute manager knows that unanimous agreement on objectives and on the appropriate weight of each is almost impossible and that this affects the acceptance of plans and control processes. Although there is a difference between controlling and directing, the manager must see the overlap between the two functions and design controls with the idea that there are many behavioral aspects of control systems. The effective manager knows that there will always be conflict among different groups and individuals but tries to reduce unintended conflict by carefully examining the behavioral aspects of managerial control systems and by making certain that controls are meaningful. Finally, although conflict can never be eliminated, the effective manager knows how to deal with it in a productive way.

Review

1. What are the relationships among decision making, establishing objectives, planning, and controlling?
2. How would you distinguish between directing and controlling?
3. What are some reasons for the importance of forward-looking controls?
4. What are the basic differences among the four basic types of controls?
5. What are the steps in the basic control process? How do they form a feedback process?
6. Explain why the characteristics of effective controls are important?
7. Describe the basic differences between direct and indirect control.
8. What can be intended and unintended consequences of controls?
9. How are effective and/or ineffective controls tied to motivation and to group dynamics? Give examples.
10. After reading this chapter, how would you explain General Lavelle's behavior? What might have motivated him?
11. Interview managers and employees of both large and small organizations. Ask them about the controls they have on their jobs and what they think about them. Do managers have the same opinions as subordinates? Explain.
12. How would you design a good control system for a course you are taking? How does the process relate to objectives and planning?

Phantoms Fill Boy Scout Lists

For most of this century, the Boy Scouts have been a tradition in the United States. The very term scouting conjures up images of camping, hikes, canoe trips, and troop meetings. After a four-month investigation, however, the *Chicago Tribune* reported another side of scouting—massive cheating on the part of paid professional staff members to make new enrollment quotas.

In 1968, the Boy Scouts of America (BSA) announced a campaign called *Boypower, 76*. The $56 million national program was to expand the BSA by more than 2 million members by 1976—to enroll one-third of all eligible boys eight to twenty years old. The program was designed to attract all nationalities and colors. Part of the campaign (programs for the poor) was federally funded.

By 1974, the program was far behind schedule, and professionals within the BSA were cheating extensively (even in the federally funded programs) to meet the Boypower quotas imposed on them. Many past and present BSA professionals claimed that, under pressure from the top, membership quotas were met with nonexistent boys in existing units or boys belonging to nonexistent units.

The investigation indicated that the cheating had little or no effect on existing Scout programs operated by adult volunteers. Once begun, the troops, packs, and posts operate almost independently of the professional organization. For example, the fifteen Cub Scouts meeting weekly in a Detroit church aren't aware that official Scout reports show their unit as having sixty-five members.

The investigation suggested that the cheating was nationwide and that the worst of it occurred in the federally funded programs. These programs pay Scout dues and fees for inner-city blacks and Latinos, many of whom live in housing projects.

In Chicago, for example, a suppressed audit of the BSA showed that while the "official" membership figure was 75,000, the actual number was less than 40,000. The Scout official who ordered the audit was quietly transferred elsewhere. An independent report in the New York area in 1971 by the Institute of Public Affairs suggested that many Scout officials believed the pressure to meet membership quotas resulted in a "numbers game and a possible cause of paper troops." The report was never released to the public.

The inflation of membership was greater in the inner city than in the suburbs. The investigation reported that a Detroit supervisor told staff members to meet quotas even if they had to register bodies in cemeteries. Another professional reported that of the three thousand Scouts on the books in Fort Dearborn in 1972, only three hundred were real.

A professional staff member received a letter indicating that enrollment at camp was below acceptable limits and that failure to show dramatic progress could result in his being fired. The individual claimed that he could not send boys to camp when they existed only on paper. He had been transferred into the district a few months earlier and had discovered that thirty-three of its forty-seven registered units did not exist.[20]

1. Assuming that the investigation was correct, what could have caused the cheating?
2. What does this case tell us about control processes?
3. Assuming you were the chief executive of the Boy Scouts, what would you do differently at the start of the campaign? After the investigation?

Footnotes

1. "Lavelle's Private War," *Time*, June 26, 1972, p. 14; "The Private War of General Lavelle," *Newsweek*, June 26, 1972, pp. 17–18; and George C. Wilson, "Washington: The Lavelle Case," *Atlantic Monthly*, December 1972, pp. 6–27.
2. P. Dauten, Jr., H. Gammil, and S. Robinson, "Our Concepts of Controlling Need Re-thinking," *Journal of the Academy of Management* 1 (December 1958): 41–55; W. Jerome, Jr., *Executive Control—The Catalyst* (New York: Wiley, 1961); E. Lawler, III, and J. Rhode, *Information and Control in Organizations* (Pacific Palisades, Calif.: Goodyear Publishing, 1976); and R. Dewelt, "Control: Key to Making Financial Strategy Work," *Management Review* 66 (March 1977): 18–25.
3. G. Giblioni and A. Bedian, "A Conspectus of Management Control Theory: 1900–1972," *Academy of Management Journal* 17 (June 1974): 293.
4. E. Strong and R. Smith, *Management Control Models* (New York: Holt, Rinehart and Winston, 1968); and H. Koontz and C. O'Donnell, *Essentials of Management* (New York: McGraw-Hill, 1974).
5. W. Newman, *Constructive Control: Design and Use of Control Systems* (Englewood Cliffs, N.J.: Prentice-Hall, 1975); and H. Koontz and R. Bradspies, "Managing through Feedforward Control," *Business Horizons* 4 (June 1972): 25–36.
6. R. Mockler, *The Management Control Process* (New York: Appleton-Century-Crofts, 1972); and W. Jerome, *Executive Control* (New York: Wiley, 1961).

7. "J. C. Penney: Getting More from the Same Space," *Business Week*, August 18, 1975, pp. 80–88.
8. Koontz and O'Donnell, *Essentials of Management*, p. 368.
9. S. Beer, *Decision and Control* (New York: Wiley, 1966).
10. R. Albanese, *Management: Toward Accountability and Performance* (Homewood, Ill.: Richard D. Irwin, 1975), p. 189.
11. Koontz and O'Donnell, *Essentials of Management*, pp. 362–365; R. Fulmer, *The New Management* (New York: Macmillan, 1974), pp. 260–261.
12. R. Fulmer, *The New Management* (New York: Macmillan, 1974), p. 259.
13. E. Caplan, *Management Accounting and Behavioral Science* (Reading, Mass.: Addison-Wesley, 1971), pp. 68–69.
14. X. Gilbert, "Does Your Control System Fit Your Business?" *European Business,* Spring 1973, pp. 69–76; A. Tannenbaum, *Control in Organizations* (New York: McGraw-Hill, 1969); and B. Reimann and A. Negandhi, "Strategies of Administrative Control and Organization Effectiveness," *Human Relations* 28 (May 1975): 475–486.
15. P. Lawrence and J. Lorsch, *Organization and Environment: Managing Differentiation and Integration* (Boston: Harvard University Graduate School of Business Administration, Division of Research, 1967).
16. Koontz and O'Donnell, *Essentials of Management*, pp. 403–413; E. Huse, "Putting in a Management Development Program That Works," *California Management Review* 9 (Winter 1966): 73–80.
17. Koontz and O'Donnell, *Essentials of Management*, p. 406.
18. C. Cammann and D. Nadler, "Fit Control Systems to Your Managerial Style," *Harvard Business Review* 54 (January–February 1976): 65–72; C. Argyris, "Human Problems with Budgets," *Harvard Business Review* 31 (January–February 1953): 108–122; Lawler and Rhode, *Information and Control in Organizations;* Newman, *Constructive Control;* and Caplan, *Management Accounting and Behavioral Science.*
19. Cammann and Nadler, "Fit Control Systems to Your Managerial Style"; and Lawler and Rhode, *Information and Control in Organizations.*
20. D. Young, "Phantoms Fill Boy Scout Rolls," *Chicago Tribune*, June 9 and 10, 1974; Lawler and Rhode, *Information and Control in Organizations;* and Cammann and Nadler, "Fit Control Systems to Your Managerial Style," p. 65.

Chapter 10

Analytical Aids to Decision Making, Planning, and Controlling

National Airlines

Models

Operations Research (OR)

Tools and Techniques Used in Operations Research
    Probability Theory
    Linear Programming
    Queuing
    Game Theory
    Time-Event-Network Analysis (PERT)
    Decision Trees

Limitations of Operations Research

Implications for the Manager

Review

Decisions at B-Mart

Learning Objectives

When you have finished reading and studying this chapter, you should be able to:

1. Define and discuss the concept of *model*.
2. Compare and contrast qualitative versus quantitative models.
3. Describe what is meant by *operations research (OR)*.
4. List organization-wide problems that OR techniques can help solve.
5. List and describe some basic tools in OR.
6. Construct a series of situations in which analytical aids can be helpful.
7. Explain why mathematical and other analytical approaches have not always lived up to their promise.
8. Specify the interrelationships among organizational objectives, plans, controls, and decision making.
9. Define and be able to use the following concepts:

model	game theory
operations research (OR)	PERT
probability theory	critical path
linear programming	decision tree
queuing theory	

Thought Starters

1. What does the term *model* mean to you?
2. How useful do you think mathematics is to a manager?
3. How comfortable do you feel using mathematics?
4. What does the term *analytical aids* mean to you? Do you think you use any such aids in making decisions?

National Airlines

The world fuel crisis in late 1973 had a dramatic impact on the airline industry. In the five months between December 1973 and May 1974, fuel prices for airlines in the United States soared from an average of 14 cents a gallon to 22 cents a gallon. Furthermore, the federal government limited each airline's monthly supply of jet fuel to a percentage of the amount used in 1972.

The result was chaos. Fuel vendors were often unable to provide fuel at specific cities. Schedules were changed, and fuel allocation did not match the revised schedules. There were excess allocations to some cities and shortages at others. In trying to plan their fuel purchases for each month, the airlines did not do well. In many cases, the monthly supply at particular fueling stations was gone by the middle of the month. This resulted in canceled flights, exorbitant prices paid for immediate purchases, and tremendous increases in operating costs. Fuel became the largest percentage costs of operations, rising to 18 percent for domestic airlines.

Using a mathematical technique (called linear programming) National Airlines was able to improve fuel availability and to reduce the cost of jet fuel. The first month National used the approach, June 1974, its fuel costs dropped to an average of 14.4 cents a gallon, compared to an average of 22.5 cents a gallon for ten other airlines (including American, United, and Trans World). The model is still being used.

Building the model was no easy task. First of all, the flight schedules and the aircraft rotation had to be considered. An aircraft rotation is a chain of flights, or "legs," that each aircraft follows. For example, a DC-10 may leave Los Angeles as Flight 36, eventually arriving at Fort Lauderdale. It may then leave Fort Lauderdale as Flight 144. After a few days, the same aircraft returns to Los Angeles to become Flight 36 again. In the meantime, other DC-10s are following the same rotation, since Flight 36 is a daily flight.

Other factors that had to be considered to get the overall lowest cost for fuel included the price, availability, and vendor allocations of fuel at each station; the minimum and maximum quantity of fuel the aircraft could carry; the maximum landing weight allowed at a station; and the fuel consumption of various planes and flights. An aircraft's fuel consumption is a function of its weight, flight altitude, speed, and the weather. If the price of fuel is lower at the first of several stations in an aircraft rotation, it seems logical to purchase the maximum amount of fuel there and then "tanker" the additional fuel for later flights (tanking can be costly). However, the extra fuel adds weight to the plane; thus more fuel is burned on the first leg than is burned when only the amount needed to reach the second station is carried. The extra fuel also results in additional consumption for all the following flight legs on which the fuel is tankered. So, it should be clear, then, that the entire flight pattern must be taken into consideration in figuring fuel costs.

Solving the problem (and building the model) involved approximately 800 constraints and 2,400 variables for a flight schedule of 350 legs, 50 station/vendor combinations, and multiple types of aircraft. But this effort was apparently worthwhile. National's fuel management and allocation model has resulted in substantial savings. For example, during price negotiations with a vendor, the model allows National to determine the effect of proposed price and supply changes on the total system. It also allows the company to analyze quickly alternative flight schedules to determine the effect of such changes on current fuel contracts and allocation levels at each station.[1]

The National Airlines case illustrates the complex interrelationships among decision making, planning, and controlling. The company's fuel management and allocation model is helping managers make decisions about how and where to schedule aircraft and how to save money on fuel—the single highest expense in operating an airline today. The model also serves as a tool in planning and controlling. Indeed, in this example—and generally—it is difficult to separate the three functions.

This chapter will describe various analytical aids that can be of value to the manager. While most managers will never become experts in all the approaches described, all managers should at least be aware of their existence. The tools to be described are operations research, time-event-network analysis, and decision trees.

Models

Models are representations of real situations or objects.[2] They can be presented in various forms. For example, a child's toy truck is a scale model of a real truck, and a *scale* model of an airplane is a representation of a real airplane. *Scale models* are physical replicas of real objects.

Another class of models is *analog models*. These models are physical in form but do not have the same appearance as the object being modeled. A thermometer, for example, is an analog model representing temperature, and an automobile speedometer is an analog model representing speed. The position of the mercury in the thermometer represents temperature, and the position of the needle on the dial represents the automobile's speed.

Models are so much a part of our relationship to the world that we carry them around in our heads. These "mental models" are the assumptions we make about people, things, and situations with which we come into contact. Everyone who has ever stood on the corner of a busy street uses a mental model of the expected situation to decide when it is safe to cross to the other side. Likewise, the manager has a mental model of how the organization and its subunits operate.

In writing descriptions of these models, we usually use a kind of shorthand—a system of symbols and mathematical relationships or expressions known as *mathematical models*. The mathematics may be simple, as in a graph or chart, or complex, requiring knowledge of, say, calculus.

The difference between a manager's mental (qualitative) model and a mathematical (quantitative) model is shown in Figure 10.1. When a problem is identified, the manager uses past experience and judgment in an attempt to solve it. If the problem is sufficiently important and complex, then quantitative analysis of it can be of great help to the manager.

In general, experimenting with models requires less time and is less expensive than experimenting with the real object or situation. Of course, the accuracy of the conclusions and decisions based on a model are dependent on how well the model fits the real situation.

Models also make it possible to infer "new" things about the real system. For example, in the National Airlines case, the model is able to account for the important factors in determining the lowest fuel cost as well as fuel availability. The number of factors involved requires the use of a computer, since calculations by hand would take far too long.

Yet another class of models useful to managers is *simulation models*. The term *simulation* generally refers to the operation of a numerical

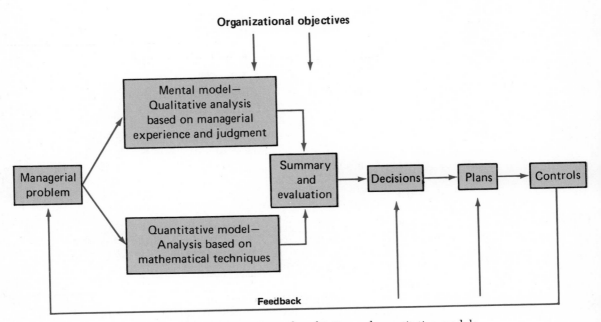

Figure 10.1 A comparison of qualitative and quantitative models

model that represents some dynamic process. When the values of starting conditions, variables, and influencing factors are given, a simulation is run to represent the behavior of the process over time. While simulations may be manually performed, the availability of computers has greatly enhanced the decision maker's capability of modeling complex problems.

Simulation models combining physical and mathematical models have been used for many years to train astronauts for moon landings. The astronaut enters a replica of the space vehicle, where he is given, by computer, a variety of situations to deal with. The computer is programmed to react to the astronaut's actions as though he were actually controlling the space vehicle. A serious mistake by the astronaut results in an automatic abort of the "mission." Some other potential simulation models are: (1) a model to simulate traffic flow in a city, (2) a model of corporate financial operations, (3) a model of a baseball game in its complete form, and (4) a model of the number of people at supermarket checkout stations and the service provided at these stations.

Operations Research (OR)

Operations research, or management science, is an approach that builds mathematical models and uses mathematical techniques to help organizations solve complex problems. The discipline developed about the time of World War II. **Operations research (OR)** can be defined as: "(1) an application of the scientific method to (2) problems arising in the operations of a system which may be represented by means of a mathematical model and (3) the solving of these problems by resolving the equations representing the system."[3]

We saw one use of OR in the case of National Airlines, which was able to save money through the development of a mathematical model. Two other applications follow:

1. A model was developed to simulate the solid waste disposal system in Cleveland, Ohio. By applying the model, Cleveland's solid waste managers were able to reduce the annual budget of $14.8 million in 1970 to a low of $8.8 million in 1972. The total savings in a four-year period, based on the 1970 budget, were $14.6 million. The solid waste work force was reduced from 1,640 to 850, and the collection routing system was completely redesigned. The management structure of the Cleveland Division of Solid Waste Collection and Disposal was completely reorganized to take advantage of and to supplement the major operational changes.[4]
2. Logs arriving at a mill making plywood were of different woods, sizes, and lengths. Intuitive judgment based on experience had been used to determine the best way to make plywoods that would be suitable for a variety of orders. But a time came when intuitive judgment was no longer sufficient. To take its place, in 1967 a linear programming model that determined the optimum balance among the different types of plywood was developed, along with an annual operating plan. The plan is implemented by scheduling the mill's production on a biweekly basis. A monthly financial report analyzes the effects of price, wood, product demand, and other variables. As a result of the program, the contribution margin of the mill—defined as sales income minus wood costs—increased by an average of $1 million per year between 1970 and 1975 as compared to the base year 1969.[5]

Operations research has been applied to a large variety of problems, including establishment of inventory levels, determination of how best to distribute advertising budgets among different products, setting of time standards as a basis for costs and labor efficiency controls, and proper distribution of warehouses. Its application requires (1) analysis of the functioning of the system, (2) construction of a mathematical model, and (3) a solution that results in greater ability to plan and control the operations of the system. The solution is obtained by solving the mathematical equations representing the system.

There appear to be at least six organization-wide problems that OR techniques can help solve: inventory, allocation, waiting lines, scheduling, replacement, and competition.[6] Although these six problems will be described independently for the sake of convenience, from a systems point of view they are usually interrelated. For example, inventory problems may be closely related to scheduling problems.

Inventory

By defining *inventory* as idle resources, *resources* can then be defined as anything usable for obtaining something of value—such as people, money, machines, and material. Inventory involves the balancing of conflicting objectives. Because of their complexity and size, many present-day organizations must maintain inventories of almost staggering size. The shortage of one critical part may halt production, and excessive shortages of goods may cause customers to find new sources of supply. However, there are costs attached to maintaining a large inventory. Storage, handling, insurance, taxes, obsolescence, and interest on capital are some of them.

Allocation

Allocation is concerned with organizing resources in order to maximize the overall efficiency of the organization. People have always been concerned with how to allocate scarce resources. The problem invades every organization and occurs whenever restricted resources have to be allocated among several groups in order to accomplish an objective.

Waiting Lines

Waiting lines are an almost universal problem. They exist at the bank teller's window, at the supermarket checkout counter, at telephone and telegraph switching stations, and at loading platforms. Airplanes wait for runways, commuters wait for buses, and machines wait for repair. Any time there is a wait, a potential waiting line problem exists.

Scheduling

The order in which operations or tasks occur can be very important. For example, many products require operations on more than one machine. When this situation exists, the material flow can be sequenced to provide maximum utilization of the different machines. One class of scheduling problems involves sequencing jobs through a succession of stations, such as grinding, polishing, and shipping.

Replacement

Parts or equipment break down or wear out over time; people leave; equipment becomes obsolete. An organized plan for repairs or replacements must be established and ready. Replacement problems involve the timing for replacement of capital equipment or other earning assets. As a unique example of this problem, consider the replacement of a television commercial as the deteriorating asset. When should it be replaced?

Competition

In many situations, there is an inherent conflict of interest among parties competing for a common resource. Examples of decision making under conditions of competition include athletic competition, collective bargaining, military deployment strategy, political campaigning, pricing strategy, and market share. In these situations, two or more units are trying to achieve conflicting objectives. When the decisions made by a competitor can materially influence a decision, the behavior of the competitor must be included as part of the decision environment. Thus the problem is to develop decisions and strategies that will minimize losses and/or maximize gains. In competitive bidding for a contract, for instance, each bidder must take into consideration the strategies of the other bidders.

Tools and Techniques Used in Operations Research

A large variety of tools and techniques have been developed in operations research, and more are constantly being created.[8] Terms and techniques used in OR are usually mathematical. The reliance on mathematics and mathematical models is based on the logical structure, precision, and convenience of the language of mathematics. This section will examine several of the techniques of OR: probability theory, linear programming, queuing, game theory, PERT, and decision trees.

Probability Theory

Probability theory, which serves as the basis for many OR applications, provides ways to measure the likelihood of occurrence (or odds) of uncertain events or environmental states. Probabilities are fundamental to decision making. Flipping a coin to see who buys the coffee is one of the simplest forms of probability. Insurance companies use a more complex form. For example, life insurance companies cannot predict the death of any particular individual. However, after careful statistical analysis of existing data, they have developed life expectancy tables. Rates for life insurance are based on these tables, which show the probable death rate for each age group in the total population.

Statistical quality control is another application of probability theory. In many organizations, inspecting each item produced would be prohibitively costly or even impossible. But a detailed inspection of a small sample makes it possible for a manager to predict the approximate number of defective products that will be produced.

The outcome of any organizational decision lies in the future. Thus most decisions involve an element of chance. However, even the most optimistic manager prefers a calculated risk to a blind gamble. Probability is a way of computing the outcomes of decision alternatives by using statistical and mathematical procedures for estimating the degree of risk. Probability theory can be used in planning the number of meals to prepare and the amount of parts to be kept in inventory as well as in airline billing, quality control, and psychological testing.

Linear Programming

Linear programming is a mathematical technique for obtaining the optimal solution in situations where the relationships among variables can be expressed as directly proportional (linear) functions. *Linearity* means that a change in one variable must produce a proportionate change in another, the result being a straight line. Generally, a number of linear functions operate at the same time.

Linear programming models are most helpful in situations where the required information is known or can be developed and the objective is an optimum allocation of resources. They are frequently used to solve allocation problems. A manufacturing plant, for instance, may have many machines that can process parts at varying rates of speed. One machine may process Part A at the rate of 2,000 pieces per hour and Part B at the rate of only 250 pieces per hour. Given a large number of machines and literally thousands of different parts, the human mind cannot work out the optimum scheduling of parts through the plant. In such cases, linear programming using complex mathematics, can be helpful.

Linear programming also helps determine the most profitable product mix, whether a product should be manufactured or bought, and what inventory levels are most economical. It has even been used for pollution control, rezoning of school districts, legislative redistricting, personnel allocation, capital budget allocation, and financial portfolio selection.[8]

Queuing

The queuing problem is that of determining the optimum amount of facilities to maintain when the need for them varies randomly, as in the case of supermarket checkout counters, where there may be long waiting lines of customers at some times and few or no customers at other times. A *queue* is a waiting line, and **queuing theory** is the study of waiting lines.

The queuing problem is a matter of economics, and it involves tradeoffs. Checkout lines cost money, but so do waiting lines. People who have to wait too long at supermarkets, drugstores, or banks may take their business elsewhere. The manager must be concerned with determining the most economical queuing system—the system of service facilities that will take care of those people who often wait for service. With enough facilities, almost all waiting could be eliminated, along with the irritation, unpleasantness, and monetary losses they engender. But extensive service facilities involve large installation, operation, and maintenance costs.

Queuing theory is concerned with balancing these opposing costs—the expected waiting costs and the expected service costs. The manager's objective is to determine the queuing system that minimizes the total expected cost. A number of different mathematical approaches provide the answers; the particular approach depends on the complexity of the problem.[9]

Game Theory

Game theory is used to develop a mathematical approach that is designed to maximize gains or minimize losses regardless of countermoves by competitors. Most organizations compete with other organizations. Their product, service, promotion, distribution, and pricing strategies usually are created in a competitive environment. Game theory attempts to predict how rational people behave in competitive situations. Its purpose is to develop long- or short-term strategies that combine low costs with high gains. Game theory is used most widely in military situations (war games). But it is also used in organizations that must adjust their actions on the basis of their competitors' actions and reactions. How will competitors respond to a price increase, a new advertising campaign, or the introduction of a new product?

By considering what competitors may do, game theorists can provide managers with guidelines for effective strategies. Unfortunately, competitive situations are often highly complex, involving a large number of variables; and game theory itself is still being developed and improved. At the present time, the mathematics have not been developed to deal with more than relatively simple problems in decision making and strategy. Still, under conditions of uncertainty, experienced managers can use game theory to supplement their own knowledge, hunches, and intuition.

Time-Event-Network Analysis (PERT)

A number of techniques have been developed for planning and controlling the time periods within which work activities are to be accomplished. The simplest scheduling method is jotting down an appointment on a calendar. More complicated methods involve complex mathematical or computer techniques for analyzing, designing, and controlling large-scale activities.

The Gantt chart, developed by Henry L. Gantt, is one of the simplest and most useful aids in scheduling activities over time. The first step in preparing the chart is to list the project's individual tasks. The second step is to plot these tasks against time. Finally, actual progress can be compared with the schedule. Figure 10.2 is a simple Gantt chart showing the construction of a small grain elevator with four silos. Actual Gantt charts are often more complicated than the one shown. In real life, such a project would be broken down into many more tasks—among them the different steps required in constructing the foundation and installing the plumbing, electrical wiring, heating system, water system, and even the office furniture.

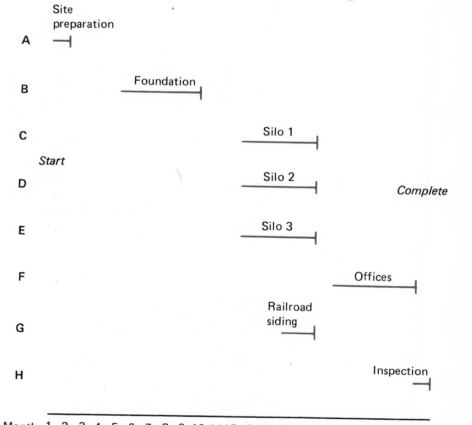

TASK

Figure 10.2 A simplified Gantt chart

An even more advanced technique is the Program Evaluation and Review Technique (PERT).[10] Developed by the navy in 1957–1958, it is a relatively new tool for planning, decision making, and control. PERT builds on the ideas of the Gantt chart but shows more clearly the interrelationship of events and activities. Specifically, **PERT** is a way of providing management with an operational network that relates the activities of a project in a time frame, thereby allowing the identification of the project's critical and subcritical stages. The navy began using PERT to plan, schedule, and control the development of the Polaris submarine. Building the submarines involved approximately 250 prime contractors, more than 9,000 subcontractors, and hundreds of thousands of individuals. The navy credits PERT with the successful completion of the Polaris two years earlier than originally scheduled. PERT and similar programs have since been adopted by many organizations, including those in the fields of manufacturing, construction, and health care.

PERT is a way to plan programs that have specific objectives and specific, measurable results. It facilitates the basic functions of decision making, planning, and control primarily by controlling time (and in some cases by also controlling cost). PERT is usually used for complicated projects requiring a great deal of coordination if they are to be completed on time. It has been used in such areas as the construction of new buildings, aircraft, missiles, and highways; the design and construction of buildings; the timing of important activities in mergers; and the development and distribution of new products. It tends to be a single-use plan, since it generally plans and controls nonrepetitive projects.

PERT plans have the following steps:

1. *Defining and listing all activities and events,* as shown in Table 10.1. An activity is defined in terms of the time and resources required to complete a specified event. An event is the actual completion of a specific, definable segment of the project. In Table 10.1 the first activity is preparing the site for the grain elevator. The elevator (the event) is scheduled to be completed two months after its beginning.
2. *Designing the PERT network,* an example of which is shown in Figure 10.3. The activities should be related to each other in order of their occurrence. As many activities as possible should be performed at the same time. For example, after the site is prepared and the foundation laid, the three silos should be started at the same time.

Table 10.1 Building a small grain elevator (times given in months)

Activity	Expected time	Minimum time	Maximum time	Preceding activities
A. Start construction	0	—	—	—
B. Prepare site	2	2	3	A
C. Complete foundation	6	5	7	B
D. Complete Silo 1	7	6	9	C
E. Complete Silo 2	8	6	9	C
F. Complete Silo 3	7	7	8	C
G. Construct offices	7	7	8	D
H. Construct railroad siding	4	2	5	C
I. Inspect	1	1.5	1	All

3. *Estimating the time between activities* (how long it will take Activity 1 to be completed before Activity 2 can be started). If desired, people familiar with the program should make three time estimates for each definable activity: (1) the minimum (or most optimistic) if eveything goes right, (2) the maximum (or most pessimistic) barring an unforeseen disaster, and (3) the likeliest. These three times can be combined using probability estimates. Thus the most probable time for site preparation in Table 10.1 is two months. (As shown by the box at the end of Figure 10.3, the project is expected to take twenty-three months to complete.)

4. *Identifying the critical path after developing the network.* The **critical path** *is the longest set of adjoining activities in the project. Delays along this path cause delays in the entire project; delays along other paths are generally not as important, since the paths are not as long as the critical path. (The critical path in Figure 10.3 is shown by the double arrows.) For example, the railroad siding for the freight cars takes only four months to complete. If construction of the siding were to begin immediately after completion of the foundation, a delay would have little effect on the entire project. But a delay in completing Silo 1 would be critical.*

Most PERT analyses have hundreds or thousands of events and require a computer to do their calculations. For instance, in real life each event shown in Table 10.1 would be broken down into a number of subevents. A number of modifications, have been made to PERT, one of which is called PERT/COST. In this application, costs as well as time are included in the network.

The main advantage of using PERT or its modifications is that it forces the planning and examination of critical areas and the use of forward-looking decisions, plans, and controls (particularly for single-use plans). PERT can also be used to study a recurring sequence of events in order to ensure that there is no time lost in the procedures. Nonetheless, it is not a cure-all. It simply establishes the conditions for the use of sound control principles.

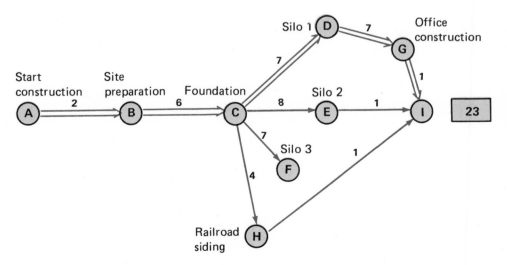

Figure 10.3 A PERT diagram for the building of a grain elevator

Time is given in months—the total being twenty-three months.

Decision Trees

The **decision tree** is a method of planning to achieve objectives by identifying and choosing among available alternatives. Probability as a help to decision making under conditions of uncertainty or risk was discussed earlier. A decision tree is a relatively simple and understandable way of using probability. It mathematically factors the degree of risk into a business decision. The decision tree helps the manager "consider various courses of action, assign financial results to them, modify these results by their probability, and then make comparisons."[11]

Perhaps the clearest way to explain decision trees is by example. Acme Hardware Stores wanted to build another store. Preliminary market research and other information indicated that the two best towns in which to build were Centerville and Easthaven. Zoning ordinances, construction costs, the price of land, and accessibility to the main warehouse were approximately the same in both towns. There was disagreement, however, among those reporting on the best location to the president. As a result, the president and his staff developed a decision tree to compare the two locations.

The usual steps in constructing a decision tree are:

1. *Identifying the possible actions and the possible outcomes (events) associated with each action.* In the Acme situation, only two alternatives existed—building the new store in Centerville or building it in Easthaven.
2. *Estimating the probability of each outcome, or payoff, and the expected value of each outcome.* The expected value of an outcome is determined by multiplying the probability event by the appropriate outcome. (Expected value is used because, under conditions of risk or uncertainty, one cannot be certain of actually reaching the outcome.) As shown in Figure 10.4, a Centerville store had a 50 percent chance of first-year profits of $400,000, for an expected value of $200,000 (0.50 × $400,000 = $200,000); a 20 percent chance of first-year profits of $300,000, for an expected value of $60,000; and a 30 percent chance of first-year profits as low as $200,000, for an expected value of $60,000. The comparable expected values for Easthaven were $160,000, $20,000 and $80,000.
3. *Analyzing the decision tree to identify which action will have the highest expected value based on its outcome and the probability that the outcome will occur.* The action with the highest expected value is usually the most attractive one. Reading from right to left on the decision tree ("rolling back") in Figure 10.4, the greatest expected value indicates that Centerville was the best choice.

Before Acme's president made a final decision, however, he received new information about projections for population growth in Easthaven. While he had more business for either store in the second year than in the first, new industry and development plans indicated that population growth would be greater in Easthaven. As a result, the president asked that the decision tree be extended for two years, as shown in Figure 10.5. At the end of that time a different situation had emerged. Based on the best probabilities available, the Easthaven location was shown to have the greatest payoff (the best outcome). Based on projected two-year profits, the greatest expected value in Easthaven was now $520,000, while the greatest expected value in Centerville was only $450,000.

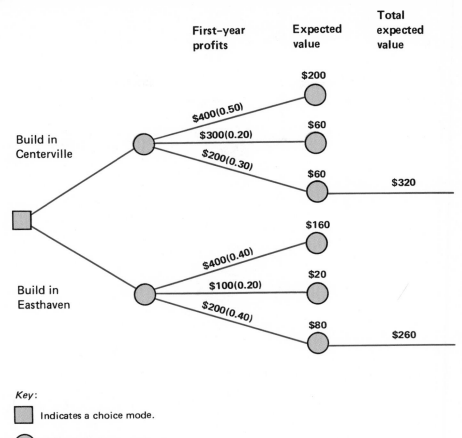

Figure 10.4 Where to build a hardware store (dollar amounts indicated are in thousands)

From these data alone, the Easthaven location appeared the most logical choice. However, the president and his advisers still had to use judgment before making the final decision, since (1) a two-year projection is more uncertain than a one-year one, (2) the company might have wanted the potential extra cash from the Centerville store during the first year, and (3) the Easthaven location also had the possibility of an expected value as low as $160,000—lower than any expected value for the Centerville location. In real life, of course, these and other variables would be included in a more complex decision tree. (The president did ultimately choose Easthaven.)

The decision tree can be used for many complex marketing, advertising, investment, equipment purchase, pricing, new venture, and other decisions. It enables the manager to see the major alternatives open and to realize that decisions should depend in part on future events. Further, by looking at the probabilities of different events, the manager can get closer to the true probability of a particular decision leading to the desired outcome. Without such an approach, the "best estimate" can turn out to be riskier than anticipated. Thus decision trees force managers to plan and to analyze alternatives carefully.

Decision trees are helpful in other ways too. Some managers tend to be conservative. They know that a single failure can generate losses that may ruin their careers, and they choose actions with low personal risk.

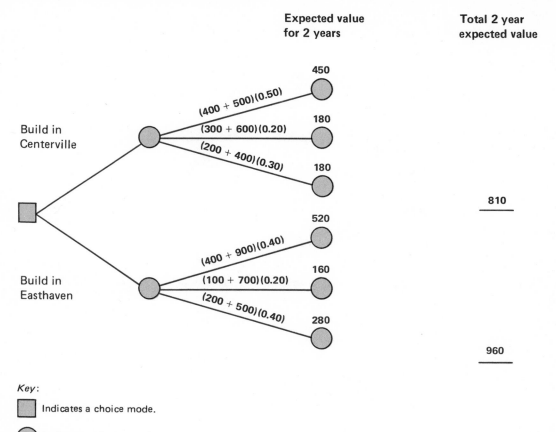

**Expected value
for 2 years**

**Total 2 year
expected value**

Build in
Centerville

$(400 + 500)(0.50)$ 450

$(300 + 600)(0.20)$ 180

$(200 + 400)(0.30)$ 180

810

Build in
Easthaven

$(400 + 900)(0.40)$ 520

$(100 + 700)(0.20)$ 160

$(200 + 500)(0.40)$ 280

960

Key:

☐ Indicates a choice mode.

⬤ Indicates a chance mode.

Figure 10.5 Two-year projections on where to build a hardware store (dollar amounts indicated are in thousands)

Other managers tend not to think through the consequences of their behavior and therefore choose actions with great risk. Using a decision tree forces both types of managers to think through the consequences of their decisions by carefully examining alternatives.

**Limitations of
Operations
Research**

As our examples have shown, operations research can be helpful in decision making, planning, and controlling. However, OR has generally been used in large organizations to solve only a limited number of problems.

One limitation of OR is the fact that organizations are complex, and attempting to determine the relationships among all the factors of a problem is a difficult task. In the case of National Airlines, thousands of variables had to be considered in minimizing the cost of jet fuel, and this was a concern of only a small part of the total organization. Another limitation is that many important managerial decisions involve factors that simply cannot be quantified. While OR can help establish the economic level of raw material inventory, individual judgment is required to estimate the consequences of an impending steel strike. Indeed, one study found that decision makers sometimes do as well, if not better, than the quantitative models developed to aid or replace them.[12]

C. Jackson Grayson, a noted practitioner of operations research, did not use OR techniques when he became head of the U.S. Price Commission, which set up and monitored price controls from 1971 to 1973. Although he was familiar with the approaches, he was in a situation requiring fast action on large-scale problems with political implications. In a thoughtful review, Grayson gives five reasons why many managers avoid the use of operations research:

1. *Time shortage*. Gathering the data and building a model for OR can be extremely time-consuming, and managers frequently need to make quick decisions.

2. *Difficulty of gathering data*. A great deal of time and effort are required to gather the data necessary for building an effective OR model.

3. *Resistance to change*. Managers have their own well-established approaches to problems and often resist novel approaches. The situation is not helped by the tendency of mathematicians (OR practitioners) to use abstract language in describing the different approaches and advantages of OR.

4. *Long response time*. Operations research is methodical, involving a number of clear-cut specified steps; and managers view OR practitioners as too slow to give them solutions to problems when they need them.

5. *Oversimplification*. Operations research deals with mathematics and mathematical models, and many organizational problems (such as politics and power struggles) are hard to quantify. In most cases, these kinds of considerations are entirely excluded from the model. When this happens, the "optimum" solution is not really optimum. Furthermore, managers tend not to look for optimum solutions but instead prefer those that "satisfice" and that account for the myriad of conflicting objectives.

Grayson suggests that OR practitioners should become considerably more sensitive to managers—to their personal styles, their immediate and quickly changing problems, and their complicated, ill-defined environments. In addition, OR practitioners should work more closely with managers in order to develop a greater understanding of managers and their immediate concerns.[13]

Implications for the Manager

This chapter has covered a few of the analytical aids available to managers: primarily probability theory, linear programming, queuing, game theory, PERT, and decision trees. (The National Airlines case demonstrated how linear programming could be used to control fuel costs and avoid disrupted flights.) Clearly, however, there are times when knowledge of specific events must override the use of sophisticated techniques.

A problem in the use of the analytical tools available today is the gap between trained mathematicians or computer experts and managers. Managers frequently have little understanding of, or appreciation for, the complexities of mathematics. They tend to be action oriented, wanting their problems to be solved quickly. Operations researchers, on the other hand, tend to have little understanding of and appreciation for the nature and urgency of managerial problems. More reflective than managers, they often seek the optimum solution and, indeed, are more concerned with the elegance of the solution than with the problem itself. Managers are primarily interested in what works and what can help make decisions based on limited data. Computerized models, however, are not very flexible; and if the important data are either unknown or cannot be measured precisely, they cannot be put on a computer.

Ultimately, managers should have a good understanding of the effectiveness and limitations of mathematical models. They should also know when to ask for help and when to rely on past experience, intuition, and personal judgment.

Review

1. Assume that no other airline besides National is using a mathematical model for reducing fuel costs. List as many reasons as you can for why such an approach is not being used. How valid do you think these reasons are? Explain.
2. After reading the chapter, how many "models" can you describe? Which of them can be helpful to managers? Explain.
3. What are the six organization-wide problems that OR techniques can help solve?
4. In what way can OR be helpful in planning? In decision making? In controlling?
5. Mathematical models are abstractions of reality. Explain how this is true with regard to linear programming and network analysis.
6. How many different uses can you think of for PERT? Describe them.
7. List some uses of a decision tree that can be helpful to a manager.
8. Describe some of the major reasons why managers will frequently not accept and effectively use quantitative methods.

Decisions at B-Mart

The manager of a local B-Mart is planning to have a sale on pocket calculators. The store has budgeted $1,250 for advertising (not including preparation of the ads) and has asked the Acme Advertising Agency to handle the job. Acme has ten days before the sale is to take place.

Acme feels that the average newspaper will produce $4,000 in sales and that the average radio spot will produce $5,000 in sales. The current standard rates are $40 for each newspaper ad and $125 for each radio spot. A newspaper ad will take about a day to prepare and a radio spot only half a day. Acme can work on only one ad at a time.

Acme informs the manager that, since radio spots produce higher dollar sales, all the B-Mart advertising monies should be spent on them. The company creates ten radio spots, which will use up the entire $1,250 budgeted for advertising. According to Acme, the radio spots should result in total sales of $50,000. The manager mentions the situation to one of the stock clerks, who returns an hour later with the following analysis:

It is clear that you want to maximize the money you will realize as a result of these newspaper and radio ads. In mathematical terms, you are saving:

Maximize $5,000R + $4,000N,

where R and N are the number of radio spots and the number of newspaper ads respectively. Now, you can't choose just any number for R and N. You have limitations. The first limitation is your budget. You have only $1,250 to spend. This limitation can be expressed mathematically as

$40N + $125R \leq $1,250,

since you would pay $40 for each newspaper ad and $125 for each radio spot. For example, if you choose to have five newspaper ads and three radio spots, the formula will be

$40(5) + $125(3) = $575,

which is less than $1,250.

This is not your only constraint, however. The advertising company needs time to prepare ads. It takes a full day for a newspaper ad to be prepared and a half day for a radio spot, and there are only ten days available. Mathematically, this can be expressed as

$N + 0.5R \le 10.$

What you must do is find the best N (number of newspaper ads) and the best R (number of radio spots) to make the following true:

$$\$40N + \$125R \le \$1,250$$
$$N + 0.5R \le 10$$

(Of course, N and R cannot be negative numbers.) You can get your answer in a variety of ways. The easiest is to find values that fulfill both the limiting inequalities. This is done by solving the two simultaneous equations—the result of which is that $N = 6$ and $R = 8$. This gives you a sales values of

$4,000(6) + $5,000(8) = $64,000.

In other words, by using six newspaper ads and eight radio spots you can top Acme's estimate of $50,000 and at the same time come in slightly under budget:

$40(6) + $125(8) = $1,240.

The manager doesn't know whom to believe. Assist him by answering the following questions.

1. Do the clerk's suggested values fulfill the constraints? Are there other values that will?
2. What would be the effect of hiring an advertising company that could do more ads in the ten-day period than Acme can?
3. Which decision-making approach is being used by Acme?
4. Which decision-making approach is being used by the clerk?
5. What if the sale nets only $42,000 as a result of the ads? Is the linear programming model wrong? Explain.

Footnotes

1. D. Darnell and C. Loflin, "National Airlines Fuel Management and Allocation Model," *Interfaces* 7 (February 1977): 1–16. This paper is a condensed version of an original paper delivered at the 16th Agifars Symposium in Miami, Florida, September 1976.
2. D. Smith, *Quantitative Business Analysis* (New York: Wiley, 1977); D. Anderson, D. Sweeney, and T. Williams, *An Introduction to Management Science: Quantitative Approaches to Decision Making* (St. Paul: West Publishing, 1976); and R. Gue and M. Thomas, *Mathematical Models in Operations Research* (New York: Macmillan, 1968).
3. C. W. Churchman, R. Ackoff, and E. L. Arnoff, *Introduction to Operations Research* (New York: Wiley, 1957), p. 18.
4. R. Clark and J. Gillean, "Analysis of Solid Waste Management Operations, Cleveland, Ohio: A Case Study," *Interfaces* 6 (November 1975): 32–42.

5. D. Kotak, "Application of Linear Programming to Plywood Manufacture," *Interfaces* 7 (November 1975): 56–68.

6. R. Ackoff and P. Rivett, *A Manager's Guide to Operations Research* (New York: Wiley, 1963).

7. Smith, *Quantitative Business Analysis*; J. Boot and E. Cox, *Statistical Analysis for Managerial Decisions* (New York: McGraw-Hill, 1970); and H. Raiffa, *Decision Analysis: Introductory Lectures on Choices under Uncertainty* (Reading, Mass.: Addison-Wesley, 1968).

8. R. Hartley, *Operations Research: A Managerial Emphasis* (Pacific Palisades, Calif.: Goodyear Publishing, 1976); and H. Lyon, J. Ivancevich, and J. Donnelly, Jr., *Management Science in Organizations* (Pacific Palisades, Calif.: Goodyear Publishing, 1976).

9. F. Hillier and G. Lieberman, *Introduction to Operations Research* (San Francisco: Holden-Day, 1967), pp. 379–471.

10. F. Levy, G. Thompson, and J. Wiest, "The ABC's of the Critical Path Method," *Harvard Business Review* 41 (September–October 1963): 99–110; D. Malcolm, J. Roseboom, C. Clark, and W. Fazar, "Applications of a Technique for Research and Development Program Evaluation," *Operations Research* 7 (September–October 1959): 646–699; and W. Merten, "PERT and Planning for Health Programs," *Public Health Reports* 81 (May 1966): 524–532.

11. E. McCreary, "How to Grow a Decision Tree," *Think Magazine*, March–April 1967, p. 13.

12. R. Woolsey, "A Candle to St. Jude, or Four Real World Applications of Integer Programming," *Interfaces* 2 (February 1972): 20–27.

13. C. J. Grayson, Jr., "Management Science and Business Practice," *Harvard Business Review* 51 (July–August 1973): 41–48.

Chapter 11   Leading

The New Captain

Managerial Authority and Sources of Power

Formal and Informal Leadership

Approaches to Leadership Behavior
    Theory X and Theory Y
    The Managerial Grid
    Personality Attribute Approaches

Contingency Models
    Fiedler's Contingency Leadership Model
    The Path-Goal Model

Similarities among Selected Concepts of Leadership

Implications for the Manager

Review

The Case of the Foundering Firm

Learning Objectives

When you have finished reading and studying this chapter, you should be able to:

1. Identify and give examples of at least five different types of power one person can exert over another in an organization.
2. Compare and contrast formal and informal leadership.
3. Compare and contrast Theory X and Theory Y.
4. Give examples of at least four different managerial styles in terms of the managerial grid.
5. Identify and give examples of the two basic factors of Fiedler's contingency leadership model.
6. Identify and give examples of the three basic concepts of the path-goal model.
7. Identify what you perceive to be your own style of leadership.
8. Define and be able to use the following concepts:

leadership	informal leadership
authority	consideration
power	initiating structure
legitimate power	Theory X
expert power	Theory Y
charismatic power	managerial grid
reward power	contingency model
coercive power	Fiedler's contingency model
formal leadership	path-goal model

Thought Starters

1. Is a leader always a manager?
2. Is a symphony conductor a manager?
3. How do you identify a good leader?
4. Who has successfully attempted to influence you? Who has unsuccessfully attempted it? What appeared to make the difference?

The New Captain

In July 1918, a young captain took over his first command. The captain was Harry S. Truman, and he later became president of the United States. The command was Battery D of the 129th Field Artillery, an outfit known as "Dizzy D" because of its bad reputation. Many of the men in the outfit were well educated, several had attended Rockhurst College, a Jesuit college in Kansas City. Nevertheless, they were "wild." Battery D had had four previous commanding officers, none of whom could control the men.

Truman reported later that he had never been so scared in his life as when he was told of the assignment. He explained to the colonel who had made the assignment that he might just as well go home, then and there. One of the men in the outfit reported that a great deal of resentment had been generated by the knowledge that Captain Truman had been assigned to them. There was talk of causing trouble, even of mutiny.

Although the men stood at attention when Captain Truman took command, their resentment and hostility were clear. They figured he could do nothing to reestablish control, and if he thought he could, he was mistaken.

From their past experience, the men in Battery D expected to get chewed out. They knew they deserved it from the new commander because of their past conduct. Captain Truman, however, did not say a single word. He walked up and down the lines about three times, looking directly at each man. Only then did he speak. His only word was, *"Dismissed."*

As the men went back to their barracks, they felt that they had been given a kind of benediction (most of them were devout Irish Catholics) and a fresh start.

Many years later, Judge Albert Ridge of the federal district court in Kansas City and a veteran of Company D said, "From that time on, I knew that Harry Truman had captured the hearts of those Irishmen in Battery D, and he never lost it. He has never lost it to this day."

As a matter of fact, Truman kept in touch with the "boys from Battery D" all the rest of his life. Of course, if he had not been a good leader, that first meeting would not have had a lasting effect. After all, Battery D had already gotten rid of four commanding officers before Truman took over.[1]

This case shows the importance of **leadership**—the ability to persuade others to get something done. Although leadership is one of the most studied aspects of management, it may be the least understood. For example, a recent book that summarizes leadership research has 150 pages of bibliography, listing over 3,000 studies. The last chapter of the book suggests that only a beginning has been made in understanding leadership.[2]

A person who has a leader's title may not have leadership ability. (Battery D "chewed up" four leaders before Truman.) Popularity is not the same as leadership ability. Sometimes, a person is popular only because he or she agrees with everyone or avoids conflict.

Managerial Authority and Sources of Power

As the Truman case indicates, there is a difference between authority and power. **Authority** is the right to command and exact obedience from others. It comes from the organization, and it allows the manager to use power. **Power** is the ability to exercise influence or control over others. Authority allows managers to make decisions that guide the actions of others. Power enables them to carry out those decisions. The four officers before Truman all had authority but no power to back it up. In contrast, terrorists who have hijacked a plane may have a great deal of power but no authority. There are at least five different types of social power: legitimate power, expert power, charismatic power, reward power, and coercive power.[3]

Legitimate power is the power that comes when the organization's authority is accepted. The manager has the authority that goes with his or her position in the organization and the power of the organization. Truman, for example, had both legitimate authority and legitimate power. Legitimate power, then, is power that stems from either implicit or explicit rules. Police, parents, teachers, managers—all have legitimate power, but only when their authority is accepted.

Expert power is the power of knowledge. It comes from specialized knowledge and skills that are important in getting the job done. Expert power includes the power of professional competence and/or knowledge. Expertise gives credibility to the manager, leading other individuals to trust that person's judgments and decisions. Physicians, lawyers, computer programmers, chemists, financial analysts, and purchasing agents are all people with expert power.

Managers do not always have expertise in every phase of their work. The dean of a university division cannot be an expert in all the subjects being taught. However, the manager can and should draw on the expert power of specialists in particular fields.

Charismatic power is the power of attraction or devotion—the desire of one person to admire another. In an organization, it is the positive attraction a subordinate feels toward a manager. On the manager's part it is identification power, relationship power, or the power to be attractive. In effect, the subordinate is saying, "I want to be like the manager; consequently, I want to act as the manager does."

The more subordinates identify with the boss, the more they internalize the boss's expectations. They then act as their own "boss," behaving in ways they think the supervisor will want.

Reward power is the present or potential ability to award something for worthy behavior. The manager has the power to give or retain tangible rewards such as promotions, raises, time off, desirable work assignments, office space, and secretarial help. Of course, the manager's awards can also be psychological: approval, praise, appreciation, and recognition, for example. For reward power to be effective, the subordinate must be confident that the manager controls access to rewards through either authority or upward influence. Reward power can increase legitimate and charismatic power.

Coercive power is the ability to threaten or punish. Tangible punishments include dismissal, demotion, a low rating, less satisfying work assignments, and poor references if the subordinate leaves. Psychological punishments include criticism, snubs, avoidance, and expressions of disapproval. To some degree, reward and coercive powers overlap, since one form of punishment is the withholding of rewards. However, evidence has shown that reward power is often more effective in getting a subordinate to *do* something, while coercive power is more effective in getting the subordinate to avoid doing something. Generally, coercive power is of less value than reward power. The latter increases the self-esteem of the individual, while the former reduces it. Overuse of coercive power can result in hostility, withdrawal, rule breaking, and a reduction of legitimate and charismatic power.

An organization dealing with precious metals had developed extremely detailed rules and severe punishments for wastage of these metals. Indeed, every fraction of an ounce of the metal had to be accounted for. Part of the manufacturing plant was built on pilings over a pond. Eventually, it became necessary to drain the pond. When the ground under the plant was exposed, it was painfully evident that literally millions of dollars of precious metals had been partially buried in the mud. For years, rather than be caught and reprimanded for making a mistake, workers had been dropping their "mistakes" into the water and falsifying records to conceal the losses.

Some types of power can be exercised by peers and groups who have no legitimate power or authority. A maintenance manager can "reward" another manager by giving high priority to that person's request. Because of expert knowledge a market research analyst can have a great deal of influence on the direction of the organization. An informal leader of a group who has more charismatic power than the manager can cause a work slowdown.

While there has been considerable research on the different formal leadership styles, there has been little research on how informal leaders gain and use power and influence. To understand how managers can do a better job of leading in a given situation, much more systematic attention must be given to the way influence is distributed among group members.[4]

The effective manager must be able to differentiate among subordinates who can work independently, those who need the participation of others, and those who need direct and forceful supervision. Furthermore, any manager who cannot be both a formal and an informal leader must learn to work with groups' informal leaders in order to accomplish organizational goals.

Formal and Informal Leadership

One of the primary reasons for distinguishing between authority and power is to show the difference between formal and informal leadership. As explained earlier, leadership is the ability to persuade others to get something done. A manager is a **formal leader** by virtue of the authority coming from the organization; that is, a formal leader is usually selected by the organization.

An **informal leader** is chosen by an individual or group. Thus all managers are leaders if their authority is accepted, but not all leaders are managers. In the book *Tom Sawyer*, Aunt Becky was acting as a manager when she told Tom to whitewash the fence. When Tom was able to get others to whitewash the fence for him—indeed, to consider the job a privilege—he was acting as an informal leader.

As a formal leader, the manager influences others to help accomplish the goals of the organization or unit. The person who leads a wildcat strike is a leader who is working against the formal goals of an organization. By defining *leadership* as influence over others, we can clearly see that most people are leaders at one time or another. Formal leadership, which comes from legitimate authority and power, may last over a long period of time. Informal leadership, leadership without "position," may shift quickly from one person to another and may last for only a brief time. The "ideal" manager is one who is simultaneously the formal leader and the informal leader.

Approaches to Leadership Behavior

Most of the better-known approaches to managerial leadership focus on one or more of four basic factors: people, task, personal attributes, and situational factors. A number of studies have examined people and task relationships under the terms of consideration and initiating structure.[5]

Consideration reflects the extent to which individuals are likely to have job relationships characterized by mutual trust, respect for subordinates' ideas, and consideration of subordinates' feelings. **Initiating structure** reflects the extent to which individuals are likely to define and structure their roles and those of their subordinates toward goal attainment.[6] Both terms will be used frequently throughout the rest of the chapter. Other factors important to leadership are the job level, subordinates' expectations of how leaders should behave, subordinates' need for information, perceived independence of the subordinate, upward influence of the leader, and task characteristics such as job clarity and job pressure.

**Theory X and
Theory Y**

One of the more influential writers on leadership is psychologist Douglas McGregor, whose primary focus is consideration. McGregor categorizes managers as having two different beliefs or assumptions about subordinates—called Theory X and Theory Y—that influence their managerial style or strategy. He believes that Theory X assumptions, which are basically authoritarian, are held by a majority of the industrial managers in our society. Theory Y assumptions, which are more egalitarian, are held by fewer managers.[7]

Typical Theory X managers believe that people dislike work and will avoid it whenever possible. Such managers feel they themselves are a small, elite group who want to lead and take responsibility but that the larger mass of people want to be directed and to avoid responsibility. Theory X managers therefore see a need for strong controls and direction achieved through coercion and punishment if people do not work properly and monetary rewards if they do.

In contrast, Theory Y managers usually assume that people will work hard and assume responsibility provided they can satisfy personal needs and organizational goals at the same time. Therefore, they do not see the clear, sharp division between leaders (elites) and followers (the masses) that Theory X posits. They feel that performance is based more on internal than on external controls. (See Table 11.1 for a comparison of the two theories.)

McGregor finds that the basic Theory X assumptions are widely used but outdated, especially given modern society's push toward increased education and desire to take on responsibility. In addition, he finds that following Theory X assumptions can "demotivate" people and become a negative self-fulfilling prophecy. McGregor points out that the Theory X and Theory Y approaches are not managerial strategies as such but tend to influence managerial styles.

An important implication of McGregor's distinction between Theory X and Theory Y is that the effective manager needs to examine carefully personal assumptions about the motivation and behavior of subordinates and others. The appropriate leadership style may depend not only on people but also on the situations. For example, McGregor was a college professor when he first described Theory X and Theory Y. After six years as president of Antioch College, he wrote:

> I believed, for example, that a leader could operate successfully as a kind of adviser to his organization. I thought I could avoid being a "boss." Unconsciously, I suspect, I hoped to duck the unpleasant necessity of making difficult decisions, of taking the responsibility for one course of action among many uncertain alternatives. I thought that maybe I could operate so that everyone would like me—that good "human relations" would eliminate all discord and disagreement.
> I couldn't have been more wrong. I took a couple of years, but I finally began to realize that a leader cannot avoid the exercise of authority any more than he can avoid responsibility for what happens to his organization.[8]

**The Managerial
Grid**

The managerial grid suggests that each manager must be concerned about both production (structure) and people (consideration).[9] Concern for production covers a wide range, including efficiency and workload,

Table 11.1   The continuum from Theory X to Theory Y

Theory X		Theory Y
Production-centered	←————————— versus —————————→	Employee-centered
Autocratic	←————————— versus —————————→	Democratic
External control	←————————— versus —————————→	Internal control
Close supervision	←————————— versus —————————→	General supervision
Initiating structure	←————————— versus —————————→	Consideration
Directive	←————————— versus —————————→	Supportive

units of output, number of creative ideas developed, quality of policy decisions, and thoroughness of staff services.

The term concern for production is not limited to things; it can also involve human accomplishment within the organization, whatever the assigned tasks or activities. Concern for people can be expressed in a number of ways: concern for the personal worth of the individual, for good working conditions, for the degree of personal commitment to completing a job, for security, for a fair salary structure and fringe benefits, and for social and other relationships.

The relationship between concern for production and concern for people is shown in Figure 11.1. The vertical axis indicates concern for people, ranging from very little (1) to a great deal (9). The horizontal axis indicates concern for production, also ranging from very little (1) to a great deal (9). A manager with little concern for production or for people (a 1,1 manager) does little except pass along orders and carry messages between subordinates and upper level managers. A manager with a great deal of concern for people and little concern for production (a 1,9 manager) tries to provide subordinates with comfortable, secure, and easy working conditions. Many 1,9 managers feel that the demands of the organization are harsh and unnecessary. Thus they try to avoid any production pressure that is high enough to reduce their personal acceptance by subordinates. In effect, they assume that by providing acceptance and understanding, they will receive loyalty; and out of loyalty, subordinates will do their jobs. Therefore, they believe, there is little direct need to be concerned with responsibility and accountability; after all, happy workers will produce well without undue pressure or coercion.

The manager with little concern for people but a great deal of concern for production (the 9,1 manager) assumes that there must be a conflict between individual needs and the organization's production needs. The 9,1 manager gives little attention to individuals. Rather, this manager concentrates mainly on getting the work done. The manager does the planning, and the subordinates follow the rules, directives, and schedules laid out for them.

The manager with a great deal of concern for both people and production (the 9,9 manager) does not assume that there is an inherent distinction between the needs of the organization and the needs of people. Believing that the two can be integrated in all cases, the basic aim of the 9,9 manager is to develop cohesive work teams that can achieve high productivity and high morale.

The Managerial Grid is perhaps the most popular of all the approaches to leadership. According to the Grid, the 9,9 style is the optimum leadership approach. Many organizations have even used training

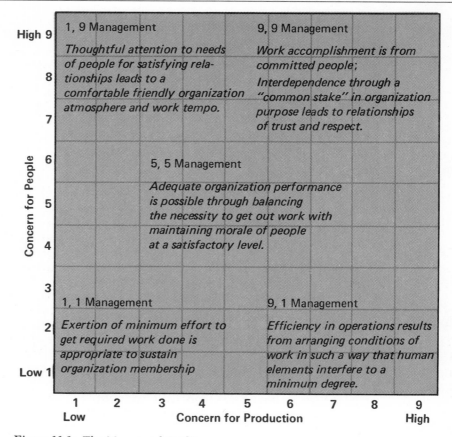

Figure 11.1 The Managerial Grid®

From Robert R. Blake and Jane S. Mouton, *The Managerial Grid* (Houston:
Gulf Publishing, 1964), p. 10. Reproduced with permission. See also *The
New Managerial Grid* (Houston: Gulf Publishing, 1978), p. 11.

programs to develop 9,9 managers. However, there is little evidence that
the most effective managers are at 9,9 or that it is desirable for all
managers to operate from this approach all the time. A further assumption in many training programs is that managers can change to a great
degree; this assumption may be unwarranted. Nevertheless, the Managerial Grid, like McGregor's Theory X and Theory Y, helps the effective
manager carefully examine underlying assumptions about human behavior that affect managerial style.

**Personality
Attribute
Approaches**

Much of the early work on leadership consisted of trying to find
personal traits inherent to "good" managers. Unfortunately, much of this
work consisted only of listing a large number of different traits with little
presentation of evidence that they were at all related to effective leadership. Although research on personal traits continues and is becoming
more sophisticated, few solid results have been obtained. The most
frequently mentioned attributes of an effective leader include "fair,"
"intelligent," "generally knowledgeable," "understanding," "perceptive," and "delegator." The most frequently mentioned traits of a poor
leader include "poor communicator," "indecisive," "lacking in leadership," and "self-centered."[10]

One of the problems with personality attribute approaches is that there is a difference between the possession of a trait and being successful as a leader. Many highly intelligent people, for example, do not make good managers; some may have the right traits but not want to be managers or not really want to be effective. Further, one comprehensive review suggests that leader characteristics and the demands of the situation combine and interact and that the combination really determines the effectiveness of a leader in a group.[11]

Contingency Models

Theories X and Y and the Managerial Grid have been, in effect, models that assume there is a best way for a manager or administrator to lead. However, no single personality trait, pattern of traits, or particular leadership style has been consistently related to effective leadership and organizational performance. An individual may be a very effective leader in one situation but ineffective in another.

Two recent leadership models have taken a different approach—that there are conditions under which one style of leadership is more appropriate than another and that those conditions can be specified. These **contingency models** suggest that effective styles are dependent (or contingent) on a number of conditions, including leader power, level and status of subordinates, and the favorableness or unfavorableness of the situation.

Fiedler's Contingency Leadership Model

Psychologist Fred Fiedler's **contingency leadership model** holds that a manager's effectiveness depends on two main factors: (1) the motivational system of the leader and (2) the extent that the situation is favorable or unfavorable to the leader.

The Leader

Leaders are motivated by satisfaction obtained from two sources—relationships with others (consideration) and task-goal accomplishment (structure). The relationship motivated manager obtains satisfaction from maintaining good interpersonal relationships with subordinates. The task-goal manager obtains satisfaction from the accomplishment of the goal. According to Fiedler, managers receive satisfaction from both relationship and task accomplishments, but the relative importance of each source varies among them. Managers can, however, vary their style, depending on the situation.

The Situation

The contingency theory suggests that relationship motivated leaders are more effective than task motivated leaders in moderately favorable situations and that task motivated leaders are more effective in highly favorable or unfavorable situations. The favorableness of the situation depends on three factors:

1. *The quality of leader-member relations*—the warmer and friendlier the relationships, the more favorable the situation.
2. *The nature of the tasks*—the more structured and routine the tasks, the more favorable the situation.
3. *The position power of the leader*—the more position power, the more favorable the situation. The leader's power includes legitimate, expert, charismatic, reward, and coercive power.

Fiedler has developed questionnaires and ratings to measure the manager's basic motivation and the favorableness of the situation. The results of the questionnaires and ratings are combined to show the

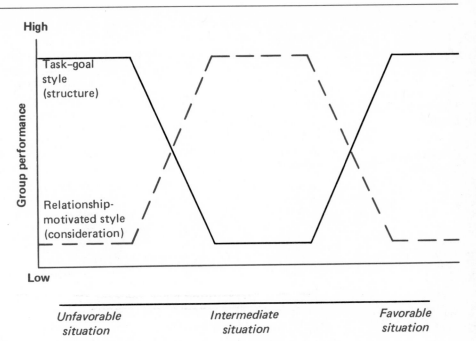

Figure 11.2   Group performance and leadership style

degree to which a situation is favorable or unfavorable. Figure 11.2 shows the appropriate leadership style for situations varying from highly unfavorable to highly favorable.

As can be seen in this figure, task-goal managers perform best in situations that are either very favorable or very unfavorable to the manager. In situations of intermediate difficulty, the relationship or people centered manager is more effective. Thus the performance of the work group is highest where the appropriate leadership style for the situation is used.

Fiedler has conducted studies of the contingency approach for such varied groups as B-29 bomber crews, open-hearth steel workers, general managers, sales display teams, service station managers, high school basketball teams, boards of directors, and church leaders. In general, his findings support the idea that task-goal managers are effective in situations that are either highly favorable or unfavorable and that relationship managers do well in situations of intermediate favorableness. The latter take something of a nondirective role, asking others in the group to share in the decision-making process and interacting with subordinates in a relatively considerate, permissive, human relations–oriented fashion.[12]

For example, a manager with good interpersonal relationships may be developing a new policy that will have a great impact on the work group. At this stage, the situation is relatively vague and unstructured but moderately favorable, and the manager may wish to consult with subordinates and consider their thoughts and ideas. Once the new policy is settled and approved, the situation becomes favorable for the manager to become more task-goal oriented in enforcing the policy.

When Truman took over Battery D, the situation was highly unfavorable. Leader-member relations were poor, and Truman had poor position power. To have asked for cooperation from the men in Company D (consideration) would have been disastrous. Rather, Truman established his position power and authority by using the single word *dismissed*, thereby turning an unfavorable situation into a favorable one.

Recent research is critical of Fiedler's model.[13] Nevertheless, the model illustrates how managers can and should vary their style to fit particular situations.

The Path-Goal Model

Psychologist Robert House has developed a path-goal model of leadership by defining the relationship between leader behavior and subordinate work attitudes and performance as situational. The essential ingredient of the **path-goal model** is that the leader smooths the path to work goals and provides rewards for achieving them. In developing the model, House returned to the expectancy model of motivation (see Chapter 4), under which people are assumed to have needs and to want to work (behave) in a way that accomplishes goals that satisfy those needs. Thus the path-goal model, like the contigency model, is based on the situation rather than on a single kind of leadership. This model also makes use of positive reinforcement (see Chapter 4).

The first concept underlying the path-goal model is that the leader motivates subordinates by clarifying the path to personal rewards that results from attaining work goals, as shown in Figure 11.3. The clarification is done by reducing the uncertainty or negative aspects of the path. It is thus the manager's task to provide the subordinate with a better "fix" on the job and on the relationship of performance to both positive and negative reinforcement.

The second concept is that when the path-to-goal relationship is clear—when the job requirements are highly structured—additional structure by the manager is unnecessary. Indeed, if too much structure is provided by the manager, the result will be decreased worker satisfaction, although not necessarily reduced performance.

The third and final concept is that managers who attempt to satisfy subordinates' needs will increase performance if the reward is related to the desirability of the effort and of the goal. That is, the manager must offer a reward only if the subordinate actually accomplishes the task. The reward can be relatively simple, such as praise, or more complex, such as a pay increase or promotion.

An individual's job satisfaction, behavior, and effort can often be predicted from (1) the degree to which the job behavior is seen as leading to various rewards, and (2) the individual's preferences for those rewards. The leadership style that motivates subordinates is the one that clarifies the kind of behavior most likely to result in goal accomplishment.

Managers should vary their style for each subordinate. For example, subordinates with high needs for affiliation will be satisfied with a considerate leader. But subordinates with a high need for achievement will probably prefer a task-oriented leader. The path-goal model forces the leader to take into consideration the individual subordinate as well as the situation itself.[14]

In one organization, when new employees showed a great deal of anxiety and a high turnover rate, an unusual training program was used to help them. The employees were told clearly what their supervisor expected of them. They were told also that they would not be expected to become immediately proficient on the job, but at the same time they were shown specific steps for becoming proficient. The results were dramatic. The workers who had been given this orientation reached job competence more quickly and made fewer errors than did those who had

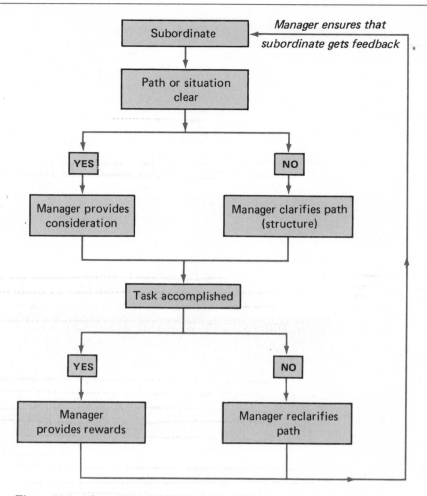

Figure 11.3 The path-goal relationship

received conventional on-the-job training. In effect, the special orientation told the new workers both what to expect and what their rewards for good performance would be. In addition the new workers were provided with a very supportive introduction to the organization.[15]

The path-goal theory of leadership is a new one, and relatively little research has been done on it. However, the early findings have been encouraging. In general, workers on highly structured tasks have reported high satisfaction when their leader uses a supportive rather than a directive style, but they are not necessarily more productive. Workers on highly unstructured tasks are more productive when the leader uses a directive style, but they do not necessarily report more satisfaction.

The path-goal approach clearly needs further refinement and additional research. Nevertheless, it appears to be one of the most promising approaches to studying the complex concept of leadership.

Similarities Among Selected Concepts of Leadership

The leadership theories and approaches studied so far do not all agree. Yet, none of them is either accepted or rejected completely as a predictor of the relationship between leader behavior and the performance or satisfaction of a work group.

Three main characteristics appear in most of the leadership approaches. The first is a concern for people, although this concern is defined and measured differently by each approach. The second is a concern with structure, an indication of the job that needs to be done. The third is a concern with situational factors. Leadership does not exist in a vacuum; the nature of the task and the organizational and societal environments are also important.

Looking at the leadership aspects only, there are four basic ways a manager can affect individual and group performance and satisfaction:

1. The manager can set goals. (The complex interrelationship of goals and leadership styles will be explored in the next section).
2. The manager can clarify how to achieve work goals. As path-goal theory suggests, initiating structure can reduce path-goal uncertainty, especially in ambiguous circumstances. Confusion among subordinates as to when and how something should be done contributes to personal frustration.
3. The manager can show consideration for subordinates. Sometimes, showing consideration may be more important than clarifying goals.
4. The manager can affect expectancies by clearly spelling out the relationship between work performed and intrinsic or extrinsic rewards (or punishments). (This assumes, of course that the manager has the power and authority to offer such rewards.) Even a manager who has little control over pay may be able to offer recognition and approval. The latter rewards can come from the group as well, but they will work only if they are important to the subordinate and are given for high performance.

Implications for the Manager

The crucial tasks of a manager are to assist, motivate, and control subordinates in order to attain organizational objectives. This can be done, in part, by helping subordinates gain personal satisfaction while accomplishing the organization's objectives.

No single factor can explain the performance of a group; nor is there a single comprehensive theory of leadership. Nevertheless, enough consistency exists among the differing approaches to offer suggestions for more effective leadership. One comprehensive review of the literature on leadership suggests two general propositions:

1. The more subordinates depend on the manager for needed or valued services, the higher the potential positive relationship between the manager's behavior and subordinate performance and satisfaction.
2. The more the manager is able to give subordinates needed, valued, or expected rewards, the higher the positive relationship between the manager's behavior and subordinate performance and satisfaction.[16]

Listed below are suggestions that will help the manager put these two propositions into effect.

Nature of Power

As has been seen, the more power managers have, the greater their potential to influence others. (Some suggestions for increasing power are spelled out in Chapter 20.) Managers can increase their expert power by becoming more knowledgeable about their own operation and by cultivating experts outside their unit. They can increase legitimate, reward, and coercive power by showing subordinates that they have influence with higher-level managers, especially by getting "payoffs," such as raises, for subordinates. They can increase charismatic power by the appropriate use of rewards and by getting to know subordinates as individuals.

Nature of the Work Task

The effective manager needs to be a good diagnostician, varying the style of supervision with the situation. When the job is simple, routine, and structured, considerate leadership may promote better job performance and satisfaction than directive leadership. For less structured tasks, more direction is usually appreciated, with consideration and appreciation following the successful completion of the task.

Provision of Feedback

Accurate and nonthreatening feedback to the individual about performance is important. Most managers cannot give complete feedback to all subordinates; therefore, effective managers must try to design tasks so that feedback is provided through the task itself or through appraisal or other approaches.

Nature of Rewards

Rewards should be part of feedback and should be closely tied to task accomplishment. Effective managers should reward successful accomplishment as soon as possible. By knowing their subordinates well, these managers can provide different types of rewards to the different types of people. Most people respond positively to praise (which is used all too little in many organizations). Opportunities for increased responsibility, achievement, and interesting work are other potential rewards.

Organizational Climate

Effective managers are aware of the organization's climate and behave in ways that do not greatly disturb it. The climate can be formal, having a number of rules and regulations, in which case the structured leader may be most effective. Or it may be permissive, having few rules and little reliance on bureaucracy, in which case a more considerate, less structured leadership style may be most effective. The leader's behavior can have a great deal of influence on the perceived climate. If employees see the leader and the organization as autocratic, they are likely to have negative attitudes and low levels of innovation and job satisfaction. If employees see them as achievement-oriented and considerate, they are more likely to respond with positive attitudes and high levels of innovation, satisfaction, and performance.

Upward Influence of Subordinates

With the exception of Fiedler's leader-member relations, relatively little attention has been given to the upward influence of subordinates. Effective leaders know when they should be influenced by subordinates—for example, when the task is complex, when the manager does not have all the expertise, and when consensus of the work group is desired.

Personal Qualities

Effective managers act naturally and try not to manipulate their subordinates. Recognizing that subordinates have a lot of other pressures, these managers try to recognize, identify, and work around the pressures.

Avoiding Value Judgments

Effective managers try to diagnose rather than use value judgments. For example, managers who classify a subordinate as "lazy" reduce their own ability to understand the individual's behavior and deal with it.

Review

1. What are the different types of power one person can exercise over another? Are they interrelated? Explain.
2. What is the difference between formal and informal leadership?
3. What are the basic differences between Theory Y and Theory X? Are their concepts oversimplified? Explain.
4. What are the two basic principles underlying the Managerial Grid? How would you compare them to McGregor's approach?
5. What are the basic differences between McGregor's and Blake's approach to leadership and the contingency approaches?
6. What distinction can be made between leading and managing?
7. What aspect of Fiedler's theory suggests that a research director should use a leadership style different from that of an accounting clerk's supervisor?
8. Interview several people, asking them to describe situations where someone's attempt to influence them was successful or unsuccessful. Analyze the reasons for the success or failure of the influence attempt.
9. Some managers reject participative approaches (such as Theory Y) as being unrealistic. Advocates of participation argue that authoritarians are afraid to change their style. What do you have to say about these views?
10. Describe how a college professor following each of the major Managerial Grid leadership styles would conduct classes.
11. Describe how a college professor using the path-goal approach would conduct classes.

The Foundering Firm

In January 1974 duPont Walston went out of business. The Wall Street stockbrokerage firm had 138 branch offices. After a merger, it had been taken over by H. Ross Perot, a naval academy graduate and data-processing multimillionaire. On the first day after the merger, all the male employees were told to get short haircuts and to wear dark suits and bow ties. Mustaches and beards were prohibited. Two black men with Afro hair styles quit immediately.

No form of dissent was tolerated. For example, eight of the directors were fired for having opposed Perot's takeover of the firm (all were employees as well as directors). Nearly all the employees in research and in certain sales and operations areas were fired. Those who made suggestions or expressed dissent were fired. Perot made it clear that he distrusted the employees, and he tried to force the staff into a paramilitary mold with strict rules and regulations that applied to everyone.

Employees were told to forget about the small investor and to go after the "elephants"—company presidents and other big investors. However, many of the big investors were already tied up with other brokers. Further, as a former executive pointed out:

> There is a big difference between the computer business and stock brokerage. In the computer business, you can make a one-time big sale to a customer and then perform service under a long-term contract. In the brokerage business, you can make a sale once, but after every sale you have to do it all over again because there are a number of other brokerage firms after the same account. Perot could not see

the difference until it was too late. You can't adapt computer-selling methods to Wall Street.

A training program was instituted, which included teaching employees how to sleep. Management forced trainees to sign an agreement to repay the organization for part of their training if they did not stay for three years. For example, a trainee who quit right after graduation would owe the organization $25,000. Trainees who did not sign were fired.

Employees were called up during off hours and asked to report to someone at work immediately for trivial matters. When the wives started complaining, that particular form of harassment stopped. More and more people objected to being treated "like plebes at the naval academy." Finally, a general exodus began. The replacements at the home office were more amenable to the paramilitary regime. However, they did not bring in the revenues. The exodus increased. In May 1973 the manager of the Decatur, Illinois, branch office, ten salesmen, and three operating workers quit to join a competitor. Only the receptionist stayed on. In Hartford, fourteen employees quit to join a competitor when a new manager was put in charge.

The firm was losing money at a faster and faster rate. After a lengthy discussion over the weekend of January 19–20, the directors voted to go out of business.[17]

1. Which approach to leadership did Perot use?
2. What motivational needs were satisfied? What needs were not satisfied?
3. What types of power was Perot using?
4. What alternative leadership approaches could Perot have used?
5. Was there a difference between authority and influence in this situation?

Footnotes

1. Adaptation by permission of Berkley Publishing Corporation from *Plain Speaking: An Oral Biography of Harry S. Truman* (p. 96) by Merle Miller. Copyright © 1973, 1974 by Merle Miller.
2. R. Stogdill, *Handbook of Leadership: A Survey of Theory and Research* (New York: Free Press, 1974).
3. J. French and B. Raven, "The Basis of Social Power," in *Group Dynamics: Research and Theory*, 3rd ed., ed. D. Cartwright and A. Zander (New York: Harper & Row, 1967).
4. G. Farris, *Leadership and Supervision in the Informal Organization*, Working Paper No. 655-73 (Cambridge, Mass.: Massachusetts Institute of Technology, 1973).
5. R. Stogdill and A. Coons, *Leader Behavior: A Description and Measurement*, Research Monogram 88 (Columbus, Ohio: Bureau of Business Research, Ohio State University, 1957); R. Stogdill, *Individual Behavior and Group Achievement* (London: Oxford University Press, 1959); A. Korman, "Consideration, Initiating Structure and Organizational Criteria—A Review," *Personnel Psychology* 19 (Winter 1966): 349–361; R. House, A. Filley, and S. Kerr, "Relation of Leader Consideration and Initiating Structure to R and D Subordinates' Satisfaction," *Administrative Science Quarterly* 16 (March 1971): 19–30; S. Kerr and C. Schriesheim, "Consideration, Initiating Structure, and Organizational Criteria—An Update of Korman's 1966 Review,"

Personnel Psychology 27 (Winter 1974): 555–568; and C. Schriesheim, R. House, and S. Kerr, "The Effects of Different Operationalizations of Leader Initiating Structure: A Reconciliation of Discrepant Results," *Academy of Management Proceedings,* New Orleans, Louisiana, August 10–17, 1975, pp. 167–170.

6. E. Fleishman and S. Peters, "Interpersonal Values, Leadership Attitudes and Managerial Success," *Personnel Psychology* 15 (Summer 1962): 43–44.

7. D. McGregor, *The Human Side of Enterprise* (New York: McGraw-Hill, 1960); and D. McGregor, *The Professional Manager*, ed. D. McGregor and W. Bennis (New York: McGraw-Hill, 1967).

8. D. McGregor, "On Leadership," *Antioch Notes*, May 1954, pp. 2–3. Used by permission of Antioch University.

9. R. Blake and J. Mouton, *The Managerial Grid* (Houston: Gulf Publishing, 1964); L. Barnes and L. Greiner, "Breakthrough in Organization Development," *Harvard Business Review* 42 (November–December 1964): 133–155; R. Blake and J. Mouton, *Corporate Excellence through Grid Organization Development: A Systems Approach* (Houston: Gulf Publishing, 1968).

10. Adapted from L. Sank, "Effective and Ineffective Managerial Traits Obtained as Naturalistic Descriptions from Executive Members from a Super-Corporation," *Personnel Psychology* 27 (Autumn 1974): 423–434.

11. Adapted from Stogdill, *Handbook of Leadership.*

12. F. Fiedler, *A Theory of Leadership Effectiveness* (New York: McGraw-Hill, 1967); G. Graen, K. Alveris, J. Orris, and J. Martella, "Contingency Model of Leadership Effectiveness: Antecedent and Evidential Results," *Psychological Bulletin* 74 (October 1970): 285–296; S. Shiftlett and S. Nealey, "The Effects of Changing Leadership Power: A Test of Situational Engineering," *Organizational Behavior and Human Performance* 7 (June 1972): 371–382; F. Fiedler, "Predicting the Effects of Leadership Training and Experience from the Contingency Model: A Clarification," *Journal of Applied Psychology* 57 (April 1973): 110–113; F. Fiedler and M. Chemers, *Leadership and Effective Management* (Glenview, Ill.: Scott, Foresman, 1974); J. Stinson and L. Tracey, "Some Disturbing Characteristics of the LPC Score," *Personnel Psychology* 27 (Autumn 1974): 477–485; D. Hovey, "The Low-Powered Leader Confronts a Messy Problem: A Test of Fiedler's Theory," *Academy of Management Journal* 17 (June 1974): 358–362; F. Fiedler, "Engineer the Job to Fit the Manager," *Harvard Business Review* 43 (September–October 1965): 118; and F. Fiedler, "The Leadership Game: Matching the Man to the Situation," *Organizational Dynamics* 4 (Winter 1976): 6–15.

13. C. Schriesheim and S. Kerr, "Theories and Measures of Leadership: A Critical Appraisal of Current and Future Directions," in *Leadership: The Cutting Edge*, ed. J. Hunt and L. Larson (Carbondale: Southern Illinois University Press, 1977).

14. R. House, "A Path Goal Theory of Leader Effectiveness," *Administrative Science Quarterly* 16 (September 1971): 321–338; R. House and T. Mitchell, "Path-Goal Theory of Leadership," *Journal of Contemporary Business* 3 (January 1974): 81–98; R. Stogdill, *Handbook of Leadership;* J. Stonson and T. Johnson, "The Path-Goal Theory of Leadership: A Partial Test and Suggested Refinement," *Academy of Management Journal* 18 (June 1975): 242–252; H. Sims, Jr., and A. Szilagyi, "Leader Structure and Subordinate Satisfaction for Two Hospital Administrative Levels: A Path Analysis Approach," *Journal of*

Applied Psychology 60 (April 1975): 194–197; and A. Downey, J. Sheridan, and J. Slocum, "Analysis of Relationships among Leader Behavior, Subordinate Job Performance and Satisfaction: A Path-Goal Approach," *Academy of Management Journal* 18 (June 1975): 252–262.

15. E. Gomersall and M. Myers, "Breakthrough in on-the-Job Training," *Harvard Business Reveiw* 44 (July–August 1966): 62–72.

16. S. Kerr, C. Schriesheim, C. Murphy, and R. Stogdill, "Toward a Contingency Theory of Leadership Based upon the Consideration and Initiating Structure Literature," *Organizational Behavior and Human Performance* 12 (August 1974): 62–82.

17. Adapted from R. Rustin, "Critics Say Heavy Hand at Helm Led to Collapse of duPont Walston," *Wall Street Journal,* February 26, 1974. Reprinted with permission of *The Wall Street Journal* © Dow Jones & Company, Inc., 1974. All rights reserved.

Chapter 12

Communications

The Plumber

The Importance of Information

What Is Communications?
    Characteristics of the Sender
    Sending the Message
    "Noise"—Communication Barriers

The Importance of Climate in Communications and Feedback

Transactional Analysis
    Structural Analysis
    Analyzing the Transaction

Implications for the Manager

Review

The Furniture Store

Learning Objectives

When you have finished reading and studying this chapter, you should be able to

1. Compare and contrast formal and informal communications.
2. Identify the basic characteristics of the sender (receiver) that affect the communications process.
3. Identify and give illustrations of the main communications channels.
4. Identify and give examples of barriers to communications.
5. List at least four ways in which climate can affect communications.
6. Use transactional analysis to diagram interpersonal interaction.
7. Give personal examples of each of the ten commandments for improving communications.
8. Define and be able to use the following concepts:

information	semantics
communications	jargon
communications channel	information overload
nonverbal communications	rumor
body language	value judgment
noise	active listening
filtering	transactional analysis (TA)
selective perception	structural analysis
empathy	transactions

Thought Starters

1. Is there a difference between clarity and effectiveness of communications? Can you give examples of each?
2. How good a communicator are you? What do you need to improve?
3. What do we mean when we say that communications have broken down?
4. What does the term *body language* mean to you?

The Plumber

A plumber from New York developed what he thought was an excellent method for cleaning drains. He wrote the Bureau of Standards to tell them that he was using hydrochloric acid and to ask them if it was harmless. The bureau replied, "The efficacy of hydrochloric acid is indisputable, but the chlorine residue is incompatible with metallic permanence."

The plumber wrote back, thanking the bureau for agreeing with him. Alarmed by his response, the bureau wrote another letter, saying, "We cannot assume responsibility for the production of toxic and noxious residues with hydrochloric acid, and suggest that you use an alternative procedure." The plumber wrote again, explaining how happy he was to learn that Washington still agreed with him.

At this stage, the bureau put the problem in simple terms: "Don't use hydrochloric acid. It eats the hell out of the pipes." Finally, the plumber understood.[1]

Both the plumber and the Bureau of Standards thought they were communicating with each other. As it turned out, communications were not effective until the bureau used words that the plumber could understand. This chapter will explore the importance of information and communications in organizations, describing (1) different types of communications, (2) barriers to effective communications, (3) ways of analyzing and better understanding the communications process, and (4) ways of improving the process.

The Importance of Information

Having the right information at the right time is of vital importance to an organization. **Information** is the knowledge or other data that are useful and pertinent to the individual or organizational unit. Decision making, establishing organizational goals and objectives, planning, and controlling cannot take place without accurate and timely information.

Information serves not only to motivate behavior but also to aim it in the proper direction.[2] For example, a truck driver receives visual information that the truck is moving off the highway onto the shoulder of the road. The information not only motivates the driver to take action but also serves to guide the action (turning the wheel in the direction that will bring the truck back onto the road). A manager receives information that the volume of bank loans is falling off and begins taking action to increase the number of loans by discussing how to do so with subordinates.

As explained in Chapter 2 and elsewhere, managers are the nerve centers of the organizational unit. In order to get the job done well, they must obtain and give information horizontally, downward, and upward. In the liaison role, managers communicate horizontally with others; they are nerve centers in touch with a variety of other nerve centers. As monitors, they must continually get information from and give information to horizontal and lower levels to ensure that the unit is operating properly. As disseminators, they must make certain that subordinates and others are informed of pertinent information. Frequently, this requires feeding the unit information that has been obtained from people at the same and higher levels. As spokespersons, managers must speak for and represent the unit to others at both the same and higher levels. All these roles require that a manager be an excellent communicator.

What Is Communications?

Communications is the process by which information is exchanged and understood by two or more people, usually with the intent to motivate or influence behavior. As people interact with others to work and to solve problems, they communicate ideas, attitudes, and feelings. If the communications are effective, the work is done better and the problems are solved more effectively. Therefore, a positive relationship exists between good communications and productivity.[3]

Communications can be either formal or informal. *Formal communications* follow lines of authority prescribed by the organization. For example, Mike gets Reports A and B but is not on the list for Report C. Chris has access to payroll information, but Leslie is not allowed such information. *Informal communications* need not follow organizationally prescribed lines of authority. Usually, they take place on a person-to-person basis. Because prescribed information channels are frequently slow and incomplete, the manager needs to develop a network of informal communications at all levels.

Most people think of communications as being rather simple. However, the process is usually quite complex, and the opportunities for sending or receiving the wrong message are great.[4] How often have you heard someone say, "But that's not what I meant"? How often have you given people directions in what you thought was a clear fashion and they still got lost?

To understand the complexity of the communications process more fully, we can look at the main elements of the process, shown in Figure 12.1. These elements are the sender, the transmitter, the message itself, noise, and the receiver. Secondary elements include the source of information, the characteristics of the sender and receiver, the type of message, the relationship between the sender and receiver, and the climate and environment within which the communications take place.

In the simplest terms, an individual has an idea. The idea exists in the person's brain and must be coded into some form of oral, written, or other language, which is then transmitted. If the coding, transmitting, or decoding process is faulty, there is "noise" in the system. When this occurs, the message may not be received, a wrong word may be used, or the right word may be misinterpreted. If and when the message is received by the other person, it must be decoded in that person's brain, where it then forms a message. If the communication has been effective, the message received is the same as the one transmitted.

A number of factors can affect the communications process, causing the message to be lost anywhere between the sender and the receiver. Considering that communications is a two-way, continuing process (the double-headed arrow in Figure 12.1), the possibilities for misunderstanding multiply.

Characteristics of the Sender

The message originates with the sender (although, as Figure 12.1 shows, the sender is often also the receiver). Since the vast majority of

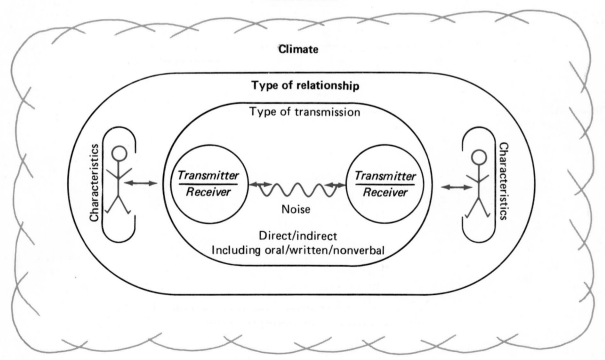

Figure 12.1 The communications process

communications are two-way, the terms *sender* and *receiver* can often be used interchangeably.

Whenever two or more people communicate with each other, the communications process is affected by their prior contacts. To make the process more effective, time and effort must be spent to create mutual trust and to identify areas of present and potential agreement. Both senders and receivers are often unaware of their actions and their impact on others. Looking for and using helpful responses from others can improve self-awareness and thereby increase the ability to send clear and inoffensive messages.

Sending the Message

Messages can be of two types. In the *overt* message, the stated idea is the only one sent to the other person. If a person says to a service station attendant, "Fill the gas tank with regular," the message is clear, simple, and direct.

Frequently, however, there is a covert, or hidden, message as well. The sender may, for example, be transmitting emotional overtones, which the receiver may or may not consciously pick up. It is important to be tuned in to both the overt message and the covert message. In many cases, the latter carries the primary weight of the entire message's meaning. Thus the covert message can seriously affect the communications process.

For example, a junior accountant may complain, "My desk is too small." The overt message is, "My work requires more space." However, since desk size may also indicate status, the covert message may well be, "I'm not getting the recognition I should be getting." Analysis only of the accountant's desk size may never get to the real problem.

As Table 12.1 shows, there are a number of methods for sending messages, the three basic ones being oral, written, and nonverbal. (Nonverbal messages also supplement and affect oral messages, often being used unconsciously or covertly.) In addition, there are a number of communications channels. (A **communications channel** is any way in which information reaches the receiver.) The choice of channel or method can affect the accuracy of communications and the degree to which the receiver responds to them. The advantages and disadvantages of the various communication methods are explained below.

Oral Communications

Oral communications have the advantage of being fast, allowing considerable two-way communication, and getting a quick response. In addition, they create an informal atmosphere, particularly if the communications are face-to-face. Probably their chief disadvantage is that they leave no written record, and people forget important messages.

The location in which oral messages are sent is important to communication. If the boss stops at the subordinate's office or desk, the two are likely to interact on a more equal basis than if the subordinate has to see the boss by appointment. Placing a telephone call personally is much more informal than having a secretary place it. In some organizations, the manager who picks up the phone first (after the secretary has placed or received the call) is considered the loser in a covert power struggle.

In most organizations, the flow of communications downward or laterally is considerably better than the flow of communications upward. Used properly, one of the chief advantages of oral communications is moving messages upward.

The president and executive vice-president of a large eastern university make it a practice to walk (separately) through the campus at least

Table 12.1   Some types of communication

Oral
   Personal—face-to-face
   Personal—telephone
   Group
   Public address system
   Closed circuit television

Written
   Personal—letters, notes
   Organizational—general announcements, newsletters
   Outside the organization

Nonverbal
   Body language—body and eye movements, facial expressions, hand signals, voice (pitch, volume), touch, smell, taste
   Mechanical—sirens, traffic lights, horns
   Symbolic—status (office size, desk size, carpet, badge), religious (bible, rosary, medal)
   Pictorial (no smoking, smoking, no trucks)

Mixed
   Most oral and written communications include nonverbal cues or components
   Written messages may be accompanied or followed by oral explanations

once a day. As the vice-president puts it, "I pick different hours of the day so that I don't run into the same people." Both also drop into the faculty dining room or one of the student dining halls on random occasions to have lunch with random groups of faculty and students. They report being able to obtain or pass on information that would be impossible to handle with more formal methods.

Written Communications

One advantage of written communications is that both sender and receiver have a record of the message. Another advantage is that written messages encourage clear thinking. Written communications are excellent for material such as policies and procedures, which remain in effect for a considerable period of time, and for technical material, such as engineering, legal, or financial data. Trying to get some of this material across orally can be a hopeless task.

One of the disadvantages of written communications is the danger of misunderstanding, especially if there is no opportunity to ask questions. A second disadvantage is the potential over-reliance on this form of communication. Some people want everything in writing so they can "prove" they have been following directions. Over-reliance frequently is a result of the lack of trust and openness in the organization. A third disadvantage is that the information contained in written messages can become accessible to the wrong people or at the wrong time.

In many cases, written and oral approaches can and should be combined. For example, a person in one department had to send a memo on a sensitive matter to a person in another department. A draft of the memo was prepared and discussed with the other person before the memo was written in final form. In this way, both individuals were able to downplay the possible negative ramifications of the memo itself.

Which is better—oral or written communications? As already suggested, written communications may be better if a formal record must be kept, but oral communications are generally faster and more interactive. Probably, a combination of the two will be appropriate under most circumstances. For example, a formal policy or procedure may be written and then orally explained to those affected; this method allows questions and answers to be exchanged. Most research studies on communication indicate that greater satisfaction, understanding, and retention occur with oral communications than with written ones.

Nonverbal Communications

Nonverbal communications are the transmission of ideas or messages without using words. As Table 12.1 shows, there are several types of nonverbal communications. A fire alarm, a police siren, a traffic light—each has its own message. A drawing of a lighted cigarette with a large X drawn through it clearly conveys the message "no smoking."

An important part of nonverbal communications is **body language,** which involves the transmittal of thoughts, actions, and feelings and how other people "read" them. Most situations require the use of words; however, often, particularly in face-to-face communications, only about 35 percent of the message's actual meaning gets across through words. The rest either gets lost or is communicated in nonverbal ways.[5]

Included in body language are voice tones, facial expressions, eye movements, and hand and body movements. For example, nodding the head up and down is the usual nonverbal sign of agreement. However, if a supervisor is communicating an unwanted message, subordinates may nod their heads to avoid verbal agreement. In this instance, the nod means "yes, boss, I hear you."

Body language varies widely among different cultures. For example, Henry Kissinger often uses one-hand gestures. To some people these gestures suggest secretiveness, that he is sending only half a message. However, European Jews commonly use one-handed gestures, and Kissinger could therefore simply be following his cultural heritage.

Middle-class Anglo-Saxons tend to use different gestures to indicate the same meanings. Frustration, for example, can be indicated by clenching hands tightly, throwing pencils, running a hand through the hair, rubbing the back of the neck, and breathing quickly and shallowly. Meditation can be indicated by stroking the face or chin, closing the eyes, and frowning or wrinkling the skin beneath the lower eyelids. Suspicion or doubt can be shown by pulling on or rubbing the ear with the index finger and/or thumb, glancing sidewise, peering over the top of glasses, frowning, and averting the eyes.

Arms and hands in sight, open, particularly palms up, usually indicate sincerity and openness. Crossed arms or legs can indicate defensiveness and "shutting people off." In one meeting, for example, the

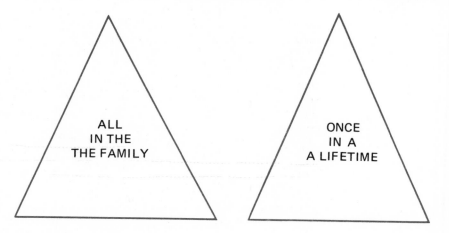

Figure 12.2 What is the message?

boss had been talking for forty-five minutes. Although the fourteen subordinates were apparently listening intently, most were leaning back in their chairs, and all had their arms crossed. Several had tightly closed fists or were tightly grasping their arms. Ten seconds after the boss said, "I want to get your opinions," all fourteen were leaning forward with their arms and hands on the table.

Nonverbal communications are often just as meaningful as words. For a number of years, Ted Williams held the record for paying the largest fine ever levied against a professional baseball player. The fine was for arguing with an umpire. During the argument, Williams never spoke a word; the entire content of his message to the umpire was through a single gesture.

Just as people learn to recognize and use words, so also do they learn to recognize and interpret body language. Consciously or unconsciously, they note whether the verbal and nonverbal signals are sending the same message. When they receive conflicting messages, they tend to rely more on the body language than on the other information. Indeed, body language is generally more accurate than other signals by its very unconsiousness. Paying closer attention to body language helps improve communications skills.

"Noise"—Communication Barriers

There are always barriers, or "noise," to communication. Communication barriers, or **"noise"** include any factors that limit or distort messages in the communications process. They include filtering, selective perception, semantics, jargon, information overload, rumors, and value judgments. Sometimes, the barriers are physical—for example, bad telephone connections or the loss of the audio on a television. However, physical barriers are much less important than others.

Filtering acts as a barrier to communication when the sender intentionally sifts or modifies the message so it will be seen more favorably by the receiver. For example, subordinates communicating with managers tend to make the information conform to what they feel the managers want to hear. Many employees feel that if they communicate openly, they will get into trouble. In addition, the more lower-level managers want to get promoted, the more they are likely to filter what is being transmitted upward.[6]

The same filtering process occurs in downward communications. Supervisors frequently avoid giving subordinates information that may be threatening. In addition, they tend to "screen" any other information moving downward. For some supervisors, knowledge equals power.

To reduce filtering, the effective manager must try to create an environment in which subordinates will not feel that they will be punished for disclosing information. In addition, the manager must give subordinates the information they need to do their jobs, must consider the characteristics of each subordinate, and must make certain that the communications process is two-way.

Selective perception is the tendency to perceive only part of a message—to screen out other information.[7] People often hear what they want to hear and see what they want to see. They tend to ignore information that conflicts with their own "knowledge," beliefs, and expectations. For example, subordinates tend to "hear" information that they think is of the most interest and/or importance to the boss.

Thus status or position can create barriers to communication. One of the most common reasons for selective perception is a poor self-concept on the part of either the sender or the receiver. Individuals with a poor self-concept tend to see communications as vaguely threatening. During a recent electrical power failure, a mother, anxious about her child, called him. The child responded, plaintively, "Mommy, I didn't do it!" The mother's concern was perceived by the child as a threat.

Figure 12.2 illustrates the tendency toward selective perception. What message is in the triangles? Most people would say "all in the family" and "once in a lifetime." But look again, saying aloud each word, one at a time. What is really written there?

One way to reduce selective perception is to develop **empathy—a better understanding of other people's viewpoints**. Managers, for example, can help subordinates see the broader picture, thereby reducing selective perception. Beyond that, each individual can strive to become more aware of inconsistencies in personal behavior.

During the energy crisis in 1973, a high level conference on energy was held at the White House on a cold day in November. Each government official arrived in a chauffeur-driven limousine. During the meeting, the engines were kept running and the heaters were kept on to keep the cars warm. After the meeting, the officials returned to their warm cars as passersby stared and news cameras clicked. These public servants were apparently unaware of the inconsistency in suggesting that other people do all they could to conserve energy while they themselves wasted it in keeping their cars warm.

Semantics is the study of meaning in language. Most messages are sent in words; and words often are not very precise, many of them carrying different meanings for different people. Actually, there are two different kinds of semantic barriers to communication. The first is the language's lack of preciseness. For example, one dictionary lists 14,000 meanings for the 500 most used words, an average of 28 meanings per word![8] As Mark Twain said, "The difference between the right word and the almost right word is the difference between lightning and a lightning bug."

The second semantic barrier is **jargon—overly specialized or technical language.** The incident at the beginning of the chapter indicates the use of jargon. It may well be that "the efficacy of hydrochloric acid is indisputable" and that "the chlorine residue is incompatible with metallic permanence," but there is no reason to assume that a plumber will know these words. Professional and other groups tend to develop specialized language that cannot easily be understood by others. A visitor to an industrial firm picked up a copy of the weekly plant newspaper and was unable to understand most of it because of the heavy use of initials, abbreviations, and technical words. When asked about the meaning of some of the terms, the editor responded, "I don't understand them either. I just print the stories as they are sent in."

Communications can be improved by using clear, simple words and by avoiding words that are emotionally loaded or highly abstract. Many states, for example, now require that insurance policies and warranties be written in clear, simple language, so their purchasers can understand them.

Information overload, another communications barrier, involves an excess of incoming information, to the point where it cannot be handled. Some managers are literally swamped with information. One study reports on a manager who received approximately six hundred pages of computer printout each day. The information detailed the location of materials, the output of each production line, and other operational information. Rather than trying to wade through the information, the manager arranged to have it removed with the trash once a month.[9]

One way to improve the overload problem is to determine which reports and messages are actually needed. Unnecessary information should not be sent or received. The person in charge of compiling a periodic, lengthy report found a unique way to convince his boss that the report was unnecessary (or at least unread). Without telling anyone, he inserted a line on page eleven of each of five reports: "I will pay fifty dollars to anyone who reads this sentence." Nobody responded. After the fifth report had been issued with this insert, he told his boss, who agreed to discontinue the lengthy report.

Yet another source of noise in the system is **rumors**—unconfirmed messages passed from person to person. Formal communications channels are often short-circuited by the "grapevine," which is an accurate and invaluable way of informally getting information to those who need it. However, many rumors passed through the grapevine are inaccurate. They are spread in two types of situations: (1) when people are confused about what is happening in the organization, and (2) when they feel powerless to affect their own future or destiny. Passing on a rumor is a means of reducing anxiety about the subject of the rumor.

Since the grapevine will always exist, and since rumors will inevitably crop up, the effective manager should use the grapevine to get information to people. A casual comment to one or more persons may take care of a problem without the need for more formal action. Also, the effective manager should be alert to inaccurate rumors and should transmit the correct information rather than allow the rumors to spread unchecked.

Value judgments, also a communications barrier, are statements or beliefs based on or reflecting the individual's personal or class values. The statements "workers aren't motivated any more" and "Jim is lazy" are judgments. They reflect someone's opinion but are not necessarily factual (even if others agree). But frequently such judgments are treated as "fact," and people do not search further for more accurate information.

Communications can sometimes literally break down; the phone may go dead or the TV may lose the audio. Most of the time, however, the term *communications breakdown* or the statement "we need better communications" is used in the value judgment sense. When two departments are feuding or two workers are not talking to each other, the communications are clear but ineffective in helping the organization reach its goals. The term *communications breakdown* shows only the symptom and avoids the more important concern—reduced effectiveness. Managers must therefore be aware of how value judgments are used as a barrier to effective communications. For example, whenever they hear the term *communications breakdown,* they should begin to examine how communications can be made more effective.

The Importance of Climate in Communications and Feedback

A number of studies have shown that the climate of an organization is important to the communications process, including feedback.[10] Especially in interpersonal communications, trust is a vital part of a good climate. There are a number of ways that the communications process can be used to build either a supportive climate (which increases trust and receptiveness to feedback) or a defensive climate (which decreases trust and increases defensiveness and resistance).

Threatening or defensive climates are usually judgmental rather than supportive. For instance, the comment, "Your typing is terrible," is more judgmental than, "There are two typing errors per page in this report." The second statement contains verifiable data, which increases the accuracy of the communication and reduces its threat.

In other areas, control can be shifted to an emphasis on problems. Strategy, or clinical detachment, can be shifted to spontaneity and empathy—an open concern for the receiver. Superiority in attitude can be shifted to equality. Certainty can be shifted to provisionalism. "You're wrong" (certainty) arouses a different reaction from "I wonder if we have thoroughly identified the problem" (provisionalism).

A supportive climate is further improved through **active listening,** which involves reflecting back to the other person not only what the person has said but also the perceived emotional tone of the message. For example, reflections of what has been said may be, "If I have heard you correctly, you are saying that . . ." or "In summary, you mean . . ." Reflections of emotional content may be, "It sounds to me like this is an important issue for you" or "Are you really saying that . . . ?"

Feedback properly given and received can increase trust and reduce dependence. Typically, feedback involves an offer by one person to another, "Here's what I think you should do . . ." The typical response is, "Thanks, but the reasons that won't work are . . ." There is a difference between simple assistance and developmental help in giving feedback. *Simple assistance* means doing the task for the other person (which tends to increase that person's dependence on the helper). Some examples are a father tying a child's shoelace, a man giving a panhandler money for a cup of coffee, or a supervisor handling a difficult problem with a subordinate's customer. *Developmental help* means working with others to help them increase their capability for handling similar problems in the future. Two examples are a mother helping a child deal with lack of acceptance by other children and a secretary helping a saleswoman see that she is hurting her chances of making a sale by calling too frequently on the secretary's boss.

Transactional Analysis

Transactional analysis (TA) is a way of improving communications by showing how the communications process can be analyzed. It focuses on four basic areas: **structural analysis,** the structure of the personality; **analyzing the transactions**—how people interact; **time structuring,** how people use their time; and **life scripts,** the roles people learn to play in life. This chapter will focus primarily on structural and transactional analysis as ways of analyzing communications. Further information on all four areas can be found in greater detail elsewhere.[11]

Structural Analysis

Structure is necessary for an understanding of transactions, which occur between ego states. In transactional analysis, each individual personality is assumed to be made up of three *ego states*—consistent patterns of experience and feeling that are directly related to observable behavior. Thus, while ego states themselves cannot be directly observed, the resulting behavior can be. The three ego states are Parent (P), Adult (A), and Child (C). As parts of the personality structure, the three can be distinguished from actual parents, adults, and children; and the capital letters P, A, and C are used to show the difference. Ego states are like cassette tapes in that people can switch easily from one to another.

The *Parent* ego state is the set of recordings or tapes developed by parents or other powerful forces in early childhood. As shown in Figure 12.3 the Parent can be divided into the Critical, Standard Setting, and Nurturing Parent. The Critical Parent disciplines and criticizes. The Standard Setting Parent sets limits, gives advice, and guides actions. (A supervisor might appear in the standard setting role by providing a new employee with the norms and rules of behavior.) The Nurturing Parent is

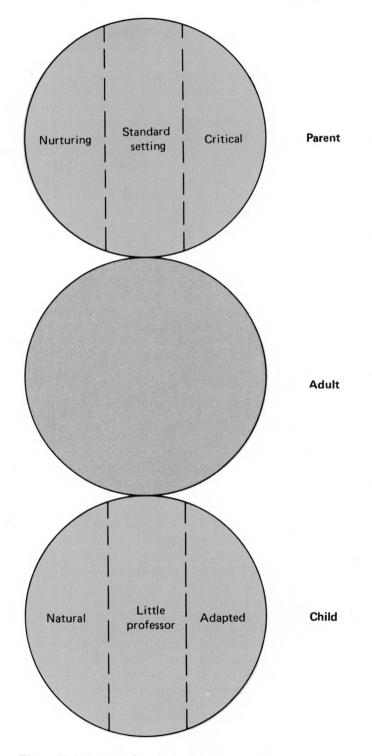

Figure 12.3   Structural analysis of the personality

warm, loving, and protective. The dotted lines in the figure show that the boundaries are movable. The Standard Setting Parent may, for example, also criticize.

The *Adult* ego state is the part of the personality that deals only with the facts. Unemotional, it computes, stores memories, and uses facts to make decisions. It is not, however, the same thing as maturity.

The *Child* ego state allows people to talk, think, or act as they did when they were children. It too is subdivided. The Natural Child is rebellious, joyful, free, and spontaneous. The Adapted Child has fully conformed to parental wishes and desires. The Little Professor is the beginning of the Adult ego state and mediates between the Adapted and Natural Child.

For the personality to be fully developed, all three ego states are necessary. None is "better" than the others. As a matter of fact, a person operating primarily from only one ego state will have serious communications and emotional problems.

Analyzing the Transaction

The three ego states affect people's behavior, especially their interactions with others. Indeed every interaction with others involves a **transaction** among ego states—a verbal and/or nonverbal message unit between two or more people. Transactions can be classified as complementary, crossed, or ulterior, as shown in Figure 12.4.

A *complementary transaction* occurs when a message sent from one person's particular ego state receives an expected response from the other person's appropriate ego state. For example, assume that a man at work receives a telephone call that his wife has been hit by a car and is being taken to the hospital. His Child ego state responds with fear and indecision about what to do. The most appropriate response his boss can make is to tell him to go immediately to the hospital; the response is that of the Nurturing Parent.

A *crossed transaction* occurs when a message sent from one person's ego state is responded to by another person's inappropriate or unexpected ego state. In the example above, the transaction will be crossed if the boss responds from his Adult ego state by saying, "That's too bad. Have you finished the Jones report?" Crossed transactions usually result in feelings of anger, hurt, or pain for at least one of the people involved in the transaction. The man whose wife has been in an accident will certainly be hurt if his boss is not sympathetic. However, crossed transactions can also be helpful, as will be shown later.

An *ulterior transaction* involves two ego states at the same time; while the content of the transaction means one thing and comes from one ego state, the underlying intent means something different and comes from another ego state. In one situation, a manager who had decided to use "participative management" assigned a group to work on a problem. When asked, "What answer will the group come up with?" the manager responded, "There's only one possible answer." The overt message the manager had sent to the group was an A-A one—"solve the problem." The underlying message, however, was P-C—"solve the problem my way."

Complementary, crossed, and ulterior transactions are, in themselves, neither good nor bad. The effective manager needs to know how to recognize and use them and how to shift from one ego state to another as appropriate. A manager who deals with subordinates primarily from the Parent ego state may find subordinates responding primarily from the Child ego state, with dependence or rebelliousness. The transactions in this situation are complementary but not very effective.

Crossed transactions can be useful when they are used appropriately. For example, it is easy to get hooked into P-C or C-P transactions, with one person always the Parent and the other always the Child. The situation can be changed, however, if, during a transaction, one person begins to respond from the Adult ego state. A high school senior

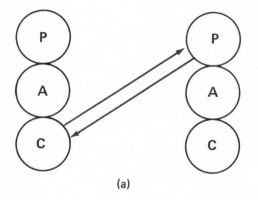

(a)

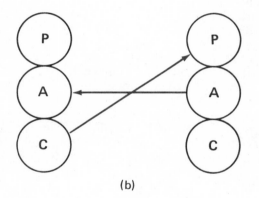

(b)

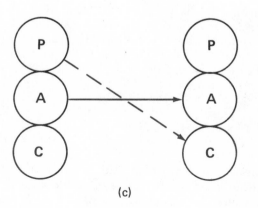

(c)

Figure 12.4 Transactions. (a) A complementary transaction (b) A crossed transaction (c) An ulterior transaction

who had had TA training was late in preparing lunch for her father. As he began to get angry, she calmly said, "You seem to be awfully upset about this." Her father blurted out, "But that's not what you're supposed to say!"

Ulterior transactions can also be useful when they are used appropriately. A manager who wants to get a message across may be uncertain about how it will be received. By using an ulterior transaction as a trial balloon, the manager may be able to learn whether a more straightforward approach will be received appropriately.

Many large organizations (such as Bank of America, Westinghouse, American Airlines, and Pan American Airlines) have trained managers and others to use TA. But although the approach seems useful, it lacks solid research evidence. Still, the effective manager can use TA primarily to understand his or her own behavior. Used this way, TA can become a framework for understanding and mentally diagramming communications.

Implications for the Manager

Managers spend a large percentage of their time communicating with others inside and outside the organizational unit. Thus communications take place upward, downward, and horizontally. As the nerve center of the unit, the effective manager develops good communications skills and a broad network of contacts on both a formal and an informal basis.

Throughout this chapter, a number of suggestions have been made to improve communications and communications skills. In doing so, the terms *sender* and *receiver* have been used almost interchangeably, since most communications are a two-way process. Further, most suggestions for improving two-way communications can also be used for improving one-way communications. The ten "commandments" for improving communications are:

1. *Develop self-awareness.* The effective manager develops awareness of actions and their impact on others. At times, nonverbal messages contradict oral or written messages. Awareness of these messages and of the ego state the messages are coming from is essential.
2. *Develop awareness of the other person.* Before sending a message, look at it from the receiver's point of view. Attempt to understand the other person and to convey something of help or value to that person in the message. Messages are usually well-received and acted upon when they contain something of either immediate or long-range value to the person receiving them.
3. *Avoid value judgments.* Value judgments such as "people are not motivated" or "communications have broken down" only add noise to the system. Since they deal with symptoms rather than causes, they should not be used.
4. *Be clear and complete.* Make certain what is to be communicated, and then make it clear to the receiver. Use simple language and concrete terms.
5. *Be concise and correct.* Get to the point, make certain the information is correct, and don't exaggerate. (The Gettysburg Address contains only 266 words.)
6. *Choose channels carefully.* Oral communications are faster than written ones, but written communications provide a permanent record. For important messages, use more than one channel.

Face-to-face oral communications, for example, can be backed up with written records.

7. *Support communications with action.* Many managers say one thing but do another. There is a tendency for people to discount a message when they believe the attitudes or actions behind it contradict it. Follow up to see how well the message has come across; ask questions. Important communications should be followed by enough feedback to make certain that appropriate action is taken.

8. *Develop a supportive climate.* Without knowing it, managers often send messages in ways that increase others' defensiveness. Description, problem orientation, spontaneity, equality, and provisionalism create a supportive climate. Evaluation, control, strategy, superiority, and dogmatism establish a defensive climate for receiving communications.

9. *Improve listening and feedback skills.* Managers have a hard time really listening. Indeed, in many interpersonal "communications," neither person is really listening to the other. Look for both overt and convert messages. Listen with empathy; that is, assume the other person's role, viewpoint, and emotions. Make sure that both the content and emotion of the message are reflected.

10. *Check the effectiveness of the messages.* Some managers can learn more effective communications techniques by tape recording themselves as they communicate with others. Generally, people do not object to being recorded if they know why the tape is being made. (Managers who tape record their communications often are amazed at some of the things they have done or said without knowing it.) Ask questions; seek feedback. One of the most important elements in human interaction is communication. Effective communication leads to good relationships and good results. Effective managers use the tools of effective communication; they are both good senders and good receivers.

Review

1. As a sender, you have an option of using either written or oral communications. Which do you prefer? Why?
2. As a receiver, do you prefer written or oral communications? Explain.
3. List what you think are the most important barriers to communications. What suggestions do you have for reducing these barriers?
4. Identify some mixed messages you have received. When have you sent mixed messages? Explain.
5. Find a group of people. Sit close enough to observe their behavior but far enough away that you cannot hear their conversation. What can you tell from the nonverbal behavior you observe?
6. Observe several people talking to each other. Diagram their transactions, using transactional analysis. What ego states are involved? Do the people shift ego states? Explain.
7. What nonverbal ways do you have of communicating? Observe yourself, and ask a friend to observe you in order to get the information. What sorts of signals do you give?
8. Do you make many value judgments? Look for others' value judgment statements. What effect do such statements have on you?

The Furniture Store

One summer, when I was in college, four other students and I worked at a furniture store having a "going out of business" sale. Although the store had sold only wholesale, when the owners decided to close the business, they opened their doors to the public.

The owners had never dealt with retail customers, so they hired professionals to run the sale for them; and the professionals hired us. Sam was our boss, Bill was Sam's boss, and Jim was Bill's boss.

At first, everything seemed basically all right. We did our work as Sam told us to. Then, Jim and Bill began to have us rearrange whatever we had just done, contradicting what Sam had told us and commenting that Sam didn't know what he was doing. This, of course, bothered us, especially when it began to happen more and more frequently.

Some days we were sent to the warehouse to uncrate merchandise and then back to the store to arrange the furniture on the sales floors. If Jim saw us resting, he would immediately ask what we were doing. Sometimes he would even peer around corners to watch us. He never let us do things on our own; he always wanted Sam to be with us, and we would have to check with him if Sam was not around. We finally reached the point where, when our work was done, we would stay out of Jim's sight. Otherwise, he would have us do some little senseless job just to keep us busy. He told us that we had been hired to work and that he would make sure we did so.

After a few weeks, I noticed that three cliques had formed; the other college students and myself were one, the men hired to run the sale were another, and the owners and original salesman were the third. The owners wanted things done one way and the professionals another. Soon they were talking behind one another's backs. This was bad for us, for we were given contradictory things to do by two or three people, and we were inevitably yelled at by those whose decisions were different from the one who first told us what to do. Once, for example, an argument arose between the owner and Jim because the owner had sent us to another one of his stores and Jim was angry that we didn't get the work done at our regular store. That time he told us not to listen to what the owners said.

Another time, one of the students got into an argument with Sam; the student had done something his own way, and Sam was angry because he had not been consulted. Eventually, the student was fired. We were told that it was because he was a bad worker, but we found out later it was because the professionals thought he was too outspoken. After that, we never offered any ideas or suggestions.

After about a month and a half, we got a small raise, thanks to Bill. But this only added to our headaches. Every time we would make a mistake, Bill would say that he had thought we were worth the raise but now he was not sure.

By summer's end the situation had deteriorated to the point where we did not talk to the bosses. We just listened to our orders, carried them out (whether they made sense or not), and left at the end of each day. The only reason I stayed on was that I needed the money and it was too late in the summer to look for another job.

1. How would you describe the climate of this organization?
2. What sorts of messages were being sent?
3. How does communication affect behavior?

Footnotes

1. Adapted from *Power of Words,* p. 259, copyright 1953, 1954, by Stuart Chase. Reprinted by permission of Harcourt Brace Jovanovich, Inc.
2. D. Nadler, *Feedback and Organization Development* (Reading, Mass.: Addison-Wesley, 1977); E. Lawler and J. Rhode, *Information and Control in Organizations* (Santa Monica, Calif.: Goodyear Publishing, 1976); and W. Newman, *Constructive Control: Design and Use of Control Systems* (Englewood Cliffs, N.J.: Prentice-Hall, 1975).
3. C. Barnard, *The Functions of the Executive* (Cambridge, Mass: Harvard University Press, 1938); R. Carter, *Communication to Organizations: A Guide to Information Sources* (Detroit: Dale Research, 1972); J. Franklin, "Down the Organization: Influence Process across Levels of Hierarchy," *Administrative Science Quarterly* 20 (June 1975): 153–163; S. Hayakawa, *Language in Thought and Action,* rev. ed. (New York: Harcourt Brace Jovanovich, 1972); R. Huseman, J. Lahiff, and J. Hatfield, *Interpersonal Communication in Organizations: A Perceptual Approach* (Boston: Holbrook Press, 1976); and E. Rogers and R. Rogers, *Communication in Organizations* (New York: Free Press, 1976).
4. V. Balachandran and S. Deshmuch, "A Stochastic Model of Persuasive Communication," *Management Science* 22 (April 1976): 829–841; G. Chapel, "Speechwriting in the Nixon Administration," *Journal of Communication* 26 (Spring 1976): 65–79; F. Roethlisberger, "Social Behavior and the Use of Words in Formal Organizations," in *Interpersonal Behavior and Administration,* ed. A. Turner and G. Lombard (New York: Free Press, 1969); C. Shannon and W. Weaver, *The Mathematical Theory of Communication* (Urbana, Ill.: University of Illinois Press, 1949); and J. Wiemann and M. Knapp, "Turn-Taking in Conversations," *Journal of Communication* 25 (Spring 1975): 75–93.
5. H. Herzfeld, "The Unspoken Message," *Small Systems World,* February 1977, 12–14; R. Harrison, "Non Verbal Communication," in *Dimensions*

in Communication, ed. J. Campbell and H. Harper (Belmont, Calif.: Wadsworth, 1970); F. Davis, *Inside Intuition: What We Know about Nonverbal Communications* (New York: McGraw-Hill, 1973); and J. Fast, *Body Language* (New York: M. Evans, 1970).

6. W. Read, "Upward Communication in Industrial Hierarchies," *Human Relations* 15 (January 1962): 3–15; and G. Gemmill, "Managing Upward Communications," *Management Review* 59 (May 1970): 26–27.

7. J. Bruner, "Social Psychology and Perception," in *Readings in Social Psychology,* 3rd ed., ed. E. Maccoby, T. Newcomb, and E. Hartley (New York: Holt, Rinehart and Winston, 1958), pp. 85–94; J. Bruner and C. Goodman, "Value and Need as Organizing Factors in Perception," *Journal of Abnormal and Social Psychology* 42 (January 1947): 33–45; M. Cook, *Interpersonal Perception* (Middlesex, England: Penguin, 1971); M. Haire and W. Grunes, "Perceptual Defenses: Processes Protecting an Organized Perception of Another Personality," *Human Relations* 3 (June 1950): 403–412; N. Maier et al., *Superior Subordinate Communication in Management* (New York: American Management Association, 1961), pp. 61–72; R. Rosenthal, *Experimenter Effects in Behavioral Research* (New York: Appleton-Century-Crofts, 1966); and S. Dornbusch et al., "The Perceiver and the Perceived: Their Relative Influence on the Categories of Interpersonal Cognition," *Journal of Personality and Social Psychology* 1 (January 1965): 433–440.

8. E. Huse and J. Bowditch, *Behavior in Organizations: A Systems Approach to Managing,* rev. ed. (Reading, Mass.: Addison-Wesley, 1977), p. 150.

9. J. Ivancevich, A. Szilagyi, and M. Wallace, *Organizational Behavior and Performance* (Santa Monica, Calif.: Goodyear Publishing, 1977), pp. 404–405.

10. J. Gibb, "Defensive Communication," *Journal of Communication* 11 (Summer 1961): 44–49; M. Greller and D. Herold, "Sources of Feedback: A Preliminary Investigation," *Organizational Behavior and Human Performance* 13 (March 1975): 244–256; D. Hellriegel and J. Slocum, Jr., "Organizational Climate: Measures, Research and Contingencies," *Academy of Management Journal* 17 (June 1974): 255–280; and C. Rogers, "Barriers and Gateways to Communication," *Harvard Business Review* 30 (July–August 1954): 44–49.

11. E. Berne, *What Do You Do after You Say Hello?* (New York: Grosset & Dunlap, 1963); E. Berne, *Games People Play* (New York: Grove Press, 1964); and M. James and D. Jongeward, *Born to Win: Transactional Analysis with Gestalt Experiments* (Reading, Mass.: Addison-Wesley, 1971).

Chapter 13

Staffing and Managing Human Resources

The Bakke and AT&T Cases

The Importance of Staffing

Civil Rights and Other Legislation

Human Resources Planning

Recruitment and Selection

Appraisal—Evaluating the Manager's Performance

Management Development
    First-Line Supervisory Training
    Middle Management Development
    Executive Development

Management Compensation
    What Is the Job Worth in Comparison to Other Internal Jobs?
    What Is the Job Worth in Comparison to External Jobs?
    What Is the Individual Worth on the Particular Job?

Promotion, Transfer, and Termination

Implications for the Manager

Review

The Promotion

Learning Objectives

When you have finished reading and studying this chapter, you should be able to:

1. Identify the effects of laws and regulations on staffing.
2. Explain the importance of having the proper managers in the proper place at the proper time.
3. Show the interrelationships of the basic steps of staffing.
4. Identify the steps in recruitment and selection.
5. Demonstrate the place of appraisal in the staffing process.
6. Compare and contrast management development programs at different levels in the organization.
7. List and give examples of at least five methods of management compensation.
8. Define and be able to use the following concepts:

    reverse discrimination   management development
    staffing   compensation
    affirmative action   transfer
    recruitment   promotion
    selection   termination
    performance appraisal

Thought Starters

1. Have you ever applied for a job? What selection methods did the organization use?
2. How might affirmative action affect you and your career?
3. How accurate are the conclusions from an interview?

The Bakke and AT&T Cases

When Allan Bakke applied to the University of California Medical School at Davis, he was turned down. At the same time, under a special quota program to help disadvantaged minority students, the school accepted sixteen Hispanic, black, and Asian-American students. According to Bakke, the sixteen minority students were less qualified than he was. Thus the school's acceptance of them was a violation of his civil rights.

Bakke sued the University of California. The case went all the way to the United States Supreme Court, which heard oral arguments in late 1977. The primary issue before the Court was whether, under the Constitution, universities can give preference to minorities over whites in order to remedy the evils of past discrimination.

The case had far wider importance, however, than the narrow question of university admissions. For example, more than fifty *amicus curiae* (friend of the court) briefs were filed by various organizations. The written argument of the U.S. government, for example, listed fifteen major programs that might be affected by the case. These ranged from grants to assist businesses owned by minorities to National Science Foundation grants to improve education in colleges with majority black and Spanish-speaking enrollments.

The Supreme Court also had under advisement another case. This one involved American Telephone & Telegraph Company, which had agreed in 1973 to make payments of $15 million to compensate 15,000 workers, mostly women, who were alleged to be victims of past salary and promotion discrimination. AT&T had also agreed with the federal government to set percentage goals in a number of job categories as well as to promote a large number of women and minorities. For example, women and minorities got more than two-thirds of the 61,000 new jobs and promotions offered by the company in 1977. Three unions challenged the quotas as **reverse discrimination**—the selection of minority persons or women for jobs or education in place of better-qualified whites and men. The unions also claimed that the affirmative action plan violated seniority rights clauses that were previously established in contracts with AT&T.

In mid-1978, the Court ruled on both cases. In the Bakke case, it decided that rigid quotas based solely on race were forbidden but that race could legitimately be an element in judging students for admission. In the AT&T case, it let stand the "model" affirmative action plan by refusing (without explanation) to review a lower-court ruling that had approved the establishment of numerical goals for employment and promotion of minorities and women. The two rulings were generally seen as supporting affirmative action programs in both education and industrial hiring and promotion policies.[1]

Although the full impact of these two cases may not be known for years, they point up some of the ways in which outside laws and regulations affect the management of human resources in almost every organization. In the discussion of the management of human resources, the term *staffing* will frequently be used. Before the term is described in detail, its importance will be established.

The Importance of Staffing

Organizations need people, and people need jobs. Every organization must select, train, and develop its workers. Voluntary organizations may not pay workers, but they still must make certain that the workers fit the jobs. Thus **staffing** is "identifying, assessing, placing, evaluating and developing individuals at work," by performing such actions as "recruiting, selecting, appraising and promoting individuals."[2] The basic function of staffing is making certain that the right people are in the right jobs at the right time and with the proper knowledge and training to do the jobs.

Organizations do not actually exist in a physical sense. A corporation, for instance, is a legal entity—a piece of paper on which are printed the articles of incorporation. Buildings and machinery do not make an organization either. What makes an organization is the people working with and for it; as one large firm advertises, "People are our most important product." There have been a number of cases of organizations, such as manufacturing plants, being completely destroyed by fire. Yet, many of them were back in operation in a few weeks with rented buildings and borrowed equipment, because the people were still there. On the other hand, the long and costly coal strike in 1977–1978 resulted in what amounted to the temporary nonexistence of the mining organizations. The mines and equipment were there, but the people were not.

For these and many other reasons, staffing is a major managerial function—one of the most important things managers can do. Although managers can get help from others, such as the personnel department, they cannot delegate the fundamental responsibility for staffing. Unfortunately, some managers (and organizations) tend to avoid the function or perform it poorly. The manager who spends a great deal of time and effort determining which machine to buy may spend relatively little time and effort making certain that the proper person is selected and trained to operate the machine.

Proper staffing is important for at least three major reasons. First, as noted above, an organization cannot function without people. Second, poor selection, appraisal, or promotion has a bad effect not only on the organization but also on individuals within it. Many people are in jobs they do not like, but they remain in them because they feel trapped. Third, there are legal and social responsibility aspects to be considered. For example, civil rights laws and regulations not only forbid discrimination against minorities but also require "affirmative action" to reduce discrimination. **Affirmative action** means that organizations must have a positive plan to reduce and/or eliminate internal minority imbalances or inequalities.[3] Failure to do so can result in fines, loss of government support or contracts, or other actions. For example, AT&T agreed to pay more than $15 million in back wages to women and other minority employees whose pay was arbitrarily low because of discriminatory practices.[4]

Civil Rights and Other Legislation

There are two broad categories of discrimination in the United States—*that against nonwhites, including blacks, Mexican-Americans, Asians, and American Indians, and that against women.* Nonwhite women are the most discriminated against. Under affirmative action legislation, organizations must show specific evidence that action has been taken to place the number of minority employees proportionate to the population at all levels. For example, in the two years after paying the back wages, AT&T increased the number of blacks and women in second-level management by 82 and 46 percent, respectively; the number of men in clerical and operator jobs by 147 percent; and the number of women in craft jobs by 119 percent. It is no longer a surprise to get directory assistance from a male operator.

In addition to civil rights legislation, many other laws and government regulations affect the staffing process. Among the relatively recent ones are:

1. The *Equal Pay Act (Fair Labor Standards Act—1963)*, which forbids unequal pay for men and women doing equal work on jobs requiring equal skill, responsibility, and effort that are performed under similar working conditions. This act was amended in 1972 to include administrative, executive, and professional employees.
2. The *Civil Rights Act* (1964), which forbids discrimination in education and employment on the basis of race, sex, color, religion, and national origin.
3. The *Age Discrimination Act* (1967), which forbids all forms of discrimination in employment for persons between forty and sixty-five years of age.
4. The *Occupational Safety and Health Act (OSHA—1970)*, which establishes mandatory safety and health standards in organizations, including work rules, job design, and the overall work environment.
5. The *Revised Order No. 4* (1971), under which the Department of Labor established detailed guidelines for affirmative action programs, including procedures and demonstration of good faith efforts.
6. The *Rehabilitation Act* (1973), which, among other rules, requires organizations to take affirmative action for employment of people

with physical or mental handicaps. Specific regulations were developed and issued by the Department of Labor in 1976.

7. The *Employment Retirement Income Security Act (ERISA—1974)*, which allows full vesting after ten years and establishes an insurance program to protect pension funds. (Vesting allows the employee to receive the employer's contributions to the pension fund if the employee terminates employment before retirement.)

8. The *Revised Guidelines for Employee Selection Procedures* (1976), which established specific rules and guidelines on employment practices for the federal government and its contractors. The Equal Employment Opportunity Commission (EEOC) provided revised and tougher guidelines for the private sector and state and local governments.

9. *Changes in mandatory retirement rules*, under which people in most jobs cannot be forced to retire before age seventy (formerly sixty-five).

These and other laws, rules, and regulations have a strong impact on all areas of staffing. Furthermore, there are a number of federal and state agencies that have been developed to police civil rights and other legislation. Among the most important federal agencies are the Equal Employment Opportunity Commission (EEOC), the Office of Federal Contract Compliance Programs (OFCCP) in the Department of Labor, and the Occupational Safety and Health Administration (OSHA) in the Department of Health, Education, and Welfare.

EEOC was created by the Civil Rights Act of 1964 to hear and investigate charges of minority discrimination. In 1972 it was given the additional power to go directly to the federal courts to enforce its decisions.

OFCCP was created in 1965 by Presidential Executive Order No. 11246 to enforce the requirement that organizations doing work for the federal government take affirmative action to reduce discrimination against women and minorities.

OSHA was created by the Occupational Safety and Health Act of 1970 to improve work rules, job design, and the work environment. It is responsible for drawing up regulations and guidelines for occupational safety and health.

Because of the complexity and importance of staffing, managers at all levels have immediate responsibility for staffing within the law. Top management must establish policy and make certain it is carried out. Middle and lower level managers must implement the policy and recommend necessary changes. As mentioned earlier, the personnel department can assist with the staffing process, but the ultimate responsibility rests with the managers.

The basic steps in staffing are: (1) the determination of needs; (2) recruitment and selection; (3) orientation, training, and development; (4) performance appraisal; (5) compensation; and (6) promotion, transfer, and termination. This chapter will be concerned primarily with the selection, development, and other staffing processes for managers and other professional employees.

Human Resources Planning

In Chapter 8 planning was shown to begin with organizational objectives and then move to the development of strategies, policies, and detailed plans to achieve those objectives. Human resources planning must be a comprehensive ongoing process tied to the overall plans of the organization. It must be continuous and systematic if it is to accomplish organizational goals.[5]

When human resources planning is haphazard or neglected, many problems emerge. For instance, one large corporation laid off a number of skilled workers on a Friday. The following Monday, another department of the same company asked the personnel department to recruit immediately a number of people with the same skills as those laid off on Friday. Unnecessary confusion and loss of productive time resulted from improper planning and coordination.

Human resources planning must start at the top of the organization and be closely monitored by top management, with each lower level of management contributing to the overall plan. Frequently, planning is relegated to the personnel department, with operating management giving little or no attention to its nature and scope. A study of 249 firms with more than 1,000 employees each showed that 96 percent of the firms assigned human resource planning to the personnel department.[6] For such planning to be done well, the head of the organization must insist that operating managers and personnel people work closely together.

What are some of the factors to consider in human resources planning? Among them are:

1. Future cost, marketing, and income projections for the organization.
2. Realistic appraisals of current and projected human resource requirements, including numbers of people and skill levels.
3. Present and future trends in terms of equipment purchase, capital expenditures, sales, and production requirements.
4. Technological and other changes.
5. Present and future trends and demands for different skills and educational backgrounds.
6. Present and future trends in general economic conditions.
7. Present and potential legislation and attitude changes in the community and the nation.

For example, the recent federal legislation raising the mandatory retirement age from sixty-five to seventy means that organizations have had to change many of their hiring, promotion, and firing procedures. Also rapid obsolescence of products or equipment cause rapid shifts in human resources requirements.

On a more specific basis, an effective program for identifying and grooming candidates for existing management positions is imperative. One way to handle this is to have each organizational department or unit develop a management replacement chart similar to the one shown in Figure 13.1. The replacement chart is simply an organization chart with all the managerial positions keyed to the promotability of each manager.

From Figure 13.1 the finance manager can easily tell the present status of the staffing function. (For the purpose of this illustration, the possibilities of someone being transferred from another division or employed from outside will be ignored.) Unless further development work is undertaken for other managers in the unit, the most likely present successor is the engineering finance manager—who in turn has a successor ready for promotion and a backup for that position. But the finance manager of military production engines represents a major problem (not all of which is indicated by the chart). He is not doing his job and should be fired. Since he took over the position eight years ago, military produc-

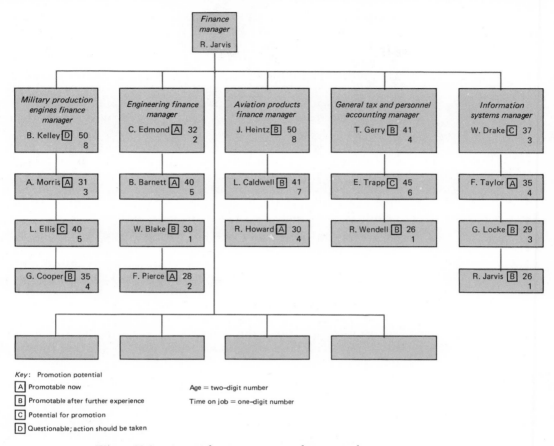

Figure 13.1   A partial management replacement chart

tion has become far more important; but he is simply not capable of handling the job. He was promoted to the position during a time of rapid expansion, when managers were scarce, but he has passed his level of competence. Since he has been with the company for many years, it will try to find him another position for which he is more suited. This will leave room for the person immediately below him to move up.

There are dangers in using a management replacement chart. Among them is the problem of confidentiality. If information of this kind is "leaked," some people will probably view themselves as "crown princes" and others will be utterly crushed. Furthermore, the simplification into four categories means that people can be stereotyped. Thus, while charts of this sort can be helpful, they must be backed up with complete data and specific plans of action for each individual.

Managers can certainly find other methods of human resource planning as well. The important thing is that such planning be done. Many organizations, both large and small, do not make such plans; and when a key person leaves, for whatever reason, they are at a loss. Some never recover. Thus human resource planning must be viewed as a continuous task of management, not left to chance.

Recruitment, and Selection

The recruitment and selection processes should be tied to the overall needs and plans of the organization. Before they begin, careful analysis should be made of specific job and skill requirements. Once these requirements have been identified, potential candidates can be recruited.

Recruitment is the process of attracting candidates from either inside or outside the organization who are qualified for and interested in the position. **Selection** is the process of choosing the most qualified person from the available pool of candidates. Many organizations like to promote from within whenever possible. Promotion from within is desirable because it creates executive continuity, career development paths, a high level of morale, and job satisfaction. However, it also entails costs. Candidates who are passed over for a promotion may become unhappy and dissatisfied, and internal candidates may not have qualifications as good as external candidates.

An important reason for recruitment outside the organization is that many organizations have systematically, even if inadvertently, discriminated against potential managers because of sex, color, age, religion, and so on. Now they must take affirmative action to ensure that women, minorities, the handicapped, and other such groups have an equal chance at becoming managers. In many organizations, the available pool of potential middle and upper level managers is primarily white men; but under existing regulations, such organizations must aggressively recruit women and minorities for positions at all levels. Thus they may have to go outside the organization for managerial candidates.

Figure 13.2 shows the recruitment and selection process in the form of a diagram. The management replacement chart, or its equivalent, is one device for assisting with recruiting and selecting from within. Another is job posting—the posting in prominent places of all open positions so that available candidates can be made aware of them.

The process of recruiting from outside the organization can include the use of colleges, private employment agencies, state employment agencies, professional associations, other employees, and newspaper advertisements. The legal requirements for all forms of recruitment are becoming stricter and stricter. For example, a 1974 law provides that certain organizations doing work for the federal government must list job openings with the local office of the state employment agency. Under other regulations, organizations may be required to advertise in minority or special group journals.

The recruiting process is also becoming more realistic. In the past, organizations tended to "sell" themselves to prospective candidates. Now they generally provide a more realistic preview of the job, so that both they and the candidates can make a better choice. Studies suggest that when clear and realistic information is given out about the job, not only are there as many applicants as before, but there is also a reduction in turnover rates among those selected.

In the early 1970s, the U.S. Army Intelligence Corps changed its description of a particular job. In the past, the job had been aimed at "an individual of high character and good intelligence with better than average ability to communicate". The new description is for "a college graduate in liberal arts who has previously demonstrated outstanding fluency and command of both spoken and written English, and can type at least 40 words a minute". This type of change leads to a better match of candidates and jobs.

In another situation, a bank personnel manager found that having applicants read job descriptions before being interviewed helped the recruitment and selection process. After reading the job description, some applicants would screen themselves out, saying, "I don't think this is the type of job I am looking for."

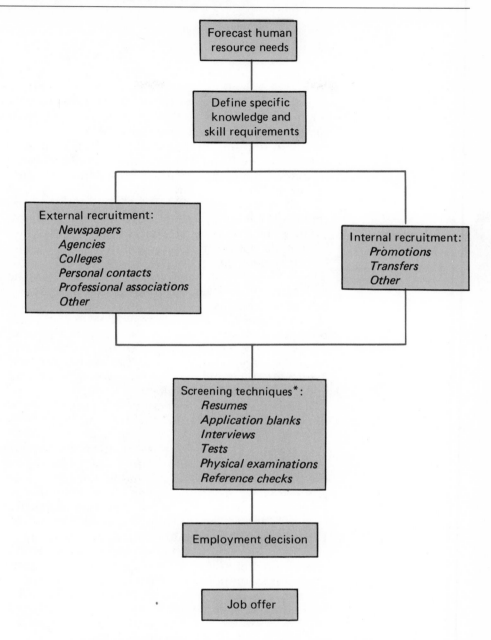

Figure 13.2   Frequently used steps in recruitment and selection

The traditional managerial selection process consists of a series of hurdles: résumés, application blanks, personal interviews, reference checks, physical examinations, and perhaps psychological testing. A sample résumé is given in Figure 13.3.

Most research on selection indicates that none of the steps in the selection process is very accurate.[7] For example, studies of the résumé suggest that impressions gathered from it are not at all related to later job success. The well-written and well-designed résumé attracts favorable attention regardless of the candidate's qualifications for the particular job.

The *application blank*, a printed form that asks for biographical or other information about a candidate, is one of the most widely used tools in outside selection. Application blanks vary considerably from organization to organization and by job level. However, few organizations have done the necessary statistical analysis to demonstrate that application blanks actually predict success on the job. These days, too, organizations are often required by law to show that the information requested is job related. Indeed, many questions about race, color, religion, age, physical or mental handicaps, marital status, and previous convictions must be either job related or left unasked.

The use of *psychological testing*, another selection tool, is being reduced. Recent Supreme Court rulings state that such tests can be used for employment decisions only if they are proven to predict job performance, do not discriminate, and are related to the job itself.

Interviews are perhaps the most widely used selection technique. They can be either relatively unstructured and nondirective or highly structured and patterned. A structured interview probes into particular predetermined areas, following a relatively detailed checklist. Most research on the interview suggests that, in itself, it is not very accurate in predicting job success but that accuracy is somewhat increased when the interviewer is well-trained and uses a structured format. Interviewer biases or stereotyping can affect the outcome of this aspect of selection. Thus more than one manager should interview and evaluate applicants, and as many different selection methods as possible should be used: *"The more carefully clues about an applicant are checked against other information, the higher the validity (accuracy) of the selection procedure is likely to be."* [8]

One way to check clues about an applicant against other information is through the assessment center. Most assessment centers are company operated, although some are independently operated. Companies usually either set aside particular offices or reserve educational or other facilities for the purpose. Many organizations (such as AT&T, IBM, Sears, General Motors, Standard Oil, General Electric, Ford, the IRS, and the U.S. Department of Agriculture) are now using this approach for selecting, identifying, and developing managers.[9] The use of such centers is spreading widely because research suggests that they are appropriate for essentially everyone—men, women, and minority groups. The centers help managers make decisions about placement, job rotation, training, and development.

There are no "best" procedures used by assessment centers. But, in general, they follow some or all of these six steps:

1. Ten to twelve people are assessed at the same time. They may be outside applicants or current employees being considered for promotion or development.
2. The people participate in a number of activities for 1½ to 3½ days.
3. The activities include interviews, leaderless group discussions, working through collections of memorandums and papers "typical" of a manager's incoming mail, business games and other simulation exercises, and a variety of aptitude or other tests.
4. The people are interviewed and observed by a trained staff, which often includes managers, personnel people, and psychologists.

A sample resume

John M. Gulick
Mill Pond Road
Chagrin Falls, Ohio 21212

Home telephone: 216/444-9393
Office telephone: 216/777-8484

Objective: To assume a position of responsibility in the financial department of a manufacturing, processing, or service organization. Ultimate goal: upper level managerial position.

Education: Case–Western Reserve University, B.A. in Finance, May 1979 (cum laude). Course work included corporate finance, investments, internal finance, management accounting, organizational studies, and computer science. Was member of University Debate Team, Academic Affairs Council, Student Governance Board.

Experience:

January 1979 to present — Western Federal Savings and Loan, Cleveland, Ohio. *Lending Officer*, responsible for managing operation of the home improvement loan department; duties include qualifying loan applications, supervising disbursement of $300,000 per month, and soliciting new accounts.

1976–1979 — Ajax Construction Company, Omar, Ohio. Four consecutive summers of increasing responsibilities. Advanced from general laborer to carpenter to detail planner and layout designer. Increasing ability to plan, organize, and control was required.

1975 — Avis Car Rental, Omar, Ohio. Summer employment, included vehicle cleaning and inspection.

1974 — Omar Market, Omar, Ohio. Summer employment as cashier and bagger.

Interests: Captain of the swimming team at Omar High School and a member of the varsity football and baseball teams. Also editor of the yearbook. Other interests include classical music, woodcraft, tennis, and softball.

References: Supplied on request.

Figure 13.3 A sample résumé

5. Observers and interviewers pool their combined judgments to develop a joint report (frequently with recommendations for development) on each individual being assessed.

6. Based on the managerial level of each participant, the staff members conduct follow-up developmental discussions with the person and frequently offer specific plans for the individual's development.

A series of studies suggest that assessment centers are generally more accurate than other selection processes in identifying and predicting managerial potential. They can also have a positive impact on the individual. For example, after a comprehensive developmental discussion, one young manager who was being assessed by General Electric remarked: "I had been thinking of leaving the company. In fact, I have an excellent job offer right now. But, I think I will stay with GE because the company shows so much interest in me as an individual".

Appraisal— Evaluating the Manager's Performance

Performance appraisal is a formal, written process for periodically evaluating managers' performance. Organizations in business, industry, and government must periodically appraise the performance of managerial and other workers in order to satisfy a variety of organizational goals.[10] Among the objectives of performance appraisal are:

1. *Work improvement*. A subordinate may need to obtain information about the improvement of personal performance.
2. *Salary administration*. The manager may need to review carefully the performance of subordinates in order to determine appropriate salary action.
3. *Information storage for administrative action*. Most organizations need data about employees to be used in future administrative actions such as promotion, demotion, or transfer.
4. *Isolation of training needs*. Clear, current information about the strengths and weakness of the organization's members is needed if the organization is to create appropriate and timely development and training programs.
5. *Selection of new employees*. Prediction of future performance is based largely on the understanding of past performance. Thus employers use appraisals of current employees to validate tests that will be applied to new employees.

These objectives of performance appraisal have been affected by recent federal legislation. Equal Employment Opportunity Commission actions and court decisions have shown organizations that they must have objective and accurate records of employee performance if they are to defend themselves against possible charges of discrimination in promotions, salary increases, and discharges. Legally, performance appraisal must be shown to be job related. Thus the appraisal rating method must be developed from comprehensive and thorough job analysis, and the ratings themselves must be free of racial, sexual, or other bias and must be collected and scored under standardized conditions.[11]

Most organizations have a formalized appraisal program that applies at least to lower and middle level management. The most common forms of programs are rating scales and essay evaluations (or a combination of the two).[12] Achievement of performance goals is a major factor in performance appraisals, most of which are conducted yearly or semi-yearly. Of the many kinds of formal appraisal approaches in use, only three will be described here: the graphic rating scale, behaviorally anchored rating scales, and management by objectives (MBO). The most frequently used approach is the *graphic rating scale*. With this method, the person doing the rating places checkmarks on the appraisal form that indicate performance in each of a number of different areas. The areas include quality of work, quantity of work, job knowledge, cooperation, and dependability. The degrees of merit being checked may run from "consistently low" to "outstanding" or from "far below standard" to "well above standard." Figures 13.4 and 13.5 show two types of rating forms. Figure 13.4 is from a large organization, and it rates managerial and administrative personnel. Figure 13.5 is a form used by the U.S. Air Force to rate officer effectiveness.

A very serious problem with graphic rating scales is that terms like *below standard* and *above standard* can mean different things to different people. The accuracy of such scales can be improved by carefully training managers and others who are doing the rating.

Attempts to improve the traditional graphic rating scale have included the development of *behaviorally anchored rating scales*, which are more job related, reduce the amount of judgment required by the rater, and are less open to the charge of discrimination.[13] A behaviorally anchored rating scale for a supermarket checker is shown in Figure 13.6.

There are basically five steps used in the development of such scales:

1. Managers (or others who know the job) describe specific incidents or examples of ineffective and effective behavior on the job.
2. Those who are developing the scales group the examples into five to ten performance categories.
3. A second group of managers (or others who know the job) sort the examples a second time into the performance categories. Examples about which people disagree are dropped.
4. The second group are then asked to rate, on a seven to nine point scale, how effective the examples are in terms of performance. Only items on which there is high agreement are kept.
5. Finally, the rating instrument is developed. Specific incidents are placed on the scale as a result of their rating in Step 4. In the supermarket study, seven dimensions were identified: conscientiousness, knowledge and judgment, skill in human relations, skill in operation of the cash register, skill in bagging, organizational ability in the checkstand work, and skill in monetary transactions.

Behaviorally anchored rating scales have not been used extensively for appraising managers. However, as more organizations find it necessary to prove the accuracy and validity of performance appraisal in terms of civil rights, the use of this approach is likely to increase.

A third type of formal appraisal is *management by objectives (MBO)*, which was described in detail in Chapter 7. An effective MBO program consists of periodic manager-subordinate meetings designed to accomplish organizational goals by mutual planning of the work, a review process, and mutual solving of problems that arise in the course of getting the job done.

The Appraisal Interview

The *appraisal interview* should be an open discussion between the manager and the subordinate regarding strengths, weaknesses, and areas for improvement. Although a majority of companies using performance appraisals report that managers conduct such interviews, these dis-

BOSTON COLLEGE
EMPLOYEE APPRAISAL AND DEVELOPMENT PLANNING

EMPLOYEE'S NAME _____
last   first   m.i.

POSITION _____ DEPARTMENT _____ DATE ENTERED POSITION _____

1. MAJOR STRENGTHS — What have been the employee's assets and chief abilities in present job? (Cite specific job accomplishments)

_____
_____
_____
_____
_____

2. AREAS NEEDING IMPROVEMENT — Where did employee exhibit need for improvement? In what specific areas is improvement needed? (Cite specific assignments which could have been more effectively performed, for example.)

_____
_____
_____
_____
_____
_____
_____

3. PERFORMANCE CHANGES — What specific performance changes have you observed over the past year? Include both positive and non-positive changes.

_____
_____
_____
_____

4. DEVELOPMENT PLANNING — What specific steps are being taken or planned to effect employee's improvement on present job and preparation for further responsibilities? What would be needed to enhance promotability?

_____
_____
_____
_____
_____
_____

5. GENERAL APPRAISAL FACTOR RATINGS — Check appropriate box for applicable factors. Empty boxes may be used to include other factors unique to position or situation (e.g. ability to meet deadlines, counseling skills, communication skills, etc.)

	UNSATIS-FACTORY	NEEDS IMPROVE-MENT	GOOD	COMMEND-ABLE	DISTIN-GUISHED
QUANTITY — Capacity for meeting workload demands of responsibilities.					
QUALITY — Accurate, complete work free of frequent or costly error, professionalism, level of work standards.					
INITIATIVE — Ability to be a self-starter, supervise self, take action on own.					
JUDGMENT — Analytical ability, common sense, ability to make sound decisions/recommendations, determine priorities and foresee ramifications.					
CREATIVENESS — Ability to come up with original thinking, new ideas, innovative suggestions.					
ATTITUDE — Degree of conscientiousness, willingness, dependability and general approach to position.					
INTERPERSONAL SKILLS — Ability to interrelate harmoniously with peers, subordinates, superiors, students, or public.					
PLANNING & ORGANIZATION — Ability to observe, analyze, plan work, organize & delegate to subordinates, utilization of time.					
LEADERSHIP — Ability to win confidence and cooperation of, and train and develop subordinates.					
CRITICAL EFFECTIVENESS — Ability/willingness to confront, control, resolve any disciplinary/remedial situations.					
OVERALL RATING —					

APPRAISED BY _____ _____ DISCUSSED WITH EMPLOYEE _____ _____
                    Supervisor   Date   Date

6. EMPLOYEE'S COMMENTS — What are your views of your performance? To what degree do you concur or not concur with this appraisal? How do you feel your supervisor or others can assist you in developing your present and/or future performance?

_____
_____
_____
_____
_____
_____
_____

EMPLOYEE'S SIGNATURE _____ DATE _____

4/78 Office of Personnel Relations

Figure 13.4 Ratings of managerial and administrative personnel

I. RATEE IDENTIFICATION DATA *(Read AFR 36–10 carefully before filling in any item)*

1. NAME *(Last, First, Middle Initial)*	3. SSN *(Include suffix)*		8. PERIOD OF REPORT FROM: THRU:
2. ORGANIZATION, COMMAND, LOCATION, PAS CODE	4. PAFSC	5. DAFSC	
	6. ACTIVE DUTY GRADE		9. DAYS OF SUPERVISION
	7. PERMANENT GRADE		10. REASON FOR REPORT

II. JOB DESCRIPTION 1. DUTY TITLE:

2. KEY DUTIES, TASKS, AND RESPONSIBILITIES:

III. PERFORMANCE FACTORS

[1] *Specific example of performance required*

	NOT OBSERVED OR NOT RELEVANT	FAR [1] BELOW STANDARD	BELOW [1] STANDARD	MEETS STANDARD	ABOVE [1] STANDARD	WELL [1] ABOVE STANDARD
1. JOB KNOWLEDGE *(Depth, currency, breadth)*	O	☐	☐	☐	☐	☐
2. JUDGMENT AND DECISIONS *(Consistent, accurate, effective)*	O	☐	☐	☐	☐	☐
3. PLAN AND ORGANIZE WORK *(Timely, creative)*	O	☐	☐	☐	☐	☐
4. MANAGEMENT OF RESOURCES *(Manpower and material)*	O	☐	☐	☐	☐	☐
5. LEADERSHIP *(Initiative, accept responsibility)*	O	☐	☐	☐	☐	☐
6. ADAPTABILITY TO STRESS *(Stable, flexible, dependable)*	O	☐	☐	☐	☐	☐
7. ORAL COMMUNICATION *(Clear, concise, confident)*	O	☐	☐	☐	☐	☐
8. WRITTEN COMMUNICATION *(Clear, concise, organized)*	O	☐	☐	☐	☐	☐
9. PROFESSIONAL QUALITIES *(Attitude, dress, cooperation, bearing)*	O	☐	☐	☐	☐	☐
10. HUMAN RELATIONS *(Equal opportunity participation, sensitivity)*		☐	☐	☐	☐	☐

AF FORM AUG 78 707 PREVIOUS EDITION IS OBSOLETE. **OFFICER EFFECTIVENESS REPORT**

IV. ASSIGNMENT RECOMMENDATION: 1. STRONGEST QUALIFICATION:

2. SUGGESTED JOB *(Include AFSC)*:

3. ORGANIZATION LEVEL: 4. TIMING:

V. EVALUATION OF POTENTIAL

~~TOP BLOCK CONTROLLED~~

~~*Evaluate the ratee's capability, relative to that of officers in the same grade in the group being evaluated, for expanded/more diverse responsibility.*~~ *Indicate your rating by placing an "X" in the designated portion of the appropriate block.*

RATER | ADDN RATER | ~~REVR~~ INDSR — RATER | ADDN RATER | ~~REVR~~ INDSR — RATER | ADDN RATER | ~~REVR~~ INDSR — RATER | ADDN RATER | ~~REVR~~ INDSR

Lowest ← → *Highest*

IF REPORT IS ABBREVIATED, "X" APPROPRIATE BLOCK
☐ REPORT CLOSES OUTSIDE CYCLE ☐ RATEE RETIRES/SEPARATES WITHIN 4 MONTHS
☐ RATEE SELECTED FOR PROMOTION ☐ LATE TO REVIEWER ☐ OTHER *(Rater explain)*

VI. RATER COMMENTS

NAME, GRADE, BRANCH OF SVC, ORGN, LOCATION	DUTY TITLE	DATE
	SSN *(Include suffix)*	SIGNATURE

VII. ADDITIONAL RATER COMMENTS ☐ CONCUR ☐ NONCONCUR

NAME, GRADE, BRANCH OF SVC, ORGN, LOCATION	DUTY TITLE	DATE
	SSN *(Include suffix)*	SIGNATURE

VIII. ~~REVIEWER COMMENTS~~ INDORSER COMMENTS ☐ CONCUR ☐ NONCONCUR

REVIEW GROUP SIZE | NO. OF | (1S) | (2S) | (3S) | (4S) | (5S) | (6S)

NAME, GRADE, BRANCH OF SVC, ORGN, LOCATION	DUTY TITLE	DATE
	SSN *(Include suffix)*	SIGNATURE

Figure 13.5 Officer effectiveness report

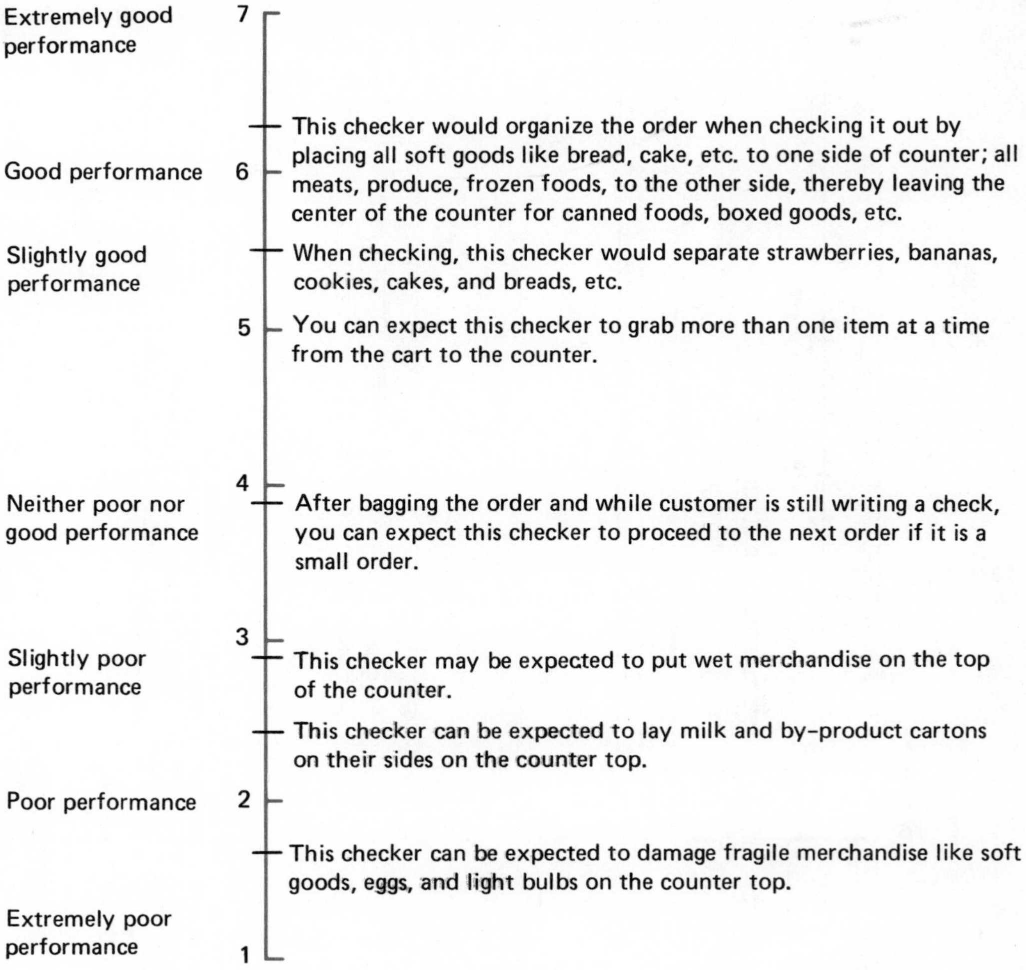

Extremely good performance	7	
Good performance	6	This checker would organize the order when checking it out by placing all soft goods like bread, cake, etc. to one side of counter; all meats, produce, frozen foods, to the other side, thereby leaving the center of the counter for canned foods, boxed goods, etc.
Slightly good performance		When checking, this checker would separate strawberries, bananas, cookies, cakes, and breads, etc.
	5	You can expect this checker to grab more than one item at a time from the cart to the counter.
	4	
Neither poor nor good performance		After bagging the order and while customer is still writing a check, you can expect this checker to proceed to the next order if it is a small order.
	3	
Slightly poor performance		This checker may be expected to put wet merchandise on the top of the counter.
		This checker can be expected to lay milk and by–product cartons on their sides on the counter top.
Poor performance	2	
		This checker can be expected to damage fragile merchandise like soft goods, eggs, and light bulbs on the counter top.
Extremely poor performance	1	

Figure 13.6 A behaviorally anchored rating scale for a supermarket checker

From L. Fogli, C. Hulin, and M. Blood, "Development of First-Level Behavioral Job Criteria," *Journal of Applied Psychology* 55 (February 1971): 7. Copyright 1971 by the American Psychological Association. Reprinted by permission.

cussions have not been very fruitful. Indeed, some studies have found that formalized performance appraisals in general do more harm than good.[14] For example, subordinates' defensiveness to criticism of their performance was shown to increase in direct proportion to the number of criticisms made.[15] Part of the problem is that performance appraisal programs developed for one purpose have been used for others. One organization instituted a "pay for performance" program with salary levels determined strictly by ratings. A young engineering graduate did an outstanding job during his first six months with the company, and at his six-month review, his manager gave him a substantial salary increase—15 percent. During the ensuing discussion, however, the young engineer found that he had received a "D" (below average) rating. Although he was doing excellent work, his manager explained, he could not be given an "A" rating, because this would force the manager to increase his pay by 50 percent—and no one in the company had ever gotten that large a raise. Although the engineer was pleased with the 15 percent increase, he soon quit, because he did not want to have a below average performance rating on his record.

Obviously, organizations need to decide carefully about the objectives of their performance appraisals. Different objectives require different methods. For example, perhaps MBO should focus on improving work performance, and graphic rating scales or other approaches should focus on promotions, salary increases, and other personnel actions. Also the appraisal interview for salary action should be separated from the appraisal interview for improving work performance. For example, if the personnel department reviews the forms or data generated by MBO to determine employees' salary levels, the data lose their usefulness for meaningful dialogue between the manager and subordinates because the objective is changed.

Accurate performance appraisals are a major tool in helping subordinates improve job performance. They also are a key to accurate and adequate management compensation (discussed later in the chapter).

Management Development

One of the reasons for using replacement charts, assessment centers, appraisal programs, and similar processes is that they help identify where job performance can be improved. In a quickly changing world, managers need continual updates on information, techniques, and skills.[16] Development should thus take place continually and throughout the entire organization.

In a sense, all development is self-development; yet the organization has a powerful effect on certain kinds of development. For example, a recent college graduate's first year in a management job can affect the person's future promotions, job success, and salary levels.[17] The higher the organization's expectations of the individual on the first job, the more likely the person is to be successful later. That the first job is important is demonstrated by an organization that had consistently high turnover among recent college graduates in their first year with the company. The organization restructured the beginning jobs to make them more challenging and found that turnover dropped to almost zero.

Management development is training or other processes to improve managers' knowledge and skills, to improve managers' performance in present jobs, and/or to prepare managers for promotion. As the term is used here, *development* can refer to the individual manager and to groups of managers.

There are a number of approaches to management development. The primary one, self-development, is explained in detail in Chapter 24. Other approaches come from the organization. They include development on the job through counseling and coaching programs and development off the job through courses, conferences, and executive seminars. As Table 13.1 indicates, management development should be tailored to the level of the position as well as to the needs and career stage of the individual manager. For example, many organizations have entry level development programs, middle management development programs, and executive development programs.

First-Line Supervisory Training

College graduates should be encouraged early in their career to develop a specialty that applies the concepts and knowledge they obtained in school Specialty provides an entrance into first-line supervisory positions. However, overspecialization can trap the individual, who may

Table 13.1 Developmental needs in early, middle, and late career

Stage	Task needs
Early career	1. Develop action skills. 2. Develop a specialty. 3. Develop creativity, innovation. 4. Rotate into new area after two–five years.
Middle career	1. Develop skills in training and coaching others (younger employees). 2. Train for updating and intergrating skills. 3. Develop broader view of work and organization. 4. Rotate into new job requiring new skills.
Late career	1. Shift from power role to consulting role; offer guidance and wisdom. 2. Begin to establish self in activities outside the organization (start on part-time basis).

Adapted and modified by permission from D. Hall, *Careers in Organizations* (Pacific Palisades, Calif.: Goodyear Publishing, 1976), p. 90.

become indispensable in a particular area. Thus, supervisors should acquire a new specialty after a few years.

When the college graduate is assigned to a first-line supervisory position, the person's practice of management begins. The individual at this career stage needs to develop action skills—skills in developing and accomplishing approved plans and programs within an established budget and in obtaining and using help from others, including staff and service groups. In addition, the individual needs information about the organization in general, the department, and the particular unit; knowledge of how to recruit, train, and motivate subordinates; and an understanding of the labor contract if there is a union and generally of how to cooperate with other departments and units.

Much of the training at this level comes directly from the immediate supervisor through example and explanation, although large organizations often have training programs for new supervisors in such areas as company policies, communications, motivation, and labor law (as it applies to the organization). The supervisor should encourage the development of creativity and innovation and should provide an atmosphere of support and freedom (including the freedom to learn from mistakes and the freedom to develop self-confidence—the feeling that one's successes are due to one's abilities). The supervisor should also help the inexperienced manager learn how to communicate with, instruct, and motivate subordinates and how to cooperate and work with peers. Thus, although each individual is responsible for personal development, upper level managers can have a great influence on the recent college graduate.

Middle Management Development

Most of those entering middle management ranks are supervisors who have had successful on-the-job experience—who have achieved specific goals in such major areas as budgeting, production, and expense control. Middle managers need to know a great deal about the practical side of management, but they move away from close contact with the day-to-day functions of workers. Managers at this level must (1) develop skills in training and coaching others, particularly young employees; (2) update and integrate their own skills; (3) develop a broader view of work and organization; and (4) know general management theory and understand the overall functions of managers.

The knowledge required at this level involves a broad background in such areas as finance, behavioral sciences, and planning for and coordinating different units. This kind of knowledge is hard to learn on the job; it can often be taught best through in-house seminars and courses, where managers can learn from give-and-take with other managers in structured situations. Another method is for managers to attend university, association, or consultant managed courses. Outside "live-in" programs have the most prestige and are the most attractive. Still another method is planned job rotation, which gives managers experience in different areas of the organization and helps them avoid overspecialization.

Executive Development

At the executive level are usually plant, functional, or division managers who are in line for management positions such as general manager, executive vice-president, or president. These people need to have the knowledge, skills, and ability to move from managing a relatively specialized area (such as marketing, production, controlling, or engineering) into managing a larger and broader area of the organization. Thus they require training and development in the management of functions with which they are not familiar. These include the strategic direction of the organization and the handling of certain functions outside the organization, such as work with trade associations, relationships with the financial community and with other countries, and lobbying.

As with middle managers, special courses and seminars and on-the-job training can be helpful to executives. Managing special task forces, sitting in on contract negotiations, and handling special assignments are among the tasks that can be used in training people at this level.

At all levels in the organization, the immediate supervisor must make certain that subordinate managers are being developed. In the press of other business, this development may not occur unless performance appraisal and reward systems (discussed in the next section) specifically ensure that managers perceive and accept their responsibility for development.

Management Compensation

Managers can receive many forms of **compensation**—direct or indirect, immediate or deferred rewards, some of which have a monetary value. One type of compensation, "psychological income," includes achievement, power, prestige, challenge, and respect. Another type of compensation is money. Most managers make enough money to satisfy their basic physiological and security needs. But money can also satisfy recognition, achievement, and growth needs. A salary increase not only helps pay the bills but also lets the manager know that good job performance is recognized and appreciated.

There are three basic and related decisions to be made about any form of wage payment:

1. What is the job worth in comparison to other jobs in the organization?
2. What is the job worth in comparison to other jobs in the community (or other areas)?
3. What is the individual worth on the particular job (what should the individual manager be paid and how)?[18]

What Is the Job Worth in Comparison to Other Internal Jobs?

All organizations have some form of job evaluation. If a manager decides that an engineer's job is worth more than a buyer's job, that is job evaluation. Of course, most organizations have a far more systematic and organized job evaluation process, generally in the following form. First, job descriptions are prepared and approved for each job in the organization. Then these descriptions are systematically compared to other jobs in terms of their importance to the organization. Finally, jobs of approximately equal importance and difficulty are placed in particular grades or levels. For example, in the federal government all jobs under civil service have been described, evaluated, and placed in grades that run from GS-1, the lowest, to GS-15, the highest. (Actually, GS ratings go all the way to 18, but beyond 15 they are presidential appointments.) Frequently, organizations have different job evaluation plans for managerial, clerical, and blue-collar workers.

What Is the Job Worth in Comparison to External Jobs?

Each job grade usually has a minimum (or starting) salary and a maximum salary. These minimums and maximums are frequently determined by salary surveys and reviews of what other organizations are doing. For hourly and clerical workers, such comparisons are often done on a community or local basis; for managers and executives, they are often done on a national or international basis. Pay scales at the World Bank, for example, are set after a survey of comparable jobs in a number of developed countries.

In the federal government, comparisons are done at a national level, since the government is in competition with employers across the country. Civil Service Grade GS-13 is the beginning of the professional, middle-to-high-level management ladder. At this grade are positions such as agricultural economist, hospital administrator, and supervisory auditor. In 1949 the beginning salary for that level was $7,600 per year. In 1969, after the first comparison salary survey, the beginning salary for the level was $16,760. In October 1977, the beginning salary was increased to $26,022. The U.S. Bureau of Labor Statistics conducts the national surveys each March, and the GS levels are adjusted on the basis of the surveys.

What Is the Individual Worth on the Particular Job?

As noted earlier, a civil service professional or manager whose job is rated GS-13 can be paid anywhere from $26,022 to $33,825. Where an individual is placed in that range is a function of the person's experience and ability. Thus performance appraisal is one method of determining the actual salary a manager is paid. In fact, most organizations try to link pay to performance. Many organizations also have a number of other ways of paying managers (in addition to straight salary). These include stock options, bonuses, consulting, and other fringe benefits.

Stock Options

Managers are often given a chance (option) to buy stock (shares in the company) at a given price, usually lower than the market value. If the shares are going up in price, a manager can buy them at the lower price, hold them for a period of time, sell them at a profit, and pay a relatively low income (capital gains) tax on the profit.

Bonuses

Bonuses are usually granted for outstanding performance. For example, the chairman of the board of Rapid-American, a retailing company, earned $916,000 in 1975. Of that amount, $555,000 was for selling a subsidiary company to another organization. Bonuses can be in the form of cash or company shares. They can be given in the current year, distributed over a period of years, or deferred until after retirement, when the executive is earning less money and will pay less tax on the income received.

Expense Accounts

In theory, expense accounts are not compensation, since managers often must use them for entertaining customers or others.

Consulting

Some organizations retain retired executives as consultants. This is a form of deferred wage payment that enables the executive to receive pay at a time when total income (and therefore the tax rate) is lower.

Additional Fringe Benefits

Pensions, life insurance, health insurance, executive dining rooms, free automobiles—all are examples of fringe benefits that add to the total compensation package. A number of organizations even have barbershops where managers can get haircuts either free or at a low price. In many executive dining rooms, meals cost less than in comparable restaurants.

Thus there are a number of ways managers can be paid in addition to straight salary. In many instances, the additional compensation is not only a performance measure but also is a way of reducing the income tax paid by managers. Top executives are very well paid, which explains why their companies try to help them minimize their taxes. (Table 13.2 shows the twenty highest paid U.S. executives in 1977.)

Table 13.2   The 20 highest paid U.S. executives in 1977

		Salary & bonus	Gains from options exercised	Gains from SARs exercised†	Total compensation*	Corporate Sales	Profits
				Thousands of dollars		Millions of dollars	
1. **Archie R. McCardell**, pres.	Int'l Harvester (Sept.-Dec.)	$1,077	—	—	$1,077	$ 5,975	$ 204
pres.	Xerox (Jan.-Aug.)	419	—	—	419	5,077	407
		1,496	—	—	1,496		
2. **Elton H. Rule**, pres.	American Broadcasting	650	$584	—	1,234	1,617	110
3. **Leonard H. Goldenson**, chmn.	American Broadcasting	800	313	—	1,113	1,617	110
4. **James E. Lee**, pres.	Gulf Oil	414	—	$685	1,099	18,040	752
5. **Henry Ford II**, chmn.	Ford Motor	992	—	—	992	37,841	1673
6. **Steven J. Ross**, chmn.	Warner Communications	990	—	—	990	1,144	71
7. **Harold S. Geneen**, chmn.	IT&T	986	—	—	986	13,194	563
8. **Lee A. Iacocca**, pres.	Ford Motor	978	—	—	978	37,841	1673
9. **Thomas A. Murphy**, chmn.	General Motors	975	—	—	975	54,961	3338
10. **Clifton C. Garvin Jr.**, chmn.	Exxon	696	—	270	966	54,851	2410
11. **Willard F. Rockwell Jr.**, chmn.	Rockwell International	636	314	—	950	5,859	144
12. **J. Edward Lundy**, exec. v-p.	Ford Motor	945	—	—	945	37,841	1673
13. **Elliott M. Estes**, pres.	General Motors	910	—	—	910	54,961	3338
14. **Robert O. Anderson**, chmn.	Atlantic Richfield	627	—	265	892	11,413	702
15. **William P. Tavoulareas**, pres.	Mobil Oil	621	—	269	890	35,700	1003
16. **Richard L. Terrell**, vice-chmn.	General Motors	885	—	—	885	54,961	3338
17. **David J. Mahoney**, chmn. & pres.	Norton Simon	800	—	—	800	1,808	102
18. **Michel C. Bergerac**, chmn. & pres.	Revlon	794	—	—	794	1,143	98
19. **Wilton E. Scott**, chmn.	Tenneco	794	—	—	794	7,440	427
20. **William F. Laporte**, chmn.	American Home Products	770	—	—	770	2,868	306

*May exclude executives whose gains from options exercised are reported for 5-year period only; may represent period other than calendar year

†SARs=stock appreciation rights   Data: Touche Ross, BW

Promotion, Transfer, and Termination

Managers do not necessarily stay in the same jobs forever; among the possibilities for change are transfers, promotions, and terminations. A **transfer** is a move to another job, usually without an increase in either status or pay. As Table 13.1 suggests, job transfer or rotation is a good way of avoiding overspecialization. Transfers also can occur when the individual and the job are not properly matched; at times, an individual may perform poorly in one job but well in another.

A **promotion** is a move to another job, usually higher in the organization and usually with an increase in status and pay. Promotion is a reward for accomplishment. It brings both higher pay and some other tangible form of recognition, such as greater challenge, prestige, and opportunities for further recognition and responsibility.

However, one problem with promotions is that, while there are usually many first-line supervisors, there is only one president. It is thus impossible for everybody to make it to the top. The Horatio Alger tradition of striving for the top has caused a great deal of psychological damage in this country, particularly among people who want to move up but are incapable of handling high level jobs. Fortunately, not everyone wants to be at the top. For example, a university school of management with almost a hundred faculty members had only two apply for the position of dean. Furthermore, one of the outside candidates for the position was the vice-president of a large industrial organization who decided that he wanted to get out of the rat race of being a top executive.

Termination is action by the organization to remove an individual from the organization. One form of termination is, of course, retirement. Most large organizations and many small ones have compulsory retirement programs. (Many also have pension programs to supplement retirees' social security income and other benefits.) The retirement age of sixty-five was established many years ago in Germany, at a time when that was the average life expectancy of a man. Now that the average life expectancy is much longer, compulsory retirement programs are being thoroughly reviewed at both federal and state levels. In fact, as mentioned earlier, recent federal legislation has raised the mandatory retirement age to seventy in most organizations. (Exceptions to the new legislation include executives with pensions of $27,000 or more; tenured faculty in institutions of higher learning—until January 1, 1982; employees of the U.S. government; and workers covered by collective bargaining agreements in effect prior to 1977—until the contract expires or until January 1, 1980.) This means that many organizations must plan another way of handling their human resources.

Some terminations come about because the work force has in general become more mobile.[19] Particularly in high technology organizations, such as electronics and aerospace industries, managers can move easily from one firm to another. In the 1960s, it was not unusual for such firms to get a contract, hire professional managers and other workers, and then lay off (terminate) workers when the contract came to an end. This process is still occurring but to a lesser degree. At times, however, an organization may simply have more managers and other employees than either work or sales can justify.

The unhappiest form of termination is dismissal or firing. There are many reasons for this action: corporate mergers, relocation of facilities, across-the-board cutbacks, poor job performance, mismatching of the job and the individual's capabilities, and so on. Sometimes, firing can be avoided by transferring the manager to another job. At other times, special development programs may be possible.

Although few managers like to fire or be fired, termination is some times a necessity. Occasionally, being fired from a job will jolt an individual into reappraising personal strengths, weaknesses, and future potential. Many organizations help those who are terminated find new jobs through the use of career placement counselors. In one follow-up of 250 managers who had been fired, it was found that 88 percent had been placed in higher-paying jobs than those they were fired from. Clearly, such results are to be found among people who have good talents and skills and who are willing to work hard at finding good jobs.[20]

Implications for the Manager

Staffing is an important managerial function, since organizations cannot exist without people. There are a number of laws, rules, and regulations affecting the selection, promotion, transfer, training, and retention of employees at all levels; and managers must be aware of them if they are to perform the staffing function well.

The effective manager makes certain that planning for human resources is closely tied to the overall long- and short-range plans of the organization or unit. In what direction is the organization going? What changes are anticipated for the future? Only when these and other questions are answered can the manager effectively plan for human resource needs. The planning can be formal or informal, but it must be systematic and ongoing.

Recruitment and selection are often done through processes that are often insufficient and sometimes even inaccurate. For example, research indicates that the results of most selection processes are not highly correlated with later job success. Thus the effective manager should not rely solely on one form of selection. Carefully developed job requirements, multiple interviews, and well-conducted reference checks are some of the ways in which the selection process can be improved. In addition, the manager must be aware of new or changed laws and regulations that affect both the recruitment and selection processes. Given all the areas that must be considered, the manager may want to use the services of an expert to improve the organization's recruitment and selection procedures.

Many organizations conduct performance appraisal in a relatively unsystematic fashion; for example, many managers report that they receive little or no feedback about their performance. The effective manager sees careful performance appraisal as an essential part of the job and uses MBO or similar approaches to coach and counsel subordinates about improving job performance. The manager then uses carefully developed rating scales for other purposes, such as salary decisions, which must be approved by others.

In one sense, all development is self-development. Yet, the manager has the responsibility for helping subordinates improve their present job knowledge and skills and prepare for possible promotions. This help can be given in the following ways: (1) by coaching and counseling, (2) by providing an example for subordinates, (3) by encouraging subordinates to attend internal or external courses, (4) by providing opportunities for job rotation, and (5) by using any other approaches that will give subordinates the opportunity to grow and develop

Compensation is an important aspect of staffing. The effective manager must make certain that the organization's plan for evaluating jobs is adequate and that the jobs themselves have salary ranges that are in line with both internal and external ranges for similar jobs. Furthermore, the manager must reward good performers and explain to others how they can improve. Studies and interviews have shown that one of the most difficult aspects of managerial jobs is explaining to subordinates the areas in which they are not performing well. Ineffective managers tend to ignore this important task.

Promotions are important, but not everyone can make it to the top. The manager must carefully review subordinates, help those who are promotable, and openly and candidly discuss with others what their opportunities are. When terminations are necessary, the manager must take the appropriate action in a humane, helpful, and caring way. Research has shown that subordinates who are fired often can be helped to find another job that better fits their qualifications.

Finally, the manager needs to review and update the entire staffing process on an ongoing basis to make certain that the human resources of the organization are used wisely.

Review

1. At the beginning of the chapter, you were asked if you had ever applied for a job. After reading this chapter, what can you say about the recruitment and selection process used?
2. How are recruitment, selection, and performance appraisals of college students similar to what the chapter has described for employees? How are they different?
3. Visit an organization's personnel office. What steps are followed in staffing?
4. Assume that you are asked to improve the recruitment and selection process of a firm. What will you want to know about the current process? What questions will you ask?
5. What are some of the effects of laws and regulations on staffing? What implications (beyond those described in the chapter) do they have for the manager?
6. Why might a manager neglect some aspects of the staffing process? Which steps are most likely to be neglected? Explain.
7. Based on your reading so far, describe some new ways to change the development process for first level, middle level, and upper level management.
8. How important is a person's first job? What effect does the supervisor have on a person's future success?

The Promotion

Maureen Thomas was a supervisor for the National Municipal Bank, one of the largest in the country. She began working for the bank as an executive secretary after receiving her bachelor's degree from the University of California. The job gave her a good insight into the bank's activities. After three years, she asked that she be considered for the next opening in management. A few months later, she was given a supervisory job in operations, where she worked with five other supervisors—all male. The six supervisors formed a cohesive group, enjoyed their work, and liked the department head, James Bedford.

After three more years, Bedford became an officer of the bank. A great deal of speculation arose as to who would succeed him as the department head. Five of the six supervisors, including Thomas, were capable of handling the job, and all five wanted it. Rumor had it that either Jim Johnson or Jack Burton would get the job; both men were highly regarded by both supervisors and employees.

However, on a Monday morning, Thomas was called into the office of the bank's executive vice-president. Much to her surprise, the vice-president told her that she would be promoted to department head as Bedford's replacement. He also said that she had been found to be as capable as any of the other supervisors and that her work had been praised by top management. Then he added that the bank had very few women in management and wanted to start promoting women as a matter of policy.

Thomas was told that as soon as her promotion was announced, she should call a meeting of the other supervisors and communicate clearly that (1) she was the boss, (2) her sex was not a factor in the promotion, and (3) she would be as objective as anyone else in the new job. The vice-president closed the meeting by explaining that success in the department head job could be the beginning of a major career with the bank and that top management and others would be closely watching her over the next few months.

1. Was Maureen Thomas promoted because she was the most qualified supervisor? Explain.
2. What might be the reactions of the other supervisors?
3. What should Thomas say and do at her first meeting with the supervisors?

Footnotes

1. C. Falk and U. Lehner, "The Bakke Ruling," *Wall Street Journal*, June 29, 1978, p. 1; and "High Court Affirms Rights of Minorities in Industry," *Christian Science Monitor*, July 5, 1978, p. 10.
2. B. Schneider, *Staffing Organizations* (Pacific Palisades, Calif.: Goodyear Publishing, 1976), p. 3.
3. G. Gery, "Hiring Minorities and Women: The Selection Process," *Personnel Journal* 53 (December 1974): 906–909; J. Straka, "Guidelines on Affirmative Action Recruiting," *Personnel Administrator* April 1975): 36–39; and W. Hubbartt, "The State Employment Service: An Aid on Affirmative Action Recruiting," *Personnel Administrator* April 1977): 289–291.
4. "Goals That Look Like Quotas," *Time*, January 29, 1973, p. 77.
5. D. Reid, "Human Resource Planning: A Tool for People Development," *Personnel 54 (March*–April 1977): 41–50; R. Fried, "Organizational Charts from Computerized Personnel Data Systems," *Personnel Journal* 56 (June 1977): 284–288; L. Tracey, "The Control Process in Personnel Management," *Personnel Journal* 55 (September 1976): 446–450; A. T. Hollingsworth and P. Preston, "Corporate Planning: A Challenge for Personnel Executives," *Personnel Journal* 55 (August 1976): 386; and J. Gilbreath, "Sex Discrimination and Title VII of the Civil Rights Act," *Personnel Journal* 56 (January 1977): 23–26.
6. A. Janger, *Personnel Administration: Changing Scope and Organization* (New York: National Industrial Conference Board, 1966), p. 25.
7. N. Schmitt, "Social and Situational Determinants of Interview Decisions: Implications for the Employment Interview," *Personnel Psychology* 29 (Spring 1976): 79–101; O. Wright, Jr., "Summary of Research on the Selection Interview since 1964," *Personnel Psychology* 22 (Winter 1969): 391–413; F. Gaudet and T. Casey, "How Much Can You Tell from a Resume?" *Personnel* 36 (July–August 1959): 62–65; and E. Burack and R. Smith, *Personnel Management: A Human Resource Systems Approach* (St. Paul: West Publishing, 1977).
8. W. French, *The Personnel Management Process* (Boston: Houghton Mifflin, 1978), p. 234.
9. J. Huck and D. Bray, "Management Assessment Center Evaluations and Subsequent Job Performance of White and Black Females," *Personnel Psychology* 29 (Spring 1976): 13–30; J. Hinrichs and S. Haanpera, "Reliability of Measurement in Situational Exercises: An Assessment of the Assessment Center Method," *Personnel Psychology* 29 (Spring 1976): 31–40; D. Bray, R. Campbell, and D. Grant, *Formative Years in Business: A Long Term AT&T Study of Managerial Lives* (New York: Wiley, 1974).

10. A. Locher and K. Teel, "Performance Appraisal—A Survey of Current Practices," *Personnel Journal* 56 (May 1977): 245; D. McGregor, "An Uneasy Look at Performance Appraisal," *Harvard Business Review* 35 (May–June 1957): 89–94; E. Huse, "Performance Appraisal—A New Look," *Personnel Administration* 30 (March–April 1967): 13–18; W. Bigoness, "Effect of Applicant's Sex, Race, and Performance on Employer's Performance Ratings—Some Additional Findings," *Journal of Applied Psychology* 61 (January 1967): 80–84; and L. Crooks, ed., *An Investigation of Sources of Bias in the Prediction of Job Performance: A Six Year Study* (Princeton, N.J.: Educational Testing Service, 1972).

11. W. Holley, H. Field, and N. Barnett, "Analyzing Performance Appraisal Systems: An Empirical Study," *Personnel Journal* 55 (September 1976): 457; and W. Holley and H. Field, "Performance Appraisal and the Law," *Labor Law Journal* 26 (July 1975): 423–430.

12. "Management Performance Appraisal Programs," *Personnel Policies Forum,* Survey No. 104 (Washington, D.C.: Bureau of National Affairs, January 1974), pp. 1–3.

13. L. Figli, C. Hulin, and M. Blood, "Development of First-Level Behavioral Job Criteria," *Journal of Applied Psychology* 55 (February 1971): 3–8; P. Smith and L. Kendall, "Retranslation of Expectations: An Approach to the Construction of Unambiguous Anchors for Rating Scales," *Journal of Applied Psychology* 47 (April 1963): 149–155.

14. "Management Performance Appraisal Programs," Huse, "Performance Appraisal."

15. E. Huse and E. Kay, "Improving Employee Productivity through Work Planning," in *The Personnel Job in a Changing World,* ed. J. Blood (New York: American Management Association, 1964), pp. 301–312; Locher and Teel, "Performance Appraisal."

16. H. Hague, *Executive Self Development* (New York: Halstead Press, 1974); D. Moment and D. Fisher, *Autonomy in Organizational Life* (Cambridge, Mass.: Schenkman Press, 1975); H. Levinson, "A Psychologist Looks at Executive Development," *Harvard Business Review* 40 (September–October 1962): 69–75; V. Walter, "Self-Motivated Personal Career Planning: A Breakthrough in Human Resource Management," *Personnel Journal* 55 (March 1976): 112; R. Howe, "Building Teams for Increased Productivity," *Personnel Journal* 56 (January 1977): 16; C. Reeser, "Managerial Obsolescence—An Organizational Dilemma," *Personnel Journal* 56 (January 1977): 27.

17. D. Berlew and D. Hall, "The Socialization of Managers: Effects of Expectations on Performance," *Administrative Science Quarterly* 11 (June 1966): 207–223.

18. "Job Evaluation Policies and Procedures," *Personnel Policies Forum,* Survey No. 113 (Washington, D.C.: Bureau of National Affairs, June 1976); D. Belcher, *Compensation Administration* (Englewood Cliffs, N.J.: Prentice-Hall, 1974); W. French, *The Personnel Management Process* (Boston: Houghton Mifflin, 1978); and E. Lawler, Jr., *Pay and Organizational Effectiveness* (New York: McGraw-Hill, 1971).

19. E. Jennings, *The Mobile Manager* (New York: McGraw-Hill, 1967).

20. M. Rogers, "Outplacement Specialists, Professional Help for Disabled Careers," *Master in Business Administration* 11 (July–August 1977): 13–15.

Part V

Organizing

Chapter 14

Systems and the Manager

The Management Information System (MIS)

Why Study Systems?

What Is a System?
 Subsystems and Suprasystems
 Inputs, Operations, and Outputs
 Open and Closed Systems
 Boundary
 Feedback
Organizations as System
 Organizations as Self-Planned
 Organizations as Process

Organizational Subsystems
 The Managerial Subsystem
 The Operations Subsystem
 Boundary Spanning Subsystems
 The Maintenance Subsystem
 The Adaptive Subsystem

Implications for the Manager

Review

The Pajama Game

Learning Objectives

When you have finished reading and studying this chapter, you should be able to:

1. Identify and give examples of a system.
2. For each example, give specific illustrations of such parts of the system as inputs, operations, outputs, boundary, and feedback.
3. Identify the basic differences among organizations as social systems and physical systems.
4. Give examples of the differences between closed system and open system thinking.
5. Compare and contrast the ideas of structure and process as applied to social organizations.
6. List and give examples of each of the five organizational subsystems.
7. Define and be able to use the following concepts:

system	structure
subsystem	process
suprasystem	managerial subsystems
inputs	operations subsystem
operations	boundary-spanning subsystem
outputs	maintenance subsystem
feedback	adaptive subsystem
organization	

Thought Starters

1. List five different ways in which you use the word *system*. Does the word have the same meaning in each of the uses?
2. How do you interpret the phrase "the whole is greater than the sum of its parts"?
3. What do the house thermostat and General Motors have in common, if anything?

The Management Information System (MIS)

A large multinational organization decided to develop an integrated, computer-based management information system (MIS) and use it in one of its plants. The plant employed approximately 7,000 people and manufactured seventeen models of highly complex equipment used for a variety of civilian and defense purposes and marketed in fourteen countries besides the United States.

The organization manufactured or bought more than 25,000 different parts each year to enable it to fill its approximately 3,200 original equipment orders and 25,000 spare parts orders. On an annual basis, it manufactured or processed almost 8 million parts. From the time an order was received, each piece of equipment required approximately twelve to fifteen months to build and ship.

As proposed, the MIS was to put customer orders for original equipment or spare parts on the computer. Through a series of fifteen major computer programs, it was to provide assembly and manufacturing schedules, inventory control, prediction of personnel and machine requirements, and other information to control the flow of work through the factory. The computer was then to provide the purchasing department with requirements for materials, other supplies, and parts from outside vendors.

The MIS was intended to replace or integrate a multitude of manual or partly computerized systems already existing at the plant. Savings from the use of the new system were expected to be more than $1 million annually. Under the old approach, approximately 18,000 work hours (nine work years) were required to make the more than 3 million hand calculations needed to develop a comprehensive planning schedule for the plant. Schedule changes, which were frequent, required about forty working days to complete. The MIS was expected to reduce this time to about four or five days, to take fewer than 100 hand calculations, and increase accuracy.

After about three years of intense effort and several million dollars, the MIS program appeared to have faded away, although it was never officially abandoned. Before its demise, the director of the program resigned to take a better job elsewhere in the organization. While the MIS was being worked on, the members of its task force condemned middle managers for not being cooperative, and the middle managers in turn complained that the task force was not generating data suitable for their needs. In the meantime, each time the programs cut across departmental boundaries, managers in one department refused to trust inputs from other departments and insisted on controlling their own information (data base). Lower level production schedulers and clerks complained that the programs contained errors. The task force maintained that it was not given sufficiently current information to put on the computer. [1]

Why did the management information system fail in spite of three years of hard work and several million dollars? The main reason is that everyone saw the problem from a different perspective. In effect, people were using single cause, or linear, thinking rather than systems thinking (described in Chapter 3). In single cause terms, each problem requires a single solution, and the solution is evaluated primarily in terms of its impact on the problem. Once found, the solution stays put. In systems thinking, each problem is part of a situation. Although the problem requires a solution, the solution will have both intended and unintended consequences that should be identified. Once found, the solution does not stay put, since the situation is bound to change.

In the case of the MIS, the members of the task force concentrated on the design of the system. Although they were aware that the system existed in a larger environment and would have a broad impact on the whole organization, they tended to lose sight of that fact in the pressure to get the MIS designed and implemented. Middle and lower level managers, on the other hand, had their own sets of pressures, primarily in the area of producing goods on a tight schedule. Although, in theory, the MIS was to help them in the future, their focus was on the here and now. Further, as in many large organizations, the managers wanted to maintain control of their individual information bases. Thus the people or groups involved were all concentrating on their own operations and neglecting to focus on the needs and demands of the larger organization.

The manager's job can be seen as one of managing systems. The manager defines the organization or its unit as a system, establishes objectives for it, creates formal subsystems if necessary, and then integrates the subsystems. In doing this, the manager recognizes the contribution and interdependence of each part to the whole system and realizes that failure to meet objectives may be due to an improper design of the system rather than to faults attributable to the system's individual components. As one management scientist phrases it: "A system is a whole that cannot be taken apart without loss of its essential characteristics, and hence it must be studied as a whole. Now, instead of explaining a whole in terms of its parts, parts began to be explained in terms of the whole."[2]

The concept of system is briefly discussed in Chapter 1. This chapter will elaborate on the concept, considering organizations as total systems composed of a number of interdependent and interrelated subsystems.

Why Study Systems?

What are the similarities and differences among a group of high school teachers working on curriculum problems, a savings bank, a group of assembly workers in a factory, and the public works department of a municipality? How do individuals interact to form groups, how do groups interact to form an organization, and how does the organization interact with its environment? In order to answer such questions, a special language is needed—the language of "general systems theory."[3] Underlying this language is the assumption that certain general laws and concepts can unify a number of different fields and show the parallels among a number of different specialties. In addition, the word *system* itself stresses the interdependence of various subparts.

What Is a System?

The concept of *system* is not a new one; it can be traced back to Aristotle, who suggested that the whole is greater than the sum of its parts. Today, the word is widely used in many different ways. There are, for example, weapons systems, highway systems, communications systems, and transportation systems, as well as the digestive system, the nervous system, and the circulatory system. The concept of system is one with which we are all familiar—perhaps too familiar, since the meaning of the term has become blurred.

In this text, system is defined generally as a series of interrelated and interdependent parts in which the interaction or interplay of any of the parts affects the whole. (The definition will be changed somewhat in the discussion of organizations.) In this definition the interdependence and interactions of subsystems are at least as important as the total system. To illustrate this importance: If an automobile's battery is dead, the auto will not start, even if the rest of the parts are in good condition.

There are a number of different levels of systems, ranging from relatively simple to highly complex. Although the MIS program described at the beginning of the chapter was a complex system, it existed in an even more complex social system—the organization. The organization, in turn, existed within yet a larger system—society.

Subsystems and Suprasystems

Subsystems are parts of a system. A change in any subsystem has an effect on the total system. A suprasystem is a series of interrelated and interdependent systems.

The passenger transportation system of an airline is an example of a complex system with subsystems. The system is designed to carry passengers between airports. Its subsystems include the aircraft; ground support equipment to supply food, sanitation, and fueling; aircraft maintenance; and passenger and baggage loading. Other subsystems include the passengers and their luggage and the people who operate the system. Any subsystem that fails to operate properly has an immediate impact on the other subsystems.

The interaction among systems can be seen clearly when an airport is closed. Planes cannot land, passengers are stranded, crowds converge on the ticket counters, and equipment is in the wrong place. Imagine what would happen if, because of a closed major airport, a jumbo jet with hundreds of passengers were forced to make a landing at a tiny airfield used only for small, private airplanes. There would be only one restroom, one telephone, a small short-order lunch counter, and an occasional taxi. The interrelatedness of the airline systems would cause enormous stresses and strains at the airport with limited systems facilities.[4] The coal strike of 1977–1978 and the blizzards in the Midwest and East in 1978 are also vivid examples of the interrelatedness of subsystems, systems, and suprasystems. The coal strike forced the shutdown of innumerable plants across the country. For example, the shutdown of plants making automobile parts forced the shutdown of plants making automobiles and may even have affected auto dealerships.

The "total system" is, of course, a matter of definition. The University of California at Los Angeles can be considered a total system with its own subsystems. However, it can also be studied and analyzed as a subsystem of the State of California system of higher education. Thus the precise definition of a particular system is often arbitrary—dependent on the purpose in studying or analyzing it. That the total system can be a matter of definition is one of the advantages of the systems approach, which allows the researcher to choose the level at which to analyze an organization while still keeping in mind that the system is interacting on many levels with other systems.

Inputs, Operations, and Outputs

Most systems and subsystems have a series of inputs, operations, and outputs, as shown in Figure 14.1. Inputs are human or other resources—such as information, energy, and materials—coming into the system or subsystem. The inputs to a computer system are data, without which the system cannot operate. Input can come from the environment or from one or more subsystems within any system. For example, the input (order) from a customer to a waiter in a restaurant is also an input to the cook; dollar deposits are inputs to a bank. Organizations have highly complex inputs; among them are information, materials, people, and energy.

Operations are the processes of transforming inputs into other forms. The refrigerator takes in electrical energy and transforms it to physical energy to operate the compressor. The customer's oral order is transformed by the waiter to a written order. Manufacturing organizations have elaborate mechanisms for transforming incoming materials into finished goods.

Outputs are the results of what is transformed by the system. Thus inputs that have been transformed represent outputs ready to leave the system or subsystem. A bank receives inputs of dollars as deposits, transforms them through the operation of record keeping, and exports them as outputs to customers in the form of loans.

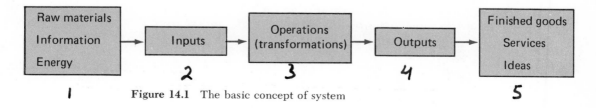

Figure 14.1   The basic concept of system

Open and Closed Systems

Systems can be viewed as relatively open or closed. A *closed system* receives no inputs from and distributes no outputs to the outside. There are very few closed systems in real life. Instead there are degrees of *openness*—the receiving of information, energy, or material from the environment. Completely closed systems are subject to *entropy*—running down. A mechanical alarm clock is a relatively closed system, since it needs to be wound periodically to keep it from running down.

Closed system thinking stems primarily from the physical sciences and is more applicable to mechanistic systems than to organizations. Traditional ideas about management were primarily closed system views, since they concentrated almost completely on the internal operation of the organization and adopted highly rationalistic approaches taken from physical science models. Each organization was thought of as sufficiently independent that its operations could be analyzed in terms of internal structure, tasks, and formal relationships—with little reference to the external environment. More modern thinking is that organizations are deeply imbedded in their environment and must be responsive to it. As shown in the MIS case at the beginning of the chapter, even the interdependence of the subsystems must be taken into account, since a change in one subsystem can have profound effects on others.

Nevertheless, there is one advantage to the concept of closed systems in analyzing organizations. It may be necessary to "create" a closed system in order to analyze a particular part of an organization. A manager may, for example, want to study in detail the accounting department or the mailroom and to do so will act as though the unit is a closed system. At the same time, of course, the manager will keep in mind that the unit is a subsystem of the larger organization and that any changes made will probably have ramifications throughout the organization.

Boundary

Boundaries—the borders or limits of the system—are easily seen in many biological and mechanical systems. In other areas, however, there are few systems that have impenetrable physical boundaries; rather, almost all systems require at least energy from outside to maintain them. Defining the boundaries of social systems is difficult, since there is a continous inflow and outflow of energy through them. For example, when a fire alarm sounds in Malmo, Sweden, a fireman puts the address of the fire into a computer terminal. A moment later, the terminal gives out a description of potential hazards at the address. The computer that stores the information is in Cleveland, Ohio.

The definition of boundary is somewhat arbitrary, since a social system has multiple subsystems, and the boundary line for one subsystem may not be the same as that for a different subsystem. As with the system itself, arbitrary boundaries may have to be assigned to any social organization, depending on the variable to be stressed. The boundaries used for studying or analyzing leadership, for instance, may be quite different from those used to study marketing strategy.

In addition, just as systems can be considered relatively open or closed, the permeability of boundaries also varies from relatively fixed to relatively diffuse. For example, the boundaries of a community's police force are probably far more rigid and sharply defined than those of the community's political parties.

Feedback

As shown in Figure 14.2, **feedback** is information regarding the actual performance or the results of the activities of a system. Not all such information is feedback, however. Only information used to control the

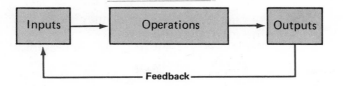

Figure 14.2   The idea of feedback

future functioning of the system is considered feedback. A frequently used example of feedback in operation is the house thermostat, which is part of the heating system. When the temperature at the thermostat drops to below the preset level, the thermostat sends a feedback signal to the furnace to begin heating the house. When the temperature goes up to the proper level, another feedback signal is sent to shut off the furnace. If the system is working properly, the house does not get too hot or too cold.

The thermostat is an example of negative, or deviation reducing, feedback; a form of feedback that serves to keep the system in a relatively steady state. For example, normal body temperature is 98.6 degrees Fahrenheit, and the body resists attempts to raise or lower this temperature.

Organizations also use deviaticn reducing feedback to collect and transmit information that will keep the system on the path of directly established goals or objectives. This is the controlling function. Howard Johnson's and McDonald's, for example, have tight, closely controlled feedback processes to make certain that a meal in one of the outlets is as similar as possible to a meal in any other outlet. Pharmaceutical companies, refineries, and similar organizations use deviation reducing feedback to ensure that medications are identical from batch to batch, that one gallon of gasoline is like another, and so on.

On the other hand, when organizations need to change direction (the planning function), they use deviation amplifying feedback. Figure 14.3 shows both deviation reducing and deviation amplifying feedback.

A salesperson in the field may report that sales are not going well and may insist on some organizational change that will improve sales. A market research group may recommend that a new product be developed and placed on the market. As styles of clothing change, clothing manufacturers must change their products.

The receiving system, also shown in Figure 14.3, can be either within the system itself or in the external environment. The salesperson wanting a change is operating within the system. A supermarket shopper who complains that a certain brand is not stocked is in the external environ-

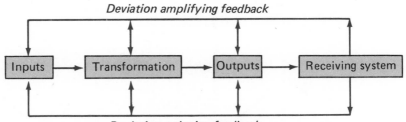

Figure 14.3   A systems model of an organization

ment rather than the system but may cause the supermarket to begin stocking the item requested.

The receiving system is important in providing feedback to the rest of the system about the quality, quantity, timeliness, and effectiveness of the system's outputs. Many organizations use elaborate mechanisms to determine how their output is received. Smaller organizations, of course, do not usually need elaborate approaches. In a small restaurant, for example, it takes only one customer pointing out that the coffee is cold for immediate action to occur.

Figure 14.4 shows how deviation amplifying and deviation reducing feedback loops can work together in an organization. The organization is moving from A to B. Shifts are caused by both deviation reducing and deviation amplifying forces. The deviation increases as the organization moves away from a planned path and decreases as it moves back toward the original path. If the system is to change direction (for example, toward C), some deviation amplifying and intervention forces are necessary. A driver proceeding toward a destination is constantly correcting the direction of the automobile. If the driver decides to change the destination, then the destination moves from B to C and the deviation is amplified.

Organizations as System

So far, the basic characteristics of systems in general—including subsystems, suprasystems, inputs, transformations, outputs, boundaries, and feedback—have been discussed. Physical and biological systems have been shown to be in some ways almost identical to organizations considered as social systems.

However, there are some fundamental differences between lower level systems and organizations as social systems. *System* was defined earlier as a series of interrelated and interdependent parts in which the interaction or interplay of any of the parts affects the whole. An **organization** as a social system is defined in a similar but somewhat different way by sociologist James Thompson: "The complex organization is a set of interdependent parts which together make up the whole because each contributes something and receives something from the whole, which in turn is interdependent with the larger environment. Survival of the system is taken to be the goal."[5]

Organizations as Self-Planned

A basic difference between the social systems of organizations and lower level systems, such as mechanical or biological systems, is in the area of structure. The **structure** of a system is the arrangement of its parts. Applied to organizations, the term *structure* refers to the arrangement of people, departments, and other subsystems within the organization. The

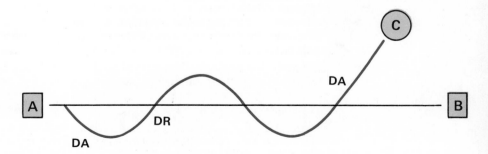

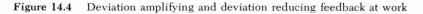

Figure 14.4   Deviation amplifying and deviation reducing feedback at work

overall structure of lower level systems is usually permanent unless it is changed or modified from the outside. For example, when a machine is redesigned, a new branch grafted onto a tree, or a heart transplanted into a human body, the change in structure comes from the outside and is imposed on the system. Each part of lower level systems usually has definite functions that do not change and that are easily indentified. For example, an automobile may wear out or rust, or its paint may fade, but the automobile cannot redesign itself to improve its functioning. It is an example of a relatively closed system.

Although a few social systems do exist in nature (ant colonies and bee hives are two examples of social systems), they are based on instinct or early learning and are relatively unchanging over time, although they are more open systems than the automobile or thermostat. Social organizations, on the other hand, are different from other social systems in that they are more open and adaptive, more easily restructured or redesigned from the inside. They are structured by members of the system and can therefore be changed by these members. According to management theorists Fremont Kast and James Rosenzweig, "The fact that social organizations are contrived by human beings suggests that they can be established for an infinite variety of purposes and do not follow the same life-cycle patterns of birth, growth, maturity and death as biological systems." [6]

Because of their openness and because of the possibility of self-design or internal restructuring, the individual parts of a social organization are less important than those in physical or biological systems. If a person's heart stops beating, the individual dies. But if an industrial plant burns down, the organization can build a new one. An organization can employ more or fewer people, buy or sell factories, and change products and still remain the same organization.

Therefore, effective managers do not accept the design of the organization or its subsystems as givens. Rather, they continually obtain feedback from both inside and outside the organization to determine whether the structure of the organization is appropriate to present conditions. Managers must maintain an open system rather than a closed system viewpoint; those in business or industry must be constantly sensitive to both change and competition.

Organizations as Process

The term *process* is widely used. In the physical sciences, chemical, biological, and physical processes are discussed. In the social sciences, psychological, group, and economic processes are dealt with. In management, decision-making, planning, and managerial processes are important. In a broad sense, a **process** is an identifiable flow of interrelated actions or events moving toward a goal or result. *Flow* suggests movement in both time and direction. *Interrelated* suggests that there is interaction between the actions or events. *Goal* suggests human objectives, while *result* suggests either human or nonhuman consequences that are either planned or unplanned. For example, the process of an automobile accident may result in damage to the automobile, but the result is usually unplanned.

When dealing with relatively simple, independent systems, such as a furnace thermostat, the focus can be primarily on structure. If the proper structure is present, the process takes place almost automatically. However, moving upward from lower level mechanical, biological, and other systems to the social system, the ties linking the subsystems become less rigid and concrete and less direct, simple, and stable. The movement of energy along unchanging and physically continous links between the subsystem change in the direction of internal variation and discontinuous subsystems with many more degrees of variation. For lower level systems, the structure is often directly observable, even when the system stops operating. For example, on a rocky beach along the seashore lies the rusted hulk of a Model T Ford, an automobile that has not been built since 1928. The structure of the car, including body, wheels, and engine, is still clearly visible.

For the social system, the structure is more abstract and theoretical and less directly observable. Often it can be inferred only by observing events over time. As sociologist Walter Buckley phrases it, "Process, then, points to the actions and interactions of the components of an ongoing system in which varying degrees of structuring arise, persist, dissolve or change."[7]

Clearly, social structures, such as organizations, are not found in a physical vacuum. Organizations consist of physical plants, material resources, and human beings—*but these physical elements do not interact naturally with each other.* As contrived and designed by humans, organizations are themselves independent of any physical or human part and can replace or remove such parts. According to social psychologists David Katz and Robert Kahn, "A social system is a structuring of events or happenings rather than of physical parts and it therefore has no structure apart from its functioning."[8] In other words, process is as important as structure to an organization. The two are interrelated and interdependent. If a biological organism stops functioning, the physical parts remain and can be examined. If an organization stops functioning, there is no longer an identifiable structure. When the process disappears, so also does the structure. It is often difficult for people to see social systems as a process of events. Instead they tend to see only the physical structure—the buildings, equipment, and people. But the effective manager must continually be aware of process and the effect it has on structure.

As social systems, organizations are not "alive." That is, they are not held together in the way plants and animals are or even in the way mechanical systems are. Automobiles are held together by nuts and bolts; organizations are held together by a kind of "psychological cement"—the managerial process that coordinates and regulates the system.

In the case at the beginning of the chapter, little attention apparently was paid to the "psychological cement" holding the organization together. That is, the MIS task force and the middle managers focused on changing the structure, ignoring motivation, personal goals and objectives, and the impact of one set of processes on another. Greater attention to process, including the needs and motivations of the system's "users," probably would have led to the successful implementation of the MIS.

Organizational Subsystems

This section will focus on subsystems existing within modern, complex organizations, particularly on their process (rather than their structure). Process is essential if the organization is to function and survive. Processes can be developed through a number of different kinds of structures. For example, the production process—a process common to all organizations—transforms inputs into outputs. But the structure of the production process varies among organizations in the same field and in different fields.

The Managerial Subsystem

Managerial subsystems are concerned with controlling, coordinating, and directing all the other subsystems of the organization. They provide the basic psychological cement that holds the organization and its subsystems together.

Chapter 1 described three basic levels of management—the operating or technical level; the managerial, coordinating, or administrative level; and the strategic or institutional level. The three levels are briefly described here.

The operating level of management is primarily concerned with such areas as production, maintenance, buying and selling, and the adaptation of the organization to its immediate environment. (Each of these processes will later be described as subsystems within the larger organization.)

As organizations get bigger and more complex, so also do their problems, especially those of coordinating people's activities, determining which products to make, and similar problems. The managerial level performs two basic functions: (1) administering, coordinating and servicing the technical level, and (2) coordinating requirements and demands outside the system with internal organizational resources and needs. The payroll department of an organization does not determine the salary of any individual; it only makes out the checks. The purchasing department does not decide on its own what to buy; nor does the production department decide what to make. All these decisions are made at the managerial level.

A formal organization must also operate in a wider social environment. It must, for example, be approved by society (the suprasystem) if it is to achieve certain goals and objectives. As a part of society, the organization is also responsible to society. The strategic level controls the managerial level and mediates between the organization and the outside community. This level is represented by the boards of directors of business corporations, school boards, and, in many cases, organization presidents or administrators.

The Operations Subsystem

The operations subsystem operates primarily at the production level and is concerned with the major transformations, operations, or work of the system. As shown in Figure 14.5, it is the technical core of the organization. The technology involves producing a product, service, or idea that can be exported outside the organization and used by the public. Many organizations are classified by the technology in which they are involved. Automobile manufacturers, banks, educational institutions, and hospitals are all classified differently because their technical subsystems are concerned with different production operations.

Every organization has an operations subsystem. Too frequently, however, production (or management operations) is seen only as manufacturing. But every organization gathers inputs from the environment in the form of materials, people, and energy and performs operations on those inputs before exporting them in the form of outputs. Insurance companies produce insurance policies and payments; educational institutions produce educated students; and law firms produce legal briefs and courtroom arguments.

The structure and technology of the operations subsystem vary from organization to organization and from the very simple to the extremely complex. Although larger organizations often have a number of different production processes, the essential process remains the same. Raw materials, energy, and other resources are transformed into something differ-

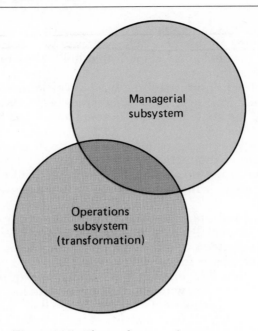

Figure 14.5   The production subsystem as process

ent. (See the Appendix for a fuller description of the operations subsystem.)

Boundary Spanning Subsystems

Organizations need to import people, raw materials, energy and other resources into the system and to export finished products, goods, services, and ideas into the environment. The subsystems that carry on transactions with the environment are called **boundary spanning subsystems.** They are boundary spanning in the sense that although their functions are carried on within the system, they are also the contact points with the external environment (as shown in Figure 14.6).

Examples of boundary spanning subsystems that import resources are the purchasing and personnel departments. The purchasing department buys the raw materials, equipment, and other supplies needed to keep the organization in operation. The personnel department recruits (imports) the human resources needed at different levels of the organization.

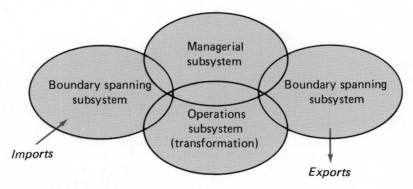

Figure 14.6   Boundary spanning subsystems as process

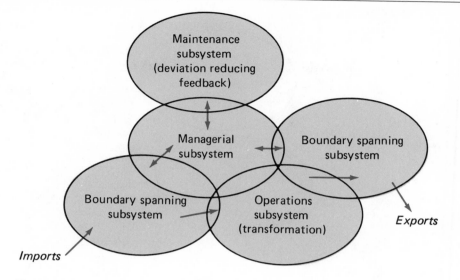

Figure 14.7 The maintenance subsystem as process

Examples of boundary spanning subsystems that export finished goods or ideas into the environment are the sales and public relations departments. The sales department sells whatever goods are produced by the organization. The public relations department exports ideas about the organization into the environment.

The Maintenance Subsystem

The **maintenance subsystem** is concerned with preserving stability and maintaining the smooth operation of the rest of the organization. It deals primarily with deviation reducing feedback—with keeping the organization on a predetermined course (as shown in Figure 14.7). This process requires monitoring and feeding back to the rest of the organization information on how well the process of inputs, transformations, and outputs is being performed.

There are many different examples of maintenance subsystems in operation. Equipment and machinery require standardized raw material. Incoming or in-process inspection and quality control are established to ensure that the raw material or goods in process meet performance standards. Policies and procedures are written to make certain that activities are carried out in established ways. Incoming workers are oriented and trained to make certain that the system works as planned. Performance appraisal, wage and salary systems, and other reward systems are established to reward or punish organization members.

Proper use of deviation reducing feedback is necessary if the organization is to remain on course with a minimum of variability. While almost all the other subsystems are subject to environmental forces, the maintenance subsystem is generally insulated from such forces. It looks inward rather than outward. As a result, the organization must establish a counterbalancing set of forces—the adaptive subsystem.

The Adaptive Subsystem

The **adaptive subsystem** is primarily concerned with the survival of the organization in a changing environment. Its purpose is to sense meaningful and relevant changes in the outside environment and to suggest necessary changes. As shown in Figure 14.8, the adaptive subsystem is concerned with deviation amplifying feedback.

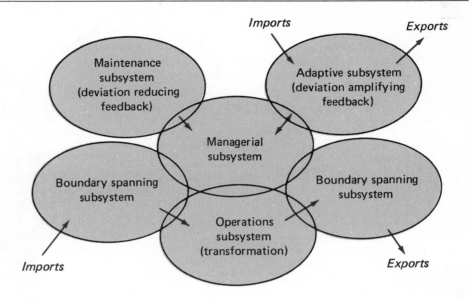

Figure 14.8   The adaptive subsystem as process

The adaptive subsystem imports information from both inside and outside the organization, evaluates it, and then suggests appropriate changes to the organization. The marketing department, for example, may receive reports about the products from customers or salespeople or may conduct surveys to acquire information that it can use in suggesting change to the organization.

The organization may carry on lobbying activities at various levels of government to bring about changes that will benefit the organization or to stop changes that will actually or potentially harm the organization. For example, as a result of lobbying activities on the part of the ski industry, the State of Vermont recently passed a law that exempts ski resorts from legal liability if a skier is injured while skiing (as opposed to using a ski lift). Adaptive process can be seen at all levels of management.

The various organizational subsystems often have different goals and objectives that need to be coordinated by the managerial subsystem. To illustrate: In many industrial organizations, there is often conflict between the manufacturing department (a production subsystem) and the quality control department (a maintenance subsystem). The people in manufacturing believe that those in quality control are out to trap them. The quality control people feel that those in manufacturing are trying to put something over on them.

To further illustrate: The finance department (an adaptive subsystem), concerned with cash flow, may want to keep parts and products inventories low. Manufacturing, on the other hand, may want to maintain a high inventory of parts so production need never be stalled. And marketing (a boundary spanning subsystem) may want to have a high inventory of several products so the company will never lose a sale by being out of stock on an item.

These conflicts are not actually caused by people; rather, they are built into the organization, because organizations are not usually designed to make proper use of the idea that their various subsystems are interrelated and interdependent. Thus these subsystems often have quite different goals and objectives.

In conclusion, an organization as a social system has five major characteristics:

→ 1. It is composed of a number of subsystems, all of which are interdependent and interrelated through both structure and process.

→ 2. It is open and dynamic, having inputs, outputs, operations, and feedback.

→ 3. It attempts to maintain a proper balance through the use of both deviation amplifying and deviation reducing feedback.

→ 4. Its subsystems serve a number of different purposes and have different functions and objectives, some of which are in actual or potential conflict.

→ 5. Its manager must strive for the optimal balance among the subsystems by paying attention to both structure and process.[9]

Implications for the Manager

Social organizations as systems differ from lower level systems in that they can be changed from within. The idea of process and the managerial subsystem serving as the psychological glue holding an organization together also separate social organizations from lower level systems.

The effective manager must be constantly aware of the continuum between closed and open system thinking. While no manager will admit to using closed system, linear thinking, many look for and settle on a single cause for an occurrence. From a systems point of view, most events have multiple causes and multiple consequences—some intended and others unintended. In the MIS case at the beginning of the chapter, everyone involved seemed to fall into the trap of closed system thinking. As a result, the system failed even though a great deal of hard work, effort, and money had been put into it.

Closed system thinking can be used deliberately as a method for *treating* a problem as an independent entity. In most circumstances, however, the manager must remain aware that the problem and all decisions are imbedded in the larger situation and that a change in one subsystem will affect other subsystems and the total system.

The effective manager must carefully choose the level of analysis for different problems or situations. At the technical or operating level, the manager may want to focus on an individual or a small group as a system (while still recognizing that this system interacts with larger systems). Improvements can be made in the organization after careful studying of such technical levels as production, buying, and selling. At the next level, the manager can focus on administering, coordinating, and servicing the operations level as well as relating its needs to other internal resources and needs. At the strategic level, the manager must focus on the interactions of the organization, as a system, with the outside community. Here, attention and concern must be directed to the present or future impact of changes in the national and international scene as well as the local one. The assembly line supervisor may need to pay little attention to the relationships among Israel, Egypt, and Saudi Arabia, but these relationships may be an important concern for the president of an oil company.

Because organizations can be modified from within, the effective manager carefully watches both structure and process. Does the structure of the production subsystem adequately fit the needs of the organization? Is the process of the adaptive subsystem being given proper weight and balance in comparison with the maintenance subsystem?

Finally, the manager's job is essentially one of managing systems. The manager defines the organization or organizational unit as a system, establishes objectives for the system, creates the necessary subsystems, and integrates the subsystems. The primary advantages of viewing the manager's job as one of managing systems are (1) the recognition of how each part contributes to and interacts with the rest of the system and (2) the realization that failure to meet objectives may be due to improper design of the organization as a system rather than to shortcomings of the system's individual components.

Review

1. Would you now use the term *system* in the same way you did before reading the chapter?
2. List five ways in which the systems approach and systems thinking can be helpful to the manager.
3. Interview several nanagers to develop a systems model of several social systems. Diagram the models, using Figure 14.3 as a guide. What are some of the similarities and differences in the diagrams?
4. List the inputs, operations, and outputs for organizations such as fast food outlets and service stations. What are the similarities among the organizations? What are the differences?
5. From your own experience or from observing organizations, identify and give examples of production, maintenance, adaptive, and boundary spanning organizational subsystems.
6. Observing yourself and others, look for specific examples of closed system and open system thinking. Describe them.
7. Explain, in your own words, why the chapter emphasized the concepts of structure and process. Give examples of the interrelatedness of these two concepts.

The Pajama Game

A pajama factory was subject to constant changes in production methods and styles. Each change was opposed by the workers, who showed their opposition in several ways. On the average, workers who transferred from one job to another took longer to learn the new job than did new employees. About 62 percent of transferred employees either failed to reach a satisfactory level of performance or quit. The types of opposition varied on the basis of the cohesiveness of the group whose work was changed. Members of noncohesive groups tended to quit; members of cohesive groups tended to restrict performance and engage in hostile acts toward management. Workers' frustration and resistance seemed to be caused by their difficulty in learning new methods, their loss of status, and their fear of never being able to regain the old rate of speed. The economics of these changes seemed less important; although the workers were paid on a piecework basis, they received a liberal learning allowance.

Four work groups became involved in an experiment the next time the work had to be changed. The change, which involved the elimination of some frills from a garment, affected less than 10 percent of the total work.

The control group's work was changed in the usual way. The workers were called together and were told that the new methods were necessary because of competition. The new piecework rate was described and the workers were allowed to ask questions.

The partial participation group were given a much fuller and more dramatic explanation. After the members of the group agreed in principle to change, they elected a committee to help management plan for the change and establish the new piecework rate.

There were two total participation groups (working on different parts of the job). All the workers in each group fully participated in planning and designing the new jobs, establishing the new production schedules, and so on.

The turnover and productivity of the "control" group were similar to those of previous groups confronted with change. There was the usual expression of hostility against management, productivity was low, and 17 percent of the workers quit in the first forty days.

The experimental groups accepted the change much more positively, particularly the total participation groups. Production was soon 40 percent higher than in the control group, and there was no turnover at all in the experimental groups.[10]

1. What was the total system in this case? What was the subsystem?
2. Using Figure 14.1 as a model, diagram the four different groups. How did the inputs, transformations, outputs, and feedback differ?
3. One of the advantages of the systems approach is the ability to choose the level of analysis or change. How does this concept apply here?

Footnotes

1. E. Huse, "The Impact of Computerized Programs on Managers and Organizations: A Case Study in an Integrated Manufacturing Company," in *The Impact of Computers on Management*, ed. C. Myers (Cambridge, Mass.: MIT Press, 1967), pp. 282–302; and E. Huse, unpublished report, 1966.
2. R. Ackoff, "A Note on Systems Science," *Interfaces* 2 (August 1972): 40.
3. C. Churchman, *The Systems Approach* (New York: Delta Books, Dell Publishing, 1968); F. Kast and J. Rosenzweig, *Organization and Management: A Systems Approach* (New York: McGraw-Hill, 1974); D. Katz and R. Kahn, *The Social Psychology of Organizations* (New York: Wiley, 1966); F. Luthans and T. Stewart, "A General Contingency Theory of Management," *Academy of Management Review* 2 (April 1977): 181–195; and J. Lorsch and J. Morse, *Organizations and Their Members: A Contingency Approach* (New York: Harper & Row, 1974).
4. W. French, *The Personnel Management Process*, 4th ed. (Boston: Houghton Mifflin, 1978), p. 34.
5. J. Thompson, *Organizations in Action* (New York: McGraw-Hill, 1967), p. 6.
6. F. Kast and J. Rosenzweig, "General Systems Theory: Applications for Organization and Management," *Academy of Management Journal* 15 (December 1972): 455.
7. W. Buckley, "Society as a Complex, Adaptive System," in *Modern Systems Research for the Behavioral Scientist*, ed. W. Buckley (Chicago: Aldine Publishing, 1968), p. 497.
8. Katz and Kahn, *Social Psychology of Organizations*, p. 31.
9. Kast and Rosenzweig, *Organization and Management*; Katz and Kahn, *Social Psychology of Organization*; and Thompson, *Organizations in Action*.
10. L. Coch and J. French, "Overcoming Resistance to Change," *Human Relations* 1 (August 1948): 522–532.

Chapter 15

Basic Propositions of Organizing

The Osage Plant

Division of Labor

Horizontal Specialization (Departmentation)

Span of Control

Authority
    Delegation
    Centralization and Decentralization

The Dynamics of Specialization and Coordination—The First Level Supervisor

Classical Principles of Vertical Coordination
    The Unity of Command Principle
    The Scalar Principle
    Line and Staff
    Functional Authority

Organization Charts and Manuals

Implications for the Manager

Review

Benton's Department Store

Learning Objectives

When you have finished reading and studying this chapter, you should be able to:

1. Demonstrate the need for structure in formal organizations.
2. Explain the reasons for division of work.
3. Identify and give examples of methods of horizontal specialization.
4. Compare and contrast these methods.
5. Identify and explain the purpose of the span of control concept.
6. List the basic reasons for the classical principles of coordination, and explain why they should be used as general guides to action.
7. Draw an organization chart, and explain what information it provides and what it does not provide.
8. Relate the concepts of the informal organization to motivation and group dynamics.
9. Show how open systems thinking affects classical approaches to managing.
10. Define and be able to use the following concepts:

division of labor	unity of command
horizontal specialization	scalar principle
departmentation	line authority
function	staff
coordination	functional authority
span of control	organization chart
delegation of authority	organization manual

Thought Starters

1. Can an organization exist without structure?
2. What are some ways in which work can be specialized?
3. How are work activities coordinated in an organization with which you are familiar?

The Osage Plant

Amco, Inc., has about seventy manufacturing plants located in the continental United States and ten other countries. One plant is located in the small town of Osage, about a hundred miles from Seattle, Washington. The plant manufactures a variety of industrial and consumer products and has about three hundred employees, including engineers, accountants, salespeople, and factory workers. Figure 15.1—the organization chart of the Osage plant—shows that six managers report to the plant manager, who, in turn, reports to a division manager.

The plant, which occupies a modern leased building, is only about two years old. The plant manager, who has been on the job about six months, was promoted from the position of manufacturing manager after the previous plant manager died. As is common for new plants, the Osage plant was losing money. The new plant manager, however, was determined to bring the plant to a profitable position as soon as possible.

With the approval of those employees directly reporting to him, he brought in a consultant. The consultant interviewed a number of people, including the manager's immediate subordinates, and gave an oral report to the plant management. The consultant reported that while the plant personnel were hardworking and dedicated, management did not seem to agree on plant objectives and mutual responsibilities.

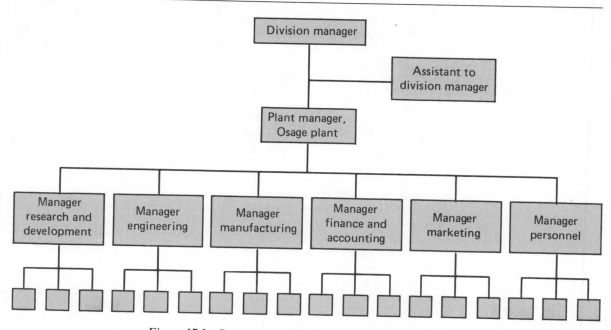

Figure 15.1 Organization chart of the Osage plant

As a result of the report, the management group decided to spend three days away from the plant to develop ways of working more effectively together. Their first task at the meeting was to identify plant objectives. Although overall objectives had been established previously, the management group either did not understand them or did not agree with them. At the meeting, the group did decide on objectives and then began to discuss mutual responsibilities.

This discussion proved difficult. The manager of finance and accounting began it by describing his job as he saw it, based primarily on Amco's carefully prepared job description. Before he got very far, several people interrupted with questions and comments. It took almost three hours for the job to be defined to the satisfaction of all seven managers and about the same amount of time for each of the other job descriptions to be worked out satisfactorily. Developed in this manner, the job descriptions looked very different from those given by the organization, which had detailed mostly relationships of subordinates rather than peers.

Next, the group redefined organizational goals on the basis of the new job descriptions. And finally, it listed the major problems facing the organization and developed approaches to solving them.

After returning to the plant, the plant manager and the other managers reported that they were working much better with each other. Clarification of each manager's role responsibilities had been difficult but useful to the functioning of the Osage plant.

The seven plant managers can be considered one system, and each manager can be seen as a subsystem. The system was faced with two fundamental problems of organizations—division of labor (specialization) and coordination of the work to ensure that the organization's objectives are accomplished. As seen in this case, even a small system has difficulty with specialization and coordination. But the larger the system, the more difficult these problems are. Consider, for example, the organizational problems of managing the federal government with its countless departments, bureaus, agencies, and services.

To function effectively, organizations must be designed so that the subsystems or units can work together. This chapter will examine classical approaches to the two problems of division of labor: (1) an individual person cannot do everything, and (2) when the work is divided, it must also be coordinated. The chapter will rely heavily on the classical proposition for dividing up and coordinating labor. The propositions are only guides, however, since organizations constantly change. As symptoms of organizational problems appear, managers study them, make adjustments, and check to see if the problems have been solved. Then, the organizational structure remains as is until another need for organizational adjustment arises. The plant manager of the Osage plant made such an adjustment by bringing in a consultant and by holding the out-of-plant meeting.

The chapter takes a relatively "closed system" approach to organizational problems; that is, it offers the basic principles of organizing *within* the organization. Chapter 16 will then move to more of an "open system" approach, including emphasis on environmental factors that affect organizational structure and design.

Division of Labor

All organizations exist for particular purposes and have limited resources—and they all strive for effectiveness in achieving their objectives. To maximize this effectiveness within the constraints of their limited resources, organizations attempt to achieve efficiency.

It has long been recognized that a necessary ingredient for achieving efficiency and effectiveness is **division of labor**—the specialization of workers, including management, in accomplishing tasks. As workers specialize, they often increase their expertise and productivity and are able to develop work methods that are well suited to the tasks they perform. Furthermore, specialized procedures and machinery can be developed to improve productivity, and new workers can be effectively trained in a specialized segment of a job.

Perhaps the most famous commentary on the division of labor and its resulting specialization is in Adam Smith's *The Wealth of Nations,* written in 1776. In that book the noted economist and philosopher described a small pin-making shop that employed ten men. Each job in the shop was specialized. One man drew out the wire, another straightened it, and a third cut it. Still others sharpened the point of the pin and put together the head. The men were able to make about 4,800 pins each day. As Smith pointed out, if each man had performed all the steps needed to make a single pin, each could have produced no more than twenty pins a day; but because of division of labor and specialization, the ten men were able to produce more pins than could 2,400 men working independently. According to Smith, division of labor increases output for three reasons:

1. The skill of the workman increases.
2. There is little time lost in moving from one type of work to another.
3. Its encouragement of the development and use of special machinery increases productivity.

Division of labor and specialization have allowed societies to produce more of what they want than would otherwise be possible. Division of labor itself provides the economic basis for advanced societies and the foundation for structuring organizations. Specialization can, however, be carried too far; and the result is reduced motivation, increased absenteeism, and other problems.

Horizontal Specialization (Departmentation)

The clustering, assignment, or grouping of work activities has been discussed for many years.[1] Clearly, organizational specialization must exist for two basic reasons:

1. Organizations take on tasks that cannot be done by one person.
2. People's mental capacity is finite; no single person can be skilled in everything.

The specialization approach most frequently discussed is that of grouping activities at a horizontal, or work flow, level. **Horizontal specialization** is the way the work of the entire organization is divided. **Departmentation** is the creation of a number of subunits, usually called departments. Departmentation can be accomplished through (1) function, (2) geographical area or location, (3) product, (4) customer or client, (5) number of persons, and (6) time. Most organizations use a combination, shifting from one approach to another as necessary.

Function—one of the most common ways of creating departmentation or specialization—is grouping activities according to similar work, skills, knowledge, and technology. For example, all the electricians may be placed in one unit, all the engineers in another, and all the salespersons in a third. The vice-president of manufacturing may supervise all manufacturing activities, as shown in Figure 15.2.

This approach, which is common in manufacturing organizations, has two major advantages. It makes certain that the power and prestige of important departments such as manufacturing, marketing, and finance are represented at the top; and it minimizes costly duplications of expensive equipment. For example, having a centralized X-ray department in a hospital is more effective than having X-ray machines scattered throughout.

The function approach has disadvantages as well. Among them are overspecialization and the development of narrow viewpoints. Given the same problem to analyze, marketing people tend to perceive marketing problems, and manufacturing people tend to perceive manufacturing problems.

Specialization by geography is a common form of departmentation among such diverse organizations as schools and sales forces (see Figure

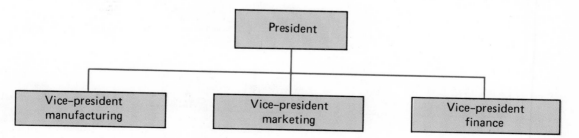

Figure 15.2 Specialization by purpose or function

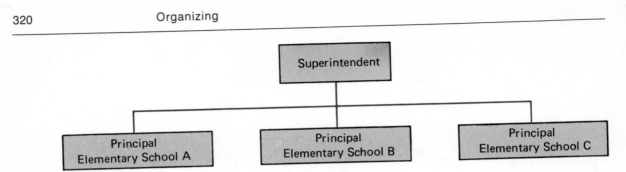

Figure 15.3 Specialization by geographic area

15.3). Elementary and junior high schools are usually established by neighborhood. A marketing department may have sales offices in various regional areas. This kind of specialization often saves time, travel, and money. For example, McDonald's found that three-quarters of their customers came into the restaurants in conjunction with some other activity, so it began to build restaurants in areas of high customer activity—sometimes within blocks of each other in order to capitalize on different traffic patterns.

Specialization by geography makes little sense for some organizational segments. For example, the overall finance function of an organization would probably suffer if split apart geographically, although geographical separation of some accounting functions might make a great deal of sense.

The product approach to departmentation (see Figure 15.4) is common to large manufacturing organizations; General Motors, for example, has separate departments for Chevrolet, Cadillac, and Oldsmobile. Each department is relatively self-contained, with its own manufacturing, purchasing, accounting, employee relations, and sales units. The advantages of this approach include being able to give more attention to the product line, improving the coordination of functional activities, and placing greater responsibility for profits and overall operations at the divisional level.

There are also disadvantages to the product approach, among them the strong possibility of duplication of effort and the difficulty of centralized management control. However, the trend in U.S. and European industry has been toward product departmentation. This is particularly true for the conglomerates, which have a number of very different products to market.

Customer or client departmentation can be helpful if an organization has clients with special or different needs (see Figure 15.5). For exam-

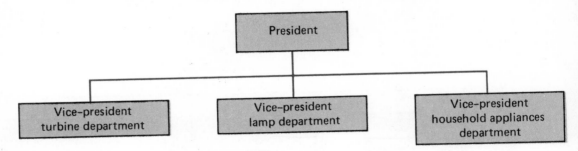

Figure 15.4 Specialization by product

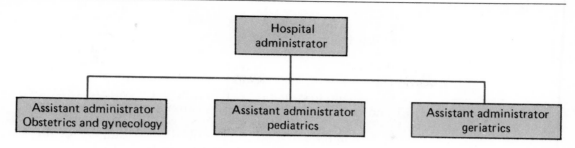

Figure 15.5   Specialization by client

ple, a sales force may be divided into those calling on private individuals, those calling on commercial accounts, those calling on industrial accounts and those calling on government agencies. Departments of the federal government are set up for businesses, farmers, educators, industrial workers, the elderly, and so on. An advantage of customer or client departmentation is being able to group activities in such a way as to meet customers' special needs. Disadvantages include increased difficulty in coordination and the possibility of underutilization of specialized groups when times or conditions change.

In summary, each of these four ways of establishing division of labor through departmentation is widely used, having performed successfully over many years. As to which is best, the decision depends on which is most capable of accomplishing the organization's objectives. If geographical specialization is essential to the existence of an organization, then it is wise to organize into geographic units that can focus on servicing the special needs of customers in various areas. This type of departmentation may operate at the expense of the potential use of the expertise available through grouping by function or technology. In the same way, if technical skills and knowledge are most critical to an organization, functional grouping makes more sense. Under this arrangement, the state of technical knowledge is advanced, but there may be a reduction of services and/or products tailored to the special needs of particular sets of customers or particular geographic locations.

Because a manager cannot be in two places at one time, departmentation is sometimes by number of persons and time. Usually, these forms of specialization occur within departments or units.

If an organization has large numbers of employees working in the same general location and doing essentially the same thing for the same clients, departmentation may be on the basis of the number of persons, as Figure 15.6 shows. In the U.S. Army, enlistees are organized into squads, platoons, companies, battalions, regiments, and divisions. In a

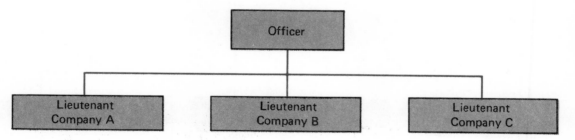

Figure 15.6   Specialization by number of persons

large office, clerks are often grouped into a number of sections with a supervisor for each section.

Many organizations cannot stop their activities at a fixed time each day. Indeed, some—for example, hospitals, steel mills, and refineries—operate around the clock. Others may work only one "shift" if sales are low but expand to two or more if production is to be increased. As Figure 15.7 shows, a hospital may have a nursing supervisor for each of three shifts.

Most complex organizations use all or a number of the six basic approaches to departmentation. The question is not which standard to use but which is the best given a particular set of circumstances. For example, a company's manufacturing unit may be designed according to function, while its sales department is specialized by geographic area. Managers must understand the uniqueness of a particular organization's (or unit's) situation and structure its resources accordingly.

Structural change is a frequent occurrence in many organizations. Large firms typically make major structural changes about every other year, and the larger the organization, the more subject it is to change. In the late 1960s, nine out of ten of the largest U.S. organizations made such changes, and sixteen out of the next twenty-five also did so. Management makes organizational changes to fit changing conditions and to increase the organization's effectiveness.[2]

Span of Control

The previous section described a number of approaches to departmentation, the first important problem of organizational structuring. Once the work has been divided (or departmentalized), the major remaining problem is coordination.[3] **Coordination** involves making certain, through the creation of specific positions and subdivisions, that individuals or groups work toward common organizational objectives. It is not difficult to realize that division of labor and the resulting specialization create a need for the coordinative function in management.

One way of providing coordination is to make one individual responsible for coordinating the work of others. If the work is simple and basically independent, a single manager can successfully orchestrate the work of many subordinates. However, if the work is interdependent and complicated, one manager can handle only a few subordinates.

The manager's **span of control** is the number of subordinates the person can efficiently supervise. (Some authors prefer the term *span of management* to *span of control*, since, from a systems viewpoint, managers have many more activities than simply controlling subordinates.) Essentially, as the number of subordinates increases arithmetically, the number of relationships between the manager and the subordinates increases geometrically. Thus, if a manager has four subordinates, the

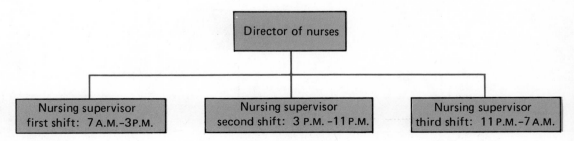

Figure 15.7 Specialization by time

theoretical number of relationships between the manager and the subordinates is 44. The addition of a fifth subordinate results in 100 potential relationships, and eight subordinates mean 1,080 potential relationships. The number of relationships, r, is computed by using the following formula:

$$r = 2^{n-1} + n - 1,$$

where n represents the number of subordinates.

Classical theorists have spent a great deal of time debating about how many subordinates should report to a single manager. Frequently, they have suggested a specific number. However, there are successful organizations where many people report to a single manager and others where managers may have only one or two subordinates reporting to them. An organization that has a small number of subordinates reporting to each manager generally has many levels of management and is thus considered "tall." An organization that has a large number of subordinates reporting to each manager has few levels and is thus considered "flat."

The proper number of subordinates for each manager ultimately depends on the individual manager, the subordinates, the type of work, and other considerations. For example, a bank manager may be able to coordinate adequately the work of twenty tellers, because each teller works almost independently of the others. But a systems programming manager may be able to manage only six programmers, because each person works on a different part of a complex computer program and each person's work must be carefully coordinated with that of everyone else. Thus the optimal span of control varies according to the nature of the task (and, of course, the skill of the manager).

Different spans of control are often found within the same organization. Most researchers, however, have examined only top managers' spans of control and have found that top managers generally supervise only five or six employees. But, as mentioned earlier, there are many factors involved in determining the proper span of control. Among them are:

1. *The manager's ability.* Some managers are more capable than others of supervising large numbers of people.
2. *The nature of the work.* The more simple, routine, and repetitive the work, the greater the possible span of control.
3. *The degree of interdependence among units.* The more interdependent the units, the greater the need for coordination and the smaller the optimal span of control.
4. *The organization's efficiency.* The more efficient the organization and the greater competence of its employees, the larger the span of control.[4]

Thus modern theorists suggest that the span of control is best determined by the situation, that there is no single "best" way for all situations. One determination of the optimal point is that if the manager appears to be harried, perhaps the span is too large. The counterpart is that if the subordinates appear to be harried, perhaps the span is too small and the manager is too closely "riding herd" on them.

In any case, it is easy to see that the smaller the span of control, the more levels of management will be needed to ensure coordination throughout the organization. Figure 15.8 shows the span of control for two hypothetical organizations. In Company A, the span of control for all

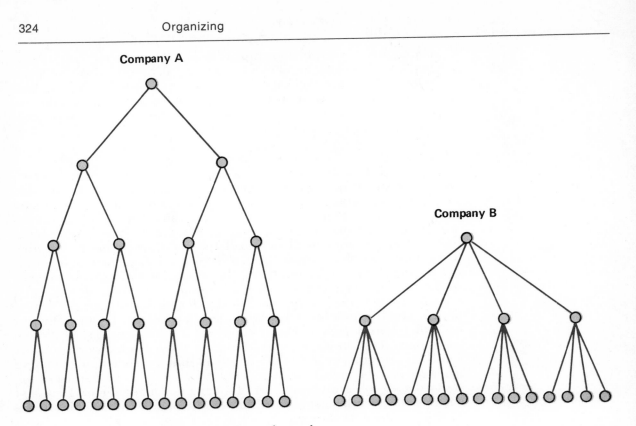

Figure 15.8 Span of control

managers is two; in Company B it is four. The number of organizational levels depends on the span of control.

Authority

So far, organizing has been viewed in part as a result of the tasks to be accomplished; that is, the need for coordination of the work influences the structure of organizations. Organizational structure viewed as a system is called the operations subsystem, because it is based on the nature of the work. But of equal importance to organizations is the matter of deciding what work to do and how to do it. This area is referred to as the managerial or authority subsystem of organization.

Authority comes from the organization; it is the right to command and exact obedience from others. Every organization has one individual who is ultimately responsible—has the final authority—for the organization's operation. That individual, often called the chief executive officer (CEO), cannot make all decisions. At the least, the person will not have the time to do so or the expertise in all decision areas. Thus in designing an organization's structure, it is necessary to identify where particular decisions will be made. Two important considerations for assigning decisions include delegation and decentralization.

Delegation

Because the CEO cannot make all the decisions, especially the day-to-day ones, it is necessary to delegate some decision-making authority to subordinates. **Delegation of authority** is the process that transfers authority from supervisor to subordinate and allows a subordinate to exercise discretion in making certain decisions. The process of delegation involves the assignment of tasks, the determination of expected results, and the granting of authority to accomplish the tasks. Two important principles of delegation are parity and accountability.

Parity means that when the responsibility for a decision is assigned to a subordinate, the individual must also receive sufficient authority to make the decision and to see that it is implemented. Two classic propositions of management are that it is meaningless to delegate responsibility without authority, and it is dangerous to delegate authority without responsibility.

Accountability means that even though decision-making authority and responsibility can be delegated, the CEO remains ultimately accountable. In one respect, this means that while the responsibility for making decisions can be delegated, the responsibility for the consequences of the decisions cannot be abdicated. As two respected management authors put it, "Likewise, *the responsibility of the subordinate to his superior for performance is absolute,* once he has accepted an assignment *and no superior can escape responsibility for the organization activities of his subordinate.*"[5]

From a closed system point of view, these statements about delegation are correct. However, from an open system point of view, it is very difficult to accept such absolute distinctions. The concept that authority must be equal to responsibility is one of the most cherished ideas of the classical management theorists. However, the responsibility of a manager operating in a subsystem within the larger system is to get a particular job done. This effort requires ongoing negotiations with subsystems over which the manager has no formal authority. Therefore, the manager's effectiveness depends, in part, on skill in negotiation, compromise, and persuasion of others.[6] Thus, while the general proposition is valid, its absolute application is difficult.

Centralization and Decentralization

An idea closely related to delegation is the decentralization of authority. Organizational *centralization* and *decentralization* refer to the degree to which authority is retained at the top of the organization (centralization) or delegated to the lower levels (decentralization). As shown in Figure 15.9, the greater the delegation of authority throughout the organization, the more decentralized the organization is.

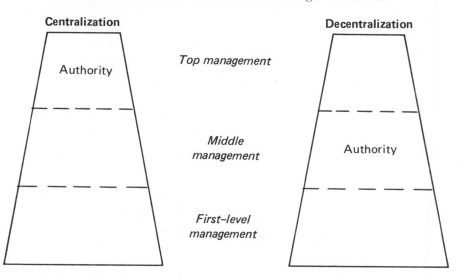

Figure 15.9 Centralization and decentralization

Decentralization often creates the need for greater coordination among decision makers, and it sometimes leads to inefficiencies due to duplication of effort. It is also difficult to determine the appropriate level of decentralization for any organization. For example, U.S. Steel reorganized its steel-related business in 1974; it took two operating divisions and five sales divisions, none of which had had profit responsibility, and converted them into five almost autonomous profit centers. The changed structure, which brought authority and power down into the divisions, was successful.[7] Of course, some organizations decentralize too far and have to reorganize to do a better job of coordination. For example, the F. W. Woolworth Company found that consolidating and centralizing its purchasing, distribution, and merchandising operations resulted in greater efficiency and reduced costs.[8] (Chapter 16 will detail some of the factors that influence the degree of decentralization that is best for organizations.)

The Dynamics of Specialization and Coordination—The First Level Supervisor

To understand more clearly the dynamics of specialization and coordination, the job of a first-level (operations) supervisor in a modern mass production organization will be examined. The supervisor is in charge of manufacturing parts for the fuel control system of a jet engine and of coordinating workers and activities at the operations level. (Although the supervisor's job is used as an example, many of the ideas described apply to other managerial levels as well.)[9] The supervisor's job is a specialized one, but it also requires interaction and coordination with a wide variety of people, including: (1) the boss to whom the supervisor formally reports; (2) a wide variety of specialists—inspectors, safety engineers, production control specialists, efficiency and standards specialists, personnel specialists, maintenance and repair specialists, methods specialists, and so on; (3) the heads of departments to which the supervisor's department relates; (4) subordinates—lower-level supervisors, group leaders, lead people, and section chiefs; (5) the workers themselves, numbering from ten to three hundred; and (6) the shop steward or other union members in a union-organized plant. All these people and groups expect certain things of the supervisor, and the supervisor expects certain things of them. The total of these expectations makes up the supervisor's role (which is described in Chapter 14). Figure 15.10 helps show the network of relationships.

The boss. The relationship with the boss is, of course, important. The first-level supervisor reports directly to a higher-level supervisor and receives approval, recognition, pay increases, and possible promotions through that person.

Specialists. The first-level supervisor's relationships with technical specialists are extremely important. The specialists originate the standards of performance that the supervisor must uphold and to which the subordinates must conform. Accountants, engineers, and other specialists frequently initiate changes at the work level. In addition, they provide information directly to higher levels of management—often before providing it to the first-level supervisor.

The heads of other departments. Because an organization is a complex interrelated set of subsystems, the first-level supervisor of one department must often work very closely with supervisors of other departments. The effective assembly line supervisor cannot wait until the time for assembly to find out if the proper parts have been manufactured elsewhere in the plant or if the scheduled purchase of parts has actually taken place. There are a variety of such lateral relations, and they are

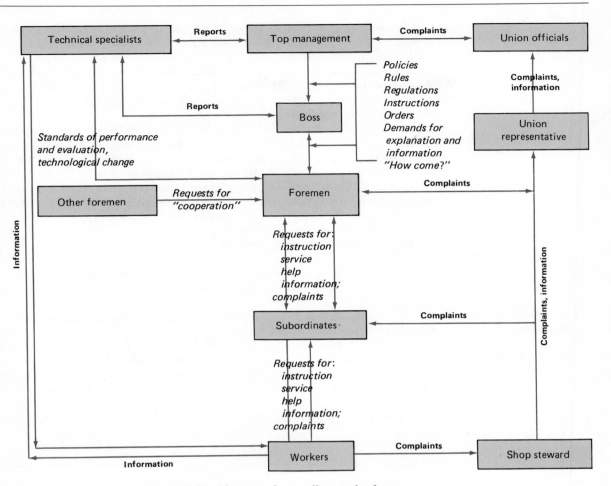

Figure 15.10   The many forces affecting the foreman

The word *foreman* is used here because it is the word used in the original
source. It corresponds to the term *first-level supervisor* used elsewhere in
the text.

Reprinted by permission of the publishers from *Man-in-Organization:
Essays of F. J. Roethlisberger*, Cambridge, Mass.: The Balknap Press of
Harvard University Press. (First published *Harvard Business Review*,
Spring 1945.) Copyright © 1945, 1973 by the President and Fellows of
Harvard College.

seldom formally defined. Their effective functioning depends in large
measure on the informal understandings that exist among supervisors.
Thus it is important for such supervisors to build and maintain good
relationships with others.

   Subordinates. The first-level supervisor must translate into action
the expectations and decisions coming from various sources and must
therefore gain the cooperation of subordinates. Cooperation at the work
level is necessary if the workers are to conform to the rules, regulations,
and standards originated by other groups. Most people do not not like to
conform, particularly when they have little to do with making the decisions that affect them. Thus the task of translating into action the plans
made by specialists is a difficult one.

The union. The role of the first-level supervisor is further complicated in a union plant. The union contract is usually signed by a top
management negotiating team and contains a comprehensive set of
rules, procedures, and policies that affect how the supervisor deals with
the unionized workers. As Figure 15.10 shows, the shop steward, the
union representative at the worker level, demands and expects many
things from the supervisor.

In the process of coordinating and dealing with these varied expectations, the first-level supervisor is constantly engaged in organizing and
reorganizing in order to "fine-tune" the department. Reorganizing includes shifting employee assignments as a result of new methods and
procedures or because of union seniority rules. It may involve training or
retraining workers in new assignments and shifting the span of control of
group leaders. It may involve borrowing material or parts from other
departments during a time of shortage or taking corrective action when
the manufactured parts are not up to standards set by quality control
experts.

Thus the first-level supervisor is constantly organizing on the basis
of ever-changing information from a variety of sources.

**Classical
Principles of
Vertical
Coordination**

The classical principles of vertical coordination, which are based
primarily on organizational hierarchy, cannot be followed rigidly, but
they can be used as a guide to managerial action. The hierarchy is often
the most visible part of an organization's structure, as is shown in Figure
15.11. The nature of the tasks to be performed and the quality of people
in the organization determine the nature of departmentation and, hence,
the horizontal differentiation. Horizontal differentiation creates the need
for coordination, which in turn creates a degree of vertical differentia-

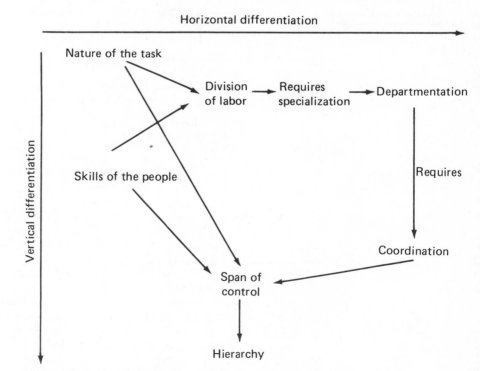

Figure 15.11 Coordination of specialization through hierarchy

tion, or hierarchy. Vertical differentiation creates a need for coordination based on systems of authority. To ensure that both vertical and horizontal coordination is accomplished, certain classical principles have been developed. They are unity of command, the scalar principle, line and staff authority, and functional authority.[10] Because organizations are complex and because each of them has unique aspects, these principles should be used only as a guide. They were developed primarily from closed systems thinking.

The Unity of Command Principle

The **unity of command** principle suggests that no organization member should report to more than one supervisor for any single function. The more clearly and completely an individual has a clear reporting relationship to a single boss, the less the chance of conflict in instructions and the greater the feeling of personal responsibility for results. However, as Chapters 1 and 2 have pointed out, managers are in contact with and are influenced by many other people. The influence process is widespread, since the organization is a subsystem with a number of subsystems interacting with each other. One of the most quoted of the classical principles, unity of command helps clarify the relationships between supervisors and subordinates—but only when it takes account of the many formal and informal relationships managers have with others. The seven managers at the Osage plant, for example, influenced each other; and the action taken by their supervisor helped clarify their relationships with each other and with the plant manager.

The Scalar Principle

Under the **scalar principle**, authority and responsibility should flow in an unbroken line from the top to the bottom of the organization. The more clearly the line of authority and responsibility flows from top management to every subordinate position, the more likely there is to be responsible decision making and organizational communication. This principle is really an extension of the unity of command principle, as Figure 15.12 shows. It suggests that an organization represents a hierarchy of authority and that lines of authority and responsibility should be as clear as possible throughout the organization. Again, this principle is helpful only as a general guideline. It does not take into consideration the idea that the organization's subsystems are interdependent and interrelated. Nor does it account for the formal and informal pressures and influences of peers and other groups. Lines of authority and responsibility are seldom clear-cut and easily identified, as Figure 15.10 shows.

Line and Staff

In the formal organization, **line authority** is that relationship in which a supervisor directs a subordinate. The function of a **staff** is to do research for and to advise a line manager. Line authority is therefore an extension of the unity of command and scalar principles.

The distinction between line and staff is confusing to many people. Frequently line functions have been seen as those directly responsible for attaining the organization's objectives. Staff functions have been seen as those assisting the line in its efforts. Thus departments such as manufacturing and sales have been described as performing line functions, while departments such as purchasing, accounting, advertising, personnel, and quality control have been described as performing staff functions.

The attempt to split up line and staff by departments augments the confusion. Take, for example, the purchasing department. Under the departmental distinction of line and staff, purchasing is considered sec-

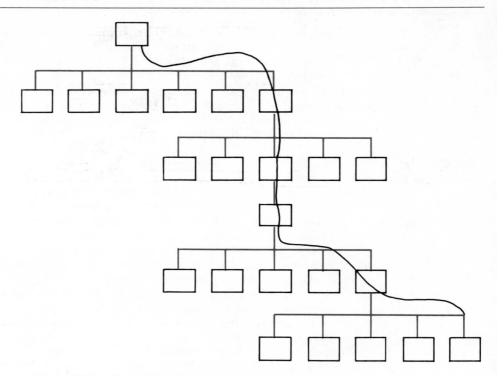

Figure 15.12   Unity of command and scalar principle

ondary to production; it is seen as advisory and inessential. But the purchase of materials, parts, and others items is just as necessary to an organization as manufacturing or other production operations. (In some organizations, the advertising department's budget is larger than that of the production department.)

Much of the confusion can be resolved if line and staff are considered from a systems viewpoint. From this viewpoint, line and staff positions reside not in the departments themselves but in the relationships among them. Using the unity of command and scalar principles, any manager is a line manager with regard to subordinates over whom the manager has legitimate authority. For example, a personnel manager may have a number of subordinate managers who in turn have subordinates. In that sense, the personnel manager is a line manager. But when the personnel manager advises the production manager, the recommendations are staff functions. If, in turn, the production manager advises the personnel manager or the chief executive, this advice is also a staff function. These relationships are shown in Figure 15.13.

Functional Authority

Functional authority is the authority to prescribe practices, procedures, policies, or other matters to units or groups not in the direct chain of command (as shown in Figure 15.13). Following the unity of command and scalar principles, such authority is delegated by higher level management. For example, the personnel department may be the delegated authority to develop and prescribe the use of an application blank to be used by all clerical applicants. In order to maintain standardized accounting practices, the controller may have the authority to prescribe how accounting records will be kept throughout a number of the organization's divisions. Although a line manager may have the authority to

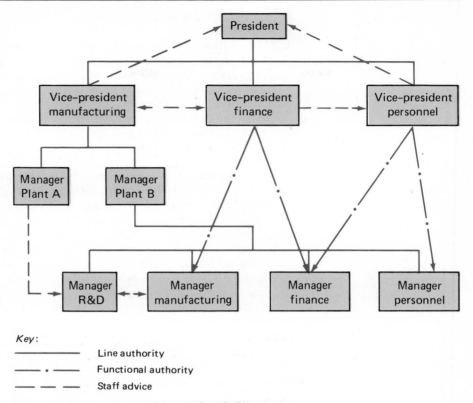

Key:

————————— Line authority

———•——— Functional authority

——— — ——— Staff advice

Figure 15.13 Line versus functional authority

employ an engineer, the personnel department may specify the salary to be paid.

Frequently, functional authority is assumed by people in "staff" jobs. For example, an assistant to a chief executive may open a request with, "The president wants . . ." The receiver of the message may not be certain whether the president really authorized the request or whether the authority was assumed by the assistant. As a result, the classic closed system approach suggests that the more clearly spelled out functional authority is, the better.

Organization Charts and Manuals

Chapter 11 described a model as being a representation of reality. An **organization chart**—a graphic model of a formal organization—has two basic purposes:

1. It shows who is accountable to whom (the scalar principle).
2. It shows, in abbreviated form, who does what in the organization.

For example, the organization chart for the Osage plant (Figure 15.1) reveals that six managers report to the plant manager. One manager is responsible for manufacturing, another for marketing, and so on. The plant manager is accountable for the operation of the entire plant and is responsible to a division manager.

Several conventions are used in preparing organization charts:

1. The individual positions on the chart are usually represented by a rectangle, although a circle or triangle is sometimes used. Com-

mittees or several executives in the same position occupy one rectangle.

2. The vertical arrangement of the rectangles usually shows relative positions in the organization's hierarchy. The most powerful position is normally at the top of the organization chart. (Some organization charts are circular or read from left to right, with the power emanating from the left.)

3. Direct organizational relationships are shown by solid lines between positions; they indicate who reports to whom.

4. Functional or advisory authority is usually shown by dotted or broken lines.

5. Lines of authority usually enter at the top center of the rectangle and leave at the bottom center; they do not run through the box. An exception is the staff assistant or "assistant to" position, which may enter the side of the rectangle (see Figure 15.1).

As a graphic model, the organization chart has a number of advantages. It is useful for showing formal work relationships among managers and others; it can help orient new members; and in the case of organizational changes, it can identify what changes have occurred and where. In this sense an organization chart can be viewed largely as a method of communication.

The **organization manual** goes even further as a model of the organization. Through its job descriptions, it shows the duties performed (thereby defining the scope and limits of the various jobs); the extent of authority held by individual managers, and the relationships of positions with each other.

There are a number of disadvantages to both organization charts and manuals, one of the chief of which is that they are expensive to develop and maintain. Perhaps more importantly, from a systems approach neither organization charts nor manuals can accurately show the dynamic, ongoing *process* of interaction among the organization's differ-

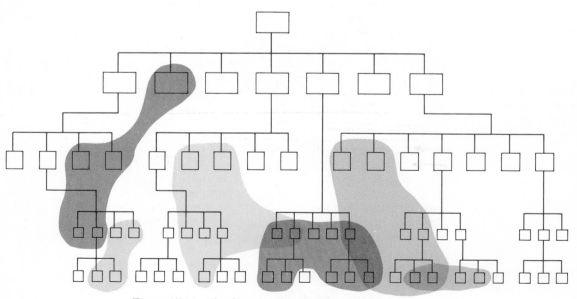

Figure 15.14   The formal and informal organization

ent subsystems. As seen in the Osage plant case, there was a great deal of misunderstanding about duties and responsibilities even though the organization had position descriptions, organization charts, manuals, and formal objectives.

Since organization charts and manuals show only the formal organization, they can be misleading. Informal organizations, or systems, evolve spontaneously from the ways in which employees at all levels interact and work with each other.[11] They help satisfy people's needs for relatedness, security, friendship, and growth. They do not have official rules or formal work managers. Indeed, sometimes they work against the organization. There are many well-documented cases of output restriction and other negative approaches used by informal organizations.

Figure 15.14 shows a hypothetical organization chart. The solid lines represent lines of authority, and the rectangles show who reports to whom. The shaded areas indicate patterns of interaction not prescribed by the formal organization that cut across formal organizational lines. Everyone knows of examples. The student whose friend works in the registrar's office may get information about grades long before the official grade notification is sent out. Knowing the mechanic at the local service station or garage may help get the work done faster and better. (Informal organizations were discussed more thoroughly in Chapter 6.)

Implications for the Manager

The effective manager is aware of the fact that, in order to accomplish objectives, organizations have two basic problems of structure or design. The first is specialization or division of work. The second is coordination of the work to ensure that the activities are accomplished. The two are highly interrelated. Different methods of dividing up the work require different methods of coordination.

The job of a first-level supervisor in a manufacturing department was used as an example to show the ongoing but constantly changing dynamics of organizing. In a specialized job at the bottom of the management hierarchy, the supervisor must coordinate the requests and expectations of a variety of individuals and groups.

The effective manager is aware that, through the years, classic principles of organizational structure based on similarities among organizations have emerged. Because each organization has some unique aspects, these principles should be used only as guides. For example, the principle of unity of command helps make clearer the relationship between supervisor and subordinate but does not take into consideration group dynamics, the power of the informal organization, and the many relationships the manager has with others.

The organization chart provides a graphic way of showing formal organization structure, but it does not reveal anything about informal organization—which has its own rules and exists concurrently with the formal organization. The effective manager makes good use of the informal organization.

The discussion of the basic principles of organizing has used a modified closed systems approach. That is, the primary emphasis has been on the organization itself, with little attention paid to other influences on the organization, such as technology and environment. Chapter 16 will provide additional material on organizational structure, using more of an open systems approach.

Review

1. What are two of the most fundamental problems facing organizations?
2. In what way might open systems thinking affect organizational structure differently than closed systems thinking?
3. List and give examples of six different methods of horizontal specialization.
4. What is the span of control? What should be considered in establishing a span of control?
5. Why is coordination necessary in organizations?
6. What are the four classical principles of coordination?
7. Give an example of each of the basic principles of coordination through use of a management hierarchy (not using any of those explained in the text).
8. In what ways is an organization chart helpful? In what ways is it misleading?
9. What are the basic differences among line, staff, and functional authority? What purpose do these differences serve?
10. What difficulties might arise if unity of command and the scalar principle were used as absolutes?
11. Can an organization exist without structure? Explain.

Benton's Department Store

Benton's Department Store was opened in 1935 by Martha Benton. Originally a small dress shop, it now carries a full line of clothing in fourteen departments, including sportswear, dresses, men's clothing, shoes, and jewelry. The store has sixty employees.

Benton's has been successful. In 1948, Martha and Henry Benton were able to finance the construction of a new building. That building has since been expanded three times, the latest expansion being in 1978. For the past five years, sales have grown steadily and are currently in excess of $5 million a year. Net profits have been averaging 4.5 percent, although last year the profit dipped to 3.8 percent. Martha Benton feels that if things were run more efficiently, the profit margin could reach 5 percent.

The store is collectively owned and managed by four people—Martha Benton, her husband, Henry, their daughter, Helen, and their son-in-law, Ken Smith. Specific duties and responsibilities have been more or less arbitrarily assigned throughout the years. Figure 15.15 shows assumed and shared responsibilities.

General management functions are performed by all four owners. For instance, Helen usually does the hiring, but often one of the other three will take the initiative to add more salespersons. The situation is usually discussed by all four before any specific action is taken. Thus each of the owner-managers is in direct touch with all phases of the business's operations.

Martha is pleased with the openness and easiness in the store management, but she is also aware of its drawbacks. At times she has heard from employees that one manager expects one thing and another something else. It also seems that every now and then certain management areas get out of hand. For instance, the payroll expense for the last six months seems extremely high.

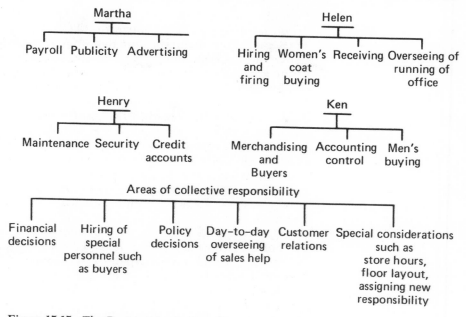

Figure 15.15 The Benton organization chart

Another problem is that often the attitudes of the four managers differ. For instance, while Martha disapproved of Henry's absences from work, Helen simply shrugged the matter off and Ken only asked Henry if he would be in on Saturday. The four managers are also stubborn; thus instances sometimes arise where the communication that is so necessary for this organization is thwarted.

Martha and Henry are now in their mid-seventies, and Martha is wondering how the organization can best be run when she and Henry leave the business. Ken and Helen each have college-age children who have expressed an interest in the family business, and Martha wonders how to incorporate them into the organization. The store functions have become increasingly complex as the company has expanded, and there are tentative expansion plans for the mid-1980s.[12]

1. How effective has the current structure been?
2. Should changes be made? If so, what should they be?
3. In what way does this organization confirm or violate some of the principles discussed in the chapter?
4. What effect might Martha's or Henry's leaving have on the organization?

Footnotes

1. H. Fayol, *General and Industrial Management* (New York: Pittman Publishing, 1949); L. Gulick and L. Urwick, eds., *Papers on the Science of Administration* (New York: Institute of Public Administration, 1937); Max Weber and Talcott Parsons, eds., *The Theory of Social and Economic Organization*, trans. A. Henderson and T. Parsons (New York: Oxford University Press, 1947); and E. Holdaway, "Dimensions of

Organizations in Complex Societies: The Educational Sector," *Administrative Science Quarterly* 20 (March 1975): 37–58.

2. D. Ronald, "Reorganizing for Results," *Harvard Business Review* 44 (November–December 1966): 96–104.

3. Urwick, ed., *The Golden Book of Management: A Historical Record of the Life and Work of Seventy Pioneers* (London: N. Neame, 1946); J. Mooney and A. Reiley, *Onward Industry* (New York: Harper & Bros., 1931); Urwick, *The Theory of Organization* (New York: American Management Association, 1952); V. Graicunus, "Relationship in Organizations," in *Papers on the Science of Administration*, ed. Urwick and Gulick (New York: Institute of Public Administration, 1937); Urwick, "The Manager's Span of Control," *Harvard Business Review* 34 (May–June 1956): 39–47; and W. Suojanen, "The Span of Control—Fact or Fable," *Advanced Management* 20 (November 1955): 5–13.

4. R. Carzo, Jr., and J. Yancuzas, "Effects of Flat and Tall Organization Structure," *Administrative Science Quarterly* 14 (June 1969): 178–191; G. Fisch, "Stretching the Span of Management," *Harvard Business Review* 41 (September–October 1963): 74–84; and G. Bell, "Determinants of Span of Control," *American Journal of Sociology* 73 (July 1967): 100–109.

5. H. Koontz and C. O'Donnell, *Essentials of Management* (New York: McGraw-Hill, 1974), p. 202.

6. E. Huse and J. Bowditch, *Behavior in Organizations: A Systems Approach to Managing*, rev. ed. (Reading, Mass.: Addison-Wesley, 1977).

7. "A Steelman Steps Up the Pace at U.S. Steel," *Business Week*, March 9, 1974, pp. 154–155.

8. "The Problems That Are Upsetting Woolworth's," *Business Week*, June 29, 1974, p. 73.

9. F. Roethlisberger, "The Foreman, Master and Victim of Double Talk," *Harvard Business Review* 43 (September–October 1965): 11–52.

10. Fayol, *General and Industrial Management*; and Urwick, *The Theory of Organization*.

11. E. Bakke, *Bonds of the Organization* (New York: Harper & Bros., 1957); D. Katz, "The Motivational Basis of Organizational Behavior," *Behavioral Sciences* 9 (April 1964): 130–145; F. Jasinski, "Adapting Organizations to New Technology," *Harvard Business Review* 37 (January–February 1959): 79–86; K. Davis, *Human Relations at Work* (New York: McGraw-Hill, 1962), p. 236; and R. Van Zelst, "Sociometrically Selected Work Teams Increase Production," *Personnel Psychology* 5 (Autumn 1952): 175–185.

12. Case originally written by Gary Eberhard under the supervision of Edgar F. Huse.

Chapter 16   Designing the Organizational Structure

The Electronic Products Division

Some Basic Factors in Organizational Design
　　Size and Structure
　　Operations Technology and Structure
　　Environment and Structure

A Contingency Model
　　Differentiation (Specialization)
　　Integration (Coordination)

A Contingency Approach to Organizational Design
　　The Strategic Level
　　The Managerial Level
　　The Operating Level

Implications for the Manager

Review

Managerial Choice

Learning Objectives

When you have finished reading and studying this chapter, you should be able to:

1. Demonstrate that organizational design depends on many factors.
2. Compare and contrast the effects of size, technology, and environment on organizational structure.
3. Compare and contrast the organic and mechanistic approaches to organizational design.
4. Explain why there is no universal "best" design for all organizations.
5. Demonstrate uses for the matrix organization other than those given in the text.
6. Demonstrate effective skills as an organizer.
7. Define and be able to use the following concepts:

contingency approach   mechanistic
size   differentiation
operations technology   integration
environmental variability   matrix organization
organic   sociotechnical approach

Thought Starters

1. Think of an organization with which you are familiar. Should it be organized differently?
2. Should a secondary school system in Great Falls, Montana, be organized the same way as one in Chicago or New York?
3. You are in charge of reorganizing the federal government. What will you change? What will you keep the same?

The Electronic Products Division

The electronic products division of Alpha Corporation, a large multinational company, was organized along functional lines. It included such departments as research, product development, manufacturing, marketing, sales (organized on a geographic basis), finance, and personnel. The division manufactured a variety of electronic instruments and components.

Because the division had experienced turbulent business conditions and poor performance for three years, its general manager called in a consultant from the home office to discuss what he saw as a problem in intergroup relations. The manager felt that there were many conflicts among the various functional groups in the division and that these were severely hampering the division's product development efforts, which required cooperation and coordination among all the functional groups.

The consultant suggested doing an analysis and examination to see if the poor intergroup relationships were a problem or a symptom. The consultant observed divisional meetings, looking at both content and process. He interviewed about forty managers, supervisors, and key individuals, and he had each of them complete a questionnaire. The problem soon became clear. The consultant found that the division was highly specialized and that the managers and others were highly motivated but that the overall design of the division needed to be improved. The primary coordination (integration) was through the division manager, who held frequent meetings with his top staff and others to discuss and coordinate all product development activities in the division. This was not sufficient, however. Poor intergroup relations were symptoms; poor organizational design was a cause.

At the suggestion of the consultant, the areas of the division that were concerned with new product development were reorganized into product teams (one for each new product) to bring about better coordination. Members of the teams were selected on the basis of the clarity and certainty of the function involved. For example, the less-known and less-certain functions of research and/or development were generally represented by a scientist and/or a development engineer. Well-established and well-known functions such as finance and manufacturing were represented by individuals at higher levels in the organization, such as the plant controller or production superintendent. Coordination of each team was the responsibility of a market development representative. The consultant trained the coordinators and served as a process observer at meetings of the project teams.

Thus the coordination was now being performed not only through the management hierarchy but also through project teams led by representatives of market development. Each of the project teams was phased out when the particular new product was developed. The initial diagnosis period lasted approximately six months. The program to change the organizational structure took approximately a year.

Follow-up studies were done eighteen months and two years after the project began. In the year after implementation of the program, nine complex products were introduced; this compared to a total of five new products in the previous five years. Intergroup friction was drastically reduced, morale was increased, and profits were up. The revised design resulted in better performance, greater commitment to the decisions made, and more professional and interpersonal competance. As a result of the success of the project, nineteen project teams were established in five major divisions of the corporation.[1]

The electronic products division is discussed here for several reasons. First, organizational design and structure is a powerful way to influence the behavior of individuals and groups. As the organizational design changed for the better, so also did the employees' behavior.

Second, organizational structure is the result of human thought; that is, organizations are designed by managers and are therefore changeable (although frequently they are not regarded that way).

Organizational design is a matter of managerial choice. To make intelligent choices, however, requires knowledge of alternative structures.[2] Given this knowledge, the manager can select the system or subsystem design that best fits the organizational strategy and managerial values.

Therefore, this chapter will examine a number of different approaches to organizational design. While Chapter 15 used a relatively closed system approach to organizations and provided some basic principles of organizing, this chapter uses a more open system approach to organizational structure and design. Many factors influence design; some of the more important are size, operations technology, and environment. This chapter offers a brief historical background and then examines the factors influencing structure. It concludes with suggestions for organizational design of the top management, coordinating, and operating levels.

Some Basic Factors in Organizational Design

The early writers on organizational design were searching for a best way to design organizations. They tended to view organizations as relatively unchangeable. But these early writers were dealing primarily with organizations that manufactured a single product. Since change in these organizations was relatively slow, design could be seen as a "given." And once the best design was created, behavior could be properly controlled by the division of labor through formal rules, management hierarchy, and span of control. In other words, structure was the key; everything else was dependent on it.

As organizations became more complex—as they moved from single products to many products and as they became multinational—managers had to worry about a number of different problems. But even then they tended to accept the organizational structure as relatively fixed. When problems occurred, they were often not viewed as the result of the firm's structure. For example, the manager of the electronic products division felt that the solution to his problem was the effort to convince his managers to "get along better." He did not question the organizational design, which was the basic problem.

Over the past thirty years, attitudes have changed, and organizational design has come to be regarded as dependent on other factors. The result of this change has been called the **contingency approach** to organization design; it suggests that there is no single best way for organizations to be designed and that each organization should be designed to fit its own circumstances. An organization making beer cans probably should be organized differently from one making electronic hand calculators. An organization operating multinationally will want to use approaches different from one operating only in the United States. The major factors affecting structure are size, technology, and environment.[3]

Size and Structure

The **size** of an organization usually is measured by the number of people working for the organization in a single location. Although the classification is arbitrary, small organizations usually have from 1 to 250 employees, medium-sized organizations have 250 to 1,000, and large organizations have more than 1,000. There are other ways to measure size—revenue, sales, assets, and so on—but the relationships among these measures are usually highly correlated with each other.

The influence of size is difficult to assess, since it is relative. A worldwide accounting firm with 4,000 to 5,000 employees is indeed large. The nature of an organization and its products also is important. For example, McDonald's is a large corporation, but it has only a few people at any single location. In contrast, the General Electric plant in Cincinnati, Ohio, has thousands of employees in a single location.

Size has an effect on structure. In general, as size increases, the organization tends to become more formal and complex—to have more rules and more formal positions, ranks, subunits, and sections within subunits. As departmentation (structural differentiation) increases, the administrative staff and the administrative hierarchy also increase.

In general, the larger the number of people, the less easy it is to relate informally. Therefore, the greater the size of the unit, the greater the need for formal procedures to deal with employee interrelationships and the flow of communications. As the number of employees increases, more formal approaches to control are necessary, including written rules, job descriptions, and increasing levels of hierarchy.[4]

C. Northcote Parkinson has developed what is known as "Parkinson's Law." In his book of that name, he suggests that there is a tendency for every unit to build up its importance by expanding the number of its employees. Indeed, Parkinson's Law states that the number of people in a given department has no relationship to the amount of work that must be done. In order to improve their own status, managers are motivated to endlessly expand their own staffs. However, this grand strategy is seldom revealed because the additional employees make work for one another through the division of labor. According to Parkinson, "An official wants to multiply subordinates, not rivals."[5]

In terms of its effect on the structure of the organization, organizational size has probably been studied more intensively than anything else. However, the effect is not clear-cut, perhaps because of the related effects of technology and environment.

Operations Technology and Structure

Most of the studies on technology have focused their attention on **operations technology,** which includes the tools, mechanical equipment, actions, knowledge, or material used in the production or distribution of a good or service. All organizations have an operations technology of one kind or another.

The definition is a broad one; it includes managerial and nonmanagerial knowledge or experience, a range of equipment from very simple to very complex, production techniques that vary widely, and a variety of different materials. An individual weaving a rug on a hand loom is using relatively simple technology, while an operator in the control room of a large automated refinery is using complex, sophisticated technology. Yet, both are involved in operations technology.

The early work dealing with the effect of technology on organizational structure was done by several management researchers, including sociologist Joan Woodward and her associates.[6] Woodward developed a scale for measuring technological complexity and found that differences in complexity accounted for differences in organizational structure.

She placed organizations into three major production categories: unit and small batch, large batch and mass production, and continuous process. The major distinction among these three operations was the extent to which the processes for manufacturing the product were standardized and automatic. She found that unit and small batch organizations were the least standardized and that continuous process organizations were the most automatic and thus the most technologically complex—as Figure 16.1 shows.

Woodward's scale is still relevant. Unit and small batch organizations are primarily involved in made-to-order items, such as custom clothing, custom furniture, and specialized electronic equipment. Their technology requires workers who are essentially experts in a given craft or who are skilled in using various simple tools. Large batch and mass production organizations include automobile companies, mass-produced clothing manufacturers, large bakeries, and industrial equipment manufacturers. Such organizations usually have highly mechanized production processes. In an automobile plant, for instance, one or more cars a minute may go past the assembly line worker. The work requires machine operators who are trained to perform very few operations. Automated, or continuous process, production involves the worker monitoring an automatic ongoing process, such as a production process in an oil refinery or a pharmaceutical or chemical plant. At an oil refinery, the product flows continuously, regulated by a set of automatic operations. Process production does not require craft workers or assembly line

Unit (craft)	Mass (mechanized)	Process (automated)
Craft workers	Machine operators, assembly line workers	Technicians, monitors

Figure 16.1   Increasing technological complexity

workers. Instead it requires technicians—workers trained to monitor operations and make adjustments as necessary.

Although Woodward saw a great deal of variation in organizational design within each of these categories, firms that were above average in commercial success tended to be organized in ways that were typical for the category. Thus Woodward concluded that (1) technology is generally related to structure, and (2) within each production category is one best way to organize, and it depends on the technology involved. Therefore, organizational structure appeared to be dependent on technology (an approach known as the "technological imperative"). For example, most successful organizations using unit or batch production technology had considerably wider spans of supervisory control and fewer levels of hierarchy than did successful firms with more stable, continuous process technologies. Woodward's pioneering study thus firmly established the importance of technology as affecting organizational design.[7]

More has been learned in recent years about the relationships between technology and organizational structure, and the effective manager should be able to experiment with different designs. Among the relationships are:

1. Technology influences organizational structure. The more routine and well-known the technology, the greater the formalization and bureaucratization of the organization. Conversely, the more uncertain and complex the technology, the less tendency there is to have rigid rules and regulations.
2. Technology has a greater effect on relatively small, production oriented units than on upper levels of organizations and on units normally considered "staff."
3. Most firms have several different technologies, and these affect the structure of the different subunits.
4. It is useful to distinguish among at least three levels of organization—the individual, the subunit, and the organization as a whole.

These recommendations may not seem particularly helpful at this point, but they will be amplified later in the chapter—after more of the structural aspects of organizations are explained.

Environment and Structure

Organizations depend on exchange with the outside environment. Their subunits must deal with both the external and the internal environment. This section will examine the effect of environmental certainty or uncertainty on organizational structure, as shown in Table 16.1.

Environmental variability, which has gained attention as a factor contributing to uncertainty among organizational decision makers, refers to the degree of change or uncertainty with which an organization or its subunits is involved.[8] It includes at least three factors: (1) the frequency of changes in the relevant environment, (2) the degree of difference

Table 16.1   A continuum from certain to highly uncertain environment

Stable, certain environment	Highly unstable, uncertain environment
Few changes in products and services	Frequent changes in products and services
Known and stable competitors and customers	Changing or new competitors
Little technological innovation	High degree of technological innovation
Formalized and centralized structure	Dynamic and flexible structure

involved in each change, and (3) the degree of predictability in the overall pattern of change.

Organizations making matches, bottles, cans, manhole covers, and toothpicks experience relatively little change. Their customers and competitors are fairly well known, and there is little technological innovation. Burlap bags and cotton twine can be made on machines that are sixty or seventy years old. But organizations involved with plastics, electronics, solar power, and nucleonics experience great uncertainty and rapid changes. Technological breakthroughs occur frequently. For example, the organizations manufacturing minicomputers are constantly changing their products.

Few organizations exist in a completely stable environment. Changes in laws and regulations, such as those on air pollution and retirement age, affect many organizations. Further, an individual organization may exist in several different environments. The General Electric division that makes electric toasters may exist in a more stable environment than the division engaged in research on solar energy. The Corning Glass division that makes hospital instruments and electronics equipment may be in a less certain environment than the division making television screens.

Nevertheless, research has suggested that successful organizations (or their subunits) existing in relatively uncertain and unpredictable environments should be structured differently from those existing in relatively known and certain environments, as shown in Figure 16.2. The two extreme types of structures are the organic and the mechanistic.[9] The **organic** type has a flexible and relaxed organization. Individuals communicate not only with immediate supervisors, subordinates, or colleagues but with anyone else in the organization with whom they need to communicate. Expert power is far more important than position power. That is, actions are dictated by the problem rather than by charts and documents specifying precise responsibilities and functions. The

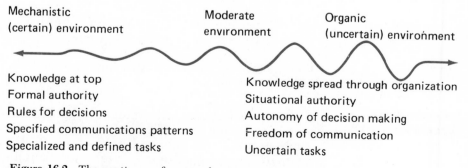

Mechanistic (certain) environment	Moderate environment	Organic (uncertain) environment
Knowledge at top		Knowledge spread through organization
Formal authority		Situational authority
Rules for decisions		Autonomy of decision making
Specified communications patterns		Freedom of communication
Specialized and defined tasks		Uncertain tasks

Figure 16.2   The continuum from mechanistic to organic organizations

organic style is most appropriate to unstable environmental conditions in which novel problems continually occur.

The **mechanistic** type of organization is highly bureaucratic. Tasks are specialized and clearly defined. Rules and procedures are emphasized, a clear hierarchy of control exists, and the responsibility for overall knowledge and coordination rests exclusively at the top of the hierarchy. This type of organization is suitable when markets and technology are well established and show little change over time. Mechanistic organizations have great difficulty adapting to technological innovation and change. Because bureaucratic values are so ingrained, managers try to use essentially bureaucratic approaches for solving organizational and technical problems created by innovation. In some cases, almost all decisions related to innovation and change are continually bucked up to the president because subordinates do not have the freedom, the confidence, or the competence to make decisions in new situations. The president is overworked, and the change process is extremely slow. Communications channels become clogged.

The organic and mechanistic styles are extremes. In real life, almost all organizations are likely to show different combinations, particularly in the organizational subunits, each of which exists in a subenvironment of its own. In the case of the electronic products division, the organizational structure was changed from mechanistic and bureaucratic to a more organic structure that was better suited to the division's rapid environmental and technical change.

A Contingency Model

The major factors of size, technology, and structure can be combined into the contingency approach described briefly earlier in the chapter. As mentioned then, the contingency approach suggests that there is no single best way to design an organization, that the design instead depends on the situation. This approach emphasizes that organizations are complex and attempts to predict the best design for various conditions and situations.[10]

An influential series of studies was conducted by sociologists Paul Lawrence and Jay Lorsch. Building primarily on previous work involving technology and environment, they developed a contingency approach to organizational design. Their model has four basic premises:

1. There is no single best way to design organizations.
2. The specific design of an organization and/or its subunits must fit both the environment and the technology.
3. The needs of individual organization members are better satisfied when the organization and its subunits are properly designed.
4. Some organizations or their subunits are improperly designed and should be changed or modified.

The model is based on two fundamental concepts—differentiation and integration.[11]

Differentiation (Specialization)

An organization's environment contains many subenvironments (for example, market, scientific, and production). Different functional units (such as sales, research, and production) deal with different subenvironments. A subenvironment is relatively certain if there is clear information regarding it, cause and effect relationships are known, and the time span of clear feedback is short. For example, cancer researchers may have to wait months or years to determine the effects of their research, while a worker doing the final assembly on a water pistol may know immediately whether the product works. Different subenvironments result in varying amounts of **differentiation**—the "difference in cognitive and emotional orientation among managers in different functional departments."[12] High uncertainty leads to more differentiation, and low uncertainty leads to less. Differentiation occurs in four basic dimensions:

1. *Formality of structure*. The degree to which an organization's subsystems have narrow span of control, rules, regulations, and other formalized procedures. Formality of structure tends to be greater in such departments as manufacturing and finance. Long-range planning units tend to have fewer rigid rules and set procedures.

2. *Interpersonal orientation*. Members of units that have either highly certain or highly uncertain tasks tend to be more concerned with the tasks than with personal relationships. Members of units with moderately uncertain tasks are concerned about establishing positive social relationships. Manufacturing people tend to be concerned with tasks; sales and marketing people tend to be concerned with relationships.

3. *Time orientation*. Subunits that have relatively immediate feedback, such as sales and production, have a much shorter time orientation than do subunits that may not get feedback for months or years, such as research and development. Manufacturing may be highly concerned with meeting daily schedules, while product development may be primarily interested in long-range thinking.

4. *Goal orientation*. Different units may have very different goal orientations. Manufacturing may prefer to have a small number of high-volume products, while sales may want a wide variety of products in order to increase the level of overall sales.

Different industries also have varying amounts of differentiation. Figure 16.3 shows the relative amount of differentiation for three major segments of the container, food, and plastics industries. The container organizations have little need for differentiation since they exist in a relatively certain environment with a stable and known technology. On the other hand, the plastics organizations exist in a relatively uncertain, high technology environment. For them, innovation is the name of the game because of their continual necessity to meet changing customer demands.

Integration (Coordination)

Integration is "the quality of the state of collaboration that exists among departments that are required to achieve unity of effort by the demands of the environment."[13] In other words, once the organization has been differentiated (specialized), it must be integrated (coordinated).

For the successful firm, the states of integration and differentiation are positively correlated. The more differentiation, the greater the need for collaboration and coordination. The effective organization needs both a level of differentiation that matches the diversity of the environment and technology and a similar level of integration.

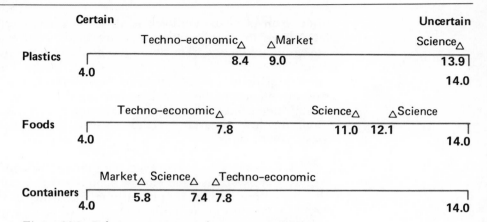

Figure 16.3 Relative uncertainty of environmental sectors

A high degree of differentiation indicates that members in different subunits view problems differently and that conflicts arise about how best to handle situations. Effective integration, on the other hand, requires that conflicts be resolved satisfactorily. How do organizations achieve high degrees of both?

In the electronic products case, individuals who had enough knowledge to make joint decisions with other departments were located at different levels in the hierarchy. In the finance subenvironment, which was relatively certain, a high-level manager had the knowledge needed to make joint decisions with other departments. But in the scientific subenvironment, with its relatively high level of uncertainty, only those working directly on a specific project had the detailed knowledge necessary for joint decision making (problem solving) with other departments.

In successful firms, the formal responsibility for achieving integration and resolving conflict is assigned to individuals located at the appropriate level in each unit or subunit. The container industry, for example, exists in a stable environment with a known technology. Thus the primary decisions involve pricing and delivery dates. In successful container firms, these decisions are made at the top and transmitted primarily through the organizational hierarchy and direct manager contact. Organizations existing in more uncertain environments or having higher technology must make decisions at lower levels. To facilitate this kind of decision making, many organizations have integrators or integrating departments formally charged with bringing about collaboration among the subunits.[14]

Of course, each industrial environment requires the appropriate degree of integration. The food industry, for example, has a less diverse and uncertain environment than the plastics industry, so its need for integration is less. Integration in stable industries with minimal differentiation can be achieved effectively through rules and managerial hierarchy. The integrative approaches are summarized in Table 16.2.

The concepts of differentiation and integration are analogous to those of division of labor and coordination. In terms of organizational

Table 16.2 Comparison of integrative devices in three high-performing organizations

	Plastics	Food	Container
Degree of differentiation	10.7	8.0	5.7
Major integrative devices	(1) Integrative department	(1) Individual integrators	(1) Direct managerial contact
	(2) Permanent cross-functional teams at three levels of management	(2) Temporary cross-functional teams	(2) Managerial hierarchy
	(3) Direct managerial contact	(3) Direct managerial contact	(3) Paper system
	(4) Managerial hierarchy	(4) Managerial hierarchy	
	(5) Paper system	(5) Paper system	

High score means greater actual differentiation.

design, however, they have been shown to be an important improvement, since more operationally defined.

The case of the electronic product division shows an application of the contingency theory. Rather than trying to change people through improving intergroup relations, the general manager made a conscious choice to change the organizational design to better fit the environment. The results were the introduction of nine complex new products in one year (as compared to a total of five in the previous five years), increased motivation and morale, and a productive handling of conflict.

A Contingency Approach to Organizational Design

As already explained, organizations are affected by size, technology, and environment, among other factors. However, some evidence indicates that these factors may not affect all levels of the organization in the same way.[15] For this reason, the effects of the factors at the three main levels of the organization—strategic, managerial, and operating—will now be examined.

The Strategic Level

At the strategic, or top management, level, size and environment may be more important than technology, since top-level managers must keep themselves informed about the external environment. From an open systems point of view, management must continually gather information about such areas as economic and energy conditions, changing attitudes toward work, social responsibility, and the growing number of environmental and civil rights groups and issues. The organization's structure should help ensure the collection of information from the external environment.

At this level, size can be controlled by departmentation or other approaches. For example, the automotive division of General Motors is decentralized into a number of operating divisions, such as Chevrolet, Buick, and Cadillac. Although the automobile names and designs are somewhat different, the Chevrolet division of General Motors is essentially the same as the Cadillac division. The organization charts of the two divisions are very similar, and the concept of function is maintained within each division. That is, the employees with the same functional specialties are grouped together—assembly workers in one subdivision, engineers in another, and so on. Overall policy and the coordination of the different automotive divisions is still centralized, however. Top management is aware that GM's subenvironments and technologies vary among the different parts of the organization. Some departments operate in fairly stable environments and with stable technologies, while others have quickly changing environments and technologies.

Departments, divisions, or other subunits operating in stable environments and with known technologies should be formalized and centralized with task-centered leadership. Those operating in uncertain environments and with changing technologies should be structured in a more organic and less bureaucratic fashion.

In the electronic products division case, the first attempt to solve the problem was through the management hierarchy, vertical information systems, and meetings at the division manager level. After the reorganization, the structure became more flexible and decentralized, allowing for self-contained tasks and reliance on lateral relationships.

The Managerial Level

The managerial, or coordinating (middle), level performs two basic functions: (1) coordinating, administering, and servicing the operating level, and (2) mediating between the operating level and those who use the products. (The products can be services as well as goods.) At this level, a number of boundary-spanning subsystems need to be established to ensure that necessary information is imported from the environment. The type of information sought is more specific than the type needed at the top level.

When the environment is uncertain and the technology complex, lateral coordinating approaches may become more important than vertical ones. In fact, a number of new approaches are being developed to handle problems that neither the functional organization (organizational units formed of different specialists) nor the product organization (different specialists in the same unit) seem capable of handling. One new approach is the **matrix organization**, a device for integrating the activities of different specialists while maintaining specialized organizational units. See Figure 16.4 for an example of this type of organization.

The matrix organization came into prominence in the 1960s, when the U.S. Department of Defense and the aerospace industry began using it.[16] Combining the functional and the project types of structure, it is often used in project, program, and product management. For example, it is often used to coordinate efforts on large, complex projects and where there are a number of product lines. It is also used for projects that have a limited time span and that need different people for each phase of the work.

Under a matrix organization, people can be shifted around as necessary while still belonging to their functional department. To illustrate: An organization may have certain people prepare bids on projects. When the contract is accepted, engineers, scientists, and other personnel may then be assigned to work on one or more of the tasks. The manager responsible for a specific project may also purchase certain needed services from elsewhere in the organization. The functional managers, in

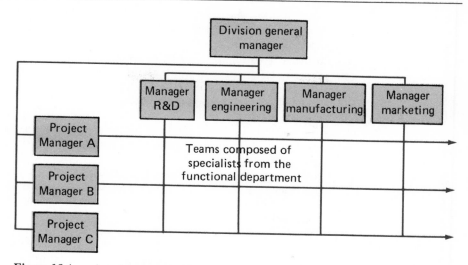

Figure 16.4   A matrix organization

turn, are dependent on this income to maintain their deparmental operations (as shown in Figure 16.4).

Modified forms of matrix organizations are often used. In the area of manufacturing, matrix approaches are followed by such industries as aerospace, chemicals, electronics, and pharmaceuticals. In the area of service, they are followed by banking, retailing, construction, health, and brokerage organizations. Even the accounting and advertising fields are using matrix organization. Hospital personnel such as nurses and social workers report to a single administrator but work in several different departments, such as obstetrics, medicine, surgery, and psychiatry.

Matrix and similar forms of organization are a powerful way to focus attention simultaneously on a specific desired goal, on complex technical issues, and on the unique requirements of customers, particularly in areas requiring a high degree of information-processing capability.

Of course, they have disadvantages too. Professionals and other employees often must be able to work for more than one boss and within teams whose existence is limited by the project itself. Collaboration and constructive conflict resolution are imperative, but they are also difficult for many people to achieve. Still, when properly used, a matrix organization can ensure that the information flow is channeled to and from the appropriate people. In one situation, an organizational redesign to take advantage of a matrix approach increased the effectiveness of designing and making hospital and medical electronic instruments. The rate of new product introduction to manufacturing more than doubled. Manufacturing efficiency, measured in terms of actual costs versus predicted costs for the first month of manufacture, rose from an average of 20 percent before the matrix organization to an average of 80 percent after its installation.[17]

The Operating Level

Every formal organization has operations subsystems to produce the goods and services. At this level, size may be important because it affects group dynamics; environment may be important because it affects the kind of work being done. And the smaller the organizational subunit, the more the structure is affected by technology, which in turn affects behavior.

Besides the matrix organization, other contingency approaches are also being used at the operating level. Among them is the **sociotechnical approach,** which is concerned with organizing and matching the technology (work flow and information flow) and the people. In most instances, it involves creating relatively autonomous groups of employees who are collectively responsible for their output.

Two early studies involved coal in England and weaving in India. In both situations, new and modern equipment had been introduced, and the change in technology had been accompanied by a change in job structure. The jobs, which were set up according to U.S. and British standards regarding the division and specialization of work, were fractionalized and did not allow a group structure to emerge. Productivity decreased sharply, and absenteeism and turnover increased.

In both instances, it was recommended that the jobs be restructured to build on work teams. Members of the newly formed teams had the necessary ability and resources to do the job itself and to coordinate efforts. In the coal mining industry, output rose from 78 percent to 95 percent; in the weaving industry, it rose from 80 percent to 95 percent. Turnover and absenteeism dropped correspondingly. In the weaving industry, a follow-up study (done sixteen years later) found that the levels of performance had remained relatively constant through the years.[18]

The results of these and similar studies made the idea of autonomous production groups popular throughout Europe, particularly in the Netherlands, Scandinavia, and Great Britain. Such groups are relatively

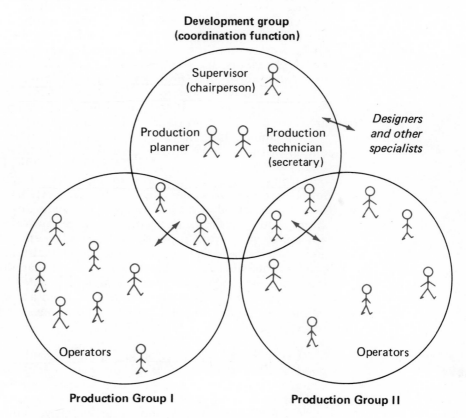

Figure 16.5 Interlocking production and development groups

self-governing in that they make many of their own decisions. A publication from Norway reports on the success of projects conducted from 1964 to 1972 for manufacturers, banks, hotels, shipyards, and other organizations. A similar publication from Sweden reports on the relative success of about five hundred different projects.[19]

Production groups should consist of persons whose work is interdependent. They should be separated from other production centers, so they can operate with relative independence. Their goals should be spelled out in clear, simple terms. Such groups enable supervisors to delegate authority and thus to devote more time to overall development and planning. Often, development groups coordinate the work of several production groups, as shown in Figure 16.5.

Extensive research on autonomous work groups has been done by Saab-Scania. The first group was established in 1969. Four years later, there were about 130 production groups and approximately 60 development groups involving 1,500 employees, and the number was still growing. Productivity increased, unplanned stoppage on the production line was reduced from 6 percent to about 2 percent, and turnover on the chassis line was reduced from over 70 percent to under 20 percent.[20]

Two of the better-known programs involve the redesign of work at Saab and Volvo plants. The widely publicized Volvo plant at Kalmar, Sweden, is designed so that different work teams are responsible for specific installations on the car (for example, the electrical system, controls, and instrumentation). One first-level supervisor and one industrial engineer or technician supervise two to four teams. Supervision focuses primarily on overall quality and on making certain that each team has the necessary equipment.

Development group at work
Courtesy of AB Volvo, Gothenburg, Sweden.

Volvo plant in Sweden
Courtesy of AB Volvo, Gothenburg, Sweden.

The Volvo plant was built to promote versatility. The outer walls are in a star-shaped pattern, which provides light and keeps the atmosphere one of a small workshop in a large factory. The teams (fifteen to twenty-five workers in each) have their own clearly defined work areas, entrances, and rest areas.

The Kalmar factory opened in July 1974. Less than a year later, the plant was working at 100 percent efficiency. In "normal" automobile plants, high productivity is 80 percent efficiency. (*Efficiency* in auto factories is defined as the number of work hours required to assemble an automobile—calculated by the engineering department—divided by the number of hours actually expended.)

A Saab engine assembly factory experimented with another type of work design. After considerable discussion, the final decision was to have teams of three or four workers completely assemble each engine. A number of engineering problems had to be solved before this approach became possible, but eventually the design shown in Figure 16.6 was developed. A large conveyor loop close to the work area brings in the engine block and takes out the completed engines. Each work group has a U-shaped guide track in the floor. Trucks can easily come in to furnish the necessary parts without disturbing the assembly group.

This plant has been criticized, however. For example, a group of U.S. workers visited the plant and reported that the work pace was too fast and the lunch breaks were too short. Immediately after the visit, a Saab executive commented that the U.S. workers had not stayed long enough to become completely proficient and that that was one reason they felt the pace was too fast. Others have criticized the team approach in general for its potential loss of accountability.[21]

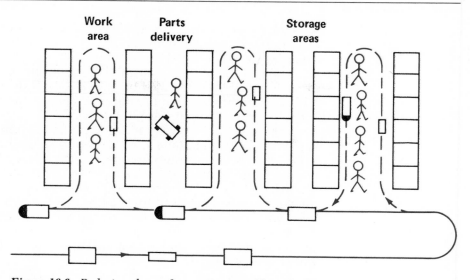

Figure 16.6   Redesigned area for engine assembly at Saab

Much more work has been done on sociotechnical systems in Europe and in Great Britain than in the United States. However, a U.S. organization making complex electronic instruments found that the introduction of autonomous work groups resulted in a 17 percent increase in productivity. Absenteeism dropped by 50 percent, quality increased 50 percent (that is, there were 50 percent fewer rejects), and employee satisfaction and morale, also increased.[22] One of the more widely publicized studies reports high levels of productivity and general satisfaction at the Gaines pet food plant in Topeka, Kansas, that occurred when autonomous work groups were introduced. However, the initial gains did not hold up—primarily because of managerial resistance. Many managers apparently feel threatened by such programs and thus resist them.[23]

Sociotechnical systems appear to be a powerful tool of organizational design, particularly at the worker level. But changes in one subsystem can have potentially negative effects on other subsystems. In this case, managers often resist the loss of their authority and responsibility. As a Swedish psychologist phrases it, "In this connection, one should pay an appropriate amount of attention to the situation of supervisors and middle managers. These categories should be given a fair chance even in the new organization to get stimulating and challenging tasks and responsibilities. It might be disastrous to the whole organization if these categories find their possibilities of performing good and qualified contributions seriously limited."[24]

Implications for the Manager

Size, technology, environment, bureaucracy—all suggest and influence ways of organizing. As open systems, organizations are highly complex. The number of inputs, transformations, and outputs of any large company almost boggles the mind. Furthermore, organizing and managing an enterprise is a constantly changing, dynamic process. Because social, economic, technical, and other conditions are changing, organizations also must change.

There is no single best kind of organization. Contingency theory suggests that relatively rigid, mechanistic, centralized approaches work well when the information and technology are well-known. Under conditions of uncertainty, more organic, open systems are better. Within this broad range is a wide degree of choice.

Thus, in the final analysis, the design of the particular organization, unit, or subsystem depends on managerial choice. At the institutional level, for example, an automobile company may need to be large for economy of manufacturing but may control size by decentralization or other methods. If it were to buy a firm making custom-made clothing, it should probably choose to keep the new firm small. As another example, organizations in uncertain environments may need to be designed in a more organic fashion than organizations in stable environments.

Finally, the use of autonomous work groups is widespread in Scandinavia but often opposed by managers in the United States. Sociotechnical systems may be chosen by only a few managers who are willing to delegate a great deal of responsibility and authority to the work force. For those managers who are unwilling or unable to do so, this is not a viable choice.

Perhaps the most important implication of this chapter is that the effective manager should not accept current organizational designs without question. Instead the manager should constantly be testing and questioning, tinkering and modifying, in order to come up with the best design possible given current knowledge, the particular situation, and the organization's values.

Review

1. Do managers really have a choice in the design of organizations and/or their subunits?
2. How important do you think personal values are in a manager's decisions regarding structure and design?
3. What does the contingency approach mean to you?
4. A paper mill that has been in operation for ten years has two identical machines making newsprint. Would you recommend a mechanistic or an organic management style for the organization?
5. What other approaches might have been considered in the case of the electronic products division?
6. Under what conditions would you recommend the use of a matrix organization? Under what conditions might it be harmful?
7. Sociotechnical systems and autonomous work groups are widely used in Norway and Sweden but very little used in the United States. What are some reasons for this difference?
8. What personal values do you hold that might make you prefer either a mechanistic or organic structure as an employee? How about as a manager?
9. What is meant by the phrase "there is no single best way to design organizations"?
10. Pick an organization with which you are familiar. Would you recommend any changes in its structure? Explain.
11. In a matrix organization, employees often work for more than one boss. Does this violate the principle of unity of command?
12. Compare and contrast differentiation and integration with division of labor and coordination.

Managerial Choice

You are the manager of the materials control department for a small plant of about three hundred people, and you report directly to the plant manager. The plant makes a variety of electronic testing instruments, some of which are used to test blood and urine samples and others to test water samples for chemical impurities. Although the plant manufactures a number of different instruments, there are only four basic types. Most of the parts used in one basic type of instrument are not used in the others, although there is some overlap.

Your department has four essential functions—purchasing, plant scheduling, inventory control, and expediting, as shown by the organization chart in Figure 16.7. (Expediting involves finishing and shipping a product faster than normally scheduled and/or speeding parts delivery.) The purchasing unit is responsible for all the plant's purchases. These include a variety of electronic parts (such as printed circuits, transistors, and resistors) as well as raw materials, clerical supplies, and everything else needed to operate the plant. There are six people in the purchasing unit, which is headed by a team leader. The people are experienced enough that each can buy almost everything needed by the plant.

The plant scheduling unit has five people, headed by a team leader. The basic responsibility of this unit is to prepare the manufacturing schedules for the plant. As orders come in, they must be scheduled to be processed through the plant. Each manufacturing area needs to know when to start production on a particular order and when to complete it.

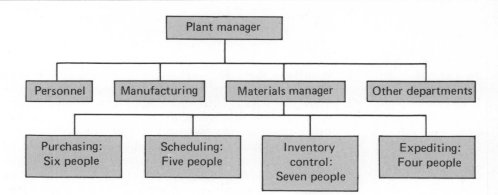

Figure 16.7 Organization chart for a small plant

The inventory control unit has four people and is headed by a team leader. There are frequent changes and modifications of the instruments made by the plant. As a result, the inventory can be overloaded with some items and understocked with others. One of the responsibilities of the inventory unit is to suggest to the manufacturing, research, and development departments that a change in an instrument might make a particular part obsolete. Then the department involved can delay the change until arrangements are made to use up the part before it becomes obsolete or to see if it can be returned to the manufacturer or used in another instrument.

The expediting unit has four people and a team leader. Because of frequent changes and because new instruments may not have detailed parts lists until just before going into manufacturing, the job of this unit is to expedite such parts. In addition, sometimes there are rush orders. Therefore, the expediters often work directly with the manufacturing people to finish an order quickly and send it out.

As the manager of the materials control department, you are aware that the way you are organized is common in your industry and in the rest of the corporation. However, there have been a number of parts shortages that have caused delays in production, and there have been frequent schedule changes because of the parts shortages or rush orders. In addition, you feel that the expediters do not like their jobs, because the work is not very challenging. Finally, you know that the different groups seem to have problems communicating across functional lines. Indeed, sometimes you wonder if any of them know what the others are doing.

You have just come from a meeting with the plant manager, who has suggested that you think of other ways of structuring the department.

1. What problems does the present organization solve? What problems does it create?
2. What are some other ways of organizing?
3. What are the advantages and disadvantages of the other approaches?

Footnotes

1. Papers presented at the Symposium on Improving Integration between Functional Groups—A Case in Organization Change and Implications

for Theory and Practice, Division of Industrial and Organizational Psychology, American Psychological Association, Washington, D.C., September 3, 1971: M. Beer, "Organizational Diagnosis: An Anatomy of Poor Integration"; G. Pieters, "Changing Organizational Structures, Roles and Processes to Enhance Integration: The Implementation of a Change Program"; A. Hundert, "Problems and Prospects for Project Teams in a Large Bureaucracy"; S. Marcus, "Findings: The Effects of Structural, Cultural, and Role Changes on Integration"; and P. Lawrence, "Comments."

2. J. Child, "Organizational Structure, Environment and Performance: The Role of Strategic Choice," *Sociology* 6 (January 1972): 2–22; P. Khandwalla, *The Design of Organizations* (New York: Harcourt Brace Jovanovich, 1977); D. Hickson, D. Pugh, and D. Pheysey, "Operations, Technology, and Organizational Structure: An Empirical Reappraisal," *Administrative Science Quarterly* 14 (September 1969): 370–397.

3. V. Sathe, "Contingency Theories of Organizational Structure," in *Managerial Accounting: The Behavioral Foundations,* ed. J. Livingstone (Columbus, Ohio: Grid, 1975), pp. 51–63; Child, "Organizational Structure, Environment and Performance"; and J. Ford and J. Slocum, Jr., "Size, Technology, Environment and the Structure of Organizations," *Academy of Management Review* 2 (October 1977): 561–575.

4. P. Blau and R. Schoenherr, *The Structure of Organizations* (New York: Basic Books, 1971); Child, "Managerial and Organizational Factors Associated with Company Performance: Part I," *Journal of Management Studies* 11 (October 1974): 175–189; Child, "Managerial and Organizational Factors Associated with Company Performance: Part II," *Journal of Management Studies* 12 (February 1975): 12–28; and M. Meyer, *Bureaucratic Structure and Authority* (New York: Harper & Row, 1972).

5. C. N. Parkinson, *Parkinson's Law* (Boston: Houghton Mifflin, 1957), p. 5.

6. J. Woodward, *Management and Technology* (London: Her Majesty's Stationery Office, 1958); J. Woodward, *Industrial Organization* (London: Oxford University Press, 1965).

7. Hickson, Pugh, and Pheysey, "Operations, Technology, and Organizational Structure: An Empirical Reappraisal," *Administrative Science Quarterly* 14 (September 1969): 370–397; E. Chapple and L. Sayles, *The Measures of Management* (New York: Macmillan, 1961); C. Perrow, *Organizational Analysis: A Sociological View* (Belmont, Calif.: Wadsworth, 1970); J. Thompson, *Organizations in Action* (New York: McGraw-Hill, 1967); P. Blau et al., "Technology and Organizations in Manufacturing," *Administrative Science Quarterly* 21 (March 1976): 21–40; D. Comstock and W. Scott, "Technology and the Structure of Subunits: Distinguishing Individual and Workgroup Effects," *Administrative Science Quarterly* 22 (June 1977): 177–202.

8. Child, "Organizational Structure, Environment and Performance."

9. T. Burns and G. Stalker, *The Management Innovation* (New York: Barnes & Noble, Social Science Paperbacks, 1961).

10. J. Ivancevich, A. Szilagyi, Jr., and M. Wallace, Jr., *Organizational Behavior and Performance* (Santa Monica, Calif.: Goodyear Publishing, 1977), p. 561.

11. P. Lawrence and J. Lorsch, *Organization and Environment: Managing Differentiation and Integration* (Boston: Harvard University, Graduate School of Business Administration, Division of Research, 1967).

12. Ibid., p. 11.

13. Ibid.

14. Comstock and Scott, "Technology and the Structure of Subunits"; C. Derr, "An Organizational Analysis of the Boston School Department" (Ph.D. diss., Harvard University, Graduate School of Business Administration, Boston, 1972); W. Brown and J. Blandin, "Coping with Uncertainty: Some Cross-Cultural Comparisons," *Journal of Business Research* 4 (May 1976): 163–174; A. Reudi, "Cultural Factors in Contingency Theory: A Comparative Study of Six U.S. and One German Plastics Producers" (Ph.D. diss., Harvard University, Graduate School of Business Administration, Boston, 1972); and E. Nielson, "Contingency Theory Applied to Small Business Organizations," *Human Relations* 27 (April 1974): 357–359.

15. R. Duncan, "Multiple Decision-Making Structures and Adapting to Environmental Uncertainty: The Impact on Organizational Effectiveness," *Human Relations* 26 (March 1974): 273–291; Galbraith, *Designing Complex Organizations* (Reading, Mass.: Addison-Wesley, 1973); Galbraith, *Organization Design* (Reading, Mass.: Addison-Wesley, 1977).

16. S. Davis and P. Lawrence, *Matrix* (Reading, Mass.: Addison-Wesley, 1977); Galbraith, *Organization Design*; T. Moore and B. Lorimer, "The Matrix Organization in Business and Health Care Institutions: A Comparison," *Hospital and Health Services Administration* 21 (Fall 1976): 26–33; and W. Goggin, "How the Multidimensional Structure Works at Dow Corning," *Harvard Business Review* 52 (January–February 1974): 54–65.

17. E. Huse and J. Bowditch, *Behavior in Organizations: A Systems Approach to Managing* (Reading, Mass.: Addison-Wesley, 1977), pp. 479–481.

18. E. Trist and K. Bamforth, "Some Social and Psychological Consequences of the Long Wall of Goal Setting," *Human Relations* 4 (January 1951): 1–8; A. Rice, *Productivity and Social Organizations: The Ahmedabad Experiment* (London: Tavistock Publications, 1958); and E. Miller, "Socio-Technical Systems in Weaving, 1953–1970: A Follow-up Study," *Human Relations* 28 (August 1975): 348–386.

19. "Work Research Institutes—Projects: 1964–1972," mimeographed (Oslo: Work Research Institutes, n.d.); and D. Jenkins, ed., *Job Reform in Sweden: Conclusions from 500 Shop Floor Projects* (Stockholm: Swedish Employer's Confederation, 1975).

20. J. Norsted and S. Aguren, *The Saab-Scania Report* (Stockholm: Swedish Employer's Confederation, 1973).

21. "Doubting Sweden's Way," *Time,* March 10, 1975, p. 40; E. Jacques, "The Importance of Accountability," *International Management* 32 (July 1977): 43–45.

22. Huse and Beer, "Eclectic Approach to Organization Development," *Harvard Business Review* 49 (September–October 1971): 103–112.

23. "The Problem with General Foods' Worker Participation Plan," *Business Week,* March 28, 1977, pp. 78–90.

24. S. Rubenowitz, *Motivational Factors Affecting Managers' Attitudes toward Industrial Democracy* (Gotesborgs: Gotesborgs Universitet, 1974), p. 10.

Part VI

Organizations and Change

Chapter 17   Managing Creativity

Pet Rock

The Importance of Managing the Creative Process

Steps in the Creative Process

Managing Creativity

Techniques for Increasing Organizational Creativity
        Establishing Special Departments
        Encouraging Individual Creativity
        Managing Group Creativity

Creativity and Stability

The Process of Implementation

Implications for the Manager

Review

The Gunnery Problem

Learning Objectives

When you have finished reading and studying this chapter, you should be able to:

1. Explain why creativity and innovation are important to organizations.
2. Describe and give examples of the basic steps in the creative process.
3. List and give examples of approaches to managing creativity.
4. Identify and give examples of techniques for increasing organizational creativity.
5. Compare and contrast interacting, Delphi, and nominal groups as ways of improving creativity.
6. Describe at least four ways in which creative ideas may be difficult to implement.
7. Explain why creativity must take place at all managerial levels.
8. Define and be able to use the following concepts:
   creativity   Delphi technique
   implementation   nominal groups
   steps in the creative process

Thought Starters

1. What does the term *creativity* mean to you?
2. Do you consider yourself a creative person?
3. Is there a difference between creativity and decision making?
4. What are some obstacles to the creative process?

Pet Rock

For a time, "Pet Rocks" were one of the hottest items going. More than a million of them were sold at $4 a rock in under three months. As late as February 1976 they were still selling at the rate of about 65,000 a month.

The "inventor," Gary Dahl, came up with the idea while in a bar south of San Francisco. The conversation had turned to the high cost of owning a pet. Dahl considers himself an expert on the subject, since he has a small menagerie of cats, dogs, chickens, and goats. As soon as he mentioned the words *pet rock*, the group he was with began to make up a number of funny one-liners, and the successor of the Hula Hoop was born.

Dahl first wrote an amusing training manual to go along with the Pet Rocks. Among the tips in the manual: "If, when you remove the rock from its box, it appears to be excited, place it on some old newspapers." The manual also suggested tricks, including "play dead" (which rocks love to practice on their own) and "roll over" (best practiced on a hill).

After writing the manual, Dahl designed an attractive carrying case, purchased several tons of egg-shaped beach rocks, and put together a package consisting of a rock, a tiny paper training manual, a handful of excelsior, and a decorated cardboard case.

Coming up with the idea was one thing; spreading the word about the item was something else. But a friend loaned Dahl $10,000 to display the Pet Rocks at a San Francisco gift show in August 1975, and trend-setting Nieman Marcus ordered five hundred. (The company was later to sell more than twenty thousand.)

Dahl also gave a press release to the San Francisco bureau of *Newsweek*, which ran a small story on Pet Rocks. Then Associated Press and United Press International did stories on them. Dahl contacted several local TV stations, and he ultimately gave more than three hundred radio interviews. Pet Rocks were plugged twice on the Tonight Show and once on The Merv Griffin Show—both times by singer John Davidson, who brought his own Pet Rock to the shows. National coverage included Dahl appearing on the Tomorrow Program with Tom Snyder. While the boom for Pet Rocks was on, the publicity did not cost a cent. Although the Pet Rock fad did not last a long time, it was long enough for Gary Dahl to become a millionaire.[1]

This case presents several important issues that will be covered in detail in the chapter. First is the idea of creativity. Pets have been around for a long time; so have rocks. Dahl's contribution was to bring these elements together, with their funny manual, thereby creating something new. Second is the idea of working to stabilize the creation. Once he had the idea, Dahl had to work hard at getting it implemented and popularizing the result. Third is the need for ongoing innovative ideas. (Once the Pet Rock fad passed, Dahl's next idea—sand breeding— did not succeed.) This chapter will examine the need for creativity as a special type of decision making and will make recommendations for effective organizational and personal creativity.

The Importance of Managing the Creative Process

Managing is itself a creative process. In a world of change, organizations cannot stand still. The effective manager must constantly come up with new approaches to policy, plans, procedures, organizational structure, and numerous other elements of the managerial task. Effective managing is thus one of the most continually creative of all jobs. Furthermore, the effective manager must encourage creativity in subordinates.

Many organizational problems require decision-making techniques that involve creativity. Chapter 6 described some standard approaches to decision making, and Chapter 10 described some mathematical and other analytical tools and aids to use in the process. This chapter deals with a special kind of decision-making—the creative process. While computers and mathematical approaches can aid immeasurably in decision making, some problems cannot be quantified. Indeed, often the creative process itself is not quantifiable. Thus qualitative approaches may be needed to achieve organizational goals and objectives.

There are a number of definitions of **creativity**.[2] It can, for example, be defined as the generation of a new idea, practice, service, or object. The invention of the wheel was a creative act, as was the invention of Pet Rocks.

Implementation is the adoption of the idea, practice, service, or object perceived as new by the relevant unit. People invent through creativity and implement through putting into practice the results of creativity and invention. Dahl had to work hard at getting the idea of Pet Rocks adopted nationwide. Therefore, he was both a creator and an implementer. Creativity, implementation, and change are highly interrelated, as Figure 17.1 shows. When the creative idea is implemented, it may bring about changes in organizational structure and policy or human attitudes and behavior in order to improve organizational performance.

Creativity is usually seen as being the product of a great mind; Edison, Beethoven, Ford, Michelangelo, and Picasso are among those considered creative. But all people are creative; all can come up with new

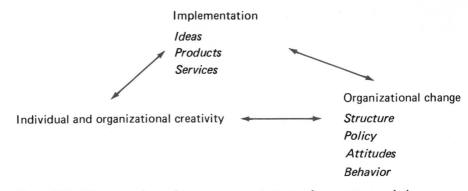

Figure 17.1   The interrelationships among creativity, implementation, and change

ideas. Of course, some are more creative than others. Where many people stop is at the implementation stage—at the point of putting the new idea into practice.

Most people think that creativity and innovation come about primarily in large organizations that have research and development departments and funds for developing new ideas. However, innovations do not occur only in large organizations. Sometimes they are made to satisfy very personal needs. To illustrate: Dr. Lucien Benoit, a dentist who lives in Woonsocket, Rhode Island, was building a paneled recreation room in his house. The wood paneling was expensive—$76 a sheet. Dr. Benoit thought he had measured properly when he cut a hole in one panel to fit an electrical outlet box. Unfortunately, the hole was not properly located, and he ruined $76 worth of paneling.

As a result, he decided to develop a template for outlet and switch boxes, telephone jacks, and the like. The template is a piece of steel cut to duplicate the shape of the intended item. On one side are four tongues that enable the template to fit into the item. On the other side are four points that stick out in front of it. The panel is positioned on the wall; when it is in place, it is given a few firm whacks with a rubber mallet in the area of the template. The points mark the back of the panel, which can then be removed. The hole can be cut by following the point marks. Templates have been built for outlet and switch boxes, junction boxes, telephone boxes, airconditioners, and other large items. Dr. Benoit's invention is now sold commercially.[3]

In this case, the creation and innovation did come from a single individual. However, there is evidence that many new developments come from large organizations because they are sufficiently complex to have the needed expertise in their subunits.[4] They also tend to have the financial resources needed to conduct large-scale research as well as the ability to obtain federal and other grants. Thus creativity can be the product of an individual, a group, or an organization. (Indeed, some organizations, such as advertising agencies and greeting card companies, have creativity as their primary focus.)

As mentioned earlier, the effective manager must be self-creative and must foster creativity in others in order to effectively accomplish organizational goals and objectives. Since creativity is a form of decision making, the basic steps in the creative process will be examined before the discussion of how the manager can encourage, improve, develop, and manage creativity in the organization.

Steps in the Creative Process

Although much research has been conducted on the creative process, there is no universally accepted theory of creativity.[5] The creative process is obscure; it is not verbalized by the creator, and it is generally not communicated to others.

Creativity and innovation range from major strategic approaches developed by large companies down to isolated, small ideas developed by single individuals (such as Dr. Benoit). Few creative ideas result in a dramatic advancement of knowledge. Most are only marginally different from existing ones, adding some new or useful element to them. Indeed, most innovation is simply the sum of a number of small improvements.

People generally go about their daily tasks in similar ways. They become creative when they attempt to do them better. Thus creativity occurs at many levels and takes a variety of forms.

Creativity is seldom a single flash of intuition. Instead it is a process that generally involves extensive analysis of a number of pieces of information and a separation of the irrelevant from the significant. Much creativity results from analyzing a variety of combinations and searching for new relationships.

As Thomas Edison, holder of more than 1,200 patents, once remarked, "Genius is 2 percent inspiration and 98 percent perspiration." When Edison set to work on a project, he first read everything available on the subject. Only after this thorough review did he begin his actual laboratory work. Then he did hundreds or thousands of experiments. If an experiment or model showed faint signs of success, he was suspicious, believing that it could be a chance event. After repeated confirmation he began to consider the project a real success. While at work on developing a filament for the electric light bulb, Edison said, "We now know a thousand things that won't work."

Ideas do sometimes come after a sudden burst of insight. Usually, however, the individual has been working on the problem for some time. To illustrate: Archimedes, a Greek mathematician of the third century B.C., is reported to have leaped out of the bath and rushed home, undressed, shouting, "Eureka! I have found it!" What he had found was that his body displaced its own volume in water. How he had found it was through his work on a problem for King Hiero II of Syracuse. The king had commissioned an artist to make a crown of pure gold, and he was concerned about whether the gold had been adulterated with a less expensive substance. Archimedes had been trying to find a way to solve the problem. His discovery about water displacement meant that if the gold had been adulterated by a lighter metal, the size of the crown would have to have been increased to equal the original weight of the gold, and the crown would displace more water than the gold had done. (The gold did prove adulterated, and the goldsmith was executed.)

The examples so far show the basic **steps in the creative process.** As Figure 17.2 shows, they include desire, preparation, experimentation, incubation, illumination, refinement, and implementation. Each of these steps will be discussed in turn. However, as the figure also shows, the steps may or may not take place sequentially. A manager may make an inductive leap or may have to go back to the drawing board. The effective manager may also have a number of creative projects in motion at the same time. A manager may start a project, drop it temporarily, and go on to something else. Meanwhile, several other projects may be waiting for time and attention. In addition, the manager may delegate improvement projects to others and periodically check on how they are coming along. In

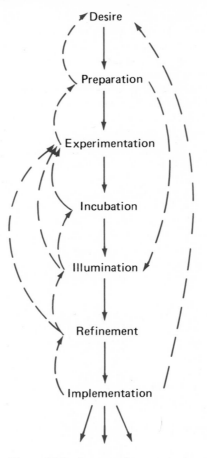

Figure 17.2 Steps in the creative process

other cases, the manager may be part of a group or task force that meets regularly to work on one or more projects.

Desire

Clearly, a creative idea can be discovered by accident. More frequently, however, the individual or group has a personal need or desire to solve a problem. Thus conscious or unconscious motivation is usually present to begin the thought process. Edison wanted to develop a working electric light bulb. The dentist wanted to prevent the waste of panels. In organizations, the desire often comes from an organizational need. The advertising department must be creative in the development of layout, copy, format, and overall design of each new advertisement. The research department must be creative in coming up with a new product. Creative thinking does not appear until there is a motivating force either from within or as a result of an external request.

Preparation

Most creative ideas do not instantly appear. Rather, they come only after an intense period of preparation, as Edison's experiments showed. Preparation involves not only gathering information and laying a foundation but also trying to see new and meaningful relationships among ideas that are already familiar. The originality of the creative idea is usually a direct result of the amount of data gathered and the information available. The more alternatives available, the more potentially creative the solution. Because of time pressure, the preparation stage can easily be slighted. Subordinates may come up with an answer that is only slightly workable because of the pressure for a quick answer.

Sometimes an individual who is relatively unfamiliar with the problem can have a flash of insight, seeing the problem from a fresh perspective. The effective manager discusses the problem with others and encourages subordinates to do so.

Experimentation

Experimentation involves trying out various alternatives. At this stage the creator begins working on the creation itself. For Edison it meant beginning the laboratory work. For Dr. Benoit it meant trying out different approaches to building the template. Sometimes experimentation follows the development of the creative solution. Archimedes arrived at his solution with no experimentation, but he then conducted experiments to determine if the solution was correct.

Managers are constantly experimenting with new approaches to problems. Will one approach to motivation work better than others? Is there a better way of arranging the work place? Can the unit's objectives be better accomplished in a different way?

Incubation

Incubation is the process of mulling the problem over, whether at a conscious or an unconscious level. Sometimes the solution to a problem is found immediately. At other times, even though there is a strong desire and adequate preparation, the solution simply does appear. Rather than becoming frustrated, the effective manager moves on to something else for a time.

Indeed, good managers usually are working on a number of development projects at the same time. The projects are often in different stages of completion, and the managers are constantly juggling them around.

Illumination

A flash of insight—an event that often occurs during the incubation period—may lead to the solution. The manager may be discussing a subject with a peer or subordinate, and suddenly a creative solution to a different problem may pop into mind. Particularly creative managers often find ways to relax that leave them open to such insights. One manager likes to go for a walk in the woods when faced with a number of difficult problems. Another likes to lie in bed for ten or fifteen minutes before getting up in the morning; she finds that this relaxed state is helpful for reviewing problems and finding possible solutions.

At other times, the illumination may not come this quickly. The individual may need to gather new data and conduct new experiments. As the manager of a Swedish steel mill remarked, "I've tried at least four different ways to solve the morale problem. I want to spend several weeks thinking about a better approach."

Refinement

Usually, the new idea is only tentative, needing to be polished and improved. In a large organization, refining a major project may be a long process, continuing almost to the end of the project's life. At other times, little or no work must be done on refinement, particularly if the innovation is a simple one. To illustrate: A complex medical instrument had to be assembled into metal boxes. Three sides of each box were closed; but the front was open, since certain controls were to be mounted on a separate piece of metal. However, the top front of each box had a steel bar welded to the two sides to give added strength and stability. This made insertion of particular subassemblies very difficult. The foreman recommended that the steel bar be attached with machine screws instead. This would allow removal of the bar during assembly and would considerably speed the assembly time. His idea was accepted.

Implementation

After the discovery is made and polished, it needs to be adopted and put into practice. Sometimes the new idea is quickly accepted, as in the case of the foreman's suggestion. Generally, the better the innovation and the fewer the people concerned, the faster the idea is adopted. However, creative ideas or products that violate accepted norms or beliefs may take years to be adopted or may even fail.

A few years ago, a new product called Analoze was developed. It was a combination pain killer and antacid that could be taken without any liquid. The pill was developed because people were known to be consuming record quantities of pain killers (analgesics), and the company reasoned that an analgesic that would dissolve in the mouth would be successful. Since antacid tablets were also being consumed in quantity, the company decided to make Analoze a combination of the two.

The company finally developed a cherry-flavored combination tablet. It gave samples of Analoze and competing products to a consumer panel for testing, and panel members overwhelmingly preferred Analoze. The company then began a massive advertising campaign, stressing that Analoze "works without water." The price was right, and the package was well designed. Prospects appeared good, and dealers were enthusiastic. There was only one problem—a mere trickle of sales in the selected test markets. After extensive probing, the company concluded that the flaw was its stress on the words *works without water.* Headache sufferers were apparently associating water with the cure of their headaches, and they had no confidence in a tablet that dissolved in the mouth.[6] The company ultimately dropped the product.

Managing Creativity

As suggested earlier, all of us are creative to some extent. One problem faced by all organizations is how to encourage constructive creativity. The way an organization is managed can help to encourage or stifle creativity. There are four important ways that effective managers can develop creativity in an organization:

1. They can develop a creative climate.
2. They can encourage independent action.
3. They can adopt a questioning attitude.
4. They can establish open communications.

Developing a Creative Climate

The climate of an organization can encourage or discourage creativity. To encourage it, management at all levels should actively encourage people to submit new ideas or suggestions. Frequently, managers say that they want new ideas, but their actions tell a different story. One or two rebuffs and subordinates learn to keep their ideas to themselves. A willingness to listen does not mean a need to adopt every idea. It does, however, mean that ideas should be given serious consideration. It also means that if an idea is not accepted, the reasons for its rejection should be carefully explained.

Encouraging Independent Action

Some organizations subtly indicate that the rules are there to be followed. Others encourage employees at all levels to use their own initiative. In one instance, the encouragement of initiative had a particularly positive result. Jim was a recent college graduate employed by a bank. The bank had made a loan to a company that was going bankrupt. One day, a bank officer casually tossed a copy of the loan agreement and related papers onto Jim's desk and said, "Close this out as a bad debt." Although the procedure was routine, Jim went through all the papers carefully. He found that, at the time of application, the company had had a bank account in another state. He called the other bank and found that the account was still open. He then made arrangements to get the loan repaid from the balance in the other bank. His innovation and creative thinking not only got the loan paid but also helped Jim himself get an early promotion.

Adopting a Questioning Attitude

Many organizations automatically accept practices that have been in existence for some time, never questioning their current utility. Both managers and workers (at all levels) should be encouraged to question why practices or customs are continued: Does an individual practice still serve the useful purpose for which it was intended?

Many organizations react to a mistake by adding a procedure to keep the mistake from reoccurring, and they never question the procedure again. To illustrate: A film company made arrangements with the British Army to use a motorized artillery unit to reproduce a World War II battle. The director watched as the gun crew loaded and fired the light artillery. Just before the guns were fired, one man stepped back a few paces and stood at attention. The crew members were asked about this procedure, but they could offer no explanation for it. The director asked a number of people in the military and finally received the answer from a retired British sergeant. The sergeant watched carefully as the gun crew fired several rounds. Then he said, "I know. He's holding the horses so they won't bolt at the sound of the guns." Horses were no longer used, but the procedure remained.

Establishing Open Communications

The more open the communications within an organization, the more likely the organization is to have a creative climate, to encourage independent action, to adopt a questioning attitude, and to share information. Lack of information is a tremendous block to creativity and change, and interdepartmental and intergroup conflicts greatly reduce information exchange.

Mechanistic organizations, with their emphasis on rules and procedures, tend to reduce creativity, while organic organizations, through their openness of communication, tend to encourage it. Even an otherwise unimportant individual can hamper the creative process by blocking information. Finally, each organization must maintain open communications with its external environment so it can sense the need for change and creativity and respond to it.

Techniques for Increasing Organizational Creativity

There are a number of techniques or approaches for increasing creativity. Among the important ones are establishing special departments, encouraging individual creativity, and managing group creativity.[7]

Establishing Special Departments

Prior to World War II, few organizations had research and development departments; now, many do. Universities often establish task forces or special departments for long-range planning and curriculum revision.

Industrial organizations establish research and development departments to develop new ideas for services or products.

Sometimes these departments do "pure" research to advance knowledge. More frequently, however, they do "applied" research—research based on "pure" research. The constant modification of the pocket calculator is an example of applied research based on the pure research of microcircuitry.

Encouraging Individual Creativity

There is evidence that less creative problem solvers get an idea, see it as a possible solution to a problem, and settle for it without further thought. More creative problem solvers are not satisfied with the first idea and are able to forego the immediate reward of applying that idea in the expectation of a better solution (greater reward). Frequently, the best idea comes late in the total production process.

The effective manager can encourage subordinates to come up with creative ideas. In the hustle and bustle of getting the job done, many managers do little to encourage individuals to come up with new ideas or approaches. But they should do so—and in a nonthreatening fashion. Direct suggestions can often be made to individuals. For example: "Mary, why don't you take a few hours this week to think about how things can be done better, about what will make your job better or improve the department?" The effective manager encourages subordinates to come up with a variety of ideas rather than just one or two.[8]

Managing Group Creativity

There is evidence that groups can be highly creative when properly used.[9] Chapter 5 described decision making in face-to-face groups. This chapter will deal with two techniques that do not require the group members to interact directly with each other—the Delphi technique and the nominal group technique. Both approaches are highly effective when properly used.

The Delphi Technique

Originally developed by the Rand Corporation, the Delphi technique, named after the oracle at Delphi in ancient Greece, involves using a group of knowledgeable people who work anonymously to improve creativity and make better decisions.[10] There are many variations, but the general process used by a manager is as follows:

1. A panel or group of experts (those generally knowledgeable about a particular problem) is selected. The members of the group never actually meet, however. The panel can have members both inside and outside the organization, and the individual members may or may not know who the other members are.
2. A questionnaire identifying the problem is sent to each member of the panel, who is asked to make anonymous suggestions and recommendations. The suggestions are then pooled, and a feedback report is developed.
3. The feedback report and a more advanced, second-stage questionnaire are sent back to the panel members.
4. Each panel member independently evaluates the feedback report, votes on the priority of the ideas contained in it, and generates new ideas based on it.
5. The process is repeated until a consensus is reached or until the manager feels that sufficient information has been received to make a decision.
6. A final summary feedback report is developed and sent back to the group members.

group never meets

A major advantage of the Delphi approach is its anonymity. In groups that interact face-to-face, one person may dominate, or everyone may watch the manager for clues to what is wanted. Further, in interacting groups, an individual may take a stand and not want to back down for fear of losing face. Frequently, experts are more concerned with defending their position than with reaching a good decision.

Many large companies use the Delphi approach to identify and solve problems. For example, TRW—a highly diversified, technically oriented company—has a number of Delphi panels. These panels suggest services and products that will have marketing potential and predict significant social, political, and economic events that will affect the company. The approach has been used successfully in a variety of areas, including the military, government, health, and education.

There are two major criticisms of the Delphi technique. It is time-consuming and costly. Thus the approach should be used to develop creative solutions in important areas where time and cost are not important.

The Nominal Group Technique

The nominal group technique involves a group of knowledgeable people who are aware of each other but who do not directly interact while they are working to improve creativity and make better decisions. Thus the technique is related to both the Delphi technique and to the interacting group approach.[11] The group differs from the Delphi group in that the members may know each other and certainly are aware of each other's presence. As with the Delphi approach, the specific techniques vary, but usually the following steps are involved:

1. The manager brings the group together and outlines the problem.
2. Each member of the group generates a number of ideas—in writing.
3. Each member then presents a single idea at a time to the entire group. The ideas are written on a blackboard or on large pieces of paper, and discussion of them is limited to clarification.
4. The "round robin" continues, with members adding to others' ideas.
5. When no further ideas are emerging, or when the manager feels the process has gone far enough, each member votes on the ideas—again in writing.
6. The final decision is the summed outcome of the individual votes, but the manager is free to accept or reject it.

The research evidence suggests that there is very little difference between the Delphi and nominal groups on the quantity of ideas generated—and both groups generate significantly more creative ideas than do interacting groups. However, the members of nominal groups appear to be more satisfied with the results than are either Delphi or interacting members.[12]

Creativity and Stability

Creativity is essential to an organization, but so are stability and conformity. Effective organizations maintain a balance between the two, and effective managers nurture creativity and ensure that the creative ideas contribute to organizational goals and objectives. To do so, they must tie creativity to both long- and short-range planning.

After creative ideas are developed, they must be put into practice. Here, less creative and more practical people may be necessary. The production supervisor who has to build a certain number of radios cannot suddenly decide to make televisions instead. However, the supervisor may be able to develop and implement an innovative idea for assembling the radios. In the earlier illustration of the metal box, the foreman performed a small creative act that helped get the job done better even within a relatively standardized production process.

The Process of Implementation

The development of a creative idea that will contribute to the objectives and plans of the organization does not automatically mean its adoption or implementation. As shown in Figure 17.3, there are many reasons why an innovation may or may not be adopted. The larger and more centralized the organization, the more likely it is that innovations coming from an established department, such as research and development, will be accepted and implemented. This is particularly true when such departments have been requested to develop a specific innovation. In larger organizations, creative ideas coming from unfamiliar sources are less likely to be implemented.

All other things being equal, the higher the degree of risk and the higher the cost of the proposal, the less likely it is to be implemented. Minor modifications to expensive equipment, for example, carry little risk and are generally inexpensive and therefore often made. Organizations tend to be resistant to innovations that upset their own technology. For example, jet aircraft engines were developed not by piston engine manufacturers but by builders of steam turbines and manufacturers of aircraft bodies. Radio and electronics organizations were more influential in developing the wireless telephone than were the telephone and telegraph utilities.

Implementation is a political process. The busy manager may resent getting ideas from an idealistic, long-haired thinker. The creative person, on the other hand, may not follow through on creative ideas. The greater the power and influence of the creator or sponsor, the more likely the innovation will be put into practice. Therefore, the creative person may need a perceptive and collaborative manager who can fight political battles.

The greater the perceived need for the proposal, the more likely it is to be accepted. For example, an innovation brought about directly to meet competition has a high chance of being accepted. Still, a number of inventions were developed by technical people before there was a perceived need. For example, when the telephone was invented, there was no perceived need for it. Photocopying was available for a number of

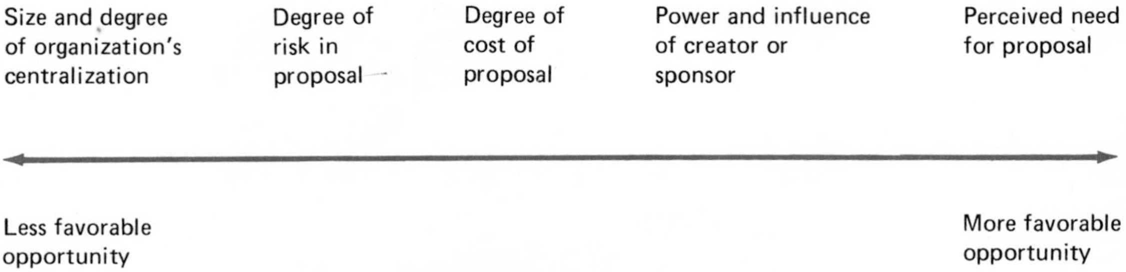

Size and degree of organization's centralization	Degree of risk in proposal	Degree of cost of proposal	Power and influence of creator or sponsor	Perceived need for proposal

Less favorable opportunity				More favorable opportunity

Figure 17.3 Some factors affecting implementation

years before it began to sell. As one manager was reported to have remarked, "Who needs it? Nothing will ever replace carbon paper."

Organizations can become myopic. The railroads resisted trucks for a long time because they perceived themselves to be in the railroad business rather than the transportation business. On the other hand, it was many years after the development of the semitrailer truck that arrangements were made to ship the trailers by rail. In like fashion, the moviemaking industry fought the coming of television. Movie makers saw themselves as being in the movie business rather than the entertainment business; as a result it was a number of years before movies were made for television. Indeed, the first of these made-for-TV movies were originated by newer, more innovative movie makers.

Finally, there is the crucial importance of taking the first step. Often there is absolutely no follow-up on a creative idea. The individual gets the idea, thinks it would be something good to try, and then goes on to something else. The Pet Rocks fad would never have been successful if Gary Dahl had not followed through on his idea.

Implications for the Manager

Organizations need to change and renew themselves constantly. Hospitals are continually purchasing new and more sophisticated equipment. Model changes in cars are routine. Last year's hand calculator is made partially obsolete by this year's model.

This chapter has described a special approach to decision making—the creative process. The effective manager must not only be personally creative but must encourage and manage the creative process in others. Creativity should not be restricted to the research department. Each individual has creative potential that can be used to help the organization reach its objectives. Managers and employees at all levels need to develop and foster new ideas and to encourage others to do so. Managers who do only what they are asked to do are not really managers but simply order takers.

Creativity is not limited to artists or to large research laboratories. Indeed, many creative ideas are deceptively simple, such as Dr. Benoit's development of a template for cutting holes in wall panels. Creativity, however, is not enough. The creative idea must be implemented. The greater the need for the creative idea and the more clearly the innovation contributes to the objectives of the organization, the more likely it is that it will be implemented.

Review

1. Discuss why Pet Rocks became so popular.
2. Was Gary Dahl a manager as well as a creator? Explain.
3. List a few ideas for items that might become as popular as Pet Rocks.
4. In what way is creativity a special form of decision making?
5. Explain why gathering information is so important to the creative process.
6. Discuss ways in which organizations can encourage creativity. Which do you find most effective?
7. What are some creative ideas that you have had but have not acted upon?
8. Visit at least two local service stations, grocery stores, or department stores. What innovations are present that may not have been there five to ten years ago? Are there any areas where you can see a possibility for further improvement?
9. If you are now attending a college or university, what innovations do you feel might be helpful to the school? To you as a student? How might you get the innovations accepted?

The Gunnery Problem

In 1899, five ships fired for five minutes each at an old lightship. After the twenty-five minutes of firing, two hits had been made. The accuracy of naval gunnery was poor. Since there was no easy way to raise and lower the cannon, the gun pointer had to fire on the roll of the ship. This meant that he had to make the decision to fire before the sights were actually on target, since he had to anticipate the speed of the ship's roll.

Telescopic sights were mounted directly on the guns, but they were seldom used because of the possible loss of an eye during the recoil. Less accurate open sights were used instead.

In 1898, Admiral Sir Percy Scott was watching gunnery practice on a British ship, the *Scylla*. He noticed that one gun pointer was more accurate than others. The pointer was partly compensating for the roll of the ship by unconsciously using his elevating gear. (At that time, elevating gear was used only for range.) After thinking about this, Scott made a number of changes on the ship. First, he had the telescopic sights mounted on sleeves so they would not be affected by the recoil. Second, he changed the gear ratio for the elevating mechanism so the gunner could move the gun to maintain sight on the target regardless of the roll. This allowed continuous aim firing. Finally, he increased the number of practice sessions, using small targets that simulated a ship and a small-caliber rifle in the gun, thereby decreasing the amount of ammunition used. In short order, the *Scylla* established remarkable records for gunnery accuracy.

A U.S. officer, William Sims, became acquainted with Admiral Scott, found out what he was doing, and made additional changes on his own ship, with corresponding increases in accuracy. Over a period of three years, Sims sent twelve lengthy official reports to Washington. Each report included: (1) an emphasis on the increased accuracy of British and U.S. ships using the new method (the report was accompanied by reams of data), (2) specific descriptions of the new methods and training procedures, and (3) an insistence on the need for continuous-aim firing, which the U.S. Navy was unable to do. The Navy was still firing "broadsides" (all the guns at once) because the men had to fire on the roll.

Washington's responses were in three stages. The first response was no response at all. In both the Bureau of Ordnance and the Bureau of Navigation the reports were simply filed because the claims and records of continuous-aim firing were simply not credible to the people in charge. Sims hated being ignored. He commented to a friend, "I want scalps or nothing and if I can't have 'em I won't play." The tone of his reports became more caustic, and he sent copies of them to other officers in the Navy. This meant that Washington had to respond.

The second response was a rebuttal from the Chief of the Bureau of Ordnance. The point-by-point rebuttal used "reason" as its basis. It said that the U.S. equipment was as good as that of other navies, and therefore the trouble had to be in the training of gun pointers, which was the responsibility of ships' officers. It also said that the bureau's own experiments (done on dry land at the Washington Navy Yard) had demonstrated that it would take more than five men to compensate for a five-degree roll in ten seconds. Therefore, Sims's reports were "mathematically impossible." As the conflict escalated, reason gave way to the third response, name-calling, and Sims was referred to as a crackpot egotist and a deliberate falsifier of evidence.

Sims finally took the only approach left to him; he wrote directly to President Theodore Roosevelt. Roosevelt's response was positive. He brought Sims back from China and in 1902 gave him the job of inspector of target practice. Sims held the job as long as Roosevelt remained in office—six years. Of course, the action created a great deal of hostility against Sims within the Navy.

In 1905, a gunner using the new methods was able to score fifteen direct hits on a target seventy-five by twenty-five feet in one minute at the standard 1,600-yard range. Even more important, half the hits were in a bull's-eye fifty inches square—a far cry from the 1899 average of two hits in the sails of a hulk after twenty-five minutes of firing.[13]

1. What creative processes were involved in the improvement in accuracy?
2. In what way did Admiral Scott differ from William Sims?
3. What are some reasons for the resistance to the implementation process?
4. Is resistance to change and innovation an isolated phenomenon?

Footnotes

1. M. Coakley, "The Anatomy of a Fad: Pet Rock," *Boston Globe,* February 26, 1976; "Pet Rocks," *Omaha World Herald,* February 27, 1976; and *The Care and Training of Your Pet Rock* (Rock Bottom Productions, 1975).
2. W. Beveridge, *The Art of Scientific Investigation* (New York: W. W. Norton, 1957); J. Bright, *Research, Development and Technological Innovation* (Homewood, Ill.: Richard D. Irwin, 1964); J. Hage and R. Dewar, "Elite Values versus Organizational Structure in Predicting Innovation," *Administrative Science Quarterly* 18 (September 3, 1973): 279–290; K. Holt, *Product Innovation* (Trondheim, Norway: Norwegian Institute of Technology, 1975); and A. Koestler, *The Act of Creation: A Study of the Conscious and Unconscious in Science and Art* (New York: Dell Publishing, 1967).

3. P. Hotton, "Now: A Way to Cut Holes in Paneling for Electrical Outlets," *Boston Globe,* July 11, 1976.

4. J. Baldridge and R. Burnham, "Organizational Innovation: Individual, Organizational, and Environmental Impacts," *Administrative Science Quarterly* 20 (June 2, 1975): 165–176.

5. J. Aram, "Innovation via the R&D Underground," *Research Management* 16 (November 6, 1973): 24–26; A. Crosby, *Creative Thinking as a Process* (London: Tavistock Publications, 1968); H. Hicks and C. Gullet, *Modern Business Management* (New York: McGraw-Hill, 1974); S. Maini and B. Nordbeck, "Critical Moments, the Creative Process and Research Motivation," *International Social Science Journal* 25 (January 1973): 190–204; and C. Taylor, *Climate for Creativity* (Elmsford, N.Y.: Pergamon Press, 1972).

6. E. Rogers, *Diffusion of Innovations* (New York: Free Press, 1962), pp. 122–223.

7. T. Alexander, "Synectics: Inventing by the Madness Method," *Fortune,* August 1965, pp. 165–168 and 190–194; A. Brief and A. Phillay, "Selling Proposals for Change," *Business Horizons* 19 (April 1976): 22–25; W. Gordon, "Operational Approach to Creativity," *Harvard Business Review* 34 (November–December 1956): 41–51; E. Huse and J. Bowditch, *Behavior in Organizations: A Systems Approach to Managing,* 2d ed. (Reading, Mass.: Addison-Wesley, 1977); A. Osborn, *Applied Imagination* (New York: Scribner's, 1953); R. Tersine and W. Riggs, "The Delphi Technique: A Long Range Planning Tool," *Business Horizons* 19 (April 1976): 51–56; and A. Vaughn, "Plan for Project Success," *Journal of Systems Management* 25 (December 12, 1974): 12–15.

8. W. Gordon, "Operational Approach to Creativity," *Harvard Business Review* 24 (November–December 1956): 41–51; C. Taylor, "A Tentative Description of the Creative Individual," in *A Source Book for Creative Thinking,* ed. S. Parnes and H. Harding (New York: Scribner's, 1962), pp. 169–191.

9. N. Maier, *Problem-Solving and Creativity in Individuals and Groups* (Belmont, Calif.: Brooks-Cole Publishing, 1970); J. Gibb, G. Platts, and L. Miller, *Dynamics of Participative Groups* (St. Louis, Mo.: Swift, 1959); and M. Shaw, *Group Dynamics* (New York: McGraw-Hill, 1976).

10. A. Delbecq, A. DeVen, and D. Gustafson, *Group Techniques for Program Planning* (Glenview, Ill.: Scott, Foresman, 1975), pp. 10–11; F. Luthans and T. Balke, "Delphi Technique Helps Set ASFSA Goals," *School Foodservice Journal* 20 (June 1974): pp. 40–41; "Forecasters Turn to Group Guesswork," *Business Week,* March 14, 1970, p. 10; and F. Luthans, *Organizational Behavior,* 2d ed. (New York: McGraw-Hill, 1977), pp. 198–199.

11. D. Taylor, P. Berry, and C. Block, "Does Group Participation When Using Brainstorming Facilitate or Inhibit Creative Thinking," *Administrative Science Quarterly* 3 (March 1958): 23–47; A. Van de Ven, *Group Decision-Making Effectiveness* (Kent, Ohio: Kent State University Press, 1974).

12. A. Van de Ven and A. Delbecq, "The Effectiveness of Delphi and Interacting Group Decision Making Processes," *Academy of Management Journal* 17 (December 1974): 605–621; and T. Bouchard, Jr., J. Barsalous, and G. Drauden, "Brainstorming Procedure, Group Size and Sex as Determinants of the Problem-Solving Effectiveness of Groups and Individuals," *Journal of Applied Psychology* 59 (April 1974): 135–138.

13. Adapted from Elting E. Morison, "A Case Study of Innovation," *Engineering and Science Magazine,* published at the California Institute of Technology, Pasadena, California, April 1950. Published by permission of the author and the publisher.

Chapter 18   Managing Conflict

The President's Decision

Changing Philosophies about Conflict

Conflict, Competition, and Cooperation

Some Sources of Organizational Conflict

Managing to Reduce Conflict
    Dominance and Forcing
    Smoothing
    Compromise
    Integrative Problem Solving
    Ensuring That Data Are Generated in Common
    Reducing Perceptual Differences
    Developing a Common Set of Goals and Objectives

Stimulating Constructive Conflict
    Communicating That Conflict Is Acceptable
    Changing Communications Channels
    Redistributing Power
    Increasing or Maintaining Perceptual Differences

Role, Role Conflict, and Role Ambiguity

Implications for the Manager

Review

The E. F. Howard Company

Learning Objectives

When you have finished reading and studying this chapter, you should be able to:

1. Compare and contrast changing philosophies about conflict.
2. Distinguish among conflict, competition, and cooperation.
3. Compare and contrast the results of cooperative and competitive outcomes of conflict.
4. Identify major sources of organizational conflict.
5. Compare and contrast the effectiveness of different approaches to conflict resolution.
6. Identify several approaches to increasing integrative problem solving.
7. Identify several approaches to stimulating constructive conflict, and describe occasions when such approaches may be helpful to the organization.
8. Show how process and structural approaches to conflict are related.
9. Show how the concept of role is important in affecting managerial behavior.
10. Demonstrate that organizational structure affects conflict.
11. Define and be able to use the following concepts:

groupthink	smoothing
conflict	compromise
conflict management	integrative problem solving
competition	role
cooperation	role conflict
dominance	role ambiguity

Thought Starters

1. Can you think of a time when conflict has been helpful? When it has been harmful?
2. How do you behave when a group to which you belong is in conflict with another group?
3. What do you do when people make conflicting demands on you?

The President's Decision

On April 17, 1961, a brigade of about fourteen hundred Cuban exiles, helped by the United States Navy, Air Force, and CIA, invaded Cuba at the Bay of Pigs. The intent was to overthrow Fidel Castro. By the third day, the battle was over, and most of the invaders were captured. The captives were later ransomed for $53 million in food and drugs. The Bay of Pigs invasion is generally considered a fiasco.

On October 16, 1962, CIA photo interpreters discovered recently finished buildings for ballistic missiles in Cuba. Intelligence estimates were that the installations would represent about one-third of the Soviet Union's current atomic warhead potential. On October 24, after the U.S. blockaded Cuba, Soviet cargo ships turned away from the country. The crisis was over on October 28, when the Soviets agreed to remove the missiles already there. The series of decisions leading up to the solution of the Cuban missile crisis are generally regarded as excellent.[1]

What made the difference? Both decisions involved President John F. Kennedy and many of the same advisers—including some of the most capable and intelligent people ever to participate in government. It has been suggested that, in the first case, those taking part in the decisions were victims of **groupthink**, a form of decision making that occurs when "the members' strivings for unanimity override their motivation to realistically appraise alternative courses of action."[2] In the second case, active disagreement was deliberately encouraged before the final alternatives were decided upon, and groupthink was thereby avoided.

Planning for a possible invasion of Cuba began before Kennedy took office. He was first briefed on the proposed invasion two days after his inauguration, in January 1961. The plan was discussed for the next eighty days and finally approved with only a few modifications. It was based on a large number of wrong assumptions, any of which could easily have been checked out. For example, one assumption was that the invasion would be widely supported by the Cuban people. Actually, an overwhelming majority of Cubans supported Castro. Another assumption was that a brigade of fourteen hundred men could defeat Castro's army, which was perceived as poorly trained and equipped. Actually, the brigade had no possibility of defeating Castro's well-trained army of two hundred thousand people.

Because of groupthink, these and other assumptions were never checked out. The need for group cohesiveness and unanimity caused the advisers not to call in experts and to ignore conflicting evidence. Doubts were quickly squelched.

Exactly the opposite approach was taken in the Cuban-Russian missile crisis. Kennedy and basically the same set of advisers were able to avoid groupthink by accepting internal conflict as the norm. Outside experts were pulled into the discussion, and the group accepted information from all sources. On occasion, Kennedy left the room to allow fuller discussion. Moral issues were explicitly discussed, and reversals of judgment were common. A wide variety of plans and possible results were examined. The final decision involved contingency plans that utilized all possible information, including predictions of how other nations might act. "The enemy" was not stereotyped.

Using this case as a base, the chapter will examine the nature and importance of conflict. **Conflict** is a struggle between two opposing forces, usually because of mutually exclusive impulses, desires, or activities. The chapter will trace the philosophical changes in conflict and distinguish between competitive and constructive conflict resolution. It will then deal with how the effective manager can reduce conflict in cooperative ways and stimulate constructive conflict when appropriate. Finally, the chapter will examine conflict within the individual that results from either too many conflicting demands on the person or from demands and expectations that are relatively ambiguous or unknown.

Changing Philosophies about Conflict

Over the years, three different philosophies that reflect different managerial attitudes toward conflict have been developed. They can arbitrarily be called the traditional, behavioral, and interactionist philosophies. Each emerged from a prevailing culture and from changing thoughts about management.[3]

The traditional, or classical, approach had a very simple attitude toward conflict: It should be eliminated. Conflict of any kind was seen as destructive, and the role of management was to rid the organization of it. If conflict appeared, it was a clear signal that something was wrong with the organization. It was assumed to develop only when managers did not apply sound management principles in designing and directing the organization or when they did not clearly communicate to subordinates that there were common interests holding management and employees together. Conflict was assumed to be quickly and easily resolvable through the management hierarchy. As Henri Fayol said, "From the instant that agreement ceases or there is no approval from supervisors direct contact comes [immediately] to an end and the scalar chain [vertical chain of command] is straightaway resumed."[4] Thus the supervisor was the final arbitrator of the conflict, and the solution to the problems causing the conflict was imposed from the top. This basic philosophy dominated management literature until about the middle 1940s. The problem with the approach, of course, was that it tended to ignore human feelings and the consequences of a solution being imposed from above.

Next came the behavioral view, which suggested that conflict is present in all organizations but that, when possible, it should be reduced or eliminated. This philosophy is still the most generally accepted approach to conflict. Its underlying rationale is that complex organizations, by their very nature, have built-in conflicts: disagreements over goals; departmental competition for prestige, status, and scarce resources; sectional competition for recognition; group competition for increased boundaries; and a constant competition by everyone for power. The behavioral view suggests that conflict can be functional at times, since it can identify problems and sometimes lead to good solutions. However, assuming that conflict is harmful, the view stresses management of its resolution and says practically nothing about its stimulation.

The interactionist view, which has emerged more recently, suggests that organizational conflict is inevitable and necessary, regardless of how organizations are designed and operated. It suggests that opposition should be encouraged and that conflict management must include conflict stimulation as well as resolution. Under this view, the management of conflict is a major responsibility of all administrators.

Thus the interactionist philosophy sees conflict as dysfunctional when it harms individuals or hinders the attainment of organizational goals. But it sees conflict as functional when it makes organizations more effective by leading to the search for better solutions, thereby bringing about innovation. The manager's task is to manage conflict—to maximize its helpful effects and to minimize its harmful ones. Appropriate management includes both conflict reduction and conflict stimulation. Established groups can develop more and better decisions when there is conflict among the members, so long as the conflict is properly handled. The conflicting opinions should be viewed as additional information rather than as threats to other group members.[5]

Organizations must change and adapt if they are to survive and prosper; those that stimulate constructive conflict are likely to examine the need for change. When the level of conflict is too low, the probability of stagnant thinking and inadequate decision making is increased, and the result is groupthink. An example of the effects of avoiding conflict is the bankruptcy of the Penn Central Railroad. There is evidence that the bankruptcy stemmed from two basic problems: mismanagement and the failure of the board of directors to question management's decisions and actions. The board, which consisted of directors from outside the company, met monthly to review and oversee the railroad's operations. Although a number of board members were uncomfortable and concerned about many major decisions made by operating management, few penetrating questions were asked. The desire to avoid friction and conflict (groupthink) allowed poor decisions to go unquestioned. Had the board

Table 18.1 Constructive versus destructive conflict

Constructive conflict	Destructive conflict
Groupthink is avoided	Cooperation is discouraged
Organizational apathy is reduced	Individuals or groups work for individual goals
Creativity is encouraged	Unnecessary stress is created
Problems are identified and clarified	Effort is spent trying to win rather than working toward common goals
Effort on the part of individuals and groups is stimulated	Deviant or "oddball" thinking is discouraged

brought conflict into the open and forced management to justify and explain key decisions, the bankruptcy might never have taken place.[6]

As Table 18.1 shows, conflict can have two contrasting outcomes. Constructive conflict is helpful to the organization; destructive conflict is harmful. The effective manager is able to diagnose the nature and type of conflict, resolve conflict cooperatively, and increase or decrease the level of constructive conflict as appropriate. The manager's goal is to manage conflict for the effective attainment of objectives rather than to have harmony and cooperation at all times.

Conflict, Competition, and Cooperation

Conflict occurs "whenever incompatible activities occur."[7] An activity that is incompatible with another one obstructs, prevents, or interferes with it in a way that makes the other less probable or less effective. Incompatible activities can involve one or more persons and can exist within and among groups or within and among organizations. This chapter will focus primarily on conflict among subunits or groups within the organization. For example, a sales department may want to get a particular customer's order out ahead of schedule, while a manufacturing department may want to reduce costs by holding to the established schedule.

Although the terms *conflict* and *competition* are often used interchangeably, they are not quite the same. Competition produces conflict, but not all conflict reflects competition. Indeed, **competition** "involves actions taken by one person to attain his or her most preferred outcome while simultaneously blocking attainment of the counterpart's most preferred outcome."[8] In other words, in competition there is an opposition in the goals of the interdependent parties so that the possibility of goal attainment for one party increases as the other's decreases.

Cooperation involves two or more parties working together to attain mutual goals. It is possible for cooperation and conflict to exist at the same time. For example, two individuals or groups may agree on goals but strongly disagree on how the goals are to be reached. The distinctions among conflict, competition, and cooperation are important, since they affect how the outcomes of conflict are managed. Conflict can occur in either a cooperative or a competitive context. The processes of conflict resolution that are likely to occur are strongly influenced by the context in which the conflict occurs. As Figure 18.1 shows, the primary issue is the mode of conflict resolution.

When conflict is resolved cooperatively, both parties gain, and the results are usually constructive. But when it is resolved competitively, the resolution can leave all parties dissatisfied, and the conflict may escalate to a win-lose stage.

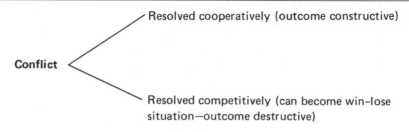

Figure 18.1 Cooperative and competitive outcomes of conflict

Organizational win-lose conflicts can be constructive. For example, in a chain of restaurants (such as McDonald's) each restaurant may compete for a bonus based on a percentage of sales. Even though only one restaurant will win the bonus, sales will probably be increased throughout the chain. More frequently, though, win-lose conflicts can reach the point where the parties involved lose sight of organizational goals and work actively at trying to destroy each other. In one situation, a manager sat behind a locked door while another manager beat and kicked on the door, screaming obscenities at the person inside the locked office. Such win-lose conflicts are destructive.

Some Sources of Organizational Conflict

Conflict can arise from many different sources, a few of which will be described here.[9] Some sources of conflict are differences in goals and in values or perceptions, allocation of scarce resources, work flow, and organization design and structure. Most of these sources involve intergroup conflict; however, they can also involve conflict among individuals and between individuals and groups.

Differences in Goals

Chapters 15 and 16 described how organization subsystems become differentiated or specialized in order to work on different tasks and problems. The differentiation frequently leads to conflict of priorities or interests, even when the parties to the conflict agree on the organization's overall goals. The marketing department, for example, may want low prices and a variety of products in order to attract more customers. The production department may want fewer products at a higher price in order to show a greater profit in manufacturing. The finance department may want a relatively low inventory of parts so the money not used for inventory can be invested in something else, such as new machinery. And the purchasing department may want to order materials in large quantities to get a discount on them. The differentiation among subsystems may be healthy for the organization but still lead to conflict because of different goals and points of view.

Allocation of Scarce Resources

Groups can function easier and goals can become easier to achieve when resources such as money, people, materials, equipment, and space are plentiful. But in most organizations these resources are limited. As a result, conflict can develop over their allocation. While there may be agreement on objectives, there may be disagreement on the use of resources to attain them. For example, a hospital's nursing department and radiology department may agree that improving patient care is a primary objective. But the nursing department may want to spend money on in-service training for nurses and on hiring nursing specialists, while the radiology department may want to purchase an expensive piece of equipment. Generally, the hospital cannot afford both.

Differences in Values or Perceptions

Each individual sees the world differently and acts on the perceptions in ways that make personal sense. Furthermore, perceptual differences are affected by group membership; those who work closely together in groups tend to have common perceptions. Indeed, a frequent source of disagreement among groups is the tendency of each one to value its own ideas and proposals more highly than those of others. Perceptual differences also arise from the tendency of individuals to evaluate things in terms of their own experiences. Since the members of any organization have different backgrounds, experiences, training, and education, they tend to perceive problems and their causes differently.[10]

Work Flow

Conflict can develop because of the work flow within an organization. When work is interdependent (two or more organizational units must depend on each other to complete their individual tasks), the potential for either conflict or cooperation exists. Conflict can occur when the groups involved are given too much to do or when the work is unevenly distributed. There is also a potential for conflict when the work is sequential—that is, when one group is unable to begin work until the other finishes its task.

Conflict can also occur because of status. If it appears that individuals from a low-status unit are giving orders to those from a high-status unit, resistance and conflict may develop. The higher-status group may find it difficult to take orders directly from lower-status people or from people whose status is unclear. Studies of the restaurant industry have shown the problems that arise when waiters or waitresses (low status) give orders to chefs (high status).[11] It is for this reason that most restaurants use written orders or other indirect approaches for the orders coming to the chef.

Organization Design and Structure

As Chapters 15 and 16 have suggested, the design and structure of the organization can have an effect on the amount of conflict generated. An organization or subunit whose design does not fit its technology and environment can generate unproductive, unnecessary, and dysfunctional conflict. An organization that is properly designed can develop constructive conflict—conflict that helps the organization attain its goals.

Organizations or subunits existing in a relatively certain environment with a stable technology should probably be organized along relatively bureaucratic lines, with clear chains of command and specific rules and regulations; that is, they should have a mechanistic structure. Those existing in a quickly-changing environment with an uncertain technology should probably be designed along relatively open lines; that is, they should have an organic structure.

Conflict frequently occurs between line managers and staff specialists.[12] This is a special instance of poor organizational design. In theory, line managers are part of a direct chain of command; they hold positions such as manufacturing manager, store manager, and area manager, and they make decisions. Staff specialists (who may also be managers) are supposed to provide advice and counsel to line managers to help their units accomplish organizational objectives; they hold positions in marketing research, the personnel department, and the computer department, and they help line managers determine the decisions to be made.

To some extent, the actual or potential conflict between these two groups (or individuals) shows the overlap of the sources of conflict already described. For example, the objective of the staff manager may be to bring about improvements, while the line manager may not want advice or suggestions from that person. A line manager in an outlying plant once said to a specialist attempting to install a company-wide job evaluation program, "Whatever you're selling, if you're from the home office, I don't want to buy."

There may be strong perceptual differences between line and staff, growing out of age and social differences. The staff specialist may be a college graduate, while the production manager may have little education and may have come up through the ranks. The staff person may have primary loyalty to a particular profession, such as research or law, while the line manager may be loyal to the organization itself.

There may also be status differences between line and staff. The staff manager may be short on experience but have the confidence of the president, and this may place the line manager in a lower-status position. A line manager with a great deal of status may resent receiving suggestions from a staff person who is viewed as lower in the hierarchy.

Managing to Reduce Conflict

To think that conflict can ever be completely eliminated is an exercise in futility. However, when conflict becomes competitive and its results become destructive, the manager must take steps to reduce it. Within organizations, there are a number of basic approaches to reducing conflict.[13] The three major types available to managers are dominance or forcing, compromise, and integrative problem solving. These approaches are quite different in the degree to which they develop cooperative versus competitive approaches to conflict resolution. They are also different in the way they establish conditions and processes for later reduction of conflict situations.

The three approaches deal primarily with interpersonal or process mechanisms, ignoring the structural/task/resource mechanisms that can also provide means of resolving or reducing conflict. (Chapter 16 described a number of structural approaches to the problem.)

Dominance and Forcing

Dominance and forcing occur when a solution to conflict is imposed or dictated. The imposing can be done by (1) the most powerful person or group in the conflict, (2) a common supervisor or other individuals within the organization who have the power and authority to enforce decisions, and (3) a neutral umpire or arbitrator. Dominance and forcing methods do not usually resolve the conflict, however. Instead they repress the conflict, forcing it underground; and they tend to establish win-lose situations in which the loser, who must give in to higher authority, ends up disappointed and hostile. The dominance-forcing solutions to conflict have two obvious problems:

1. There is no guarantee that the winning side will make a decision that is best for the organization. The decision generally is in the best interests of the winning side.
2. The losing side generally remains unconvinced and frustrated and looks for opportunities to win at some other time.

The classical theorists were clear about the best way to eliminate conflict: The common supervisor of the two parties in conflict should be the arbitrator.[14] Of course, this solution doesn't always work. In one situation, for example, three managers who worked together reported to different upper-level managers. The conflict among the three was particularly destructive. After a company reorganization, these managers were to report to a single individual. When their new boss found out about the conflict, he called the managers together and announced to them that from that day forward they would cooperate closely with each other. All three nodded their heads. What they meant was, "Yes, boss, we hear you—but we don't agree with you." The conflict was thus driven underground and emerged in more subtle ways than before.

Smoothing

Smoothing deals with conflict by denying it or avoiding it. It is a subtle and diplomatic kind of dominance. Instead of dealing openly with the conflict, it denies or hides it. The manager may emphasize common interests, minimize differences, and avoid known areas of disagreement. Problems are not raised; indeed, they are ignored in the hope they will go away.

Smoothing was visible in President Kennedy's approach to the Bay of Pigs fiasco. People were polite, conflicting views were not brought up, and groupthink became evident. Smoothing was also obvious in the actions of the Penn Central's board of directors before the railroad went bankrupt. Rather than upset the applecart, the directors did not intensively question management about its actions.

Majority rule is the attempt to resolve group conflict by a majority vote. This approach can be satisfactory if the process is seen as fair; however, if one party consistently outvotes the other, the losing side tends to feel dominated or forced.

Dominance and forcing do tend to eliminate conflict, at least in the short run. Clearly, there are times when the boss has to make a decision for opposing groups. However, the primary weakness of the approach is that is usually deals with symptoms rather than the root of the problem.

Compromise

Compromise is the attempt to obtain agreement through mutual concessions—by having each party modify their point of view to achieve a workable solution. It is the attempt to find a middle ground among two or more positions. The compromise approach is less likely to generate hostility than the dominance and forcing approaches. However, from the viewpoint of the organization, compromise is not a highly effective conflict resolution method, since it does not necessarily attempt to reach a solution that will best achieve organizational goals. Rather, the pressure is to reach a solution that all parties to the conflict can at least minimally subscribe to and live with. If the manager has more information than any of the parties involved, a compromise can usually be reached. But if the manager is seen as favoring one side over the other, the loser is likely to feel resentful.

Integrative Problem Solving

Integrative problem solving involves the open, complete, and rapid sharing of information concerning the problem and a joint search through the shared information to arrive at a decision that best accomplishes organizational goals. The term *confrontation* has also been used for this approach.[15] All the relevant facts are brought into the open, and conflicting viewpoints and opposition are encouraged. Integrative problem solving was the method of conflict resolution used in the Cuban-Russian missile crisis discussed earlier.

Managers almost unanimously see this kind of problem solving as the most desirable mode of conflict resolution. Yet, according to sociologists Paul Lawrence and Jay Lorsch, "it is used much less than it is recommended."[16] One of the reasons confrontation is seen as desirable but seldom used is that many people avoid sharply highlighting differences. Dominance, smoothing, and compromise are often easier to deal with. Also, confrontation tends to be more time-consuming, and it assumes a degree of trust and a lack of alienation or withdrawal on the parts of the people involved. It also requires skilled leadership and a willingness to accept additional stress and tension while the problem is being worked through. Finally, it encourages unusual ideas.

In one factory, the quality of manufactured parts was poor. Dominance, smoothing, and compromise had been tried without success. A number of different groups were involved, and each was in conflict with the others. Finally, the manager suggested a weekly meeting to explore the reasons for poor quality. The emphasis at these meetings was on integrative problem solving and confrontation rather than defensiveness. Over a period of six months, quality improved by 62 percent, for an annual savings of approximately $100,000.[17]

Integrative problem solving, which is usually superior to the other approaches to conflict resolution, is most effective when the conflict can be resolved through face-to-face meetings of the parties. The approach can also involve examining and changing the organization's structure, as described in Chapter 16. Actually, both structural and interpersonal approaches to conflict resolution may be necessary to deal successfully with the sources of conflict.

Three specific methods of integrated problem solving will be discussed: ensuring that data for problem solving are generated in common, reducing perceptual differences, and developing a common set of goals and objectives.

Ensuring That Data Are Generated in Common

Many organizational problems involve more than one subsystem or group. If only one develops a solution to the problem, the odds are that the others will reject it. From a systems point of view, no single group has all the information. In addition, a solution developed by one group may be excellent from its point of view but may be less than optimal from the others' viewpoints. When representatives of different groups are brought together to study the problem and develop joint decisions, the chances of pooling all relevant information, solving the problem, and reducing the conflict are improved.

More and more, organizations are using task forces to solve problems that affect several groups and the organization as a whole. To be successful, the task force generally has to include representatives from each group involved with the problem. For example, one organization was having difficulty moving new products through the development, manufacturing, and marketing stages. The managers involved decided to appoint a task force of representatives from research and development, marketing, production, and purchasing. The task force met to integrate the work of the units and departments. It referred policy questions to higher management, but it thrashed out operating problems within the group—through confrontation. All the relevant facts were brought out as each issue was openly debated. Finally, a decision was reached on each of the problems. Conflicting viewpoints and opposition were encouraged. As a result, new products were designed, developed, and manufactured much more quickly and effectively than ever before.[18]

Reducing Perceptual Differences

Earlier in the chapter, perceptual differences were described as a source of conflict. One method of resolving this conflict is to bring the conflicting groups together so they can share their perceptions of each other, clear up misunderstandings, and make certain that each has a better understanding of the purposes and objectives of the others. Sometimes, a single meeting can do much to clear the air, and follow-up meetings can be used to iron out persistent differences.

This approach has been used to reduce conflict between union and management prior to bargaining. The formalized version of the approach involves each group writing down its self-perceptions and its perceptions of the other group and then discussing these perceptions. Frequently, the process demonstrates that the perceptions are incorrect but that they have nonetheless considerably influenced behavior.[19]

Developing a Common Set of Goals and Objectives

Subsystems within an organization frequently have differing goals (as indicated in Chapter 7), and conflict among these subsystems can develop because of them. Many managers are rewarded on the basis of their success in attaining the objectives and goals of their particular subsystems. But when a subsystem is concerned about making itself look good—sometimes at the expense of other groups—competitive conflict is generated.

The organization confrontation meeting is one method of encouraging groups to establish and work toward common goals. The method consists of several steps. First, groups of ten to fifteen people are formed. Each group is a representative sample of the organization; its members are drawn from functional areas and hierarchical levels of the organization. The groups are assembled in one place and told that their task is to identify problems whose solution would be helpful to individuals or to the entire organization. Each group meets separately to determine the problems and then returns to the common meeting place to report on them. The problems are then categorized, and new groups are formed to begin working on their solution. The individual groups meet periodically either with the manager or with the larger group to report on their progress.[20]

The approach has been used with engineers, managers, nurses, clerical staffs, and entire organizations. In one unionized plant of about three hundred employees, the approach involved everyone in the plant, including guards, janitors, secretaries, engineers, and managers. As Figure 18.2 shows, the program was started in manufacturing period 7; and by the last period indicated, manufacturing costs had been reduced by about 45 percent, representing a savings of more than $1 million per year. Productivity also climbed sharply, and morale and job satisfaction increased.[21]

Stimulating Constructive Conflict

As explained at the beginning of the chapter, conflict is essentially neutral; indeed, constructive conflict contributes to the organization's aims and goals. Rather than always trying to minimize conflict, the effective manager diagnoses each situation to determine the most effective level of constructive conflict for the organization or subsystem.

Although many writers have discussed ways of reducing conflict, relatively few have written about ways of stimulating it.[22] Many organizations do not have enough functional, purposeful, constructive conflict; and the effective manager must therefore create such conflict. Some effective ways of stimulating conflict are simple; the easiest method is not to apply any of the conflict reduction techniques already described. For example, the manager may choose not to mediate or not to have each group develop solutions that can be discussed among all the groups. When conflict is not mediated, it escalates. Other approaches to stimulat-

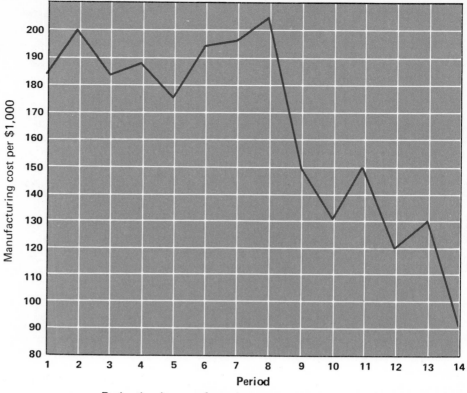

Reduction in manufacturing costs per accounting period

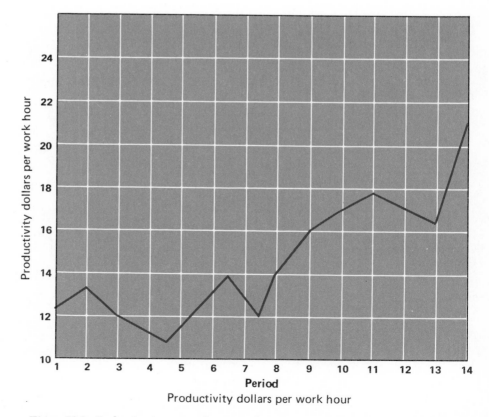

Productivity dollars per work hour

Figure 18.2 Reduction in costs and increased productivity using the organization confrontation approach

ing conflict include communicating that conflict is acceptable, changing communications channels, redistributing power, and increasing or maintaining perceptual differences.

Communicating That Conflict Is Acceptable

In many organizations, the role of conflict is clear; it is supposed to be nonexistent. Such organizations want peace and harmony, not conflict and disagreement. Employees get the message and respond to it by downplaying their differences of opinion, especially to their supervisors.

The single most effective way of increasing managed conflict is to let subordinates know that constructive conflict and disagreement have their place. One way of doing this is for the manager to show subordinates that problem identification is valued and that original thinking will be rewarded. The effective manager allows all ideas to be challenged and encourages different points of view and opinions.

To illustrate: A number of groups were asked to analyze and develop a solution to a problem. In some of the groups there was one person who challenged and questioned the group's analyses and solutions; in other groups no one challenged anything. In each situation, the group having a challenging person was better able to handle conflict and developed better analyses and solutions.[23]

Changing Communications Channels

Communicating that constructive conflict is acceptable is probably the single most effective way of stimulating that conflict. Once that communication has been received by subordinates, a second way of stimulating conflict is by changing the communications process. A basic way of changing the process is to alter the formal channels of communication. For example, a manager who sends information to individuals or groups in regular communications may decide not to do so. Or a manager who normally does not send information to certain groups or individuals may begin doing so. A manager who wants to stimulate tension and conflict may send a memorandum to the usual people but omit one or two from the list. The omission will bring about reexamination of the situation.

On the informal level, a manager may carefully select which messages should go through the grapevine and who should get them. Changes in the traditional channels redistribute knowledge inside the organization. Since knowledge represents power, changing communication channels shifts the balance of power.

In addition, a manager seeking to stimulate conflict can send out ambiguous information. Ambiguous information deliberately communicated results in conflict. Suppose a memorandum has some implicit contradictions. Subordinates and others receiving it will question it, seek out more information, and take other actions to reduce the ambiguity.

Redistributing Power

Those who possess power (described more fully in Chapter 20) can deliberately use it to bring about the results they want. A manager who wants to bring about change through constructive conflict may decide to redistribute power among the organization's members. Power is obtained from the activities that take place in the organization, and a reshuffling of responsibility for such activities can serve to stimulate both conflict and the desired change.

Often, new managers entering an organization bring in subordinates with whom they have worked in the past. This kind of redistribution of power brings about a careful examination of present and past practices. Those who have been somewhat apathetic in the past frequently become much more active and energetic as the power is redistributed.

Increasing or Maintaining Perceptual Differences

In the Electronic Products Division Case described in Chapter 16, top management initially diagnosed a conflict situation as arising from poor intergroup relations. The division's general manager determined that there were many internal conflicts among the various functional groups, and he felt that these conflicts were severely hampering product development efforts. He decided at first to attempt to reduce the perceptual differences among the groups. Further study of the problem, however, suggested that reducing perceptual differences was not the answer. The organization existed in a turbulent and uncertain environment and actually required a high degree of differentiation or perceptual variation in the areas of formality of structure, interpersonal orientation, and goal and time orientation. Under the circumstances, it was good that the scientists saw the world differently from the assembly managers. In this situation, getting greater perceptual agreement would actually have been a disservice to the organization. Instead, the company reorganized the groups into project teams, thereby maintaining the perceptual differences and lessening conflict. Thus, in some cases, managers must actively work at maintaining or increasing perceptual differences.

Role, Role Conflict, and Role Ambiguity

So far, conflict, conflict resolution, and conflict stimulation have been described as primarily occurring among individuals, groups, or subsystems of the organization. This section will confront conflicts within the individual. Chapters 1 and 2 stressed the crucial importance of the manager's job and the critical position of the manager as a nerve center for a variety of other individuals and groups, and Chapter 14 described the concept of systems and the interrelatedness of subsystems. An important characteristic of an organization as a system is the concept of role.[24] Chapter 2 defined a **role** as a set of systematically interrelated and observable behaviors that belong to an identifiable job or position—the sum total of the activities the manager is expected to perform. The expectations are those of both the individual manager and those with whom the manager is in contact.

The manager's role constitutes a link among the manager, the manager's unit, the rest of the organization, and contacts outside the organization. Figure 18.3 shows who the manager associates with in performing the organizational role and which other people are linked to the manager outside the organization.

Role behavior is caused not only by the characteristics and personality of the manager but also by the expectations of others, including subordinates, peers, supervisors, vendors, and customers. A manager may have contact with hundreds of people or groups each month, and each of these individuals and groups may have a different set of expectations. The manager must be able to integrate these expectations as well as personal ones into a coherent and organized set in order to perform successfully. **Role conflict** occurs when the manager experiences conflicting expectations about how to perform the role. In other words, the manager knows what is expected but is not able to comply with all the expectations. For example, a plant manager may be under pressure from the accounting department manager to cut personnel costs while the personnel manager is pushing for the speedy employment of more people from minority groups.

Role ambiguity occurs when the manager receives an inadequate amount of role related information—that is, when the manager does not clearly understand all the expectations. One common cause of role ambiguity is the individual's hesitation to show ignorance by asking ques-

Boundaries of the organization

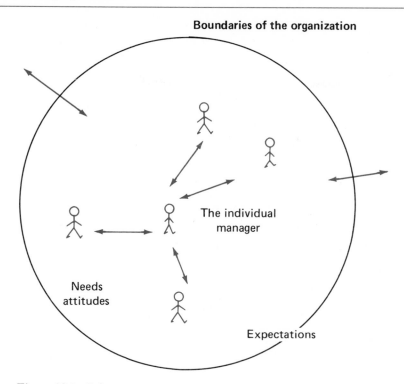

Figure 18.3 Role expectations, conflict, and ambiguity

tions of those higher in the organization. Another is the tendency to restrict the information flow upward through the organization's hierarchy.

Role conflict and role ambiguity cause job stress and tension, some of which is healthy and stimulating. A job without excitement and challenge can be boring. However, too much tension reduces job satisfaction and increases the possibility of sickness, high turnover, and decreased job performance.[25]

Although the evidence is not yet clear, it appears that under conditions of role conflict, the manager tends to respond first to the individual or group who has the most power. If the power is approximately equal, or if the individuals or groups have relatively little power, the manager tends to make an independent decision and take independent action.[26]

Implications for the Manager

Conflict in organizations is inevitable. It stems from a number of sources—people and their differences, jobs, interacting groups, and the inevitability of organizational change, among others. The effective manager understands the changing philosophy about conflict and distinguishes between conflict resolution that is helpful to the organization and conflict resolution that is not helpful.

Given that conflict is inevitable, the effective manage recognizes that it must be managed. The manager must diagnose the nature and source of conflict before deciding whether to increase or decrease its level in order to attain the aims, goals, and objectives of the organization.

When conflict must be reduced, the effective manager uses forcing or dominance if necessary but strives for integrative problem solving. Approaches to integrative problem-solving include ensuring that the data for solving the problem are generated in common, that perceptual differences are reduced, and that a common set of goals and objectives is developed. The manager also reviews the design and strucuture of the organization, since structural and process changes go hand in hand in resolving conflict cooperatively and constructively.

Given that conflict must be managed, the effective manager first examines his or her personal style of working with others. Is that style such that conflict can develop when appropriate? If not, the style needs to be changed. After examining personal style, the manager should attempt to understand how conflict comes about, to diagnose the situation, and then to determine whether the level of conflict should be increased or reduced. If conflict should be reduced, the manager should work for cooperative rather than competitive conflict resolution.

Internal conflicts resulting from role conflict and role ambiguity occur frequently in organizations. The effective manager can use problem-solving techniques to reduce both role conflict and role ambiguity and can avoid placing subordinates in situations that will cause undue stress of this nature.

Review

1. Explain how the thinking about conflict has changed over the years.
2. Compare and contrast the classical and interactionist views of conflict.
3. What are the differences among conflict, cooperation, and competition?
4. Identify and describe five sources of organizational conflict.
5. What are the conditions under which these types of conflict might emerge?
6. What are some consequences of a low conflict level in an organization?
7. Describe how managers can stimulate conflict.
8. What are the major types of conflict resolution?
9. Rank the different types of conflict resolution in order of their long-term effectiveness.
10. What are the differences between role conflict and role ambiguity?
11. Is role conflict necessarily bad? How about role ambiguity? Explain.
12. If you were a manager, how would you feel about deliberately increasing the level of conflict within or among groups?
13. In terms of your own verbal and nonverbal communication, do you indicate that conflict is acceptable or not acceptable? Does this vary with the circumstances?
14. What is your personal response to role conflict, especially when there are many conflicting demands? Is yours the best reaction? Explain.
15. How can organizational design affect conflict, conflict resolution, and conflict stimulation?

The E. F. Howard Company

Richard Wise, corporate quality control manager for the E. F. Howard Company, hung up the phone and stared blankly out the window, thinking about his alternatives. The phone call had been from Art Johnson, a Howard vice-president and Wise's boss, and it was both reassuring and troubling. Wise was happy to know that he had his boss's support of whatever decisions he might make in the present situation. Nevertheless, he was unhappy with the available alternatives and would have appreciated some additional advice.

The E. F. Howard Company is a small manufacturer, established in 1920; annual sales are approximately $40 million. The company employs approximately four hundred people. Howard's two plants are located in small midwestern towns, and its corporate headquarters is in Denver. Wise has been corporate quality manager for one year. The position is a relatively new one. Until two years ago, the quality control staff reported directly to the production manager. Now, all plant quality control people report to the plant quality control manager, who in turn reports to Wise. The man who held the position before Wise had been on the job about a year, until he was fired by the president for being unqualified for the job.

The president of Howard had said to Wise, "Put in a tough quality control program. Don't worry about stepping on toes. I want you to make certain that our products are of the highest quality." Keeping that direction in mind, Wise had taken a hard look at the quality control staff of several plants. He now felt that the quality control manager of the Drysdale plant simply was not effective. Wise realized that the small town location of the plant might be contributing to the slow pace of the plant personnel. He also appreciated the plant personnel manager's desire to keep the plant nonunion. But Wise was convinced nonetheless that the quality control program in the plant could be vastly improved.

When a Drysdale quality control technician retired, Wise hired a competent young woman, Lois Carroll, to take his place. He believed this would keep people on their toes. Also, Carroll's dedication to a career in quality control impressed Wise and created a strong bond between them. Carroll reported to Wise by phone on a daily basis to keep him aware of impending problems. After six months with Howard, she was producing more work than Ralph Burgess, the quality control manager, and all the other technicians combined. She was never absent, she worked many hours of overtime, and she had changed a number of procedures, which substantially increased efficiency and quality.

Wise, delighted with Carroll's progress, was finally becoming optimistic about developing the "tough" quality control program the president had requested. The minor complaints he received about Carroll's strained relationships with other members of the department and with production personnel were, he felt, based on their own lack of initiative and on envy of her superior performance.

When Wise received a request for a conference call, he had no idea what the topic of discussion might be. The call included Bill Lewis, the plant manager; Ralph Burgess, the plant quality control manager, and Bob Franklin, the plant personnel manager. Burgess told Wise that Franklin had received a serious complaint about Lois Carroll from one of the other technicians. Carroll was accused of intentionally disrupting their work by giving the other technicians instructions and claiming she had Wise's permission to do so. The other technicians believed this was an attempt by Carroll to undermine Lewis's authority. They also believed that Carroll, as the junior member of the department, was challenging the authority they had earned by virtue of their longer tenure with the company. The production people agreed and demanded that Carroll be fired because she was a disruptive force interfering with the work of two departments.

Burgess told Wise that he, Franklin, and Lewis all agreed that Carroll should be fired. Not to do so would cause trouble in the plant and might bring about unionization (which the president had told them to avoid at any cost), the ill will of several long-term employees, and the interruption of the smooth production flow. The three felt that Carroll, who had been with the company only six months, was certainly less valuable than the long-term employees in the quality control department. Burgess told Wise that he expected suitable action to be taken by the end of the week.

Stunned by this telephone conversation, Wise had immediately placed his call to Art Johnson.

1. What seems to be the problem at the Howard Company?
2. How did it develop?
3. What recommendations do you have for Richard Wise?

Footnotes

1. This case is adapted with permission from I. Janis, *Victims of Groupthink* (Boston: Houghton Mifflin, 1972).
2. Ibid., p. 9.
3. S. Robbins, *Managing Organizational Conflict: A Nontraditional Approach* (Englewood Cliffs, N.J.: Prentice-Hall, 1974).

4. H. Fayol, *General and Industrial Management,* trans. C. Storrs (London: Pitman Publishing, 1949), p. 35.
5. J. Hall and M. Williams, "A Comparison of Decision-Making Performances in Established and Ad Hoc Groups," *Journal of Personality and Social Psychology* 3 (February 1966): 217.
6. P. Binxen and J. Daughen, *Wreck of the Penn Central* (Boston: Little, Brown, 1971).
7. M. Deutsch, *The Resolution of Conflict* (New Haven, Conn.: Yale University Press, 1973), p. 19.
8. R. Cosier and G. Rose, "Cognitive Conflict and Goal Conflict Effects on Task Peformance," *Organizational Behavior and Human Performance* 19 (August 1977): 379.
9. J. Harvey, "The Abilene Paradox: The Management of Agreement," *Organizational Dynamics* 3 (Summer 1974): 63–80; A. Negandhi, ed., *Conflict and Power in Complex Organizations: An Interinstitutional Perspective* (Kent, Ohio: Kent State University Press, 1972); G. Strauss, "Tactics of Lateral Relationship," *Administrative Science Quarterly* 7 (September 1962): 161–186; R. Walton and R. McKersie, *A Behavioral Theory of Labor Negotiations* (New York: McGraw-Hill, 1965); and C. Argyris, "Human Problems with Budgets," *Harvard Business Review* 31 (January–February 1953): 1–14.
10. D. Dearborn and H. Simon, "Selective Perception: A Note on the Departmental Identification of Executives," *Sociometry* 21 (June 1958): 140–144.
11. W. Whyte, *Human Relations in the Restaurant Industry* (New York: Harper & Bros., 1948).
12. J. Belasco and J. Alutto, "Line and Staff Conflicts: Some Empirical Insights," *Academy of Managment Journal* 12 (January 1969): 469–477; and M. Dalton, *Men Who Manage* (New York: Wiley, 1959).
13. R. Blake and J. Mouton, *The Managerial Grid* (Houston: Gulf Publishing, 1964); P. Lawrence and J. Lorsch, *Organization and Environment* (Homewood, Ill.: Richard D. Irwin, 1967); and R. Walton and J. Dutton, "The Management of Interdepartmental Conflict: A Model and Review," *Administrative Science Quarterly* 14 (March 1969): 73–84.
14. F. Taylor, *Principles of Scientific Management* (New York: Harper & Bros., 1911); and L. Urwick, *The Elements of Administration* (New York: Harper & Bros., 1943).
15. Lawrence and Lorsch, *Organization and Environment,* p. 220.
16. Ibid., p. 222.
17. E. Huse, "The Behavioral Scientist in the Shop," *Personnel* 42 (May–June 1965): 50–57.
18. E. Huse and M. Beer, "Eclectic Approach to Organizational Development," *Harvard Business Review* 49 (September–October 1971): 103–112.
19. R. Blake, H. Shepard, and J. Mouton, *Managing Intergroup Conflict in Industry* (Houston: Gulf Publishing, 1974).
20. R. Beckhard, *Organization Development: Strategies and Models* (Reading, Mass.: Addison-Wesley, 1969); and Huse, *Organization Development and Change* (St. Paul, Minn.: West Publishing, 1975).
21. E. Huse and J. Bowditch, *Behavior in Organizations: A Systems Approach to Managing,* rev. ed. (Reading, Mass.: Addison-Wesley, 1977), pp. 451–455; Huse, *Organization Development and Change,* pp. 140–142; and C. Barebo, personal communication.
22. R. Dubin, "Theory Building in Applied Areas," in *Handbook of Industrial and Organizational Psychology,* ed. M. Dunette (Chicago:

Rand-McNally, 1975), pp. 17–39; S. Robbins, G. Salanick, and J. Pfeffer, "Who Gets Power—and How They Hold onto It: A Strategic-Contingency Model of Power," *Organizational Dynamics* 5 (Winter 1977): 3–21; D. Nightengale, "Conflict and Conflict Resolution," in *Organizational Behavior: Research and Issues*, ed. G. Strauss (Belmont, Calif.: Wadsworth Publishing, 1976); and A. Zaleznik, "Power and Politics in Organizational Life," *Harvard Business Review* 48 (May–June 1970): 47–60.

23. R. Kahn and E. Boulding, *Power and Conflict in Organizations* (New York: Basic Books, 1964).

24. D. Katz and R. Kahn, *The Social Psychology of Organizations* (New York: Wiley, 1966); R. Kahn et al., *Organizational Stress: Studies in Role Conflict and Ambiguity* (New York: Wiley, 1964).

25. R. House and J. Rizzo, "Role Conflict and Ambiguity as Critical Variables in a Model of Organizational Behavior," *Organizational Behavior and Human Performance* 7 (June 1972): 467–505; D. Hall, "A Model of Coping with Role Conflict: The Role Behavior of College Educated Women," *Administrative Science Quarterly* 17 (December 1972): 471–486; and R. Schuler, "Role Perceptions, Satisfaction, and Performance: A Partial Reconciliation," *Journal of Applied Psychology* 60 (December 1975): 683–687.

26. G. Ritzer, *Working: Conflict and Change* (Englewood Cliffs, N.J.: Prentice-Hall, 1977); R. Hatley and B. Pennington, "Role Conflict Resolution Behavior of High School Principals," *Education Administration Quarterly* 11 (Autumn 1975): 67–84; and N. Gross, W. Mason, and A. McEachern, *Explorations in Role Analysis: Studies of the School Superintendency Role* (New York: Wiley, 1958).

Chapter 19   Managing Change

The Instrument Department

The Accelerating Pace of Change
    The Knowledge Explosion
    Rapid Product Obsolescence
    The Changing Composition of the Labor Force
    Growing Concern over Personal and Social Issues
    Increasing Internationalization of Business

Structural and Process Change
    Structural Change
    Change as a Process

Change and Organization Development
    Assumptions in Organization Development
    The Need for Proper Diagnosis

Managing Change through Organization Development (OD)
    Organizational Structure
    Intergroup Relationships
    Improving Group Relationships
    Improving Intrapersonal Relationships

Some Problems with Managing Change

Implications for the Manager

Review

A New Approach to Making Pet Food

Learning Objectives

When you have finished reading and studying this chapter, you should be able to:

1. Illustrate how change is a continuing fact of life.
2. Compare and contrast structural and process change.
3. Describe the assumptions underlying organization development efforts.
4. Demonstrate the need for proper diagnosis of change attempts.
5. Identify the major phases or steps in successful change attempts.
6. Name and differentiate the broad classifications of organization development approaches.
7. Identify and demonstrate the use of specific tools or techniques for organization development.
8. Define and use the concept of organization development within the context of a total system.
9. Identify and discuss specific problems with organization development.
10. Define and be able to use the following concepts:

competent organization	organization development
organizational effectiveness	job enrichment
organizational efficiency	core job dimensions
structural change	team building
process approach to change	sensitivity training

Thought Starters

1. What are the implications of the statement that 90 percent of all scientists that have ever lived are still living?
2. Under what conditions will people accept change? Under what conditions will they resist it?
3. How can change be managed?

The Instrument Department

The Medford Company makes a variety of medical testing equipment. Its instrument department assembles electronic instruments designed to conduct blood tests and other tests in hospitals and doctors' offices. Some of the instruments are highly complex, costing up to a hundred thousand dollars. About thirty men and women work in the department.

When the supervisor of the instrument department was promoted, Lou Barnes, an engineering technician, took over the job. It was his first supervisory job; in fact, he had not yet finished the work on his bachelor's degree in management and was attending night school to do so. Several of Barnes's courses had covered areas such as motivation, group dynamics, and the management of change; and working with one of his professors, Barnes decided to try out some of the ideas he had learned.

He began by being frank and open with his people in explaining why schedule and other changes were necessary. Holding team meetings, he involved his subordinates in the planning process by discussing with them how schedules could be met. When he took over the job, each assembler was performing limited tasks based on detailed, written instructions. Barnes began encouraging workers to exchange tasks and to help each other out.

As the workers became more skilled and versatile, he tried having single workers assemble the less complex instruments; and as the workers gained confidence in their abilities, he kept expanding their jobs. Within a year, individuals were undertaking the complete assembly of complex instrument systems. For the most complex instruments, Barnes had groups of workers do the assembly. The workers themselves could decide who would perform which tasks. Since everyone in the department knew the schedule, the workers could shift from one set of instruments to another if there were parts shortages or other complications.

During the next year, four new instruments were introduced into the department for assembly. In contrast to the usual large drop in productivity when new products entered the traditional assembly line process, the introduction of the new instruments caused only a slight drop. Because of delays and other problems, one major instrument was brought into the department without any instructions or drawings. Using an instrument that had been built in the development department as a guide, the workers were told, "Make it like this one."

To determine the effectiveness of Barnes's approach, the plant accountant studied the costs of several instruments that had been in production for at least two years before Barnes's entry into the department. The average productivity for the eight months preceding the change was used as a base. The accountant found that during Barnes's tenure, productivity had risen by 17 percent, or approximately $1,500 per year per worker. Quality also had improved; the number of rejects had decreased from an average of 25 percent to an average of 13 percent, an increase in quality of about 50 percent. Absenteeism had been reduced from 8.5 percent per month to 3.4 percent, a reduction of about 50 percent.[1]

This case describes a situation of planned change. Although the instrument department's productivity had been satisfactory when Barnes took over, he was able to substantially improve both productivity and employee morale.

This chapter will examine the need for planned change that comes in part from the accelerated pace of change throughout the world. Change can occur in many ways. Some needs for change develop outside the organization: New laws are passed; the competition develops a better product; the organization is taken over by another one. Other changes arise from within the organization: A new building must be built; a new machine is purchased; conflict among groups becomes destructive.

Change has become almost a way of life—a norm. The effective manager is able to manage change rather than simply reacting to it. This chapter therefore explores a number of ways in which managers can bring about planned and managed change.

The Accelerating Pace of Change

Change is accelerating rapidly in our society; revolutions are occurring in technological, communications, political, scientific, and institutional areas. Because the changes are so rapid, new and improved methods need to be developed to deal with them. Both cultural and technological changes appear to be irreversible. In the past twenty-five years, the amount of technological change has been greater than in the past two hundred thousand years. At least five areas of rapidly accelerating change are having an impact on today's organizations. They are the knowledge explosion, rapid product obsolescence, the changing composition of the labor force, the growing concern over personal and social issues, and the increasing internationalization of business.

The Knowledge Explosion

It has been said that more than 90 percent of all the scientists that have ever lived are still living. Particularly since World War II, we have seen a tremendous explosion in the development of knowledge. For thousands of years, the wheel was the most advanced invention in transportation. During that time, relatively little improvement was made on it. It evolved from being solid to having spokes; then, a few years ago, the tubeless rubber tire was invented. Yet, in about eighty years, transportation progressed from buggies to automobiles and even to rockets to the moon and probes to Mars and Venus. These days, knowledge quickly becomes obsolete, and organizations can become obsolete just as quickly.

Rapid Product Obsolescence

As new knowledge is developed, old knowledge and products become obsolete. The vacuum tube was replaced by the transistor, which was replaced even more rapidly by "chip" technology, in which entire circuits can be viewed only with the aid of a microscope. This has allowed the development of the modern computers. Organizations in the medical instrumentation field that bring out new, complex instruments soon discover that other companies are bringing out better instruments at lower cost.

The Changing Composition of the Labor Force

A dramatic shift in the labor force is occurring in the United States as the country becomes increasingly urbanized. The educational level of the population is steadily rising. More than 60 percent of the urban population is involved in some form of education beyond high school. Another major change is the decrease in the median age of the work force. Managers are now dealing with better-educated and younger workers who do not readily accept outmoded styles of management.

Finally, the work force that once consisted of laborers and semi-skilled workers (so-called blue-collar workers) is shifting. There are many more managerial, professional, sales, and clerical workers (white-collar workers). In 1956, white-collar workers outnumbered blue-collar workers for the first time, and the trend is increasing. Agricultural and manufacturing jobs are decreasing, while jobs in government, service, and health care are increasing.

Growing Concern over Personal and Social Issues

The younger, more mobile, more highly-educated labor force has shown an increasing desire to "do its own thing." Many workers are less interested in money as such and more concerned about opportunities for autonomy, personal choice, and freedom—about the quality of work life. The rising educational levels and younger age of workers have also raised the level of worker discontent. An absenteeism rate of 40 percent is not uncommon in automobile plants where the traditional assembly line has remained relatively unchanged.

New college graduates expect to be able to use and apply their training in their first jobs, but they often are told not to rock the boat. Discouraged, they quit. According to consultant Richard Beckhard, "Over 70 percent of the masters graduates of the Sloan School of Management [Massachusetts Institute of Technology] are in their second companies within two years . . . and this statistic is not exclusive to our school. It's pretty expensive recruiting."[2]

The same kinds of dissatisfaction are being seen in middle and top management. One large consumer products company had openings for regional marketing managers. These jobs, which paid over $40,000 and included other incentives, were offered to two of the company's best men. Both refused, even though the job would have included a pay increase of at least $8,000 per year. Neither man wanted to move and disrupt his family.[3]

Increasing Internationalization of Business

The increasing internationalization of business can be seen by a glance at the front page of almost any urban newspaper. The oil crisis in 1973 and the continuing dependence of the United States on outside energy are only two examples of this interdependence and growing internationalization. One report suggests that "60 percent of all the world's business will eventually be done by international firms."[4]

The fact of change seems clear. It is part of the personal experience and common observation of almost everyone. For example, in about three years, more than sixty of the hundred largest industrial companies in the United States publicly reported organizational changes; and this was only the visible tip of the proverbial iceberg.[5] Organizations that are not adaptive and flexible quickly become obsolete.

Immediately after Prohibition, there were more than 700 breweries. That number was reduced to 118 in 1965 and to 47 in 1977. By 1985, there may be only about 15. The message is clear. Organizations that do not change and adapt disappear or are taken over by more progressive ones.

In order to stay healthy, adaptive, and flexible, organizations must be competent. The **competent organization** is both effective and efficient.[6] **Organizational effectiveness** is the degree to which a specific organization attains its objectives and goals. **Organizational efficiency** is the amount of resources used by an organization to produce a unit of output. An organization may be very efficient in attaining its goals of making high-quality buggy whips but if no one wants buggy whips, the organization's goals need to be changed. On the other hand, even if the goals are right and proper, the organization may be inefficient in reaching them. It thus may go out of business because its products are too costly and it cannot meet the competition's prices. Many breweries went out of business simply because they were inefficient.

Structural and Process Change

There are two overlapping and related ways of bringing about change. One is through **structural change,** or changes in the various functions or activities performed in an organization. At the strategic top level, these changes can involve changing objectives, redesigning the organization, or purchasing another company. At the managerial level, they can involve shifting lines of authority or communications or shifting policies and procedures. At the operations level, they can involve the purchase of new and improved machinery and the development of new products. At all three levels, some formal aspect of the organization is modified to bring about improved organizational effectiveness and efficiency.

The **process approach to change** focuses on how things are done rather than on what is done. It is concerned with such areas as interpersonal interactions, group dynamics, and the relationships among workers and machines. Rather than focusing on the purchase of a new machine (a structural approach), the process approach may focus on making a job more interesting and challenging. While the structural approach may involve firing or transferring people who are quarreling, the process approach may try to determine the reason for the conflict.

Structural Change

The structural approach can be traced back to classical management theory, with its emphasis on worker efficiency. The process approach stems more from the behavioral sciences, with its interest in and concern about both personal and interpersonal attitudes. In the structural approach, the question is not whether workers will like the new machine but whether the machine will improve productivity. In the process approach, the question is how well workers will adapt to the new machine and what the content of their work experience will be. Although a philosophical distinction can be made between these two approaches, they do overlap, as Figure 19.1 shows.

Both structure and process need to be considered in managing change, since each affects the other. Structural change affects the process of people working together. For example, the purchase or acquisition of another organization may affect many managers. The purchase of a new machine may affect group and interpersonal relationships. On the other hand, shifts in interpersonal or group relationships may affect the organization's structure. In the case at the beginning of the chapter, for example, the first actions Lou Barnes took were process changes, including group meetings and greater worker involvement in planning. Later changes were structural and included changes in the design of the jobs.

The two approaches are practically inseparable, since changing the organization eventually means changing the behavior of people as they work together to accomplish the organization's goals. Efforts at change can take many different forms. "In the final analysis, however, all organizational change efforts, regardless of initial focus, must take account of the fact that *people are called on to do things differently.*"[7] Properly managing people in the change process is one of the most important tasks a manager can perform.

Change as a Process

Although managers can discuss the idea of process in the abstract, they cannot work directly upon a process. Rather, they must work with specific individuals and groups to change the behaviors that created the

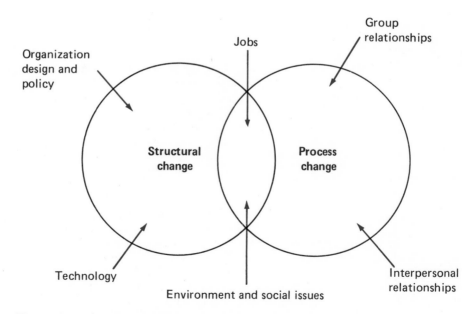

Figure 19.1 The interdependence of structure and process

ineffective processes. Unless they are highly motivated, most people do not make significant changes in their work behavior overnight. Instead, they must first recognize that their current work behavior or practices are ineffective or inappropriate and that alternatives are possible. Then they can begin to change. Thus change can be considered a process that involves individuals or groups and their behavior.

Kurt Lewin, a sociologist, has developed a process model for change that consists of three basic steps—unfreezing, changing or moving, and refreezing.[8]

Unfreezing is a reduction in the strength of old values, attitudes, or behaviors. Before people become willing to change their behavior, they must understand that the behavior is no longer effective or is somehow inadequate to the demands of their particular situation or problem. Unfreezing is a disturbance of equilibrium that makes people receptive to new ideas or behaviors.

Changing, or moving, is the bringing about of specific changes through the development of new values, attitudes, and/or behaviors. Unfreezing creates a vacuum unless alternatives that are realistic, known, and possible are available.

Refreezing is the stabilization change at a new state of equilibrium. The people accept the new values, attitudes, and behaviors. For example, a person may experiment with new behaviors, see that they are better than the old ones, and make the change permanent.

A review of eighteen studies of change in large organizations found that the more successful change attempts involved six major phases: pressure and arousal, intervention and reorientation, diagnosis and recognition, intervention and commitment, experimentation and search, and reinforcement and acceptance.[9] Thus the process of unfreezing, changing, and refreezing is a continuum rather than a series of discrete steps (as shown in Figure 19.2).

Pressure and arousal. A need for change is felt as a result of stress. Many people, including at least a senior manager, are dissatisfied with present behavior and performance. The stress can come from internal forces such as interdepartmental conflict, decreased productivity, or a strike, or from external forces such as stockholder discontent or a technological breakthrough by a competitor.

Intervention and reorientation. An influential and respected person, frequently a newcomer, acts as a change agent. Newcomers often have a more objective viewpoint, can size up organizational needs, and can begin to help managers change their thinking by getting them to reexamine their practices and procedures. Often, the "problem" is only a symptom.

Unfreezing		Pressure and arousal
		Intervention and reorientation
		Diagnosis and recognition
Changing	↓	Intervention and commitment
		Experimentation and search
Refreezing		Reinforcement and acceptance

Figure 19.2 The change process

Diagnosis and recognition. The change agent/manager helps the organization examine past and present policies and practices in order to identify problems and their causes. In the more successful change approaches, this is a shared rather than a unilateral or delegated process.

Intervention and commitment. Using a participative approach to obtain full commitment, effective solutions are found. The more successful change approaches involve intensive searches for innovative ideas and solutions with many people working together. None of the less successful change attempts ever reached this phase. Their attempts at change created too much resistance for the proposed changes to be adopted.

Experimentation and search. Those whose change approaches were successful tried out the new problem solutions and changes on a small scale before making any large-scale changes. They checked tentative solutions with personnel at different levels to discover problems or flaws. This sharing of power makes certain that these minor decisions can be rescinded if they turn out wrong.

Reinforcement and acceptance. The success of small, tentative changes establishes a climate for further change—a support for change at all levels of the organization. An increasing number of people begin to see their personal interests as being served by the organizational change. This reinforces the impact of the change and rewards people for experimenting.

This study and others suggest that successful organizational changes require four positive notions:

1. Managers must assume that change is not only for those lower in the hierarchy than they are. Change can also come from the bottom up.
2. The myth that organizational change consists of a master blueprint designed and executed from the top down by an expert manager or consultant must be put to rest.
3. Change is more successful when many people participate than when it is unilateral or delegated.
4. Those involved in the change must be given the opportunity to develop a broad perspective and become less parochial in their approach to change.[10]

Change and Organization Development

In one sense, almost every chapter in this book deals with change. The process of motivating and working with groups involves change. Decision making and establishing or modifying organizational goals and objectives involves change. Planning and establishing or reestablishing control systems to accomplish organizational goals involves change. Organizing and dealing with the staffing process involves change. One of the basic purposes of communications is to ensure that proper change is accomplished. Creativity and the management of conflict certainly involve change.

In this chapter, the primary focus is on managing change through **organization development(OD)**—the application of behavioral science knowledge in a long-range effort to improve an organization's ability to cope with changes in its external environment and increase its internal problem-solving capabilities.[11] Several parts of this definition need to be explored in order to distinguish OD from a change such as the purchase of a new machine. The application of behavioral science knowledge implies that the primary focus is on integrating the needs of individual employees for involvement, growth, and development on the job with the goals and objectives of the organization. OD tends to be a long-range effort; planned change comes about gradually. The effort to improve an organization's ability to cope with change implies that the human resources of many organizations can be better used by improving the problem-solving capabilities of the people in the organization.

Assumptions in Organization Development

An explicit part of the OD approach concerns humanistic values and the quality of people's work life. The focus is on both improving the organization's competence and providing the opportunity for individuals to develop and grow in the organizational setting. OD is based on a number of assumptions:

1. Most people want and need opportunities for growth and achievement.
2. When the basic needs have been satisfied, most people will respond to opportunities for responsibility, challenge, and interesting work.
3. Organizational effectiveness and efficiency are increased when work is organized to meet individual needs for responsibility, challenge, and interesting work.
4. Personal growth and the accomplishment of organizational goals are better attained by shifting the emphasis of conflict resolution from smoothing to open confrontation.
5. The design of individual jobs, group tasks, and organizational structure can be modified to more effectively satisfy the needs of the organization, the group, and the individual.
6. Many assumptions that people have about individuals, groups, and organizations need to be reconsidered.
7. Many so-called personality clashes result from problems of incorrect organizational design.

The basic difference between OD programs and other planned change programs is that OD programs are directed toward both the health and growth of the organization and the health and growth of the individual, while other planned change programs focus on either the individual or the organization.

The Need for Proper Diagnosis

A wide variety of OD techniques have been developed to bring about change; many of them have been highly effective, at least in some situations. Of course, some techniques are more effective than others. But perhaps more important than the technique itself is the need for clear diagnosis of the problem. If the problem or situation is clearly identified, then the correct approach can be determined in a relatively easy way. Some techniques are effective in one set of circumstances but totally ineffective in another.

Although a large number of OD tools are currently available, some OD practitioners cherish a particular tool and use it without careful consideration of whether it is right for the situation. For example, one large organization has a group of internal consultants who use only attitude surveys in all situations. After they survey the workers, each work group discusses the results and develops plans for corrective action. By now, the organization has used attitude surveys at least three times for every work group. Indeed, one consultant commented, "We now know which managers will become defensive and will not really

Table 19.1 Different approaches to planned change

Modifying organizational structure
   Contingency approaches to organization design
   Job enrichment
   Sociotechnical systems

Improving intergroup relationships
   The organizational confrontation meeting
   Changing intergroup perceptions

Improving group relationships
   Process consultation
   Team building

Improving intrapersonal relationships
   Laboratory training
   Life- and career-planning interventions
   Management by objectives

use the results of the survey." But he did not question whether the survey approach should be used with every manager or whether there were more appropriate techniques to be used in different situations. In the meantime many of the work groups are not responding with good plans.

Managing Change through Organization Development (OD)

There are a number of different ways to classify OD approaches.[12] One is to view them as being directed toward organizational structure, intergroup relationships, group relationships, and intrapersonal relationships, as shown in Table 19.1. From a systems point of view, these four broad classifications are interrelated and interdependent, but they will be discussed separately.

Organizational Structure

Structural change focuses on the roles and functions to be performed in the organization. The change strategy may involve specifying organization design, defining jobs for individuals and groups in the organization, and identifying overall organizational problems.

Organizations or subunits in an uncertain, quickly changing environment need to be designed differently from those in a stable, known environment. Individuals can be highly motivated and have feelings of achievement, accomplishment, and competence when there is a good fit between the organization design and the environment, even when the organization is highly bureaucratic in nature.

Another structural design is **job enrichment**—a way of making jobs more satisfying by providing workers with more opportunity for meaningfulness, responsibility, growth, achievement, and challenge.[13] For a time, the terms *job enrichment* and *job enlargement* were used almost interchangeably. Today, most people use *job enlargement* to refer to job rotation or activities added to a job (such as putting on both the front and rear wheels of a car rather than just one wheel). Recent research indicates that this approach can have a negative effect on workers.[14] *Job enrichment*, on the other hand, refers to adding both horizontal and vertical activities to a job, thereby providing the whole person with a whole job.

There are three basic elements in a whole job: (1) planning—deciding how it is to be done; (2) doing—actually performing the task; and (3) evaluating—obtaining feedback and taking appropriate actions. Many clerical and blue-collar jobs involve only the "doing" aspects.

Work on job enrichment has taken two separate but overlapping approaches. The first focuses on the individual. It stems from Herzberg's stress on the growth factors of recognition, achievement, and responsibility (described in Chapter 4). The second focuses on the job and job tasks.[15]

A Job Diagnostic Survey (JDS) has been developed to measure the level of jobs on five core dimensions, the reactions of individuals to their work, and the readiness of individuals to take on enriched jobs.[16] Some individuals have strong growth needs and respond positively to enriched jobs. Others have weak growth needs and will not react positively.

The five core dimensions of work reflect the second approach and lead to three critical psychological states. These in turn have personal and work outcomes, such as internal work motivation, work performance, work satisfaction and low absenteeism and turnover (see Figure 19.3). The **core job dimensions** are:

1. *Skill variety*—the greater the number of different skills involved, the more the potential for a meaningful job.
2. *Task identity*—the extent to which the job allows for a whole piece of work that is clear to the worker. Assembling an entire toaster is more meaningful than only attaching the electric cord to it.

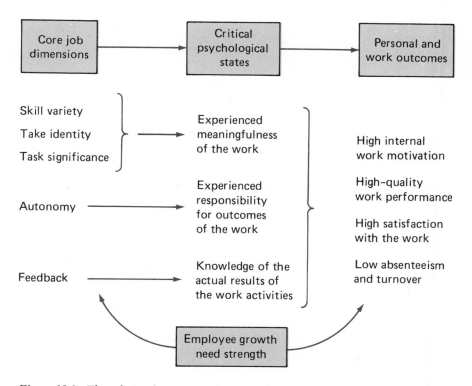

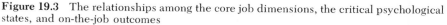

Figure 19.3 The relationships among the core job dimensions, the critical psychological states, and on-the-job outcomes

From J. Hackman and G. Oldham, "Development of the Job Diagnostic Survey," *Journal of Applied Psychology* 60 (April 1975): 161. Copyright 1975 by the American Psychological Association. Reprinted by permission.

3. *Task significance*—having a perceivable impact on others. A nurse working in an intensive care unit is more likely to see the impact on others than a person who fills small boxes with paperclips.
4. *Autonomy*—the degree to which the job gives the worker freedom, independence, and discretion in scheduling and carrying out the task. Greater autonomy leads to a greater sense of responsibility.
5. *Feedback*—the degree that a worker is able to obtain information about the effectiveness, quality, and quantity of the work performed. The best feedback comes directly from the work itself rather than from other sources.

The two basic uses of the JDS are to diagnose existing jobs on the core dimensions and to determine the effects of job changes on employees. Generally, a job must be high on all five core dimensions for the worker to be motivated by the job itself.

The instrument department case at the beginning of this chapter illustrates a successful job enrichment program for both individuals and groups. Skill variety was increased by allowing individual workers to assemble entire instruments themselves or to work as a group on more complex instruments. Task identity was increased by the workers doing a "whole" piece of work. Task significance increased, because the workers were able to see the impact of their jobs more clearly. Autonomy was increased with the workers' greater opportunity to plan and organize their jobs. Feedback was increased by the immediate testing of each instrument, so the workers knew at once whether it worked.

There are a large number of positive reports on job enrichment. One book summarizes more than thirty studies showing increased productivity and job satisfaction, and other reports show the same positive results.[17] Job enrichment also has been criticized, however. One criticism is that most job enrichment programs have not used scientific controls. Another is that job enrichment is used in a faddish way or as a tool for management to manipulate workers. For example, many union officials are opposed to it on the ground that it is only another way to speed up production. Yet other criticisms are that job enrichment reduces the number of jobs and that most workers are happy on their jobs and do not want the increased variety and challenge.[18]

Despite the criticisms, there is abundant evidence that effective managers use this approach when conditions are appropriate for it. As the JDS is further developed, it may become an extremely useful tool for determining the proper conditions for job enrichment and for identifying those individuals who will respond positively to such a program.[19]

Intergroup Relationships

Chapter 16 pointed out that conflict among groups can sometimes be positive, although often it is destructive. At times, conflict becomes so great that groups try to destroy each other—at least in a symbolic way. Each views the other as "the enemy." The long and bitter coal strike in 1977 and 1978 is an example of groups locked in conflict.

Steps can be taken to improve such adversary relationships. Chapter 17 described the organizational confrontation meeting, where groups are brought together to identify and work on organizational problems. Another basic strategy for improving interdepartmental or intergroup relationships is to change the perceptions (or, more accurately, the misperceptions) that the groups have of each other. A formal approach for accomplishing this change consists of a six-step procedure. The steps are:

1. The managers of the conflicting groups choose a neutral third party, often a consultant, to assist them in improving the inter-group relationships. The use of a third party is highly recommended, because without such a person the groups usually become deadlocked and the conflict escalates.

2. The groups meet together. The managers, together with the third party, describe the purpose of the meeting—to develop better understanding and improved relationships. The groups are asked to consider questions such as the following: What qualities best fit our group? What qualities best fit the other group? How do we think the other group will describe us?

3. The groups go to separate rooms and write down their answers to these questions. The third party works with them to help them become more open and develop lists that accurately reflect their perceptions of both their own image and that of the other group.

4. The groups are brought together again after completing their lists. A representative from each group presents the written perceptions. Only the representatives are allowed to speak, since the primary objective is to make certain that the perceptions, attitudes, and images are presented as accurately as possible. Arguments, hostility, and defensiveness might arise if the groups were allowed to argue with each other. Questions are allowed in order to make certain that the groups clearly understand the written lists. At this stage, the groups begin to understand the different perceptions they have of each other.

5. Once the lists have been presented and clearly understood, the groups again separate. Now each group's task is to analyze and review the reasons for the different perceptions. The emphasis is not on whether the perceptions are right or wrong but on how they came into being. It is essential at this point for each group to focus on the basic question: How have we contributed to these perceptions?

6. The next step is a joint meeting to share the identified reasons for differences and the approaches that will be taken to work on the problems. The primary focus is on the behavior leading up to the perceptions and the development of specific plans for solving individual problems and for improving future relationships. Then, a follow-up meeting is scheduled so the two groups can report on actions, identify further problems that have emerged, and formulate additional action plans.[20]

This approach was first used to get a union and management to work together rather than having frequent and bitter strikes. Since then, the technique has been used in a variety of situations. The approach need not always be as formal as described above. For example, on one occasion, the first-level supervisors of a manufacturing plant and the members of the engineering department were brought together. One of the biggest perceptual differences identified was that the engineers felt that the supervisors were stupid and could not solve problems. The supervisors, on the other hand, felt strongly that the engineers were lazy and had nothing to do.

Over time, these perceptions had become exaggerated by the behavior of both groups. Believing that the engineers had nothing to do, the first-level supervisors had taken to sending them problems that they could have easily solved themselves. This contributed to the engineers' belief that the supervisors were stupid and could not solve problems. They in turn put off working on some of the supervisors' requests in order to concentrate on what they perceived as more pressing problems. Getting little response, the supervisors sent still more requests, and the cycle continued. After an intergroup meeting, the engineers and first-level supervisors gained a better understanding of their dynamics. The supervisors began solving more of their own problems, and the engineers began to be more responsive to the problems that the supervisors really could not solve.

Improving Group Relationships

Although managers spend much of their time in meetings, they frequently feel unhappy and dissatisfied about the progress of these meetings. There are, however, ways of making groups more effective and improving working relationships among individuals and groups so that time spent in meetings is more productive. The emphasis is on improving communication, collaboration, and methods for stimulating or reducing present and future conflicts in a productive way; in short, it is an effort to determine how people can work together more effectively. A typical approach at this level is **team building**—helping a work group become more effective in accomplishing its tasks and in satisfying the needs of group members.

Many work groups distinguish among group task, group building, and self-serving activities (as described in Chapter 5). Group task activities are those directed at helping the group accomplish its goals. Group building activities are those that allow the group to maintain itself by helping to satisfy members' needs and by fostering cooperation among group members. Self-serving activities satisfy other individual needs.

Team building is a deliberate attempt to help groups become more productive by achieving the proper mix of these three activities. Among the many variations of team building is process consultation, which examines how groups go about their work (usually through actual observation) and then helps the groups understand, diagnose, and improve their behavior.[21] For example, a manager may ask someone skilled in group dynamics to sit in and observe regular staff meetings. The process observer pays much more attention to how the meeting is being conducted than to what is being discussed. During the meeting or later, the observer "feeds back" the observations in order to help the group better understand what it is doing so it can ultimately make its own diagnosis.

In one situation, a manager held meetings in order to obtain ideas from his subordinates. But without realizing what was happening, he consistently interrupted others when they tried to speak. During an hour and a half meeting, no one else was able to speak for more than thirty-five seconds at a time. The average amount of time people were able to talk before being interrupted by the manager was about eighteen seconds. The observer simply kept a time log in which he recorded who spoke, when, and how much. During the feedback session (conducted privately with the manager) the manager was astonished to find out what had happened. Without realizing it, by constantly interrupting others, he had completely cut himself off from the ideas he was trying to get.

Eventually, most groups become better able to use their own resources to identify and solve the interpersonal problems that block their work-related problems; then they are better able to handle work-related problems. In the situation above, the manager became considerably more capable of observing for himself when he was interrupting others. At the same time, the other group members began to point out when they were being interrupted.

To be most effective, groups must pay close attention to group task and building roles. These roles enable them to improve communication and become more open to dissenting points of view.

Improving Intrapersonal Relationships

The manager is the center of a series of communications networks involving superiors, subordinates, and people outside the work unit. Approximately a third to a half of the manager's time is spent with subordinates, and about 10 percent of the time is spent with supervisors. Most of the work day is spent with peers and others outside the actual work unit. The average manager may be in daily contact with twenty-five to fifty individuals or groups. At the lower levels, the contact may be for a period of seconds; at the higher levels, it may be somewhat longer. For chief executives, half their activities are completed in less than nine minutes, and only a tenth of them take more than an hour. Thus managers at all levels are in almost constant contact with others.[22]

Because of these fleeting and frequent contacts, the effective manager must use time effectively; and this means the person must gain understanding of his or her style and how it affects others. The manager described in the last section did not realize at first that he was constantly cutting others off, thereby reducing his effectiveness in bringing about change.

Management by objectives (MBO), described in Chapter 11, is a way of involving subordinates in the setting of performance objectives and the evaluation of their attainment. The effective manager uses MBO to improve intrapersonal relationships and bring about change.

Sensitivity training is a method of helping managers become more sensitive to their effect on others. Managers learn by interacting with other members of their group. (Other terms for *sensitivity training* are *laboratory training* and *T-group*.)[23] A typical sensitivity training group consists of ten to twelve members and a professional trainer. The group meets periodically for two days to two weeks. At the beginning of the first session, the trainer tells the group that his or her role is to serve as a resource. Then, after a brief introduction, the trainer lapses into silence. Since the trainer has not taken on a leadership role, the group must work out its own methods of proceeding. Individual members usually try out different roles or approaches, many of which are unsuccessful. In one training group, a member made a number of direct, forceful, and unsuccessful attempts to take over the leadership role. Finally, he conspicuously withdrew from the group and began to work a crossword puzzle. This person had two basic styles of working with others—dominance and withdrawal; he had never learned to collaborate.

When appropriate, the trainer will intervene or comment on the proceedings. Usually, the trainer encourages individuals to understand the group's activities, their own feelings, and the impact of their behavior on themselves and others. The primary emphasis is on the "here and now" experience rather than on past experiences.

Learning from a sensitivity training group is different for each member, but it is usually described as learning more about oneself as a person, learning to be more competent in interpersonal relationships, learning how others react to managers' behavior, and learning about the dynamics of group formation, norms, and growth.

Sensitivity training is being used less often as other techniques are developed, but it can be useful for personal growth and development. The technique has been criticized as being potentially dangerous to the participants. But if the trainers are carefully selected and the participants thoroughly briefed on what to expect, the danger can be minimized.

This section has provided an overview of a number of approaches to managing change or preparing managers for it. No attempt has been made to describe all the OD techniques currently available; instead, a representative sample has been provided. Each of these techniques has both positive and negative effects, and these depend in large measure on the circumstances in which they have been used. Careful diagnosis of the situation and of the actual problems should be made before applying any of them.

Some Problems with Managing Change

Earlier in the chapter, some conditions that improve the chances of planned and managed change were listed. When these conditions are violated, the potential success of the planned change is reduced, and additional problems can occur. One problem is the failure of many OD practitioners to deal with the concept of power. Indeed, many of them deliberately ignore the problem of power and the politics of change.

Organizations are essentially political in nature. To expect openness and trust in an autocratic organization is to be unrealistic. To expect managers to give up power willingly is also unrealistic. In some circumstances, the best way for the effective manager to bring about change is through the strategic use of power. (This issue will be discussed in more detail in Chapter 20.)

Another major problem lies with change itself. Change may challenge deeply rooted assumptions held by managers or others regarding the nature of managerial and worker responsibilities and skills. People do not resist change that they see as having a positive effect, but they do resist change that they believe will be negative or threatening. As a matter of fact, resistance to change should not be seen as necessarily bad. Often, it is a sign that something is going wrong.[24] Resistance can thus be viewed as showing a need for more effective communications or for better approaches to implementing change. On occasion, the *lack* of overt resistance to change can also be a sign that something is wrong; it may indicate the presence of fear and suspicion.

On occasion, change will be harmful to an individual but must be implemented anyway. For example, it may be necessary to fire an incompetent worker. When such occasions occur, the manager must make the best decision possible under the circumstances, explain the reasoning as carefully as possible, and implement the decision.

A final problem with change is that it may occur in a system that has complex, interrelated subsystems. A change in one subsystem can cause both intended and unintended consequences for the others. It may, for example, upset established norms and values elsewhere in the organization. Giving workers more responsibility may create bureaucratic barriers regarding pay or other factors. Numerous approval channels may be involved. Top management, staff groups, supervisors, unions, and the workers themselves are tied together. Opposition from any subsystem may cause a program to fail. In one situation, autonomous work groups had developed considerably higher productivity than other work groups; but the corporate wage and salary administration group "killed" the program because their traditional pay system did not reflect the increased responsibility of a group operating without a supervisor.

Implications for the Manager

Most managers know that change, like conflict, is both necessary and inevitable. With this knowledge, the effective manager actively works to develop and maintain competence in the organization. This effort requires an ongoing attempt to strike the best possible balance between maintaining the status quo and bringing about, or responding to, change. Thus the effective manager constantly shifts between the entrepreneurial and disturbance handling roles. To maintain the proper balance, the manager must be both a good diagnostician and a good change agent.

Perhaps the most important aspect of planned change is diagnosis. The manager should constantly ask, "Is this a problem or a symptom?" Clearly, separating structure and process can be helpful in problem identification.

The people in an organization can either help or hinder the change process. Therefore, the effective manager brings about necessary change in ways that satisfy both organizational and individual needs. Proper use of organization development requires the diagnosis and identification of problems. Then, the best OD tools or techniques can be selected to handle the situation. For example, a good manager would not try to install a job enrichment program in an organization or subunit that had a hostile and bitter union. Such an approach would be attacking a symptom before solving the more basic problem—developing better union-management relations.

Finally, the effective manager recognizes that there are problems with managing change. Many managers look for quick and easy answers, but this is seldom effective. When resistance to change occurs, the manager must explore the reasons for it. Using a systems approach, the manager can recognize that a change in one subsystem has had an impact on others. Thus the effective manager works hard at trying to see and understand the broad implications of any change.

Review

1. List and give examples of some major forces that are bringing about accelerated change.
2. How would you define *structural change*? Give examples of it.
3. How would you define *process change*? Give examples of it.
4. In what ways are structural and process change related?
5. What are the characteristics of a competent organization?
6. What are the assumptions underlying organization development? Explain.
7. What are the major steps or phases in successful change attempts?
8. In your opinion, what is the key factor in the six phases of successful planned change programs? Defend your position.
9. Elaborate on the importance of proper diagnosis.
10. What is job enrichment? How does it relate to the assumptions regarding organization development?
11. Under what circumstances might team building be helpful? Not helpful?
12. Under what circumstances might the procedure for improving intergroup relationships be most helpful?
13. What are some major problems associated with planned change?
14. Interview several managers. What are their assumptions about people? About change? How might their assumptions affect their behavior?
15. From your own experience or from other sources, describe a failure of an attempt at planned change. What do you think caused the failure?
16. If you have held a job, give suggestions as to how that job could be enriched.

A New Approach to Making Pet Food

In the late 1960s, the pet foods division of a large corporation was facing serious trouble. Its manufacturing plant had low productivity, high absenteeism, and negative employee attitudes. Acts of sabotage and violence were occurring.

As a result, the organization decided to build a new plant that would combine improved technology with behavioral science knowledge. Four managers and their supervisor worked with a behavioral science consultant, visited other plants, and came up with an innovative plan. The new plant, designed to balance the needs of people with the needs of the business, opened in the early 1970s. As planned, many functions that had been the responsibility of management were performed by the workers themselves. These functions included making job assignments, interviewing prospective employees, and even deciding on pay raises.

The new plant eliminated layers of management and supervisory personnel. Its self-managing teams had three areas of responsibility: processing, packaging and shipping, and office work. Each shift had teams of seven to fourteen members who shared the responsibility for tasks in their area. For example, the processing team not only manufactured the pet food but was also responsible for unloading raw material and maintaining equipment and quality. The team was large enough to perform highly interdependent tasks and small enough to allow for effective face-to-face meetings to make joint decisions. Each team had a team leader rather than a supervisor, and this person acted more as a guide than a boss.

What were the results? Engineers had estimated that at least 110 employees would be needed to run the plant. But using teams, the plant was able to operate with only 70 people—40 fewer than anticipated. After eighteen months, the reduction in manufacturing costs and the low absenteeism had resulted in savings of approximately $1 million a year when compared to the traditional factory system. Morale appeared to be high, and managers, team leaders, and operators all seemed highly involved in their work. The plant's safety record was outstanding, and absenteeism was below the industry average.

However, some difficulties began to emerge. There were reports that the system was working too well and that some management and staff people were seeing their long-term positions as threatened. The bureaucracy of the larger corporation apparently did not support the new ideas. Fearing possible negative reactions from the National Labor Relations Board, company lawyers opposed the idea of having team members vote on pay raises. Personnel managers opposed having team members make hiring decisions. Engineers resented the idea of workers doing their own engineering work. Accountants did not like the idea of workers keeping records. The plant eventually added seven management positions, including a plant engineering manager, a controller, and a manufacturing services manager.

Pay became a sticky issue. Besides the lawyers' opposition to team members voting on pay increases for fellow employees, such decisions were inherently difficult. Workers also began to feel that they should share in the plant's financial success, but a bonus system at one plant could cause problems elsewhere.

There were subtle problems also. A vendor was initially surprised and disappointed to find himself talking with a worker rather than with a manager. At a corporation-wide meeting of safety officials, nearly all the participants were managers. The only nonmanager was the representative from the new plant, and his presence was at least potentially threatening to the status and self-esteem of the other participants.

Although the corporation has officially announced that the program is a success, there is evidence that the new concepts are slowly being eroded away. Several of the original managers have quit. One of them said: "They saw we had created something the company couldn't handle, so they put their boys in. By being involved, I ruined my career with the company."[25]

1. What evidence would you need in order to determine whether the new plant was successful?
2. What assumptions and practices of organization development were used in the design and operation of the plant?
3. What factors might cause the plant to be successful? Unsuccessful?
4. Could some of the problems have been predicted from what you know about the systems framework (Chapter 14)? Explain.

Footnotes

1.   M. Beer and E. Huse, "A Systems Approach to Organization Development," *Journal of Applied Behavioral Science* 8 (January–February 1972): 79–101; Huse and Beer, "Eclectic Approach to Organizational Development," *Harvard Business Review*

49 (September–October 1971): 103–112; and L. Marcarelli, personal communication.

2. R. Beckhard, "The New Pressures on the Corporation," paper presented to Innovation Group, 3rd Conference, Harrison House, October 3, 1971, p. 3.

3. Ibid.

4. B. Bass, "Panel: Implications of the Behavioral Sciences on Management Practices in the Year 2000," in *Management 2000* (New York: American Foundation for Management Research, American Management Association, 1969), p. 10.

5. A. Toffler, *Future Shock* (New York: Random House, 1970).

6. A. Etzioni, *Modern Organizations* (Englewood Cliffs, N.J.: Prentice-Hall, 1964); E. Huse and J. Bowditch, *Behavior in Organizations: A Systems Approach to Managing*, 2d ed. (Reading, Mass.: Addison-Wesley, 1977); and E. Schein, *Organizational Psychology*, 2d. ed. (Englewood Cliffs, N.J.: Prentice-Hall, 1970).

7. N. Margulies and J. Wallace, *Organizational Change—Techniques and Applications* (Glenview, Ill.: Scott, Foresman, 1973), p. 2.

8. K. Lewin, *Field Theory in Social Science* (New York: Harper & Bros., 1951).

9. L. Greiner, "Patterns of Organizational Change," *Harvard Business Review* 45 (May–June 1967): 119–130.

10. W. Dinn and F. Swierczek, "Planned Organizational Change: Toward Grounded Theory," *Journal of Applied Behavioral Science* 13 (June 1977): 135–157; T. Qvale, "A Norwegian Strategy for Democratization of Industry," *Human Relations* 29 (May 1976): 453–469; and R. Golembiewski, K. Billingsley, and S. Yeager, "Measuring Change and Persistence in Human Affairs: Types of Change Generated by OD Designs," *Journal of Applied Behavioral Science* 12 (June 1976): 133–157.

11. E. Huse, "Organization Development," *American Personnel and Guidance Journal* 56 (March 1978): 403–407; Huse, *Organization Development and Change* (St. Paul, Minn.: West Publishing, 1975).

12. W. Bennis, *Organization Development: Its Nature, Origins, and Prospects* (Reading, Mass.: Addison-Wesley, 1969); W. French and C. Bell, Jr., *Organization Development: Behavioral Science Interventions for Organization Improvement*, 2d ed. (Englewood Cliffs, N.J.: Prentice-Hall, 1978); and R. Harrison, "Choosing the Depth of Organizational Intervention," *Journal of Applied Behavioral Science* 6 (March–April 1970): 181–202.

13. L. Davis and J. Taylor, eds., *Design of Jobs: Selected Readings* (New York: Penguin, 1973); R. Ford, *Motivation through the Work Itself* (New York: American Management Association, 1969); and M. Myers, *Every Employee a Manager* (New York: McGraw-Hill, 1970).

14. S. Orelius, University of Gothenburg, Sweden, personal communication.

15. A. Turner and P. Lawrence, *Industrial Jobs and the Worker* (Boston: Harvard University Graduate School of Business Administration, Division of Research, 1965); J. Hackman et al., *A New Strategy for Job Enrichment*, Technical Report No. 3 (New Haven, Conn.: Yale University, Department of Administrative Sciences, May 1974); and J. Hackman and G. Oldham, "Development of the Job Diagnostic Survey," *Journal of Applied Psychology* 60 (April 1975): 159–165.

16. Hackman et al., *A New Strategy for Job Enrichment*.

17. *Work in America: The Report of a Special Task Force to the Secretary of Health, Education and Welfare* (Cambridge, Mass.: MIT Press, 1972);

Huse and Beer, "Eclectic Approach to Organizational Development"; W. Paul, K. Robertson, and F. Herzberg, "Job Enrichment Pays Off," *Harvard Business Review* 41 (March–April 1969): 61–78; and W. Roche and N. McKinnon, "Motivating People with Meaningful Work," *Harvard Business Review* 48 (May–June 1970): 97–110.

18. C. Hulin and M. Blood, "Job Enlargement, Individual Differences, and Worker Responses," *Psychological Bulletin* 69 (January 1968): 41–51; M. Fein, "Job Enrichment: A Reevaluation," *Sloan Management Review* 15 (Winter 1974): 69–88; and F. Luthans and W. Reif, "Job Enrichment: Long on Theory, Short on Practice," *Organizational Dynamics* 2 (Winter 1974): 30–38.

19. J. Pierce and R. Dunham, "Task Design: A Literature Review," *Academy of Management Review* 1 (October 1976): 83–97.

20. R. Blake, H. Shepard, and J. Mouton, *Managing Intergroup Conflict in Industry* (Houston: Gulf Publishing, 1954); Huse, *Organization Development and Change;* and R. Beckhard, *Organization Development: Strategies and Models* (Reading, Mass.: Addison-Wesley, 1969).

21. E. Schein, *Process Consultation: Its Role in Organization Development* (Reading, Mass.: Addison-Wesley, 1969); C. Argyris, *Intervention Theory and Method* (Reading, Mass.: Addison-Wesley, 1970); and R. Walton, *Interpersonal Peacemaking: Confrontations and Third-Party Consultation* (Reading, Mass.: Addison-Wesley, 1969).

22. H. Mintzberg, *The Nature of Managerial Work* (New York: Harper & Row, 1973); and R. Guest, "Of Time and the Foreman," *Personnel* 32 (May 1956): 478–486.

23. L. Bradford, J. Gibb, and K. Benne, *T-Group Theory and Laboratory Methods* (New York: Wiley, 1964); R. House, "T-Group Education and Leadership Effectiveness: A Review of the Empiric Literature and a Critical Evaluation," *Personnel Psychology* 20 (Spring 1967): 1–33; J. Campdell and M. Dunette, "Effectiveness of T-Group Experiences in Managerial Training and Development," *Psychological Bulletin* 70 (August 1969): 73–104; and G. Cooper, "How Psychologically Dangerous Are T-Groups and Encounter Groups?" *Human Relations* 28 (June 1975): 255–268.

24. P. Lawrence, "How to Deal with Resistance to Change," *Harvard Business Review* 32 (May–June 1954): 50–61.

25. R. Walton, "How to Counter Alienation in the Plant," *Harvard Business Review* 50 (November–December 1972): 70–81; and "Stonewalling Plant Democracy," *Business Week,* March 28, 1977, pp. 78–82.

Part VII

The Organization and the Environment

Chapter 20

Values, Power, and Ethics

A Crisis of Conscience

The Importance of Values
    The Role of Values
    Values as Influence

The Importance of Power and Politics
    The Two Faces of Power
    Power and Politics

The Importance of Ethics
    Influences on Ethics
    Encouraging Ethical Behavior

Implications for the Manager

Review

To Tell or Not to Tell

Learning Objectives

When you have finished reading and studying this chapter, you should be able to:

1. Identify why many "people problems" have their basis in the area of values.
2. Show how value systems affect behavior.
3. Compare and contrast behavior channeling and perceptual screening.
4. Explain the concept of power, and identify sources of power.
5. Compare and contrast the two faces of power.
6. Show how a manager uses politics to gain power.
7. Compare and contrast ethical and legal behavior or misbehavior.
8. Identify some major influences on ethical behavior.
9. Give illustrations of how ethical behavior can be encouraged.
10. Define and be able to use the following concepts:

values	two faces of power
behavior channeling	politics
perceptual screening	illegal behavior
power	ethics

Thought Starters

1. What does power mean to you?
2. Is politics always bad? Explain.
3. Are business people more or less ethical than the population as a whole? Explain.
4. Do you have a personal standard of ethics? Explain.

A Crisis of Conscience

Universal Neucleonics was the parent company for a number of wholly owned smaller companies, among them Quasar Stellar. The president and the controller of Quasar Stellar sent regular monthly reports to the parent company. Over a period of time, they began to distort the reports to reflect their operation more favorably. The status of projects was inaccurately reported, and actual and projected earnings were grossly inflated. In fact, when the truth became known, the year-end report of Universal Neucleonics showed earnings considerably lower than had been previously predicted. Shortly thereafter, Quasar's president and controller resigned and were replaced.

What had happened? To find out, corporate headquarters decided to interview five of the company's key managers: George Kessler, vice-president of manufacturing; William Heller, vice-president of engineering; Peter Loomis, vice-president of marketing; Paul Brown, vice-president of industrial relations; and Donald Morgan, chief accountant. The first four men had all reported directly to the ex-president; the fifth had reported directly to the controller. All five had had access to information showing that the monthly reports were distorted, but none had reported the true state of affairs to corporate management.

Following is a brief summary of the interviews.

William Heller, vice-president of engineering: I was initially skeptical when the decision was made to shift from a subcontractor approach to bidding on primary contracts. Then I became very enthusiastic. The really big ones we tried for were the Apollo and LEM (lunar landing craft) contracts. If we had gotten one or both of these contracts, the engineering department would have been right out in front. Looking back, I was shortsighted and did not take into consideration the potential impact on both engineering and other parts of the company. I am an engineering manager, not a business manager. As a result, when things went wrong, I accepted the business decision to modify the reports. Actually, I tried not to know what was in the reports. I wouldn't want a subordinate of mine second-guessing me and going around me. Perhaps the solution would be to have the corporation use an internal audit team.

George Kessler, vice-president of manufacturing: I was opposed from the beginning. Not long after we had a series of meetings, I was no longer involved in what went into the reports. I knew they were padded, but I wanted to work within the system. No self-respecting manager would go around his boss. Perhaps a solution would be to have the monthly report routinely include minority reports as the Supreme Court does. Another solution might be to have each manager report routinely to his counterpart at corporate headquarters.

Peter Loomis, vice-president of marketing: I had only been with the company nine months and perhaps I was overly optimistic about our odds of getting those two contracts. But there was a lot of pressure from corporate headquarters to try for both. Once the decision was made, we couldn't back down or we would lose face. Headquarters decided that this was the direction we would go. When things went wrong, they looked for scapegoats to sacrifice. I had to support my boss and be loyal to him. Besides, how much should personal morality enter into business decisions?

Donald Morgan, chief accountant: We report only on data given to us. Our job is not to set policy or to question management decisions. Our job is to follow instructions.

Paul Brown, vice-president of industrial relations: At first, people were really enthusiastic. It was like they were smoking pot. Then, when the trouble began to show up, a lot of people began to leave. I think that some of the people stayed only out of loyalty to their boss and the company.[1]

This case, which shows real managers in a real situation, demonstrates how values can affect behavior and how managers can exercise power. For example, what might have happened if the chief accountant had reported to the parent company that the figures were incorrect? How ethical was the managers' behavior?

This chapter will critically examine the influence of values, power, political tactics, and ethics on managerial behavior, focusing primarily on the individual. The larger issue of the social responsibility of organizations will be discussed in Chapter 21.

The Importance of Values

Many managers feel that their behavior is completely objective—that they gather the facts and then make completely rational decisions. This attitude is valid, however, only if the managers understand that their personal values and beliefs are among the "facts." One of the most pervasive values learned in early childhood is that "tattling" or "squealing" is wrong. G. Gordon Liddy, one of the first people sentenced as a result of the Watergate burglary, marched off to jail proud of the fact that he had not squealed. There was evidence that, had he chosen to talk, he would have received a shorter jail sentence. The message in the case at the beginning of this chapter is that some managers will refuse to squeal even if their refusal may harm the company. This is clear evidence of behavior being affected by values rather than being completely objective.

There are, of course, people who blow the whistle—for example, A. Earnest Fitzgerald, a deputy for management systems in the air force. In 1965, Fitzgerald was earning $31,000 a year. He blew the whistle on a $2 billion cost overrun on the C-5A (a transport plane), a fact that the Pentagon was apparently trying to conceal from Congress. He soon lost his job. In 1969, General Motors recalled 2.4 million Chevrolets to repair a faulty design that let carbon monoxide into the automobile. The recall cost was reported to be over $100 million. Edward Gregory is the safety inspector who repeatedly warned the company that the autos were unsafe. When he got no results from GM, he contacted Ralph Nader. After several reported deaths from carbon monoxide poisoning, the automobiles were recalled. At last report, Gregory was still working for General Motors (perhaps because he is a member of the autoworkers' union).

Relatively little is known about whistle blowers, but they seem to have a high degree of personal responsibility and ethics. Frequently, they suffer retaliation by being transferred, demoted, isolated, cut off from responsibility, or fired. For example, shortly after Fitzgerald reported on the C-5A overrun, he was transferred to examining the cost problems of bowling alleys in Thailand; and he was no longer invited to management meetings.[2]

Values are relatively permanent ideals (or ideas) that influence and shape the general nature of people's behavior and determine what they will consider desirable or undesirable, good or bad. People use values as a guidance system when they are faced with a choice among various actions. Values are usually acquired early in life; they reflect family and educational background and are influenced by peers, teachers, and the culture.[3]

The Role of Values

In stressing the role of values in influencing behavior, psychologist Robert McMurray has suggested that many "people problems" arise in the area of values. These problems involve people such as (1) the factory owner who is usually rational but who will go out of business rather than be forced to negotiate with a union, (2) the scientist who becomes a poor security risk because of misguided idealism, (3) the factory worker who welds pop bottles inside the body of the automobile just for kicks, (4) the labor leader who starts a costly strike just to show his muscle, and (5) the intellectuals and politicians who push for confiscatory taxes because they believe that profits are unethical.[4]

A study of more than a thousand managers concludes that:

1. Most managers are pragmatic; that is, they have values that contribute to success. A smaller number of managers have ethical-moral values. For them, the important ideas are those that are "right" rather than "successful."
2. Value systems can vary widely among managers.
3. Personal values affect both corporate strategy and goals and day-to-day decisions.

4. The personal values of individual managers have both a direct and an indirect effect on organizations.
5. Personal values are in turn influenced by organizations.
6. Differences and similarities of values help explain both conflict and cooperation among managers.[5]

According to a twelve-year study, values appear to be related to success. The more successful managers stick with the values they learned in early life. They place importance on integrity and a sense of fairness to others, they have a sense of their own personal worth and value, and they promote the general welfare of the organization. The less successful managers are less interested in helping humanity or the organization than in helping themselves. They are more concerned about their financial security and immediate work situation.[6] (The managers in the case at the beginning of the chapter appeared to be much more highly involved in keeping their jobs and staying out of trouble than in promoting the general welfare of the organization.)

Values as Influence

Values often influence behavior through behavior channeling and perceptual screening, as shown in Figure 20.1.[7] **Behavior channeling** is the idea that actual behavior is consistent with values. Behavior is channeled toward or away from particular actions as a result of the direct influence of values on behavior. If morality is an important value to a manager, then the manager will be channeled away from immoral behavior, however he or she defines it.

Behavior channeling affects managerial behavior in the following areas: decisions and solutions to problems, determination of ethical behavior, acceptance or resistance to organizational goals and pressures. Strong behavior channeling values prevented the managers in the case at the beginning of the chapter from reporting the distortions.

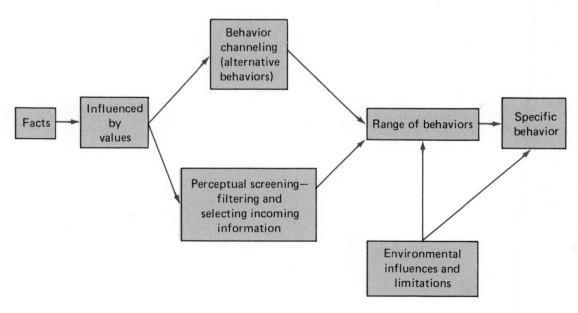

Figure 20.1   Values as influence

Values have a more indirect effect on behavior through **perceptual screening,** the idea that values influence what the individual sees and hears. Perceptions can be highly inaccurate. Personal values often cause the individual to filter out or select incoming information. A story is told about three managers who heard their work groups laughing. The first manager thought, "They are laughing because they are happy and productive." The second manager thought, "They are laughing because they are goofing off." The third manager thought, "They are laughing at *me*." Depending on their values, then, each manager will behave and react differently to the same input.

Perceptual screening influences how managers "see" interpersonal relationships, definitions of situations and problems, and their own or their organization's success or failure. Evidence of perceptual screening can be seen in the case at the beginning of the chapter—particularly in the chief accountant's statement, "Our job is to follow instructions," and the engineering vice-president's statement, "Actually, I tried not to know what was in the reports."

The Importance of Power and Politics

Power is "the ability of a person or group, for whatever reason, to affect another person's or group's ability to achieve its goals (personal or collective)."[8] In simpler terms, it is the ability to exercise influence or control over others.

As Chapter 11 pointed out, there is a difference between power and authority. Authority is the right to command and exact obedience from others, and it comes from the organization. Indeed, organizations have a hierarchy of authority. Power, however, is a broader concept than authority.[9] Power comes from many sources, including expert knowledge and friendship. Authority comes only from the organization. Some managers, for example, have much more power then others. Power is often seen as being immoral. The statement "power corrupts, and absolute power corrupts absolutely" summarizes what many people feel about it. Those with power even tend to deny that they have it. Whether or not they admit it, managers value power more than other people; and better managers tend to value it more highly than poorer ones.

Many nonmanagers have little or no authority but a great deal of power. For example, a particularly insensitive person was hired by a medium-sized organization to be the manufacturing manager. Within a short period of time, he was able to alienate all the secretaries, including the president's secretary. He never understood why it took so long to get an appointment with the president, why he didn't receive important information, why memos to him were lost, and why telephone calls were not returned. Needless to say, he did not last very long in the organization. Secretaries often have a great deal of power, as every good manager knows. Unfortunately, many managers are reluctant to openly admit the importance of power as it affects both individual behavior and organizational relationships.

The Two Faces of Power

One of the reasons emigrants came to the United States was to escape oppression. In a pluralist society, people become uneasy when a political party becomes too strong or when an individual is seen as taking on too much power. There was a public outcry, for example, when President Nixon attempted to change the uniforms of White House guards into something resembling the uniforms of the Swiss Guards at the Vatican. The uniforms were soon quietly withdrawn.

A way to avoid seeing power only in a negative light is to realize that there are **two faces of power.**[10] The *negative face* involves personal domination of others. If one person wins, another loses. The most direct and least socialized form of power is seen in direct physical aggression, where the loser is forced to submit to the winner. At the managerial level, the negative face of power is much more subtle. In an extreme case, the powerful individual may be seen as superhuman, and those over whom the power is exercised may feel loyalty, devotion, and submissiveness. One characteristic of both Hitler and Lenin was their ability to sway their audiences in mass meetings. When they established their power, the masses followed loyally and obediently.

The *positive face* is much more socially desirable. Power is exercised not for personal advancement or benefit but for the good of the organization or society. The person exercising power in the positive sense attempts to clarify the goals the group should achieve and then help the group members gain the confidence to achieve them. Rather than submission, there is a greater sense of unity; rather than powerlessness, there is the feeling that the group and individual followers are powerful and can accomplish things on their own. Power is socialized rather than personalized.

One of the reasons for the frequent misunderstanding and misperception of power is that the successful manager balances upon a knife edge between expressing personal dominance and the more socialized type of leadership.[11] Managers must take initiative—but not too much. They must take counsel—but not to the point of seeming weak and helpless.

Power can be used either directly or indirectly. In the case at the beginning of the chapter, none of the managers interviewed mentioned that squealing on the boss might cause the loss of their job or other possible negative consequences. The president of their company did not have to use his power in a direct fashion; somehow, the message got communicated.

Power and Politics

The effective manager gains additional power through the judicious use of **politics**—that is, the use of resources, both physical and human, to achieve more power over others.[12] In other words, politics deals with the methods, approaches, and tactics used to increase power and control. Although *politics* is another word that has negative meanings, both power and politics are integral parts of organizations and managerial behavior. Organizations are political structures: "People will readily admit that governments are organizations. The converse—that organizations are governments—is equally true but rarely considered."[13]

What are some of the political techniques by which managers gain and use power? Biographies of such well-known leaders as Alexander the Great and Franklin D. Roosevelt and interviews with successful managers suggest that there are some political tactics practiced by those whose success rests on the ability to control and direct the actions of others. Some of these tactics are explained below. They include alliances, taking counsel, maneuverability, communication, compromise, proper timing, self-dramatization, confidence, and "always the boss."[14]

Alliances

The effective manager is able to form political relationships with others. Few organizations are ruled by a single person, and power coalitions are necessary to make and implement decisions. Even fewer organizations are pure democracies in which the majority rules. Most organizations require strong and skillful coalitions to bring about common action. Without them, power often is fractionalized and actions are divisive. Lyndon Johnson was able to get more programs through Congress than was John F. Kennedy. One reason for this is that, as a senator, Johnson had developed better political alliances than had Kennedy.

Taking Counsel

The capable manager asks for advice only when it is necessary. Many decisions do not need the involvement of others, and asking for it too frequently can be seen as a sign of weakness. The effective manager also knows whom to ask for advice. The right person can be extremely helpful in determining when an idea or recommendation has a possibility of being accepted and when to wait for another time.

Many decisions are made in committee meetings. A certain politically astute manager makes a point of never bringing up a recommendation before a group until he has sounded out its more influential members and gotten the go-ahead from them.

Maneuverability

The capable manager never gets caught in a situation that does not have plenty of escape hatches. And since situations keep changing, the manager must maintain flexibility. Inflexible managers cannot adapt to changing circumstances.

Communication

The smart manager/politician sometimes holds back on information or carefully times its release. This is particularly important for plans for the future, which often are tentative and may need to be changed when new information comes in or when the situation changes.

At the same time, the manager needs to develop excellent communications networks. As the nerve center of the unit, the manager must continually scan the environment to collect information. The effective manager designs a personal communications system that is largely informal rather than formal, largely oral rather than written. The manager then pieces together all the incoming information into a mental image or model of the unit and its interaction with the external environment or with other units of the organization.

Information is power and an important tactical weapon, and it should be treated as such. Rather than thinking only of increasing the information flow to subordinates, the capable manager considers the important questions: Who should get to know what, when, and for what purpose? and what information should be withheld?

Compromise

Politics is the art of the possible. The capable manager thus accepts compromise when necessary while continually keeping in mind a clear-cut sense of direction and the goals to work toward. One politically astute manager makes a practice of never speaking at the beginning of a meeting. When she has specific ideas, she waits until a number of people have offered their thoughts and suggestions. She has noticed that the first few suggestions often are not accepted, since others also have ideas that they want to explain. As a result, she does not make her suggestions until she can weave her ideas in with others, thereby picking up their support.

Proper Timing

Managers are frequently urged to take action immediately, but sometimes immediate action is not wise. A delay may be more appropriate in a particular situation. Indeed, it may be wise for the manager to appear to be in the process of doing something even though it never quite gets done.

Self-Dramatization

Successful actors are able to influence audiences by both verbal and nonverbal communications. Successful managers consider self-dramatization as a way of getting messages across. The first step in this process is observing how others successfully portray themselves. Formal classes in speech and drama can be helpful in learning better communications skills. The effective manager should have a well-trained and well-disciplined voice and body so that the message will convince others.

Confidence

The successful politician/manager needs to look and act confident, especially when a decision has been made. If the manager lacks confidence about a decision, perhaps it should be put off. In any case, the manager who maintains an attitude of confidence and certainty is simultaneously using power and increasing it.

Always the Boss

Managers should get along well with subordinates; this adds to their referent (charismatic) power. At the same time, they should not get so involved with subordinates that their personal feelings become a basis for either positive or negative action.

The political tactics described above are neutral; they have no inherent moral value. They take on moral qualities only in the way they are used. Power can be used for either good or bad, but those who have power have a moral obligation to use it responsibly. Good managers have the wisdom, knowledge, and skill to use it well.

The Importance of Ethics

One of the most important values for a manager is a good sense of ethics. But the almost daily disclosures of illegal political contributions, juggled books, overseas payoffs, wiretapping, and similar activities have raised questions about the morality of all types of leadership in our society.[15]

Consider, for example, the following list of events reported in the news media:

1. Watergate
2. Marvin Mandell, the governor of Maryland, was convicted in 1977 on seventeen counts of mail fraud and one count of racketeering.
3. Southwestern Bell Telephone lost a $1 million suit for illegally tapping the telephone of a Southwestern Bell manager.
4. Gulf Oil admitted paying over $12 million—including $4 million to the party backing President Park Ching Hee of Korea—to national and international political figures.
5. United Brands (Chiquita Banana) admitted spending $4 million to bribe government officials and others in the Honduras to lower taxes on bananas.
6. Braniff Airways admitted to the Civil Aeronautics Board that travel agents had been given $750,000 worth of free tickets to promote Braniff. It also admitted to illegally contributing $40,000 to the Nixon campaign out of a much larger fund developed by selling unrecorded air tickets.
7. In 1976, the Air Line Pilots Association suspended Frontier Airlines pilots after the pilots had agreed to fly Frontier's twin-engined Boeing 137s with only two men in the cockpit instead of three, although a similar aircraft, the DC-9, is flown with two.

This list consists only of items that either hit newspaper headlines or made national television news. But ethical and legal issues do not always involve top corporate or governmental officials and large sums of money. What about the college student who passes the word to a friend about an upcoming exam? Or the manager who hires an engineer from a company that has just developed a technical breakthrough? Or the purchasing agent who buys from a particular vendor and receives a case of bourbon? Or the salesman who pads the expense account to buy a toy for his child? Or the manager who has a long, three-martini lunch? Or the worker who stretches out the job? Or the salesclerk who waits on a friend before a stranger? Or the politician who shows favoritism in employment? What is ethical or unethical behavior? How does it differ from legal or illegal behavior?

There are, of course, many instances of ethical behavior, but these usually do not hit the headlines. There are the purchasing agent who repeatedly refuses gifts of any kind from suppliers and the manager who always charges personal calls made from the office to his home number. There are the large number of managers who turn in scrupulously honest expense accounts. And there are the many managers who feel that acting only in the interest of shareholders, without considering employees and consumers, is unethical behavior.

The term *ethics* is a slippery one. For example, an early study on ethics found that all people believed they were behaving ethically, according to their own standards.[16] Furthermore, society's ideas about laws and ethics keep changing. Almost everyone would agree that child labor in factories is not only illegal but unethical. Yet, when the U.S. Congress passed the Child Labor Act in 1937, the act was bitterly contested and was not upheld as constitutional by the Supreme Court until 1941.

Laws and ethics are related but not identical. **Illegal behavior** is behavior that violates a law in a particular jurisdiction or area. For example, political contributions by corporations are illegal in the United States but legal in Canada and Italy. Ethical behavior stems from values and is affected by laws. Thus behavior can be legal but unethical. Lavish entertainment of and gifts to customers is an accepted business practice in the United States. At what point, however, does the practice remain legal but become unethical?

While values influence a person's beliefs and behavior, ethics is concerned with moral rights and wrongs and with the individual's moral obligations to society. From the viewpoint of the manager, **ethics** is "the rules or standards governing the moral conduct of the organization management profession."[17] In simple terms, ethical behavior is behavior that society considers right. But determining specific rights and wrongs is complicated, since moral concepts, like other ideas, change over time. A minimal guide to ethics is the recommendation made by the chairman of the board of a large organization: "Possibly the best test—for a person with a family—might be to think whether you would be happy to tell your spouse and children the details of the action you are contemplating or whether you would be willing to appear on television and to explain your actions in detail."[18]

Under this definition, disclosure is the key to whether behavior is ethical. Thus a reasonable and practical standard is whether the behavior, if disclosed, would be embarrassing to the individual, the person's family, or the organization.

The definition of *ethics* suggests that only individuals can act ethically or unethically. Indeed, to talk of corporate ethics is misleading in a way, since most organizations are really only pieces of paper. Ethics applies instead to the individual men and women who give life to the organizations. Bob Dorsey, the chief executive of Gulf Oil, was the individual who gave $3 million to S. K. Kim, the Korean fund raiser, for the 1971 Korean election. In the case at the beginning of the chapter, the president and the vice-president of finance were the two individuals who sent the distorted reports to the parent company.

Ethics cannot be considered remote; instead, ethical behavior must be viewed as the guiding principles that help individuals retain a sense of identity and self-respect while still taking the interests of others into account. Ethics, then, is a personal responsibility that each individual has to others.

Influences on Ethics

There have been many surveys and reports on ethics, and they generally agree on the following:

1. Managers at all levels face ethical problems daily.
2. A majority of managers believe strongly that organizations should be more ethical.
3. Most managers want to be honest and ethical, but a majority of them (in both business and government) feel that they are under pressure to lower their personal ethical standards in order to achieve organizational goals. The pressure is felt more strongly by lower- and middle-level managers than by upper-level ones.
4. Managers are aware of a number of commonly accepted practices that they consider unethical—practices such as bribery and gift giving, price discrimination, dishonest or misleading advertising, dishonesty, or shadiness in making or keeping contracts, unfair credit practices, unfairness to employees, and prejudice in hiring.[19]

There is also evidence that many people operate under a "double ethic"; that is, they use one standard with friends and another with strangers. A librarian may charge one person but not another a fine for overdue books. Managers with inside information about a stock may tell their friends but not their stockbroker.

A series of questions intended to determine the causes of ethical behavior were asked of 1,700 managers. As Figure 20.2 shows, each manager's own code of ethics is most likely to influence that person's ethical behavior. The behavior of immediate supervisors and formal company policy are tied for the next most likely influences. The behavior of immediate supervisors is most influential in terms of influence toward unethical behavior. The ethical climate of the industry also has a high impact on the tendency toward unethical behavior.[20]

In one study, applicants for supervisory positions at a juvenile corrections institution completed an anonymous questionnaire. Their responses showed that they all considered punitive attitudes toward delinquency and delinquents unethical.[21] Some of the applicants were hired. After working several months, they again completed the same questionnaire. These newly-hired workers had changed their opinions to conform with the views of the institution's other personnel. Now they saw punitive and negative behavior toward the care and handling of

What influences an executive to make ethical decisions?

Rank or importance

	Most
Personal code of ethics	1
Behavior of superiors	2.5
Formal company policy	2.5
Ethical climate of industry	4
Behavior of equals in company	5
	Least

What influences an executive to make unethical decisions?

Rank or importance

	Most
Behavior of superiors	1
Ethical climate of industry	2
Behavior of equals in company	3.5
Lack of company policy	3.5
Personal finances	5
	Least

Figure 20.2   Influences on managerial behavior

delinquents as a way of life. (One manager has commented that the best advice for a young person entering an organization is to find a good boss. Indeed, there is evidence that someone who wants to act ethically should go to work for an ethical boss.)

Similar results were found in a study that compared the responses of both business and government managers to a series of questions on ethics. For example, 64 percent of business managers and 60 percent of government managers reported feeling pressure to achieve organizational goals. The pressure was strongest at the low- and middle-management levels.

As 78 percent of business and 76 percent of public sector (government) managers report, this pressure from the top can cause persons farther down the line to behave unethically, even if the organization itself is ethical. Indeed, managers at the top may not know that subordinates are acting unethically out of loyalty to or fear of either the organization or their bosses. One of the questions asked in the study had to do with whether young managers in business would show their loyalty by behaving like the junior members of the Nixon reelection committee. The responses are shown in Figure 20.3. Approximately 72 percent of the managers in government and 60 percent of the managers in the private sector felt that younger managers in business would behave unethically out of loyalty to their supervisors.[22] Apparently, the managers at Quasar Stellar were not alone in being loyal to their boss.

Encouraging Ethical Behavior

To assume that everyone behaves ethically and legally all the time is unrealistic. Human nature is imperfect. Nevertheless, there are a number of ways in which business ethics can be improved. Perhaps the most important approach is for top management to carefully examine

Respondents were asked to agree or disagree with the following statement:
The junior members of the Nixon reelection committee who went
along with their bosses to show their loyalty did just what
young managers would done in business.

Response	Private sector	Public sector
Agree	59.3%	72.3%
Disagree	40.7	11.0
Undecided	—	16.7

Figure 20.3   The influence of loyalty

Adapted from J. Bowman, "Managerial Ethics in Business and Government," *Business Horizons* 19 (October 1976): 52. Copyright, 1976, by the
Foundation for the School of Business at Indiana University. Reprinted by
permission.

such management practices as reward systems, managerial style, and
decision-making processes. For example, in some organizations the reward system promotes unethical behavior by creating the pressure to
achieve organizational goals at almost any cost. Ethical behavior thus
depends on complex and highly interrelated factors.

In one situation, two general foremen were in charge of producing
and shipping two almost identical products. Foreman A had ordered a
railroad car and planned to load the product on the car at the beginning
of the next workday. Foreman B had forgotten to order a railroad car and
was going to have to wait several days to ship the product. Rather than
wait, he took his crew out and, under cover of darkness, physically
moved the railroad car ordered by Foreman A to his own area and
loaded the product immediately. The next morning, Foreman A had no
car and could not ship his product. In the prevailing climate of the
organization, Foreman B was seen as resourceful and shrewd, and
Foreman A was seen as having been caught unprepared. What sort of
ethical message was management communicating in this organization?

Clearly, top management must set a good example. Development
and enforcement of a code of ethics is one way for management to do
this. However, such codes are often something like overall organization
objectives in that they are written by a blue-ribbon panel and then
ignored.

A third approach is for boards of directors and top management to
examine their own practices and to regularly conduct internal audits to
ensure that business is being conducted ethically. For example, the
success of the Nixon Committee to Reelect the President was due in part
to finding organizations that had slush funds. These organizations may
have already been acting unethically when they were approached by the
committee.

A fourth approach is careful law enforcement. Increasingly, managers are being held responsible for preventing or correcting violations

when they have the necessary power and responsibility to do so. Furthermore, a number of organizations are being sued by stockholders or other organizations for acting illegally.

Nevertheless, in the last analysis, ethical behavior results from personal decisions. Reducing the pressure from the top, establishing codes of ethics, conducting internal audits, and more carefully enforcing laws may make it easier to behave ethically, but the individual manager must still make a personal decision to act in an ethical or unethical manner. The junior manager who is working for an unethical supervisor may want to look for another job or a different boss.

From a practical point of view, speaking directly about ethics may not be as valuable as a more indirect approach. The effective manager may want to express ethical ideas in a way that points out how ethical behavior contributes to the long-term good of the organization.

Implications for the Manager

The effective manager is aware that decisions are made not only on facts but on personal values as well. Personal value systems influence both behavior and how people see the world. The effective manager is aware of both self-values and the values of others.

Many people feel that the term *power* is a dirty word. Yet, whether they admit it or not, good managers are those who know how to gain and use power effectively. They understand that there are two sides or "faces" of power, and they use each of them at different times.

Politics is the art of gaining and using power. Effective managers have no choice but to be effective politicians. They know how to pick and choose among political tactics in order to effectively wield their power.

But power and politics need to be used ethically. Few managers are unethical as a matter of policy. Yet they all share the problem of determining what is ethical or unethical when they are faced with unexpected dilemmas. In many organizations there is constant pressure to behave in unethical ways. Evidence exists that the pressure is greater at lower levels of the organization than at higher levels. Evidence also exists that the higher levels of management may not be aware of the pressures that lower-level managers perceive. While ethics is a personal responsibility, it is heavily influenced by higher management. The effective manager must fight daily battles with regard to ethical standards. Winning these battles is essential if individuals and organizations are to survive and be respected.

Review

1. How can values cause "people problems"?
2. How does a value system affect behavior?
3. What is behavior channeling? How does it affect behavior?
4. What is perceptual screening? How does it affect behavior?
5. What is power? List some sources of power.
6. How do the two faces of power differ? Explain.
7. What is politics? List ways in which managers use politics to gain power.
8. What is ethics? What are some criteria for ethical behavior?
9. What are some major influences on ethical behavior?
10. How can ethical behavior be encouraged?
11. What are your values systems? List three or four terms or words that affect you strongly.
12. Observe other people. See if you can find evidence of behavior channeling and perceptual screening stemming from individual values.
13. How do you use power? Observe others to see how they obtain and use power. Describe them.
14. Does the case at the beginning of the chapter relate to anything in your own experience? Explain.
15. Interview managers about common practices in their areas that they feel are unethical. What do you recommend they do?
16. Interview a physician, a lawyer, a psychologist, or a similar person in the professions. How much influence do you think ethical codes have on the behavior of such people?
17. Are the nine political tactics of obtaining power ethical? Explain.

To Tell or Not to Tell

- A senior in her last semester at college has a straight "A" average and is looking forward to graduating summa cum laude. She observes another student cheating on a final examination. The instructor grades on the curve, and noncheaters' grades can be affected if the cheater gets an "A" in the course.

- In 1967 (before it became illegal), a key manufacturer sold master keys for automobiles to mail-order customers, although it was clear that some of the purchasers might be automobile thieves.

- A highly influential politician holds a "no show" job (one where the employee draws a salary but does not have to put in the work expected of others for the same salary) in a state agency. Other employees are aware of the situation.

- A cosmetics company advertises and sells a skin moisturizer that has a money-back guarantee. The moisturizer is 98 percent water and 2 percent alcohol, has a pleasing fragrance, and is packaged in an attractive bottle. It does "moisten" the skin.

- A college professor is aware of the fact that another professor has not kept up with the times and as a result is teaching material that is out of date and misleading.

- A technician in an aircraft factory is asked to adjust some test figures so that an aircraft brake will pass a military qualifications test. The brake will be unsafe if it is used on the aircraft.

- The export manager of a large company is asked by an important overseas customer to word sales invoices in a certain way. The wording will not violate U.S. laws, but it will clearly help the customer evade taxes in the other country.

- A serious proposal has been made that business ethics should be different from personal ethics, that bluffing and similar approaches should be usable as long as they do not involve outright cheating.

1. In each of these situations, what is ethical behavior? What is unethical behavior?
2. What would you do or recommend in each situation?

Footnotes

1. Adapted by permission from John J. Fendrock, "Crisis in Conscience at Quasar," *Harvard Business Review* 46 (March–April 1968): 112–120. Copyright © 1968 by the President and Fellows of Harvard College; all rights reserved.
2. R. Nader, P. Petkas, and K. Blackwell, eds., *Whistle Blowing: The Report of the Conference on Professional Responsibility* (New York: Grossman Publishers, 1972).
3. G. England, "Personal Value Systems of American Managers," *Journal of the Academy of Management* 10 (March 1967): 53–68; W. Guth and R. Tagiuri, "Personal Values and Corporate Strategy," *Harvard Business Review* 43 (September–October 1965): 123–132; and H. Bunke, "Heroes, Values and the Organization," *Business Horizons* 19 (October 1976): 33–41.
4. R. McMurray, "Conflicts in Human Values," *Harvard Business Review* 41 (May–June 1963): 130–145.
5. England, "Personal Value Systems of American Managers."
6. H. Singer, "Human Values and Leadership," *Business Horizons* 18 (August 1975): 85–88.
7. England, "Personal Value Systems of American Managers."
8. M. Zald, "Political Economy: A Framework for Comparative Analysis," in *Power in Organizations*, ed. M. Zald (Nashville, Tenn.: Vanderbilt University Press, 1970), p. 238.
9. C. Burck, "The Intricate 'Politics' of the Corporation," *Fortune*, April 1975, p. 109; R. Goodwin, "The Art of Assuming Power," *New York Times Magazine*, December 26, 1976, p. 7; G. Kelley, "Seducing the Elites: The Politics of Decision Making and Innovation in Organizational Networks," *Academy of Management Review* 1 (July 1976): 66–73; D. Mechanic, "Sources of Power of Lower Participants in Complex Organizations," *Administrative Science Quarterly* 7 (June 1962): 349–364; and A. Zaleznick, "Power and Politics in Organizational Life," *Harvard Business Review* 48 (May–June 1970): 47–60.
10. N. Long, "The Local Community as a Project of Games," *American Journal of Sociology* 64 (November 1958): 110.
11. D. McClelland and D. Burnham, "Power Is the Great Motivator," *Harvard Business Review* 54 (March–April 1976): 100–110. See also D. McClelland, "The Dynamics of Power and Affiliation Motivation," in

Organizational Psychology: A Book of Readings, ed. D. Kolb, I. Rubin, and J. McIntyre (Englewood Cliffs, N.J.: Prentice-Hall, 1971), pp. 141–154.

12. McClelland, "The Dynamics of Power and Affiliation Motivation," p. 150.

13. T. Burns, "Micropolitics: Mechanisms of Institutional Change," *Administrative Science Quarterly* 6 (September 1961): 259.

14. N. Martin and J. Simms, "Approaches to Power," *Harvard Business Review* 34 (November–December 1956): p. 25.

15. M. Korda, *Success* (New York: Random House, 1977).

16. J. McCloy, "John J. McCloy on Corporate Pay-offs," *Harvard Business Review* 54 (July–August 1976): p. 45; "Payoff Is Not 'Accepted Practice,'" *Fortune,* August 1975, p. 123; J. Kaikati, "The Phenomenon of International Bribery," *Business Horizons* 20 (February 1977): 25–37; A. Carr, "Can an Executive Afford a Conscience?" *Harvard Business Review* 48 (July–August 1970): 48–64; W. Robertson, "The Directors Woke Up Too Late at Gulf," *Fortune,* June 1976, p. 121; R. Bauer and D. Fend, Jr., "What Is a Corporate Social Audit?" *Harvard Business Review* 51 (January–February 1973): 37–49; and S. Sethi, *Up Against the Corporate Wall,* 2nd ed. (Englewood Cliffs, N.J.: Prentice-Hall, 1974).

17. M. Hurley, "Ethical Problems of the Association Executive," *Study Guide for Institutes of Organization Management* (Washington, D.C.: Chamber of Commerce of the United States, 1972), p. 8.

18. C. Walton, ed., *The Ethics of Corporate Conduct* (Englewood Cliffs, N.J.: Prentice-Hall, 1977), p. 5.

19. R. Baumhart, "How Ethical Are Businessmen?" *Harvard Business Review* 39 (July–August 1961): p. 6; Baumhart, *Ethics in Business* (New York: Holt, Rinehart and Winston, 1968); J. Bowman, "Managerial Ethics in Business and Government," *Business Horizons* 19 (October 1976): 48–54; A. Carroll, "Managerial Ethics: A Post-Watergate View," *Business Horizons* 18 (April 1975): 75–80; and W. Blumenthal, "Rx for Reducing the Occasion of 'Corporate Sin,'" *SAM Advanced Management Journal* 42 (Winter 1977): 4–13.

20. Baumhart, "How Ethical Are Businessmen?"

21. C. Perrow, *Organizational Analysis: A Sociological View* (Belmont, Calif.: Brooks/Cole Publishing, 1970), p. 4.

22. Bowman, "Managerial Ethics in Business and Government."

Chapter 21   Managers and the Environment

The Alaskan Pipeline

The Corporate Dilemma

Changing Concepts of the Economic System
    Profit-Maximizing Management
    Trusteeship Management
    "Quality-of-Life" Management

The Interpenetrating Systems Model
    Special Interest Groups
    Shareholders
    Boards of Directors
    Lobbying

Corporate Social Responsibility and the Social Audit
    Social Responsibility
    Social Measurement and the Social Audit

Implications for the Manager

Review

The Chevymobile

445

Learning Objectives

When you have finished reading and studying this chapter, you should be able to:

1. Identify the causes of the corporate dilemma.
2. Identify stages in the changing economic system.
3. Compare and contrast profit-maximizing management, trusteeship management, and quality-of-life management.
4. Describe the interpenetrating systems model of corporation and society.
5. Give illustrations of influences on the organization.
6. Compare and contrast social involvement and social responsibility.
7. Identify and give examples of social responsibility.
8. Define and be able to use the following concepts:

profit-maximizing management   environmentalism
trusteeship management   consumerism
quality-of-life management   lobbying
social involvement   social responsibility
interpenetrating system   social audit
special interest group

Thought Starters

1. Can you influence organizations? If so, what kinds? In what ways?
2. How do organizations affect you?
3. What are some state and federal rules and regulations that influence organizations?
4. How do organizations influence state and federal agencies?

The Alaskan Pipeline

In 1969 the Standard Oil Company of Ohio (SOHIO) and six other large oil companies, who would later form the ALYESKA Pipeline Service Company, began what was eventually to become the largest business venture ever undertaken by private enterprise. The eight hundred mile pipeline was planned to eventually carry 1.2 million barrels of crude oil a day from Alaska's North Slope to the Port of Valdez on its south coast. The original plan called for the oil to be transported by tanker to the California coast, where it would be unloaded and either refined or moved through a pipeline system to refineries lying east of the Rocky Mountains. These refineries have the greatest shortage of crude oil and represent 65 percent of the industry's total refining capacity.

SOHIO executives originally estimated that the Trans-Alaska Pipeline System (TAPS) would be completed by 1973 and would cost approximately $900 million. By mid-1977 TAPS was finally completed at a cost of more than $9 billion, ten times the original estimate. There were many reasons for the increased cost. Because of environmental and other concerns, construction of the pipeline was delayed until it was specifically authorized by Congress in 1973, after the Arab oil embargo. Because of increased equipment costs, the size of the line was doubled. There were endless hassles with regulatory bodies, delays due to weather, technical foul-ups, and accidents. An important cost factor was the need to protect the fragile Arctic environment—including the caribou and moose migration patterns and the fish streams.

Financing was hard to get, partly because of the uncertainties of the project and partly because it was not clear where the oil would actually go. A number of major institutional investors chose not to participate in the TAPS financing. Some investors were concerned about the risk that the government would not permit Alaskan crude oil to compete with world oil in the marketplace and thus would limit the rate of return the oil companies could pay to their investors.[1]

When the pipeline finally opened in 1977, the destination of the oil it would carry was still uncertain. There was a glut of oil on the West Coast, and permits to build a new terminal and connecting links to existing pipelines were still not available. Alternatives included selling the oil to Japan or shipping it to the Gulf Coast by tanker through the Panama Canal, which would be more expensive than a pipeline.

In Alaska, there appeared to be evidence that many environmental concerns were justified. There were reports that ALYESKA had frequently violated state and federal environmental rules agreed to when the right-of-way lease agreement was signed in 1974. Apparently, the pipeline took priority over the environment. For example, nearly 40 percent of the moose and caribou crossings built in 1975 were reported to be too low or wrongly located. Reports of environmental damage include erosion of tundra, water pollution resulting from improperly run sewage treatment plants, massive oil spills at construction sites, damage to fish spawning beds, and blocked fish streams. Some problems had been corrected, but it was too early to know just how permanent and serious the overall environmental impact would be, especially on wildlife and fish.[2]

The Trans-Alaskan Pipeline System is a vivid example of the complex interplay of forces outside the organization. This chapter will examine the interfaces between organizations and their environment. Many management texts have not recognized the impact groups both within the organization and outside it have on managerial decision making. While middle- and lower-level managers can be responsible for the coordinating and production functions of organizations, top management must spend a great deal of time making decisions that relate to political issues and problems. Furthermore, managers at all levels affect and are affected by such issues, among them affirmative action, pollution abatement, and federal and state laws, rules, and regulations.

The Corporate Dilemma

At the beginning of the century, it was possible for a company president to state that business executives were "Christian men to whom God in his infinite wisdom has given control of the property interests of the country."[3] Although William Vanderbilt, the president of the New York Central Railroad, may or may not have said, "the public be damned" (in about 1883), historians have confirmed that his father, responding to the possibility that he had acted illegally, exploded, "Law? What do I care about the law? Ain't I got the power?"[4]

In contrast, Daniel McNaughton, the chairman and chief executive officer of the Prudential Insurance Company of America, very recently wrote, "Business belongs to the people. Business has, in effect, a franchise granted to it by society, and the franchise will be continued only as long as society is satisfied with the way it is handled."[5] He went on to say that business needed to be responsive to a wide variety of constituencies—for example, suppliers, consumers, employees, stockholders, and the general public—rather than to only one or two.

These remarks point up two extreme viewpoints, both of which have their followers.[6] One extreme insists that business exists only to maximize long-run profit and that no other decision-making criteria are to be used. Thus economist Milton Friedman contends that the only business of business is profits and that even corporate gifts to charitable organizations such as the Community Fund or the Girl Scouts are wrong. Friedman says, "If the corporation makes a contribution, it prevents the individual stockholder from himself deciding how he should dispose of his funds. . . . There is no justification for permitting deductions for contributions to charitable and educational institutions."[7] Those who take this position argue forcefully that the role of government should be strictly limited to the major functions of preserving law and order, enforcing private contracts, and fostering competitive markets.

Others argue, just as forcefully, that as corporations become larger, they must be controlled in ways that make them work more closely with society. Their point is that business and industry have not been sufficiently responsive to society and as a result, "public anger at corporations is beginning to well up at a frightening rate, bringing with it a dizzying variety of protest movements."[8] The protests stem from concern over air and water pollution, misleading advertising, low product quality, and meaningless warranties. The Committee for Economic Development, a leading business group, has strongly urged management to involve itself in a wide variety of social issues, such as urban renewal, job opportunities for minorities and women, aid to education, and training of the disadvantaged.[9] The argument is that the traditional economic model of business has worked well, and business does not need to apologize for its important role in bringing economic plenty to much of the world but that there have been so many significant changes in the world that the traditional business model must now be modified to more closely fit today's social environment and society's expectations.[10]

The result of these conflicting viewpoints is what has become known as the "corporate dilemma."[11] The dilemma is how to determine the proper balance between long-run profits and social responsibility. Clearly, businesses must be responsive to the larger society. But individual corporations cannot sacrifice a large portion of their profits in order to take an active role in every area of social and economic life. Thus, neither complete concentration on profits nor full response to every societal demand is possible.

In the case of SOHIO, environmental concerns and hassles with regulatory agencies played a part in the high cost of the pipeline. This chapter will attempt to deal with the issues surrounding this kind of situation. It will attempt to answer questions such as: What were the responsibilities of the regulatory agencies and environmentalists in protecting the Arctic environment? What was SOHIO's responsibility in tapping the Alaskan North Slope oil reserves to bring needed oil to the United States? What was SOHIO's responsibility to its stockholders and to the environment?

One extreme viewpoint would be that SOHIO should have remained within the law but done nothing more. The other extreme would be that SOHIO should have protected the environment even if it had gone under as a company in its own right. Rather than debate the merits of the two extremes, this chapter will first briefly examine the origins of the economic system in the United States to determine how the opposing schools of thought emerged and then describe how external forces in the environment can significantly affect the success of business and industrial organizations.

Changing Concepts of the Economic System

The suggestion has been made that laws, regulations, and concepts regarding businesses' social involvement have gone through at least three phases: profit-maximizing management, trusteeship management, and quality-of-life management [12].

Profit-Maximizing Management

The industrial revolution swept through the United States in the nineteenth century, carrying with it new attitudes toward business. **Profit-maximizing** management emerged at the same time. It had but a single objective—to maximize profits. The only constraints on them were legal ones, and these were frequently ignored.

In the nineteenth century, and in the first third of the twentieth century, U.S. society had a lot of room to expand, but at the same time it experienced economic scarcity. Its primary national goals were economic growth and the accumulation of wealth. Giant corporations began to dominate the economy. By the end of the nineteenth century, the two hundred largest manufacturing organizations had added more to the Gross National Product than had the hundred thousand next largest.

Massive trusts with immense power were developed. These trusts showed their power through such practices as lockouts of labor, manipulation of commodity prices, discriminatory pricing, kickbacks, and a lack of concern for employees and customers. In the cigar manufacturing industry, almost three-fourths of all employees became ill after six months on the job. In the food industry, milk was commonly preserved with formaldehyde. *Caveat emptor* (let the buyer beware) characterized decisions and actions in dealing with customers. These practices led to the development of federal antitrust legislation, railroad rate regulation, and fair trade laws. For example, Standard Oil, duPont, and American Tobacco were divided into smaller companies.

Profit-maximizing values were based on Calvinist philosophy, which stressed that the road to salvation was through hard work and the accumulation of wealth. Thus managers adhering to that philosophy believed that self-interest was an absolute good.

During the 1920s the relationships between business and government were amicable. As Secretary of Commerce, Herbert Hoover was so strongly pro business that he intervened to prevent an inquiry about the antitrust consequences of a proposed acquisition.[13]

Then came the crash of 1929, when the bottom fell out of the stock market. By 1932, a quarter of all U.S. workers were unemployed. In effect, U.S. business was "offered the choice between rugged individualism and business autonomy or economic security. The generation raised on the gospel of wealth gladly forfeited the former."[14] Franklin Roosevelt defeated Herbert Hoover for president in 1932, and the age of profit-maximizing management was ushered out.

Trusteeship Management

Trustee management emerged from the nature and thrust of the larger society and from structural changes in business organizations themselves. The idea of **trustee management** is that the corporate manager is responsible not only for profits but also for maintaining a proper balance among the competing claims of stockholders, employees, suppliers, customers, and the broader community.

The two structural trends largely responsible for this concept of management were the increasingly broad ownership of U.S. corporations and the development of a more pluralistic society. By the early 1930s, the largest stockholders in corporations such as U.S. Steel, the Pennsylvania Railroad, and American Telephone & Telegraph owned less than 1 percent of the total outstanding shares. Although many large organizations were still closely controlled, others had such diversified ownership that management was firmly in control of them and could maintain that control through the use of voting proxies (a procedure allowing top management to vote the shares of many stockholders).

The term *pluralistic society* has been defined as "one which has many semi-autonomous and autonomous groups through which power is diffused. No one group has overwhelming power over all others, and each has direct or indirect impact on all others."[15] Since the depression and the resulting legal and social changes, the corporation has been increasingly regarded as an institution that has a social obligation to fulfill in a pluralistic society. The government has restated the responsibility of business toward a variety of groups through such actions as collective bargaining and minimum wage laws and regulations, requiring disclosure of corporation information, civil rights and fair employment practice laws, and the establishment of agencies to promote nondestructive competition. In the 1930s, the major pressure groups were the labor unions and the government. Now, the list includes numerous environmental, minority, and consumer groups. Thus the task of the modern manager is to balance the claims of all these groups and still make a profit for the business.

The values of trusteeship managers have changed. The new generation of corporate managers, includes many who are college-educated and heavily influenced by liberal arts humanism. These new managers recognize that self-interest is important but that it must be balanced, at least partially, against the interests of the many groups involved with and affected by the organization. Rather than resisting government and governmental regulations, they pragmatically accept them as a way of life.

Quality-of-Life Management

Around the turn of the century and later, society assumed that business would produce increasing amounts of goods and services and thus continue to raise the standard of living of its citizens. Since then, the United States has become an "affluent society" with other needs and issues as well. There is increasing concern about air and water pollution, poverty, and urban blight. A new set of national priorities seems to be emerging, one that stresses the overall quality of life. Some believe that business should assume broader responsibilities—that its financial resources and technological and managerial skills should be directed more specifically toward the solution of society's major problems. John F. Kennedy said in his inaugural speech, "Ask not what your country can do for you; ask what you can do for your country."

Under the trusteeship management developed in the 1930s, a relatively harmonious accord existed between government and business. In the late 1960s and the 1970s, however, the accord was disturbed. There was an increasing emphasis on consumerism, environmentalism, and similar issues. Government began to impose new responsibilities on business, including consumer protection measures such as truth in advertising, truth in finance, and product assurance standards; environmental legislation to protect water and air quality; and campaign financing legislation to reveal the magnitude of corporate political contributions. From all these changes emerged a new kind of management—**quality-of-life management**. In quality-of-life management, managers are responsible for enhancing the organization, the society, the environment, and the dignity of employees.

Quality-of-life managers believe that society's interests are important, that although profits are essential to the organization's survival, they are not the only objective of the organization. They believe that people are more important than money and therefore that employment of minorities and the handicapped is essential. They believe in the dignity of each employee and feel that people are worth more than machines.

Such managers also see that the environment must be preserved, since an adequate environment is not only good in itself but also benefits those who want to lead a high-quality life. Overall, they believe they are accountable to the organization's owners, to the others who contribute to the organization, and to society as a whole. They believe that government and politicians are necessary contributors to society and to the quality of life and that business and government need to cooperate in solving society's problems.

The growing feeling that a change has occurred in the social contract organizations have with society—and that when the social purpose changes, so do the activities of corporations—is expressed by Fletcher Byrom, chairman of the board of Koppers Company, a large manufacturing corporation: "You can't continue a business without profit, but profits are not the be-all and end-all of the corporation. . . . If it does not at the same time serve the needs of society, then the corporation as an instrumentality of accomplishment will surely perish, and deserves to perish."[16]

The Interpenetrating Systems Model

The debate among proponents of each of the models—profit-maximizing, trusteeship, and quality-of-life—has been extended and heated. Rather than further discuss the merits of any of the positions, however, this section of the chapter will describe how organizations exist in, influence, and are influenced by society and many subsystems within its environment.

Organizations and the society are inherently interrelated. The scope of managerial responsibility extends to activities beyond those mediated by market contacts. **Social involvement** is the interaction of the organization, as a system, with other organizations and individuals and with society as a whole.[17] It is a neutral term; the degree of any organization's involvement can be large or small, specific or general, benign or harmful.

Interpenetrating systems are two or more systems, neither of which totally contains or is contained by the other, that are involved in particular events or processes. Figure 21.1 shows two interpenetrating systems.

For example, the federal government's efforts to raise the mandatory retirement age from sixty-five to seventy has created an interpenetrating

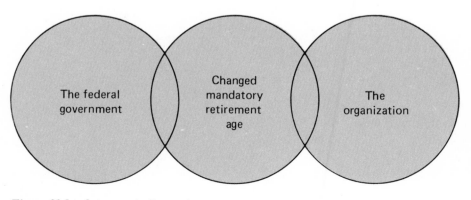

Figure 21.1   Interpenetrating systems

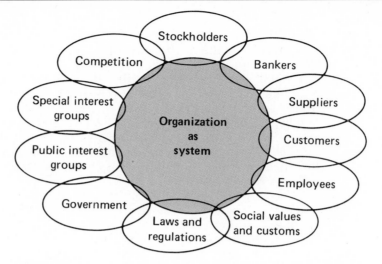

Figure 21.2   The many influences on the organizational system

system where the event (passing the law) penetrates organizations (which must create new retirement policies, change pension plans, and the like).

In the interpenetrating systems model, the organization can be considered a micro unit of the larger society, but both the organization and society can also be considered separate systems. Thus organizations and society neither completely control nor are completely controlled by the broad social environment. The model provides the possibility "which has, in fact, become a necessity—of considering the potential differences, conflicts, and compatabilities among the goals of micro-organizations and those of society at large."[18] A vice-president of General Electric has commented, "The social and economic responsibilities of the corporation have been so broadened and interwoven in the public's expectations . . . that it no longer makes sense, if indeed it ever did, to talk as if they could be separated.[19]

Some of the other systems the organization must interact with and, in many cases, compete with or try to influence are shown in Figure 21.2. They include customers, bankers, suppliers, stockholders, employees, and government.

The diagram is misleading in that it does not show the complex interrelationships of the various influences on the organization. For example, laws are affected by customs and in turn affect special interest groups. A change in laws may affect a special interest group, which may in turn allow a minority person to sue an organization. Civil rights and other movements profoundly affect legislation and government regulations. As stockholders become more active in the affairs of an enterprise, their activity may influence employees, customers, unions, and special interest groups.

Special Interest Groups

Thus the effective manager is constantly trying to balance the actions of many **special interest groups**—groups that attempt to exert influence over someone in order to benefit one or a few specific causes that are important to them. The manager's decision making must therefore take into account not only the organization itself but the many and varied competitors for its scarce resources.

Although Figure 21.2 shows a number of influences on the organization, the text will discuss only a few—minorities, environmentalists, consumerists, shareholders, boards of directors, and lobbyists.

Minorities

Minority pressure on businesses, especially against discrimination in employment and promotion, has been steadily increasing. There is now stricter enforcement of state and federal antidiscrimination laws (some of which were briefly described in Chapter 13). In 1973, for example, AT&T agreed to upgrade the jobs of approximately 50,000 women and 7,000 minority group members and to employ approximately 4,000 men to fill positions that had been traditionally handled by women (such as telephone operator and clerk). The company also agreed to pay approximately $15 million to women and other minorities who had not been given equal pay for their work. In 1978, the Supreme Court essentially upheld the lower court decision that had forced AT&T to change its policies by refusing to hear the company's appeal.

A number of organizations have taken antidiscriminatory steps beyond those required by law; among them are Atlantic Richfield, General Electric, and Standard Oil of Indiana.[20] Standard Oil, for example, has affirmative action programs to promote jobs for minority construction workers in the organization's new construction.

Environmentalists

Environmentalists are special interest groups that focus on the physical environment and the changes people have made in it. For many years, only a few seemed to worry about the environment; now, almost every day there are headlines about oil tanker spills, pollution of air and water, and danger from pesticides. According to the National Institute for Occupational Safety and Health, about 20,000 manufactured products need to be federally regulated because they contain toxic substances; more than 400 of these products contain cancer-causing agents.

Sometimes, special interest groups become frustrated by inaction and seek to dramatize their concern. A few years ago, a mystery person called "The Fox" won the approval of many people when he stopped up the drainpipes and smokestacks of companies that he thought were polluting the environment. On one occasion, he left a dead fish and sludge on the ivory-colored rug of a steel company executive. In 1977, more than 1,400 protestors were arrested and jailed for attempting to stop the building of a nuclear power plant in Seabrook, New Hampshire. In 1978, more than 8,000 farmers and students destroyed the control tower and other facilities of the new $4 billion Tokyo International Airport the day before it was to be opened (five years late). When the airport finally "officially" opened, it did so under extreme emergency conditions, with a security force of 14,000 guarding it.[21]

Consumerists

Consumerists are special interest groups that focus on the safety and quality of products bought by consumers. Although there have always been consumer groups, consumerism first made major headlines with the publicity that Ralph Nader generated with his book, *Unsafe at Any Speed*, and his head-on confrontation with General Motors regarding automotive safety. Perhaps the confrontation would not have generated so much publicity if General Motors had not hired a private detective to check on Nader and his purposes. Eventually, the president of GM had to appear before Congress and apologize to Nader. Congress has since passed a number of laws regarding the safety, reliability, side effects, and prices of products. Today, we accept automobile call-backs as a matter of course; but before the rise of consumerism, such events were unlikely to occur.

Nader is only one illustration of how government and the environment interact. Another occurred in 1978. In a landmark case, the Supreme Court, upheld the Federal Trade Commission's order that the makers of Listerine (Warner-Lambert) pay for $10 million in advertising to correct false claims that Listerine was effective against colds and sore throats. The court fight had lasted for almost seven years. The American Advertising Federation strongly objected to the decision, calling it "drastic" and "probably the most far-reaching advertising order ever issued by the commission."[22]

On the positive side, Lees Carpets has run advertisements that provide information to persons thinking about buying carpets. Hunt-Wesson Foods has decided to avoid discussing relatively unimportant product differences in its advertising. Many other national advertisers are becoming interested in conducting educational campaigns and using more informative, specific copy than they were using a few years ago.[23]

Shareholders

Shareholders are part owners of businesses; they become part owners by buying shares of stocks issued by corporations. Some organizations have only a few owners of their stock; others have many. General Motors, for instance, has approximately 1,500,000 individual shareholders. Traditionally, the chief executive of an organization has worried primarily about the reactions of the major group of stockholders—the people who own large blocks of stock and the members of the board of directors. And for a long time, the primary concern has been whether the price of the stock or the dividend is high enough. If it is, management has little to worry about. For example, the majority of the stockholders of General Motors do not control, direct, or bear much responsibility for the company; and the vast majority have little ability to influence it. Rather, many are concerned only about the price of the stock and the rate of return on their investments.

As a result, the annual stockholders' meeting is usually a relatively sedate and quiet affair. In recent years, however, things have begun to change. There have been confrontations at annual meetings between environmentalists and other interest groups. Questions have been raised and protests have been made by shareholders about such social issues as discrimination, pricing policies, pollution, and hiring practices in South Africa. More and more resolutions have been filed to influence social, political, and environmental decisions. Activist groups have involved such diverse shareholders as universities, churches, and labor unions (including the United Auto Workers). These organizations have put pressure on many large companies, including Johnson & Johnson, Coca-Cola, and Eastman Kodak.

Managers are reacting differently to shareholder questions and concerns than they were a few years ago. In the past, questions were seen as disruptive and impertinent. Now, managers carefully prepare for meetings and treat questions respectfully. John Bunting, chairman and chief executive officer of the First Pennsylvania Corporation, says, "Now there is greater recognition that the shareholder has the right to know." Another chief executive points out that "shareholders are becoming less lethargic about what they can do. They are making it clear that they will not put up with any nonsense during meetings."[24]

Boards of Directors

Social involvement is also affecting boards of directors.[25] Membership on a board of directors used to be far more comfortable than it is now. Under state laws of incorporation, boards of directors are charged with protecting the interests of the companies' owners. For a long time, this meant taking a relatively narrow view of stockholder interests. Now, however, critics are suggesting, or demanding, that directors take a wider view. In addition, boards are being asked to examine more carefully the operation of the organizations themselves. For example, the Securities and Exchange Commission (SEC) recently criticized the outside directors of National Telephone, a telephone equipment supplier that went bankrupt. The SEC claimed that the directors did not sufficiently question or correct the overly optimistic statements of the organization's managers.

Often, boards of directors are composed primarily of insiders—those who were already employees of the company when they joined the board. Currently, however, business is moving toward the use of outside directors—people who are not members of management and who do not have strong ties to management. The move toward using outside directors is being forced by a recent New York Stock Exchange ruling that all companies listed on the exchange must have audit committees and that the members of these committees must be outside directors. Such committees were being used even before the NYSE's ruling, partly because of scandals involving political payoffs in the early 1970s. In fact, many organizations have had audit committees for years. General Motors, for example, has had an audit committee since the late 1930s.

More and more organizations are establishing other active committees in such areas as wages, benefits, and other kinds of compensation; public affairs; and ethics. Furthermore, since they have become increasingly subject to lawsuits and other harassments, board members are taking their responsibilities more seriously than they did before. Some noted people have recently turned down appointments because they felt they did not have the time to properly handle the job of director.

Lobbying

Lobbying involves actions taken by individuals or organizations to influence government agencies and federal, state, or local legislation. The term *lobbyist* need not have a negative connotation. Indeed, in most political systems, lobbyists and lobbies are essential. Legislators and government agents often work better when a variety of information is presented to them. The Sierra Club may lobby for more environmental protection. The National Association for the Advancement of Colored People (NAACP) may lobby for more civil rights legislation or enforcement of such legislation. The local Parent-Teachers Association may lobby for or against a new school building. Unions may lobby for a higher minimum wage. Union political action committees raised and contributed over $17 million dollars to political parties and candidates in the 1976 elections. Business political action committees raised and contributed over $12 million in the same elections.[26]

Management must also present clear and accurate information to government bodies in order to get legislation or rulings favorable to their organizations. Lobbying is thus a critical function. Organizations that fail to lobby or that do it ineffectively are almost always hurt in a political system that has many competitive and diverse interests.

Organizations usually have a trade association (such as the American Bankers Association or the National Association of Realtors) to lobby for their special causes. Most large firms, such as General Electric and General Motors, also have their own representatives in Washington and/or the state capitals to lobby for their interests. Smaller firms frequently hire an organization that specializes in lobbying, usually a law firm. Other organizations may directly approach regulatory agencies, local members of Congress, or state legislators.

Industry and other special interest groups sometimes work together to lobby in areas in which they have common interests. At other times, they may lobby intensively on opposite sides of an issue. Top management may lobby directly to get favorable action for an organization. For example, J. Paul Austin, the head of Coca-Cola, spends at least half his time traveling from one country to another lobbying to open up new markets for his company.[27]

Other heads of business firms are becoming more involved in direct lobbying. In 1972, the Business Roundtable, an organization of about two hundred of the chief executives of the country's major corporations, was formed. The primary purpose of the Roundtable is to give business more political clout. As issues arise, members are organized into task forces that analyze the issues, take specific positions, and then argue these positions with regulatory agencies, the White House, or the Congress.

The Roundtable was formed as a direct result of increased government regulation and taxation and the growth of special interest groups in the late 1960s and early 1970s. Ralph Nader has been an effective lobbyist because he and his organization provide Congress and government officials with lists of facts. The Roundtable now does the same thing. As an illustration, the proposal to create a federal agency for consumer protection was strongly sponsored by Nader, but when the Roundtable mustered its own facts, the proposal to create the new agency was roundly defeated by Congress in early 1977.[28]

Corporate Social Responsibility and the Social Audit

The previous section indicated that organizations are involved in the larger environment through interpenetrating systems. In addition to this social involvement, organizations are becoming more aware of their social responsibilities. The awareness is due in part to changing values of the society. The public is always concerned with issues. Some of these issues lead to increased public good, such as Medicare. Others lead to government action to eliminate problems, such as the Occupational Safety and Health Act or the many laws and regulations affecting air, water, and other pollution. Because an organization's legitimacy depends on its acceptance by the public, many managers have found it desirable to pay attention to the public's attitudes on important issues. Thus social responsibility and the social audit came about.

Social Responsibility

Social responsibility is behavior for the social good beyond the law or common custom demanded. For example, a certain amount of pollution control is required by law and is therefore expected behavior. When a firm goes beyond the requirements, it is showing social responsibility. The U.S. Chamber of Commerce suggests that voluntary social action can be viewed at four levels, shown in Figure 21.3.

The first level is conformity to existing legal requirements in fulfilling the economic function of the business. A profit-maximizing manager would probably follow this course. The second level is meeting recognized public expectations and social demands over and above what is required by law, a position the trusteeship manager might take. The third level is anticipating new social demands and preparing in advance to meet them, a position the quality-of-life manager would take. The fourth level is serving as a leader in setting new standards of business social performance.[29]

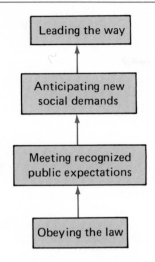

Figure 21.3   Levels of corporate social action

In order to show how the organization is fulfilling its social respon-sibilities, more and more organizations and authorities are considering the use of social audits. A **social audit** is generally an ongoing evaluation of performance measured against established goals in selected areas of social responsibility. For example, ABT Associates, a social research and consulting firm, includes in its annual report a listing, in dollar terms, of its social assets and liabilities.

To successfully develop and implement a social audit or social mea-surement of some kind, a firm must evaluate the environment in which it functions, establish improvement objectives, make resource allocations to the identified needs, and measure and evaluate its progress on an ongoing basis. Although most annual reports touch on the subject of social responsibility, few do so in statistical terms in their financial review sections. Their reporting tends to be sporadic and disjointed rather than comprehensive. But for the benefit of outsiders looking in, of company executives on the inside, and of society as a whole, some form of social accounting is needed.[30]

Most current reporting on company social performance has resulted from responses to pressures from outside groups, such as product safety and environmental protection agencies. Some of it has been simply a form of advertising aimed at preventing outside interference in company policy making. Other reporting has been on progress made in meeting legal requirements in areas such as minority hiring and product safety. However, these haphazard reporting efforts often ignore areas of good performance and overlook areas in which the organization has performed poorly.

Because there is a significant investment today in social overhead—from automobile safety to pollution to day care centers—a more rational management of this investment is needed, both within and outside the organization. A recent study of 185 firms from *Fortune*'s lists of the top 500 and second 500 largest U.S. corporations indicated that only about half the organizations had established objectives in the area of exter-nal affairs. Those that had established even broad objectives saw them-selves as being more successful than organizations not having objectives in such areas as environmental affairs, stockholder relations, and good citizenship.[31]

Without clear objectives, however, there can be little systematic comparison made of the returns of one social investment against the returns of another. By systematically comparing all current and other possible social costs, an organization can replace less efficient ones with those that are more efficient. An optimum mix of social programs that will either give maximum benefits for a fixed cost or that will cost the minimum amount for some fixed level of responsibility needs to be achieved.

More balance must also be given to the external optimum mix. For example, in 1974, approximately $1 billion was spent to develop and install a complex "interlock" system of seat belts for automobiles. The car would not start unless the belts were connected. The belts irritated drivers and passengers, and Congress eventually withdrew the requirement. Perhaps all the money spent on this project could have been better spent on developing good road signs, intensive driver training, more thorough vehicle inspections, or other safety approaches.[32] The cost of social responsibility must thus be carefully considered, both within and outside the organization.

Social Measurement and the Social Audit

The social audit must consider two opposing approaches to social responsibility. The first results from a desire to respond to the demands of outside pressure groups. With this approach, social responsibility will probably be equated with the public's expectations. The second is based on management's desire to assess its own social performance. The likely result here is an internal management report used to determine the company's strengths and weaknesses in the area of social responsibility.

The external audit approach may result in attempts by the organization to make itself look good without actually achieving a high level of performance. It may also result in an unwise use of resources and may limit management's discretion in the selection and execution of social programs. An internally generated report, if issued to outsiders, may indicate only what the organization considers socially relevant and may deal with only those areas where the organization's performance is good. As a result, neither approach should be used to the exclusion of the other.

There are four general approaches suggested for reporting the results of a social audit. The first is a *straight inventory approach*, where a company lists all its social activities. The second is a *cost approach;* in addition to listing social activities, the company indicates the amount spent on each. The third approach is *program management;* here, cost information is given along with a statement about whether the organization met its objectives for each activity. The fourth approach is a *cost-benefit* one; it includes the cost information and the real worth or benefits of each expenditure.[33]

Clearly, the inventory approach is the simplest and easiest method, since it lists only what is being done to meet social responsibilities. The most difficult is the cost-benefit approach, which will show up many inefficiencies due to an undersupply of social program services and/or an oversupply of services that are not strongly demanded. For example, an organization may support a bowling league even though relatively few employees like to bowl. At the same time, it may have a large population of working mothers but no day care center.

There are many problems in trying to report on social responsibility. One of the major ones is definition. Business and social planners sharply disagree over the elements of social responsibility—what it includes and how far it should go. Another major problem is the actual measurement of social costs and benefits. Out-of-pocket costs are relatively easy to establish for many activities. But the true costs—such as managerial time spent on a project—may be impossible to determine. Indeed, social benefits are nearly impossible to measure. A case in point is the benefit to society from pollution control. Although it is possible to measure the reduction in the amount of pollutants in the air, this reduction cannot be quantified in dollar terms. Still, there are a number of quantitative and qualitative approaches to measuring social performance. For example, one can count the number of minority group members hired.

At present, there is little agreement on what a social audit is, who should do it, or how it should be undertaken. The only general agreement is that standards are needed. Without some sort of agreed-upon standards, managers are understandably reluctant to discuss social programs and plans. Without accepted guidelines for performing a social audit, there is the added problem of credibility. If the report is conducted primarily by an internal company group, there can be doubt as to how much negative performance is being reported. Even if outside auditors prepare the report, it is questionable whether they can rely on internal sources to generate negative data regarding the organization's social performance.

Some advances have been made in the area of social measurement. For example, the American Institute of Certified Public Accountants has established a committee on social accounting, and the American Accounting Association has set up a committee on measurement of social costs. The National Association of Accountants has organized a task force to establish goals for the accounting profession in setting forth principles of social accounting and improving the social performance of the business community. The Securities and Exchange Commission offered guidelines in late 1975 on how organizations should report their environmental performance to investors. Although the SEC declined to make suggestions for reporting in other social performance areas, the guidelines are at least a beginning. All in all, it looks like the next few years will show a growing awareness of social responsibility and more effective techniques for measuring how well organizations are meeting their social responsibilities.

Implications for the Manager

The manager of today faces a dilemma. As the culture and values of society have changed through the years, so also have the manager's responsibilities. Under profit-maximizing management, the responsibility was clear—to make a profit. Now, however, the larger society is looking to organizations, particularly the larger corporations, to assume a larger responsibility for social goals. While many managers still believe in profit maximization, there are others who reject this idea as being too simplistic.

Therein lies the dilemma. With rapidly shifting cultural values, what is the real responsibility of the manager to the organization, to the stockholders, and to the larger community? Should the manager adopt a trusteeship style and attempt to balance the conflicting interests of varied groups, or should the manager take up a quality-of-life approach and become a leader?

One thing has emerged clearly from the discussion in the chapter. If managers can organize with other businesses or special interest groups, their lobbying attempts stand a good chance of success. The unanswered question is: What is the proper balance?

Another implication is that managers who are hoping to successfully operate a business must be much more aware of the influences and interests of a wide range of special interest groups. Through interpenetrating systems, these special interest groups are able to influence many business organizations. Thus consideration of issues ranging from racial discrimination in the job market to environmental pollution or corporate contributions to the arts is vital to today's corporate managers.

Social changes involve organizations of all types. Particularly in the past twenty years, a number of federal, state, and local laws and regulations have had a large impact on organizations. Simply obeying the law today is much more complicated than it was around the turn of the century.

Although many people, including some economists, would disagree, it appears that trusteeship management is taking the place of profit-maximizing management. The concept of interpenetrating systems make this abundantly clear. For example, the recent change in the mandatory retirement age from sixty-five to seventy will force managers to rethink their position on many related issues, such as performance appraisal and pension plans.

More and more organizations are moving beyond simple social involvement and toward acceptance of social responsibility and the social audit. However, the thinking in this area is as yet relatively unsystematic. Some organizations have moved a long way in this direction. Others have ignored the whole idea of social responsibility.

In conclusion, it must be suggested that the effective manager realizes that an organization's legitimacy depends ultimately on its acceptance by the public. Thus many managers have found it desirable to pay attention to the public's attitudes on important issues and to evaluate the organization's actual performance in those areas.

Review

1. Describe the changing concepts of the economic system. What has been the influence of the larger environment?
2. Is *social involvement* a more neutral term than *social responsibility*? Explain.
3. How does the interpenetrating systems model help in understanding the current influences on organizations?
4. What is the corporate dilemma, and what are some of its causes?
5. How would you now answer the question, "Do organizations affect state and federal agencies?"
6. Visit a local or other regulatory agency, such as a board of zoning appeals or a liquor licensing commission. Interview the chairperson or a member of the commission to determine the individual's views about the purpose of the agency.
7. Interview several local business managers. Describe their opinions about regulatory agencies.
8. Compare and contrast the answers you get from the two groups (regulatory agencies and business managers). If there are differences, what causes them?
9. Suggest some ways in which organizations can or should take action regarding social responsibility. What is *your* social responsibility?

The Chevymobile

A Chicago man took his new 1977 Oldsmobile back to his dealer to replace the fan belt on the engine. The dealer did not have the proper belt in stock, and when the owner took a look at the engine, he discovered that the new Oldsmobile did not have an Oldsmobile engine. Instead it had a less expensive engine made by Chevrolet. The owner demanded a "pure Oldsmobile" and was turned down. At this point he took his case to the Illinois attorney general.

As the case unfolded, it became obvious that the man from Chicago was not the only person to get a cheaper engine. General Motors had put Chevrolet engines not only into Oldsmobiles but also into 1977 Buicks and Pontiacs. As a result, GM became the target of about 250 private and state lawsuits.

In late December 1977, the company settled out of court with forty-four states that had banded together to sue for all "Chevymobile" owners in their states. (Six states—California, Iowa, Kentucky, Louisiana, New York, and Tennessee—did not join in the settlement.)

Under the terms of the settlement, all 75,000 owners in the forty-four states would receive a $200 cash rebate—about $120 more than the estimated difference between the value of the Chevrolet engine and the other engines. In addition, each owner would receive a transferable three-year or 36,000-mile warranty estimated to be worth about $200 per car. If all the owners of the "Chevymobiles" in all fifty states were to agree to those terms, the total dollar cost to GM would be about $37 million, not including the costs of the lawsuits, the damage to the company's reputation, and other intangibles.

In making the announcement that the company had agreed to settle the dispute out of court to save the cost of many lawsuits, GM denied any wrongdoing or liability. The chairman of the board said:

The interdivisional usage of engines is not new with General Motors or the automobile industry generally. General Motors used V-8 engines produced in a plant operated by its Chevrolet Motor Division in Buick, Oldsmobile and Pontiac cars because it sought to satisfy consumer demand for V-8 engines in its 1977 cars. Those engines were part of the General Motors family of engines and offer quality performance and durability. General Motors stands proudly behind those engines and all of its products.

He pointed out that car buyers who paid for a 350 cubic inch, 170 horsepower engine got exactly that. However, some owners have experienced delays in getting their cars repaired because parts from Buick, Oldsmobile, and Pontiac engines do not always fit the Chevrolet engine. GM now warns buyers in its advertising that its automobiles may come equipped with equivalent components produced in GM plants.

There are two notable side effects of the GM case: (1) that the settlement may be one of the largest awards ever in a consumer protection case, and (2) that this is the first time so many state attorneys general have banded together to fight for consumers against a single company. In effect, a national public service law firm was formed.[34]

1. Do you agree with the Chicago owner who demanded a "pure Oldsmobile"?
2. Do you agree with the statement of the chairman of the board of GM that the switch in engines was to satisfy consumer demand?
3. What are the legal, moral, and social responsibilities of GM in this case?
4. What are the implications of this case for the future?

Footnotes

1. "Testimony during Hearings on Alaskan North Slope Pricing, Entitlement Issues before the Federal Energy Administration," March 21, 1977. (Statement of Avid P. Goodman, managing director of Morgan Stanley & Co., Inc.)
2. Information about the pipeline came from the following sources: A. Morner, "For SOHIO, It Was Alaskan Oil—Or Bust," *Fortune*, August 1977, pp. 173–184; "Pipeline to Mid-America," *The Sohioan*, February 1977, p. 10; R. James, "Alaska Pipeline Opens on Time, but Shortcuts Scar the Environment," *Wall Street Journal*, June 20, 1977, p. 1; H. Ellis, "Alaska Oil May Be a 'Mixed Blessing,'" *Christian Science Monitor*, June 21, 1977, p. 1.
3. L. Canfield, *The United States in the Making* (Boston: Houghton Mifflin, 1949), p. 552.
4. N. Eberstadt, "What History Tells Us about Corporate Responsibilities," in *Managing Corporate Social Responsibility,* ed. A. Carroll (Boston: Little, Brown, 1977), p. 21.
5. D. MacNaughton, "Managing Social Responsiveness," *Business Horizons* 19 (December 1976): 19.
6. B. Nanus, "The Future-Oriented Corporation," *Business Horizons* 18 (February 1975): 5–12; C. Burck, "The Intricate 'Politics' of the Corporation," *Fortune*, April 1975, pp. 109–192.

7. M. Friedman, *Capitalism and Freedom* (Chicago: University of Chicago Press, 1962), p. 135.

8. D. Ewing, "The Corporation as Public Enemy No. 1," *Saturday Review*, January 21, 1978, p. 12.

9. *Social Responsibility of Business Corporations* (New York: Committee for Economic Development, 1971).

10. K. Davis, "Social Responsibility Is Inevitable," *California Management Review* 19 (Fall 1976): 14–20.

11. D. Votaw and S. Sethi, *The Corporate Dilemma* (Englewood Cliffs, N.J.: Prentice-Hall, 1973).

12. R. Hay and E. Gray, "Social Responsibilities of Business Managers," *Academy of Management Journal* 18 (March 1974): 135–143.

13. F. Sturdivant, *Business and Society* (Homewood, Ill.: Richard D. Irwin, 1977), p. 67.

14. Eberstadt, "What History Tells Us about Corporate Responsibilities," p. 22.

15. G. Steiner, *Business and Society* (New York: Random House, 1971), pp. 70–71.

16. F. Byrom, *Koppers Foundation* (Pittsburgh, Pa.: Koppers Company, n.d.), p. 2.

17. L. Preston and J. Post, *Private Management and Public Policy* (Englewood Cliffs, N.J.: Prentice-Hall, 1975).

18. Preston and Post, *Private Management and Public Policy,* p. 26.

19. V. Day, "Management and Society: An Insider's View," *Management and Public Policy,* proceedings of the Conference, School of Management, State University of New York at Buffalo, September 1971, p. 157.

20. C. Stabler, "For Many Corporations, Social Responsibility Is Now a Major Concern," *Wall Street Journal,* October 26, 1971, p. 1.

21. "Tokyo Airport Opens after Years of Strife," *Boston Globe,* May 20, 1978; E. and P. MacInnis, "Showdown at Narita," *Boston Globe*, May 20, 1978.

22. R. McLean, "Gargle Go-Round Has Ad Industry Gagging," *Boston Globe,* April 9, 1978.

23. D. Aker and G. Day, "Corporate Responses to Consumerism Pressures," *Harvard Business Review* 50 (November–December 1972): 110–121.

24. Y. Ibrahim, "The Metamorphosis of the Shareholders' Meeting," *New York Times,* April 9, 1978, sec. 3, p. 9.

25. L. Smith, "The Boardroom Is Becoming a Different Scene," *Fortune*, May 8, 1978, p. 151.

26. W. Guzzardi, Jr., "Business Is Learning How to Win in Washington," *Fortune,* March 27, 1978, pp. 53–58.

27. M. Jensen, "A Market Thirst Never Quenched," *New York Times,* April 8, 1978, sec. 3.

28. Guzzardi, "Business Is Learning How to Win In Washington."

29. Chamber of Commerce of the United States, Council on Trends and Perspective, *The Corporation in Transition* (Washington, D.C.: Chamber of Commerce of the United States, 1971).

30. D. Linowes, *The Corporate Conscience* (New York: Hawthorne Books, 1974); J. Paluszek, *Business and Society: 1976–2000* (New York: American Management Association, 1976); A. Carroll, ed., *Managing Corporate Social Responsibility* (Boston: Little, Brown, 1977).

31. W. Hegarty, J. Aplin, and R. Cosier, "Achieving Corporate Success in External Affairs: A Management Challenge," *Business Horizons,* in press.

32.   M. Weidenbaum, "The High Cost of Government Regulation," *Business Horizons* 18 (August 1975): 43–51.

33.   D. Fetyko, "The Company Social Audit," *Management Accounting* 10 (April 1975): 135–148.

34.   "End of the Great Engine Flap," *Time*, January 2, 1978, p. 66; "GM Settles Engine Cases in 44 States," *Boston Globe*, December 20, 1977; "Costly Auto Troubles," *Business Week*, January 9, 1978, p. 30.

Chapter 22

The International Environment

Coca-Cola

International and Multinational Firms
    Reasons for International and Multinational Operations
    Forms of International Involvement

Comparative Management versus International Management
    Comparative Management Adjustments
    International Management Adjustments

Environmental Constraints
    Legal Constraints
    Political Constraints
    Economic Constraints
    Cultural Constraints

Foreign Management Assignments

Implications for the Manager

Review

Laker's Skytrain

This chapter contributed by
PROFESSOR JOHN D. DANIELS,
The Pennsylvania State University

Learning Objectives

When you have finished reading and studying this chapter, you should be able to:

1. Identify and give reasons for international and multinational involvement.
2. Compare and contrast domestic, international, and multinational forms of operation.
3. Identify and show the differences among different forms of international involvement.
4. Identify and contrast comparative and international management adjustments.
5. Identify and give examples of the various environmental constraints affecting international operations.
6. List several ways of staffing international and multinational operations.
7. Define and be able to use the following concepts:

domestic organization	consortium
international organization	constraints
multinational organization	comparative management
subsidiary	international management

Thought Starters

1. What effect do other parts of the world have on your life?
2. How much is your life affected by multinational companies?
3. Name five products that have been produced or distributed in the United States by multinational companies based elsewhere.

The Coca-Cola Company

The Coca-Cola Company has been in business for about ninety years. It has annual sales of over $3 billion and operates in about 150 different countries. In 1976, some 55 percent of its profits came from foreign operations. Much of the company's growth is due to its secret formula for producing Coke; the formula is the basis for a syrup that is sold to wholesalers and bottlers.

Coca-Cola also has many other products besides Coke. For example, it owns Taylor and Great Western wines, Tab, Fresca, and Sprite. It produces orange juice and instant coffee and tea products, including Minute Maid and Butter-Nut. One of its wholly-owned subsidiaries is Aqua-Chem, a company that designs and manufactures equipment for desalting sea water and other related equipment.

For Coca-Cola, the world is divided into three parts, with an executive vice-president in charge of each. One part involves operations in the United States and Central and South America. Another involves Europe, Africa, Southeast Asia, and the Indian subcontinent. The third involves Canada, the Pacific, and the Far East.

Dealing in the multinational market requires decisions and strategies considerably different from those made by organizations operating only in one country. For example, when Coca-Cola gave an Israeli firm a franchise to bottle and sell Coke in Israel, in 1967, Coke was promptly boycotted in the Arab countries. However, Coca-Cola has technology and know-how that the Arab countries need. Aqua-Chem, for example, is expert in water desalination, and Saudi Arabia alone is planning to spend billions of dollars in desalting over the next few years. Coca-Cola's foods division has expertise in agriculture, and the Arabs are interested in developing their agricultural know-how. The company hopes that this expertise will re-open the door to selling Coke to the Arab world.

India has posed a different kind of problem. The Indian government insists that multinationals transfer some of their knowledge and ownership to Indian nationals. Coca-Cola refuses to give up the confidentiality of its secret formula and has thus discontinued selling Coke in India. Refusal has meant the loss of the lucrative Indian market, but management feels that disclosure of the secret formula would be even more adverse to the company's interests.

Even if Coca-Cola had no foreign sales or production facilities, its operations would still be highly affected by the international environment. Imports are essential for two of the company's major products— soft drinks and coffee. Almost all coffee must be imported, and about half the sugar used in soft drinks comes from foreign sources.[1]

The Coca-Cola case shows the increasing importance of the international environment for both imports and exports. This importance is further demonstrated by the fact that approximately one-third of U.S. corporate profits now come from foreign operations of U.S. firms. Projections also indicate that by the turn of the century the United States will be completely dependent on foreign suppliers for such scarce resources as aluminum, manganese, tin, cobalt, and tungsten.[2] Conditions such as rising wages in the United States and the rise and fall of the dollar are other illustrations of how the U.S. economy is linked to an international economy.

The Coca-Cola case also shows the conflicts of interests between company and national interests. The decision to franchise in Israel led to the boycott in the Arab countries. India's desire to help its nationals become knowledgeable resulted in Coca-Cola's withdrawal from that country. The 1973 oil embargo is another illustration of conflicts of interests. The Arab embargo was directed primarily at the United States. The major U.S. oil companies had to enforce (at least partially) an embargo of their own country in order to satisfy both the Arab countries and their other customers around the world. Clearly, this was not a pleasing prospect for them.

This chapter will explore the reasons for international and multinational involvement, the different forms of such involvement, management practices in various countries, and environmental constraints on international management. Organizations become multinational in order to expand the alternatives open to them, to obtain scarce resources, or to compete more effectively with other organizations. Dealing in the international arena requires managerial strategies and decisions considerably different from those used by organizations operating in only one country.

International and Multinational Firms

A continuum exists from the domestic company to the international company to the multinational company, as Figure 22.1 shows. A **domestic organization** limits its purchases and sales to a single country. An **international organization** has interests that cut across national boundaries; it imports or exports goods, services, or products. Examples of such organizations are firms that buy uncut diamonds from Amsterdam or that import Oriental rugs from Iraq or India. Even a small U.S. bakery located close to the Canadian border that sells some of its bread in Canada is

Domestic	International	Multinational
Purchases and sales only within one country	Direct purchases and/or sales in home country and one or more host countries	Usually, one or more subsidiaries in host countries

Figure 22.1   Domestic, international, and multinational operations

considered an international organization. The term *multinational firm,* which did not appear in any dictionary until the 1970s, has been defined several ways in both textbooks and common usage.[3] As will be seen later, a **multinational organization** usually is a company that has one or more subsidiaries abroad and that is willing to go anyplace in the world to secure resources and to make sales. This chapter will pay more attention to multinational than to international organizations, since multinationals often have their objectives set on a global rather than a national basis.

There has been no worldwide census to determine the exact sizes and characteristics of international companies; however, the many fragments of information available all indicate that they are a large and growing influence.[4] Indeed, it is fairly safe to say that nearly all large companies headquartered in the free world are either international or multinational. The only general exceptions are utility companies and certain transportation firms; most countries simply do not allow foreign ownership of such industries.

Not all international companies are large; in fact, some companies with yearly sales of less than $1 million have acquired international status. However, the large firms receive most of the publicity because of the enormous power they wield. One rather startling fact is that if the hundred largest world organizations were ranked in terms of output, forty-nine of the top hundred would be nations (as measured by their gross national product), and the other fifty-one would be international companies (as measured by their yearly sales).

Today, most people will at some time work for an international company, unless they are exclusively employed throughout their career by a government agency or nonprofit organization. This means that many people will have to make decisions about operations in countries that have different operating environments and conditions than those in the United States. It may also mean the weighing of decisions that are best for the company as a whole but not necessarily for either the company's U.S. operations or the economic, political, and social objectives of the United States.

U.S. citizens working in the United States for foreign-owned companies may come to question some operating and management practices imported from abroad. They may also question whether they can aspire to top-level management positions or whether these will be reserved to citizens of the country that has set up operations in the United States.

There is a considerable difference among multinationals on the degree to which they are known as foreign entities in their overseas operating locales. At one extreme are companies such as Volkswagen and Honda, which were well-known as being German and Japanese long before they announced that they were setting up manufacturing facilities in the United States. Many other companies, however, have developed such a local profile that most people are unaware of their foreign ownership. Few people in the United States, for example, realize that Nescafé is a Swiss firm, Norelco a Dutch firm, and Bic a French firm—all with manufacturing facilities in the United States. Likewise some U.S. companies operating abroad are equally unknown as such in some of their foreign markets. In England, for instance, Hoover, Heinz, and Woolworth are so deeply entrenched that they are generally thought of as British rather than American. It is even common in England for people to say that a carpet has been Hoovered rather than vacuumed.

Reasons for International and Multinational Operations

Foreign operations expand the alternatives available to domestic companies. Since markets abroad imply additional people and income, companies should usually be able to expect a greater sales potential by operating internationally rather than only domestically. By selling abroad, companies can take greater advantage of market opportunities and can effect various internal economies by being able to cover fixed costs more readily and to recoup research and development expenditures before competitors have an opportunity to emulate advancements in the market.

There are many other ways in which costs can be reduced through foreign operations. One method is to acquire cheaper inputs to production in the form of labor, raw materials, power, or capital. The French firm, Pechiney, for example, mines bauxite in New Caledonia but processes it in the northwestern part of the United States, where electric power is relatively cheap. Another method is to develop risk aversion strategies by acquiring scarce resources or buying existing sales outlets abroad so that competitors are prevented from gaining control over essential supplies or markets. Since business cycles vary among countries, the dependence on multiple rather than one-country markets may help stabilize a company's earnings as well.[5]

Forms of International Involvement

Companies that use international markets usually follow multiple strategies for their operations. Some of these strategies are unique to international operations and require personnel with specialized knowledge to advise on and manage the needed functions. For example, exporting goods from one country to another involves special transportation, packaging, documentation, and financing, as well as knowledge of the laws and customs in the host country. In terms of exporting, there are six general methods: individual sales, exclusive sales agreements, independent agents, branch offices, subsidiary companies, and joint export organizations.

Individual Sales

The first step in exporting is often individual sales to host company buyers. However, this approach may pose problems in terms of collecting payment, and it does not usually secure a steady flow of export orders. Usually, intensive exports can be achieved only if a permanent sales organization is established in the host country to create and maintain a demand for the goods and to provide the home organization with firsthand information on the special requirements of the market and the actions of the competition. Thus establishing a permanent sales organization is strongly favored, and a company that wants to export on a permanent basis usually chooses one or more of the other five possibilities.[6]

Exclusive Sales Agreements

Under exclusive sales agreements the exporter or seller grants the buyer in the host country sole rights to handle specific goods, products, or services in a particular geographical area. The buyer agrees to rely on the seller as the sole source of supply from the home country. The contract usually provides the general terms on which individual sales will be made. For example, suppose a typewriter manufacturer in the United States signs an exclusive sales contract with an importer in India. The agreement may provide that the U.S. manufacturer cannot sell typewriters to other firms in India and that the Indian purchaser cannot purchase typewriters made by other firms in the United States.

Independent Agents

Independent agents sell goods or services in the host country and receive commissions on the sales. They frequently have the authority to give credit and to receive direct payments for the goods. Companies that use independent agents must rely heavily on their judgment and discretion. Thus they must choose such agents carefully.

Branch Offices

In some cases, exporters establish branch offices abroad and staff them with their own employees. Many organizations prefer this arrangement because it gives them direct control over the company's foreign market activities. This arrangement requires sufficient sales volume to warrant the expense of having employees in host companies. Furthermore, if the employees are of the same nationality as the exporter, two sets of laws must be followed—those of the home country and those of the host country. Of course, if the employees are residents of the host country, the exporters usually must comply only with the local employment laws.

Subsidiary Companies

The most favored form of modern export trading is the establishment of a subsidiary company in the country into which the exports are directed. The **subsidiary** is wholly owned by the parent company but is incorporated under the laws of the host country. It possesses separate and independent legal rights and has the same status in the host country as any other firm in that country. The subsidiary is controlled by the parent firm, which may hold a majority of its shares. In some countries (such as Nigeria) foreign companies can carry on business only through the incorporation of a domestic company.[7] By establishing one or more subsidiaries abroad, a parent company becomes a multinational enterprise—"a combination of companies of different nationality, connected by means of shareholdings, managerial control, or contract and constituting an economic unit."[8]

There are a number of legal and other problems involving multinational organizations. For example, the interests of the host country in which the subsidiary is formed may conflict with those of the home country of the multinational. In such cases, the laws and public policies of the host country prevail over those of the home country. As another example, in the European Community—also known as the European Common Market—the various subsidiaries of the multinational are treated as a single unit, even when they are in different countries of the Common Market.

Joint Export Organization

Increasing attention is being paid in modern export trade to combined exporting. The basic characteristics of this method are that a number of economically independent manufacturers or merchants set up a joint organization in order to coordinate their exports, but they keep their freedom of action in other respects. The cooperation may be very tight or relatively loose. The two most important forms of cooperative exporting are joint selling organizations and consortiums.

Joint selling organizations can take many forms. In one, a group of manufacturers or other companies form a marketing company to operate in a particular foreign territory; the expenses are shared by the members in some agreed-on way. Another involves an independent company with overseas branches that acts as the selling organization for a limited number of manufacturers. The manufacturers contribute as a group to the overhead expenses of the sales organization and are charged individually with any costs that are unique to an individual company.[9]

Consortium

A **consortium** is an organization created when two or more companies cooperate so as to act as a single entity for a specific and usually limited purpose. For example, the Society of Lloyds, better-known as Lloyds of London, is a group of insurance underwriters who join together to cover certain insurance risks that are too great for any individual underwriter.

Other forms of international involvement include *international licensing*—the sale to an organization in a host country of the right to use patents, trademarks, or other intangible assets. For these transactions, it is especially important to have personnel with specialized legal knowledge, since each country treats these assets and their transfer differently. Another form of involvement abroad is the foreign management (for a fee) of a facility in a host country. Finally, in what is known as a turnkey operation, an organization or a consortium will build facilities in a host country for a local organization to eventually own and run. In theory, all the host country has to do after the preliminary agreements is to "turn the key" to start the facility. Often these facilities are automobile, cement, or fertilizer plants. Management contracts and turnkey operations have been growing in importance, because countries such as Iran, Saudi Arabia, and the Soviet Union wish to use Western management and technological expertise while maintaining ownership for themselves.

Comparative Management versus International Management

Comparative management is the study of differences among management practices in various countries, usually with an attempt to determine which environmental conditions have been responsible for the different norms of managerial behavior. **International management** focuses on practices at the worldwide corporate level, since coordination of the activities in each of the countries where the multinational company operates usually occurs at this level. Both comparative and international management are, of course, important to multinational companies.

Comparative Management Adjustments

Comparative management is useful in that it helps identify the areas in which a firm may need to alter its operating methods for a particular country. When an multinational firm observes that management practices in a given foreign country are different from those at home, this should alert the firm to the possibility that it may have to adapt its operations to fit the local norm. Of course, the multinational company operating abroad should not necessarily operate exactly the same as local firms. To do so risks the possibility that competitive innovations will not be adopted. Indeed, an important advantage of a multinational may be its efficient management techniques, which competitors may not be following. However, to assume on entering a host country that one can do there exactly what has been done at home is also not wise. There may be legal, political, or cultural obstacles to the introduction of such methods that could result in failure.

How do multinational companies react to comparative management differences? Over the past decade, a large number of studies have confirmed what has long been suspected—that management and personnel practices vary substantially from country to country. Some of these studies describe practices on a country to country basis, and some compare attitudes of managers from different countries.[10] Studies of multinationals' reactions to the differences indicate an overall attempt to infuse into foreign operations many of the multinationals' previous practices.

Many managers think they can reduce the risk of failure by managing their foreign operations in a manner similar to their home operations. Many others believe that differences from country to country are so inconsequential that they can make their home country practices work anywhere. For example, a good deal of evidence exists that U.S. firms (more so than Japanese or French ones) tend to replace labor with capital intensive operating methods because of the traditionally high labor costs and labor scarcity in the United States. These companies are often criticized for using inappropriate technology in the labor abundant less-developed countries.

The implementation of home country practices does not mean that multinationals transfer all their practices intact to their host country subsidiaries. Most of such operations tend to be hybrids of home country practices and local ones. This is true for multinational companies from other countries as well as the United States. There are a number of reasons for this. One is that for a long time (until the late 1960s) many of the developed nations revered U.S. management practices. Now, more and more managers in host countries have graduate degrees in management and are as well-versed in good management practices as U.S. managers. In some countries—such as West Germany, France, Sweden, and Japan—managers are somewhat critical and unaccepting of U.S. managerial practices.

A second reason for hybridization is that when a firm establishes a subsidiary in a host country, the parent organization frequently sends a whole battery of personnel. But as time goes on, these people are replaced with more and more citizens of the host country—especially in countries requiring work permits. Even when U.S. managers remain in foreign operations, they tend to shift their management styles to conform to local styles.

There is some evidence that the larger and more experienced multinational firms can use similar management techniques in all countries because of their size and/or the oligopolistic nature of their worldwide markets.[11] For example, a large U.S. automobile manufacturer wanted to construct a new plant in England. Because of the impact the plant would have on England's economy, the company was able to get the government to modify a number of rules, regulations, and policies as an inducement for it to build there. These modifications allowed the foreign subsidiary to operate with management techniques similar to those in the United States. Thus large multinationals can have a great deal of influence on host countries, particularly if these countries are relatively small ones.

**International
Management
Adjustments**

From a corporate standpoint, the operations in foreign countries have to be coordinated and controlled. Although constraints are placed on management because of the diverse country-to-country environments in which their companies operate, the parent firm still has to determine which decisions will be made by managers in the foreign country and which by managers at some regional or corporate headquarters. The corporate organization must thus establish the location of decision making, communications flow, and integration of activities.

Management policies and practices should be looked at from the corporate viewpoint as well as the country-by-country one because many decisions that are optimal for a given subsidiary are not optimal for overall corporate objectives. Corporate management is therefore particularly prone to control decision making that will affect more than one operating unit or that will minimize profits for a subsidiary in order to maximize profits for the corporation itself. Suppose a company is manufacturing the same product in both Canada and England. Corporate management may dictate that the two operations either can or cannot export the product to the other's market. Only at the corporate level can the overall repercussions of the decision be seen.

International management therefore includes the study of the transfer of resources (including managers) among entities in different countries where the companies are operating, organizational structures to cover multinational activities, and strategy development in a global context. Multinational companies need to study management from both a comparative and an international perspective. Comparative studies help them learn how to operate better in the countries where they have facilities. International management helps them learn how to coordinate and control the activities among these countries.

Environmental Constraints

Constraints are restrictions or limitations on managerial actions. Environmental conditions are one reason that management practices differ from country to country. Although these practices involve every aspect of business operations—including marketing, finance, and accounting—the following discussion will center primarily on the ones involving overall policy questions and interpersonal relationships. The number of environmental constraints is great; thus the discussion is representative rather than conclusive.

Legal Constraints

Each country has its own set of laws, and these laws are a combination of formalized and traditional practices. It is often difficult for multinational companies to recognize that all countries have certain laws that are either not enforced or are enforced unevenly and certain practices that, although not specified in the written law, are nevertheless so customary that all companies are expected to follow them. Multinationals are apt to face more difficulties than domestic companies because their managers may lack the long-term experience of recognizing the subtle differences between law and practice. Furthermore, multinationals may receive a great deal more criticism than domestic companies for not following the letter of the law. For example, in many countries, the tax law is something to be circumvented rather than followed by most individuals and organizations. However, if the multinational circumvents it to the extent that local firms do, it may cause a public outcry or even be expelled from the country.

There is also a great deal of variation among countries concerning who can be hired by a firm. In the United States, for example, there has been a move toward nondiscrimination by sex, religion, race, and national origin. At the other extreme is South Africa, a country that specifies by race who can legally take which job. As another example, at the same time that the retirement age in the United States has been moved up to seventy, in Japan it has been forced down to fifty-five—a radical departure from decades of Japanese practice under which older people were revered and kept in positions until they reached a very advanced age. Most Western European countries have also been moving toward a lower mandated retirement age.

Most countries do not recognize the practice of laying off workers during slack periods. Instead, if a company wishes to reduce the work force, it must fire people and pay them settlement sums required by law. A number of countries actually prohibit the firing of employees after they have worked a specified period of time. In these countries, the only way a company can fire people is by declaring bankruptcy—and then the employees have priority over creditors or stockholders to the assets of the business. In these sorts of situations there is great pressure on management to stabilize production output.

Another area of marked contrast to U.S. practice is the policy of codetermination now followed in most Western European countries and being introduced in parts of Latin America. Under this policy, labor representatives are included in management or on boards of directors. The inclusion ensures not only that workers gain information that normally is kept from them but also that they share in policy-making decisions. Some of the countries that include workers on boards of directors are Sweden, Norway, and West Germany. The concept has also been proposed in Great Britain.

Political Constraints

Multinational companies usually must receive permission from political authorities in the country where they plan to operate before setting up facilities. In order to get the permission, they may have to agree in advance to follow certain practices. Recent negotiations with foreign governments have dealt with such issues as what a firm will do about pollution, whose ships will carry its merchandise, how much of its earnings will be reinvested, and who will serve in its management and on its board of directors. Once these issues are resolved, the multinationals may find themselves operating under a political system very different from their own. Today, companies operate in communist as well as capitalist countries and in dictatorial as well as democratic ones.

Because of the large size of multinational companies in relation to the small size of some host countries, their operations often are scrutinized at the highest level of government. Even in the Soviet Union, corporate leaders such as Armand Hammer of Occidental Petroleum or Henry Ford II of Ford Motor Company talk directly to top-level officials at the Kremlin. This can have some adverse effects on the company. It often forces managers to deal directly with systems with which they do not agree personally, and the close connections with foreign government leaders often results in adverse public opinion at home about the firm's foreign operations. A growing problem is the development of joint operations between a company and a government. Standard Oil of Indiana, for example, shares ownership of fertilizer plants with the government of India. Often, such governments have as their objectives the maximization of employment or minimization of prices, and these objectives must take precedence over the maximization of profits.

Economic Constraints

Each country has its own economic and social conditions. For example, small countries often are plagued by low levels of education, poor social services, inadequate transportation facilities and utilities, high levels of unemployment, and small markets. These conditions may necessitate a substantial alteration in the production process. For example, a high unemployment rate leads to both low wage rates and a desire by government authorities to absorb as many people as possible into the work force. The result is that companies may have to use labor-intensive types of production instead of the machine-oriented production common to industrialized countries.[12]

While this seems to be a logical move, it is not without drawbacks. The low levels of education may necessitate additional training and supervision, and qualified supervisors are usually in short supply. Quality control and product uniformity are additional problems when people are used instead of machines. In Costa Rica, McDonald's is using people rather than machines to cut up the potatoes used for french fries. The potatoes are, of course, less uniform; but this creates no problem, since they are sold only within Costa Rica. If a company is trying to export and compete in world markets, however, quality control and consistency assume greater importance.

The economic system may also prohibit many of the practices that keep firms competitive on the world market. In the Soviet Union, for example, multinational companies are prohibited from owning production facilities and from promoting their products as they do at home. Some U.S. steel producers have argued that the very close connection between Japanese firms and their government makes it almost impossible to export products into that market because locally owned firms are favored regardless of price. In other countries, certain areas are heavily controlled by government agencies. Pharmaceuticals, for example, may be sold almost entirely through government agencies as part of a national health plan.

By controlling the economy, governments can substantially affect the control that an individual company has on its decision making. If, for example, a company is prohibited from remitting back home most of its profits from an overseas operation, its funds must be reinvested abroad to a great extent. This can lead the company to engage in new lines of endeavor in order to use up the funds and, in the process, to shift the location of decision making elsewhere.

Cultural Constraints

Norms, or standards of behavior, vary from country to country. They are difficult to assess and thus are one of the more subtle environmental constraints facing companies as they expand abroad. There is growing evidence that a certain few behavioral variables have the greatest effect on these companies. The most important variables are:

1. *The prestige of work and of particular occupations within the society.* Some societies, for example, hold the pursuit of leisure in much higher esteem than do other societies. Thus the axiom that some people live to work and others work to live has considerable validity for international comparisons. For the workers themselves, there are also differences in the types of occupations to which they aspire. Most people want to work in occupations that have higher prestige than others. Since business and management are held in fairly high esteem in the United States, highly qualified persons are prone to seek careers in them, whereas in, say, Argentina, large numbers of qualified persons shirk business in favor of other professions.

2. *How managers react on the job.* Studies comparing managers from different countries have indicated that there are significant differences in willingness to take personal responsibility for solving problems, in setting achievement goals, in taking calculated risks, and in requesting concrete feedback about performance.

3. *The desire for individual versus group oriented compensation.* In societies where individual achievement is revered, the work force tends to be mobile in terms of changing employers and locations. The workers also tend to prefer monetary compensation as a direct form of feedback on their perceived worth. In other societies, such as Japan and parts of Latin America, fringe benefits may substantially exceed the amount of direct compensation given to employees. These benefits often include transportation to and from work, lunches at work, bonuses at Christmas, time off for the funerals of even distant relatives, and gifts to employees' children when they are married or graduated from school. This attitude also affects decision making. In group oriented societies, workers and managers frown on individual decision making, preferring group consensus.

4. *The identification of individuals with certain groups.* The group affiliations are based on such things as sex, family, age, caste, religion, political preference, membership in associations, ethnic background, race, and occupation. Membership in the various groups often reflects the degree of access to economic resources, prestige, social relations, and power. If a company does not understand the subtle or overt manifestations of these group affiliations, it may hire people who will be unacceptable to their peers and subordinates.

5. *Social mobility.* The more open or mobile the society, the more likely it is that anyone can be chosen to fill a position strictly on the basis of qualifications for the job. Of course, even in the mobile and open society of the United States, it has been only in the last few years that certain occupations have become open to various groups. For example, nurses, elementary school teachers, and secretaries are almost always women; and airline pilots, religious ministers, and trash collectors are almost always men. There is certainly no innate ability that makes either group more qualified than the other for these occupations. It is simply that tradition or culture has dictated certain occupational norms. Other countries deviate from the U.S. norm in many areas, including occupation.

These are but a few examples of cultural differences that affect foreign business operations. They do indicate, however, that when a multinational company operates abroad, it should proceed with caution. Before introducing any change into the environment, it should determine if the benefits of that change are worth the costs that will be incurred. Then, if the change is still thought to be a good one, the company should take care to assure that local persons participate in the actual decision making and in the rewards brought about by it. There may, however, be obstacles because of the importance of the change to people in the host society, because social structures may be upset, or because the time is simply not right for modifying practices or implementing new ones.

Foreign Management Assignments

When a multinational company sets up operating facilities, management contracts, or turnkey operations abroad, one major problem is staffing the foreign operation. Most positions are filled by nationals of the host country. This is done for many reasons, among them: (1) it is usually less expensive to hire local people than to bring in people from the outside, (2) governments often prohibit the hiring of foreigners, and (3) local people are familiar with the environment in which the business is to be conducted.

Besides using local people, multinational companies also transfer large numbers of U.S. citizens from one country to another. It is estimated that there are as many as one hundred thousand U.S. employees working for multinational companies outside the United States. Most of them are managers who have been transferred to foreign operations in order to implement certain management practices abroad or to ensure that corporate policy is followed. Those who are not managers are largely engineers and technicians who have been hired to work on turnkey projects in remote areas of the world.

Two other types of expatriate management are of growing importance to multinational companies. One is transferring a foreign national in a foreign operation to another foreign country (for example, transferring a British manager to an Australian operation because that person may know the culture better than a U.S. manager would). The other is transferring a foreign manager at a foreign operation to U.S. corporate headquarters. IBM and Mobil Oil, for example, now have non-U.S. managers of proven ability filling some of their top-level positions in the United States.

Regardless of the type of foreign assignment, the expatriate and his or her family must face some substantial adjustments. If they do not make these adjustments satisfactorily, then the person's ability to manage abroad may be hampered.[13] Since it is extremely costly to move a manager with family to a foreign assignment, the company should do everything possible to assure that the person will be accepted by other employees and will view foreign living conditions as satisfactory. There is near consensus among such companies that an important attribute for someone being considered for a foreign assignment is the technical mastery of the job, because this proficiency can help the person become accepted by other employees. Of course, the expatriate manager may still face problems on the job, not only because of the changed operating environment but also because the distance from the home office makes it difficult to get staff assistance.

In terms of living conditions, spouses are sometimes prevented by local regulations from accepting any type of employment, which can make foreign assignments cumbersome for husbands and wives who both want careers. Children may have to go to very different types of schools. Housing is usually difficult to find and is expensive, and managers are usually forced to rent rather than purchase a home. Changes in language and eating habits may necessitate further adjustments. It is generally agreed that these adjustments in living conditions make it difficult for managers to perform their tasks successfully. There is little consensus, however, on how to cope with the adjustment problem.

Implications for the Manager

International and multinational firms are becoming increasingly important to the world's economy. Organizations expand to multinationals in order to widen the alternatives open to them, to obtain scarce resources, or to deal more effectively with competition. Coca-Cola, one of the largest multinationals, operates in about 150 different countries.

International and multinational organizations can use a number of management strategies. For example, they can sell or purchase directly, have exclusive sales agreements, deal with independent agents, or establish branch offices in host countries. They can establish subsidiary companies controlled by the parent company but subject to the laws and regulations of the host country. They can use joint export organizations for large projects. (The Organization of Petroleum Exporting Countries [OPEC] has had a tremendous influence on the Western world, and this influence may well increase.) They can provide technical advice and services—for example, building a facility such as a cement or fertilizer plant that will be operated by the host country. In theory, all the other country has to do is begin operations. In the majority of cases, however, the country manages the operation until local managers and workers can be trained to take over.

Management practices can and do vary widely from country to country, usually because of legal, political, economic, and cultural constraints. But some similarities exist too. The effective manager must be sensitive to both the similarities and the differences. A U.S. manager working for a Japanese or German company that operates in the United States must also be sensitive to the different norms and values of the particular organization.

Because of differing laws and customs and of other variables, the effective manager who wants to become involved in international or multinational operations must become thoroughly familiar with the specific host country. Operations management in the international environment is a highly complex process.

Review

1. Discuss the reasons for the growth of multinational firms. Do you think this growth will continue? Explain.
2. Discuss the differences among domestic, international, and multinational forms of operation.
3. Identify and give examples of six basic forms of international involvement.
4. In what ways might legal, political, economic, and cultural constraints affect international or multinational operations?
5. Reread the Radio Shack case in Chapter 8. What suggestions do you have for the management of Radio Shack?
6. What is the difference between a subsidiary and a consortium?
7. Several examples of foreign-owned organizations with manufacturing operations in the United States are given in the chapter. Using personal experience, the library, or any other sources, list at least five more of these organizations.
8. List five foreign countries. In what ways might managing in these countries be the same as managing in the United States? In what ways might it be different?
9. Interview a manager working for a multinational company (for example, a foreign car dealer). What advantages and disadvantages does the manager see in working for a multinational?

The Laker Skytrain

Laker Airlines flew its first daily Skytrain from London to New York on September 26, 1977. The Skytrain is a new approach to international travel—no frills and no reservations; tickets are sold on a first-come, first-served basis. The cost of a round trip from New York to London is approximately $236. On other airlines, such as British Airways or American Airlines, the cost for an economy class ticket with no restrictions on the purchase of the ticket or on the stay at the destination is approximately $626 for reserved seats. On Laker's Skytrain there are no free meals and coffee. Passengers pay $3 for dinner and $2 for breakfast; coffee costs 30 cents.

Skytrain is a personal victory for Frederick A. Laker, the president of Laker Airways. An operator of charter flights, he battled the British and American governments, the International Air Transportation Association (IATA), and every major airline flying planes between the United States and Europe. The battle took six years, and part of it continues. Laker is now battling for approval to operate unlimited flights across the Atlantic—essentially a continuous trans-Atlantic shuttle service. He also wants to start a Skytrain service from London to Australia at sharply reduced fares.

The other airlines initially opposed Laker's plan because they felt the reduced fares would cut sharply into their own business. Laker, however, argued that the reduced fares would actually attract more passengers, especially those who could not afford the higher cost of either the charter flights or the regularly scheduled flights. Studies made since the Skytrain was introduced have proven Laker right. New business has been generated for both Laker and the other airlines that have lowered fares under special conditions.

When Laker's first plane landed at Kennedy Airport, Laker blasted the IATA, whose approval must be gotten for any changes in fares by the member airlines. Among other things, he said: "The purpose of IATA is to keep lazy airline executives in a job where they don't have to think. All the airlines are flying the same aircraft, on the same routes, at practically the same time and are spending money advertising their plastic sandwiches." Suggesting that the IATA should be abolished, he added: "Thirty years ago, the big carriers got together and wrote a charter which said air travel should be for the benefit of mankind. I assure you that was the last time those carriers, or any others, gave any thought to mankind . . . until today."

The breakthrough in the struggle came in February 1977, when the British government decided to drop its long-running court battle with Laker Airlines. Laker had already won two earlier court victories. The U.S. Civil Aeronautics Board (CAB) also approved Skytrain.

Now, a number of airlines have a variety of reduced air fares. For example, passengers can fly standby from New York to London on some other airlines for $256. Tickets for these trips can be purchased in advance, but seats are assigned only on the day of departure on a first-come, first-served basis. Budget flights on the other airlines for the same amount of money allow passengers to buy tickets three weeks in advance. The airlines then notify passengers at least seven days in advance of their flight date.

1. What types of constraints were operating in this case?
2. What impact might reduced air fares have on charter flight airlines?
3. What purposes should associations such as the IATA have?
4. What managerial roles do you think Laker was following during the six years of his dispute with other airlines and the government?
5. What assumptions were being made by Laker? By the IATA?

Footnotes

1. *Moody's OTC Industrial Manual,* (New York: Moody's Investors Services, 1977); "The Graying of the Soft-Drink Company," *Business Week*, May 23, 1977, pp. 68–72; "Coca-Cola Co. Seeking Access to Soviet Union, China and Middle East," *Wall Street Journal*, November 8, 1977, p. 21; M. Jensen, "The American Corporate Presence in South Africa," *New York Times*, December 4, 1977, p. D1; K. Rangan, "Give Up Knowhow or Leave Country," *New York Times*, August 9, 1977, p. 45.
2. C. Bergstein and W. Cline, "Increasing International Interdependence," *American Economic Review* 66 (May 1976): 155–162.
3. J. Behrman, *Some Patterns in the Rise of the Multinational Enterprise* (Chapel Hill, N.C.: University of North Carolina Press, 1969).
4. Department of Economic and Social Affairs of the United Nations, *Multinational Corporations in World Development* (New York: United Nations, 1973).
5. E. Daniels, E. Ogram, Jr., and L. Radebaugh, *International Business: Environments and Operations* (Reading, Mass.: Addison-Wesley, 1976), chaps. 3 and 25.
6. C. Schmitthoff, *The Export Trade: The Law and Practice of International Trade,* 6th ed. (London: Stevens and Sons, 1975); I.

Brownlie, *Principles of Public International Law*, 2d ed. (Oxford, England: Oxford University Press, 1973).

7. Nigerian Decree No. 51 of 1968.
8. Schmitthoff, *The Export Trade*, p. 169.
9. G. MacEwan, *Overseas Trade and Export Practice* (London: Macdonald and Evans, 1938).
10. N. Farmer and B. Richman, *Comparative Management and Economic Progress*, rev. ed. (Bloomington, Ind.: Cedarwood Publishing, 1970).
11. J. D. Daniels and J. Arpan, "Comparative Home Country Influences on Management Practices Abroad," *Academy of Management Journal* 15 (Fall 1972): 305–315.
12. L. F. Wells, Jr., "Don't Overautomate Your Foreign Plant," *Harvard Business Review* 52 (January–February 1974): 111–118.
13. C. Arensberg and A. Niehoff, *Introducing Social Change: A Manual for Americans Overseas* (Chicago: Aldine Publishing, 1964).

Part VIII

A Conclusion and a Beginning

Chapter 23

Effective Managing —A Comparison and a Summary

The Bureau of Vital Statistics

Managing Business Organizations (the Private Sector)
    Why Large Businesses Exist
    Why Small Businesses Exist
    Managing in Different-Size Organizations

Managing in the Public Sector
    Reasons for the Existence of Organizations in the Public Sector
    Managing in Profit-Making and Government Organizations—A
    Comparative Approach

Managing Third Sector Organizations

Managing—Some Common Functions

Effective Managing—A Review and a Summary

Implications for the Manager

Review

The College President

Learning Objectives

When you have finished reading and studying this chapter, you should be able to:

1. Identify the differences between large and small organizations.
2. Compare and contrast managing in large and small organizations.
3. Compare and contrast managing in the private and public sectors.
4. Define and give examples of third sector organizations.
5. Give illustrations of managing in private, public, and third sector organizations.
6. Give illustrations of some common functions of managing.
7. Give illustrations of the unique functions of organizations.
8. Define and be able to use the following concepts:

private sector   third sector
public sector   entrepreneur

Thought Starters

1. What percentage of managers are in public administration?
2. What is a small business?
3. What does the term *third sector* mean to you?

The Bureau of Vital Statistics

A number of years ago, the director of a bureau of vital statistics faced a problem. The bureau, in the health department of a large city, had a number of tasks to perform. The three most important were (1) the receiving, recording, and issuing of birth certificates; (2) the receiving, recording, and issuing of death certificates; and (3) the maintenance of vital statistics dealing with births, deaths, hospital admissions, gunshot wounds, child abuse, and the like.

The new director was appalled to learn that it took three months for the bureau to issue a birth certificate and the same amount of time for it to issue a death certificate. The bureau had come under fire from state and federal agencies because of its six-month delay in reporting out the city's vital statistics. It had come under fire from parents each fall because of its delay in issuing birth certificates for children's admission to kindergarten. And it had come under fire from those who needed death certificates in order to collect survivor benefits from Social Security. The twelve clerks in the bureau were constantly being berated by unhappy citizens, and they felt themselves to be in a constant state of crisis.

The director first asked for funds to hire three more clerks to reduce the backlog. When the funds were denied (because of a lack of money in the budget), he discussed the problem with someone in the personnel department. Together, they decided to see if they could simplify the work—by studying tasks to see if any could be eliminated and by combining tasks to make the work flow easier.

At a meeting with the clerks, it was decided to thoroughly analyze the receiving and issuing of birth certificates, since this task caused the most problems. The clerks were enthusiastic about the possibility of reducing the pressure they all felt. Since there was no time for studying and analyzing the tasks during the day, the group decided to work extra hours two afternoons a week. Provided with forms and procedures, they began to analyze the work flow process. Since the process had evolved over the years, many overlaps, duplications, and unnecessary procedures were found and eliminated. Elated with their success, the group went on to study all the bureau's tasks.

Six months later, the bureau looked very different. The work was caught up, and it was common for a request for a birth or death certificate to be honored the same day it was received. The number of employees in the bureau had dropped from twelve to ten (two clerks had transferred to other departments), and the group knew that the bureau could actually manage with one person less. Three months later, an opportunity for a promotion occurred, and the total staff of the bureau was reduced to nine clerks and the director.

This case illustrates a dilemma that almost all managers face—how to plan, organize, and control the work with available resources. Although the problem concerned a large municipality, the approaches used to solve it can be applied to almost any type of organization. The case also shows that managers do not exist only in manufacturing firms. As Chapter 1 pointed out, only 14 percent of all managers work in manufacturing, while about 20 percent work in public administration.

This chapter has two major thrusts:

1. To focus on some of the similarities and differences in managing different but related types of organizations: the private sector, the public sector, and the third sector.
2. To highlight some basic functions that managers perform in formal organizations of all kinds.

The **private sector** consists basically of profit-making organizations. The **public sector** consists of federal, state, and local government bodies. The **third sector** includes voluntary, semi-public, and semi-private organizations (such as private colleges, the Girl Scouts, the Postal Service, Amtrak, voting leagues, and so on).

Managing Business Organizations (the Private Sector)

Business firms come in numerous sizes and types. Because national and multinational firms are written about so often, we frequently think of them as the predominant kind of business firm. Actually, there are many small organizations. In fact, as Chapter 1 pointed out, approximately 98 percent of all U.S. firms employ fewer than fifty people. Some of the advantages and disadvantages of small and large firms will be discussed before similarities and differences in managing them are dealt with.

No single definition of *small business* is completely satisfactory. However, for loan purposes, the Small Business Administration (SBA) defines a *small business* as one that is independently owned and operated, is not dominant in its field, and has the following characteristics:

- Manufacturing—250 or fewer employees
- Retailing and service—$1 million or less annual sales
- Wholesaling—$5 million or less annual sales.[1]

Even with the SBA-developed guidelines for distinguishing between large and small businesses, the distinctions are not always clear (as was pointed out in Chapter 16). Nevertheless, the guidelines can be helpful in understanding some of the reasons for the existence of large and small businesses.[2]

Why Large Businesses Exist

Organizations have many advantages in being large and complex. Among them are technological ability, increased competition, and the maintenance of financial strength and stability. For example, General Motors and General Electric can spend an enormous amount of money on research and development and are probably more financially stable than most small organizations. Of course, the temporary bankruptcy of Lockheed and the failure of the Penn Central railroad indicate that these advantages do not always hold.

Technology. Mass production of automobiles is a good example of the effect of technology on size. In order to reach economy of scale, an organization must invest millions of dollars in highly specialized equipment. The cost would be prohibitively high if automobiles were to be manufactured by a small organization. In the same fashion, a modern oil refinery requires millions of dollars in capital equipment.

Competition. The economy of scale in manufacturing or purchasing frequently gives larger companies an edge over smaller ones. For example, a large food or grocery chain can usually buy its products more cheaply than can a small grocery store, since discounts are usually given for purchases over a given amount.

Financial strength. In many cases large firms have greater financial strength and stability than smaller ones. For example, Westinghouse makes a large variety of products. A reduced demand for one product does not necessarily mean a reduced demand for another. Sears, Roebuck can afford to take a loss on some of its merchandise while it makes a profit on other merchandise. A smaller firm might not be able to continue in business if demand for its products fell off.

Why Small Businesses Exist

There are many reasons for some organizations remaining small. These include greater flexibility, more personalized or specialized service, and limited demand for particular products. For example, a local garage can be much more effective than a large automobile company at "customizing" automobiles.

Greater flexibility. Large firms have much more of a management hierarchy and many more checks and balances than do small ones. As a result, smaller firms can shift to new products or services more easily. The suggestion has been made that had the originator of Pet Rocks been affiliated with a large firm, the product would never have been developed.

More personalized service. Many small firms, such as barber and beauty shops, are local. Their owners get to know the customers and can give personalized service. A local butcher shop or record shop will often have a much better understanding of the needs and wants of customers than will a large organization servicing many cities.

Limited demand. Some products are not needed on a large scale. While most men's and women's clothing is "ready to wear," a demand does exist for tailor-made or one-of-a-kind suits and dresses for which people are willing to pay extra. The gourmet or health food store is another example of a specialty firm that provides products unavailable elsewhere.

Managing in Different-Size Organizations

Although the distinction so far has been between large and small organizations, this is an oversimplification. Clearly, there exists a range of organizations from the very small (such as the corner grocery store) to the very large (such as General Motors). In addition, some organizations begin small and then grow. Of course, not all organizations grow, and not

Table 23.1 Managing in different-sized organizations

	Characteristics of company growth		
Organizational characteristic	Patterns of the first stage	Patterns of the second stage	Patterns of the third stage
Core problem	Survival	Management of growth	Managerial control and allocation of resources
Central function	Fusion of diverse talents and purposes into a unified company	Fission of general authority into specialized functions	Fusion of independent units into an interdependent union of companies
Control systems	Personal (inside); survival in marketplace (outside)	Cost centers and policy formulation (inside); growth potential (outside)	Profit centers and abstract performance criteria (inside); capital expansion potential (outisde)
Reward and motivation	Ownership, membership in the family	Salary, opportunities and problems of growth	Salary, performance bonus, stock options, peer prestige
Management style	Individualistic; direct management	Integrating specialists; collaborative management	Integrating generalists; collective management
Organization			
Structure	Informal	Functional specialists	Division organizations
CEO's primary task	Direct supervision of employees	Managing specialized managers	Managing generalist managers
Levels of management	Two	At least three	At least four

Table reproduced by permission from Louis B. Barnes and Simon A. Hershon, "Transferring Power in the Family Business," *Harvard Business Review*, July–August 1976): 109. Copyright © 1976 by the President and Fellows of Harvard College; all rights reserved.

all continue growing. Nevertheless, management approaches and management problems are somewhat different at different levels of growth or size, as shown in Table 23.1. Organizations do grow in stages, and each stage needs to be managed differently.[3]

Assume that an individual is starting a new business as an **entrepreneur**—a person who organizes and manages a business, taking a risk for the possibility of making a profit.

In Stage 1, the first problem is determining the specific niche that the organization is to fill in terms of products or services. If this is done properly, the organization will survive. Then, the central function of management is bringing together people with different talents and purposes and getting them to work together. Control systems are relatively simple and usually highly personal, and the managerial style is highly individualistic and direct, since all the employees are working for the chief executive officer—the person who has started the business. The structure of the organization is relatively informal, with few written rules and procedures. In the absence of formal policies, many decisions are made on an ad hoc basis. For example, how much sick leave an individual should get may be clearly stated in a large organization but determined on a personalized basis in a smaller firm.

Stage 2 presents different problems, and the managerial approach must be different. This stage usually has a steadily growing and perhaps diversified product line and a growing market for the products. Managing for survival is no longer a problem; instead, the core problem is managing for growth.

The increasing size and complexity of the organization leads to increasing specialization. Second-level management is involved in such specialized activities or departments as marketing, finance, engineering production, and personnel. Authority is split apart into the different functions.

The chief operating officer can no longer know as intimately as before all the details of the organization. Therefore, the management style is more collaborative. The top manager is working with specialists in a cooperative fashion, since one of the primary tasks is integrating their work. At the same time, their expert help is an aid in the decision-making process. The control function has also changed. Rather than being personal, it is exercised more through the development of cost centers and the establishment of policies.

For example, the top manager usually no longer knows the names of all the employees. Formal personnel policies, such as those involving vacations, sick leave, salary, and fringe benefits begin to emerge. Time clocks may be installed for hourly workers.

Planning has now changed. Rather than the more immediate and ad hoc planning that may have characterized the first stage, planning is now becoming formalized. Longer-range plans need to be developed and implemented throughout the organization. This implementation is done through the management hierarchy, and it requires more formalized rules and procedures.

At Stage 3, as shown in Table 23.1, the core problem shifts again. Now, it is one of overall control and allocation of resources throughout the organization—which now consists of at least four (and perhaps many more) levels.

The structure of the organization at this stage may be vastly different from the structure in the first and second stages. There may be divisional or other structures. Different product lines may have become different divisions or subsidiary companies. If the organization has become multinational, the divisionalization may be on an area basis as well (for example, North America, Latin America, Europe, and the Middle East).

The organization may have general managers in the main office and in decentralized units or divisions. These managers must work with other general managers and with functional specialists.

Thus, the control function shifts as well. At the first stage, control can be directly exercised by the individual manager. At the second stage, it requires the separation of general authority into specialized functions. At the third stage, it requires further coordination through such approaches as profit centers (for example, the Chevrolet division versus the Cadillac division of General Motors).

Planning is now highly formalized, with planning units set up at different levels of the organization to assist both top management and division management. Policies and procedures are established to help maintain common practices among the various departments and divisions.

The task of the top manager is now that of managing generalist managers. It requires the ability to integrate the work of managers who are themselves generalists but who are managing such specialized functions as marketing, finance, production, engineering, and personnel.

Of course, as Chapter 16 pointed out, many other factors besides size affect management style. Indeed, a consulting firm with 500 employees may be quite large in comparison with most other such firms. American Motors, on the other hand, has more than 29,000 employees but is actually close to being too small a firm to efficiently produce automobiles. As a matter of fact, its automotive operations were losing about $90 million a year in 1978 and it was seriously considering merging with other organizations.[4]

The franchise business is another one where the distinction between large and small firms becomes blurred. The franchiser is a company that licenses others to sell its services or products. Some examples are McDonald's, Midas Muffler, Holiday Inn, Dunkin Donuts, and Pizza Hut. One of the chief advantages of franchising is instant recognition and standardized operation. For example, a Midas Muffler shop in New York City is very similar in appearance, operation, and product to one in Denver, Colorado. Another advantage of the franchise is that the individual franchisee tends to be his or her own boss managing a small business. A disadvantage is that the individual may be tightly controlled by the parent corporation.

McDonald's is a large corporation in terms of total sales, but the manager of the local McDonald's is actually a small business person of a sort. McDonald's gives the individual franchisee the exclusive right to sell its products in a specified location. Each franchisee pays an initial fee and yearly sums for the right to use the trade name and to get managerial and financial help. Franchisees can be sure of getting a standardized product from the parent corporation. For example, the production of McDonald's hamburgers is computerized to make certain that each 4¾-inch hamburgers patty contains precisely the "right" amounts of moisture (65 percent), protein (17 percent), and fat (18 percent). When cooked, the hamburger patty slips precisely into the standardized 4-inch bun.[5]

Among the fastest growing franchise businesses are computer stores.[6] They sell microcomputers—not only to hobbyists but also to small business people, who find them powerful, effective tools. Business people can purchase components that fit their individual businesses, such as small insurance offices and retail stores. In one instance, a Franciscian order of priests bought a microcomputer to keep track of its nine hundred brothers around the world. Computer stores are expanding by chains as well as by franchises. Industrial giants such as IBM are now opening their own stores across the country. One franchise operation, Computerland Corporation, is expanding even faster than did McDonald's in its early days.

Managing in the Public Sector

As mentioned earlier, the *public sector* refers to government bodies. These bodies incorporate at least five levels of government: commissions and boards, municipalities (cities or towns), counties; states (in Canada, provinces), and the federal government.[7] Since there are so many different types of public organizations, primary emphasis in this section will be on the federal government; but mention will be made of other levels to illustrate specific points.

There is no doubt that government is a "growth industry." While manufacturing employment remained relatively stable or even dropped a little between 1961 and 1976, the number of government workers increased from 8.7 million to more than 15 million in the same time period. In 1976, approximately 1.8 million managers and administrators were employed by governments, while approximately 1.2 million managers were employed by manufacturers. In addition, about 18 percent of all government workers were classified as professional or technical (nonmanagerial), while only about 10 percent were so classified in manufacturing.[8] Government is certainly big business.

Over the years, there has also been a steady increase in interaction between the public and private sectors, with the two becoming interdependent. For example, the U.S. Department of Defense is heavily dependent on private enterprise for the development, design, and manufacture of weapons. In turn, many private organizations are heavily dependent on the Department of Defense for much of their business. (Chapter 21 called this interdependence the interpenetrating systems model and used it to show the marked increase in public regulation of private firms in such areas as automobile safety and air and water pollution.)

However, despite the increasing interdependence, there still exist some major differences between the two sectors. These differences come about partly from the reasons for the existence of organizations in the public sector.

Reasons for the Existence of Organizations in the Public Sector

There are a number of reasons for the existence of government organizations, a few of which will be briefly discussed here.

Laws, rules, and regulations. Laws that are passed are often unclear or ambiguous. Therefore, many federal, state, and municipal organizations exist to interpret and enforce them for the public welfare through rules and regulations. To illustrate: The Interstate Commerce Commission regulates all commerce across state lines. The Federal Communications Commission oversees the activities of radio and television companies. The local school committee ensures that children get a proper education.

Protection of resources. A major function of many government agencies is the protection of life, property, and resources. Local fire and police departments offer protection from fire and theft. The National Park Service and the Environmental Protection Agency both protect the nation's resources.

The problem of indivisibility. Many problems cannot be divided into pieces that can be handled by individuals or individual profit-making organizations. National defense, for example, cannot be provided by individuals or individual firms, although individual firms can make products required for defense purposes. Building streets and highways is another example of an activity that requires funding and coordination by a government organization. Although an individual firm can contract to plow snow or clean streets, the decision of whether or not to use the service cannot be left to individuals.

Providing special aid. Help often is needed by the elderly, the young, the sick, and the unemployed. Medicare, Medicaid, welfare, and aid to dependent children are examples of special aid to individuals and groups. The Small Business Administration provides loans, assistance, and advice to small businesses.

Managing in Profit-Making and Government Organizations—A Comparative Approach

Relatively little solid research has been done on the similarities and differences between managing in the private sector and managing in the public sector. Thus a respected professor at Harvard University argues that public management is different from corporate management in both degree and quality.[9] At the same time—and in the same journal—the chief administrative and management officer of the Department of Health, Education, and Welfare (HEW) argues just as strongly that the differences in the approaches to management are heavily outweighed by the similarities.[10] The argument itself may never be settled. For the purposes of this text, however, it will be sufficient to demonstrate ways in which managements in the private and public sectors are both similar and different.

The Problem of Objectives

In the private sector, the primary objective, as defined by stockholders and boards of directors, has usually been to maximize return on investment. There are usually individual goals intended to help reach the main objective. These goals include increasing the company's growth rate, developing new products, increasing market standing, and contributing to society. Most of these goals are usually compatible with maximizing the return on investment. It is possible to translate both the primary objective and each of its smaller goals into measurable units and to accurately measure them with sophisticated accounting tools.

Unfortunately, unanimously agreed-upon objectives and measurements do not exist so clearly in the public sector. Frequently, little agreement exists between the public and the members of a government agency on what the primary objective should be, and often there is even less agreement on the subobjectives, many of which are nebulous, difficult to measure, and lacking in precision.

It is easy for the Chevrolet Division of General Motors to count the number of automobiles it has manufactured and sold. However, the typical federal department is itself a conglomerate organization. For example, the Secretary of HEW is responsible for directing such diverse programs as delivering hot meals to the elderly, determining eligibility for Medicaid benefits, and funding cancer research. Individual managers in the public sector thus find it difficult to see a connection between their work effort and its results; and direct verification of these results is often unlikely to be available for them.[11]

The Problem of Benefits

Measuring the ratio of costs to benefits in the public sector is more difficult than it is in the private sector. For example, although the dollar cost of teaching a disadvantaged child to read can be measured, how is the "profitability" of this service to society to be measured? Furthermore, in the private sector, the customer may refuse to buy the product; in the public sector, the customer is usually "built in." There is relatively little competition or substitution for Medicare, the post office, or police and fire departments.

The Problem of Politics

The political climate of the two sectors is quite different. Private industry is affected by politics, but public agencies react much more strongly to the political climate. The result is that the public sector has a shorter and more dynamic operating cycle than the private sector. Many appointed officials, for example, may be replaced after an election; and this leads to a higher rate of turnover among top-level decision-making personnel in the government than in the private sector. Further, objectives established by public sector managers in today's political setting may be changed to something entirely different in tomorrow's political climate. In addition, federal agencies are budgeted annually, and the budget may change with the political climate.[12]

Given these and many other difficulties, how do effective managers accomplish anything in the public sector? In effect, good managers learn to use the difficulties to their advantage. To show how this is accomplished, some common elements will be drawn from two examples: the reform of New York City's welfare program and the establishment of the U.S. Environmental Protection Agency (EPA). Most attention will be paid to the reform of the welfare system, which in two years increased staff productivity by 16 percent, reduced the error rate by 50 percent, and resulted in a $200 million savings in welfare payments.[13]

Much of the success of a top government manager is determined by the first three months in office. The individual may be replaced in the next election, and only a finite number of improvements can be made while resources are still available. Furthermore, resources are more easily obtained at the beginning than later. To be effective, the administrator must quickly develop well-defined targets and clear priorities. There is little time to thoroughly analyze and study problems in detail. Thus the administrator must pick problems that are pressing and create programs that will show early results. For example, New York City's welfare department director, Arthur Spiegel III, used two criteria for setting priorities—public expectations and simplicity of the problem. Three of his earliest projects were stopping welfare check fraud, establishing a central registry to identify and track down drug addicts, and issuing a photographic ID card to every welfare client. (The latter reduced fraud and sharpened client scheduling skills.) The head of the EPA, William Ruckelshaus, had to bring together a collection of previously independent agencies; he chose air pollution as a primary issue because it was a "hot" item and everyone in the organization could identify with fighting it.

Often, people simply do their best in the absence of tangible goals. But in both situations mentioned earlier, the administrators established tight timetables and specific performance measures. For example, within sixty days after taking office, Ruckelshaus took steps to send out guidelines that would affect the entire U.S. auto industry. In New York, Spiegel began by reducing six lines of command to one, instituting time-keeping and absenteeism records that were strictly kept, and developing a set of productivity reports that provided a way of ranking the forty-five welfare centers.

In both cases, the press was used as an accountability tool. For example, Spiegel publicly issued agency-wide performance objectives and published regular reports on progress. Ruckelshaus kept the press fully informed in the same way in order to gain public support for actions and to make needed changes. He also enlisted the help of the environmental lobby (including the Sierra Club and the Audubon Society) in establishing goals and in determining the organization's position and measuring its accomplishments. This helped keep pressure on the agency and enabled it to obtain support for further efforts.

Gaining the support of civil servants was a problem for both the EPA and the New York City welfare department. Spiegel, for example, found that there was a great deal of untapped talent among New York's civil service employees, and he won their support on the basis of four factors: "proof of our [his immediate staff's] competence, the mayor's backing of our effort, our respect for their [civil service employees'] standard bureaucratic procedures, and insight into the mutuality of our objectives. Their support was not difficult to obtain."[14] Although he brought in a number of outsiders, they were carefully matched with people who had a thorough knowledge of standard agency problems and procedures. In one instance, a revised procedure was not accepted by the civil service employees because it had been written by an "outsider" and was therefore not understood. A civil service supervisor rewrote it, referencing old procedures, and it was immediately implemented.

Rather than trying to fight the civil service employees who had been around a long time, both Ruckelshaus and Spiegel were able to gain their support and thus make use of their richness of experience and vast knowledge of procedures and regulations. Civil service workers are used to a constantly changing top management and constantly changing regulations. Thus they can be a force for continuity in the changing operations.

In the two situations being discussed here, the new top administrator was able to bring about progress and change by using good management skills. Each was willing to lead, make decisions, and take responsibility; and each was able to turn difficulties into advantages. For example, the short time they had in which to establish themselves enabled the two administrators to set early, simple, and measurable goals that oriented the organization to a common cause and protected it politically. Private sector business managers avoid publicity. But in the open political arena, Spiegel and Ruckelshaus were able to use publicity to gain support for their programs. And rather than decrying the bureaucracy and putting down the civil servants, both Spiegel and Ruckelshaus were able to find and use these people's potential.

Managing Third Sector Organizations

Descriptions of the public and private sectors leave out a large group of organizations that are neither profit making nor government bodies. Organizations in the public sector rely on *law* for their existence, and organizations in the private sector rely on *capital* for theirs. Writers on management and public administration used to describe primarily these two sectors of the economy. Almost all other organizations were treated as relatively unimportant. As a result, little attention was paid to the growing importance of and increased need for proper management of third sector organizations. Indeed, the government reports cited earlier in this chapter do not yet identify the third sector as such.

Third sector organizations are developed to conduct both the social and the economic "business" of mature capitalism. "Some are created out of a mix of private business and governmental elements. Others take the form of voluntary organizations (e.g., Red Cross or League of Women Voters) and the non-profit corporations (e.g., the Ford Foundation)."[15]

Third sector organizations originally were voluntary organizations such as churches, community groups, and consumer groups. In recent years, however, the third sector has expanded and grown more political. Organizations such as Common Cause and the American Civil Liberties Union, for example, have "goals of either confronting large bureaucratic organizations in hope of making them more responsive, or of organizing around certain functions that established organizations will not or cannot perform."[16]

In addition, the differences of the public and private sectors are becoming blurred through greater cooperation between government and business. At least three broad areas of public and private sector cooperation have expanded the activities of third sector organizations beyond those of volunteer organizations. One area involves the government essentially in partnership with the private sector. For example, the key to the effectiveness of the NASA Apollo project was the cooperation of a variety of organizations to achieve a specific function. The federal government has also asked U.S. physicians to set up professional standards review organizations (PSROs) to review and monitor the medical care given under federally supported programs. The PRSOs are third sector organizations with authority over programs created by federal law. The physicians are not employed by the government but instead work with it to achieve certain goals.

The second form of third sector expansion is that established by government edict. In this form, the government establishes quasi-public corporations to handle certain functions. Amtrak and the U.S. Postal Service are examples of third sector organizations established by government edict. The concept behind this form is that certain organizations can operate more effectively as private businesses free of government red tape. The question of whether this is an effective form of organization is still unsettled.

The third form of third sector expansion is that of public organizations that are quasi-private. Examples are the Federal National Mortgage Association (FNMA—also known as Fannie Mae) and the Communication Satellite Corporation (COMSAT). These organizations are not actually private, but they issue stocks that are held by investors who exercise some of the rights shared by stockholders in other private corporations. Thus they differ from, say, the U.S. Postal Service and Amtrak, which do not issue any stock.

Fannie Mae, which was originally a government agency, is supposed to meet the public's need for housing by providing a secondary market for government-insured mortgages. It was "privatized" in 1968, and its shares of stock were sold to the public. The people owning its stock can elect ten of the fifteen members of the board of directors. The other five are appointed by the Secretary of Housing and Urban Development. Fannie Mae is now one of the larger corporations in the United States.

COMSAT was created in 1962 through an act of Congress expressly to maintain communications satellites. It represents a unique blend of federal money and private technology. Federal funds were used in the development of the technology, and civilian participation was made possible by a corporation financed half by the U.S. government and half by the commercial communications companies. The board of directors of COMSAT includes public officials, representatives of the communications industries, and directors appointed by the public.

Third sector organizations tend to be as diverse as public and private sector organizations. Indeed, there is little solid research characterizing the activities, responsibilities, and duties of managers in this sector.

Although the third sector is growing rapidly in the United States, it is growing even faster in other countries, particularly in the developing nations. Many of these nations refuse to leave development efforts totally in the hands of private enterprise. Instead they require interaction between the public and private sectors. In many highly industrialized parts of the world, such as Scandinavia, public policy has such strong influence on the economic activities of organizations that third sector organizations are becoming even more important than they were in the past.

Managing—Some Common Functions

Managers often claim that their organizations and their problems are unique. There is evidence that this claim has some validity, but there is also evidence that organizations have a great deal in common, regardless of their sector.

Figure 23.1 shows the overlap of organizations in the private, public, and third sectors. The black area is the one that formal organizations have in common with each other. For example, every formal organization exists as a system within an environment. Each has goals, objectives, structure, rules, people, and procedures for handling recurrent activities. While some organizations have more rules and procedures than others, the chances of an organization having none are doubtful.

The striped areas are the dimensions in which organizations are both similar to and generally unlike others. In the striped areas are dimensions in which organizations do not have complete overlap but do have some things in common with some, but not all, organizations. For example, consider two third sector organizations—the Postal Service and COMSAT. The Postal Service appears to have much more in common with the government than with private enterprise. COMSAT, on the other hand, appears to have more in common with private enterprise than with the public sector. Thus, while in the black area all dimensions overlap, in the striped area only some of them overlap.

The white areas are those unique to particular organizations. An organization may have a unique product, physical location, or history of

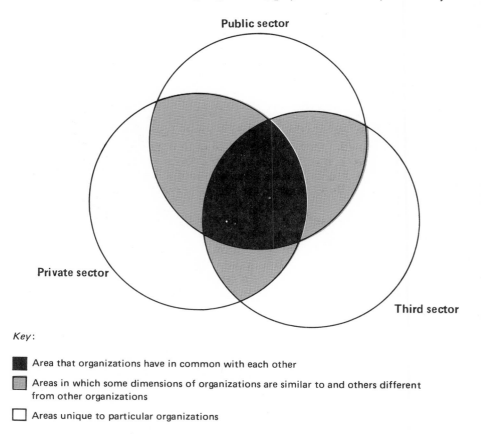

Key:

■ Area that organizations have in common with each other

▨ Areas in which some dimensions of organizations are similar to and others different from other organizations

□ Areas unique to particular organizations

Figure 23.1 Similarities and differences among organizations

development. The personality of the top manager may be different from that of top managers in other organizations. These and other differences create a combination of factors not found in any other organization.

The figure is intended to illustrate the relative importance of these three areas. If the white area is predominant, then relatively little can be said about the organizations and their management. If the striped and black areas are predominant, then there can be some common functions of managing that can cut across most, if not all, organizations. There is no solid information regarding the relative overlap of these areas in organizations, but the best current evidence is that about 50 to 75 percent of these areas are common to most organizations. This percentage is shown by the combination of black and striped areas.[17]

Effective Managing—A Review and a Summary

This section will focus on some common tasks and challenges that managers face in all organizations and will point out how these tasks vary in different types of organizations. (Chapter 2 described specific working roles or activities that managers must engage in if the organization is to accomplish its objectives. A review of these roles may be helpful in understanding this section.) The basic roles are shown in Figure 23.2. In interpersonal roles, the manager must deal with others at all levels of the organization. In informational roles, the manager must obtain and distribute information to others. In decisional roles, the manager must act to improve the unit, to reduce disturbances, to allocate resources, and to negotiate for needed resources.

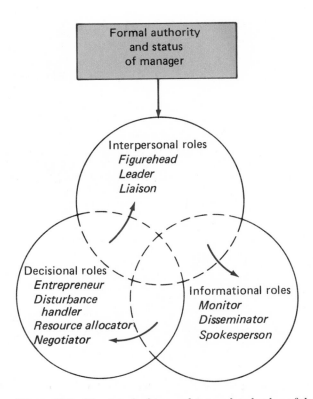

Figure 23.2 The interlocking and interrelated roles of the manager

By acting in one or more of these roles, the manager performs functions that are common to organizations of any type. These functions involve determining the needs of the environment, establishing objectives, developing clear plans, dividing and coordinating the work, controlling, motivating, and decision making. The specific ways that these functions are performed vary from organization to organization and from situation to situation, but all of them must be performed.

Determining the Needs of the Environment

As systems, organizations take in raw materials, people, and other resources. They then transform the resources into outputs that fit the needs and wants of the receiving system. Thus managers must develop boundary-spanning subsystems that gather information from the environment in order to assess the needs and wants of the receiving system. Clearly, this approach is not one-way, since large organizations can also create "needs" through advertising and other methods.

In gathering information from the environment, managers must perform two related tasks—monitoring and disseminating information. In the monitor role, the manager's "radar" is constantly in use, gathering information of all kinds. In the disseminator role, the manager transmits that information to subordinates and others as necessary. Establishing the wants and needs of the environment may be easier in a private organization than in a public one. However, the classic failure of the Edsel (a project that cost Ford millions of dollars) shows the difficulty of getting a real reading on needs. The company spent enormous sums on market surveys and other kinds of information gathering that showed the need for the Edsel—but the public simply would not buy it.

Establishing Objectives

The overall mission of any organization is to meet the needs and wants of the receiving system. One of the most common causes of organizational failure is the lack of carefully considered and clear-cut objectives. An effectively functioning organization must know in an explicit way what it is doing and why it exists.

In the leadership role, the manager must establish adaptive subsystems to make certain that the organization's objectives are in line with the needs of the receiving subsystem. Since the organization's mission can change with changing environments, the manager needs to make certain not only that the objectives are met but also that the objectives are changed when necessary.

The objectives of a private sector organization may be easier to define and put into operation than those of a public sector organization. The challenge to the manager as leader is to make these objectives specific and tangible.

Developing Clear Plans

As discussed in Chapter 8, planning involves the statement of objectives, strategies, and policies and detailed plans to achieve them. Well-designed and functioning organizations have plans that are clearly communicated, realistic, worthwhile, measurable (or at least verifiable), and adequate.

The manager as leader must develop and communicate plans and change or modify them as necessary; as entrepreneur, the manager must improve the performance of the unit; and as disturbance handler, the manager must control and modify plans to meet unexpected changes. Because of laws, rules, and regulations, plans may have to be modified or changed more quickly in a private enterprise than in a public one. Nevertheless, the task needs to be accomplished effectively.

Structure—Dividing and Coordinating the Work

Since most organizations have many tasks, the work must be divided and coordinated. *Structure* refers to how work is specialized (differentiated) and coordinated (integrated). It is dependent on size, on technology, and on environment. Thus there is no universal best way to design organizations or their subunits. The proper structure is contingent on the situation.

Frequently, the structure of a public agency is determined at least in part by laws and regulations. For example, the reorganization of the executive office of the President can be disallowed by either house of Congress. Thus reorganization in any public agency may be more difficult and more time-consuming than reorganization in the private sector.

Controlling

Control is what makes certain that activities are producing the desired results. The manager must evaluate the desired outcomes of activities and make adjustments when necessary. The basic purpose of control is positive in that it focuses on achieving organizational objectives. Controlling is usually easier in the private sector than in the public sector. It is easier to control the production of tangible goods than the provision of, say, mental health care. First, the goals and objectives can be more clearly defined, and the measurements can be more specific and tangible. Second, human service delivery requires a relatively high proportion of professionals such as lawyers, physicians, teachers, and social workers. Often these professionals preserve their autonomy and the confidentiality of their relationships with "clients." This means that they often have relatively little concern about what others in the system are doing. Thus, although the effective manager must establish and maintain controls, the controls may vary according to the type of organization. In an organization producing an intangible product, the control may be more directly related to the proper selection of professionals and the way in which they use their time.

Motivating

Organizations of all types have employees. A significant function of managers in any organization is to establish the conditions under which both individuals and groups will be selected, trained, motivated, and committed to accomplishing the organization's objectives. Therefore, the effective manager has a working knowledge of and respect for the basic principles of individual and group behavior and the ability to apply these principles in every area of the structure and functioning of the unit.

Decision Making

All the areas described above require decision making. Thus a common denominator for managers in all types of organizations is the ability to make good decisions. Managers may make literally hundreds of decisions a week. Some will be very minor, taking only a few seconds to make; others may be major decisions that require a great deal of analysis. Because there is a lot to be done, managers seldom try for the "best" decision. Instead they tend to satisfice—picking a solution that is satisfactory, although not necessarily the best.

From a systems point of view, decision making is not an isolated process. Frequently, decisions affect other people in the organizational unit or in other units. As a result, the decision-making process is one of constant renegotiation. A number of analytical aids to decision making exist—among them linear programming, probability theory, queuing theory, PERT, and decision trees. They can be used most effectively when the decisions can be programmed. Other decisions require new, creative, and innovative processes.

Managers in private enterprise often have more freedom to make decisions than managers working in the public sector. For example, Civil Service rules and regulations that protect employees also reduce managers' freedom of action.

Implications for the Manager

Although the basic functions of small and large organizations are essentially the same, the larger the organization, the greater its tendency to change structure and to formalize such functions as planning, control, and decision making.

Although more and more interaction between the public and private sectors is occurring, there remains disagreement as to whether the three sectors should be managed differently. Certainly, their reasons for existence are different, but until better comparative research is done, the "right" answer cannot be provided. Nevertheless, evidence does exist that organizations of all types have a large number of characteristics in common and that generalizations about them often have a valid base. Of course, different organizations also have different problems.

Although the emphasis may differ, the manager must still perform some common functions. Regardless of the organization or the sector, people must be hired, trained, and motivated. Organizational goals and objectives must be established. Planning and controlling must be done carefully if the organization is to be effective. The internal climate and the external environment affect the manager, who in turn affects them.

Most people are in constant contact with a large variety of organizations, all of which need to be well managed in order for them to be effective. Thus effective managing is an important, challenging, and exciting job that provides rewards such as achievement, recognition, and responsibility.

Review

1. What are some reasons for the existence of large businesses? For the existence of small businesses?
2. How might managing in large and small businesses be similar? How might it be different?
3. Describe the stages in the growth of a small business to a large one.
4. Can you think of any managerial functions that might be performed only in large organizations? Only in small ones?
5. Using the working roles of a manager as a guide (see Chapter 2 if necessary), identify organizations where one or more roles might be emphasized more than they are in other organizations.
6. List some basic reasons for the existence of public sector organizations.
7. Would the approaches to managing used by Spiegel and Ruckelshaus be appropriate to the private sector? Explain.
8. What are some functions common to most organizations?
9. List ways in which a particular organization might be unique.
10. List third sector organizations you have heard about (not in the text).
11. How much contact have you had with small firms as opposed to large ones? Explain.
12. Visit at least two organizations. Interview or observe several managers. Can you describe how they spend their time? What are their roles?

The College President

Donald Kirk has arrived early at his book-lined office. As president of Jefferson College, a small, private, liberal arts college, he has spent the last two days with business executives in Chicago designing a capital funds campaign for a group of private colleges. He knows that a number of pressing matters await him even though his absence has been brief.

Jefferson College can pass as the ideal of a small Midwest college. It has modest but adequate facilities, a competent faculty, a dedicated staff, and a good suburban location. However, each year a smaller number of middle-income students can afford the high tuition and fees charged by Jefferson. Thus the full-time students enrolled at the college are starting to be drawn from two disparate socioeconomic classes. Extensive federal and state aid to students through scholarship grants, loans, and work-study programs has attracted students whose parents' incomes are low. These funds, along with internally generated scholarship funds, have permitted Jefferson to compete with state universities for such students. The other students came from affluent homes, where the parents are usually college educated professionals.

Although the diversity of backgrounds does not create any unusual social problems, an extensive program of remedial teaching has been necessary for many of the disadvantaged students, both black and white.

The complexity of the aid programs has required a full-time staff of three to handle all the paperwork. Additional admissions counselors have also been necessary because of the intense competition for students who qualify for federal support.

Students actually pay for about 75 percent of the cost of running the college. The remainder comes from gifts or federal support programs (see Table 23.2). Up till now, the college has operated in the black, but any surplus generated in the short term quickly goes to cover unanticipated maintenance, utility, or personnel costs.

Table 23.2 Report on revenues and gifts from all sources, 1976–77

Student revenue	$5,150,000
Federal support grants	300,000
Annual fund (alumni/friends)	450,000
Endowment income	400,000
Church support	75,000
Foundations	400,000
Corporate support	55,000
Miscellaneous sources	45,000
Total revenue for operating purposes	$6,875,000
Capital support (consortium share)	$ 125,000
Gifts to endowment	100,000
Total revenue for capital/endowment purposes	$ 225,000

Kirk's concerns for the college's future are twofold—the potential loss of students and increases in costs. Demographic studies have forecasted a decline (5 percent per year for the next four years) in the number of traditional prospective college students. Furthermore, increases in the cost of operating the college cannot be completely offset by raising tuition. Kirk feels that the college is being confronted by an elastic demand curve. If it raises the price of tuition, student enrollment will drop.

As Table 23.3 shows, in spite of the foreboding trends, Jefferson's enrollment has remained stable so far at 1,200 full-time equivalent students (FTEs). (FTEs are an accepted measure of students; two half-time students equal one FTE.) This stability has been the result of a number of programs to attract nontraditional students. Several years ago, Jefferson initiated an evening degree program for adults, and enrollment in that program has exceeded the college's expectations. Because of the way the program is priced, four part-time evening students are considered to equal one FTE. A new one-year program for teaching English to foreign (particularly Middle Eastern) students has also been instituted, but it has been less successful. Programs stressing vocational majors such as nursing and business have been expanded with apparent success. These programs alone attract one-third of the students as majors. A cooperative off-campus/on-campus work-study program has also been initiated with temporary government funding.

Table 23.3 Jefferson College enrollment

Full-time day students		1,065
Scholarship/grant equivalents	210	
Full-pay equivalents	855	
Special program students		465
Co-op work/study	30	
English for foreigners	15	
Adult evening program	420	
Other		15
overseas semester	10	
Nondegree, special	5	
Total head-count enrollment*		1,545

* This is not the same as FTE enrollment because of part-time/partial tuition enrollments in the special program and other student categories.

The college has other programs in the planning stages, but their diversity will create large additions to the nonteaching staff, increasing overhead, and some anguish on the part of senior faculty concerning the fundamental purpose of the college. Many of the programs are the result of development grants from government and foundations. Kirk is worried about whether these programs can even pay their own way after the external funding runs out. Along with three other presidents of local private colleges, he has just completed a grant application for funding a cooperative computer operation; and two other internally generated proposals await signature.

Kirk glances at his calendar for the rest of the month. It includes a trip to Russia with an alumni group, a meeting in Washington with HEW officials, a meeting with a generous benefactor, and two alumni club functions that will require more off-campus travel. He is scanning one of the documents on his desk when the intercom interrupts the reading: "Dr. Kirk, Mr. Myers [the business manager] is here with the proposal for the maintenance workers' union."

"Thanks Betty. Ask him in," Kirk replies, as he muses over the fact that weeks have passed since he has confronted a problem concerning education of the students.[18]

1. As a manager of a third sector organization, does Kirk engage in activities significantly different from those of managers of profit-seeking or government organizations?
2. What roles must a college president such as Kirk assume?
3. What problems may arise from the expansion-by-grant strategy? What solutions can you recommend?
4. Do you feel that Kirk's activities are concerned with educating students? Explain.

Footnotes

1. U.S. Small Business Administration, *SBA Business Loans* (Washington, D.C.: Government Printing Office, February 1975), p. 3.
2. H. Mintzberg, *The Nature of Managerial Work* (New York: Harper & Row, 1973); R. Stewart, "Studies of Managerial Jobs," *International Studies of Management and Organization* 2 (Spring 1972): 7–37; A. Filley and R. House, *Managerial Process and Organizational Behavior* (Glenview, Ill.: Scott, Foresman, 1976); J. Carrington and L. Aurelio, "Survival Tactics for Small Business," *Business Horizons* 19 (February 1976): 13–24; L. Barnes and S. Hershon, "Transferring Power in the Family Business," *Harvard Business Review* 54 (July–August 1976): 105–114; and W. Copulsky and H. McNulty, "Finding and Keeping the Entrepreneur," *Management Review* 63 (April 1974): 5–11.
3. Barnes and Hershon, "Transferring Power in the Family Business."
4. J. Emshwiller, "AMC's Bid to Remain an Auto Maker Is Seen Linked to Non-Car Lines," *Wall Street Journal,* March 23, 1978, p. 1.
5. D. Anable, "Computerization of Hamburgers," *Christian Science Monitor,* July 6, 1977, p. 2.
6. G. Bylinsky, "The Computer Stores Have Arrived," *Fortune,* April 24, 1978, pp. 52–57.

7. M. Murray, "Comparing Public and Private Management: An Exploratory Essay," *Public Administration Review* 35 (July–August 1975): 364–371; N. Long, "Public Policy and Administration: The Goals of Rationality and Responsibility," *Public Administration Review* 14 (Winter 1954): 18–34; D. Pearlman, ed., *The Future of the American Government* (Boston: Houghton Mifflin, 1968); D. Ink, "The President as Manager," *Public Administration Review* 36 (September–October 1976): 508–515; L. Lynn, Jr., and J. Siedl," 'Bottom-line' Management for Public Agencies," *Harvard Business Review* 55 (January–February 1955): 145–153; W. Turcotte, "Control Systems, Performance, and Satisfaction in Two State Agencies," *Administrative Science Quarterly* 19 (March 1974) 60–73; and R. Golembiewski and M. Cohen, eds., *People in Public Service* (Itaska, Ill.: F. E. Peacock, 1976).

8. U.S. Department of Labor, Bureau of Labor Statistics, *Handbook of Labor Statistics, 1977* (Washington, D.C.: Government Printing Office, 1966).

9. J. Bauer, "Effective Public Management," *Harvard Business Review* 55 (March–April 1977): 131–140.

10. R. Brady, "MBO Goes to Work in the Public Sector," *Harvard Business Review* 51 (March–April 1973): 65–74.

11. B. Buchanan, II, "Government Managers, Business Executives, and Organizational Commitment," *Public Administration Review* 34 (July–August 1974): 339–347.

12. L. Goodstein, "Organization Development in Bureaucracies: Some Caveats and Cautions," paper presented to OD 78, a Conference on Current Theory and Practice in Organizational Development, University Associates, San Francisco, California, March 16–17, 1978.

13. Bauer, "Effective Public Management"; C. Grayson, Jr., "Management Science and Business Practice," *Harvard Business Review* 51 (July–August 1973): 41–49; and A. Spiegel, III, "How Outsiders Overhauled a Public Agency," *Harvard Business Review* 53 (January–February 1975): 116–124.

14. Spiegel, "How Outsiders Overhauled a Public Agency," p. 120.

15. A. Etzioni, "The Third Sector and Domestic Missions," *Public Administration Review* 35 (July–August 1973): 315; T. Leavitt, *The Third Sector* (New York: AMACOM, 1973), pp. 28–29; M. McGill and L. Wooten, "Management in the Third Sector," *Public Administration Review* 35 (September–October 1975): p. 445.

16. Etzioni, "The Third Sector and Domestic Missions," p. 315.

17. J. Galbraith, *Organization Design* (Reading, Mass.: Addison-Wesley, 1977); and G. Egan, "Model A: The Logic of Systems as OD Instrument," paper presented to OD 78, a Conference on Current Theory and Practice in Organizational Development, University Associates, San Francisco, California, March 16–17, 1978.

18. Case written by Gail Miller, Otterbein College. Reproduced by permission.

Chapter 24

Career Planning and Development

The Interview

Career Consciousness

Career Stages
    The Broad Stages
    The Levinson Model

The Dalton, Thompson, and Price Model

The First Job
    Reality Shock
    The First Supervisor

Organizational Socialization

Equal Employment and Careers

The Dual-Career Family

Developing Initial Personal Career Plans
    Developing Self-awareness
    Learning About Jobs and Organizations
    Determining Initial Career Plans

Implications for the Individual

Review

The Raymond Chemical Company

Careers: An Annotated Bibliography

This chapter contributed by
PROFESSOR HAROLD G. KAUFMAN,
Polytechnic Institute of New York

Learning Objectives

When you have finished reading and studying this chapter, you should be able to:

1. Give reasons for the growing importance of career consciousness.
2. Identify needs and desires satisfied by a proper career.
3. Identify the broad stages of a career.
4. Compare and contrast the Levinson and Dalton models of careers.
5. List and give examples of aspects of the first job that can potentially affect a career.
6. Demonstrate how the importance of the first job is tied to the career models.
7. Compare and contrast pivotal and relevant norms.
8. Describe problems in equal opportunity and its effect on career development.
9. Compare and contrast different strategies for dealing with problems in the dual-career family.
10. Outline steps you would take to develop your own career plan for maximum satisfaction and use of your potential.
11. Define and be able to use the following concepts:

career	organizational socialization
career development	anticipatory socialization
novice phase	pivotal norms
mentor relationship	relevant norms
apprentice stage	tokenism
reality shock	

Thought Starters

1. How well formulated are your own career goals? Explain.
2. If you were to write a feature story about yourself to appear in a local paper fifteen years from now, what would you want it to say?
3. What advice would you give a college student who is about to pick a major? What advice would you give to one who is looking for a job?

The Interview

Every spring, recruiters from a variety of organizations visit college campuses to interview students for possible jobs with their organizations. Table 24.1 lists typical questions asked by these recruiters. Many of the questions, or variations on them, are also asked by interviewers when an employee is thinking about changing jobs or moving from one organization to another.

A number of the questions suggest that students should have relatively good insight into their abilities and motivations. They also suggest the wisdom of having at least a tentative career plan that will assist students in answering the questions and guide them in the direction they want to go. As a matter of fact, answering the questions can help in formulating a career plan or in sharpening or focusing an existing one.

Career planning and development is important for a number of reasons. From the personal point of view, it can help people best use their abilities, interests, and motivations. From an organizational point of view, it can help managers do a good job of managing and developing

Table 24.1 Typical questions asked by interviewers

1. *What do you want to do, and why?*
   (Employers want to know long- and short-range objectives and career plans.)

2. *How and why did you choose your major field?*
   (They want to know what stimulated you in the particular direction.)

3. *Tell me about yourself.*
   (They want only important points, such as key influences of your early home environment, why you chose the university you are attending and what is motivating you to choose a career.)

4. *Why are you interested in our organization?*
   (They want you to know something about their organization, such as whether it is expanding or the key products or services it provides. They would like to see you tie this in with your own vocational objectives and in other ways show that you are interested in their particular organization.)

5. *Why isn't your grade record better? Or, for students with a B or higher average: Why didn't you participate in more extracurricular activities?*
   (They don't want alibis or rationalizations. Instead, they prefer that you tell them where you rank in class and why you are involved or not involved in extracurricular activities.)

6. *What courses did you like best, and why? What courses did you like least, and why?*
   (Again, they want you to tie your answer in with your objectives. The answer "I don't know why" shows no ability to discriminate, evaluate, or make decisions.)

7. *What are the three most important characteristics for success in your chosen field?*
   (It is best to think out in advance the characteristics that fit in with your own strengths and to show how you possess these characteristics.)

8. *What do you see as your particular strengths and weaknesses?*
   (Your answers should be tied to Questions 1 and 7. Be honest and specific without telling the interviewer everything about yourself.)

9. *What have you learned from previous job experiences?*
   (If you have no job experience, discuss what you have learned from volunteer work, campus activities, and other sources. Don't be afraid to admit that there is still a lot for you to learn. As much as possible, relate this question to Questions 1 and 7.)

10. *How do you expect to achieve your job and career objectives?*
    (Bring out what you hope to learn on the first job, how long you expect to stay at that level, and what you think is the next job level you should move to. Be as realistic as possible.)

11. *Why should we hire you?*
    (Summarize your interests and assets and show how they fit the employer's job requirements. An effective closing will help you get an invitation to visit the employer or an offer for employment.)

Note: Each interviewer is different. Some interviewers may ask none of these questions, but most will ask questions that are closely related to them.

Adapted and modified from J. Steele, Director, Career Planning and
Placement, Boston College, personal communication.

subordinates. This chapter does not answer all possible questions about careers, but it does provide a general overview of them. An annotated bibliography at the end of the chapter will be of further help in developing personal career goals.

Career Consciousness

The choice of a career is more important to college students today than it was in the 1960s, when activism over social issues was more common. Then, only about half the college students viewed their education as preparation for a successful career. But by 1973 the proportion had jumped to two-thirds, and it has continued to increase.

There are many reasons for this increased concern about careers. One of the most important is that the job market for college graduates changed quite suddenly. During the 1960s, the rapidly growing economy stimulated a demand for college graduates to fill an increasing number of professional and managerial positions. In some fields, the shortages were so great that high-level positions often had to be filled with less-qualified individuals. With the economic slowdown beginning in the early 1970s, the growth in demand for professionals and managers came to a halt just as the annual supply of college graduates was growing at a rapid pace.[1]

The relative oversupply of graduates is likely to continue. In 1970, there were about 30 million workers in the "prime" 25 to 44 age range; they constituted about 35 percent of the work force. In 1990, about 60.5 million workers are expected to be in this age range, and they will constitute about 60 percent of the work force. The 25 to 44 age range is called prime because people of these ages are perceived as being ambitious, wanting advancement, and having skill. The tremendous increase of people in this age range will mean increasing competition for scarce jobs, particularly since these workers will, on the average, be better educated than many of their superiors.[2]

Given the difficulties of finding jobs appropriate to their abilities, knowledge, and skills, it is understandable why college students have become career conscious. However, a career is much more important than finding a first job. For the purposes of this text, a **career** is "the sequence of behaviors and attitudes associated with past, present and anticipated future work-related experiences and role activities as perceived by either the individual or some other observer."[3] Thus a career is work-related and lifelong. As Table 24.1 shows, it has to do with both short- and long-range objectives, with particular choices, with the development and achievement of career choices, and with past and future experiences. It does not have to do with success or failure, the type of work in which a person is engaged, or activities engaged in outside of work.

Careers are important for most people because work itself is important. People want not only to make their own living but also to work at something that gives meaning to their lives. They want a sense of worth and uniqueness from their career. Generally, a career should meet a number of psychological needs and desires (as described in Chapters 4 and 5). These include:

1. The need for mastery or achievement over ideas, situations, people, or other aspects of work.
2. The need for the approval and recognition of supervisors, fellow workers, spouses, and other who are significant in one's life.
3. The need for social relationships. People at work are usually members of social units and can feel they are part of a group.
4. The need for prestige or status. If properly chosen to fit the individual, a career can allow feelings of accomplishment, prestige, and status.
5. The desire for social equality and personal liberation. This desire seems particularly important for women and minorities. The first woman airline pilot in the United States was employed in 1973. Before then, pilots were always men. Recently, under pressure from the Equal Employment Opportunity Commis-

sion, United Airlines agreed to actively recruit and hire qualified women and minorities.[4]

If these needs and desires are to be met, careful planning is necessary to ensure proper career development. **Career development** is "a developing, progressing process whereby an individual proceeds from a point of having no career direction to that of attaining a career consistent with his or her interests, abilities, and aspirations."[5] Many people think of career development as taking place very early in life, usually by the age of 20. As will be seen in the next section, however, career development is actually a long-term process.

Career Stages

Just as there are stages people go through when growing up, so there are stages in careers. Generally, career stages follow a broad pattern.[6]

The Broad Stages

Although different researchers use different models, there appear to be three broad career stages—establishment, advancement, and maintenance.

Establishment. When young managers first enter an organization, becoming established and integrated is of primary concern to them. Their entry can be a very stressful experience, and those who adjust best during this stage are those who can most easily deal with the insecurity and uncertainty of their new environment.

Advancement. Once the young managers are established and integrated into the organization, they become concerned with achievement and promotion. Successful advancement during this stage is very important for satisfying their need for achievement and a positive self-image.

Maintenance. Many managers reach a limit to advancement, and the limit can be either organizational or personal. In some organizations, there is little turnover and therefore little chance for promotion or advancement. On the personal side, some managers continue to grow while others reach a plateau, stagnate, or even decline. Many managers whose growth has ceased encounter a mid-career crisis when they realize that their goals either have been achieved or are unattainable. Some older managers feel that their knowledge and skills are obsolescent, that their mobility is limited, and that they cannot compete in the job market. Therefore, they become more concerned about security than growth.

The Levinson Model

Psychologist Donald Levinson has suggested that there are a number of basic stages and transitions in life: childhood and adolescence, novice stage, early adulthood, middle adulthood, and late adulthood. These are shown in Table 24.2.

Each stage begins as another one is being terminated. Thus there is a transition (and usually a crisis) period between stages. This section will

Table 24.2   Career stages and transitions

Stages	Transitions
0–22 Childhood and adolescence	17–22 Early adult transition
17–45 Early adulthood	17–33 The novice phase
40–65 Middle adulthood	40–45 Midlife transition
65–? Late adulthood	60–65 Late adult transition

briefly describe the stages, focusing primarily on the tasks to be performed in the transition between childhood and early adulthood—the novice stage.[7]

Age 0–22: Childhood and Adolescence

At the stage from childhood to adolescence, the individual becomes a person and begins to explore the world. The early adult transition, beginning at about age 17 and lasting to about age 22, marks the time the individual is beginning to form the adult self and to make choices that will establish the initial membership in the adult world. The stage involves pulling up roots and breaking away from family ties. Those who assert their independence become gradually more self-sufficient and confident than those who prolong family ties.

Age 17–45: Early Adulthood

The second and probably most dramatic stage of the life cycle is early adulthood. The body is at its peak functioning. In the early part of this period, major choices are made in areas such as occupation, marriage, and style of living—all of which form the preliminary adult identity. In terms of a career, the individual first becomes established at a junior level and then advances up formal or informal ladders until about age 40, when, if progress has been satisfactory, a new stage begins. If progress has not been satisfactory, the individual may become involved in radical job changes, different geographical locations, or divorce.

Age 17–33: The Novice Phase

Critical to successfully moving from the adolescent to the early adulthood stage is the **novice phase,** during which the individual explores the adult world and makes important choices about work, marriage, and family. There are many tasks common to this period; among them are learning to relate to authority figures, forming peer relationship with adults of both sexes, and relating as an adult to people of different ages. Four developmental tasks are critical. They are:

1. Forming a dream—that is, developing an idea or vision of the kind of adult life the individual wants to lead. The dream usually starts out in a vague fashion and becomes sharper and clearer with age. Individuals who have a clear idea of the dream and who attain it are likely to feel successful. Those who have vague ideas about it or who fail to attain it are likely to have career difficulties or to feel unsuccessful, regardless of their actual attainments.
2. Forming **mentor relationships**—that is, finding a person, usually several years older, who can help the individual facilitate the realization of the dream. The relationship, which can be formal or informal, involves teaching, counseling, guidance, advising, and sponsoring. A major function of the mentor is to help the individual move away from dependency on parents and toward interaction as a peer with other adults.
3. Forming an occupation (rather than choosing an occupation, since the "formation" usually occurs over a number of years). Some individuals make early initial choices and become physicians, lawyers, and the like. Most make their initial serious choice somewhere between the ages of 17 and 29 but try several different directions to sort out interests, discover various occupations, and eventually commit themselves to one of them. Occupational skills, credentials, and values must be developed.

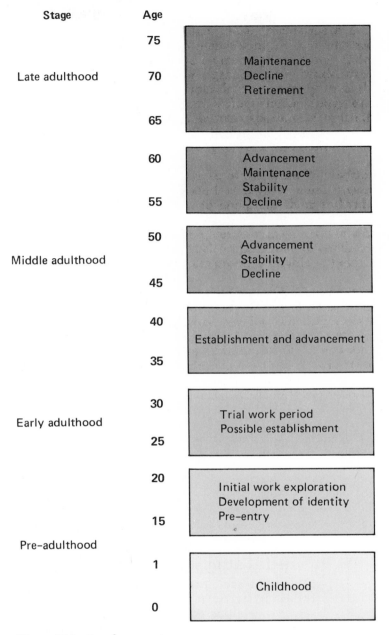

Figure 24.1 Broad career stages

4. Forming love relationships. Establishing such relationships, which usually involves marriage, is one of the tasks that appears to be important in moving into the adult world.

Age 40–65: Middle Adulthood

The midlife transition, lasting from about age 40 to age 45, involves the termination of early adulthood and the beginning of middle adulthood. It marks a potential midlife crisis, depending on the completion of the novice phase. Managers who are satisfied with their career to date will generally continue to be effective, developing pride in their achievements and experience. If the novice stage has not been satisfactorily worked through—if the dream has not been accomplished—a mid-life crisis may emerge. Feelings of sadness, resentment, and frustration may develop. The crisis can often be seen in such behavior as a sudden job change, excessive drinking, a dramatic change in life-style, or other dramatic breaks with the past.

Age 56–?: Late Adulthood

The late adulthood stage usually involves retiring from formal employment and (if the earlier stages have been worked through properly) satisfying individual needs and desires. Frequently, this stage requires finding a new balance of involvement with society and the self. Many creative and intellectual works have been produced by people in their sixties, seventies, and eighties. (See Figure 24.1 for an indication of all the stages.)

The Dalton, Thompson, and Price Model

Three business professors—Gene Dalton, Paul Thompson, and Raymond Price—have developed a model that suggests there are four successive career stages: apprentice, colleague, mentor, and sponsor. Each stage involves different tasks, types of relationships, and psychological adjustments.[8]

Apprentice

A young professional who enters an organization is an **apprentice**—a beginner or learner under the direction of others. The individual must learn to perform some of the organization's tasks competently and must learn how to get things done through formal and informal channels. Many activities are routine, so the individual must be aggressive in searching out new and more challenging tasks.

The primary relationship is that of a subordinate to others. Thus, in the ideal situation, the new employee will work with a mentor who can counsel, advise, and sponsor. The presence or absence of a mentor can have a strong effect on later career development.

Psychologically, the individual must adjust to the dependence involved in being a subordinate and be able to take supervision while at the same time exercising directed initiative and creativity. Many new employees expect to head their own projects or be able to work without taking orders and are psychologically unprepared for the apprentice role. A young, newly-employed engineer was shocked to find out he would not even have a desk of his own.

Colleague

The individual who develops a reputation for being technically competent and able to work independently has entered Stage 2 (the colleague stage). At this stage, the individual should develop a particular set of specialties that will gain him or her a reputation for knowledge and skill. For example, someone working in a bank may concentrate on loans to utilities or show effectiveness in systems analysis and computer programming or develop skills in dealing with customers or clients. The individual should avoid becoming overly specialized but should develop a solid base of competence and expertise visible to those higher in the organization. At this stage, the individual also needs to develop ongoing peer relationships that can be used to get the job done better. The critical psychological issues are the move from dependence to independence and the development of self-confidence.

Mentor

Successful entry into Stage 3 (the mentor stage) means assuming responsibility for directing, guiding, influencing, and developing others, either directly as a manager or more informally as part of the work process. Interests and capabilities are broadened, and contact with others inside and outside the organization and its subunits may be increased. Activities may involve helping others get salary increases, obtaining contracts, and getting budgets approved.

The relationships with others change as a result of the changed activities. At this stage, the individual needs to take care of others, assuming responsibility for their work. Interpersonal skills become highly important in supervising, coordinating, delegating, and setting objectives. The psychological issues are being able to build the confidence of junior people and to take the responsibility for the output of others. Some very competent people do not want to take on supervisory responsibility and prefer to remain in the second stage in a situation that will still allow them to exercise broad influence.

Sponsor

Not all individuals reach Stage 4 (the sponsor stage). The clearest characteristic of the sponsor stage is the influence the individual has in defining the direction of the organization or a major subunit of it. This influence does not need to come directly through line management positions. Instead it can be exercised by developing new ideas, products, markets, or services and by interfacing and negotiating with key people in the environment.

At this stage, individuals usually are engaged in at least one of three roles: manager, idea innovator, and internal entrepreneur. Many upper-level managers are in this stage, and so are idea innovators. The latter may be individual contributors who come forth with innovative ideas that affect the organization. Internal entrepreneurs are people who have new ideas or who get ideas from the innovator and then have sufficient influence to bring people, resources, and money together to further the ideas and affect the direction in which the organization will go.

Key work relationships can involve the selection and development of others. Outside relationships are critical both for gathering current information and for giving the organization visibility. An essential psychological issue at this stage is learning how not to second-guess subordinates and others on operating decisions and how to use power successfully to form strong political alliances.

An important feature of the Dalton, Thompson, and Price model is that it avoids the trap of suggesting that career development consists only of moving up the managerial hierarchy. The model suggests instead that individuals can be successful at the colleague, mentor, and sponsor levels, depending on their own needs and aspirations.

The First Job

Since a career involves a sequence of jobs or stages, the most logical place to begin is at the first job. Several aspects of the initial job experience can pose both problems and opportunities and can have potentially far-reaching effects on the career.

Reality Shock

Many new college graduates enter the world of work with unrealistic information or expectations. The result is **reality shock,** a situation where the actuality does not agree with the expectations. One factor contributing to reality shock is the overly rosy view of the organization painted by recruiters. Another factor is the lack of work challenge. Many new graduates expect to have a great deal of challenge and responsibility on their first job and find that they are really apprentices working under close supervision, their abilities underutilized.[9]

There are a number of ways in which reality shock can be reduced. From the organization's viewpoint, recruiters and others can provide a more realistic view of the organization and more challenging work. The new employee, on the other hand, can more carefully explore the organization before entering it and, once there, can seek out innovative, challenging work. Students also need to understand that accepting a particular job means that they may idealize it while downgrading other jobs. Thus students need to make themselves aware of the perceptual distortion (reality shock) that can occur.[10]

The First Supervisor

As mentioned earlier, the first supervisor can be an important influence on the career of the new recruit. The supervisor has a great deal of control not only over job assignments but also over organizational rewards and therefore is in a key position to launch and direct career development.

The first supervisor can be a positive influence by serving as a mentor and role model. The degree to which supervisors serve as achievement role models has been found to strongly affect subordinates' management career progress.[11] In fact, the influence of the supervisor as a mentor and role model is just as important as the influence of job assignments on the later careers of managers. The supervisor who acts as a mentor, who demonstrates competence, who has influence on superiors, and who provides stimulation, support, and feedback to subordinates is an ideal role model for the new recruit.

The first boss can also have a negative effect on the career of the new employee. Many managers have a stereotyped image of college graduates, viewing them as overly ambitious and unrealistic in their expectations, too theoretical and naive to be given a challenging initial assignment, too immature and inexperienced to be given much responsibility, and unskilled in communications. If the supervisor treats the new recruit in accord with these assumptions, the stereotype can become a self-fulfilling prophecy, stifling the career development of the young subordinate.[12]

In such a situation, the new recruit should find a mentor elsewhere in the organization, transfer to a department that has a more open supervisor, or think about finding another job. In one situation, a new employee found a mentor who was manager of another department. She was able to go to the other manager to discuss work assignments and to get advice and criticism. Eventually, the other manager acted as a sponsor to get the new employee transferred to another unit in the organization. Thus the individual was able to overcome the initial handicap by exercising her own initiative.

Organizational Socialization

A person's life history and career can be seen as a series of passages from one role or level to another, with each passage stimulating a change or adjustment that can affect the person's identity, values, attitudes, and behavior. The discussion of the first job makes it clear that the passage from the role of college student to that of employee can be crucial to career development. It is primarily during the first job experience that the new employee undergoes **organizational socialization**, which means learning not only the role requirements of the job but also the values and behavior norms considered important in the organization.[13]

Work organizations typically have a unique and well-defined subculture with shared values and norms that govern patterns of behavior and interaction of the employees. For example, employees of one organization are fond of saying, "There is a right way, a wrong way, and the X Company way." Knowing about these norms of behavior is important for those who want to make it in the particular company or, sometimes, even to get a job with it. A college student wearing a three-piece suit, white shirt, and tie to a morning class probably has a job interview later in the day. A man applying for a high-level administrative position in a large, conservative organization had two strikes against him when he appeared in a checked suit and flowered shirt and tie.

The process of socialization can start before the first job even begins. Called **anticipatory socialization,** it involves the adoption of attitudes, values, and identity perceived to be associated with an anticipated role before ever entering it. During the course of their education, students learn some attitudes, values, and identities associated with particular occupational or organizational roles. They can learn more about particular organizations by talking to other students and by interviewing with recruiters from a number of organizations before taking the first job. Anticipatory socialization helps smooth the passage from the student role to the first work role.[14]

Organizations attach varying degrees of importance to different values and norms. Some are **pivotal**—absolutely necessary for anyone who intends to remain in the organization. For example, belief in the values of the competitive free enterprise system or in the hierarchy of authority is pivotal for managers in most U.S. business organizations. Other values or norms are less important but still **relevant**—important but not absolutely necessary to accept. Examples of relevant norms and values can include standards of dress and decorum, holding of certain political views, and belonging to the right clubs. Of course, organizations differ in their values and norms. For example, a few years ago, when bow ties were popular, a new employee came to work wearing one. His boss hinted for several days and finally said: "Please don't wear bow ties any more. The president doesn't like them, and it would look bad if he suddenly paid us a visit." In this case, the norm was close to being pivotal.

A new employee has several options for behavior. One response is *rebellion*—the rejection of all the organization's values and norms. A second is *creative individualism*—the acceptance of pivotal norms and the rejection of some or all relevant ones. A third choice is *conformity*—the acceptance of all of the organization's values and norms. Rebellion results in the individual's either leaving the organization (or being fired) or working toward its goals and objectives without believing in them. Complete conformity results in a curbing of the individual's creativity, and valuable information and other inputs may be lost to the organization. The complete conformist also gives up many personal values, becoming an "organization type." Creative individualism is probably best for both the individual and the organization. (Chapter 20 described some techniques of power and politics that organization members can use to further their creative individualism.)

Equal Employment and Careers

In many U.S. organizations, entry to and advancement in the management hierarchy has been limited to white Anglo-Saxon men. Many capable people have been excluded from pursuing careers in management because they do not conform to pivotal norms regarding race, religion, or sex. To some extent, this situation is changing. Largely stimulated by federal and state equal employment legislation, organizations have begun to alter their hiring and promotion practices to comply with affirmative action programs. A major goal of such programs is to move more women and minorities into management-level positions. However, radical changes in employment practices have created new problems—not only for organizations but also for the careers of those directly affected by the changes.[15]

Tokenism

Some minorities or women are hired simply as an effort at **tokenism**—a way of meeting the organization's obligations to affirmative action programs. The token person is usually put in a highly visible or specially created position but has little power or opportunity for advancement. Thus career success is, even now, difficult for women and minorities. The burdens carried by token employees take their toll in terms of extreme psychological stress even if they have some career success. Tokenism will likely diminish as a problem when minorities and women come to hold a substantial percentage of management positions. An increase in their numbers will not only reduce tokenism but will also provide a support group to deal with stress producing situations.[16]

Lack of Mentors or Role Models

A factor contributing to the stress associated with tokenism is that the token person rarely has a mentor or role model to assist with the management career. As already seen, a mentor is vitally important to career success. Only recently, however, have management programs for women been developed to help socialize them into their new roles. Without a role model, the token person is a pioneer of sorts, breaking through barriers to gain recognition and respect. The task is especially difficult when the token person is a new college graduate with little previous experience. However, in time this difficulty too will ease, as minorities and women rise in the management hierarchy.[17]

Leadership Problems

Stereotyped and prejudiced attitudes still operate against women and minorities in management. These attitudes are manifested not only by superiors but also by peers and subordinates. The result is a lack of influence over decision making and decision implementation in the work group—and thus a limitation on the exercise of leadership. Here again, it is the recent minority and women college graduates who are most likely to encounter this problem, although it also exists at higher levels.[18] In an unguarded moment, a hospital administrator recently told a women manager that she could never become an assistant administrator, in spite of her obvious qualifications, because "people don't like to work for a woman."

The Dual-Career Family

With ever-increasing numbers of women responding to career opportunities, the number of dual-career families is also increasing rapidly. In the dual-career family, both spouses have careers, and this situation may bring on problems beyond those associated with the stresses of their work. There is no single best strategy for coping with dual-career problems. Instead, the most important ingredient of success is that the spouses discuss and agree on a common strategy. For example, two college professors who are married to each other have decided that if they must leave a particular geographic area, they will take turns in picking the new location. If it is the wife's turn and she takes a teaching job in another geographic area, the husband will follow and will attempt to find work there. Some concrete strategies for dealing with actual or potential problems created by the dual-career family include:

1. *Limiting either family or career demands.* This can mean having no children or having only one child, thereby placing greater emphasis on the career. On the other hand, a couple may decide to emphasize the family and limit the career growth for both husband and wife. Availability of day-care centers for children and of flexible or part-time work schedules can help limit the demands of the family.

2. *Shifting the stages of work and family events.* The family, as well as the career, develops in stages, and the demands change during each stage. Thus husband and wife can postpone the child rearing stage until after they are both established in their careers, or they can postpone their periods of maximum work involvement until the children have grown up enough to be somewhat independent.

3. *Segmenting or compartmentalizing work and family activities so that both need not be dealt with at the same time.* There can be a total concentration on the career during working hours and a total involvement with the family the rest of the time. This is not new for women. What is new is the meshing of both partners' schedules in the dual-career family.

4. *Husband and wife participating in a joint venture.* Establishing a small family business is one way in which both husband and wife can work toward career success. However, in a joint venture it may be difficult to segment work and family concerns (not to mention the possible problem of personal competitiveness).

5. *Pursuing completely independent careers.* Adaptations to this career strategy include the use of full-time child care and long-distance commuting. The strategy can be satisfactory for those who do not need to form close relationships but may not work well for people who are dependent. Some commuting couples who are separated because of geographically distant jobs appear to have successful marriages despite (or because of) the separation, but for many others the separation seems to increase the stress.[19]

Clearly, there are many strategies that can be used to cope with dual-career problems. The best approach, of course, is to have an open strategy that can be modified as necessary. In one situation, for example, the husband received a lucrative job offer requiring a move to an area where the wife would have had little opportunity to move up in her own career. A few years earlier, there would probably have been little discussion, and the family would probably have moved to the new location. In this instance, however, the husband turned down the job offer. Both spouses feel that the decision has strengthened their marriage.

Developing Initial Personal Career Plans

Careers often tend to evolve more out of accident than design. Even managers have been found to be remarkably lax in making major career decisions, passively letting the changes and demands in the external environment determine the organization they work for or the types of jobs they accept.[20] As one manager in a large organization put it: "Why should I worry? The company knows about me and will advance me when I am ready." Far too many people are like this manager. They fail to take the initiative in career planning, preferring to wait for someone else to act or for something to happen before they make a move. One modern text on career planning suggests that "most people spend less time gathering and consciously analyzing data on possible occupations to enter than they do on the cars they buy."[21]

Another problem is that many people feel that once having chosen a career, the decision is immutable. Frequently, however, the ages of 17 to 30 or 35 are exploratory. One woman who had a master's degree in social work left a successful career in that field at the age of 34 to become a caterer. Her catering business is highly successful, and she is enjoying her new career.

Developing Self-Awareness

Self-knowledge is central to developing a personal career plan. In fact, career choice is often determined primarily by one's self-concept.[22] One good way to start developing a career plan is to obtain career counseling and guidance. This service, or information about it, is often provided on campus. Self-administered career planning exercises can also be useful. Two of the best known of these exercises are writing an obituary for yourself, saying what you would like to have said at some specific time in the future, and writing a feature article about yourself for the front page of your local newspaper, saying what you would like to have said about yourself ten years from now. Many of the questions in Table 24.1 can be helpful, as can talking to instructors and friends about your strengths and weaknesses. Finally, many universities are now offering courses in career planning and development. Whatever approach you use, the key objective is to find out your capabilities and your interests.

Learning about Jobs and Organizations

The other kind of necessary knowledge is about jobs and organizations. As with increasing self-awareness, the kind of knowledge involves a learning process. Specific information about many organizations and the types of graduates they hire can be obtained from the *College Placement Annual,* a publication that is usually available in the college placement office. Another source of information about the job market is the U.S. Department of Labor *Monthly Labor Review,* which details the industries where jobs are most (and least) abundant. For example, the number of accountants, bank and finance managers, health administrators, and computer systems analysts is expected to increase by 1985, while the number of college teachers, postmasters, and funeral directors is expected to decrease.[23]

Personal work experience in part-time, summer, or volunteer jobs can be invaluable in choosing the type of job or organization most appropriate for a specific career. Before even going to college, one young woman took a volunteer job at a day-care center for abused children to help her decide whether her thoughts about becoming a child psychologist were realistic. The experience confirmed her dream and made her more certain about her career.

The job hunter should acquire as much information as possible about prospective employers and types of organizations. Interviews with recruiters can begin even before there is serious interest in a job. People who actively learn about jobs and organizations before completing college are in a good position to begin career planning. In addition, questions asked by recruiters and other interviewers help students formulate questions about themselves and their careers.

**Determining Initial
Career Plans**

For some, formulating career plans is relatively easy and quick. For others, it is a complicated process that can last a number of years. As pointed out earlier in the chapter, the assumption that most people have made firm career choices in their early twenties is misleading. The first serious choice sometimes occurs between 17 and 29, but even when the preliminary choice appears to be definite, it is frequently only the beginning. An individual may take several years to determine interests, to discover the most suitable occupations, and to become committed to one of them.

As also mentioned earlier, the first job is highly important, since it is there that the individual begins the process of actual, rather than anticipatory, socialization. It is also there that the individual begins, as an apprentice, to perform organizational tasks competently. Competence in critical tasks of the organization are essential for an individual to begin developing a reputation for knowledge and ability.

There is disagreement as to whether people should specialize early. A *Business Week* article suggests that experience should be sought in several fields, such as manufacturing, sales, and finance. It adds: "Get out of your specialty fast, unless you decide that's all you ever want to do. This means rapid rejection of the notion that you are a professional engineer, lawyer, scientist, or anything but a manager." [24] More formal research suggests that "it is often advisable to become a specialist, at least temporarily, and gain a reputation for competence within that specialty. . . . A person who has done outstanding work in one area is more likely than a jack-of-all-trades to gain visibility in a large organization." [25]

This contrasting advice points up most vividly the importance of a mentor who can guide, counsel, and support the new college graduate. Almost all the research agrees that the first supervisor is highly important in career development or planning. Should this person be unable or unwilling to undertake the mentor role, the individual just starting out should actively look for someone else to do so on either a formal or an informal basis.

Career planning and development clearly extends beyond the first job. Many individuals shift from one job and organization to another in the search for opportunities to fulfill the dream and to advance. But many managers settle in to their job and give little thought to the importance of ongoing career planning. In fact, "most managers, when asked how much time they spend on their own career planning, are surprised to realize how little they do. Usually they spend far more time managing their subordinates' careers than their own." [26]

Choosing a career and becoming successful in it involves a number of important steps, including self-knowledge and organizational knowledge, skills in interviewing and resume writing, socialization without the loss of independence, finding a mentor, and plotting a continuing career path. This chapter cannot do justice to all of these and other important topics. Thus an annotated bibliography that can serve as a beginning library for self-study appears at the end of the chapter. More and more material is being developed on career planning and development, so the bibliography should be seen as only a starting point on the career path.

**Implications for
the Individual**

As Table 24.1 noted, people should have a certain degree of self-awareness and at least a tentative career plan before looking for a job.

The tentative career plan is also helpful in determining which courses to take in college and which types of jobs to look for after college. The evidence is clear that proper career planning allows an individual to make the best use of abilities, values, interests, and motivations. Those who do not plan properly may wind up living lives of quiet desperation.

The evidence is also clear, as stated earlier, that career development depends heavily on the first job and the first supervisor. It is here that organizational socialization takes place and that the new employee has the opportunity to look for, and work with, a mentor. The individual who does not have a good mentor is less likely to satisfy the dream and to become successful in a chosen career.

The process also works the other way. The effective manager is one who can serve as a mentor to newer, younger subordinates. The manager who is on the wrong career track finds it difficult to serve as a role model, since he or she is likely to feel frustrated and unhappy rather than calm and confident.

Career planning and development is an extended process. Managers need to think about their own careers as well as those of their subordinates. One of the most important characteristics of the effective organization is the ability to select, develop, and place good people in the right jobs.

Review

1. How clear are you about your own career? What steps should you take to make certain you are headed in the right direction?
2. Interview friends and acquaintances. How well do they know what they want to do? How well thought out and realistic are their career plans?
3. How do you feel about a working spouse? How might your feelings and attitudes affect your dual-career family if you had one?
4. What are your expectations about your first job? How can you check to see if they are realistic?
5. Go to the alumni office and find the names of five recent graduates of your school. Call them and ask about their experiences after they accepted their first job.
6. Discuss your career plans with the placement director, a professor, or some other knowledgeable person. What have you learned about your career possibilities?
7. What problems do women and members of minority groups face in their careers with organizations? Discuss.

The Raymond Chemical Company

After receiving B.S. and M.S. degrees in industrial engineering from a well-known eastern university, Larry Jones joined the Buffalo plant of the Raymond Chemical Company. Larry, who had been the top man in his graduating class, was considered to be a very promising addition to the staff, and the plant manager felt that his knowledge of mathematical techniques would be extremely valuable in solving a number of pressing problems.

Larry was assigned initially to an experimental group that had earned a reputation of being able to solve the toughest of technical problems. Larry fit in well with the group, and he soon gained the reputation of being a first-rate idea man in a very idea-conscious group. One of Larry's early contributions, a mathematical model of materials flows, caught the attention of factory manager Charlie Jenison. Jenison, who was second in command at the Buffalo plant, asked Larry to become his assistant, and Larry accepted.

As Jenison's assistant Larry came up with a number of interesting ideas. Though his suggestions were not always immediately workable, they were invariably thought-provoking. Jenison felt that with more practical experience Larry would soon be ready for a top-level management job. He proposed to Larry that he transfer to the inventory-control department where he could serve as assistant to the manager, Allan Wilkinson. Though it was never mentioned by Jenison, Larry knew that Mr. Wilkinson had only four years to go until retirement, and he believed that he was being groomed to be Wilkinson's successor.

In the inventory-control group things went poorly from the start. Mr. Wilkinson rode Larry at every turn and delighted in posing problems almost impossible to solve. Wilkinson then taunted him with comments such as, "Your bright ideas aren't too good under real conditions." When Larry tried to develop new approaches, Wilkinson blocked their use by saying that they were not practical. He did allow Larry to introduce one system, but it contained some costly bugs. Wilkinson ordered it removed with the comment, "I told you it wouldn't work." After a few months on the job, Larry felt that Wilkinson was either ignoring him or giving him only routine work.

One evening Larry decided he had had enough. He waited for Charlie Jenison after work and told him about his difficulties with Wilkinson. When Larry asked to be reassigned, Jenison assented and suggested a transfer to the job of assistant manager of production control. Larry agreed, and left Jenison's office feeling much less frustrated.

The following morning Larry learned that the production control department was headed by Phil Burgess, a man who had only five years left until retirement, and who, for all practical purposes, was another Wilkinson. Larry was quite upset. He wondered why Jenison, whose judgment he respected, had transferred him to Burgess' department.[27]

1. Why do you think Jenison did what he did?
2. Assuming Larry wishes to stay with the Raymond Chemical Company, what do you suggest he do to make his new assignment less frustrating?
3. If you were Larry, would you stay with the Raymond Chemical Company? Why or why not?

Footnotes

1. D. Yankelovich, "Turbulence in the Working World—Angry Workers, Happy Grads," *Psychology Today*, December 1974, pp. 81–87.
2. J. Flint, "Oversupply of Young Workers Expected to Tighten Jobs Race," *New York Times*, June 25, 1978, p. 1.
3. R. Kopelman, Baruch College, City Univeristy of New York, personal communication.
4. M. Satchell, "Now Women Pilots Get Their Turn with the Airlines," *Parade*, June 25, 1978, pp. 4–5.
5. T. Bachhuber and R. Harwood, *Directions: A Guide to Career Planning* (Boston: Houghton Mifflin, 1978), p. 2.
6. E. Erickson, *Childhood and Society*, 2d ed. (New York: Norton, 1963); D. Super, *The Psychology of Careers* (New York: Harper & Bros., 1957); and E. Schein, *Career Dynamics: Matching Individual and Organizational Needs* (Reading, Mass.: Addison-Wesley, 1978).
7. D. Levinson, *The Seasons of a Man's Life* (New York: Knopf, 1978); D. Levinson, "Growing Up with the Dream," *Psychology Today*, January 1978, p. 20; and G. Sheehy, *Passages* (New York: Dutton, 1976).
8. G. Dalton, P. Thompson, and R. Price, "The Four Stages of Professional Careers—A New Look at Performance by Professionals," *Organizational Dynamics* 6 (Summer 1977): 19–42; G. Dalton and P. Thompson, "Accelerating Obsolescence of Older Engineers," *Harvard Business Review* 49 (September–October 1971): 57–68; and P. Thompson and G. Dalton, "Are R&D Organizations Obsolete?" *Harvard Business Review* 54 (November–December 1976): 105–117.
9. A. G. Athos and L. B. Ward, *Student Expectations of Corporate Life: Implications for Managerial Recruiting* (Boston: Harvard University, Graduate School of Business Administration, 1972); J. P. Wanous, "Realistic Job Previews for Organizational Recruitment," *Personnel* 52 (April 1975): 50–60. J. P. Wanous, "Organizational Entry: Newcomers Moving from Outside to Inside," *Psychological Bulletin* 84 (July 1977): 601–618; P. J. Manhardt, "Job Orientation of Male and Female College

Graduates in Business," *Personnel Psychology* 25 (July 1972): 361–368; and D. A. Ondrack, "Emerging Occupational Values: A Review and Some Findings," *Academy of Management Journal* 16 (September 1973): 423–432.

10. D. E. Berlow and D. T. Hall, "The Socialization of Managers: Effects of Expectations on Performance," *Administrative Science Quarterly* 11 (June 1966): 207–229; R. J. Campbell, "Career Development: The Young Business Manager," paper presented at Longitudinal Approaches to Career Development symposium, American Psychological Association annual meeting, San Francisco, 1968.

11. D. W. Bray, R. J. Campbell, and D. L. Grant, *Formative Years in Business: A Long-Term AT&T Study of Managerial Lives* (New York: Wiley-Interscience, 1974).

12. E. E. Jennings, *Routes to the Executive Suite* (New York: McGraw-Hill, 1971); E. H. Schein, "How to Break In the College Graduate," *Harvard Business Review* 42 (November–December 1964): 68–76; and J. S. Livingstone, "Pygmalion in Management," *Harvard Business Review* 47 (July–August 1969): 81–89.

13. E. H. Schein, "Organizational Socialization and the Profession of Management," *Industrial Management Review* 9 (Winter 1968): 1–15; J. Van Maanen and E. H. Schein, "Career Development," in *Improving Life at Work: Behavioral Science Approaches to Organizational Change,* ed. J. R. Hackman and J. L. Suttle (Santa Monica, Calif.: Goodyear Publishing, 1977).

14. D. T. Hall, *Careers in Organizations* (Pacific Palisades, Calif.: Goodyear Publishing, 1976).

15. G. W. Bowman, "What Helps or Harms Promotability?" *Harvard Business Review* 42 (January–February 1964): 6–26; and R. M. Powell, *Race, Religion and the Promotion of the American Executive,* Monograph No. AA-3 (Columbus: Ohio State University, College of Administrative Science, 1969).

16. R. M. Kanter, "Tokenism: Opportunity or Trap?" *MBA* 12 (January 1978): 15–21; S. E. Taylor, "Structural Aspects of Prejudice Reduction: The Case of Token Integration," in *Psychology and Politics,* ed. J. Sweeney (New Haven: Yale University Press, in press); and B. Rosen and T. H. Jerdee, "Sex Stereotyping in the Executive Suite," *Harvard Business Review,* 52 (March–April 1974); 45–48.

17. "Why Women Need Their Own MBA Programs," *Business Week,* February 23, 1974, pp. 102, 107; and Kanter, "Tokenism: Opportunity or Trap?"

18. J. E. Haefner, "Sources of Discrimination among Employees: A Survey Investigation," *Journal of Applied Psychology* 62 (June 1977): 265–270; W. C. Hamner et al., "Race and Sex as Determinants of Ratings by Potential Employers in a Simulated Work Sampling Task," *Journal of Applied Psychology* 59 (December 1974): 705–711; S. A. Richards and C. L. Jaffee, "Blacks Supervising Whites: A Study of Interracial Difficulties in Working Together in a Simulated Organization," *Journal of Applied Psychology* 56 (June 1972): 234–240; and Rosen and Jerdee, "Sex Stereotyping in the Executive Suite."

19. L. Bailyn, "Accommodation of Work to Family: An Analysis of Couples with Two Careers," in *Working Couples,* ed. R. Rappoport et al. (New York: Harper & Row, in press); D. T. Hall, "A Model of Coping with Role Conflict: The Role Behavior of College Educated Women," *Administrative Science Quarterly* 17 (December 1972): 471–486; and L. Bailyn, "Career and Family Orientations of Husbands and Wives in

Relation to Marital Happiness," *Human Relations* 23 (February 1970): 97–113.

20. A. Roe and R. Baruch, "Occupational Changes in the Adult Years," *Personnel Administration* 30 (July–August 1967): 26–32.

21. Hall, *Careers in Organizations,* p. 39.

22. A. Korman, "Self-Esteem as a Moderator of the Relationship between Self-Perceived Abilities and Vocational Choice," *Journal of Applied Psychology* 51 (February 1967): 65–67; and A. Korman, "Toward a Hypothesis of Work Behavior," *Journal of Applied Psychology* 54 (February 1970): 31–41.

23. "Where the Jobs Will Open Up over the Next Decade," *U.S. News & World Report,* December 27, 1976, pp. 82–83.

24. "Plotting a Route to the Top," *Business Week,* October 12, 1974, p. 128.

25. Dalton, Thompson, and Price, "The Four Stages of Professional Careers—A New Look at Performance by Professionals," p. 26.

26. Hall, *Careers in Organizations,* p. 40.

27. The case of the Raymond Chemical Company and the questions following it are from J. Hutchinson, *Organizations: Theory and Classical Concepts* (New York: Holt, Rinehart and Winston, 1967), pp. 32–33. Reprinted by permission of Jean M. Hutchinson, executor, estate of Prof. John G. Hutchinson, deceased, Graduate School of Business, Columbia University.

Careers: An Annotated Bibliography

Bolles, Richard. *What Color Is Your Parachute? A Practical Manual for Job-Hunters and Career Changers.* Rev. ed. Berkeley, Calif.: Ten Speed Press, 1977.

One of the most down-to-earth, practical, and specific books written on how to find or change jobs. Full of helpful hints regarding resumes, interviews, finding the right people to interview, and so on. The book has an excellent bibliography at the end to help further the search for a career.

Crystal, John, and Bolles, Richard. *Where Do I Go from Here with My Life?* New York: Seabury Press, 1974.

A handbook to accompany Richard Bolles's What Color Is Your Parachute? *The book provides a systematic, practical, and effective life and work planning manual for students of all ages. It includes specific suggestions regarding career planning, job hunting, and interviewing.*

Hall, Douglas. *Careers in Organizations.* Pacific Palisades, Calif.: Goodyear Publishing, 1976.

A good research-based overview of concepts about careers in organizations. The book applies to both men and women and discusses the dual-career family; it also is somewhat abstract but can help students understand both the personal and the organizational approach to career planning and development. The bibliography is excellent.

Holmstrom, Lynda. *The Two-Career Family.* Cambridge, Mass.: Schenkman Publishing, 1973.

A description of research and findings regarding the two-career family. The book includes a discussion of problems and ways of resolving them in a constructive fashion.

Kanter, Rosabeth. *Men and Women of the Corporation.* New York: Basic Books, 1977.

A detailed look at a particular organization that shows how the careers and self-images of male and female managers, professionals, secretaries, spouses of managers, and others are affected by the distribution and exercise of power. The book contains a number of specific examples and incidents.

Kaufman, Harold, *Obsolescence and Professional Career Development,* New York: Amacon, 1974.

The most comprehensive book on the causes and cures of career deterioration resulting from individual obsolescence. Written from a management perspective, the book provides clear insight into how one's work and organization can contribute to career deterioration. A comprehensive bibliography is provided.

Kotter, John; Faux, Victor; and McArthur, Charles. *Self-assessment and Career Development.* Englewood Cliffs, N.J.: Prentice-Hall, 1978.

An excellent, research-based manual designed to help people manage their own careers by developing concrete skills at assessing themselves and their opportunities, making career and job related choices, and maintaining the assessment process over the long run. The book contains a number of specific exercises and learning assignments in self-assessment, job campaigns, job offers, and career stages. It provides extensive information on organizations, careers, and job opportunities.

Lewis, Adele. *How to Write Better Resumes.* Woodbury, N.Y.: Barrons Educational Series, 1977.

    A step-by-step approach to writing individualized resumes. The book includes suggestions about cover letters, interviews, and follow-ups and provides a number of examples and illustrations.

Moment, David, and Fisher, Dalmar. *Autonomy in Organizational Life.* Cambridge, Mass.: Schenkman Publishing, 1975.

    A good book with a number of excellent illustrations about how individuals can enter organizations and still maintain their own autonomy and independence.

Nutter, Carolyn. *The Resume Workbook.* 5th ed. Cranston, R.I.: Carroll Press, 1978.

    Suggestions and recommendations regarding resumes, cover letters, and job campaigns. The book offers suggestions for self-analysis in career planning and a guide to writing good resumes.

Ritti, R. Richard, and Funkhouser, G. Ray. *The Ropes to Skip and the Ropes to Know: Studies in Organizational Behavior.* Columbus, Ohio: Grid Publishing, 1977.

    A fun book to read and an excellent description of what it is really like inside an organization. The book shows career situations within a fictionalized large bureaucratic organization. As a guide to career development, it provides homey examples of how professional people in organizations can interpret and understand what is going on around them. Although fiction, the book is true to life.

Schein, Edgar. *Career Dynamics: Matching Individual and Organizational Needs.* Reading, Mass.: Addison-Wesley, 1978.

    A personal and an organizational view of career development in organizations. The book presents both theoretical and applied aspects of career planning and contains many helpful hints for thinking about and acting on careers. It has excellent chapters on self-diagnosis, on the tasks to be performed at the entry stage, and on the tasks to be performed in order to be effectively socialized into the organization. The bibliography is excellent.

Sheehy, Gail. *Passages: Predictable Crises of Adult Life.* New York: Dutton, 1976.

    A description of some major and predictable crises of adult life and ways in which they can be handled, it contains many excellent true-to-life examples. The book was on the best seller lists for over a year and has been very popular at college bookstores.

Shertzer, Bruce. *Career Planning: Freedom to Choose.* Boston: Houghton Mifflin, 1977.

    A practical, relatively low-level, down-to-earth handbook to help people understand work, occupations, and personal development. The book discusses ways to plan educational development, resumes, job interviews, and the like. It has many review items for self-study.

Valliant, George. *Adaptation to Life.* Boston: Little, Brown, 1977.

    A follow-up study of over two hundred Harvard graduates. Through the case history method, the book demonstrates many adaptive mechanisms used by adult males in more than forty years of coping with life and careers. The study is limited to males but is an excellent source book of what actually happens to people in organizational life.

Appendix

Operations Management

Throughout the text there are references to and discussions of certain functions, processes, and systems that combined, though seemingly unrelated, make up what is termed *operations management*. Operations management envelops various production systems that together transform a set of inputs, with some kind of processing, into outputs—be they of goods or of services. Operations management, as such, entails close interrelationships between departments in the selection, design, planning and control, finance, and marketing areas, with decision making within these systems. Therefore, operations management is the core of production as it touches on or directs the many facets of creating products. The purpose of this Appendix is to pull together the activities involved in these areas of production and to demonstrate the force of this managerial field in enterprises of all dimensions—culminating with a discussion of an actual operations system (a book publishing company) in action.

The Operations Function

Organizations (schools, hospitals, manufacturing plants, restaurants, department stores, and others) exist for a purpose. The basic purpose underlying all organizations is providing goods, services, or ideas. The *operations function* is concerned with the development, use, and interaction of resources (people, facilities, information, materials, and money) to provide the goods, services, or ideas for which the organization was established. A bank, for example, takes in money in the form of deposits and provides such services as automobile and personal loans. A manufacturing organization may produce such goods as automobiles and electric carving knives. A consulting company may not produce a tangible service or product but may, instead, produce ideas that will help another organization to function more effectively.

The *operations manager* is involved in the managerial activities of selecting, designing, operating, controlling, and updating the production processes. Thus, the operations manager is concerned with developing the best allocation and combination of resources in order to produce the desired product, service, or idea, in the proper amount, and at the desired quality level.

Chapter 1 describes the operations function as the subsystem that concentrates on performing effectively at the technical level. The operations manager may be called the first-level manager, first-level supervisor, or a related title. Above this level in the organization are middle management (the coordinating level) and top management (the strategic level).

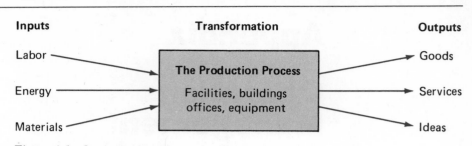

Figure A.1 Operations management as a system

Operations as a System

Chapter 14 describes the organization as a set of interdependent parts that together make up the whole. Each part contributes something to and receives something from the whole, which in turn is interdependent with the larger environment. The production or operations subsystem operates primarily at the technical level and is concerned with the major transformations, operations, or work of the system. It is the technical core of the organization. The technology involves producing a product, service, or idea that is exported into the environment and used by the public, as shown in Figure A.1. As Figure A.1 shows, the organization receives such inputs as labor, energy, and materials. In the operations subsystem, these inputs are then transformed into a modified or different form. For example, the customer's oral order is transformed by the waiter to a written order. Manufacturing organizations have elaborate mechanisms for transforming incoming materials into finished goods.

Outputs are the results of what is transformed by the system. When the inputs have been transformed, they represent outputs and are ready to leave the system or subsystem. In the restaurant example, the raw food (and the order) are transformed into an output—the finished meal. A bank may receive inputs (dollars as deposits), transform these inputs (record keeping), and export (output) the money to customers in the form of automobile and mortgage loans. A body shop takes in an automobile damaged in an accident, repairs it, and returns the automobile to the owner.

Types of Operations

Inputs can be transformed into outputs in many different ways. The most commonly known type of operation is manufacturing. Operations in manufacturing are usually called production systems. The term *operations* has only relatively recently been substituted for the term *production* to indicate that production occurs in many organizations other than manufacturing. In manufacturing production operations, the inputs are primarily physical, as are the outputs. For example, in an automobile factory, inputs can consist of raw materials. Tools, equipment, and workers are used in the fabrication and assembly (transformation) of cars; the complete automobile is the output.

As Figure A.2 shows, the production or operation function may be primarily physical. Operations can also include exchange, transportation and storage, communications, and gratification. Figure A.2 can be misleading, since the operations are not mutually exclusive. As an illustration, a department store allows shoppers to compare both prices and quality (informational); to purchase items (exchange); and to hold merchandise in inventory until needed (storage). Further, many department stores will deliver items to the home of the shopper (transportation).

Type	Illustrative Organizations
Physical	Manufacturing, health care, publishing, construction
Exchange	Retailing, wholesaling, legal firms, auto rental, banks
Transportation and storage	Warehousing, railroads, trucking firms, Postal Service
Communications	Newspapers, radio stations, news magazines
Gratification	Motion pictures, television, dance bands

Figure A.2 Operations systems classified by types of operations

There are some major differences between a manufacturing system and, for example, a service system. First, as Figure 14.9 in the text suggests, the operations subsystem of a manufacturing organization is usually protected from the external environment by boundary-spanning subsystems that handle the actual imports and exports. Only on relatively rare occasions will a representative from operations be involved in meetings with suppliers or customers. These functions are usually performed by individuals in the purchasing or sales departments. In a service function, on the other hand, the production or operations manager may directly interrelate with the customer. For example, the manager of a restaurant, or a high school principal may, and usually does, have a great deal of contact with the public.

A second major difference between the operations system in manufacturing and its counterpart in service is that most service organizations deal directly with the consumer, whereas manufacturing managers frequently do not. Department stores, supermarkets, and banks deal directly with the public. Furniture manufacturers, refineries, and automobile firms typically have wholesalers, retailers, or other producers as customers. For example, a refinery does not sell its gasoline or heating oil directly to the public. Gasoline is purchased at the local service station, which may or may not be owned or operated by the oil company operating the refinery.

Finally, the production function is much easier to locate and pinpoint in a manufacturing organization than in a service organization. Many service organizations do not perceive themselves as having a production function and frequently do not clearly identify or formalize it on their organization charts. The director of nurses in a hospital or the dean of a college might object to being called the head of a production function. Thus, the term *operations* is more acceptable.

Nevertheless, service and other organizations are adopting some methods and techniques from manufacturing to increase effectiveness and productivity. Productivity has been a major problem for service organizations. The concept of "providing a service" has traditionally portrayed an image of personal attendance on others, and thus the operations function in service organizations has also usually been highly labor-intensive, with a greater percentage of the operations cost resulting from labor rather than from materials or other expenses. The application of manufacturing techniques reduces cost, but at a price of less personal service and humanism.

A number of manufacturing concepts are being applied to service organizations to increase productivity. Four will be described here: mechanization, assembly-line standardization, specialization, and organizational expansion.

Mechanization, or the use of machines or other mechanical approaches to increase output, can be seen in laundry and dry-cleaning organizations. The use of such machines as commerical dishwashers, paint sprayers, floor and wall scrubbers, and automobile washers has increased output per labor hour in other service areas. Air wrenches and pressurized greasing machines are prevalent in service stations and garages.

Standardization developed for the assembly-line has been useful in a variety of different service fields. Fast-food outlets such as McDonald's, Burger King, and Kentucky Fried Chicken have adopted such methods. Corporations and labor unions have sponsored mass physical examinations, using automated test equipment and mobile health units.

Specialization of effort has made labor more productive in service organizations. Specialization has long been practiced in the medical profession. Automobile repair firms specialize in such areas as rustproofing, body repair, and the installation or repair of brakes, mufflers, and transmissions. Midas Muffler Shops can install an automobile muffler at less cost than can an automobile dealer's garage, in many instances. Self-service gasoline stations are on the increase, selling gasoline at less per gallon.

Organizational expansion improves productivity by consolidation, as when oil companies add restaurants and motels to their service mix; or major airlines such as TWA and United add hotels; or automobile rental agencies develop a credit card business; and large retailing organizations such as Sears develop broader lines—automobile insurance, for instance.

Organizational Processes

Operations processes can be classified in a number of different ways. Three will be briefly described here: classification by the way material inputs are handled, classification by time or flow, and classification by the amount of human input needed.

Classification by Material Inputs

Material inputs can involve the combination of materials, breaking them down, or treating them. Combination involves putting different parts together to form a more valuable whole. Automobiles, ball-point pens, pumps, and typewriters must go through the combination process. Breaking down involves removing or at least separating some of the original input, usually a raw material, to smaller quantities that are of greater value. Examples of the breaking-down process are metal shops that make smaller parts from larger sheets of metal, and butcher shops that cut up a beef carcass into smaller quantities that can be sold in a market. Treating inputs involves doing something to them to make them more useful or valuable. Universities provide knowledge to students. Social work agencies treat clients. Physically, the treatment process may involve reshaping, hardening, or softening an object. Smoking bacon or molding the plastic for a ball-point pen are examples of the treatment process. In most cases, the production process involves all three of these processes, as in the production of a typewriter.

Classification by Time

The time of operations processes can be either continuous or intermittent—either for stock or to order. The flow of a continuous production process goes on and on. Examples of continuous flow processes include cola bottling plants, assembly lines, petroleum refineries, and fast-food outlets with standardized products, such as McDonald's. Many continuous flow processes, such as refineries, are highly automated.

An intermittent production process starts, stops, and starts again. Examples of such flow systems are hospitals, universities, physicians' offices, and special-order fabrication shops. Most continuous production processes produce goods for stock; that is, the goods are produced and kept in inventory until there is a demand. For example, the petroleum refinery or the cola bottling plant can anticipate a fairly steady demand. Keeping goods in inventory or storage is expensive, since such goods take up space, may become obsolete, damaged, or stolen, and may require financing.

Producing to order is an alternative to producing to stock. The organization waits until there is a specific order before starting the manufacturing process. Hand-made clothing originals, customized automobiles, Diesel locomotives, and gourmet restaurants make items to order.

Classification by the Amount of Human Input

Operations or production processes also vary in the amount of human input they need and use. A labor-intensive process depends more on people than on machines. Universities, hospitals, department stores, custom women's apparel manufacturing, automobile body shops, and law firms are highly labor-intensive. Capital-intensive processes are those in which machines can do the job better than people. Indeed, in a petroleum refinery, people may have relatively little to do with the actual production process, which is highly automated.

The basic design of the operations system is partly established by the type of organizational process. For example, if there is a high demand for a standardized product or service, then the continuous flow process is usually more effective. If the volume is low, or if the product or service must be customized, an intermittent process may be more effective.

Because of high volume, specialization of labor, high equipment usage, and economies of scale, the unit cost of the continuous flow system is usually lower than that of the intermittent flow process. However, a continuous flow process usually requires a larger capital investment than an intermittent flow process and thus is more capital-intensive.

The Operations Function in Context

A primary function of operations management in the context of the larger system is to contribute to the overall goals and strategic plans of the organization. For most organizations, the operations function lies at the basic core of the organization. For operations managers to do their job successfully, they must interact constantly with other functions of the organization, especially marketing and finance. Many manufacturing and other organizations require an engineering function as well.

**Planning and
Operations
Management**

Planning in organizations is an essential activity. Only after direction has been established can managers decide what is to be done, when it is to be done, how it is to be done, and who is to do it. Planning looks to the future to determine the direction in which an organization or its subunits should be going. It helps bridge the gap from where we are to where we want to be by raising and answering three basic questions:

1. Where are we now?
2. Where do we want to be (short-term, long-term)?
3. How can we get there from here?

In the simplest sense, a plan is anything that involves selecting a course for the future by answering these questions. All managers plan, and planning is done at all levels of the organization, as shown in Figure A.3. At the top level of the organization, the planning is strategic, directed toward the general position of the organization in the environment. Chapter 8 defines strategic planning as a process that begins with goals and objectives and that creates strategies, policies, and detailed plans and controls to achieve them. In Chapter 7, organizational goals are described as states of affairs that the organization attempts to realize, and organizational objectives are defined as ideas or statements that help steer the activities of the organization toward the attainment of those goals.

Thus, strategic planning is directed toward answering questions such as: What should be the overall goals of the organization? What is its basic mission or purpose? What is its overall strategy? What should be its continuing objectives?

Tactical planning involves deciding specifically how the resources of the organization will be used to help the organization achieve its strategic plans and goals. As Figure A.3 suggests, the operations planning cycle includes not only the actual operations but also the control and evaluation of the operations or actual production. Control is the process that allows managers to determine whether activities conform to the plan and the objectives and then to make adjustments when necessary. Thus, in the planning stage, operations management is concerned with such questions as: What should be the design of the product or service? How should the actual process take place? What should be the physical layout of the process? How should the operation be scheduled? Who should perform the operations? How should these people be selected, trained, assigned, and motivated? The operations control pro-

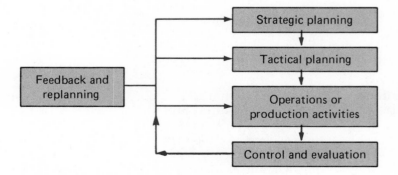

Figure A.3 Operations management planning cycle

cess involves such questions as: What is the relationship between operations scheduling and control? How will the quality of the goods and/or services be controlled? What types of cost control should be established and used?

As seen in Figure A.3 and in the questions that strategic and tactical plans are designed to answer, there are some fundamental differences between strategic and tactical plans. The first has to do with time spans. Usually, short-range plans are tactical, such as operations schedules and day-to-day actions. The second major difference involves the number of different organizational functions that are affected by the plan. The more strategic the plan, the more functions are involved. Strategic plans tend to be broad in scope, whereas tactical plans are narrow and focused on more specific targets. For example, a corporate level plan is more likely to be broad and strategic (what widgets should be made?) than a production plan (how many of the X-type of widget should be made?). The third major difference is concerned with the establishment of goals. Strategic planning is involved with the formulation of overall organizational goals and the selection of the means and approaches by which those goals are to be attained. Tactical planning is based on a set of goals established by higher levels in the organization and is concerned with specific ways of reaching them.

Operations Management in Relation to Other Functions

For many organizations, the operations function is the most important one and lies at the basic core of the organization. A brewery must be able to manufacture a beer with a given taste and at a price that customers will pay. A restaurant must produce a well-cooked meal or customers will not return. The product must periodically be updated or it can become obsolete. Electronic hand calculators are a prime example of a product that can become obsolete very quickly.

Thus, in addition to the actual production of goods and services, most organizations need a marketing function and a finance function. Most manufacturing organizations require an engineering function as well. The organization must determine customers' needs, and the product must be designed before it can be built. After manufacture, the organization needs to sell and distribute the goods or services produced by the operating system. The finance function needs to provide the funds necessary to support the activities of the engineering, operations, and marketing activities. Funds can come from the sale of the organization's goods or services but can also be obtained through the sale of stock, retained earnings, investment income, and loans.

Chapters 15 and 16 describe not only the basic functions of specialization and coordination but also contingency approaches to organizing the work of an organization. For example, the organization chart, described in Chapter 15, can show such basic departments as marketing, engineering, operations, and finance, as demonstrated here in Figure A.4. From a systems viewpoint, however, a particular production problem, project, or process, may have a dynamic effect on more than one department, as shown in Figure A.5. For this particular problem, each department (marketing, engineering, operations, and finance) contributes its own area of specialization and expertise to solving the problem. No operations manager can perform a job effectively without a great deal of cooperation and help from colleagues. For another, the analysis and methodology that are brought to bear on operations problems must necessarily include elements of financial or market analysis and planning. Among other things, an operations manager needs to know how

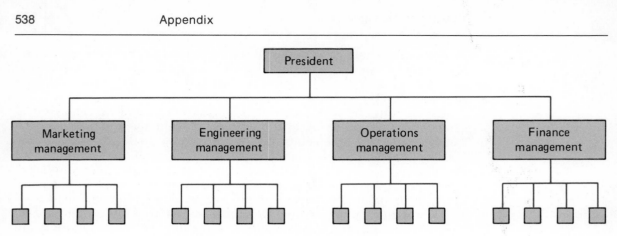

Figure A.4 Basic approach to departmentation

operations decisions affect corporate financial plans—and how financial plans affect operations decisions.

Thus, whether it is realized or not, the operations manager is necessarily part of the financial management "team." One of the most important and most difficult functions of an operations manager is providing the data that are important for arriving at good financial plans. An operations manager needs to make strong recommendations to the finance management about investment opportunities that have high profit-making opportunities.

In addition to financing, close interrelationship is required between departments in the design, production, and marketing of a product, especially a physical one. For example, marketing, as a subsystem of the organization, involves the activities and processes required to find, build, and serve markets for products and services. Marketing both precedes and follows the operations function. Prior to production of goods or services, marketing must frequently find out what products or services people already want or need and then help to determine what their proper design should be. At times, this part of the marketing function involves trying to satisfy old and established wants and desires. At other times, marketing involves stimulating or creating new wants

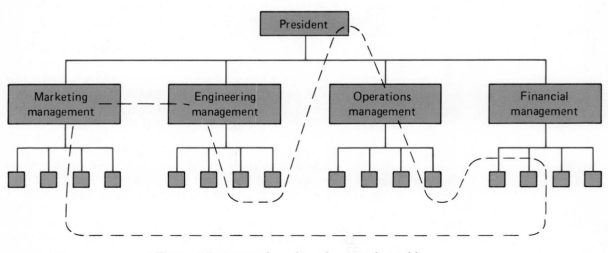

Figure A.5 Systems boundary of a particular problem

and desires. After the goods or services have actually been produced, they must be sold and distributed. Thus, marketing involves such activities as marketing research, retailing, managing the sales force, advertising, and transportation.

What happens when marketing, manufacturing, finance, and engineering do not work together as a team? One actual situation involved a high technology company that did a great deal of governmental defense work, which emphasized performance. The company was dominated by engineers. The president of the company, himself an engineer, decided that the organization should expand and go into television manufacturing. The engineering department designed an outstanding television set, which was then sent to manufacturing for actual production. After a few hundred sets had been made, the marketing department was asked to set up sales and distribution outlets. Unfortunately, the set, although well built, had not been designed with the consumer in mind. The sets did not sell for one simple reason—they cost approximately five times as much as comparable sets. Consumers resisted buying them, primarily on the basis of cost. As a result, the company's venture was prohibitively costly. There was no way that the company could make and sell the sets at a profit.

To avoid mistakes of this kind, many organizations, particularly high technology organizations in such fields as electronics, are using a "design-to-cost" approach. Design-to-cost establishes, as a goal, a unit production cost that is obtained from the price that the marketplace is willing to pay for a given product volume and performance. Most of the world's customers do not want technology for the sake of technology; they want high performance at the lowest possible price. Thus, marketing determines what product is needed and the price customers are willing to pay. Finance determines which particular product, as opposed to another one, the organization is to produce. Then, the operations manager must decide what performance-versus-cost ratio makes the most salable product. If additions to performance are made in one area of the product, the cost of such increased performance must be offset by reduced cost elsewhere. Thus, the manager must constantly make trade-offs to maintain both the cost and price ceilings. This approach is particularly useful in high-volume electronic products organizations where the life-cycles are relatively brief—three to five years.

To explore design-to-cost further, it may be helpful to look at the major phases of a product's life. First, basic performance requirements are determined. What does the potential customer want the product to do? Next, volume projections are made after a careful study of the market. Price is also determined by the same careful study: What is the customer willing to pay for the product and how will the market expand as the price of the product is lowered? Profit margins are then determined to finance growth. In this way, working backwards from price, unit production costs for the entire product can be determined for each major element of the product. The process of estimating what the potential customer wants the product to do and estimating how many dollars the customer is willing to pay for it gives a definite target for product design and manufacture.

When a particular product first enters the marketplace, the organization may lose money on it until a particular volume is reached. The break-even point is the point at which costs are covered and the organization begins to make a profit. Volume, in turn, is partly determined by competitors who may quickly alter their products or even enter new ones to compete with the new product. Volume also is partly determined by the consumer, whose judgment of the product is determined partly by performance and partly by price.

Thus, the operations manager faces a constant challenge—that of cost reduction, which will continue throughout the life of the product. On-going attempts must be made to realize cost reduction, whether through product simplification, new methods of manufacturing, training of employees, or other methods.

Some organizations suggest that training production workers, together with tooling simplification, will allow about a 5 to 15 percent reduction in costs. Additional reductions can occur through product redesign or simplification of the manufacturing process. Such approaches can result in cost reductions of 10 to 25 percent. When volume justifies the capital investment, automation can result in cost reductions ranging from 10 to 20 percent. Attempts at cost reduction through the interaction of marketing, design, and operations managers continue until the product is phased out.

Designing Operating Systems

The format of an operations system involves designing the product or service that is going to be produced, selecting the process that will be used in producing the goods or services, selecting the location for the physical facilities, determining the layout of the facility, and organizing for the actual production. Clearly, these different activities overlap considerably, and different steps may be taken, or omitted, at different stages in time. For example, relatively seldom does an organization actually build a new plant. Some organizations have been making essentially the same product or offering the same service for a number of years, so that designing a product really means continuing product improvement.

Product or Service Design

The operations manager usually does not become involved with the actual product or service design until many preliminary design decisions have been made. The first step in product design usually involves the marketing and engineering departments in preparing basic specifications for the product so that the product will meet functional requirements that will satisfy potential customers or users. The operations manager gets involved at the stage when the basic overall design has been established. The operations manager then begins to determine what material will be used, the manufacturing process that will be used, the equipment or facilities necessary, and the like.

Marketing, design engineering, and operations need to work together closely to ensure that the product or service meets market requirements and that the processes used will minimize the production costs consistent with both quality and quantity. In many instances, the design needs to be altered from the original in order to make the product easier to manufacture. Even when a product has been in manufacturing for a considerable period of time, both engineering and manufacturing process changes are made to improve the product or reduce the cost. Changes made by the engineering department are usually labeled Engineering Change Requests (ECRs); changes initiated by the manufacturing department are usually called Manufacturing Change Requests (MCRs). Usually, both departments need to approve the change before the actual change is made in the manufacturing process.

Traditionally, there has been conflict between design engineers and operations managers. Such conflict can frequently be useful. At times, however, conflict can result in less effective approaches to problem solving. Chapter 16 describes some ways in which such conflict can come about because of differences in viewpoints—called **differentiation**. The concept of **integration** describes some ways in which conflict can be resolved productively. Chapter 18 describes additional ways of managing conflict.

Process Selection

A number of decisions must be made in process selection. These include the different transformation processes that are available; specific component decisions, which determine the equipment and procedures to be used; and specific process flow decisions.

The alternative transformation processes can include decisions regarding the choice between using special-purpose or general-purpose equipment, the degree of mechanization, automation, or use of human labor, and make-or-buy decisions. For example, one question that often arises in process selection is whether to make a particular product or component part or to buy the product or part from someone else—the make-or-buy decision. Many firms, particularly those in the exchange type of transformation (Figure A.2), are organized in such a way that they make more money by buying a product and then reselling it or using it. Automobile rental firms, for instance, do not make their own automobiles, but they do service the automobile while they own it.

A number of other factors are involved in the make-or-buy decision. Is there a reliable source from which to buy the product or part? Can a supplier meet needs for quantity, quality, and delivery schedules? Is it cheaper to buy? Does buying rather than making allow for more flexibility? The major automobile manufacturers usually buy many of the different parts of the automobile they make. Construction firms often use a number of different subcontractors for such parts of the project as plumbing, heating, and electrical work.

Facility Location and Construction

Operations management also must be concerned with the location of the facility. Facilities include offices, the production operation itself, warehouses, service centers, and branches. The location of the facility or facilities can affect such factors as overall cost, number of customers, ease of operations, employee morale, and transportation. For example, a chemical plant requires large amounts of water for processing and thus may need to be located along a large river. An oil refinery needs ways of transporting the crude oil into the refinery and the finished products away from the refinery, and thus needs to be located in areas where there are pipelines or other sources of transportation, such as ships or barges. Fast-food shops, such as McDonald's and Burger King, need to be located in areas of relatively high traffic density in order to attract customers.

Two major decisions need to be made regarding the location of a particular facility; the general area and the specific site. Questions that should be asked about the general area include: Will the finished products be transported to customers or will the customers take or consume the products on the premises? What is the quantity and quality of the available labor supply? What is the adequacy of power and water supplies? Where are competitors located? Customers? Suppliers? Questions that should be asked about the specific site location include: Is the

Table A.1   Questions for plant design and layout

Is the process capital- or labor-intensive?
Is the process continuous or intermittent?
What are the sizes of the units?
Are the units perishable?
What are total output expectations?
Will production be year-round or seasonal?
What financing will be necessary?
Will machines be arranged by product or process?
Will future expansion be necessary?

area of sufficient size? What is the accessibility of highways, railways, or other means of transport? What are the restrictions on land use? On waste disposal? What are the costs of land? What is the availability of leased facilities?

After the actual selection of a site, the building then must be designed. At this stage, architects, engineers, and operations experts plan the capacity and design of the building. The capacity of the plant is the maximum output possible, using existing technology. A plant assembling pocket calculators may need 12,000 square feet of space in order to assemble a maximum of 2,500 units a day.

The design of the building depends not only on the capacity but also on the layout of the plant—the planned location of the different aspects of the production process. Some of the factors to be considered are listed in Table A.1. For example, a plant layout for a chemical processing plant will look very different than for the calculator assembly plant mentioned above. Assembly of calculators is labor-intensive, continuous, and for stock. Thus, it might well be laid out in a straight line. Incoming parts could be checked and stored at one end, the different steps in assembly could take place in the center, and the other end of the building could contain the inspection, packing, and shipping processes. The physical layout of a fast-food restaurant, such as Kentucky Fried Chicken, would look very different from the physical layout of a gourmet restaurant, where much more space is devoted to food preparation and leisurely dining.

Operations managers must not only consider the location of new facilities but must also continuously reexamine the location of present facilities to ensure the most effective production-distribution mix. For example, oil companies that have their own service stations continuously reexamine not only the location of present stations but also the possible location of new stations. A refinery is impossible to move after it has been built. Therefore, facility decisions are involved with the renovation, closure, or expansion of the facility. Gasoline service stations may be opened or closed much more easily than refineries.

Decisions made regarding site location might be made more easily using a decision tree, as shown in Figure 10.5. After the site has been located, decisions regarding the actual construction of the building might be made more easily by using a Gantt or PERT chart. Examples of both are shown in Figures 10.2 and 10.3.

Organizing for Production

Organizing the operations process system involves a complex interrelationship of workers, equipment, machinery, product, and other resources in the production subsystem, as well as relationships with the larger system. Chapters 15 and 16 cover the basic priciples and processes of organizing; here, three important considerations will be briefly discussed as they apply to the operations process: organizing by function or product, staffing, and job design.

Organizing by Function or Product

As shown in Figure 15.2, one of the most common ways of organizing is by function, which involves grouping activities according to similar work, skills, knowledge, and technology. A function-oriented layout is usually used when the work flow is intermittent. In such an arrangement, equipment or procedures that are similar are grouped together. Thus, all grinding machines are grouped in one place, all x-ray machines are grouped together, all buffing machines are grouped together. Restaurants, hospitals, and custom fabrication shops frequently use this approach. For example, in a restaurant, all salads may be prepared in one location, and desserts in another.

In the product type of organization, as shown in Figure 15.4, each unit is relatively self-contained. For example, product-organized plants might have one department for making mechanical pencils and another for ball-point pens. Product layouts have the equipment or services placed according to the different steps by which a product is manufactured or a customer serviced. Product layouts can be seen most clearly in assembly lines where a standardized product is made in large quantities. Chapter 15 summarizes some of the reasons for both product and function organizations.

Staffing

The operations manager is responsible for staffing and motivating the work force. Staffing for production is frequently complicated by the requirements for highly trained and specialized personnel. Chapter 3 describes basic approaches to individual motivation, and Chapter 5 shows the interplay and influence of groups on individuals. Chapter 13 describes the basic steps in the recruitment, selection, and development of people. The job of the operations manager is complicated by the role played by unions in many organizations, particularly manufacturing. Union contracts and other factors frequently influence the way in which the operations manager can hire and promote personnel, as well as assign people to jobs.

Job Design

The operations manager, particularly in manufacturing, faces the classic problem of combining human resources together with a high degree of capital investment in equipment. The operations manager cannot consider only the motivation and satisfaction of personnel, nor can the manager concentrate only on the capital equipment necessary to do the job. Chapter 19 provides some recommendations for job design, including the concept of sociotechnical systems, which provides a way of interrelating both the technical and the social system in designing jobs.

Planning and Control of Operations

Because an operations system is properly designed is no assurance that the system will operate either efficiently or effectively. An old adage, known as Murphy's Law, states that "Whatever can go wrong, will." Therefore, an essential part of operations management is directed toward planning and controlling day-to-day operations. The production must be planned and scheduled, material and other resources must be ordered, the products or services must be guided through the system, quality must be maintained, inventories controlled and managed, and cost constraints followed.

Planning and control concepts and principles which are discussed in Chapters 8 and 9, need to be effectively applied by the manager to the operations function. For example, good planning and scheduling minimizes the wasting of time, equipment, and material. Good inventory control reduces the cost of investment in both inventories and space. Costs also are reduced by good quality control that reduces scrap and wasted materials.

Operations Planning and Control

Although the terms **operations planning** and **control** are not synonomous, they are used almost synonomously since they are so closely related. Operations planning involves developing specific plans and courses of action for the operations system over an extended time period. Operations controlling is the process that allows managers to determine whether activities conform to the plan.

Operations planning is sometimes called **aggregate planning** or scheduling so that it can be more clearly differentiated from the day-to-day scheduling by which the actual production plan is carried out. Aggregate operations planning involves forecasting the demand for the organization's products or services and choosing the combination of human and material resources to produce the goods or services to meet the demand in the most effective and efficient fashion, including minimizing work force costs and inventory fluctuations.

The first step in developing an operations plan is to develop a demand forecast for the goods or services of the organization. Next, the demand forecasts are evaluated in terms of the impact on the organization's resources. The last step is to develop the best plan for using the current and expected resources to meet the expected demand. Thus, the operations plan results in the determination of actual production rates, work force needs, and inventory levels for the operations system over a specified time period. The plan must allow for the ordering of materials, distributing work to the different operations departments and work stations, establishing personnel requirements, and establishing production times for each stage of the process.

A number of mathematical and other tools are available to assist with operations planning. Forecasting can be done through statistical techniques, customer surveys, correlation with economic or consumer trends, and salesmen's estimates. In the operations planning itself, a number of graphical and charting approaches, such as the Gantt chart (shown in Figure 10.2), linear programming (described in Chapter 10), and other related mathematical techniques have been applied to almost every activity of operations management. Linear programming is particularly helpful in determining the best routing of the product through the facility in order to make optimum use of existing equipment and personnel.

Operations control is concerned with the conformance of the actual activities to the plan. Much of the same information generated in the operations planning process is used in the control process. For example, if actual sales do not conform to the forecasts, a warning signal is raised. Linear programming is not only a planning device but is also used as a control device, as in the case of National Airlines, at the beginning of Chapter 10.

Controls in other types of organizations may be less sophisticated, but still necessary. For example, the director of a well-managed social work agency receives each month a series of computerized reports. The reports describe how and where each social worker has spent time during the month, the number of cases seen, the number of contract versus unpaid hours, progress against contracts, and the like. To get a

Table A.2 Client distribution within program (*Partial Report*)

A. Doe, Social worker

Type of Client	Total	Open	Terminate	New	Direct Time (Monthly)
Counseling	2	2			8.00
Unwed parent	25	8	7	3	42.25
Foster care	5	2	3	1	18.25
Children's protective service	14	11	3	4	94.50
Total	46	23			163.00

quick estimate of the productivity of a given worker, the director would first review the total number of cases assigned to the worker, the time per case (compared with previous activities), the number of direct client hours in comparison with administrative time, and the like.

As shown in Table A.2, for example, the social worker, A. Doe, has stopped working with seven unwed parents and has picked up only three new cases—thus, it may be possible to assign additional cases to the worker.

Proceeding to another worker, the director notices that, as shown in Table A.3, A. Black appears to be spending a reasonable amount of time in administrative activities. However, knowing the territory that the social worker has to cover, the director wonders if the worker is spending too much time in the office and not enough time in the field. The director then makes a note to check further on this particular activity. In addition, other reports have suggested that Code 87, the grant project, is behind schedule. Black may need to spend more time on the project next month.

Quality Control

Quality control is concerned with the quality of goods and services provided. It ranges from the relatively simple to the highly complex. A relatively simple quality control model is a student's grade point average. At the more complex end of the quality control spectrum, every part of the Apollo, Mariner, and Viking space vehicles was examined rigorously before assembly to make certain that the parts work properly. Fail-

Table A.3 Monthly administrative activity (*Does not include time with clients*)

A. Black, Social worker

Code	Activity	Hours	Percent
55	Case management	10.00	
60	Telephone	2.50	
63	Staff development	.50	
80	Staff supervision	1.00	
83	Staff/unit meeting	15.00	
85	Conference and outside meetings	3.00	
87	Grant Project	3.50	
88	Travel	1.75	
**	Total administration	38.75	24.07
91	Holiday	7.00	
92	Sick leave	3.25	
**	Total lost time	10.25	6.37
	Total hours:	168.00	

ure of one part could abort the entire mission. Some of the parts, when finally completed, were more expensive per ounce than gold.

Earlier in the Appendix, the concept of design-to-cost was described. Under such a concept, the amount of quality designed and built into a product is, in part, determined by the price that customers are willing to pay. For example, the tolerances and specifications for a common water glass may be relatively "loose." That is, the shape of the glasses do not have to be identical, since they do not have to fit together. Indeed, as one manufacturing manager put it, "They are designed to 'fit the air.'" On the other hand, quality control for medical and related equipment must be much higher and more accurate, since mistakes could result in patients' deaths. Mistakes in quality assurance and control can be extremely costly, as automobile callbacks have demonstrated.

Operations quality control applies to raw materials or parts coming into the plant, the finished product, and to critical stages in the production process. The usual process is to inspect materials coming into the organization to ensure that they are as specified and ordered. During the work process, the organization usually has established inspection processes at critical stages or at steps in the production operation that might cover up or hide defects or other problems. For example, a particular part might be inspected just before it is placed inside another part that would cover it over. Parts and other materials are usually inspected just before painting, which may temporarily cover a defect.

Before the product or service is distributed to the customer or wholesaler, it is usually given a final inspection. For example, new cars are test driven before being released; radios and other small applicances are given a final inspection before being packaged. The number of actual checkpoints and inspections depends on the cost of inspection and the cost of passing a defective unit or part.

In many instances, a 100 percent final inspection is necessary because of the serious results that might occur if one defective unit was produced and sold. In most instances, however, 100 percent quality of all inputs and outputs is impossible. One reason is cost. To check every light bulb before it was put into the carton would increase the cost of bulbs. Thus, only a sample of light bulbs is actually tested. Another reason is that inspecting some products will destroy them, such as dynamite, gun powder, and detonating caps. Thus, many organizations perform the inspection operations by using a sampling process based on probability. Highly accurate sampling techniques have been developed to reduce cost and to keep the quality of the product at the desired level.

Inventory Control

Inventory control is concerned with making certain that the right amount of raw materials, work in progress, and finished goods are available. A supermarket manager who orders too little milk runs the risk of losing sales; one who orders too much milk runs the risk of spoilage and waste. Airlines, hotels, and motels have a complex inventory control process to ensure maximum use of facilities.

From a systems point of view, inventories can be very useful as a buffer between different subsystems with different rates of work flow. Inventories are generally classified into three broad areas: raw material, in-process inventory, or finished goods. Raw material inventories are helpful as a buffer between purchasing and the actual production process. In-process inventories are helpful to buffer differences in flow rates through the different production departments, processes, or areas.

Finished goods are helpful as a buffer between the last stages of production and the customer.

Thus, there are some reasons for keeping inventory levels high. The buffering process means that an organization is not so likely to run out of parts and have down time. A supply of finished goods makes it less likely that a customer will be told that the organization will be out of stock.

The reasons for keeping inventories low are equally as good. High inventories mean tie-up of funds. The lower the inventory, the more money available for other purposes. Inventories take up space, which may be scarce and expensive. In addition, inventories of incoming material or of finished goods may deteriorate or become obsolete as products or markets change.

There are a number of mathematical aids to improve inventory control. The formulas are usually based on such factors as expected delivery time; price, which may vary by amount purchased; insurance costs; storage and storage costs; deterioration or obsolescence; and taxes. Inventory costs and levels may vary widely, depending on the organization and the product or service. For example, a municipality in the northeastern part of the United States might not be very concerned about having several carloads of sand left over after the winter season—the sand can always be put on the streets next winter. However, a manufacturer of high-fashion women's dresses might worry far more about having excess inventory.

Keeping close track of proper inventory levels is essential to good operations management. As a specific illustration, the manager of a relatively small bicycle store had an opportunity to purchase a relatively large number of a particular model imported bicycle at a greatly reduced price. Because of the number, some of the bicycles remained in inventory for almost a year. Only at the end of the year, when the books were closed, did the store manager learn to his chagrin that he had actually lost money on the bicycles because of interest rates, storage costs, insurance, and other costs.

An Operating System in Action—Book Publishing

A production system can be relatively simple, such as making sandwiches in Joe's Bar and Grill, which is a labor-intensive, intermittent process. Refineries and chemical plants are highly capital-intensive, continuous-flow production processes. However, intermittent processes can also be highly complex. Many different examples or illustrations might be given of production processes. This section describes the work flow involved in publishing a book. The accompanying flow chart (Figure A.6) illustrates in minute detail the many operations processes involved in book production—in this case, a college textbook. It further puts into perspective the coordination of planning systems, preliminary selection and design decisions, the various controls required as production goes forward, and the interrelationship between departments. As a graphic review of the overall discussions in the text, it is appropriately placed as the finale of this book.

Producing a textbook is a complicated process. Each textbook (like each model of an automobile) is different in design and content; in other words, it is a custom item that is prepared for manufacturing.

Before a textbook can actually go into production, its author is signed (or hired) to write a book by an acquisition editor. After the actual writing process, the manuscript is reviewed and analyzed to determine manufac-

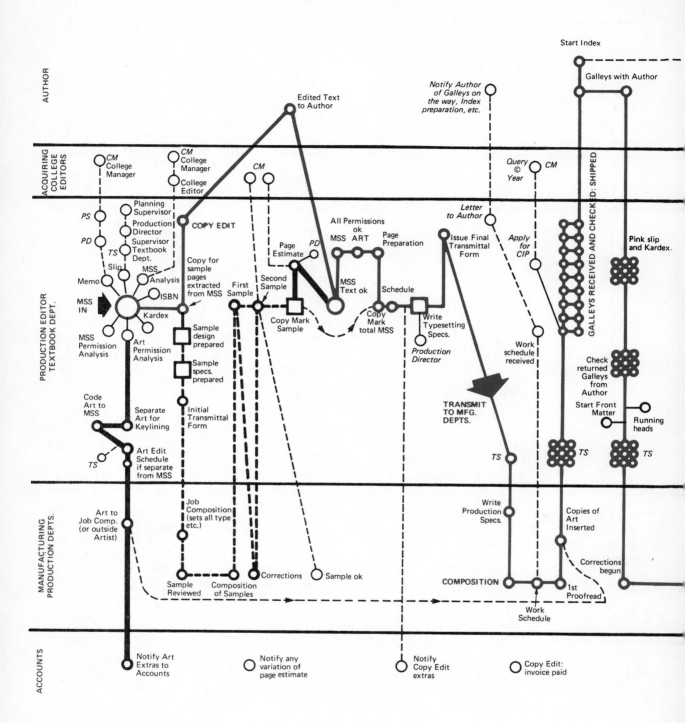

Legend of Terms:

CIP: Cataloging in Publication (Library of Congress)
CM: College Manager
F and G's: Folded and gathered pages
ISBN: International Standard Book Number
Kardex: Internal record-keeping system

MSS: Manuscript
PD: Production Director
PS: Production Supervisor
Specs: Specifications of the book
TS: Textbook Department Supervisor

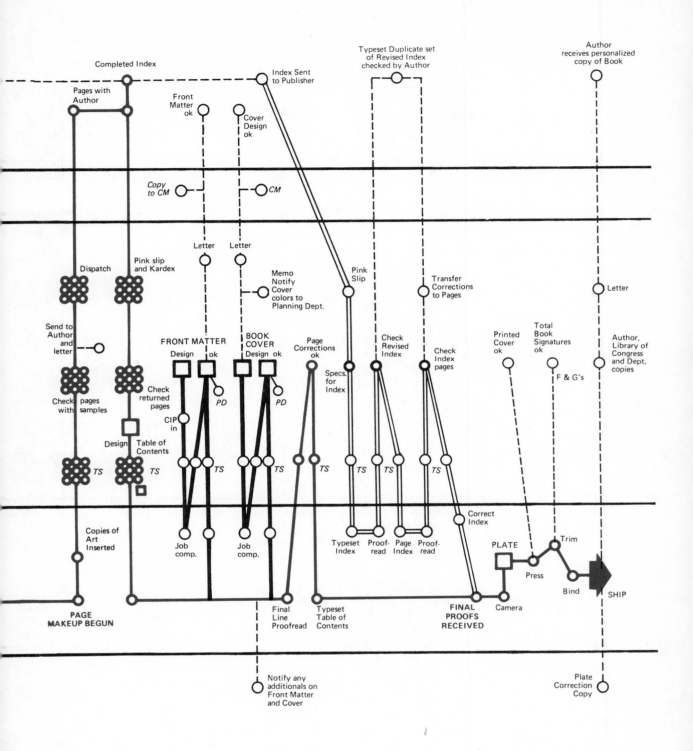

Figure A.6 The work flow of an operating system: Book production

turing costs. Market research is also involved before the manuscript enters the production process.

Transmittal is the method by which an editorial department releases the manuscript to the operations management. In most publishing houses, the acquisition editor either meets with editorial, marketing, and operations people, or prepares a transmittal document for them, with details of the results of market research and reviews, as they pertain to production (production planning). Such information is essential to the operations staff, because it ultimately affects the final manufacturing process.

The flow chart on pages 548–49 (Figure A.6), illustrates how a textbook is produced following transmittal. The basic steps that most publishers follow in the production process are:

1. Administrative staff notifies concerned departments—editorial, marketing, operations, planning, and so forth—that the manuscript has been transmitted for production.
2. A production editor, who in essence is the operations manager-supervisor of production from manuscript to bound (or finished) book, is assigned. After reviewing the manuscript, the production editor selects, hires, supervises, and coordinates the work of the various related publication specialists—copy editor, book designer, artist, photographer or photo researcher, technical illustrator, compositor (often called typesetter). This is a production planning stage.
3. The copy editor is usually the first to work on the manuscript. This is a quality-control measure. Spelling, punctuation, syntax, and style are checked, after which the author reviews the copy editor's suggestions and changes.
4. The production, or managing, editor codes the manuscript for the typesetter, according to the typesetting specifications drawn up by the book designer. This is a production control measure.
5. The compositor, or typesetter, sets the manuscript into type. The author and the production editor review the typeset material, which first appears in a form called *galley* proofs. These are long sheets of paper that usually do not contain any illustrations, nor is the type broken up into pages. This is the beginning of the actual physical production of the book.
6. After the galleys are proofread (production control) and the compositor makes the corrections indicated, the type is broken up into pages. The compositor groups footnotes on the pages on which they belong, inserts illustrations, and adds any credit lines or captions necessary. This second set of proofs is called *page proofs*. The author sees the pages arranged as they will appear in the book, proofreads them, and notes any corrections that must be made by the compositor.
7. After the compositor completes page proof corrections, the camera-ready pages are sent to the production editor for a final review.
8. The production editor writes a set of specifications (production control) to guide the press, bindery, and shipping departments. The press department prints the book pages and the accompanying covers, which are sent to the bindery to be trimmed and bound (covered). They are then ready for shipment from the warehouse and the manufacturing process is completed.

9. The operations process does not end when the books are published and ready for distribution. A copy of the first printing of the book is retained in the operations department. It is called the *plate correction* copy and serves as the master record for corrections to be incorporated into subsequent printings.

The accompanying chart (Figure A.6) illustrates the main functions that constitute the complex operations process in the production of a textbook for publication.

Glossary

Active listening
Reflecting back to the other person not only what the person has said but also the perceived emotional tone of the message.

Actual objectives
Shifting and uneasy compromises among the individuals within the organization and the changing demands made by the outside environment. They are the result of a continuing series of negotiations among constituencies.

Adaptive subsystem
The adaptive subsystem is primarily concerned with the survival of the organization in a changing environment. Its purpose is to sense meaningful and relevant changes in the outside environment and to suggest necessary changes.

Affirmative action
Organizations must have a positive plan to reduce and/or eliminate internal minority imbalances or inequalities.

Alternatives
The possible courses of action from which choices can be made. If there are no alternatives, there is no choice and, therefore, no decision.

Anticipatory socialization
A process that involves the adoption of attitudes, values, and identity perceived to be associated with an anticipated role before ever entering it.

Apprentice stage
A career stage in which a young professional entering an organization is a beginner or learner under the direction of others.

Authority
The right to command and exact obedience from others. It comes from the organization and it allows the manager to use power.

Behavior channeling
The idea that actual behavior is consistent with values. Behavior is channeled toward or away from particular actions as a result of the direct influence of values on behavior.

Body language
An important part of nonverbal communications which involves the transmittal of thoughts, actions, and feelings through bodily movements and how other people "read" them.

553

Boundary spanning subsystems
These are the subsystems of the organization that carry on transactions with the environment.

Bounded rationality
This is a technique that reduces the complexity of a problem to the level at which a manager can handle the possible alternatives. Bounded rationality is a natural limit on the human ability to handle complex situations.

Branch office
In international management, a sales office established by an exporter in a host country and staffed with the exporter's own employees.

Budget
Plans for a given future period that are stated in numerical (usually financial) terms. To some degree, budgets are a control device, since they govern a variety of different activities.

Budgeting
Handling budgets, fiscal planning, accounting, and control.

Career
The sequence of behaviors and attitudes associated with past, present, and anticipated future work-related experiences and role activities as perceived by either the individual or some other observer. Thus a career is work-related and lifelong.

Career development
A developing, progressing process whereby an individual proceeds from a point of having no career direction to that of attaining a career consistent with his or her interests, abilities, and aspirations.

Changing
The bringing about of specific changes through the development of new values, attitudes, and/or behavior.

Charismatic power
The power of attraction or devotion, the desire of one person to admire another.

Choice
The opportunity to select among alternatives; if there is no choice, there is no decision to be made.

Coercive power
The ability to threaten or punish.

Command groups
Formal groups that consist of managers and their direct subordinates.

Committee
A formal group that is created to carry out specific organizational assignments or activities.

Communications
The process by which information is exchanged and understood by two or more people, usually with the intent to motivate or influence behavior.

Communications channel
Any way in which information reaches the receiver.

Comparative management
The study of differences among management practices in various countries, usually with an attempt to determine which environmental

conditions have been responsible for the different norms of managerial behavior.

Compensation
Direct or indirect, immediate or deferred rewards, some of which have a monetary value.

Competent organization
An organization which is both effective and efficient.

Competition
A process involving actions taken by one person to attain his or her most preferred outcome while simultaneously blocking attainment of the counterpart's most preferred outcome.

Compromise
An attempt to attain mutual concessions by having each party modify their point of view to achieve a workable solution.

Conditions of certainty
Under such conditions, the manager has enough information to be able to closely predict the outcome of decisions. The alternatives are known and the decision can maximize the outcome desired by the manager.

Conditions of risk
Under such conditions, the manager can develop alternatives and estimate the probability of their leading to the desired outcomes.

Conditions of uncertainty
Under such conditions, the probabilities attached to the available alternatives are even less well known than those for risk.

Conflict
Occurs whenever incompatible activities occur. An activity that is incompatible with another one obstructs, prevents, or interferes in a way that makes the other less probable or less effective.

Conflict management
Management's task is to manage conflict by reducing or stimulating it, depending on the situation, in order to develop the highest level of organizational performance.

Conformity
The acceptance of all of the organization's values and norms.

Consequences
Consequences are the result of decisions made from a selection of alternative courses of action.

Consideration
Reflects the extent to which individuals are likely to have job relationships characterized by mutual trust, respect for subordinates' ideas, and consideration of subordinates' feelings.

Consortium
An organization created when two or more companies cooperate so as to act as a single entity for a specific and usually limited purpose.

Constraints
Restrictions or limitations on managerial actions.

Consumerism
A cause pertaining to special interest groups that focuses on the safety and quality of products bought by consumers.

Content
The subject of the meeting or of the task being performed.

Content models
Motivation models that tend to focus primarily on the wants and needs that individuals are trying to satisfy within the situation.

Contingency approach
This approach suggests that there is no single best way to design an organization, that the design instead depends on the situation.
Contingency model of leadership
Effective styles are dependent (or contingent) on a number of conditions, including leader power, level and status of subordinates and the favorableness or unfavorableness of the situation.
Continuing objective
An objective that is relatively unchangeable over time.
Continuous reinforcement
The employee is reinforced every time the correct performance occurs.
Control
The process that allows managers to determine whether activities conform to the plan and the objectives and to make adjustments when necessary.
Cooperation
A process involving two or more parties working together to attain mutual goals.
Coordinating
The functional activity of interrelating the various parts of the work to be done so it will flow smoothly.
Coordination
Involves making certain, through the creation of specific positions and subdivisions, that individuals or groups work toward common organizational objectives.
Core job dimensions
These are the five dimensions of work including skill variety, task identity, task significance, autonomy, and feedback.
Cottage industry
Work done in the home by a domestic artisan who generally owned all the tools of the trade.
Creative individualism
The acceptance of pivotal norms and the rejection of some or all relevant ones.
Creativity
The generation of a new idea, practice, service, or object.
Critical path
The longest set of adjoining activities in a project. Delays along this path cause delays in an entire project.
Cultural constraints
Norms or standards of behavior that vary from country to country and restrict or limit managerial action.
Culture
The totality of socially transmitted ideas, beliefs, and values within a society.

Decision
A choice made from among alternative courses of action that are available. The purpose of making a decision is to establish and achieve organizational goals and objectives.
Decision tree
A method of planning to achieve objectives by identifying and

choosing among available alternatives. A decision tree is a relatively simple and understandable way of using probability.

Decisional roles
Includes entrepreneur, disturbance handler, resource allocator, and negotiator roles.

Delegation of authority
The process that transfers authority from supervisor to subordinate and allows a subordinate to exercise discretion in making specific decisions.

Delphi technique
A future-predicting technique which involves using a group of knowledgeable people working separately and anonymously to improve creatively and make better decisions.

Departmentation
The creation of a number of subunits, usually called departments.

Deviations
Variations from a plan. Measurement of results against standards would allow deviations to be detected in time to make corrections.

Differentiation
The difference in cognitive and emotional orientation among managers in different functional departments. High uncertainty leads to more differentiation and low uncertainty leads to less.

Direct control
The process of developing better managers to more skillfully use concepts, principles, and techniques to reduce the amount and degree of undesirable results.

Directing
A task which includes leading, developing, training, and motivating subordinates.

Disseminator role
Involves passing along special or privileged information that subordinates would not otherwise be able to obtain.

Disturbance handler
A manager who takes corrective action in response to unforeseen problems which are beyond personal control.

Division of labor
The specialization of workers, including management in accomplishing tasks.

Domestic organization
A firm that limits its purchases and sales to a single country.

Dominance
A state which occurs when a solution to conflict is imposed or dictated.

Dual-career family
Both spouses have careers, and this situation may bring on problems beyond those associated with the stresses of their work.

E.R.G.
Consists of three levels of core needs: existence, relatedness, and growth.

Economic constraints
A country's economic and social conditions that restrict or limit managerial action.

Emergent activities
Informal actions beyond those required that result from changed
sentiments.
Emergent interactions
Informal interactions beyond those required resulting from changed
activities and sentiments.
Emotional decisions
Decisions based primarily on intuition with little real data to back
them up. These decisions are made from an emotional state, such as
fear, anger, or joy.
Empathy
The development of a better understanding of other people's
viewpoints.
Entrepreneur
A person who organizes and manages a business, taking a risk for the
possibility of making a profit.
Entrepreneur role
The manager works to improve the unit, and bring about planned,
voluntary, controlled change for the better.
Environmentalism
A cause pertaining to special interest groups that focus on the
physical environment and the changes that people have made in it.
Environmental variability
Refers to the degree of change or uncertainty with which an
organization or its subunits is involved.
Ethics
The rules or standards governing the moral conduct of the
organization management profession.
Exclusive sales agreement
A policy under which the buyer in the host country has sole rights in
a particular geographic area to handle specific goods, products, or
services.
Expectancy
The belief, expressed as a subjective estimate or odds, that a
particular act will or will not be successful.
Expectancy model
A process model of motivation suggesting that people are motivated
at work to choose among different behaviors or intensities of effort if
they believe their efforts will be rewarded and if the rewards they
expect to get are important to them.
Expert power
The power of knowledge. It comes from specialized knowledge and
skills that are important in getting the job done.
Extrinsic rewards
Rewards given by the organization, such as pay, promotion, praise,
tenure, and status symbols.

Feedback
Feedback is information regarding the actual performance or the
results of the activities of a system.
Feedback
In communications, looking for and using helpful responses from
others. Feedback can improve self-awareness and thereby increase
the ability to send clear and inoffensive messages.

Fiedler's contingency model
The model suggests that a manager's effectiveness depends on two main factors: (1) the motivational system of the leader and (2) the extent that the situation is favorable or unfavorable to the leader.

Figurehead role
All managerial jobs require some duties that are symbolic in nature. As head of the organization or organizational subunit, the manager represents the unit in formal matters, including ceremonies and symbolic activities.

Filtering
A barrier to communication which occurs when the sender intentionally sifts or modifies the message so it will be seen more favorably by the receiver.

Formal group
A unit established by the organization to accomplish specific tasks. Individuals are usually assigned to formal groups.

Formal leadership
A manager is a formal leader by virtue of authority coming from the organization; that is, a formal leader is usually selected by the organization.

Function
One of the most common ways of creating departmentation or specialization is grouping activities according to similar functions, such as work, skills, knowledge, and technology.

Functional authority
The authority to prescribe practices, procedures, policies, or other matters to units or groups not in the direct chain of command.

Game theory
Used to develop a mathematical approach that is designed to maximize gains or minimize losses regardless of countermoves by competitors. Its purpose is to develop long or short-term strategies that combine low costs with high gains.

Goals
Desired states of affairs which the organization attempts to realize. They are levels of aspiration that are relatively timeless.

Group
Any number of people who: (1) have a common purpose or objective, (2) interact with each other to accomplish their objective, (3) are aware of one another, and (4) perceive themselves to be a part of the group.

Group building activities
Those activities that allow the group to maintain itself by helping to satisfy members' needs and by fostering cooperation among members.

Group cohesiveness
The degree to which group members are motivated to remain within the group and, in consequence, to behave in similar ways.

Group task activities
Activities directed at helping the group accomplish its goals.

Groupthink
A form of decision making that occurs when the members' striving for unanimity overrides their motivation to realistically appraise alternative courses of action.

Hawthorne effect
When workers' behavior changes and productivity increases because the workers are aware that persons important in their lives are taking an interest in them. (A myth.)

Hierarchy of objectives
Various levels of objectives that correspond with the three broad managerial levels.

Horizontal specialization
The way the work of the entire organization is divided across the organization to accomplish organizational goals.

Illegal behavior
Behavior that violates a law in a particular jurisdiction or area.

Implementation
Adopting and putting a new idea into practice.

Independent agent
A seller of goods or services (in a host country) who receives commissions on sales. The agent frequently has the authority to give credit and receive direct payments for goods.

Indirect control
Traces the cause of an unsatisfactory result to the responsible person so that activities or practices can be corrected.

Industrial Revolution
Economic and social changes brought about when the mechanization of production resulted in a major shift from home manufacturing to large-scale factory production.

Influence group
Any person or persons who exert pressure on an organization.

Informal group
A group formed within the organizational structure by the individuals rather than by management.

Informal leadership
An informal leader is chosen by an individual or group.

Information
The knowledge or other data that are useful and pertinent to the individual or organizational unit.

Information overload
A communications barrier which involves an excess of incoming information, to the point where it cannot be handled.

Informational roles
The manager is the central focus for the receiving and sending of non-routine information. As a nerve center, three roles characterize the manager: monitor, disseminator, and spokesman. In these roles, information is received, transmitted or recombined.

Initiating structure
Reflects the extent to which individuals are likely to define and structure their roles and those of their subordinates toward goal attainment.

Inputs
Human or other resources such as information, energy, and materials coming into the system or subsystem.

Integration
The quality of the state of collaboration that exists among departments that are required to achieve unity of effort by the demands of the environment.

Integrative problem solving
A process that involves the open, complete, and rapid sharing of information concerning the problem and a joint search through the shared information to arrive at a decision that best accomplishes organizational goals.

International licensing
The sale to an organization in a host country of the right to use patents, trademarks, or other assets.

International management
Focuses on management practices at the worldwide corporate level including the study of the transfer of resources among entities in different countries where the companies are operating.

International organization
A firm whose interests cut across national boundaries; it imports or exports goods, services, or products.

Interpenetrating system
Two or more systems, neither of which totally contains or is contained by the other, that are involved in particular events or processes.

Interpersonal roles
The manager has formal authority and status, from which the three interpersonal roles develop. They are the manager as figurehead, as leader, as liaison.

Intrinsic rewards
Rewards that must originate and be felt within the person. Intrinsic rewards include feelings of accomplishment, achievement, and self-esteem.

Inventory control
Concerned with making certain that the right amount of raw materials, work in progress, and finished goods are available.

Jargon
Overly specialized or technical language.

Job enrichment
A way of making jobs more satisfying by providing workers with more opportunity for meaningfulness, responsibility, growth, achievement, and challenge.

Key performance areas
Eight areas that directly and vitally affect the survival and prosperity of the business. These eight key performance areas are the following: (1) market standing, (2) productivity, (3) profitability, (4) physical and financial resources, (5) innovation, (6) manager performance and development, (7) worker performance and attitudes, (8) public and social responsibility.

Law of effect
Behavior that leads to a positive result tends to be repeated, while behavior that leads to a neutral or negative result tends not to be repeated.

Leadership
The ability to influence the behavior of others. The task of the leader is to help the group reach both organizational and personal goals.

Leadership role

Involves responsibility for directing and coordinating the activities of subordinates to accomplish organizational goals.

Legal constraints

A set of laws which are a combination of coded and common law practices that restrict or limit managerial action.

Legitimate power

The power that comes when the organization's authority is accepted. It is power that stems from either implicit or explicit rules.

Liaison role

The manager makes contacts outside the vertical chain of command in an effort to bring information into the unit and gain favors from others. The role includes interacting in a network of contacts with peers and others in order to get that information.

Linear programming

A mathematical technique for obtaining the optimal solution in situations where the relationships among variables can be expressed as directly proportional (linear) functions. Linearity means that a change in one variable must produce a proportionate change in another, the result being a straight line.

Line authority

That relationship in which a supervisor directs a subordinate.

Lobbying

A process involving actions taken by individuals or organizations to influence government agencies and federal, state, or local legislation.

Maintenance subsystem

The maintenance subsystem is concerned with preserving stability and maintaining the smooth operation of the rest of the organization.

Management by objectives (MBO)

Management by objectives consists of periodic manager-subordinate meetings designed to accomplish organizational goals by mutual planning of the work, periodic review of accomplishments and mutual solving of problems that arise in the course of getting the job done.

Management development

Training or other processes to improve managers' knowledge and skills to improve managers' performance in present jobs and/or to prepare them for promotion.

Manager

A person who works to accomplish the goals of the organization and directly supervises one or more people in a formal organization.

Managerial Grid

The Managerial Grid suggests that each manager must be concerned about both production (structure) and people (consideration).

Managerial subsystems

Managerial subsystems are concerned with controlling, coordinating, and directing all the other subsystems of the organization.

Managing level

Also called the administrative level, it performs two functions: administering and servicing the technical level and mediating between the technical level and those who use the products. Decisions made at this level determine how the technical level operates.

Matrix organization
A device for integrating the activities of different specialists while maintaining specialized organizational units.

Mechanistic organization
This type of organization is highly bureaucratic. Tasks are specialized and clearly defined. This type of organization is suitable when markets and technology are well established and show little change over time.

Mentor relationship
A relationship which can be formal or informal that involves teaching, counseling, guidance, advising, and sponsoring. It involves finding a person, usually several years older, who can help the individual facilitate the realization of the career dream.

Monitor role
An informational role in which the manager continually scans the environment to receive and collect information pertinent to the organization or unit he manages.

Motivation
The conditions responsible for variation in the intensity, quality, and direction of ongoing behavior.

Motivation-hygiene model
Describes factors in the work-place that dissatisfy people and factors that motivate them.

Multinational organization
A firm having one or more subsidiaries abroad and willing to go worldwide to secure resources and to make sales.

Need hierarchy
A model of motivation that describes a hierarchy of needs existing within people. The five need levels are psychological, safety, social, ego, and self-actualization.

Negative response
The individual or group activity resists the control process. The resistance need not be overt or blatant.

Negotiator role
The manager discusses and bargains with other units to obtain advantages for his or her own unit.

Noise
Any factor that limits or distorts messages in the communications process.

Nominal groups
Involves using a group of knowledgeable people who are aware of each other but who do not directly interact while they are working to improve creativity and make better decisions.

Nonverbal communications
The transmission of ideas or messages without using words.

Norm
A rule that tells the individual how to behave in a particular group.

Novice stage
A career stage during which the individual explores the adult world and makes important choices about work, marriage, and family.

Objectives
Ideas or statements that help steer the activities of the organization toward the attainment of goals.

Official objectives
The "general purpose" of the organization. They are used in annual reports and other authoritative pronouncements.

Operating goals
Goals that guide the activities of the organization, regardless of what the official goals say are the aims.

Operations
The processes of transforming inputs into other forms.

Operations level
A suborganization which concentrates on performing the technical function effectively.

Operations management
The development, use, and interaction of resources (people, facilities, information, materials, money, and ideas) to provide the goods, services or ideas for which the organization was established.

Operations research
An application of the scientific method to problems arising in the operations of a system which may be represented by means of a mathematical model and the solving of these problems by resolving the equations representing the system.

Operations subsystem
Operates primarily at the production level and is concerned with the major transformations, operations or work of the system.

Operations technology
Includes the tools, mechanical equipment, actions, knowledge or material used in the production or distribution of a good or service.

Organic organization
This type of organization is relatively flexible and relaxed. The organic style is most appropriate to unstable environmental conditions in which novel problems continually occur.

Organization
An organization is composed of individuals and groups consisting of human, financial, and other resources existing over time to achieve common goals and objectives by operating as a complex system.

Organization chart
A graphic model of a formal organization with two basic purposes: (1) it shows who is accountable to whom (the scalar principle), and (2) it shows, in abbreviated form, who does what in the organization.

Organization development
The application of behavioral science knowledge in a long-range effort to improve an organization's ability to cope with changes in its external environment and increase its internal problem-solving capabilities.

Organization manual
The organization manual goes even further (than the organization chart) as a model of the organization. It shows the duties performed thereby defining the scope and limits of the various jobs; the extent of authority held by individual managers, and the relationships of positions with each other.

Organizational effectiveness
The degree to which a specific organization attains its objectives and goals.

Organizational efficiency
The amount of resources used by an organization to produce a unit of output.

Organizational goal
An end or a state of affairs the organization seeks to reach.
Organizational policy
A "standing decision" made in advance and covering a set of prescribed circumstances that form the limitations and/or guidelines for action.
Organizational socialization
A process that involves learning not only the role requirements of the job but also the values and behavior norms considered important in the organization.
Organizational strategy
A broad course of action selected from among alternatives as the best way to obtain major objectives, with due regard for relative capabilities, major functions, policies, and resources. The purpose of the strategy is to maintain an advantageous position by capitalizing on strengths and minimizing weaknesses.
Organizing
The activities necessary to develop the formal structure of authority through which work is subdivided, defined, and coordinated to accomplish the organization's objectives.
Outputs
The results of what is transformed by the system. Imputs that have been transformed represent outputs ready to leave the system or subsystem.

Partial reinforcement
The employee is rewarded for correct behavior only part of the time the correct behavior occurs.
Passive response
The individual recognizes the objective of the control as being part of the job responsibility but is personally indifferent about the actual or desired results.
Path-goal model
This contingency model of leadership defines the relationship between leader behavior and subordinate work attitudes and performance as situational. The essential ingredient of the path-goal model is that the leader smooths the path to work goals and provides rewards for achieving them.
Perceptual screening
Personal values influence what the individual sees and hears.
Performance
The behavior that a person selects on the job to meet or achieve personal goals.
Performance appraisal
A formal written process for periodically evaluating managers' performance.
PERT (Program Evaluation and Review Technique)
A way of providing management with an operational network that relates the activities of a project in a time frame, thereby allowing the identification of the project's critical and subcritical stages. PERT is a way to plan programs that have specific objectives and specific, measurable results.
Pivotal group norm
A norm to which every member of the group must conform.

Pivotal norms
Organizational values absolutely necessary to accept for anyone who intends to remain in the organization.

Plan
Anything that involves selecting a course of action for the future.

Planning
Developing in broad outline the things that need to be done and ways of doing them that will accomplish the objectives of the organization.

Policies
Standing decisions intended to serve as overall guidelines to thinking and decision making.

Political constraints
Restrictions or limits on managerial action derived from the political authorities and conditions of a country.

Politics
The use of resources, both physical and human, to achieve more power over others. Politics deals with the methods, approaches, and tactics used to increase power and control.

Positive Reinforcement Model
A model of motivation that involves the use of positive rewards to increase the frequency or probability of the occurrence of the desired performance.

Positive response
The control process is accepted because the individual feels that the goals and plans are worthy, relevant, and appropriate or that they may bring rewards or punishments.

Post-action controls
Those which compare results to a standard when the action or task is completed.

Power
The ability of a person or group, for whatever reason, to affect another person's or group's ability to achieve its goals (personal or collective).

Pre-controls
Forward-looking controls established before an activity takes place.

Preferences
The valuing of some rewards more highly than others and avoiding punishment.

Private sector
Types of organizations that are oriented toward profit-making.

Probability theory
The likelihood (or odds) of occurrence of uncertain events or environmental states.

Procedures
Plans that establish a customary method of handling future activities.

Process
How the content is handled or discussed by the group.

Process (organizations)
An identifiable flow of interrelated actions or events moving toward a goal or result.

Process approach to change
A focus on how things are done rather than on what is done. It is concerned with such areas as interpersonal interactions, group dynamics, and the relationships among workers and machines.

Process models
Motivation models that focus on how managers can change the situation to better tie need satisfaction to performance.
Production control
An activity concerned with the timing and routing of any product.
Profit-maximizing management
A theory of business management based solely on the objective of profit maximization.
Program
A single-use plan that involves a large number of interrelated and interdependent activities.
Programmed decisions
Repetitive and routine because definite systematic procedures have been established for making the choice.
Project
A single-use plan that is either a subset of a program or less complex than a program.
Promotion
A move to another position, usually higher in the organization and usually with an increase in status and pay. Promotion is a reward for accomplishment.
Public Sector
Types of organizations consisting of federal, state, and local government bodies.

Quality control
Concerned with controlling the quality of goods and services provided.
Quality-of-life management
A type of management where managers are responsible for enhancing the organization, the society, the environment, and the dignity of employees.
Queuing theory
The study of waiting lines or queues to minimize total expected cost.

Rational decisions
Decisions are based primarily on facts and positive data or proof.
Reality shock
A situation where the actuality does not agree with the expectations.
Rebellion
The rejection of all the organization's values and norms.
Recruitment
The process of attracting candidates from either inside or outside the organization who are qualified for and interested in the position.
Refreezing
The stabilization of change at a new state of equilibrium.
Relevant group norm
Not as central as a pivotal norm; following it is seen as not absolutely essential but considered as worthwhile and desirable.
Relevant norms
Organizational values that are important but not absolutely necessary to accept.

Reporting
Keeping supervisors, managers, and subordinates informed as to what is going on within the manager's area of responsibility through records, research, inspection, or other methods.

Required activity
Assigned tasks performed by the individual.

Required interaction
Occurs when a person's activity follows or is influenced by the activity of another; interaction can be verbal or non-verbal.

Resource allocator role
The manager decides who will get what resources in the unit. The resources can include time, money, material, equipment, people, and the unit's reputation.

Reverse discrimination
The selection of minority persons or women for jobs or education in place of better qualified whites or men.

Reward power
The present or potential ability to award something for worthy behavior.

Role
A set of systematically interrelated and observable behaviors that belong to an identifiable job or position.

Role ambiguity
A result of inadequate information regarding role related expectation and understanding—when the manager does not clearly understand all the expectations.

Role conflict
A result of the conflict between managerial expectations and managerial experiences with regard to performance of the role.

Rules
The simplest type of plan and the narrowest in scope; they describe or require that definite, specific actions be taken (or not taken) in a given situation.

Rumor
An unconfirmed message passed from person to person.

Satisfice
The practice of striving for a "satisfactory" rather than an "optimum" decision.

Scalar principle
This principle suggests that authority and responsibility should flow in an unbroken line from the top to the bottom of the organization.

Scenario
A contingency plan based upon a specific set of assumptions about the future.

Scientific management
Observe the separate elements of each task performed. Carefully analyze and redefine the job to develop the "one best way" for all workers. Select and train the workers.

Selection
The process of choosing the most qualified person from the available pool of candidates.

Selective perception
The tendency to perceive only a part of a message, to screen out other information.

Self-actualization
Development of the full potential of the individual through self-development, creativity, and psychological health.
Self-serving activities
Activities that satisfy individual needs at the expense of the group.
Semantics
The study of meaning in language.
Sensitivity training
A method of helping managers become more sensitive to their effect on others. Managers learn by interaction with other members of their group.
Sentiments
The feelings or attitudes a person has about others such as like or dislike and approval or disapproval.
Shareholders
Part owners of businesses; they become part owners by buying shares of stocks issued by corporation.
Single-use plan
Plans specifically developed to carry out courses of action that are relatively unique and unlikely to be repeated.
Situation
Some areas of motivation are controlled by individuals, each of whom comes into any situation with different needs and abilities. Managers influence the conditions under which the people work, and changing the work situation frequently has a powerful effect on performance.
Size
The size of an organization usually is measured by the number of people working for the organization in a single location.
Smoothing
Dealing with conflict by denying it or avoiding it.
Social audit
An ongoing evaluation of performance measured against established goals in selected areas of social responsibility.
Social involvement
The interaction of the organization, as a system, with other organizations and individuals and with society as a whole.
Social responsibility
Behavior for the social good beyond the law or common custom demanded.
Society
The totality of social relationships among human beings.
Sociotechnical approach
This approach is concerned with organizing and matching the technology (work flow and information flow) and the people.
Span of control
The number of subordinates a manager can efficiently supervise.
Special interest group
A group that attempts to exert influence for one or more specific issues important to them.
Spokesperson role
The manager speaks for the unit and represents it to others. A key concept of the spokesperson role is that of representation. The manager must act as an advocate for subordinates.
Stable environment
Little or no unexpected or sudden change; that is, the few product or

other changes that do occur generally can be predicted well in advance.

Staff
The function of a staff is to do research for and to advise a line manager.

Staffing
Identifying, assessing, placing, evaluating, and developing individuals at work by performing such actions as recruiting, selecting, appraising, and promoting individuals.

Standards
The units of measurement that serve as reference points against which actual results can be compared.

Standing plan
A plan established to guide organizational actions that are repeated frequently.

Steering controls
Controls in which results are predicted and corrective action is taken while the operation or task is being performed.

Steps in creativity
The basic steps include desire, preparation, experimentation, incubation, illumination, refinement, and implementation.

Strategic level
Controls the managerial level and mediates between the organization and the broader community served by the organization.

Strategic planning
A process that begins with goals and objectives and that creates strategies, policies, and detailed plans, and controls to achieve them.

Structural analysis
A way of analyzing communications through the structure of the communicator's personality.

Structural change
Changes in the various functions or activities performed in an organization.

Structure
The structure of a system is the arrangement of its parts.

Subsidiary
A company established in a host country by an exporting organization. It is incorporated under the law of the host country.

Subsystem
A part of a system. A change in any subsystem has an effect on the total system.

Suprasystem
A series of interrelated and interdependent systems.

System
A set of interdependent parts which together make up the whole because each contributes something and receives something from the whole, which in turn is interdependent with the larger environment.

Tactical planning
Deciding specifically how the resources of the organization will be used to help the organization achieve its strategic goals.

Task force
A group established to solve a particular problem.

Team building
The process of helping a work group become more effective in accomplishing its tasks and in satisfying the needs of group members.

Termination
Action by the organization to remove an individual from the organization.

Theory X
Typical Theory X managers believe that people dislike work and will avoid it whenever possible. Such managers feel they themselves are a small, elite group who want to lead and take responsibility but that the larger mass of people want to be directed and to avoid responsibility.

Theory Y
Typical Theory Y managers usually assume that people will work hard and assume responsibility provided they can satisfy personal needs and organizational goals at the same time.

Therbligs
Seventeen basic motions or thought processes by which a job can be analyzed (such as search, find, grasp, transport, and position).

Third sector
Types of organizations that include voluntary, semi-public, and semi-private organizations (such as private colleges, the Girl Scouts, railroads, voting leagues, and so on).

Tokenism
A way of meeting the organization's obligations to affirmative action programs. The token person is usually put in a highly visible or specially created position but has little power or opportunity for advancement.

Transactional analysis (TA)
A way of improving communications by analyzing how people interact. It includes structural analysis, analysis of transactions, time structuring, and life scripts.

Transactions
Verbal and/or nonverbal message units between two or more people. Transactions can be classified as complementary, crossed, or ulterior.

Transfer
A move to another job, usually without an increase in either status or pay.

Trusteeship management
A type of business management where the corporate manager is responsible not only for profits but also for maintaining a proper balance among the competing claims of stockholders, employees, suppliers, customers, and the broader community.

Turbulent environment
Many sudden, rapid, and frequently unpredictable product or other changes.

Two faces of power
(1) the negative face involves personal domination of others. (2) the positive face involves power being exercised not for personal advancement or benefit but for the good of the organization or society.

Types of technology
There are three types of technology which vary with the techniques and type of production. These are: (1) unit and small-batch

production, (2) mass or large-batch production, and (3) continuous of process production.

Unfreezing
A reduction in the strength of old values, attitudes, or behaviors.
Unity of command
This principle suggests that no organization member should report to more than one supervisor for any single function.
Unprogrammed decision
Unprogrammed decisions have few rules, procedures, regulations, and other guidelines; they require considerable judgment on the part of the manager. Often the objectives or goals are not clear.

Value judgment
Statements or beliefs based on or reflecting the individual's personal or class values.
Values
Relatively permanent ideals (or ideas) that influence and shape the general nature of people's behavior.

Yes-no controls
Controls that indicate that the work is either acceptable or unacceptable.

Name Index

A

Aaker, D., 145
Abt Associates, 457
Ackoff, R., 207, 208, 298
Acme Hardware Store, 214
Addleman, R., 114
Aguilar, F., 34
Aguren, S., 353
Air Line Pilots Association, 435
Aker, D., 454
Albanese, R., 188
Alderfer, C., 68
Aldrich, H., 117
Alexander, T., 371
Alexander the Great, 433
Alger, Horatio, 286
Allstate Insurance Company, 158
Alveris, K., 233
Alyeska Pipeline Service Company, 466–467
American Accounting Association, 459
American Advertising Federation, 454
American Airlines, 54, 204, 259, 481
American Bankers Association, 455
American Civil Liberties Union, 497
American Institute of Certified Public Accountants, 459
American Motors Company, 493
American Telephone and Telegraph Co., 141, 164, 266–267, 268, 274, 449, 453
American Tobacco Co., 449
Anable, D., 493
Anderson, D., 205
Anthony, R., 162
Aplin, J., 457
Aqua-Chem, Inc., 468
Aram, J., 367

Archer, S., 115
Archimedes, 367
Arensberg, C., 479
Aristotle, 298
Arizona Public Service Co., 172
Argyris, C., 125, 194, 386, 416
Arlutto, J., 387
Arnoff, E. L., 207
Arpan, J., 474
Associated Press, 364
Atlantic Monthly, 70
Atlantic Richfield Corporation, 453
Athos, A. G., 517
Audubon Society, 496
Aurelio, L., 138, 489
Austin, J. Paul, 456

B

Backhuber, T., 513
Bailyn, L., 521
Baker, B., 125
Bakke, Allan, 266–267
Bakke, E., 333
Balachandran, V., 247
Baldridge, J., 366
Balke, T., 372
Bamforth, K., 352
Bandura, A., 71
Bank of America, 259
Barebo, C., 391
Barnard, C., 247
Barnes, L., 9, 143, 230, 489, 491
Barnett, N., 276
Barsalous, J., 373
Baruch, R., 521
Bass, B., 407
Bauer, J., 436, 495, 496
Baumhart, R., 437, 438
Beame, Abraham, 28
Beatty, R., 71
Beckhard, R., 391, 406, 407, 415
Bechtel Corporation, 9
Bedian, A., 184

Beer, M., 81, 341, 355, 390, 405, 414
Beer, S., 114, 188
Beeson, Richard, 172, 173
Beethoven, Ludwig Van, 365
Bergstein, C., 469
Berlew, D., 281
Berlow, D. E., 518
Berne, E., 255
Bernstein, P., 161
Behrman, J., 470
Belasco, J., 387
Belcher, D., 283
Bell, C., Jr., 412
Bell, G., 323
Benne, K., 100, 417
Bennis, W., 146, 230, 412
Benoit, Lucien, 366, 367, 369, 375
Berry, P., 373
Bethlehem Steel Corporation, 47
Beveridge, W., 365
B. F. Goodrich Co., 117
Bic Pen Co., 471
Bigoness, W., 276
Billingsley, K., 410
Binxen, P., 385
Blackwell, K., 430
Blake, R., 230–232, 388, 391, 415
Blandin, J., 348
Blau, P., 342, 344
Block, C., 373
Blood, J., 146
Blood, M., 277, 414
Blumenthal, W., 437
Bolles, Richard, 529
Boot, J., 209
Boston Globe, 462, 453
Bouchard, T., Jr., 373
Boulding, E., 393
Bowditch, James, 90, 253, 325, 351, 371, 391, 407

Bowman, J., 437, 438, 439
Bowman, G., 519, 520
Boy Scouts of America, 198–199
Bradford, L., 417
Bradspies, R., 185
Brady, R., 495
Braniff Airways, 435
Bratton, F., 42
Bray, D., 274–276, 518
Braybrooke, D., 26
Brayfield, A., 79
Brief, A., 371
Bright, J., 365
British Airways, 481
Brown, W., 348
Brownlie, I., 471
Bruner, J., 252
Bucalo, J., 148
Buchanan, B., II, 143, 495
Buckley, W., 304
Bunke, H., 430
Bunting, John, 454
Burack, E., 273
Burck, C., 432, 448
Bureau of National Affairs, 276
Burnham, D., 433
Burnham, R., 366
Burns, T., 53–54, 114, 345, 433
Business Roundtable, 456
Business Week, 19, 164, 165,
　　172, 174–175, 187, 285, 326,
　　372, 421, 462, 468–469, 520,
　　523
Bylinski, G., 493
Byrd, R., 149
Byrom, F., 451

C

Cammann, C., 194, 196, 198–
　　199
Campbell, J., 251, 417
Campbell, R., 274–276
Campbell, R. J., 518
Canada Dry, 172
Canfield, L., 447
Caplan, E., 191, 194
Capulski, W., 489
*The Care and Training of Your
　　Pet Rock,* 365
Carey, A., 50
Carey, E., 47–48
Carey, Hugh, 28
Cargill Corporation, 9
Carlson, S., 12
Carr, A., 436
Carrington, J., 138, 489
Carroll, A., 437, 457
Carroll, S., 147
Carter, R., 247
Cartwright, D., 91

Carzo, R., Jr., 323
Casey, T., 273
Castro, Fidel, 382, 383
Cazes, B., 169
Central Intelligence Agency,
　　382
Chapel, G., 247
Chapple, E., 344
Chase, Stuart, 246
Chemers, M., 233
Cheops, 42
Chicago Tribune, 198
Child, J., 341, 342, 344
Childe, M., 44
Choran, I., 35
Christian Science Monitor, 267
Churchman, C. W., 207, 298
Civil Aeronautics Board, 435,
　　481
Clark, C., 212
Clark, J., 117
Clark, R., 207
Clarkson, G., 115
Cleland, C., 170
Cline, W., 469
*Close Encounters of the Third
　　Kind,* 5
Coakley, M., 365
Coca-Cola Co., 12, 30, 454, 456,
　　468–469
Coch, L., 311–312
Cohen, A., 95
Cohen, M., 493
Coleman, William T., 28
College Placement Annual,
　　522
Committee for Economic De-
　　velopment, 448
Committee on Industrial Light-
　　ing, 49
Communications Satellite Corp.
　　(COMSAT), 498–499
Community Fund, 448
Computerland Corporation,
　　493
Comstock, D., 344, 348
Contenau, G., 44–45
Cook, M., 252
Coons, A., 229
Cooper, G., 417
Corning Glass Works, 345
Cosier, R., 144, 385, 451
Cowan, J., 149
Cox, E., 209
Crittenden, A., 114
Crockett, W., 79
Crooks, L., 276
Crosby, A., 367
Crystal, John, 529
Cummings, L., 114, 144

D

Dahl, Gary, 364–365, 375, 376
Dalton, G., 516, 523
Dalton, M., 387
Daniels, E., 471
Daniels, J. D., 474
Darnell, D., 205
Daughen, J., 385
Dauten, P., Jr., 183
Davidson, John, 365
Davies, C., 137
Davis, F., 251
Davis, K., 333, 448
Davis, L., 412
Davis, R., 34
Davis, S., 350
Day, G., 145, 454
Day, V., 452
Dean, W., 94
Dearborn, D., 113, 387
DeFee, D., 146
Delbecq, A., 114, 372, 373
Dembard, L., 7
Dermer, J., 79
Derr, C., 348
Deshmuel, S., 247
Deutsch, M., 385
Dewalt, R., 183
Dewar, R., 365
Dickson, J., 122
Dickson, W., 48–49, 73
Diffenbach, J., 169
Dinn, W., 410
Donnelly, J., Jr., 210
Dornbusch, S., 252
Dorsey, Robert, 437
Downey, A., 235
Drauden, G., 373
Drucker, P., 112, 141–142
Dubin, R., 391
Duncan, R., 349
Duncan, W., 47
Dunnette, M., 417
Dunham, R., 414
Dunkin' Donuts, 493
DuPont Walston, 239–240
Dutton, J., 388

E

Eastern Airlines, 32
Eastlack, J., 164
Eastman Kodak, 454
Eberhard, G., 334–335
Eberstadt, N., 447, 449
Edison, Thomas, 49, 365, 367,
　　368, 369
Edmonds, C., III, 146
Egan, G., 500
E. I. DuPont, 163, 449
Elbing, A., 121–122

Elion, S., 138
Ellis, H., 447
Emery Air Freight Corp., 72, 74, 78
Emery, D., 122
England, G., 113, 138, 430–431
Enshwiller, J., 493
Environmental Protection Agency (EPA), 494, 496–497
Equal Employment Opportunity Commission (EEOC), 269, 276, 512
Erickson, E., 513
Erman, A., 42
Etzioni, A., 138, 407, 497
European Common Market, 472
Ewing, D., 448

F
Falk, C., 267
Farmer, N., 474
Farris, G., 91, 229
Fast, J., 251
Faux, V., 529
Fayol, Henri, 25, 50, 51, 57, 319, 329, 384
Fazar, W., 212
Federal National Mortgage Association (Fanny Mae), 498–499
Federal Trade Commission, 454
Feeney, E., 72, 74
Fein, M., 414
Fend, D., Jr., 436
Fendrock, John J., 429
Ferrero, G., 59
Fetyko, D., 459
Fiedler, F., 12, 34, 233–234
Field, H., 276
Figli, L., 277
Filley, A., 99, 229, 489
Filipetti, G., 45
First Pennsylvania Corporation, 454
Fisch, G., 323
Fisher, D., 125, 281, 530
Fitzgerald, A. Earnest, 430
Fleishman, E., 229, 241
Flint, J., 512
Forbes, 173
Ford Foundation, 497
Ford, Henry, 54, 365
Ford, Henry, II, 476
Ford, J., 342
Ford Motor Co., 121, 170, 274, 476, 501
Ford, R., 70, 412
Foreland, F., 169
Form, W., 50

Forrester, J., 112
Fortune, 19, 436, 457
Francis, A., 137
Frank, A., 138, 143
Franklin, J., 247
French, J., 227, 274, 283, 299, 311, 312
French, W., 412
Fried, R., 269–270
Friedman, M., 448
Frontier Airlines, 435
Frye Shoe Co., 2, 19, 20
Funkhauser, G., 530
Fulmer, R., 190
F. W. Woolworth, 326, 371

G
Galbraith, J., 349, 350, 500
Gammil, H., 183
Gantt, Henry L., 211
Gaudet, F., 273
Gemmill, G., 252
General Electric Co., 8, 142, 164, 165, 170, 274, 276, 342, 345, 350, 452, 453, 455, 490
General Motors Corporation, 5, 8, 12, 140, 274, 320, 349–350, 430, 453, 454, 455, 461, 462, 490, 492, 495
George, C., Jr., 45
Gershenfeld, M., 91
Gerstner, L., 168
Gery, G., 268
Gibb, J., 125, 254, 372, 417
Giblioni, G., 184
Gilbert, X., 191
Gilbreath, J., 269–270
Gilbreth, Franklin, 47–48
Gilbreth, Lillian, 47–48
Gillean, J., 207
Gillespie, J., 47
Gilmore, F., 170
Girl Scouts of America, 448
Givenchy, 19
Goetz, Del, 24–25
Goggin, W., 350
Golembiewski, R., 410, 493
Gomersall, E., 235–236
Goodman, Avid P., 447
Goodman, C., 252
Goodstein, L., 496
Goodwin, R., 432
Gordon, W., 371, 372
Gottlieb, C., 5
Grace, J. Peter, 160, 161
Graen, G., 233
Graicunus, V., 322
Granger, C., 138
Grant, D., 274–276, 518
Gray, E., 449

Grayson, C. J., Jr., 217, 496
Greiner, L., 230–231, 409
Greller, M., 254
Gremion, C., 114
Greve, F., 142
Gross, N., 395
Grunes, W., 252
Gue, R., 205
Guest, R., 12
Gulick, Luther, 25, 26, 51, 319, 322
Gullet, C., 367
Gustafson, D., 372
Gulf Oil Co., 435, 437
Guth, W., 430
Guzzardi, W., Jr., 455, 456

H
Haanpera, S., 274–276
Hackman, J., 413
Haefner, J. E., 520
Hage, J., 365
Hague, H., 281
Haire, M., 252
Hall, D. T., 68, 281, 395, 518–519, 521–522, 523, 529
Hall, J., 384
Hall, R., 117
Hallmark Cards, 9
Hammer, A., 476
Hammurabi, 44
Hamner, W. C., 71, 74, 520
Hand, J., 146
Handbook of Labor Statistics, 494
Harper, H., 251
Harrison, R., 251, 412
Hartford Courant, 48
Hartley, R., 210
Harvard School of Business Administration, 48
Harvard University, 495
Harvey, J., 386
Harwood, R., 513
Hatfield, J., 247
Hatley, R., 395
Hawthorne Plant, 90
Hay, R., 449
Hayakawa, S., 247
Hearst Corporation, 9
Heenan, D., 114
Hegarty, W., 457
Hellriegel, D., 254
H. J. Heinz and Company, 9, 471
Hemphill, J., 12
Henderson, A., 319
Herold, D., 164, 254
Hershon, S., 9, 143, 489, 491
Herzberg, F., 69–71, 413–414

Herzfeld, H., 251
Hicks, H., 367
Hickson, D., 341, 344
Hill, N., 122
Hiller, F., 210
Hinton, B., 70
Hitler, Adolf, 433
Holdaway, E., 319
Holiday Inns of America, 493
Holley, E., 276
Hollingsworth, A. T., 269–270
Holmstrom, L., 529
Holt, K., 365
Hotton, P., 366
Homans, G., 92
Honda Motors Corporation, 470
Hoover, Herbert, 449
Hoover Vacuum Cleaner Co., 471
Horne, J., 12
House, R., 149, 164, 229, 235–236, 395, 417, 489
Household Furniture Daily, 159
Hovey, D., 233
Hovey and Beard Co., 88–89, 92, 100–101
Howard Johnson's, 301
Howe, R., 281
Hubbartt, W., 268
Huber, G., 144
Huck, J., 274–276
Hulin, C., 277, 414
Hundert, A., 341
Hunt, S., 145
Hunt-Wesson Foods, 454
Hurley, M., 436
Huse, E., 81, 90, 126, 146, 147, 193, 253, 276, 280, 296–297, 325, 351, 371, 390–391, 405, 407, 410, 414, 415
Huseman, R., 247
Hutchinson, J., 525–526

I
Ibrahim, Y., 454
Ink, D., 493
International Air Transportation Association, 481
International Business Machines Corp. (IBM), 17, 274, 479
Internal Revenue Service (IRS), 10, 274
Ireland, Donald, 19
Ivancevich, J., 147, 210, 253, 346

J
Jacques, E., 354
Jaffee, C. L., 520
James, M., 255
James, R., 447

Janger, A., 270
Jangeward, D., 255
Janis, I., 382, 383
Jasinski, F., 333
Jaws, 3, 4, 5, 20, 30
J. C. Penney, 158–159, 187
Jennings, E. E., 286, 518
Jensen, M., 12, 456, 468–469
Jerdee, T., 520
Jerome, W., Jr., 183, 186
Johnson & Johnson, 454
Johnson, Lyndon B., 16, 434
Johnson, T., 235

K
Kahn, R., 298, 304, 309, 393, 394
Kaikati, J., 436
Kaiser Industries, 9
Kanter, R. M., 520, 529
Karagianis, M., 20
Kast, R., 298, 303, 309
Katz, D., 298, 304, 309, 333, 394
Katz, R., 144
Kaufman, H., 529
Kay, E., 146, 147, 280
Kelley, G., 432
Kerr, S., 149
Kendall, L., 277
Kennedy, John F., 16, 382–383, 389, 434, 450
Kennell, J., 170
Kepner, C., 114, 118
Kerr, S., 229, 235, 237
Khandwalla, P., 341
Kim, S. K., 437
King Hiero, II, 367
King, W., 170
Kinkead, E., 94
Kin-Sun Hung, 45
Kissinger, Henry, 183, 251
K-mart, 159
Knapp, M., 247
Knowles, M., 90
Kochan, T., 144
Koestler, A., 365
Koontz, H., 166, 174, 185, 188, 189, 193, 194, 325
Kopelman, R., 512
Koppers, Co., Inc., 451
Korda, M., 435
Korman, A., 229, 522
Kotak, D., 207
Kotter, J., 529
Kuo-Cheng, U., 45

L
Lahiff, J., 247
Laker, Fredrick, A., 115, 481
Laker Airlines, 481–482
Laker's Skytrain, 115
Lorange, P., 162, 163

Latham, G., 138
Lauer, R., 122
Lavelle, General John, 182–183, 188
Lawler, E., III, 9, 66, 75, 166, 183, 194, 198–199, 247, 283
Lawrence, P., 191, 341, 346, 347, 350, 388–389, 413, 418
League of Women Voters, 497
Leavitt, T., 138, 497
Leblebici, H., 122
Lee's Carpets, 454
Lenin, I. I., 433
Lepawsky, A., 45
Levinson, D., 513–514
Levinson, H., 148, 281
Levy, F., 212
Lewin, Kurt, 409
Lewis, A., 530
Libman, J., 24–25
Liddy, G. Gordon, 429
Lieberman, G., 210
Likert, R., 91
Lindblom, C., 117
Linneman, R., 170
Linowes, D., 457
Lippitt, D., 91
Livingstone, J. S., 518
Locher, A., 276, 280
Locke, E., 70
Lockheed Aircraft Corporation, 17, 490
Loflin, C., 205
Lombard, G., 247
Long, N., 141, 433, 493
Lorimer, B., 350
Lorsch, J., 191, 298, 346–347, 388–89
Lupton, T., 12
Luthans, F., 56, 298, 372, 414
Lynn, L., Jr., 141
Lyon, H., 210

M
MacCrimmon, K., 115
MacEwan, G., 473
MacInnis, P., 453
Mahler, W., 149
Mahoney, David, 172–173
Maier, N., 123, 125, 252, 372
Maini, S., 367
Malcolm, D., 212
Mandell, Martin, 435
Manhardt, P., 517
Marcarelli, L., 405
Marcus, S., 341
Margulies, N., 408
Marius, Caius, 58
Marsh, F., 59
Martella, J., 233

Martin, N., 433
Maslow, A., 67, 68, 71
Mason, W., 395
Massachusetts Institute of Technology (MIT), 49, 406
Mausner, B., 70
Mayo, Elton, 48, 49, 50
McArthur, C., 529
McClelland, D., 149, 433
McCloy, J., 436
McCreary, E., 214
McDonald, P., 164
McDonald's, 193, 301, 320, 342, 386, 493
McEachern, A., 395
McLean, R., 454
McNaughten, Daniel, 447
Murray, M., 493
McGill, M., 497
McGregor, D., 67, 71, 230, 276
McKersie, R., 386
McKinnon, 77, 414
McMurray, Robert, 430
McNulty, H., 489
Mechanic, D., 432
Merten, W., 212
Meyer, M., 342
Michelangelo, 365
Midas Muffler Co., 493
Midlin, S., 117
Miller, D., 50, 90, 114
Miller, E., 352
Miller, Gail, 504–506
Miller, L., 125, 372
Miller, Merle, 226–227
Minrichs, J., 274–276
Mintzberg, H., 12, 15, 26–36, 114, 170, 489
Mitchell, T., 235–236
Mobil Oil Corp., 479
Mockler, R., 186
Moment, D., 281, 530
Montgomery Ward, 158
Monthly Labor Review, 522
Moody's OTC Industrial Manual, 468–469
Mooney, J., 322
Moore, T., 350
Morison, E., 377
Morner, A., 447
Morning Telegraph, 9
Morrell, R., 114
Morrisey, G., 148
Morse, J., 298
Mouton, J., 230–232, 388, 391, 415
Multinational Corporations in World Development, 470
Murphy, C., 237
Murphy, D., 125

Murray, M., 141
Myers, M., 70, 235, 236, 412

N
Nadar, Ralph, 430, 453, 456
Nadler, D., 194, 196, 198–199, 247
Nanus, B., 169, 448
Napier, R., 91
Nord, W., 71, 78
National Academy of Sciences, 49
National Airlines, 203, 204, 205, 206, 207, 216, 217, 219
National Association for the Advancement of Colored People (NAACP), 455
National Association of Accountants, 459
National Association of Realtors, 455
National Association of Social Workers, 37
National Institute for Occupational Safety and Health (NIOSH), 453
National Park Service, 494
National Research Council, 49
National Telephone, 455
Nealy, S., 12, 34, 233, 234
Nebuchadnezzar, 45
Negandhi, A., 191, 386
Newman, W., 166, 185, 194, 247
Neustadt, R., 29
Newsweek, 364
New York Central Railroad, 447
New York City Welfare Department, 496–497
New York Stock Exchange (NYSE), 91, 455
Niehoff, A., 479
Nielson, E., 348
Nieman Marcus, 364
Nightengale, D., 391
Nixon Committee to Reelect the President, 438, 439
Nixon, Richard M., 16, 432
Nordbeck, B., 367
Norelco, 471
Norsted, J., 353
Norton Simon, Inc., 172
Nougaim, K., 68
Nutter, C., 530

O
Occidental Petroleum Co., 476
Occupational Safety and Health Administration (OSHA), 269

O'Donnell, C., 99, 100, 166, 185, 188, 189, 193, 194, 325
Office of Federal Contract Compliance Programs (OFCCP), 269
Ogram, E., Jr., 471
Oldham, G., 413
Omaha World Herald, 365
Ondrack, D. A., 70, 517
Orelius, S., 412
Organization of Petroleum Exporting Countries (OPEC), 163
Orris, J., 233
Osborn, A., 371

P
Paluszek, J., 145, 457
Pan American Airlines, 259
Parent's and Teachers Association (PTA), 91, 455
Park Ching Hee, 435
Parkinson, C. N., 342
Parsons, H., 49, 73
Parsons, T., 9, 319
Paul, W., 70, 414
Pearlman, D., 493
Penn-Central Railroad, 17, 384, 389, 490
Pennington, B., 395
Pennsylvania Railroad, 449
Perroni, A., 47
Perrow, C., 144, 344, 437
Peters, S., 229
Petkas, P., 430
Pet Rocks, 363–365, 375, 376
Pfeffer, J., 122, 391
Pheysey, D., 341, 344
Philco, Inc., 170
Phillay, A., 371
Picasso, Pablo, 365
Pierce, J., 414
Pieters, G., 341
Pinto, P., 26
Pizza Hut, 493
Platts, G., 125, 372
Polaroid Land Corporation, 17
Pompey, 59
Ponder, Q., 12
Porter, L., 75
Post, J., 451, 452
Pounds, W., 118
Powell, R. M., 519–520
Preston, L., 451, 452
Preston, P., 269–270
Price, R., 516, 523
Professional Standards Review Organizations, 498
Prudential Insurance Co., 447
Pugh, D., 341, 344

Q
Quale, T., 410

R
Radebaugh, L., 471
Radio Shack International, 176–177
Rados, D., 114
Raia, A., 147
Raiffa, H., 209
Raisinghani, D., 114
Ralston Purina Co., 172
Rand Corporation, 372
Rangan, K., 468–469
Raven, B., 95, 227, 228
Read, W., 252
Red Cross, 497
Reid, D., 269–270
Reiff, W., 414
Reiley, A., 322
Reimann, B., 191
Resser, C., 281
Reudi, A., 348
Rivett, P., 208
Rhode, J., 9, 66, 166, 183, 194, 198, 199, 247
Rice, A., 352
Richards, S., 520
Richman, B., 474
Ridgway, V., 148
Rietsema, J., 95
Riggs, W., 371
Ritti, R., 530
Ritzer, G., 395
Rizzo, J., 395
R. J. Reynolds Tobacco Company, 114
Roach, D., 68
Robbins, S., 383, 391
Robertson, K., 70, 414
Robertson, W., 140, 159, 436
Robinson Crusoe, 94
Robinson, S., 183
Roche, W., 414
Roe, A., 521
Roethlisberger, F., 48–49, 73, 247, 326, 327, 328
Rogers, C., 254
Rogers, E., 247, 370
Rogers, M., 287
Rogers, R., 247
Rolls-Royce, 17
Ronald, D., 322
Roosevelt, Franklin D., 29, 433
Roosevelt, Theodore, 19, 377
Rose, G., 144, 385
Roseboom, J., 212
Rosen, B., 520
Rosenthal, R., 252
Rosenweig, J., 298, 303, 309

Rubenowitz, S., 355
Ruckelshaus, W., 496–497
Rustin, R., 239–240

S
Saab-Scandia, 353, 354
Salancik, G., 122, 391
Soelberg, P., 114
Sank, L., 232
Satchell, M., 513
Sathe, V., 342
Sayles, L., 12, 32, 33, 34, 344
Schein, E., 94, 96, 407, 416, 513, 518, 530
Schmitt, N., 273
Schmitthoff, C., 471, 472
Schneider, B., 267
Schneider, C., 71
Schoen, C., 170
Schoenherr, R., 342
Schoeffler, S., 164
Schriesheim, C., 229, 235, 237
Schuler, R., 395
Scott, Admiral Percy, 376, 377
Scott, W., 344, 348
Sears, Roebuck & Company, 158–159, 490
Securities and Exchange Commission, 455, 459
Seiler, J., 55, 92
Serrin, W., 70
Sethi, S. P., 117, 436, 448
Seventeen, 9
Shannon, C., 247
Shartle, C., 34
Shaw, M., 92, 125, 372
Sheats, P., 100
Sheehy, Gail, 514, 530
Shepard, H., 391, 415
Sheridan, J., 235
Shertzer, B., 530
Shiftlett, S., 233–234
Shils, E., 94
Shull, F., 114
Siedl, J., 141, 493
Siekman, P., 173
Sierra Club, 455, 496
Simms, J., 433
Simon, H., 112, 113, 117, 387
Sims, H., Jr., 235
Sims, William, 376, 377
Singer, H., 431
Sloan School of Management, 406
Slocum, J., Jr., 235, 254, 342
Small Business Administration, 489, 490, 494
Small Business Administration Loans, 489
Smith, Adam, 50, 518

Smith, D., 205, 209
Smith, L., 454
Smith, P., 277
Smith, R., 185, 273
Snyder, Tom, 365
Snyderman, B., 70
Social Security Administration, 10, 11
Society of Lloyds (Lloyds of London), 473
The Sohioan, 447
Southwestern Bell Telephone, 435
Spiegel, A., III, 496–497
Spielberg, Steven, 4, 5, 12, 19, 30
Stabler, C., 453
Stagner, R., 164
Stalker, G., 53–54, 114, 345
Standard Oil Co., 274, 449
Standard Oil of Indiana, 453, 476
Standard Oil Co. of Ohio (SOHIO), 446, 448
Starr, M., 114
Steele, J., 511
Steiner, G., 159, 160, 162, 168, 173, 450
Stewart, R., 12, 26, 35, 489
Stewart, T., 298
Stieglitz, H., 35
Stinson, J., 233, 235
Stogdill, R., 227, 229, 233, 235, 237
Stover, J., 173
Stonich, P., 173
Stouffer, S., 94
Straka, J., 268
Strauss, G., 386
Strauss, H., 37–38
Strong, E., 185
Sturdivant, F., 449
The Sugarland Express, 4
Suojanen, W., 322
Super, D., 513
Sweeney, D., 205
Swierczek, F., 410
Szilagyi, A., Jr., 235, 253, 346

T
TRW, 373
Tagiuri, R., 113, 430
Tandy, Charles D., 176, 177
Tannenbaum, A., 191
Taylor, C., 367, 372
Taylor, D., 373
Taylor, Fredrick, 46, 47, 56, 388
Taylor, J., 412
Taylor, S. E., 520

Teel, K., 276, 280
Tehner, U., 267
Tersine, R., 371
Theoret, A., 114
Thomas, M., 205
Thomas, R., 122
Thompson, G., 212
Thompson, J., 6, 117, 302, 309, 344
Thompson, P., 516, 523
Thune, S., 164
Tillman, R., 91
Time, 5, 163, 182, 183, 268, 462
Toffler, A., 407
Tom Sawyer, 229
Tosi, H., 147
Tornow, W., 26
Tracey, L., 233, 269, 270
Trans World Airlines, 204
Trego, B., 114, 118
Triangle Publications, 9
Trist, E., 352
Truden, A., 117
Truman, Harry S, 226–227, 234
Tuggle, F., 121–122
Turcotte, W., 143, 493
Turner, A., 247, 413
TV Guide, 9
Twain, Mark, 252

U

United Airlines, 204, 513
United Auto Workers, 454
United Brands, 435
United Press International, 364
U.S. Army Intelligence, 272
U.S. Bureau of Labor Statistics, 284
U.S. Bureau of Navigation, 377
U.S. Bureau of Ordance, 377
U.S. Chamber of Commerce, 456
U.S. Department of Agriculture, 274
U.S. Department of Defense, 494
U.S. Department of Health,

Education and Welfare (HEW), 141, 146, 269, 495
U.S. Department of Labor, 269, 522
U.S. Environmental Protection Agency, 496–497
U.S. Federal Communications Commission, 494
U.S. News and World Report, 81, 522
U.S. Postal Service, 498–499
U.S. Price Commission, 217
U. S. Steel Corporation, 326, 449
University of California at Los Angeles, 299
University of California Medical School (Davis), 266
University of Pennsylvania, 48
Unsafe at Any Speed, 453
Urwick, 139, 319, 322, 329, 388

V

Valliant, G., 530
Vancil, R., 162, 163
Vanderbilt, William, 447
Van de Ven, A., 372, 373
Vandivier, K., 117, 122
Van Maanen, J., 518
Van Zelst, R., 333
Vaughn, A., 371
Veterans Administration, 38
Vinake, W., 66
Volkswagen of America Corporation, 470
Volvo of America Corporation, 353
Votaw, D., 448
Vroom, V., 75, 125, 140

W

Wallace, J., 408
Wallace, M., Jr., 253, 346
Wall Street Journal, 159, 447, 468, 469
Walter, V., 281

Walton, R., 386, 388, 416, 421, 436
Wanous, J., 79, 517
Ward, L. B., 517
Warner Lambert, 454
Warren, E., 173
Waters, L., 68
Watson, C., 118
The Wealth of Nations, 518
Weaver, W., 247
Weber, Max, 51, 52
Weeks, R., 20
Weidenbaum, M., 459
Weihrich, H., 146, 148
Wells, L. F., Jr., 477
Western Electric Co., 48, 49, 90
Westinghouse Electric Co., 8, 164, 259
Whyte, W., 88, 95, 387
Wiard, H., 71
Wiemann, J., 247
Wiest, J., 212
Williams, M., 384
Williams, T., 205, 252
Wilson, G., 182–183
Wolle, H., 47
Woodward, Joan, 52, 53, 343 344
Woolsey, R., 217
Wooten, L., 497
Wrapp, E., 170
Wrege, C., 47, 49, 50
W. R. Grace Co., 160–161
Wren, D., 45
Wright, O., Jr., 273
W. T. Grant Co., 17

XYZ

Xerox Corporation, 17
Yancuzas, 323
Yankelovich, D., 512
Yeager, S., 410
Yetton, P., 125
Young, D., 198–199
Yuhl, G., 138
Zald, M., 432
Zaleznick, A., 391, 432
Zenger, J., 90

Subject Index

A

Accountability, definition of, 325
Accounting, 44
Activities, required, 92
Adult ego state, 257
Affirmative action, 268
Allocation, 208
Alternatives, definition of, 112
  developing, 120
  evaluating, 120–121
  solutions, 120
Anticipatory socialization, 519
Assessment center, approach for selection, 274–276
Authority, definition of, 227, 325
  delegation of, 325–326
  functional, 330–331
  managerial, 227
Autonomous work groups, 352–355

B

Behavior, ethical, 438–440
Behavior channeling, 431–432
Behavioral aspects, of control, 194–196
Behaviorally anchored rating scale, 277–280
  See also Performance appraisal
Board of directors, 455
Body language, 251–252
  See also Communication
Book publishing, as operations, 547–551
Boundary, 6
  definition of, 300
Bounded rationality, 117
Branch office, 472
Breadth of plans, 166
Budget, 168
Budget control, 192

Budgets, types of, 192–193
Bureaucracy, 51–52

C

Capital budget, 192
Career, definition of, 512
  dual-career family, 520
  importance of, 512–513
  planning of, 521–523
  stages of, 513–517
Career consciousness, 511–517
Career stages, apprentice, 516
  colleague, 516
  mentor relationships, 514
  novice phase, 514
  sponsor stage, 517
Certainty, conditions of, 115–116
Challenge, 17
Change, accelerating pace, 405–406
Child ego state, 257
Choice, definition of, 112
Civil Rights legislation, 268–269
Civil Service, 45
Classical management, 50–52
Classical principles, as closed system, 329
  line, 329–330
  scalar, 329
  staff, 329–330
  unity of command, 329
Climate, in creativity, 370–371
  organizational, 238
Command groups, 91
Committee, 91
Common functions, of management, 499–503
Communication, 246–259
  active listening, 255
  body language, 251–252
  breakdown, 254

characteristics of the sender, 248–249
  definition of, 247
  feedback in, 254–255
  formal, 247
  informal, 247
  nonverbal, 251–252
  oral, 14–16, 249–250
  political use of, 434
  supportive climate, 254–255
  ten commandments of, 259–260
  types of, 249–252
  written, 14–15, 250
Communication barriers, filtering, 252
  information overload, 253–254
  jargon, 253
  noise, 252
  selective perception, 252–253
  semantics, 253
  value judgment, 254
Communication improvement, ten key steps, 259–260
Communication network, 14–17
Communications channel, defined, 249
Comparative management, 473–475
Compensation, 283–285
  highest paid executives, 285
  job evaluation, 284
  salary, 284
Competent organization, 407
Competition, 209, 385
Compromise, 389
Concern for people, in leadership, 230–231
Concern for production, in leadership, 230–232
Conflict, 197
  behavioral view, 384–385

classical view, 383–384
constructive, 385–386
constructive stimulation of,
    391–394
definition of, 385
destructive, 385–386
interactionist view, 384
managerial implications,
    395–396
perceptual differences, 390
philosophies of, 383–385
power redistribution, 370–371
reduction of, 388–391
role, 394–395
sources of, 386–387
Confrontation, 389
    See also Conflict
Consideration, 229–231
Consortium, 473
Constraints, 140
    cultural, 477–478
    definition of, 475
    economic, 476–477
    legal, 475–476
    political, 476
Consumerists, 453
Content models, comparison of,
    70–71
Contingency approach, 54–56
    sociotechnical, 352–354
    See also Management
Contingency model, leadership,
    233–236
    of organization, 346–355
Contingency planning, 168–169
    See also Planning
Contingent strategic planning,
    168–169
Continuous reinforcement,
    definition of, 73
Continuum in decision making,
    123–124
Control, 183–197
    acceptance of, 194–195
    analytical aids to, 205–217
    behavioral aspects of, 194–
        195
    budgetary, 192–193
    definition of, 184
    deviations, 187
    direct, 195
    extent of, 191
    feedback in, 196
    indirect, 193
    inventory, 192
    managerial, 161
    managerial implications, 197
    post-action, 186
    pre-controls, 185
    process of, 185–186

production, 191–192
quality, 192
relationship to planning,
    183–184
standards, 186–187
steering, 185–186
ten basic characteristics,
    189–191
types of, 185–186
yes–no, 186
Control process, steps in, 186–
    188
Control systems, 188–189
Cooperation, 385
Coordination, through hierar-
    chy, 328
Coordinative management, 11
Corporate dilemma, 447–448
Cost, 188–189
Cottage industry, 46
Creative organizational climate,
    370–371
Creative process, steps in,
    367–370
Creativity, 365–375
    Delphi technique, 372–373
    development of, 366
    implementation of, 370
    incubation process, 369
    management of, 372–373
    managerial implications of,
        375–376
    nominal group technique,
        373
    techniques for increasing,
        371–373
Critical path, definition of, 213
Culture, 43–46

D

Decision, alternatives, 112
    definition of, 112
    emotional, 122–125
    evaluating results of, 121–122
    importance of, 114
    implementing, 121–122
    objective quality of, 122
    personal nature of, 123
    politics, 117–118
    programmed, 114–115
    rational, 122–125
    rejection of, 122
    steps in making, 118–122
    unprogrammed, 115
Decision making, 111–128, 138
    analytical aids to, 205–217
    and planning, 164–165
    bounded rationality, 117
    choice, 112
    decision tree, 126–127

descriptive model, 124–125
group, 116
involving subordinates, 125–
    127
limits of, 117
multiple consequences, 113
planning, 165–166
politics of, 117–118
problems multiply caused,
    113
psychological factors, 122–
    123
rational model, 118–122
satisficing, 117
styles of, 125–127
systems viewpoint, 113–114
under certainty, 115–116
under risk, 116
under uncertainty, 116–117
use of groups, 125–127
Decision tree, 126–127, 214–
    216
Decisional roles, 31–34
Delegation, 324–325
Delphi method, 116, 372–373
Departmentation, 319–322
    See also Specialization
Design-to-cost, 539–540
Designing operations systems,
    540–542
Development groups, 353
Deviations, 187
    See also Control
Diagnosis, in decision making,
    119–120
Differentiation, 346–347
    influence of environment,
        347–349
Direct supervision, 8
Directing, 184–185
Discrimination, categories, 268
Disseminator role, 30–31
Disturbance handler role, 32–33
Division of Labor, definition
    of, 318
    reasons for, 318–319
Domestic organization, 469
Dominance, 388
Dual-career family, 520

E

E.R.G., definition of, 68
Economic system, 449–452
Ego states, 255–258
Emergent activities, 93
Emergent interactions, defini-
    tion of, 92–93
Empathy, 253
Entrepreneur, definition of, 491
    role of, 32

Environment, effects on organizational structure, 344–349
  organizational differentiation, 346–347
  stable, 53–54, 345–346
  turbulent, 53–54
Environmental variability, 344–345
Environmentalists, 453
Equal employment, 519–520
Ethics, encouraging, 438–440
  importance of, 435–436
  influence on, 437–438
Executives, highest paid, 285
Existence, definition of, 68
Expectancy, definition of, 75
Expectancy model, of motivation, 75–77
  three primary factors, 75
Expense budget, 192
Extrinsic rewards, definition of, 66

F
Facility location and construction, 541
Feedback, 6, 72–73
  as control, 188
  deviation-amplifying, 301
  deviation-reducing, 301
  in communications, 254–255
  in systems, 300–301
Figurehead role, 28
Filtering, 252
  See also Communication barriers
Financial budget, 192
First level supervisor, dynamics of, 326–328
Forcing, 388
Formal groups, definition of, 91
Franchise, 493
Functional manager, 12

G
Game theory, application of, 210
  definition of, 210
Gantt chart, application of, 211–213
  definition of, 211
General manager, 12
Goals, operating, 144
  organizational, 138
Graphic rating scale, 277
  See also Performance appraisal
Group, accomplishing organizational objectives, 95
  building activities, 101
  cohesiveness, 97–99

command, 91
committees, 91
content, 100
decision-making, 125–127
definition of, 90
Delphi, 116
effectiveness, 95
formal, 91
formal leadership, 99–100
goal clarity, 95
goal-path clarity, 95
informal, 91
informal leadership, 99
leadership, 99
manager as formal leader, 97
managers' effectiveness, 101
need satisfaction, 94–95
nominal, 116–117
norms, 95–97
pivotal norms, 96
process, 100
relatedness, 94
relevant norms, 96
self-serving activities, 101
support, 94
task activities, 100–101
task force, 91
training new members, 95
Group cohesiveness, accomplishing group goals, 98
  definition of, 97
  geography, 97–98
  groupthink, 98–99
  outside pressure, 98
  proximity, 97–98
  size, 97
  unanimity, 98
Group effectiveness, content, 100
  process, 100–101
Group leadership, definition of, 99
  informal, 99
  social, 99
  task of, 99
Group norms, characteristics of, 95–97
  conformity, 96–97
  creative individualism, 96
  definition of, 95
  importance to the manager, 97
  pivotal, 96
  range of possible deviation, 96
  relevant, 96
Groups, consumerist, 453
  environmentalist, 453
  improving group relationships, 414–416
  influence, 145–146
  managers' membership, 101

minority, 453
shareholders, 454
special interest, 452
task activities, 100–101
Groupthink, 98, 382–383
  avoidance of, 99
Growth, definition of, 68

H
Hawthorne effect, 49–50
  See also Hawthorne Studies
Hawthorne Studies, 48–50
  effect of feedback on, 73
  groups effect on human behavior, 90
Hierarchy of objectives, 142–143
Horizontal specialization, definition of, 319
Human relations, 48–49
Human resources planning, 269–270
  management replacement chart, 271

I
Implementation, 365
Improving intergroup relationships, 414–416
Independent agents, 472
Industrial Revolution, 45–46
Influence groups, 145
Informal groups, 91
Information overload, 253–254
  See also Communication barriers
Informational roles, 29–31
Initiating structure, in leadership, 229
Inputs, 6
  definition of, 299
Integration, organizational, 347–349
Integrative problem solving, 389–390
Interaction, definition of, 92
  emergent, 92–93
  required, 92
International involvement, forms of, 471–473
International management assignments, 479
International organization, 469–470
International sales, 471–473
Interpenetrating systems, 451–452
Interpersonal roles, 28–29
Intrinsic rewards, definition of, 66

Inventory, 208
Inventory control, 192, 546–547

J
Jargon, 253
    See also Communication barriers
Job enlargement, 412
Job enrichment, 412–414
    core job dimensions, 413–414
    criticism of, 414
Job grades, Civil Service, 284
Job satisfaction, relationship to productivity, 79

K
Key performance areas, defined, 141–142

L
Labor, division of, 318–324
Laws and rules, 44–45
Leader, formal, 229
    informal, 229
    personality attributes of, 233
Leadership, 28
    common approach characteristics, 236–237
    consideration, 229–231
    contingency models, 233–236
    Fiedler's contingency model, 233–235
    influence, 236–237
    influence of subordinates, 238
    Managerial Grid, 230–232
    managerial implications of, 237–239
    path-goal model, 235–236
    personality attributes, 232–233
    similarities between models, 236–237
    Theory X and Theory Y, 230
    traits, 232–233
Levels of management, 43–44
Liaison role, 28–29
Linear programming, 204, 209–210
Line authority, 329–331
Long-range planning, steps in, 169–172

M
Management, 9–12
    common functions, 499–503
    comparative, 473–475
    contingency approach, 54–56

decision making, 502
    employee motivation, 502
    integrative trends, 54–56
    international, 473–475
    interrelated roles, 500–501
    levels of, 43–44
    managerial level, 305, 350–351
    operations, 142, 305–306, 351–352
    principles of, 51–52
    private sector, 489–493
    profit-maximizing, 419
    public sector, 493–494
    quality-of-life, 450–451
    scientific approach, 46–48
    sociotechnical approach, 352–354
    strategic, 142, 305, 349–350
    systems concept, 54–56
    third sector, 497–498
    trusteeship, 419–420
    use of control, 502
Management assignments, international, 479
Management by objectives, 146–149, 194, 277, 417
    criteria, 149
    historical forms of, 147–148
    motivational benefits of, 149
    principles of, 147
    problems in, 148–149
Management development, 281–284
Management principles, 51–52
Manager, 5–18
    activity preferences, 13–16
    functional, 12
    functions of, 25–26
    general, 12
    levels and titles, 7–12
    operations, 10–11
    rewards of, 16–18
    role of, 394–395
    styles of, 16
    titles, 8–12
Managerial employees, 9–10
Managerial Grid, 230–232
Managerial influence, 236–237
    See also Leadership
Managerial roles, 26–36
    categories and subdivision, 27–35
    contingency of, 34
    integration of, 34
Managerial subsystems, 305–309
Managing, a comparative approach, 495–497
Manufacturing manager, 35
Matrix organization, 350–351

Meetings, 14–15
Message, 249
    covert, 249
    overt, 249
Middle management, and planning, 162–163
Minorities, 453
    and careers, 519–520
Models, analog, 205–206
    comparison of, 205–207
    content, 67–71
    definition of, 66, 205
    expectancy, 75–77
    mathematical, 206
    mental, 206
    need hierarchy, 67–69
    process, 71–77
    scale, 205
    simulation, 206–207
Models of motivation, relationships among, 78
Monitor role, 29–30
Motivation, changes in, 66
    definition of, 66
Motivation-hygiene model, 67–70
Motivation models, content, 67–71
    expectancy, 75–77
    guidelines for the manager, 79–80
    motivation-hygiene, 69–70
    overlap of, 78–79
    positive reinforcement, 71–74
    process, 71–77
Multinational operations, reasons for, 471–472
Multinational organization, 469–479
Myths, Hawthorne effect, 49–50
    scientific management, 47

N
Need hierarchy, motivation, 67–69
Negotiator role, 34
Nerve center, 16, 36
Network of communications, 14–17
Noise, 252–254
    in communications, 252–254
    See also Communication barriers
Nominal group technique, 116–117, 373
Nonverbal communications, 251–252
Norms, conformity to, 519
    creative individualism, 519
    international, 477–478
    pivotal, 519

rebellion against, 519
relevant, 519
Number of employees, managerial, 9–10
professional, 9–10
technical, 9–10

O

Objectives, 11
actual, 143–145
changing, 145–146
characteristics of, 138–140
conflict over, 144
continuing, 140–142
hierarchy of, 142–143
importance of, 137–138
influence of regulations, 146
management by, 146–149
multiple, 140–142, 145
official, 143–145
organizational, 136–150
Operating system, book publishing, 547–551
Operations, 6, 9–11, 13, 299, 531–551
relations to other functions, 535–540
types of, 532–533
Operations budget, 192
Operations function, 531–533
Operations in context, 535–537
Operations level, 44
Operations management, 326–328, 531–551
Operations manager, 11
Operations management, and planning, 162–163
Operations, planning and control, 543–547
Operations research, applications of, 207–209
decision trees, 214–216
definition, 207
game theory, 210
limitations of, 216–217
linear programming, 209–210
managerial implications, 217–218
probability theory, 209
queuing theory, 210
reasons for avoidance, 217
time-event-network analysis (PERT), 211–213
Operations technology, 343–344
Oral communications, 14–16, 249–250
Organization, as system, 302–309
autonomous work groups, 352–355
centralization, 325–326

competent, 407
decentralization, 325–326
definition, 6
development groups, 353
domestic, 469
influencing factors, 355–356
influence of size, 343–344
influence of technology, 343–344
integration, 347–348
interpenetrating systems model, 451–452
managerial level, 350–351
matrix, 350–351
mechanistic, 53, 345–346
international, 469–470
multinational, 469–479
operating level, 351–352
operations, 10–11
See also Appendix
organic, 54, 345–346
self-planned, 302
size of, 342–343
social system characteristics, 309
specialization of, 319–322
strategic level, 349–350
structure, 50
structural change, 322
system, 5–7
tasks and structure, 502
Organization development, 410–418
approaches to, 412–418
assumptions in, 411
Organizational change, components of, 409–410
managerial problems with, 418–419
planned approaches to, 412
process approach, 407–408
refreezing behavior, 409–410
structural approach, 407–408
unfreezing behavior, 409
Organizational climate, 238
Organizational design, basic factors, 342–345
Organizational goals, 112, 138
Organizational objectives, 136–150
Organizational policy, 161
Organizational processes, in operations, 532–535
Organizational socialization, 518–519
Organizational strategy defined, 160
Organizational structure, contingency approaches, 346–355
Organization chart, 331–332

Organization manual, 332–333
Organizing, for production, 542–543
Outputs, 6, 299–300

P

Parent ego state, 255–256
Parity, 325
Parkinson's Law, 342–343
Partial reinforcement, definition of, 73
Path-goal leadership model, 235–236
See also Leadership
Path-goal model, 235–236
Perceptual screening, 432
Personality attributes, in leadership, 232–233
Politics, problem of, 495–496
Performance, 238
feedback, 238
Performance appraisal, appraisal interview, 277–281
behaviorally anchored rating scale, 277–280
definition of, 276
graphic rating scale, 277
management by objectives (MBO), 277
objectives of, 276
use in compensation, 284
Performance audit, 72
conducting, 72
Performance standards, 72
Pivotal group norm, definition of, 96
Plan, 159
Planning, 158–174, 543–547
analytical aids to, 205–217
contingency, 168–169
and control operations, 543–547
and coordinative management, 162–163
decision making, 165–166
difficulties with, 173–174
environmental forecast, 164–165
framework of, 165
importance of, 163
managerial implications of, 174–175
operational, 162
and operations management, 162–163
relation to control, 161
scenarios, 167–168
short and long range, 168
steps in, 169–172
strategic, 160–174
tactical, 162

and top management, 162–163
Plans, budget, 168
    types of, 166–167
    types of single-use, 167–168
Policy, organizational, 161
Politics, approaches to gain
    power, 433–435
    in decision making, 117
    use of, 432–433
Positive reinforcement model,
    71–75
Positive rewards, 73
Power, 17, 432, 433
    charismatic, 228
    coercive, 228
    expert, 227–228
    legitimate, 227
    political approaches, 432–435
    redistribution of, 370–371
    reward, 228
    sources of, 227–228
    two faces of, 432–433
Preferences, 75
Prestige, 17
Principles of management,
    51–52
Private sector management,
    489–493
Probability theory, 209
Problem identification, 118–120
Procedures, 167
Process, definition of, 303
Process selection, 541
Processes, in operations, 532–
    535
Product or service design, 540
Production, organizing for,
    542–543
Production categories, 343–344
Production control, 45, 191,
    543–547
    See also Appendix
Productivity, relationship to
    satisfaction, 79
Professional employees, 9–10
Profit-maximizing management,
    419
Profits, 188
Program, 167–168
Program Evaluation and Review
    Technique (PERT), 212–
    214
Programmed decisions, 114–115
Progressive career, 17–18
Project, 167–168
Promotion, 286
Psychological income, 283
Public sector management,
    493–494

Q
Quality control, 192, 545–546
Quality-of-life management,
    450–451
Queuing theory, 210

R
Reality shock, 517–518
Receiver, 248–249
Recruitment, affirmative action,
    272
    legal requirements, 272
    process of, 272–276
Regulations, impact on objec-
    tives, 146
Reinforcement, continuous, 73
    definition of, 71
    partial, 73
    six basic rules, 74
    use of, 73–74
Relatedness, definition of, 68
Relevant group norm, definition
    of, 96
Reorganization, Roman Army,
    58–59
Replacement, 208
Required activities, definition
    of, 92
Resource allocator role, 33–34
Return on investment (ROI),
    122, 123, 188
Revenue budget, 192
Reverse discrimination, 267
Reward, financial, 18
Rewards, 66, 238
    See also Performance
Risk, conditions of, 115–116
Role, definition of, 394
    level, 36
    managerial, 394–395
    type of organization, 35–36
Role ambiguity, 394–395
Role conflict, 394–395
Roles, decisional, 31–34
    interpersonal, 28–29
    managerial, 26–36
    See also Managerial roles
    informational, 29–31
Rules, 167
Rumors, 254
    See also Communication bar-
    riers

S
Sales, international, 471–473
Satisficing, 117
Scalar principle, 329
Scenarios, definition of, 168–
    169
Scheduling, 208

Scientific management, 46–48
Selection, application blank,
    274
    assessment center, 274–276
    definition of, 272
    interview, 274
    psychological testing, 274
    resume, 273–274
    validity, 273–274
Selective perception, 252–253
    See also Communication bar-
    riers
Self-development, 281
Semantics, 253
    See also Communication bar-
    riers
Sender, 248–249
Sentiment, definition of, 92
    emergent, 92–93
    required, 92
Shareholders, 454
Shuttle service, 32
Single-use plan, 167
Simulation, definition, 206–207
Single-cause thinking, 54
Size, influence on structure,
    342–344
Smoothing, 389
Social audit, 457–459
Social responsibility, 456–459
Socialization, anticipatory, 519
    organizational, 518–519
Society, 43–46
Sociotechnical systems, 352–
    355
Span of control, 322–323
Special interest groups, 452
Specialists, 326
Specialization by client, 320–
    321
    by function, 319
    by geography, 319–320
    by number of persons, 321–
    322
    by product, 320–321
    by time, 322
Spokesperson role, 31
Staff, 329–331
Staffing, 267–288
    affirmative action, 268
    civil rights legislation, 268–
    269
    importance of, 267
    managerial function, 270, 287
Stages of career, 513–517
Standards, definition of, 72
Standards of control, 186–187
    See also Control
Standing plan, 167
Strategic management, 11–13

Strategic plan, defined, 160
Strategic planning, contingent
    approaches, 168–169
Strategy, 160–161
    organizational, 160
    See also Planning
Structural analysis, 255–256
    See also Transactional
        analysis
Structural change, 407–408
Structure, and environment,
    344–346
    as control, 191
    in leadership, 229–231
    and size, 342
    and technology, 343–344
Suboptimization, 113
Subordinates, decision making
    with, 125–127
Subsidiary, 472
Subsystem, 6
    adaptive, 307–308
    boundary-spanning, 306–307
    definition of, 298
    maintenance, 307
    managerial, 305–309
    operations, 305–306
Supervision, direct, 8
Suprasystem, definition of, 298
Synergism, 6
System, 6–7, 298–310
    boundary, 6, 300
    closed, 300, 318
    closed approach, 318
    definition of, 298
    deviation-amplifying feed-
        back, 301
    deviation-reducing feedback,
        301

feedback, 6, 302–303
inputs, 6, 299
interaction among, 298
interpenetrating, 451–452
levels of, 298
open, 300
operations, 6, 299
as organization, 302–309
organization as, 302
outputs, 6, 299–300
as process, 303–304
social, 303
structure, 302–303
synergism, 6
types of subsystems, 304–309
Systems thinking, 54–56
Systems concept, 54–56

T
Tactical planning, defined, 162
Task force, 91
Team building, 416–417
Technical employees, 9–10
Technology, influence on struc-
    ture, 343–344
    types of, 53–54
Termination, dismissal, 286–
    287
    retirement, 286
Theory X, 230
    See also Leadership
Theory Y, 230
Therbligs, 47–48
Thinking, multiple-cause,
    55–56
    single-cause, 54
    systems, 54–56
Third sector management,
    497–498

Time study, 47–48
Titles of a manager, 8–12
Tokenism, 520
Top management, and planning,
    162–163
Transaction, types of, 257–258
Transactional analysis (TA),
    255–259
Transfer, definition of, 286
Trusteeship management,
    419–420

U
Uncertainty, conditions of,
    115–117
Union, 328
Unity of command, 329
Unprogrammed decisions, 115

V
Value judgment, 254
    See also Communication bar-
        riers
Values, perceptual screening,
    432
    role of, 430–432
Vertical coordination, principles
    of, 328–331

W
Waiting lines, 208
Whistle blowing, 430
Women, and careers, 519–520
Work situation, behavior
    changes, 66, 78–79
    choice, 75
    managers control over, 78–79
Written communications, 14–15,
    250–251